Contents

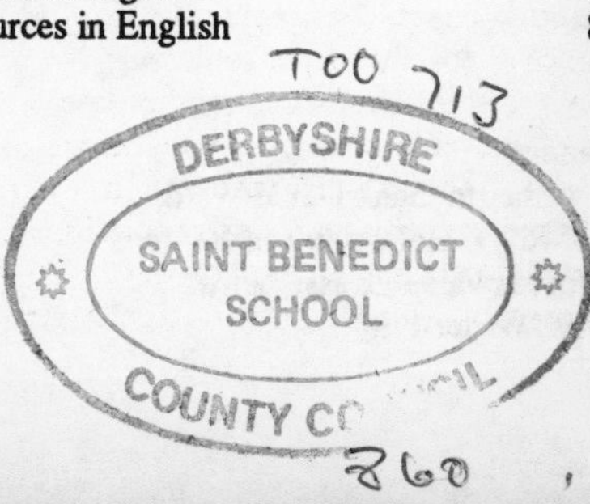

Acknowledgement
The Compiler wishes to thank David Ward, at the Library of Royal Holloway and Bedford New College, for his valuable assistance in compiling this 'Writer-File'.

The theatre is, by its nature, an ephemeral art: yet it is a daunting task to track down the newspaper reviews, or contemporary statements from the writer or his director, which are often all that remain to help us recreate some sense of what a particular production was like. This series is therefore intended to make readily available a selection of the comments that the critics made about the plays of leading modern dramatists at the time of their production — and to trace, too, the course of each writer's own views about his work and his world.

In addition to combining a uniquely convenient source of such elusive *documentation*, the 'Writer-Files' series also assembles the *information* necessary for readers to pursue further their interest in a particular writer or work. Variations in quantity between one writer's output and another's, differences in temperament which make some readier than others to talk about their work, and the variety of critical response, all mean that the presentation and balance of material shifts between one volume and another: but we have tried to arrive at a format for the series which will nevertheless enable users of one volume readily to find their way around any other.

Section 1, 'A Brief Chronology', provides a quick conspective overview of each playwright's life and career. *Section 2* deals with the plays themselves, arranged chronologically in the order of their composition: information on first performances, major revivals, and publication is followed by a brief synopsis (for quick reference set in slightly larger, italic type), then by a representative selection of the critical response, and of the dramatist's own comments on the play and its theme.

Section 3 offers concise guidance to each writer's work in non-dramatic forms, while *Section 4*, 'The Writer on His Work', brings together comments from the playwright himself on more general matters of construction, opinion, and artistic development. Finally, *Section 5* provides a bibliographical guide to other primary and secondary sources of further reading, among which full details will be found of works cited elsewhere under short titles, and of collected editions of the plays — but not of individual titles, particulars of which will be found with the other factual data in Section 2.

The 'Writer-Files' hope by striking this kind of balance between information and a wide range of opinion to offer 'companions' to the study of major playwrights in the modern repertoire — not in that dangerous pre-digested fashion which can too readily quench the desire to read the plays themselves, nor so prescriptively as to allow any single line of approach to predominate, but rather to encourage readers to form their own judgements of the plays in a wide-ranging context.

Federico Garcia Lorca fits oddly into this series, since so many of his plays were censored out of existence in Spain almost as soon as they were written — while his reputation abroad has been based on just one or two works, squeezing critical expectations into an ill-fitting strait-jacket of dour Iberian cut. Happily, the last few years have seen a controlled explosion of new productions — as of the actable translations on which these depend: so it may be that the function of this 'Writer-File' will not so much be to introduce the full range of Lorca's work as to provide a context for understanding the short lifetime's achievement of this dedicated but haunted man.

The material on *The House of Bernarda Alba*, as sampled in this volume, suggests both the problems and the potential. It documents the childhood recollections from which the play's situation and characters derive — yet it also enables us to contrast, at one extreme, the assumption that Bernarda herself is a detested embodiment of fascist repression, with, at the other, the belief that she is herself a hapless symbol of oppressed Spanish womanhood. Into the tensions created by this web of possible responses we may mix the personal subtext of a homosexual writer whose best-known characters are unequivocally female, bearing as they do all the tragic dignity of their degradation in a society whose brute machismo Lorca recognized only too well. It was, finally, to cut short his own life when, five years to the day after he had completed a play called *When Five Years Pass*, he was shot dead by assassins, like his own author-persona in that play.

The expected themes are of course brought out in this volume — the frustrations of unfulfilled need, the fear of time passing, the certainty of death — as is what Lorca himself describes on page 71 as the 'agrarian complex' which roots his work so firmly in the soil of his nation. But no less important is the revelation of the generic range — from cinematic surrealism to folk-puppetry, from Brechtian dialectic to proto-absurdism — through which he expressed the characteristic concern summed up by one critic on page 39 as 'the clash between unexpressed inner need and imposed external control'. Here, we may find how some of Lorca's 'inner needs' were energized, albeit elliptically expressed: but no less helpfully can we begin to realize the range of the man's *expressed* needs — not the least of these the desire to create a truly responsive people's theatre, such as La Barraca so tantalizingly set out to be.

Simon Trussler

1: A Brief Chronology

1898 5 June, Federico Garcia Lorca born in Fuente Vaqueros, near Granada. Eldest of four children of Don Federico Garcia Rodriguez, a prosperous farmer, and Dona Vicenta Lorca Romero, a schoolteacher.

1909 Family moves to Granada where Federico and his brother Francisco attend the College of the Sacred Heart of Jesus (an institution free from clerical influence).

1914 Despite his desire to continue music studies, Lorca's parents send him to University of Granada where he studies in Faculties of Arts and Law.

1915 Lorca comes under the influence of Fernando de los Rios and Martin Dominguez Berrueta (both liberal educationalists). Joins Granada Arts Club and gains reputation as pianist, guitarist and poet. Also active in the 'rinconcillo' of the Cafe Alameda, a literary gathering of unconventional Granadans.

1915-17 Accompanies Berrueta on a series of educational tours of Spain.

1917 Early poetry and prose writings express a rejection of patriotism and conventional Catholicism.

1917-18 Writes first draft of unfinished play, *Christ, a Religious Tragedy*, in which Christ's alleged sexual frustration bears a close resemblance to his own.

1918 With financial assistance from his father, Lorca publishes *Impressions and Landscapes*, a prose collection based on experiences of travels with Berrueta.

1919 Lorca enrols at Madrid University and lodges at the Residencia de Estudiantes, an institution renowned for its promotion of liberal educational principles, where he meets Luis Bunuel and, later, Salvador Dali. Writes poem about an injured butterfly which Gregorio Martinez Sierra, a leading anti-realist playwright, invites him to dramatize. Begins friendship with the composer Manuel de Falla.

1920 *The Butterfly's Evil Spell* staged at the Teatro Eslava, Madrid, ridiculed by audiences and taken off after four nights.

1921 Publication of his first collection of poetry, *Book of Poems.*

1922 Completes *The Tragicomedy of Don Cristobal and Senorita Rosita.* With Manuel de Falla, helps to organize the Festival of Deep Song (a festival of flamenco) in Granada.

1923 Finishes Law degree. Begins friendship with Salvador Dali. Presents puppet show, with Manuel de Falla, at the Lorca household, which includes his short puppet play *The Girl who Waters the Pot of Basil* and *The Inquisitive Prince*. Starts work on libretto for comic opera *Lola, the Actress*, but Manuel de Falla fails to produce the music. Primo de Rivera's coup begins seven-year period of military dictatorship and censorship in Spain.

1924 Meets the poet Rafael Alberti, with whom he is to develop a close personal relationship. Works on poems influenced by the Festival of Deep Song, to be published later as *Gypsy Ballads*, one of the most celebrated books of poetry in Spanish literature.

1925 Completes final version of *Mariana Pineda*. Influenced by the surrealist movement, writes *Buster Keaton's Stroll.*

1926 Delivers lecture on poetic theory, 'The Poetic Image in Don Luis de Gongora'. Publication of *Ode to Salvador Dali*.

1927 Publishes *Songs*, his second collection of poetry. Edits the first edition of literary review *Gallo (The Cockerel)*. *Mariana Pineda* opens in Barcelona with Margarita Xirgu, later transfers to Teatro Fontalbo, Madrid. Collection of drawings exhibited in Barcelona.

1928 Publication of *Gypsy Ballads*. Delivers two lectures to the Athenaeum Club in Granada, 'Imagination, Inspiration, and Escape in Poetry' and 'Sketch of the New Painting'. Has affair with a sculptor, Emilio Aladren, followed by period of depression.

1929 Chamber version of *The Love of Don Perlimplin for Belisa in His Garden* banned from performance in Madrid. Margarita Xirgu's production of *Mariana Pineda* opens at Teatro Cervantes, Granada. Travels with Fernando de los Rios to New York via Paris and London. Witnesses effects of Wall Street Crash. Writes poem 'The King of Harlem', and surrealist filmscript *Trip to the Moon*, influenced by Bunuel's *Un Chien Andalou*.

1930 Travels to Cuba. Delivers highly successful series of lectures, in

Havana, on Spanish poetry. Finishes first version of *The Public*. *The Shoemaker's Prodigious Wife* opens at Teatro Espanol, Madrid. Returns to Spain at end of June. Primo de Rivera replaced by the more moderate General Damaso Berenguer in January. Republican coup attempt in December fails.

1931 Publication of *Deep Song*. Completes *When Five Years Pass*. Starts work on *Blood Wedding* and *The Puppet Play of Don Cristobal*. Second Republic proclaimed: Lorca's friend and former teacher Fernando de los Rios becomes Minister of Justice. With students from Madrid University, sets up touring theatre company La Barraca, which receives official support from the new government.

1932 La Barraca tours Spain with productions of interludes by Cervantes and Calderon's *Life is a Dream*, but comes under attack from right-wing opposition. Completes *Blood Wedding*.

1933 Highly successful premiere of *Blood Wedding*, directed by Lorca, at Teatro Beatriz, Madrid. Premiere of *The Love of Don Perlimplin for Belisa in His Garden*, at Teatro Espanol. Travels to Buenos Aires where he sees successful productions of *Blood Wedding* and *The Shoemaker's Wonderful Wife*. La Barraca tours production of Lope de Vega's *Fuente Ovejuna*, adapted and directed by Lorca.

1934 Productions in Buenos Aires of *Mariana Pineda* and Lope de Vega's *The Simple-Minded Lady*, adapted and co-directed by Lorca. Writes poem on the death of famous bull-fighter, 'Lament for Ignacio Sanchez Mejias'. Right wing gains control of key government ministries. La Barraca's grant cut by half. Premiere of *Yerma*, at Teatro Espanol, interrupted by hecklers.

1935 *Yerma*, *Blood Wedding*, and *The Shoemaker's Wonderful Wife* all performed in Madrid. *Yerma* opens in Barcelona and Valencia. New York production of *Blood Wedding*. Highly acclaimed premiere of *Dona Rosita the Spinster* at Teatro Principal Palace. La Barraca's grant cut entirely. Political instability moving towards crisis.

1936 Completes *The House of Bernarda Alba* and works on new plays, *Comedy without Title*, *The Dreams of My Cousin Aurelia*, and *Blood Has No Voice* (all unfinished). Increasingly publicizes his left-wing sympathies. Civil war breaks out. Goes into hiding in Granada, but is captured and shot at Viznar by paramilitary forces loyal to Franco.

a: Stage Plays

The Butterfly's Evil Spell

'A comedy in two acts and a prologue.'
Written: 1919-20.
First production: Eslava Theatre, Madrid, 22 March 1920 (dir. Gregorio Martinez Sierra).

A verse drama influenced by the symbolist tradition. Sylvia, a female cockroach, is in love with Curianito, a cockroach with a poetic disposition. She implores Curianito's mother, Dona Beetle, to persuade him to marry her. Dona Beetle complies at once, for Sylvia is rich and this is an opportunity for financial gain. However, Curianito cannot be persuaded to marry, and when Mariposa, a wounded butterfly, falls from the sky he is transfixed by her. A witch beetle warns him that falling in love with Mariposa will mean certain death. Mariposa is nursed back to health by the cockroaches with the help of the witch beetle and protected from Scorpy, a woodcutter who enjoys terrorizing the cockroaches. In the last scene of this unfinished play Curianito woos Mariposa in vain and laments his inability to fly while she performs a dance to show how she is regaining the strength of her wings.

The poet was twenty-one years old when the work was first performed. The Eslava Theatre was then one of the most prestigious in Spain. Catalina Barcena, the leading lady, was famous all over the Spanish-speaking world, and the director of the theatre, Gregorio Martinez Sierra . . . was a vital part of the Modernist movement. Martinez Sierra's interest in reforming the theatre helps to explain the attention he paid to my brother, who was very young and totally unknown.

Martinez Sierra, who felt a noble desire to promote new talent, had also written the text of Falla's *El amor brujo* (*Bewitched Love*), the work which made the great composer universally popular. The part of the Butterfly, which includes a dance we might call 'the dance of the wounded butterfly', was performed by Encarnacion Lopez ('La Argentinita'), who was just beginning her career. I mention this because, later on, both Federico and Manuel de Falla would collaborate closely with her.

Francisco Garcia Lorca,
In the Green Morning, trans. C. Maurer,
1989, p. 135-6

The Teatro Eslava was responsible for the presentation of works by Shakespeare, Molière, Goldoni, Dumas, Ibsen, Shaw, and Barrie to Spanish audiences between 1917 and 1924, while, at the same time, it was Martinez Sierra's initiative that brought Lorca's ill-fated *Butterfly's Evil Spell* to the stage in 1920. And while both Lorca and his producer were distinctly mistaken in their estimation of the receptivity of the Madrid public for such fanciful and poetic theatre, there was no other impresario in the capital at the time who would have taken the risk of encouraging and producing such a piece.

Reed Anderson, *Federico Garcia Lorca*, 1984, p. 27

The general symbolism of *El maleficio de la mariposa* (*The Butterfly's Evil Spell*) is clearly in the tradition of Maeterlinck, for while the characters are cockroaches, glow-worms, and a butterfly, they are essentially generic figures, the embodiment of universal experiences, attitudes, and feelings which anticipate the human characters of Lorca's mature drama.

Gwynne Edwards,
Spanish Theatre in the Twentieth Century, 1985, p. 78

The last pages of the manuscript of *The Butterfly's Evil Spell* are lacking. This is not surprising — and it is why other manuscripts, as well, are incomplete or missing — for after the murder of Federico Garcia Lorca his papers were avidly sought by the insurgent authorities in Granada. To avoid seizure these were removed from place to place, and at least once were hidden in a haystack. Those who saw the play have conflicting descriptions of the final action, but all agree that the play ended with the death of the protagonist, Poet Beetle.

Francisco Garcia Lorca, Introduction to
Lorca, *Five Plays*, 1970, p. 19-20

When, on the night of 22 March 1920, the curtain went up on *The*

Butterfly's Evil Spell, neither 'La Argentinita', nor Catalina Barcena (in the role of the Cockroach), nor Grieg, nor Mignoni's colourful set, nor Barradas's costumes, nor Martinez Sierra's direction, nor the several merits of the little verse play itself, could overcome the rooted hostility of the audience. . . . The performance of Federico's first dramatic work was a fiasco. From the moment the actors began to speak the protests erupted, and it soon became clear that a section of the audience was determined to wreck the show. Boos, catcalls, insults and witticisms, foot-stamping — the hullaballoo was deafening. . . . When the final curtain fell it was clear that Madrid was not yet ready (and no doubt never would be) for a verse play concerning the amorous misfortunes of cockroaches. . . . Next day almost all the Madrid press referred, in a few dismissive lines, to the failure of *The Butterfly's Evil Spell* . . . . The poet Rafael Alberti, whose friendship with Lorca began a few years later, recalled that Federico told him in fits of laughter about the disastrous first night; while as late as 1935 Lorca was still insisting that his reaction to the misfortune had been to have a good laugh. It may well be, however, that, deep down, the evening left its mark, for afterwards the poet stated publicly on various occasions that his first play was *Mariana Pineda*, which had its premiere in 1927, conveniently forgetting to mention his unpleasant experience at the Eslava seven years earlier.

Ian Gibson, *Federico Garcia Lorca*, 1989, p. 97-8

Mariana Pineda

'A popular ballad in three engravings.'
Written: 1923-25.
First production: Teatro Goya, Barcelona, 24 June 1927 (dir. Margarita Xirgu; des. Salvador Dali).
British production: Loose Change Theatre, Oval House, London, 20 May 1987 (trans. Caroline Mylon; dir. Tessa Schneideman).

Loosely based on the true story of a popular national heroine, who rebelled against the tyrannical rule of King Ferdinand VII in the early nineteenth century, Mariana, a widow and mother of two, is a martyr to the causes of love and liberty. Her tragic commitment to these ideals is symbolized by her association with the rebels' red banner. After her arrest for conspiracy she retains her honour and integrity by fending off the sexual advances of the villainous Pedrosa and refusing to betray her lover, the rebel leader Pedro de Sotomayor, even though he deserts her to save his skin. In the final scene she goes to her death on the scaffold, a solitary but defiant and heroic figure.

I wish to write a 'processional' drama, a simple and hieratic narrative, permeated by evocations, mysterious breezes, like an old-fashioned Madonna with her arc of cherubims . . . the red of the blood will become confused with the red of the curtains. Mariana is a passionate woman to her very core, a person 'possessed'. . . . She is a Juliet without her Romeo, and [my treatment of her] is closer to that of a madrigal than an ode. In the final act she will be dressed in white, and the entire stage will be set in the same colour.

Lorca, letter to Fernandez Almagro, 1923,
trans. Reed Anderson, in *Federico Garcia Lorca*, 1984, p. 71

I'm convinced that the work's success won't lie, and should not lie, as Don Fernando [de los Rios] would wish, in its political aspects, because it's a work of pure art, a tragedy I've written, as you know, without a political slant. I want its success to be a poetical one — and it will be! — no matter when it is produced.

Lorca, letter to his parents, Nov. 1924,
trans. Ian Gibson, in *Federico Garcia Lorca*, 1989, p. 138

In order to create this fabulous creature, it was absolutely necessary to falsify history, and history is an unassailable fact that doesn't allow the imagination any out except to adorn it with poetry in its language, and with emotion in its silences and in all the things that form their background. . . . For I sincerely believe that theatre is, nor can it be anything other than, emotion and poetry in its words, in its action, and in its gestures.

Lorca, *Obras Completas*, III, 1986, p. 587-8,
trans. Reed Anderson, p. 68

Surrounded by a multitude of poetic shades, Mariana had been asking for justice from the mouth of a poet. . . . They compared her to Judith, and she searched in the shadows for the hand of her sister Juliet. Around her wounded neck they placed the golden necklace of the ode, but she was asking for the freedom of the madrigal. While everyone sang of the eagle that cuts through the iron bars with one sweep of its wing, Mariana was bleating like a lamb, abandoned by all, sustained only by the stars.

Fulfilling my duty as a poet, I have contrasted a living, Christian Mariana, resplendent with heroism, to the cold one on the pedestal, dressed as a foreigner and a freethinker.

Margarita [Xirgu] has fulfilled her duty as an actress, and by means of her voice and her gestures has given substance to this lovely, torn shade, marrow and symbol of Liberty. . . .

I am not saying that my work belongs to the vanguard . . . it falls somewhere in the second line. But I believe that it has certain unusual vibrations. My play is naive, like the soul of Mariana Pineda, and I wanted to give it the atmosphere of an engraving, using all the lovely commonplaces of Romanticism. It is obviously not a Romantic drama because today one can no longer seriously do a pastiche, that is, a drama of the past. I saw two ways to carry out my intentions. The first was by treating the theme with the truculency and crude colouration of the broadside ballad, but of course no one could do this better than Don Ramon [de Valle-Inclan]; the other, the one which I followed, answers to my own vision, a nocturnal, lunar, childish vision.

Lorca, quoted in Francisco Garcia Lorca,
In the Green Morning, trans. C. Maurer, 1989, p. 158-60

Referring in 1927 to the early drafts of the play, Lorca said that he had 'three completely different versions of the drama, the first of them absolutely unviable as theatre', and went on: 'The one I'm staging implies a fusion, a synchronization. It has two planes: the first is broad, synthetic, and over it the attention of the audience can hover without complications. The second — the deep meaning — will be grasped only by part of the audience.'

Ian Gibson, *Federico Garcia Lorca*, 1989, p. 142

One of the methods which Federico selected to give his work a Romantic atmosphere was the renewed use of verse. This is the only play except *The Butterfly's Evil Spell* written entirely in verse. The language has an elevated, lyrical tone. The critics have pointed out, and perhaps they are right, that the theatre of Lope de Vega may have served as a distant model, especially the work where his lyricism flows most freely, *The Knight of Olmedo*. It is true that among all the works of that fabulously prolific creator of the Spanish theatre, this was Federico's favourite.

Francisco Garcia Lorca, *In the Green Morning*,
trans. C. Maurer, 1989, p. 161

In *Mariana* we can also hear echoes of the superior, more perfect tonality of *Book of Poems*. And this is not surprising, given the fact that many poems in that book are in dialogue. . . . We also find the direct popular inspiration of children's ballads, the passionate, sensual, dramatic emotion the poet feels towards the themes of love and death, the flight towards pure song that has not been trimmed down into particular poems — song that seems more appropriate for extroverted expression than for other more intimate lyrical forms.

Francisco Garcia Lorca, as above, p. 166

The detailed naturalism of the stage production, on the one hand, is played off constantly against the artificiality of the verse dialogue, the framing effect of the ballad prologue and epilogue, and the intensification of the drama's emotional projection by symbolic means on the other hand. Lorca's interest in exploring this most fundamental and characteristic contradiction in theatre — the creation of experience that is at once real and artificial — is indicative of his keen awareness of the possibilities and limitations of the form even as he started out as a writer for the stage.

Reed Anderson, *Federico Garcia Lorca*, 1984, p. 70

The yellow of a dress plays off the black of a backdrop. The curves of a sofa are picked up in the curves of a chair. The clock on the wall extends the line of a window. The stripes of a costume play with the stripes on a doorway. And thus on to infinity. A total symphony, a constant orchestration.

Sebastian Gasch, trans. Reed Anderson,
Federico Garcia Lorca, p. 72

The play is not only an eerie premonition of Lorca's own murder at the hands of the fascists, but has the first of his frustrated and doomed heroines. Mariana resembles Dona Rosita, Yerma, and the heroine of *Blood Wedding* in her frustrated and doomed love. And she manifests the same passivity in the face of circumstances she cannot resist. Although the play is supposed to rest upon her political martyrdom, her death is instigated by her refusal to fall in sexually with the corrupt king's representative, Pedrosa.

And Lorca shows the way in which her passion for her lover is not fully requited.

Although written partly in prose, the play prefigures later Lorca in its use of theatrical metaphor, and its emphasis upon the private or coded language of colour: Mariana walks to her death like a bride in white with the black garbed Pedrosa.

Sadly the actors are simply not up to the demands of the play. Miss Schneideman's production tends to be rumbustious and over-rhetorical, while Isabel Hernandez, though looking every inch a Spaniard, manages to pass through the play in a calm mood of nonchalant languor. . . .

Nicholas de Jongh, *The Guardian*, 23 May 1987

While occasionally you feel that this British premiere suffers a little in translation, the production itself more than makes up for it. Loose Change has put together a riveting and moving show with outstanding performances by Josephine Welcome and Leon Herbert as the rebel lovers. Their main love scene is played with a passion that genuinely has you wondering where the embrace on the sofa is going to end — if at all! The set, particularly for the final scene, is a beautifully crafted use of space and light and the measured pace of the production does not let up for a moment. The whole effort is a delight.

Andrew Bell, *Time Out*, 22 May 1987

Buster Keaton's Stroll

A surreal playlet, first published in the avant-garde magazine *Gallo*, May 1928.

Written: 1928.

First British production: Ragazzi Theatre Company, Battersea Arts Centre, 18 April 1990 (trans. Gwynne Edwards; dir. Robert Delamere).

Buster Keaton kills his children and then takes a cycle ride across a bizarre landscape near Philadelphia, where a black man stands by a tyre dump eating a straw hat. Buster falls off his bicycle, then meets a young girl and says enigmatically, 'I would love to be a swan but I can never be what I want. Where would I put my hat?' The play ends as he kneels down and kisses the girl.

Dali and Lorca, like Rafael Alberti and other friends more or less connected to the Residencia de Estudiantes, were avid cinema-goers, and passionate admirers of Buster. 'It seems that Buster has made a film on the sea-bed with his straw hat on top of his diver's helmet', Dali wrote to Lorca. . . . The reference was to *The Navigator*. . . . With another letter Dali sent Federico a charming collage entitled 'The Marriage of Buster Keaton', comprising a series of press cuttings (photos of Buster and accounts of his courtship of Natalia Talmadge), snippets from works on astronomy, and Dalinian additions. Some years later Salvador was to attempt an emulation of Keaton's sub-aquatic feat when, in July 1936, at the International Surrealist Exhibition in London, he attempted to give a lecture wearing a diver's suit, and was almost asphyxiated in the process. . . .

Buster Keaton's Stroll, despite its extreme brevity, can be seen with hindsight to have been an important landmark in Lorca's development as a writer, looking forward in various ways to *Poet in New York*, *The Public*, and *When Five Years Pass*. The setting (the outskirts of Philadelphia), the Pathé News cockerel, the Black who chews a straw hat among old tyres and petrol tins, the aggressively liberated Modern Woman, the insensitivity of an immense, materialistic country — all of this is an intimation of what was to come a few years later when Lorca escaped to New York.

Ian Gibson, *Federico Garcia Lorca*, 1989, p. 150-1

Recent translations by Gwynne Edwards of the comedies, if that is what they are, and the puppet plays reveal the same strange viewpoint and cursory dialogue familiar from the tragedies. Three of these short pieces make up the programme presented at the BAC Studio by the Ragazzi Theatre Company, a new group whose clear talent in the directorial and design areas is more thinly spread in their acting.

As an aperitif they give us *Buster Keaton's Spin*, a surrealist poem that Lindsay Kemp once choreographed and made no more sense of than Robert Delamere's staging here. Keaton kills his children with a wooden sword, cycles off on his penny-farthing, and meets a wasp-waisted girl in bridal white who fairly soon dies. Played on a weirdly pretty landscape spattered with projection-room cog wheels, and crisply performed by Bruno Roubicek (Keaton) and Vernon Douglas, it really does not add up to much.

Jeremy Kingston, *The Times*, 23 April 1990

Buster Keaton's Spin is a surreal nightmare, with the innocent white-faced hero cycling through a hostile urban landscape of 'geometry and anguish' peopled with mysterious figures.

Nick Curtis, *Time Out*, 25 April 1990

Eschewing the confines of realism, *Buster Keaton's Spin* is a surreal cinematic evocation of frustrated optimism adrift in an antagonistic world. . . .

Louise Kingsley, *The Independent*, 25 April 1990

The Maiden, the Sailor, and the Student

A playlet, first published in the avant-garde magazine *Gallo*, May 1928.
Written: 1928.

A girl full of the idealism of youth is contrasted with an old woman dressed in rags who sells snails. The girl embroiders the letters of the alphabet while dreaming of the different names that her lovers may call her, but her brief encounters with the Sailor and the Student reveal that love is frustrated both by authority and the passing of time.

The final suggestion is one of despair as [the Maiden] thinks of suicide. The sea, the symbol of death, dominates the ending of the play. And the reference to the three fog horns which deceive the coastguards, evoking the Sirens of classical mythology through the double meaning of the Spanish word 'sirenas' (fog horns/Sirens), points to the deceptive nature of illusion and dream, so attractive and yet so fatal. In its characters and themes, as well as in its final pessimism, *The Maiden, the Sailor, and the Student* is a rehearsal for the major plays that were soon to follow it and, for all its brevity, an effective piece.

Gwynne Edwards,
Lorca: the Theatre Beneath the Sand, 1980, p. 51

If *Buster Keaton's Stroll* constitutes a little tribute to the silent screen (and heralds Lorca's New York filmscript, *Trip to the Moon*), *The Maiden, the Sailor, and the Student* conjures up Malaga. . . . The balcony where the 'dialogues' take place recalls the window of the Dalis' villa, as it does a work by Salvador, 'Venus and the Sailor', painted that year; while the indication 'a motorboat bedecked with flags crosses the bay, leaving behind its stuttering song' evokes not only this painting, as well as many of Dali's drawings of the period, but, more concretely, Lorca's letter of May 1925 to Ana Maria Dali in which the poet 'imagines' the scene on the village shore: 'The silver fish come up to take the moon and you bathe your tresses in the water while the stuttering song of the motorboats comes and goes.' The days in Cadaques, and the constant contact with Dali, were already influencing Lorca's approach to his work.

Ian Gibson,
Federico Garcia Lorca, 1989, p. 151-2

Dream

A playlet intended for publication in the third edition of the avant-garde magazine, *Gallo*.
Written: 1928.

Enrique is leaving his wife and six children. He meets an old man, a former retainer of his wife's family, who tells him about his fear of horses and hints at the danger of the sea. But Enrique hurries to catch a train, saddened by the departure from his family. His children cry out for the presents they wish him to bring back and his wife describes the loneliness and loss which she now faces.

The third playlet, *Dream* (*Quimera*) was to have appeared in the third number of *El Gallo*, but the magazine was discontinued. Like *The Girl, the Sailor, and the Student*, this is a piece which in its themes seems to anticipate in particular *When Five Years Pass*. Of the three short plays it is the least successful, less inventive than *Buster Keaton's Spin* and less memorable as an image than *The Girl, the Sailor, and the Student*.

Enrique's departure from his wife and his six children suggests at once the theme of a journey and of passing time, an idea reinforced by the presence of the familiar Lorquian figure of the Old Man. . . . His wife and children face the terrible loneliness of the widows and the fatherless children of *Blood Wedding*. About their lives there blows a cold wind and upon them there descends a darkness that are as symbolic as they are literal — the chill and the blackness of despair in which the Lorquian tragic figure is inevitably cast adrift. . . .

Gwynne Edwards,
The Theatre Beneath the Sand, 1980, p. 53

The Shoemaker's Wonderful Wife

'A Violent Farce in Two Acts and a Prologue.'
Written: 1926-30, revised 1933.
First production (first version): Teatro Espanol, Madrid, 24 Dec. 1930 (dir. Cipriano Rivas Cherif; with Margarita Xirgu).
First production (second version): Teatro Avenida, Buenos Aires, 30 Nov. 1933 (dir. Lola Membrives), transferred to Teatro Coliseum, Madrid, 18 March 1935.
British productions: Cambridge Amateur Dramatic Club, 7 Feb. 1956 (trans. George Leeson; dir. Michael Marland); Unity Theatre, London, 12 Oct. 1956 (trans. George Leeson; dir. Dan Kedar); Ragazzi Theatre Company, Battersea Arts Centre, 18 April 1990 (trans. Gwynne Edwards; dir. Robert Delamere).

A hard-working but somewhat dull shoemaker is unhappily married to a volatile and fanciful woman much younger than himself. No longer able to bear their constant rows, and the gossip of the villagers about her flirtations with other men, he leaves. The bad news is relayed to the shoemaker's wife by a young boy with whom she has a close, almost erotic, relationship. Abandoned by the shoemaker, the wife runs a bar where she is pursued by a number of the local men including the mayor; she is also taunted by the villagers for supposedly leading the men on. The shoemaker returns disguised as a puppeteer and tells a story about an unhappy marriage in which a shoemaker's wife encourages one of her many suitors to kill her husband. During the story a knife-fight breaks out offstage, and the villagers claim that the shoemaker's wife is the cause of it. Meanwhile the shoemaker, still disguised, is left alone with his wife and she tells him how much she loves her husband. He reveals his true identity, and she is at once delighted and horrified, but despite her renewed scolding they stand together united against the villagers.

The troubled letters I was getting from my friends in Paris during their beautiful and bitter struggle with abstract art led me to write, by way of reaction, this almost vulgar fable, with its direct version of reality, wherein I wanted to weave an invisible thread of poetry, but where the comic gesture and the humour would stand out clear and undisguised at the surface. . . . [The play] is a simple farce, of a purely classical tone wherein is depicted the spirit of a woman who is just like all other women, and who becomes at the same time, and in a gentle way, an apology for the human soul. Thus it is, then, that the Shoemaker's Wife is at once a type and an archetype; she is a fundamental [*primaria*] creature and a myth of our own pure and unsatisfied idealism.

Lorca, *La Nacion*, Buenos Aires, 30 November 1933,
trans. Reed Anderson, in *Federico Garcia Lorca*, 1984, p. 48 and 51

The Shoemaker's Wonderful Wife is a farce, but more than that it is a poem about the human spirit and the latter is the only really important character in the play. . . .

After all, the shoemaker's wife is not a particular woman but all women. . . . The whole audience has a shoemaker's wife within its bosom. . . .

Lorca, 1933, trans. Gwynne Edwards, in
Spanish Theatre in the Twentieth Century, 1985, p. 89

Lorca's first version of *The Shoemaker's Wonderful Wife* was written in 1926, but the play was not completed until 1930, receiving its premiere at the Teatro Espanol in Madrid on 24 December, the part of the Wife played by the famous Spanish actress, Margarita Xirgu, the costumes designed by Picasso. Sub-titled 'a violent farce', the play is a good example both of a well-established theatrical tradition and an important direction in Lorca's theatre. The tradition of farce in Spain extends from the fifteenth to the twentieth century, embracing such writers as Lope de Rueda and Cervantes in earlier times, and more recently Carlos Arniches and, in particular, Ramon del Valle-Inclan. . . .

As far as style is concerned, *The Shoemaker's Wonderful Wife* embraces both the bold, simplified character of farce and the poetic stylization of symbolism. The setting for Act One, for instance, with its white walls and large window and doors, owes much to the puppet-play tradition in which the sets are frames for exaggerated and vigorous action. On the other hand, the creation of mood and lighting belongs quite clearly to the symbolist theatre of Maeterlinck, W. B. Yeats, and Edward Gordon Craig. When, for example, the butterfly is pursued by the Boy and the Wife, the fading light, the hushed dialogue, and the lovely song addressed to the butterfly evoke a magical, poetic mood that is quite removed from the world of farce, looking back to *The Butterfly's Evil Spell* and forward to moments when Yerma and the daughters of Bernarda Alba dream impossible dreams. . . .

Given these highly poetic moments, the greater influence remains that of farce, and costume, movement, gesture, and language largely contribute to that end through their boldness and exaggeration. . . .

Lorca's achievement in *The Shoemaker's Wonderful Wife* is both to have given a comic form an underlying seriousness and to have created characters who move us both to laughter and to tears.

Gwynne Edwards, Introduction to Lorca, *Plays: Two*, 1990, p. xviii-xxi

The theme of an elderly man married to a young, attractive wife is, of course, an old one, and Lorca was no doubt familiar with many of the precedents, Spanish and otherwise. A manuscript that appears to be an early sketch of the play, written in the style of a folk tale . . . suggests . . . that in his mind were echoing, particularly, reminiscences of Cervantes's *Exemplary Novels* and of Alarcon's novel *The Three-Cornered Hat*: reminiscences most likely prompted by the poet's close knowledge of Falla's ballet *The Three-Cornered Hat* and his tiny opera *Master Peter's Puppet Show*. . . .

The Shoemaker's Prodigious Wife was destined to be one of the poet's most successful works and to be produced, in his lifetime, more than any other of his plays. In it Lorca connected again . . . with the Andalusian popular tradition within which his childhood had developed. And the result was a work of perfect balance and symmetry. Music and snatches of verse taken directly from folk tradition, or invented in accordance with that tradition, and the richly metaphorical language of the Vega: these were to be fundamental elements in the later rural tragedies. As for the theme of the work, here again, despite the guignolesque, farcical aspects and the humour of the play, we find yet another variant of Lorca's omnipresent obsession with amorous frustration and sterility.

Ian Gibson, *Federico Garcia Lorca*, 1989, p. 137-8

On 24 December [1930] the curtain of the Teatro Espanol went up on *The Shoemaker's Prodigious Wife*. That morning the poet explained in a newspaper interview his intentions in the play, stressing the function therein of the chorus (the neighbours who comment on the action), which, he said, now seemed to him an essential element of the theatre. The observation sugggests that Lorca had been reading ancient Greek drama as well as listening to Rivas Cherif, for whom the return of the chorus was a matter of vital importance, and in this respect the play can be seen to look forward to *Blood Wedding* and *Yerma*, where the device is given a much fuller treatment. Lorca was careful to stress that *The*

Shoemaker's Prodigious Wife, whose first version he had begun several years earlier, did not represent his current theatrical practice. 'No', he said in the same interview, 'it isn't my real work. My real work will come later. . . . I've already got something. . . . What's coming later will be my real work. Do you know what I've called it? *The Public*. That's it . . . that's it . . . powerfully, powerfully dramatic. . . .'

The premiere was a success. Lorca himself read the witty prologue to the play ('He could be a splendid actor if he decided to', commented one paper), decked out in a resplendent star-spangled cape, and the audience loved Margarita Xirgu's vivacious Zapatera [Shoemaker's Wife]. Next day Enrique Diez-Canedo, perhaps the most distinguished drama critic in the country, noted the influence of the Andalusian puppet tradition on the work, and praised Salvador Bartolozzi's sets and costumes, which were based on drawings by the poet, themselves in turn influenced by Picasso's for Falla's *Three-Cornered Hat*. In general the other critics were indulgent, although Juan Olmedilla of the *Heraldo de Madrid* was disappointed that after a year in America Lorca had not put on something more modern.

Ian Gibson, *Federico Garcia Lorca*, 1989, p. 307

When Federico visited Argentina [in 1933] . . . the play was presented again, in a new version. Federico modified the 'violent farce' . . . adding songs and dances written especially for the leading lady, Lola Membrives. These additions brought out the play's vaguely ballet-like air, the musical line of its plot, and its stylization in the manner of comic opera, and also sharpened the profiles of the characters. On the occasion of this new production, Federico remarked in an interview (*La Nacion*, 30 November 1933):

'The work which I put on in the Teatro Espanol in Madrid was a chamber version. That production was a more intimate one, but it robbed the play of its true rhythmic perspectives. In reality the true premiere is here in Buenos Aires. The play is now bound together with songs from the eighteenth and nineteenth centuries, danced with extraordinary charm by Lola Membrives and her company.'

Francisco Garcia Lorca, *In the Green Morning*, 1989, p. 171-2

The Shoemaker's Wonderful Wife is the main offering, again cleverly staged against distorted doors and windows, and punctuated by demonic trills from offstage violin and flute. A piercing performance by Penelope Dimond as an all-too-tempestuous wife reduces the pleasures of this modest farce, a sort of *Yerma* with laughs. Delamere's direction of the crowd of village gossips is finely stylized and his company has skills in plenty; Victoria Willmott's shy child singing to a butterfly is a charming moment.

Jeremy Kingston, *The Times*, 23 April 1990

The Billy-Club Puppets

'The Tragicomedy of Don Cristobal and Senorita Rosita, a guignolesque farce in six scenes and an announcement.'
Written: 1928.
First production: Teatro de la Zarzuela, Madrid, 10 Sept. 1937 (dir. Felipe Lluch Garin).

The play is set in an Andalusian town, where the young and romantic Rosita is in love with Cocoliche and plans to marry him. Her impoverished father has, however, arranged for her to marry the brutal braggart Don Cristobita, in exchange for a hundred gold pieces. Cocoliche laments the loss of Rosita and drowns his sorrows in a tavern. Cristobita arrives and beats up Quakeboots, the tavern keeper. Meanwhile Currito, a former lover of Rosita, visits her disguised as a cobbler who has come to try out her wedding shoes. He attempts to elope with Rosita, but Cristobita turns up and he has to hide in a wardrobe. Shortly afterwards Cocoliche arrives and he too has to hide, in another wardrobe. The marriage of Rosita to Cristobita goes ahead but, in the farcical conclusion to the play, Cristobita discovers Rosita in the same room as Cocoliche and Currito. He literally explodes with rage and dies, revealing that he was not in fact a 'real' person but a puppet. Cristobita is given a mock funeral and Rosita, who has rejected the advances of Currito, is left in the arms of Cocoliche.

I'd like, if you can and it's possible, if you could do me the favour of modelling the little puppet heads. Time is running out and I wouldn't like to be on the bad side of those people from my old Residencia.

The head of Cristobal is energetic, brutal, like the club.

Currito el der Puerto is young with a very melancholy character.

Cocoliche is the beautiful child, the singer.

The Mosquito is Shakespeare's Puck, half sprite, half child, half insect.

Figaro is a Figaro.

I ask you not to forget me and to tell me where we could sketch them out. . . .

Lorca, letter to Angel Ferrant, 1935 trans. David Gershator,
in *Federico Garcia Lorca: Selected Letters*, 1983

The Billy-Club Puppets does not contain any clear indication as to the nature of the characters, and more than once I have been asked if it was best to perform the play with marionettes or with people. In the final version the poet seems to want the little characters to be performed by people, and this would mean inverting the procedure typical of the traditional puppet theatre — instead of puppets playing the roles of people, people would act as puppets. This inversion would be much to Federico's liking. When MS. A and MS. B were combined, the plot became much more complex, and perhaps this is why in the final version the characters are apparently to be played by people. But there is no reason why the play cannot be done by puppets. At certain moments, two expert puppeteers would be required.

Of the two manuscripts, A seems more intended for puppets than B. In the sixth and final scene (which comes from MS. A), shortly before the work ends, the stage notes indicate that the characters are indeed puppets. . . . There are no previous indications of this sort, although the situation, movements, and acting have a certain puppet-like quality. Those who have read the work will remember that its denouement revolves around the fact that Don Cristobal is nothing but a mortal puppet, i.e., his mechanism is capable of breaking down. The other characters recognize objectively that he is only a puppet, and automatically place themselves on another level of reality. But, on the whole, the author has given the tragicomedy an ambiguous quality, allowing for both possibilities. This is part of its charm. It is interesting that in the first scenes of MS. A and MS. B there are never more than two characters on stage at the same time. The play grows progressively more complicated but not so much as to be unworkable in a simple puppet theatre.

Francisco Garcia Lorca, *In the Green Morning*,
trans. C. Maurer, 1989, p. 148-9

During the summer of 1922 the Garcia Lorcas made their annual visit out to Asquerosa where, on 5 August, the poet finished the first draft of his 'guignolesque farce' *The Tragicomedy of Don Cristobal and Senorita Rosita*, begun the previous year. Federico wrote excitedly to

Falla, who, it seems, had agreed to write the music for the play, about their projected puppet theatre which now, more realistically, they planned to take to the Alpujarras, the high mountain region south of Granada. . . .

The Tragicomedy of Don Cristobal and Senorita Rosita, which the poet later reworked considerably, was a notable advance on *The Butterfly's Evil Spell.* Lorca, now writing within the Andalusian tradition, had begun to find his authentic voice as a dramatist. The play contains several elements characteristic of the poet's mature work: the subtle exploitation of folk songs; witty, incisive dialogue modelled on the speech habits of the countryfolk of the Granadine plain; the theme of society's suppression of individual liberty. Despite the happy ending of the puppet farce, Rosita's words on love (as she embroiders) anticipate those of Lorca's great protagonists, while looking back to his earliest prose and poems:

'Between priests and fathers we girls have a miserable life. *(She sits down to embroider.)* Every afternoon — three, four — the priest tells us: You're going to be sent to Hell! You'll be done to a frizzle! Worse than dogs. . . . But I say dogs marry whom they wish and have a good time! How I'd like to be a dog! If I obey my father — four, five — life will be a hell on earth, and if I don't, I'll be sent to the other one up there. . . . The priests also could shut up and not talk so much.'

Currito, too, foreshadows Lorca's later protagonists. Because he is a rover he loses Rosita, his great love, for ever. In Lorca, he who hesitates in matters of the heart is lost — always.

Ian Gibson, *Federico Garcia Lorca,* 1989, p. 117-8

The Love of Don Perlimplin and Belisa in the Garden

'An Erotic Print in Four Scenes.'

Written: 1928.

First production: Club Anfistora, Teatro Espanol, Madrid, 5 April 1933 (dir. Lorca).

British productions: Theatre Workshop, St. George's Hall, Kendal, 22 Oct. 1945, then touring nationally until 1949 (trans. Luis Meana and Joan Littlewood; dir. Joan Littlewood).

Don Perlimplin, a confirmed bachelor of fifty, is persuaded by his servant Marcolfa to marry the young and beautiful Belisa.

He is afraid of women and totally inexperienced, but once married he is overwhelmed by Belisa's sexuality. The entry of two sprites marks a transition to a world of fantasy and they reveal a scene of Don Perlimplin in bed with Belisa with golden horns on his head. Don Perlimplin encourages Belisa to discuss her infatuation with a mysterious stranger who sends her erotic letters. Far from being outraged, Don Perlimplin takes on the role of go-between. A secret garden assignation is arranged between Belisa and her lover but Don Perlimplin arrives and she reveals that she is uncontrollably in love with the stranger. Enigmatically, Perlimplin offers to kill her lover so that she can 'feel the eternal love of the dead' and he can be free from his infatuation with her body. He leaves the stage and shortly afterwards the lover appears in a red cape dying of a knife wound in the chest. Belisa embraces him and he removes the red cape from his face to reveal that he is Don Perlimplin himself.

In Fall, 1935, a Spanish jounalist asked Lorca which was his most successful play.

'Successful? None of them! Or perhaps I should say, the ones I haven't yet written. If you ask me which one I like best, I can tell you it's a little play whose true lyricism has scared away professional theatre groups. It is called *The Love of Don Perlimplin. . . .*'

Francisco Garcia Lorca, *In the Green Morning*,
trans. C. Maurer, 1989, p. 185

What I try to do . . . is to bring out the contrast between the lyrical and the grotesque, and to blend one element with the other. This work is supported by music, like a little chamber opera. Its brief scenes are tied together with sonatinas of Scarlatti, and the dialogue is continually interrupted by chords and background music.

Lorca, 1933, quoted in Francisco Garcia Lorca,
In the Green Morning, trans. C. Maurer, 1989, p. 187

At some point, if we can believe Bunuel's memoirs, Dali, who was wildly enthusiastic about *Don Perlimplin*, persuaded a reluctant Lorca to read the play to the budding film director during one of the latter's visits to Madrid. Halfway through Bunuel could stomach no more. 'It's a load of rubbish!' he exclaimed, banging on the table. 'Bunuel's right', Dali now agreed. 'It's a load of rubbish.' According to Bunuel's account, Lorca turned pale and closed the manuscript.

Ian Gibson, *Federico Garcia Lorca*, 1989, p. 157

In *Don Perlimplin*, the poet has delicately woven together the lyrical and the grotesque, cruelty and tenderness, the world of the flesh and the world of the spirit. In these shifting lights we see the timid soul of Perlimplin reach the proportions of a dramatic hero.

Francisco Garcia Lorca, *In the Green Morning*,
trans. C. Maurer, 1989, p. 188

Perhaps *Don Perlimplin*, with its merging of the pathetic and the grotesque, and its disregard for the strictures of surface realism, bears a closer resemblance to Lorca's experimental works than do any of the other comedies. Logical discourse begins to break down in these works and is replaced by sequences of scenes that produce the symbolic quality of dreams, both in their content and in their relationships to one another. The 'logic' of the subjective mind or of the dream prevails though we do not see the same abolition of all logic that was later to characterize European absurdist drama.

Reed Anderson, *Federico Garcia Lorca*, 1984, p. 134

According to a statement of Garcia Lorca this play was already finished in December 1928. Any performance of it, however, was forbidden during the dictatorship of Primo de Rivera, which continued until 1930, not so much because of the sensual exuberance of Belisa but because the protagonist was an officer of the army and it was considered damaging to military dignity for him to be a cuckold, betrayed by the 'five races of the earth'. The play was first performed in April 1933, by the theatrical club 'Anfistora' in Madrid.

Francisco Garcia Lorca, Introduction to Lorca,
Five Plays, 1965, p. 16

Don Perlimplin is lyrical and tragic — it does not belong to the picturesque world of [castanets] and fans but to the world of passions . . . and it realizes its full dramatic quality in the last scene of nocturnal reminiscence. Here the imagination triumphs and the man of flesh and blood perishes whom, in the earlier scenes, we have seen treading the delicate line between the foolish and the poetic. . . . The audience received the work favourably, impressed moreover by Ontanon's design, whose sensitivity to colour and light revealed the deftness of his artistry. Each scene's design lent an appropriate atmosphere, as did the sonatinas of Scarlatti. . . . Ontanon himself played the central role. . . .

M. Fernandez Almagro, *El Sol*, 6 April 1933

Don Perlimplin opened . . . at the end of October [1945] in St. George's Hall, Kendal, and at once became a *cause celèbre*, dividing the theatregoers of the town. Some were so disgusted they crossed the street to avoid me — I was playing Don Perlimplin. Others came up to congratulate me. Today, even Mary Whitehouse would let it go without comment, but I suppose it's not surprising that in that time and place some people were disturbed by an old man's obsession for a woman young enough to be his daughter and by lines like 'between my thighs the sun swims like a fish', sung by a beautiful Swedish actress Kristin Lind.

Howard Goorney, *The Theatre Workshop Story*, 1981, p. 49

The production by Joan Littlewood was excellent, as was the acting of Howard Goorney, Kristin Lind, and Rosalie Williams in the major parts. Mr. Goorney, in particular, worked hard to give a thoughtful study of the elderly Perlimplin stricken by erotomania. What then, was amiss? Was it the translation, which seemed to stress too strongly the desire and sense of frustration which Perlimplin felt, rather than the beautiful sacrifice which he was prepared to make for his young and lovely bride? Or are we in this island less erotic than the Spanish and, therefore, less appreciative of the theme with which this play is concerned?

Westmorland Gazette, 27 Oct. 1945

When Five Years Pass

'A Legend of Time in Three Acts and Five Scenes.'
Written: 1931.
First production: Provincetown Playhouse, New York, 5 April 1945.
First production in Spanish: University of Puerto Rico, Puerto Rico, 22 Nov. 1954 (dir. Victoria Espinosa de Maisonet).
British production: National Student Theatre Company, Edinburgh Festival, 14 Aug. 1989 (trans. Gwynne Edwards; dir. Robert Delamere and Maria Delgado), transferred to Battersea Arts Centre, London, 13 Sept. 1989.

A surrealistic drama about time. The first act is set in a library where the central character, known only as Young Man, reveals to an Old Man that he must wait five years to marry his lover. The Secretary is in love with Young Man, but he rejects her advances. Young Man also meets First Friend, whose approach to life is unashamedly hedonistic, and Second Friend who is afraid of growing old. The act is interrupted by a short scene between a dead child and a dead cat, revealing the transience and cruelty of life. References to time indicate that all the action of Act One takes place at six o'clock. Act Two is set in the bedroom of Young Man's would-be lover. She is seen embracing a silent football player, who unceasingly smokes cigars. When Young Man arrives, she refuses to marry him, and he is forced to confront the illusory nature of his view of her as his willing lover. He then meets a Manikin dressed in a wedding gown, symbol of an unattainable fertility. Young Man now turns his desire to the Secretary. The third act is controlled by Harlequin and a Clown, who offer to help Young Man and the Secretary at the same time as mocking them. The Secretary then declares that she will not be able to marry Young Man until five years have passed. The final scene returns to the library, where three Card Players enter and play out the last moments of Young Man's life. When Young Man plays the ace of hearts, one of the Card Players shoots a silent arrow at a huge image of a heart which appears on the library wall. At this moment Young Man is mortally wounded and the Card Players leave him to die alone. He calls out for help but hears only the echo of his own voice.

When Five Years Pass astonished the group of friends to whom Lorca read it on 4 October 1931, and in an interview in 1936 was described by him as 'unplayable' and 'impossible'. The Spanish premiere did not take place until 1954, at the University of Puerto Rico, and the play was not performed in Spain until 1978 when it opened at the Teatro Eslava in Madrid. Lorca would have been delighted by the kind of critical reaction it then received in the Spanish newspaper *ABC*: 'It seems to me that in *When Five Years Pass* we see the true depth of the great theatrical personality that Garcia Lorca would have become and, probably, his most original and experimental contribution to the theatre.' In expressing his reservations in 1936 Lorca was, of course, acknowledging the limitations created by an extremely conservative theatrical tradition and a theatregoing public that at that time would have howled from the stage a play which had its roots in Surrealism.

Gwynne Edwards, Introduction to Lorca, *Plays: Two*, 1989, p. xxiv-xxv

Though convinced that the extant version of this play is not the final one, it is easy to realize that, even in its present form, we are in the presence of one of the most original poetic dramas in the modern theatre.

Rafael Martinez Nadal, *Lorca's 'The Public'*, 1974, p. 99

We possess very little information about the gestation of *When Five Years Pass*, and only the vaguest indications as to the poet's intentions in the play. On one of the rare occasions on which it appears he talked about these, he was reported as saying: 'It's a mystery play with the characteristics of this genre, a mystery play about time, written in prose and verse.'

Procrastination in love is always, for Lorca, a crime against Nature, as is the masking of true feeling, and it inevitably brings death in its train. The echoes of Lorca's first poems, with their obsessive allusions to lost love, can be heard in all the poet's later work, but perhaps nowhere as insistently as in this modern mystery play, this 'legend about time', as it is subtitled. *When Five Years Pass*, where the traditional and the ultra-modern in Lorca fuse more completely than in any of his other plays, expresses with supreme artistry the poet's anguish about the future, the certainty of death and the impossibility of sexual fulfilment.

Ian Gibson, *Federico Garcia Lorca*, 1989, p. 315

Its direct source was clearly Bunuel's *Un Chien Andalou*, and many points of contact can be discerned between the film and the play in relation both to theme and technique. . . . The themes of both *The Public* and *When Five Years Pass* are typically Lorquian — the characteristic themes of passion, frustration, passing time, and death — but a knowledge of surrealism and of Bunuel's film in particular allowed Lorca to express those themes in an altogether freer and more fluid manner.

Gwynne Edwards, *Spanish Theatre in the Twentieth Century*, 1985, p. 97-8

In *Five Years*, Lorca has used the space of the stage to play out in concrete terms the mystery drama of his protagonist's interior life in its dialectical relationship to his life in the world of other people. The empirical tests for separating interior from exterior, and imaginary from real, no longer apply from the standpoint of the spectator. Though the interpretation of the symbolic roles played by the generically-named figures in this drama may well be done through the methodologies of contemporary literary criticism, Lorca's conception of this work was thoroughly theatrical. The illusory but seductive comforts of fantasy and regressive escapism are symbolically played out onstage, as are the contrastive roles of those who live in time, in the 'real' world, and in constant struggle to seize the moment against the arrival of death.

Reed Anderson, *Federico Garcia Lorca*, 1984, p. 141

Both *When Five Years Pass* and these poems from ten years earlier ['Suite of the Return' and 'Moments of Song'] conjure up a pre-adolescent, almost infantile setting, and suggest once again that in the Young Man Lorca was expressing his own sense of heterosexual failure.

Complementing the frustration that racks both the Young Man and the Typist is their shared obsession with sterility, which looks forward to *Yerma* . . . and back to *Book of Poems* and *Suites*. As for Lorca's ever-present concern with death, in none of his plays is it as insistent as here. And how can we fail to be impressed by the fact that Lorca was killed exactly five years after the day on which he finished a play with this title, and in a manner not dissimilar to that of the Young Man — the victim of a bullet rather than an arrow?

Ian Gibson, *Federico Garcia Lorca*, 1989, p. 317

Much has changed in the theatre since Garcia Lorca wrote (with the apparent freedom of poetry and the rigorous logic of drama) of the vital anguish caused by the passage of time. The simultaneity of temporal planes and the tense poetic language that bring home that idea create a plot in which drama and poetry fuse with rare intensity. I am referring to *When Five Years Have Passed*. The work is inaccessible to 'the many', but this hardly justifies the ineptitude of journalistic critics who have entirely overlooked its far-reaching implications and have found its connection with later authors to be a mere coincidence, both amusing and inexplicable.

Francisco Garcia Lorca, *In the Green Morning*,
trans. C. Maurer, 1989, p. 234

It seems to me that in *When Five Years Have Passed* we see the true depth of the great theatrical personality that Garcia Lorca would have become and, probably, his most original and experimental contribution to the theatre. The Teatro Estable Castellano has embarked boldly, with literary and artistic fervour, on its theatrical adventure. The first production soars above the level of mediocrity in which, with our new freedom, we see our theatre immersed.

ABC, 28 Sept. 1978, trans. Gwynne Edwards,
The Theatre Beneath the Sand, 1980 p. 94

This British premiere of Lorca's haunting prose-poem is beautifully handled. The surreal, dream-like quality of the piece is magically evoked by Gwynne Edwards's taut, lyrical translation; . . . Nick Barnes's designs (empty trunks, dust-covered windows and surreal clocks); David Stewart's exquisite lighting, and measured and effective use of violin and clarinet. Time ticks inexorably by, as love is lost and found, and destiny and malevolent human nature extinguish life and hope. Robert Delamere and Maria Delgado's production doesn't quite sustain the two-hour duration of the piece, but this is mature, life-enhancing work. . . .

Lyn Gardner, *City Limits*, 7 Sept. 1989

The Puppet Play of Don Cristobal

'A farce for puppets.'
Written: 1931.
First production: Book Fair, Madrid, 11 May 1935 (with Lorca as the puppeteer).
British production: Ragazzi Theatre Company, Battersea Arts Centre, 18 April 1990 (trans. Gwynne Edwards; dir. Robert Delamere).

After a dispute between the poet and the director, the brutish Don Cristobal is called on stage and told to play a doctor. He then beats up a patient and steals his money so that he can buy off Dona Rosita from her mother. Once married, Cristobal gets drunk and falls asleep while Dona Rosita, whose essential characteristic is an insatiable desire for sex, has brief assignations with Currito, the poet and the patient. Rosita then gives birth to quins and Cristobal kills her mother in fury, at which point the director stops the play and delivers an epilogue in praise of the Andalusian puppet-play.

In the puppet figure Lorca saw an opportunity for that freedom of expression, spontaneity, and vitality which he felt to be the vital ingredients of a living theatre. The puppets could, in short, express action and emotion in a simple, bold, direct, and dramatic manner that for Lorca was the very essence of theatre. In the prologue to [*The Puppet Play of Don Cristobal*] he has the poet refer to 'el delicioso y duro lenguaje de los munecos' ('the delicious and hard language of the puppets'). . . . And when, at the end of the play, the director gathers in the puppets, he draws a revealing distinction between the liveliness of puppet-theatre and the stale naturalism of contemporary Spanish theatre:

Gwynne Edwards,
Spanish Theatre in the Twentieth Century, 1985, p. 87

Ladies and Gentlemen. The peasants of Andalusia often watch this kind of play beneath the grey branches of the olive trees, or in the darkness of abandoned stables. Amongst the eyes of mules, as hard as fists, embroidered leather harnesses from Cordoba, and heaps of damp and tender ears of corn, the words we wouldn't tolerate in cities where the air is thick with alcohol and games of cards explode, with joy and charming innocence. Those bad and vulgar words take on a fresh simplicity when spoken by the puppets as they recreate the magic of this ancient rural farce. So let us fill the theatre with fresh and pure wheat and hear upon the stage vulgarities that overwhelm the tedious triviality to which it is condemned. Let us honour today in the puppet-show the Andalusian Don Cristobal, cousin to the Galician Bululu and brother-in-law to Aunt Norica from Cadiz; brother of Monsieur Guignol from Paris, and uncle to Don Arlechino from Bergamo. He is a character in whom the pure ancient spirit of the theatre still survives.

Concluding speech of the Director from
The Puppet Play of Don Cristobal,
trans. Gwynne Edwards, in Lorca, *Plays: Two*, 1990

Don Cristobal, you are a mainstay of the theatre, all theatre originates from you. There was once a poet in England called Shaespeare who created a character called Falstaff, who is your son.

Lorca, 'Dialogue between the Poet and Don Cristobal',
Obras Completas, III, 1986, p. 455-6

What the poet now prefers is crude, raw, even salacious language. This style is closer to genuine popular theatre. The author does not even construct a plot; the play is no more than a series of scenes held together by the main character. There are more authentic expressions and an increase in the amount of verse. The poet makes use of the absurd chains of verse that are often found in children's rhymes.

Francisco Garcia Lorca, *In the Green Morning*, trans. C. Maurer, 1989, p. 152-3

Lorca's interest in puppet theatre began at an early age and continued into adult life. His own puppet-play, *The Girl Who Waters the Basil Plant*, was presented at the children's festival in Granada in 1923. A second puppet-play, *Tragicomedy of Don Cristobal and Miss Rosita*, may even have preceded this, while the third, *The Puppet Play of Don Cristobal*, was completed in 1931 and presented at the Book Fair in Madrid in 1935 with Lorca himself manipulating the puppets.

Like farce, the puppet-play belongs to an old Spanish tradition, while in the early part of the twentieth century Ramon del Valle-Inclan and Jacinta Grau wrote interesting and significant plays for puppets. . . . Outside Spain the view of man as a puppet-figure manipulated by forces outside himself was strong throughout the 'twenties, finding expression, for example, in the plays of Pirandello, and revealing the extent to which a comic tradition could be used to express serious ideas.

Gwynne Edwards, Introduction to Lorca, *Plays: Two*, 1990, p. xxiii

The Puppet Play of Don Cristobal permits a crude portrayal of voraciousness, both physical and financial. Like the frenzied farce of *The Shoemaker's Wonderful Wife*, it is an unsentimental attack on the conflicts arising from outmoded social constraints in a mutating society.

Louise Kingsley, *The Independent*, 25 April 1990

Blood Wedding

'A tragedy in three acts and seven scenes.'
Written: 1932.
First production: Teatro Beatriz, Madrid, 8 March 1933 (dir. Lorca).
British productions: Arts Theatre, London, 3 March 1954 (trans. Richard L. O'Connell and James Graham-Lujan; dir. Peter Hall); Nottingham Playhouse, 19 March 1956 (trans. Richard L. O'Connell and James Graham-Lujan; dir. Kosta Spaic of Yugoslav National Drama Theatre); Leeds Playhouse, 14 Feb. 1973 (trans. and dir. David Carson); Edinburgh Festival, 23 Aug. 1982 (flamenco interpretation by Antonio Gades Ballet of Spain); Royal Lyceum

Theatre, Edinburgh, 22 Aug. 1986 (dir. Jose Luis Gomez for Teatro de la Plaza); Contact Theatre, Manchester, 11 Nov. 1987 (trans. Gwynne Edwards; dir. Anthony Clark); Communicado Theatre Company, Lyceum Studio, Edinburgh, 14 Aug. 1988 (trans. David Johnston; dir. Gerard Mulgrew), transferred to Donmar Warehouse, London, 26 Sept. 1988; National Youth Theatre, Bloomsbury Theatre, London, 15 Sept. 1988 (trans. Michael Dewell and Carmen Zapata; dir. Edward Wilson); Asian Co-operative Theatre, Half Moon Theatre, London, 6 Oct. 1989 (trans. Jonathan Martin and Mary Ann Vargas; dir. Jonathan Martin).

Film version: as *Bodas de sangre*, 1976 (dir. Irene Papas); based on the flamenco interpretation by Antonio Gades Ballet Company, 1981 (dir. Carlos Saura).

In the arid hinterland of southern Spain a wedding is planned between two peasant families. With the exception of one character, Leonardo Felix, all participants in the drama remain nameless. The Mother of the Bridegroom has forebodings about the marriage when she learns from a neighbour that her son's fiancee was formerly engaged to Leonardo Felix, since both the husband and elder son of the Mother were killed in a long-running feud with the Felixes. Leonardo himself is now married with a baby, and another is on the way, but by the end of Act One it is evident that he is secretly visiting the Bride. The wedding celebrations begin in Act Two, but the Bride's attitude to the Bridegroom is cold. Leonardo is one of the guests and his presence reawakens her old passion for him. The tension increases until news suddenly breaks that the Bride has neglected her 'duty' and run off with Leonardo. The two families immediately set out in pursuit of the elopers through a forest. The Bridegroom is led to Leonardo by the figure of Death, disguised as an Old Beggar Woman, and both Leonardo and the Bridegroom are killed in an ensuing knife fight, which takes place offstage but is revealed by a conversation between the Old Beggar Woman and the Moon. Finally, the Bride returns to the house of the Bridegroom's Mother and declares, in a bitter confrontation, that her son's honour is still intact, since she is still a virgin and Leonardo is dead. The play concludes with the Mother, the Bride, and Leonardo's Wife united in their grief.

The more general problem of mixing prose and poetry throughout the play had been an overriding concern of Lorca's in rehearsals. . . . He had his own vision of the balance that should be sought:

'[*Blood Wedding* is] no more than a dramatic work put together with the rhythmic hammer blows of verse from the first to the last scenes. Free and solid prose can attain high levels of expressiveness, allowing us an outpouring that would be impossible within the rigidity of metrical forms. Poetry is welcome at those moments where the development and the tension of the theme require it. Never at any other time. In accord with that formula, you can see in *Blood Wedding* that up until the epithalamic scene, verse does not appear with any of the breadth and intensity one might expect, and it dominates absolutely the scene in the forest and the drama's final scene.'

When asked what he would call the most gratifying part of the drama, Lorca said, 'The one where the Moon and Death intervene as elements and symbols of fate. The realism that predominates in the tragedy up to that point is broken and disappears to give way to poetic fantasy where I naturally feel as comfortable as a fish in water.'

Reed Anderson, *Federico Garcia Lorca*, 1984, p. 102-3

To some critics this is the play which best achieves an integration of poetry and drama. It is the most spontaneous and simple because the poet does not struggle against his poetic instinct; he gives himself over to it, but without forgetfulness of his previous experiences.

Francisco Garcia Lorca,
Introduction to Lorca, *Three Tragedies*, 1961, p. 24-25

Those who recall certain ballads of Garcia Lorca will not have failed to recognize last night, in each and every one of the seven scenes which comprise *Blood Wedding*, the same violent, electric atmosphere, an analogous landscape — presented rather than written — a similar game with effects by means of simple language or passion which overwhelms movement. . . . The Spanish of Andalusia, wild and passionate people in a difficult landscape . . . doubtless, their geographical situation is a great influence upon them. It controls them and is, ultimately, their tragedy. What happens is that scene and characters fuse into a single accord of violence, love and hate. . . . What most impressed me, in *Blood Wedding*, was just this: the spirit which moves it all, a breath which comes from very far and very deep, the soul of a primitive people. The same soul of *Gypsy Ballads* which doesn't refer to the Andalusians of the East or the West, of inland or coast, but to the Andalusians in their deepest historical and psychological perspective. . . . From scene to scene the effects are executed with magisterial skill, harmonizing those which are purely literary with those of the [dramatic] situation, served by certain mural or choral equivalents, as in the first scene of Act Two which certainly turned the expectant attitude of the audience into real enthusiasm.

M. Fernandez Almagro, *El Sol*, 9 March 1933

The premiere of *Blood Wedding* took place in the Beatriz Theatre, Madrid, on 8 March 1933, a month or so before the fleeting presentation of *Perlimplin.* I attended the rehearsals directed by Federico, in which he showed he was already a skilled director. He had to struggle with actors unaccustomed to a style entirely opposed to ordinary theatre, for in *Blood Wedding* stage movement and language have a depth of music that is brought out by the verse. The actor who played the Bridegroom seemed an almost insurmountable obstacle. He was an excellent actor, but he had made his name in light comedy, and was hardly able to conquer the image that the public — and he himself — had formed of his talent. There were other problems with the Woodcutters in the forest scene: Federico had to resign himself to letting the actors (mediocre ones, who had probably never spoken a line of verse on stage) play their roles in their own manner. It is the only time I ever saw my brother lose patience as a director. But of course later on, after the premiere, he congratulated them warmly. . . .

Blood Wedding was Federico's first great success as a playwright. It seemed to confirm his potential as a dramatic poet, and it showed that the public was capable of accepting a theatre with noble artistic intentions and room for poetry and fantasy. At the end of the second act, on the night of the premiere, Federico was called onstage by the audience. I would rather narrate this in someone else's words: 'The whole theatre bursts into a frenzied ovation, calling for the author. . . . Once they have fallen silent, and their enthusiasm has been calmed, the play continues.' It was the success of *Blood Wedding* which led to the poet's triumphal visit to Buenos Aires and Montevideo [1933-34].

Francisco Garcia Lorca, *In the Green Morning*, 1989, p. 201-2

Before *Blood Wedding* was a play, it was a short newspaper account in *El Defensor de Granada*, one of the local papers. I remember Federico reading to me an account of a bride from Almeria who, on her wedding day, ran off with her former lover. The bridegroom followed them and the two men killed each other. . . . Apparently, after this, the newspaper account was forgotten; yet some time later Federico told me of an idea he had for a tragedy — it was based on the incident in Almeria. Then, for some time, the play would seem to have been forgotten again. This process of letting a play write itself was my brother's method. He never consciously wrote down a play's outline.

Francisco Garcia Lorca, 'From Granada to Bleeker Street', *New York Times*, 30 Jan. 1949

Communicado, under the direction of Gerard Mulgrew, has always been known for its willingness to mingle moods and to blend discordant styles, but never has their talent been put to better use than in their passionate, deeply felt, and brilliantly executed staging of Lorca's tragedy with its poetic speech and appearance of the Moon and Death on stage. It would be easy to set this work in some fairyland forlorn, but Barbara Rafferty, as the Mother who moves from the affectionate, couth, hearty figure to the desolate female facing despair, and Alyxsis Daly as the bustling, gossipy, nosey maid endow their characters with a down-to-earth, familiar feel and these two marvellous performances provide a context and a sense of felt experience, and from that base in reality the work can move beyond all periods and place.

It may be that the play dramatizes a clash between unexpressed inner need and imposed external control, and the production conveys these overwhelming passions by a switch between peasant chatter and a solemn liturgy. I could never have imagined that there is any humour at all in this piece, but the laughter fades before the brooding presence of Leonardo (Benny Young), or the urgent, frustrated sensuality so well caught by Alison Peebles's performance and most of all by the music (composed by Karen Wimhurst and sung by Judah Collins and Moyra Paterson) or by the choral movements of the whole company which transform this from an individual to a collective tragedy.

It is a pity, and a little confusing, that it is necessary to double up for the characters of Moon and Death however powerfully Graham Vallentine and Alyxsis Daly perform the roles.

David Johnston's translation has, in turns, the lilt of song and the flint of peasant speech, and the production, which opens vistas and touches the heart, indicates how poetic drama can be done with powerful effect on the modern stage.

Joseph Farrell, *The Scotsman*, 17 Aug. 1988

'A bit funny to have Scottish voices' — an English voice overheard at the interval. By the end of the play such quibbles were stilled.

It is pointless to compare Communicado's *Blood Wedding* to the haunting Spanish version seen at the official festival two years ago. This production of Lorca's stark tragedy of sexual passion lacks a little polish, and the sense of authenticity wavers — but not the inventiveness of Gerry Mulgrew's direction and the commitment of the seven actors and two singers.

The outline is spare: a bride is carried away by the man she once loved, a member of the family who killed the groom's father and brother in a blood feud. Swift revenge is inevitable. There are moments when the tension flags (I can't make up my mind about Karen Wimhurst's music, which sometimes I found distracting) but the emotional force built up in the final scenes is overwhelming. From the wit of the dumb-show wedding speeches to the savagely brief double killing (via the soliloquy of the watching moon — surprisingly, male — and the intervention of a Highland speywife), the tension hardly slackens, and the final moments of stillness and poetry are devastating. The thin blood-scarred skein of wool wound up at the end is one of many effective visual symbols.

Barbara Rafferty gives a fine performance of controlled anguish as the mother whose life is left in ashes, and when the control breaks she is electrifying, Alyxsis Daly's servant, in a nice contrast, is solidly down to earth. I admired David Johnston's lean resonant translation.

John Fowler, *Glasgow Herald*, 18 Aug. 1988

The Half Moon's production of *Blood Wedding* finds a suitable correlative for Lorca's Spanish peasants. The Asian Co-operative Theatre transports the play to a vaguely Asian location, and this transportation makes the rigidities and conventions of Lorca's peasants seem freshly appropriate.

The choral passages, sung rather than declaimed to the haunting, ominous accompaniment of Akintayo Akinbode's music, no longer sound arch. But Ashley Martin Davies's setting — a bald open space, with an occasional silvered tree brought on — and Jonathan Martin's production lack erotic voltage and tension or devices to deal with the culminating symbolism. And the acting — particularly Mona Hammond's tragedy-queen Mother — is often out of key.

Nicholas de Jongh, *The Guardian*, 16 Oct. 1989

Lorca's powerful and poetic tale of a smouldering passion which leaps into brief life in the barren lands of rural Spain is a finely tuned work of restraint and abandon, the stiff tradition of duty and honour against the hot, consuming longing of the lovers' desire. When a bride abandons her groom at the wedding feast to run away with her lover, family honour dictates that the pair be hunted down and vengeance swiftly and bloodily satisfied. The Asian Co-operative Theatre and Half Moon's staging only fleetingly captures the unique fluid rhythms of Lorca's writing and fails to achieve the heights of a passion which surges with the sudden unstoppable force of a broken dam. In Jonathan Martin's production, strains of the sitar blend eloquently with the sound of Spain and Peggy Phango lends her rich voice to moving effect, but of the rest of the cast only Mona Hammond stands out as the mother who mourns in hatred and bitterness but whose spirit blazes through in brilliant glimpses of the woman she could have been.

Helen Rose, *Time Out*, 11 Oct. 1989

Lorca's masterpiece is simple and robust enough to stand anything I have ever seen a director do to it, and Martin's sturdy, sure production is among the most convincing. A joint effort from the Half Moon and the Asian Co-operative Theatre, it is somewhat tenuously justified by the fact that Western Europe's Gypsies are said to have originated in Rajasthan. More to the point are the similarities between the rigorous codes of honour of Lorca's Andalusia, and those of traditional Asian culture. . . . Martin uses the width of the Half Moon stage to create an airy Andalusia of baked terracotta walls and cruel white light, an arena of suitable aridity for the gory tragedy. Performances are stark and precisely delineated; properly, there is never much doubt in their purpose or the outcome. Nor do you detect much indecision in the early scenes between Leonardo (Okon Jones) and the Bride (Janet Steel): their love is a fact as remorseless as the harsh world they inhabit.

This severity makes Lorca's graceful notes ring out with shocking clarity. Martin and the Peruvian actor Mary Ann Vargas have provided a new translation that is sober and beautiful, using simple, earthy epithets: the Bride 'as soft as wool', the Bridegroom leaving to hunt her down 'like a raging star'.

But the great pleasure is the pacing: from a disconcertingly leisured start the rush towards disaster is an obsessedly determined acceleration: the ritual of the wedding feast slips easily into the ritual of the hunt, the villagers brandishing their hoes and sickles like sacrificial knives then rushing to the woods like maenads. . . .

Alex Renton,
The Independent, 17 Oct. 1989

Yerma

'Tragic Poem in Three Acts and Six Scenes.'
Written: 1934.

First production: Teatro Espanol, Madrid, 29 Dec. 1934 (dir. Cipriano Rivas Cherif; with Margarita Xirgu).
British productions: Arts Theatre, London, 31 July 1957 (trans. James Graham-Lujan and Richard L. O'Connell); Aldwych Theatre, London, 17 April 1972 (dir. Victor Garcia; with Nuria Espert), revived Aldwych Theatre, London, 2 April 1973, and Royal Lyceum Theatre, Edinburgh, 19 August 1986; People's Theatre, Newcastle-upon-Tyne, 10 Oct. 1978 (trans. Ian Macpherson and Jacqueline Minett; dir. David Hankin); National Theatre, London, 26 March 1987 (trans. Peter Luke; dir. Di Trevis; with Juliet Stevenson); Cracked Mirror Theatre Company, touring production, Jan.-April 1990 (trans. David Johnston; dir. Olivia Fuchs).
Radio productions: BBC Third Programme, 12 Nov. 1950 (trans. Roy Campbell; revised and adapted E. A. Harding and R. M. Nadal; dir. E. A. Harding); BBC Radio 3, 17 Dec. 1961 (operatic version by Denis ApIvor; prod. Dennis Arundell; libretto Montagu Slater).

Yerma (the name derives from the word 'yermo' meaning barren) passionately longs for a son, but her husband is more interested in making money from his farm than making love. Although she is sexually attracted to Victor, a neighbouring shepherd, her sense of honour prevents her from following her instincts. Yerma's apparent infertility is contrasted with signs of natural vitality all around her. She seeks a cure for her apparent sterility from Dolores, a sorceress, but her absences from home only serve to further her estrangement from Juan. Mocked for her childlessness and suspected of infidelity, she is finally driven to despair and, in a climactic frenzy, she murders Juan, thereby destroying the son she longs for.

I am working hard. Now I shall finish *Yerma*, a second tragedy. The first was *Bodas de sangre* [*Blood Wedding*]. *Yerma* will be the tragedy of the barren woman. The theme, as you know, is a classical one. But I want to develop it in a new way. A tragedy with four main characters and a chorus, as tragedies should be. It is necessary to return to tragedy. The tradition of our theatre compels us to do so.

Lorca, interviewed in 1934, trans. Gwynne Edwards, in *Spanish Theatre in the Twentieth Century*, 1985, p. 103

'*Yerma* is a tragedy. A tragedy based on honour. From the very outset, the audience supposes that something awful is going to happen.'

'And what happens?'

'What happens? *Yerma* has no plot. Yerma is a character who develops in the six scenes that make up the work. As befits a tragedy, I have supplied a chorus which comments on the action, or the theme of the tragedy, which is always the same. Notice that I said "theme". I repeat, *Yerma* has no plot.'

Lorca, interviewed in Sept. 1935,
In the Green Morning, trans. C. Maurer, 1989, p. 211

Yerma, an essentially tragic figure that I have put in modern dress, is above all else the image of fertility condemned to remain sterile. A soul singled out by Destiny to be a victim of sterility. . . . And it is this contrast between sterile and life-giving principles which gives the play its tragic tension. . . . Six scenes. Of these, three are interiors with an intensely concentrated, dramatic mood charged with silent emotion, and which materially reflect a state of spiritual torment. The other three scenes, with their natural atmosphere and colour, are like bright candles burning in the darkness of the tragedy. The main characters take a subordinate role in these latter scenes, in which the sole protagonists are the choruses, conceived in the Greek manner. These choruses, which I used for the first time in *Bodas de sangre* [*Blood Wedding*] are more fully developed in *Yerma*, where they acquire greater importance.

Lorca, *Obras Completas*, III, 1986 p. 616-17,
trans. Jacqueline Minett, in *Yerma*, 1987, p. 34

A confluence of traditional Spanish theatre tendencies, plastic and musical, is brought about in this play. This is achieved in a purer classical conception, toward which the poet turned his eyes in search for simplicity and sobriety.

Francisco Garcia Lorca,
Introduction to Lorca, *Three Tragedies*, 1961, p. 26

As for the final dance in the pilgrimage scene of *Yerma*, it comes from a dance of northern Spain, from Asturias I think, and perhaps it is bacchic in origin. It is danced by a man and a woman. He carries a horn, and she, I seem to recall, a wreath of flowers. I do remember very clearly the dialect names of the two objects carried by the dancers: the *pilueta* and the *tronaor*. Federico has brought out the erotic character of the dance and has given masks to the couple.

From this pagan feeling, placed in a poetic social setting (where religious ceremony acquires the character of an ancient rite); from the mixture of instinct and tradition; from the blind, individual passion, punctuated by cries of collective encouragement — from all this is woven the central character — a poetic, tragically solitary creature, born amid the almost miraculous fertility of our lands in the Vega of Granada.

Francisco Garcia Lorca, *In the Green Morning*,
trans. C. Maurer, 1989, p. 218-19

The language of the play, far from being realistic, corresponds to the characters' obsessions and is distinguished throughout by its highly patterned and structured character. Quite apart from the songs, which occur at moments of great emotional intensity, the prose dialogue itself often has the rhythm and the emotional quality of music, as much expressive of Yerma's joy and enthusiasm as of her despair. Indeed, in its closely integrated pattern of stage settings, costumes, movement, lighting, dialogue, and music, *Yerma* illustrates supremely well the theory and practice of European symbolist producers and writers like Craig, Appia, Maeterlinck, Yeats, and Wilde. It is surely no coincidence that when the play was presented in Madrid in December 1934, it was directed by Cipriano Rivas Cherif, who had studied the work of Gordon Craig in Italy.

Gwynne Edwards,
Spanish Theatre in the Twentieth Century, 1985, p. 113

As early as 1918 Lorca had evoked in the poem 'Elegy' . . . the plight of a Granada spinster . . . whom he imagined to be waiting in vain not only for a husband but for the day when she would be a mother; and, where his theatre was concerned, he had already touched on the theme of maternal frustration in *When Five Years Pass*. Moreover, on a personal level, Lorca was poignantly aware of his own 'sterility' as a homosexual, as can be seen from some of the *Suites*, poems in *Songs*, and the sonnet 'Adam', written in New York. . . . It was almost inevitable, therefore, that sooner or later he should have written a play exclusively devoted to the theme of infecundity. . . .

Lorca explained that Yerma is a victim of the Spanish code of honour which is almost part of her blood and bone, and which, once she has made the fatal mistake of marrying a man for whom she does not feel passion, prevents her from opting out and looking for a suitable partner. Implicit in *Yerma* is the rejection of the rigidities of Spanish Catholicism, as the Right was quick to see when the play was produced in December 1934. And the rejection, too, of machismo, which relegates women to the category of second-rate citizens, of penned-up sheep.

Ian Gibson, *Federico Garcia Lorca*, 1989, p. 356

Victor Garcia, the producer, abolished all literal details of scene and stage furniture, and put in their place a dirt-coloured trampoline on which characters moved as though walking on thick sand. The setting was of no colour; its lifelessness became the symbolic background against which the tragic drama took on added strength and meaning. By mechanical means, in the Romeria scene, this device was raised to become a mural background for the hanging vision of Yerma's inflamed dream. The performance brilliantly justified Federico's confidence in the powers of imagination when making use of surrealist means. In literal productions, *Yerma* had been poetic but not convincing. Here, with an avant-garde setting and interpretation, decades after its author had felt the first force of that theory, *Yerma* came into its own.

Mildred Adams,
Garcia Lorca: Playwright and Poet, p. 198-9

In rhythmically structured dialogue, Lorca returns again and again in the play to the same themes: female frustration and oppression, the life-denying Spanish code of honour, the stale conventions of a society that equates fertility with moral virtue.

What gives the play its power, however, is the tension between Yerma's physical longing for motherhood and the forces that deny it: the dry sexlessness of her husband, the rigid code that prevents her absconding with the shepherd Victor by whom she is profoundly stirred, the fearful ethic that 'a woman who doesn't bear children is as useless as a bunch of thistles'.

The subject of the play is Yerma's barrenness; but beyond that Lorca is attacking (as much as Ibsen in *Ghosts*) the barrenness of a society in thrall to dead ideas and the stranglehold of the past. Realizing this on stage is no easy matter since Lorca's six scenes cut from the bottled-up hell of Yerma's home to washerwomen at work in the streams, and pagan fertility rights before a mountain shrine.

To accommodate this the designer Pamela Howard, with Bunny Christie, has transformed the Cottesloe into a rectangular, stone-floored playing area with the audience on four sides and linen draped from the galleries. But . . . I feel that Di Trevis doesn't always make best use of the space she has been offered. The scene with the washerwomen singing of fertility as they pound the floor with wet clothes has exactly the right earthy vitality. But the Bacchanalian ritual in the hills, embodied by some tasteful gipsy dancing accompanied by a decorous trio on guitar and violin, is about as far from pagan sexuality as a night in an ethnic Spanish eaterie in West London.

Ms. Trevis captures perfectly well the puritan restrictiveness of Spanish rural life: I liked the treatment of Yerma's two dried-up sisters-in-law as a couple of silently gliding house detectives in black and also Roger Lloyd Pack's haggard, haunted watchfulness as Yerma's suspicious husband. What I missed is any visual suggestion of the mocking vitality of nature and much real sense of passion lurking beneath the surface.

About Juliet Stevenson's Yerma (which has to carry much of the play) I also feel equivocal. She conveys grief, waste and the self-censorship of a woman bound by honour: Ms. Stevenson is very good . . . at unflinching moral integrity. But however dutifully she massages her thighs or talks of sticking needles in her eyeballs, I don't get much feeling (until she strangles her husband) of a woman of overwhelming and implacable passion. . . .

Ms. Trevis's production has the vitue of clarity but, because wedded to the English naturalistic style, misses the fierce, imaginative quality at the heart of Lorca's tragic poem.

Michael Billington, *The Guardian*, 28 March 1987

The Cottesloe auditorium, hung on four sides with washing, encloses audience and performers in an intimate and claustrophobic world dominated by women and by the suppressed passions of their lives. It ironically suggests a womb — a hidden, secret, life-giving place — and Di Trevis's exciting production is suffused with the earthy atmosphere of nature and the rhythms of peasant life. Yerma is a woman who understands these rhythms, who loves the rain on her face, the earth beneath her feet; who feels the intuitive sensuality of her body but is cursed with a dry, passionless husband and an empty womb. Her tragedy is that first her innocence and later her honour prevent her from fulfilling her spiritual and physical desires with her childhood sweetheart Victor. Instead she remains resolutely faithful to Juan (cold, hard control from Roger Lloyd-Pack) who, sensing her desperate need for the children he refuses to give her, locks her up with his pinched, frigid, spectral sisters as guardians.

As Yerma, Juliet Stevenson is totally compelling; whether caressing a young pregnant girl's belly in awe or reaching between her thighs for the cursed menstrual blood of her despair, she tears at the heart with the depth of her anguish. This is an excellent production: intuitive, intelligent, and moving.

Helen Rose, *Time Out*, 1 April 1987

Director Di Trevis has cleverly rearranged the Cottesloe so that the audience represents the sides of two mountains and the action unfolds in the valleys below.

There's more than a touch of the films of Carlos Saura in this rendering of Lorca's earthy, rural tragedy, and if, overall, the production never quite achieves the heights of sensuality, poetry, and hot-blooded passion one would hope for, never mind, for Juliet Stevenson in the title role will set the heart racing. It is an extraordinary performance — a heady mix of instinct and intelligence that is convincing physically, vocally, and psychologically.

Lyn Gardner, *City Limits*, 2 April 1987

At the Cottesloe Theatre, *Yerma*, Lorca's meditation on the theme of female fecundity and the tragic consequences of its denial, proves rather intractable to Di Trevis's company. Here is a lot of intelligent work, a lot of effortful adaptation — but I never could forget the intelligence and the effort, nor the stubborn Englishness of the enterprise. Juliet Stevenson, so good at playing women in whom passion and probity run in equal measure, never convinced me as the peasant woman who is all passion; nor the lanky and thoughtful-featured Roger Lloyd-Pack, whom I last saw playing Kafka, as her simple shepherd husband. There is a telling moment when he lets his arms hang limply by his side as she embraces him: she picks one of them up and puts it round her. The gesture seemed to sum up the futility of her febrile pleas for any kind of love.

Victoria Radin, *New Statesman*, 3 April 1987

Images of water lap refreshingly through his play's verse speeches while metaphors of heat, dryness, and parching convey menace and misery. Illustrating the everyday naturalness of such imagery to his Andalusian peasants, this production emphasizes the carrying of pitchers of water from the well, the white-hot sun baking down on black-shawled women, the river-bank where laundresses splash and pound linen.

The laundresses' scene, one of the set pieces, is staged with particular vigour at the Cottesloe. Brimming with animal vitality, folk lore, and raucous realism, it provides an exuberant epitome of Lorca's dramatic world — and, like many of the play's episodes, is entirely female. The men in *Yerma* are in fact rather lacklustre — and at the Cottesloe receive lacklustre renderings. Where Di Trevis excels is in recreating a community of peasant women as vividly as Juliet Stevenson displays the unused maternal energies tearing her apart.

Peter Kemp, *The Independent*, 28 March 1987

As a homosexual in a very intolerant society, Lorca was always concerned with the problems of social pressures and expectations. *Yerma* . . . can be seen as an allegory of his own predicament. The play has been well translated by Peter Luke, who spent ten years as a farmer in Andalusia, and is obviously familiar not just with the Spanish language but also with country life in Spain.

As the play opens, Yerma — the adjective *yermo* means 'waste', 'uncultivated' — has been married for two years and is still childless. This is the rural Spain of the 1930s, where women are expected to be childbearers, and she feels profoundly that she has failed. Her friends and husband are affectionately reassuring, but as the years go by her obsession provides a second reason for setting her apart from others.

Juliet Stevenson, in the title role, is memorable, her face and body expressing her gathering absorption in the one desire. Her movements become stiffer, rigid with longing, as she pleads with her husband, who is more interested in making money for his sheep and not really concerned at having a family, to spend more time with her. Di Trevis's production was largely successful in creating a credible ambience, but some momentum was lost in the final scenes of bacchanalian revels, so that the intensity essential for the play's shocking end was missing.

Della Couling, *The Tablet*, 18 April 1987

Dona Rosita the Spinster

Subtitled 'A poem of 1900 Granada, divided into various gardens, with scenes of song and dance' and 'The Language of Flowers'.

Written: 1935.

First production: Teatro Principal Palace, Barcelona, 12 Dec. 1935 (dir. Cipriano Rivas Cherif; with Margarita Xirgu).

British productions: RADA, London, 30 April 1956 (trans. C. A. Rossner; dir. Ellen Pollock); Hampstead Theatre Club, London, 7 March 1965 (adapt. Selma Vas Diaz, from trans. C. A. Rossner); Nuria Espert Company, Royal Lyceum Theatre, Edinburgh, 30 Aug. 1983 (dir. Jorge Lavelli); Theatre Royal, Bristol, 12 Oct. 1989 (trans. Gwynne Edwards; dir. Phyllida Lloyd).

Radio productions: BBC Third Programme, 10 Feb. 1957 (adapt. Selma Vas Diaz, from trans. C. A. Rossner).

In the romantic city of Granada, in the late nineteenth century, the orphan Dona Rosita lives with her uncle, aunt, and nurse.

She falls in love with her cousin, but he is called away to Argentina on family business, though he promises that he will come back and marry her. Fifteen years later, in one of his infrequent letters, he proposes marriage by proxy, and Dona Rosita agrees. However, he fails to return and marries in Argentina. After the uncle's death, the family are forced to move home and Dona Rosita is doomed to end her days a spinster.

In *Dona Rosita* I wanted to create a poem about my childhood in Granada in which there appear characters and settings which I knew and felt deeply about.

This is the moving drama of Andalusian and Spanish spinsterhood in general. Spain is the country of respectable spinsters, of pure women, victims of the sociey in which they live.

As a change from *Yerma* and *Blood Wedding*, both of them tragedies, I wanted to write a simple and pleasing comedy; but I have failed to achieve it, because what I have achieved is a poem that is even sadder than my previous two plays. . . .

Lorca, quoted in programme note,
Theatre Royal, Bristol, production, Oct. 1989

It will be a piece full of gentle ironies and touches of tender caricature; a comedy of middle-class manners, soft-toned, imbued with the charm and delicacy of past moments and periods. I think that people will be surprised by this evocation of time past, when the nightingales really sang and the gardens and flowers were topics for novels. That wonderful period when our parents were young. First the days of the hooped skirt; then, bell-shaped skirts and the hobble: 1890, 1900, 1910.

Lorca, quoted in Ian Gibson,
Federico Garcia Lorca, 1989, p. 395

It is not simply another good play amongst the few that exist in the modern Spanish theatre. . . . It is an extraordinary play by a writer who combines his great talent as a poet with his equally outstanding gifts as a dramatist.

Antonio Espina, *El Sol*, 15 Dec. 1935, trans. Gwynne Edwards,
in *The Theatre Beneath the Sand*, 1980, p. 208

The poet Garcia Lorca has moved away decisively from the general thrust of his earlier work. In *Dona Rosita* you will not find neither the tragic boldness of *Blood Wedding* nor the deep and tangible humanity of *Yerma*, but rather the delicate tones of those pinks and blues of the period he was evoking. . . . *Dona Rosita* has its own unique character . . . and expands the limitless possibilities for this poet-dramatist. It is a work of true literary merit, its essence — I repeat — theatrical, worthy of comparison with the very best European plays.

Maria Luz Morales, on the Spanish premiere, 1935

This play haunted the poet's imagination for many years and was the longest in maturing among all that he wrote. Its conception was such a task to him that I know that when he saw it finished it was a load off his shoulders. . . . I believe that with *Dona Rosita*, written with great care, he overcame the private failure of *Mariana Pineda*.

Francisco Garcia Lorca, Introduction to Lorca, *Three Tragedies*, 1961, p. 22-3

Dona Rosita the Spinster is, to all appearances, the most 'realistic' of all Lorca's plays, for here the simple, stylized settings of plays like *Blood Wedding* and *Yerma* become, in a manner reminiscent of Chekhov, the representation of real rooms in all their detail. The photographs of the Barcelona premiere of 1935 depict, for example, the three settings of the play — three rooms in Rosita's house — complete with chairs, sofa, sideboard, table, pictures, wallpapered walls, curtains, and French windows. Lorca's stage directions in the published version of the play are themselves very brief and convey no sense of detail. . . . On the other hand, his indications for the costumes of the characters are detailed and precise, and their aim in every case is to emphasize the sense of period of each act and thus the sense of passing time that is central to the play in general. It is clear, therefore, that the set for each act should be seen not as a piece of realism but as something stylized, its purpose not simply to present on stage an accurate picture of the time in question but, in selecting and highlighting particular characteristics of that time, to capture its essence.

Gwynne Edwards, *The Theatre Beneath the Sand*, 1980, p. 228

Lorca's elegy for a beautiful girl in turn-of-the-century Granada condemned to spinsterhood and a society watching its own time running out, is brought to Edinburgh by Nuria Espert's company. . . . Prodigally, Lorca brings on stage a host of characters who intensify pressure on both the spinster and her social group, starving and pathetically genteel unmarriables a few steps below, careless *nouveau riche* above (and how a drawing room's atmosphere crackles with those two classes facing each other), and a sweetly dignified old poet turned schoolteacher suffering humiliation from rich brats. . . . Espert herself is mesmerizing. She ages in convincing departure from Lorca's direction, largely by tightening her hair in a bun, and finally by a faintly hunched shuffle in a white shift that answers Lorca's image of the rose changing from morning red to white death at night. Already, in Act Two, she allows herself an arresting, apprehensive glance at breasts, face, and waistline. In the great speech recognizing her despair, she tiptoes as if dreaming. Jorge Lavelli's production uses unorthodox stage placings with creative assurance, and Max Bignen's set has the same flair. His gauze front curtains and cyclorama frame an austerity suggesting rather a museum than a salon with real rooms beyond, but embrace the widows and spinsters in the white of the dying rose, the trousseau, and the shroud.

Anthony Masters, *The Times*, 1 Sept. 1983

There is no tragic impetus, and not much sense of the stifling, inverted atmosphere of middle-class Granadan society; instead Lorca fashions an affectionate, lightly mocking impression of conservative Spanish suburbia. Rosita's uncle is interested in little but his sumptuous flowers; her aunt basks in a gentility which is forever subverted by an earthy housekeeper. But Rosita herself is mirror to the play's growing desolation and symbolism: a dashing young woman in the first act, dressed in red, she is still faithfully waiting aimlessly for marriage ten years on, though by then arrayed in pale pink. By the third act, when her fiancé's betrayal cannot be ignored, and attired in pale white, she has declined into a despairing, withered middle age.

The symbolism, however naive it is, emphasizes Lorca's idea of love as the most fragile and transient of emotions. Rosita's great arias of regret, her sense of being stranded barrenly in anachronistic youthfulness, and the final Chekhovian scene in which she, her aunt, and servant totter out of their deserted home, combine to achieve a quiet but fierce pathos.

Nicholas de Jongh, *The Guardian*, 16 Oct. 1989.

The House of Bernarda Alba

'A Drama of Women in the Villages of Spain.'
Written: 1936.

First production: Teatro Avenida, Buenos Aires, 8 March 1945 (dir. Margarita Xirgu; with herself as Bernarda).
First Spanish production: Teatro Goya, Madrid, 10 Jan. 1964 (dir. Juan Antonio Bardem).
British productions: French version by Studio des Champs Elysées, Paris, Mercury Theatre, London, 17 June 1946 (trans. and dir. M. Jean-Marie Creach); Greenwich Theatre, London, 21 March 1973 (adapt. Tom Stoppard; dir. Robin Phillips; with Mia Farrow); Lyric Theatre, Hammersmith, 8 Sept. 1986 (trans. Robert David Macdonald; dir. Nuria Espert; with Glenda Jackson and Joan Plowright), transferred to Globe Theatre, London, 16 Jan. 1987.
Film version: as *La Casa de Bernarda Alba*, 1987 (dir. Mario Camus).

Bernarda's second husband has just died and she demands a period of eight years mourning. Her obsession with status and a perverse notion of family honour lead her to dominate her five daughters, aged between twenty and thirty-nine, with tyrannical authority. Poncia, the family maid, despises Bernarda and takes pity on the daughters, but also recognizes that, as a servant, she has no option but to obey Bernarda's orders. Locked away upstairs is the demented grandmother, Maria Josefa, a grotesque representation of sexuality destroyed by age. A marriage is arranged between the eldest daughter, Angustias, and Pepe el Romano (a much younger character, whom we never actually see), but the youngest daughter, Adela, is passionately in love with him and rebellious to the point of recklessness. Her sister Martirio is also a rival for the love of Pepe el Romano and jealousy between them ferments until a furious quarrel breaks out, leading to Bernarda's discovery that Adela is secretly meeting Pepe el Romano. Bernarda rushes after him with a gun, and Martirio then falsely informs Adela that Pepe el Romano has been killed. Adela runs to her room, where she hangs herself. Finally, Bernarda seeks to maintain family honour by suppressing the truth and declaring that Adela died a virgin.

It was like this. Not far from Granada, there is a tiny village where my parents owned a small estate: Valderrubio. In the neighbouring house lived an old widow Dona Bernarda, who practised a tyrannical and relentless control over her unmarried daughters. They were like prisoners, deprived of any free will; I never spoke to them at all but I used to see them going by like shadows, always silent and always dressed in black. . . . At the end of the courtyard there was an interconnecting well, which didn't have any water in it. I used to go down into it to spy on this strange family whose curious behaviour intrigued me. From there I could observe them. It was a cold and silent hell in the middle of the African sun, like a tomb of living people under the iron rod of their warden. And this is how *The House of Bernarda Alba* was born. The women locked in there are Andalusian but they are coloured by the ochre lands more in keeping with the women of Castille.

Lorca, quoted in Carlos Morla Lynch,
In Spain with Federico Garcia Lorca, 1958, p. 488-9

The afternoon that Federico read *Asi que pasen cinco anos* [*When Five Years Pass*] to Margarita Xirgu, who had always been the best actress in the interpretation of his work and a great support to him, he listened to her cold words and must have reached some profound conclusions. The surrealist genre, which he liked so much, ran the risk of only appealing to minorities, to literary elites. What Federico wanted — it is well known now, he even died for it — was to be understood by the people in the 'gods', the audience in the cheapest seats, the people living in the smallest Castillian villages. For this experiment, he modelled himself on Lope de Vega, undoubtedly because this classic Spanish writer made people his protagonists, bringing them on to the stage and talking about their problems, their hopes, and their struggles with the powerful. In the same sense that he was developing a political consciousness, so it was no accident that Federico's dramatic work was becoming more naturalistic, increasingly tied to the observation of Andalusian society.

The House of Bernarda Alba, premiered in Buenos Aires by Margarita Xirgu nine years after the poet's murder, is the culmination of this growing identification between Federico and Andalusian people. Surrealist elements still exist in the play and there are ambiguities, as is the case with all great plays, but the author's intention, both to achieve a 'photographic document' and to avoid a poetic interpretation which would detract from the recognition of repressive forces and ideas within the play, is evident. Federico wanted to write about a recognizable society, about the overwhelming power of money, about sacrifice of the inner self to outward appearances, and about the imprisonment of living beings within the most wretched aspects of Catholic morality. Once more, he wanted to discover the conflict between the world as it is presented by those in power and this same world as it is suffered by Bernarda's daughters.

As I said before, 'photography' in the hands of a poet is very much more than a snapshot. Audiences of all times find references in *The*

House of Bernarda Alba not only to a real world in a specific time and place, but also to a conflict which is, perhaps, still the most important in modern society: the conflict between the imposition of order and liberty, between rules and regulations and personal freedom. In short, it is the pursuit of a utopia, not inconceivable, in which the social being and the individual being are in harmony — a world in which, not only would Adela not die, but in which her very existence would be incomprehensible. Federico was speaking of these things very shortly before Fascism — Bernarda — murdered him under the olive trees at Viznar.

Jose Monleon, programme note for
Lyric Theatre, Hammersmith, production, Sept.1986

The over-valuation of *Bernarda Alba* in relation to the poet's other works is easy to explain. For one thing, it is a final point of reference. People have always seen in it something like the rectification of a poetical vision of the theatre, and a step toward the type of realism that has come to be considered appropriate to 'normal' theatre, theatre *par excellence*, as opposed to 'poetic theatre.' *Bernarda Alba* would be the final triumph of the playwright over the poet. To me this means that neither Bernarda nor the rest of Garcia Lorca's theatre has been properly understood.

Francisco Garcia Lorca, *In the Green Morning*,
trans. C. Maurer, 1989, p. 233-4

The House of Bernarda Alba, of these plays [*Blood Wedding*, *Yerma*, and *The House of Bernarda Alba*), is the one which has the most direct inspiration in reality. . . . And in spite of this basic reality, I would say that this is his most artful play and the one which is most disciplined in technique. In a certain way, it is the most artistic in its strangeness. His tendency of making female characters the most important ones in his theatre is accentuated until he produces a drama of women only.

Francisco Garcia Lorca, Introduction to Lorca,
Three Tragedies, 1961, p. 22-3

It cannot have been by chance that Lorca wrote a play on the theme of despotism at a time when everyone with any sense knew that there was a very real possibility of a right-wing coup in Spain. Bernarda, with her hypocrisy, her inquisitorial Catholicism, and her determination to suppress other people's freedom, represents a mentality known only too well to the poet. Reading the play against the context in which it was written, it is impossible not to think of *El Debate*, Spain's leading

Catholic newspaper, which had attacked the Barraca and *Yerma* and, during the 1936 election campaign, presented Gil Robles as a Spanish equivalent of Mussolini.

In calling the play *The House of Bernarda Alba* and not simply *Bernarda Alba*, moreover, Lorca put the emphasis on the environment within which the tyrant moves and has her being, making such an intention explicit in the subtitle, 'A Drama of Women in the Villages of Spain'. When he termed the play 'a photographic documentary', the poet was indicating that it constituted a sort of report, with black-and-white illustrations, on the intolerant Spain always ready to crush the vital impulses of the people, represented here not only by Bernarda's daughters but by the servants. 'The poor are like animals,' Bernarda pronounces. 'They seem to be made of different materials from the rest of us.'

Writing out of his own experience of conditions in the Spanish countryside, Lorca must have been bitterly aware of the failure of the agrarian reform promised by the Republic — a reform initiated during the first two years of democratic rule, paralyzed when the Right came to power in 1933, and still to be implemented in 1936 when he finished the work.

Ian Gibson, *Federico Garcia Lorca*, 1989, p. 437-8

The House of Bernarda Alba, with this relentless examination of the dynamics of oppression and the tragic consequences of a systematic suffocation of the human spirit, is Lorca's most highly-developed response to his own call for a theatre committed to the exposure of the struggles and conflicts of his times. During the Franco regime in Spain, a great deal was made of Lorca's non-involvement in politics; the non-political nature of his writings was asserted again and again. In some cases, this constituted a well-intentioned effort to 'rehabilitate' Lorca by 'neutralizing' him in such a way that he could not continue to be attacked and censored for political reasons by the dictatorship.

Reed Anderson, *Federico Garcia Lorca*, 1984, p. 131

Onto a design by Antonio Saura in which there is only voluminous whiteness, thus serving the indications of the author, J. A. Bardem has directed an excellent cast and enabled them to achieve a perfect naturalism. Personally I don't like this manner of dealing with the play. I would have preferred a more poetic tone and rhythm. For me, naturalism destroys certain qualities of the work. But I recognize that the performance was perfect. Candida Losada was astonishing in her gestures and voice, her realization of the character very reflective and internalized. . . . The audience followed the work with fervour. They applauded frequently before the appropriately bare stage and afterwards gave ovations to the actors, director, and producer.

Enrique Llovet, *ABC*, 11 Jan. 1964

Together with the Spanish productions of *Yerma* and *Blood Wedding*, seen in Edinburgh last month, Espert's *Bernarda Alba* brings a great twentieth-century dramatist within our accessible common heritage and ken. Lorca has been rescued from the people who take themselves too solemnly, which he did not; we no longer need to accept his reputation on trust or nod in agreement when told that he does not survive in translation. His dramaturgy is superb, and he does.

Robert David Macdonald has done this *Bernarda Alba*, which means that the task is undertaken in a spirit of humility and bravura. His English for Lorca is sardonic, robust, and austere. The play stands in its own hard, bright light, its tension precisely sprung, its images never merely decorative but packing a dramatic resonance and poetic sharpness throughout: a photograph hidden in a bed; an improperly frivolous fan; a jug of fresh water; a stallion kicking a door; stars hanging like fists in the Andalusian sky. Such things energize the action of the play.

Ezio Frigerio's courtyard setting of whitewashed rough-cast, brick, and stone soars out of sight like a fortress wall, broken only by the uneven fenestration of centuries; the sun beats down from above; the windows are barred like those of an enclosed order. . . .

Michael Ratcliffe, *The Observer*, 14 Sept. 1986

Lorca was a homosexual who wrote very feelingly about women who were denied their womanhood, and was particularly gripped by 'that grotesque and moving spectacle, an old maid in Spain'. Here there are five of them and three widows. With no private, non-rational, easing, erotic love about, the household becomes a vicious prison of hypocrisy and secretiveness, in which all the members — from Bernarda, thwacking her daughters, to the maid, striking a beggar woman — try to establish a pecking order made up of nothing better than social convention. As the social conventions themselves were established by men, and as the unseen fiancé Pepe is the real ruler of the roost, the spectacle we see is one of slaves enslaving themselves further and adopting the measures of their masters with even greater brutality.

The process is deforming, and the big image that one carries away from this production is one of women travestying themselves. Clothed in their black weeds, all the sisters are ungainly: Julie Legrand's eldest, over-sized and loping, has a hint of the pantomime dame, while Deborah

Findlay's waspish and physically twisted Martirio, lame and glittery-eyed, echoes Richard III. Amanda Root as the youngest almost suggests a young, passionate girl driven to suicide. Joan Plowright's housekeeper is shrewd, if not quite earthy. Over all of them stands, ramrod-straight and often (and puzzlingly) with her back to us, Glenda Jackson's Bernarda: a compelling and intelligent portrait, but one which seems to reveal, as Lorca never quite did, that the tyrant's viciousness is the product of her own demons. It makes her more palatable, but I never quite believed it.

Victoria Radin, *New Statesman*, 12 Sept. 1986

One of the greatest artistic tragedies of this century was the murder in 1936 of Federico Garcia Lorca, by Falangists in Granada, while Lorca was preparing for a trip to Mexico. At 38, Lorca was at the height of his enormous powers as a dramatist who successfully reconciled the seemingly irreconcilable elements of poetry and drama in modern theatre.

This, his last work, avoids the verse form of early masterworks like *Yerma* and *Blood Wedding* for the prose of Andalusia, splendidly Anglicized here by Robert David MacDonald, but is painted in the same vivid colours: the red of blood and sexuality (inseparable in his work); the blackness of Catholic piety, in the veils of its woundedly faded and unloved women; white for purity and grace and for the towering, windowed walls of Bernarda Alba's fortress home where five daughters of varying natural fortune dream of men from the fields and are stained with the curse of money, inheritance, and social oppression.

More than all this there is the heat, an intolerable force in Lorca's plays, a heat which saps the strength and tears at his characters in this brilliant production by one of the Spanish theatre's gratifyingly blooming legends, Nuria Espert. Both the pace and almost all the individual performances are perfect, form Amanda Root's doomed Adela to Joan Plowright's bustling and worldly Poncia, to Patricia Hayes's deranged Maria Josefa, an old lady driven crazy by half-remembered passions and left to wander the yard like some steamy version of Miss Haversham.

Sadly the only flaw is smack bang at the top, in Glenda Jackson's interpretation of Bernarda as if she were some starchy headmistress at a minor girls' convent school, and with a delivery which does for intonation and emphasis what e e cummings did for the full stop. Sod it, though, this is one production that Spain and Great Britain can be very proud of — in fact, whoever persuaded Espert to come to Hammersmith deserves an immediate knighthood for services to theatre.

Steve Grant, *Time Out*, 17 Oct. 1986

Long absent from the British stage, Lorca's marvellous prophetic work on the nature of repression is most welcome. The play works both as pure narrative and as poetic-political symbol. Bernarda Alba (Glenda Jackson) guards her five daughters like a gaoler, and her obsession with honour, nobility, class, and respectability results in the youngest daughter, Adela's suicide. 'My daughter died a virgin', she laments as she sees her hanging from a tree. And, in this final moment, the play's use of the virgin sacrifice which it also mocks — it is apparent that Adela (Amanda Root) has lost her virginity with her sister's fiancé — links codes of family honour and Catholicism with Spain's pagan past.

The play was written in 1936, just before Lorca was murdered by Franco's army, and is haunted by the issue of freedom. Bernarda's five daughters hunger for a man; sexuality is the anarchic force which threatens this society. A sexual woman is threatened by the disgrace of prostitution, dishonour, or death; a sexual man must be allowed what he wants. Lorca's women express their frustrations and inequalities with a defiance which is timeless. 'Even my eyes do not belong to myself', says one daughter. Nuria Espert's production is handsome and high pitched. Joan Plowright as the servant Poncia encapsulates the edgy mood of Lorca's poetry most vividly and brings a real humanity to the stage which is not always integrated within the whole company.

Julia Pascal,
City Limits, 18 Oct. 1986

How is it that Lorca has excited so little enthusiasm in this country? Apart from his greatness as a dramatist, surely his homosexuality and his socialist politics ought to have made him an almost obligatory object of interest at least in certain quarters of the subsidized theatre. In his plays he raises a highly persuasive voice against traditionalist forces in Spanish society, especially the Catholic Church. And apart from his work in the theatre his poetry too is highly esteemed — although again not widely in this country. Now, in this compelling production at the Lyric, Hammersmith, directed by the celebrated Spanish classical actress Nuria Espert, we have a chance to see what we have been missing.

Although intensely Spanish and located in a national tradition that includes Lope de Vega and Calderon, Lorca's themes — it might be more accurate to call them obsessions — sound instantly in the northern European tradition as well. His drama, with its focal points of passion, honour, and blood, also enacts fundamental human conflicts that transcend the purely local Spanish context. As has been well remarked, if anyone doubts this they should go from Strindberg's *Lady Julie* to *Blood Wedding*, or from Ibsen's *Ghosts* to this work at the Lyric. And if the climax of *The House of Bernarda Alba* seems melodramatic (and it *is* melodramatic) then this too is a limitation we have become used to — certainly in Ibsen's work. . . .

The power of the production springs from several sources. Not least there is a superbly suggestive set by Ezio Frigerio — a white, baking cauldron of a courtyard under whose sheer, peeling walls the daughters appear more and more to resemble scurrying black inmates deprived of fresh air. Against the prevailing tones of black and white Adela flounces on in a riotously flamboyant green flamenco dress and leaps onto a table. Such is the claustrophobia generated by the production that this small gesture really does strike us as rebellious and extravagant.

There is also a likely and highly speakable translation by Robert David Macdonald — quite the best English text of the play we have come across. The cast, too, is especially strong, including Joan Plowright as Poncia, Bernarda's worldly peasant servant, and Patricia Hayes as Bernarda's demented eighty-year-old mother whose sole wish — a symbolic parallel of Adela's behaviour — is to return to her village on the coast to get married again.

One criticism of the production is its failure adequately to distinguish between the characters' class — a point central to Lorca's political intentions. Bernarda and her daughters do not sound much different from Joan Plowright's earthy but rather plummy peasant, Poncia (and Adela sounds altogether more common than even the beggar woman, which is a pity). But these are minor blemishes bearing in mind the overall achievement of the production. Here is a rare chance to see a distinguished staging of a little-known European classic.

Christopher Edwards, *The Spectator*, 20 Oct. 1986

The Public

Written: 1930-36.
First production: University of Texas, 1972.
British production: Theatre Royal, Stratford East, London, 3 Oct. 1988 (trans. Henry Livings; dir. and des. Ultz).

Sometimes called The Audience (El Publico, *the Spanish title, means both 'audience' and 'public'), this play is an exploration of reality, illusion, and subconscious sexual desire. The play is fragmentary and dream-like, and its disjointed nature is compounded by the fact that no final manuscript was ever written. The central character, called simply the Director, is visited by four horses and then by three identical Gentlemen with whom he discusses the function of theatre. The Gentlemen argue in favour of a 'theatre beneath the sand', which will subvert conventional theatre. The Director, transformed into an effeminate Harlequin figure, becomes a character in the Gentlemen's 'play', and it becomes apparent that he has had sex with all three Gentlemen. The Director's own homosexuality had been disguised previously by his relationship with Helen, who is shown to be an idealistic mythical creation of men. A contest for the Director takes place between the Third Gentleman and Helen, with the Third Gentleman appearing in studded leather and beating the Director for failing to be honest about his sexuality. It is then agreed that the play 'proper' should begin. Two sylph figures enact a kind of Genetesque scene of mutual attraction and hate, and one of them is chosen by a Roman Emperor to be his lover. The Director, who has been watching this allegorical 'play', embraces and then fights with the First Gentleman. A performance of* Romeo and Juliet, *in which the two central characters are played by men, provokes a furious debate among the audience. Members of the cast are killed in a riot. Back in his study, the Director meets Death in the form of a Magician, who suggests that* A Midsummer Night's Dream *might have been a better choice for an allegory about sexuality.*

It is the mirror of the public. That is to say, it parades on the stage the real drama which each spectator may have at the back of his mind while looking absentmindedly at the performance, often without paying the slightest attention to what is going on. And since usually the personal drama within each one of us is very poignant and generally nothing to be proud of . . . the spectators will immediately rise in fury from their seats and prevent the perfomance from continuing. Yes. My play is not to be performed but, as I have already said, it is 'A poem to be booed'.

Lorca, interviewed in *La Nacion*, Buenos Aires, 14 Oct. 1933,
trans. Rafael Martinez Nadal,
in *Lorca's The Public*, 1974, p. 229

The title of Lorca's strangest and most ambitious play, *El Publico*, means both 'audience' and 'public', and of these two meanings the first is the one that we should primarily accord it (though out of the amorphous, heterogenous public an audience comes). Possibly following

Pirandello in *Six Characters in Search of an Author*, Lorca makes *El Publico* invert that sense of illusion customarily imparted by the theatre. Here, for much of the time, we in the theatre are looking at a theatre (indeed, in a deeper sense, we are doing this for the whole duration of the work); we are concerned with a director and his three actors, and we hear discussions, practical and theoretical, about the production of drama, the real nature of theatre; in particular we are occupied with a performance of *Romeo and Juliet*. . . . Lorca certainly saw the idea of the audience as not merely central to, but determining his play; any artist, however maverick, enters into a collusion with the outside world (if it is only in his own mind a very limited segment of it); more, he can be said to be its servant, even its creation, since the art form in which he works (perhaps the drama pre-eminently) is an expression, an embodiment of the wishes of society. Lorca wanted to show in *El Publico* how art often, and at the highest level, mirrors thoughts, desires which we prefer not to admit to in our conventional social existences. And in particular he was intent on demonstrating the variety of homosexual desires that exists — particularly among men who would never admit to this.

Paul Binding, *The Gay Imagination*, 1985, p. 151-2

It is extremely brave of the Theatre Royal, Stratford East, to give Lorca's *The Public*, with its surreal imagery and cast of forty characters, its British premiere. But any notion that the play might be prosecuted under Clause 28 for its promotion of homosexuality is preposterous. Lorca is as much concerned with a Pirandellian quest for the nature of theatrical reality as he is with the advocacy of sexual freedom.

What Lorca has to say about love is candid, uncontroversial, and backed up by Shakespearean reference: that love is a matter of chance rather than will and that if Titania can fall for an ass, then there is no earthly reason why man should not be sexually attracted by man. . . .

This is theatre about theatre: faintly jejune, often incoherent, looking back to Pirandello and forwards to Genet, but always redeemed by Lorca's capacity to pull another surprising image out of the hat. And even if Ultz's production sometimes sends the whole thing up (a suffering, crucified Christ, for instance, has a satin pillow to prop up his head), his designs are imaginative and often beautiful: the final scene in which the walls of the director's office part to reveal the white hands of the public raining down from the sky has a mysterious potency that reminds you of Magritte.

Michael Billington, *The Guardian*, 4 Oct. 1988

Far from 'promoting' homosexuality *The Public* rather depressingly demonstrates how social strictures can entangle homosexuals with guilt and humiliation.

Though there are a few lines proclaiming that it does not matter who or what you love, the play's themes do not back this up very inspiringly. The dominant feeling is of bravado masking ambivalence and even shame. . . . Lack of manliness is a charge the play's male lovers contemptuously fling at each other. . . . Besides testifying to the crippling sexual assumptions of 1930s Spain, the play brims with evidence of the surrealism then in vogue. Studiously inconsequential, its dialogue is rife with mention of wombs, tombs, spiders, prayer books, worms, and numerous other phallic lookalikes. Fetishistic fitments, such as whips and shoes, are waved around. Blasphemy is religiously set up in the form of a burlesque Calvary.

Ultz's production revels in the opportunities for the visually bizarre the play affords: empty garments cavort across the stage; a quartet of horses hoof through a dance routine; a creature with a face blank as an egg totters on. But, despite all the panache brought to this premiere, it always seems less an effective play in its own right than a garish sidelight on Lorca's masterpieces.

Peter Kemp, *The Independent*, 5 Oct. 1988

Rumours that the vigilant Mrs. Whitehouse and the Clause 28 heavy mob might descend on Joan Littlewood's old East End stomping ground and turn Ultz's exotic players into pillars of salt will no doubt prove as premature as the appearance of this extraordinary play has proved tardy.

Lorca wrote *El Publico* shortly before his murder at the hands of Franco's Nationalists in 1936. It was, he said to the friend with whom he entrusted the manuscript, 'for the theatre years from now'. He also described it as 'a poem to be hissed at'.

And on both accounts he was probably right. Whether or not the theatre is ready even yet for its wild surreal extremes is debatable. But what is certain is that those most inclined to hiss at his poetry will be far too baffled by its much vaunted homosexual flights of fantasy to risk exposing their bewilderment to the cold light of a court prosecution.

Jack Tinker, *Daily Mail*, 13 Oct. 1988

Repression is a theme that recurs time and again in the work of the Spanish playwright Lorca. Anyone who saw the recent London productions of *The House of Bernarda Alba* or *Yerma* will know this. Characteristically in Lorca's plays, the life of instinctual passion is blocked, often by harsh social conventions. Writing in the Spain of the 'twenties and 'thirties, the straitjacket of bourgeois conformity pinched tightly on Lorca. But it also generated the creative tension that inspired his bold and often innovative kind of theatre. . . .

Chunks of it come over as homages to Dali and Bunuel, and perhaps if the production had stuck in that groove it would have found a coherence it sadly lacks. We encounter a theatre director (Gerard Murphy) in his study. An X-ray of the human body is flashed before us, signifying inwardness. A large painted hand towers over the desk, signifying, perhaps, propriety — the dead hand of. Perhaps, but perhaps not. Much of the imagery is mysterious in a jokey, knowing way that trivializes Lorca's voyage into the unknown.

Enter four white horses, announced as 'the public'. The Director sends them away. Enter three identically dressed men with identical beards, also announced as 'the public'. The Director speaks about his theatre beneath the open skies. The men with beards want a theatre beneath the sand. This makes the Director anxious. He clearly has something to hide.

What follows is a series of transformation scenes: an allegorical tableau, part of a version of *Romeo and Juliet*, a symbolic uprising by an audience, and a visit by Death, dressed as a conjurer. Much of it is visually very striking, some of it brilliantly and imaginatively to the point (both direction and design are by Ultz). The struggle in the drama is the Director's. He reappears dressed as Harlequin, then in a ballet gown. He discards the Harlequin suit and then the gown; both costumes return incarnated as independent forms and seem to chase him. This is superb to watch and perfectly intelligible. The Director is investigating his own repressed sexuality, along with the masks that are used to conceal and transform desire. Unfortunately not all Lorca's deep engagement with the truth of sexuality is handled with the same flair or respect.

Camp triviality creeps in. An allegorical tableau between two classical lovers vying for the Emperor's favour becomes an opportunity for a display of mincing bitchiness. Titters all round almost manage to conceal the debate about love and aggression. Furthermore, this kind of revue-bar posturing tends to perpetuate a misleading idea of nancy, effeminate homosexuality. Then the extract from *Romeo and Juliet* — which is supposed to provoke its stage audience to murder — sinks into archness. Gowned students burst in and embark upon an earnest debate about dramatic truth. We learn, to our surprise, that what provoked the audience into riot was the discovery that Juliet was being played by a boy. Such, however, is the lack of aesthetic and thematic coherence that we are past caring. Boy, horse, man with beard, naked Christ on the cross waiting for the curtain to go up on His performance — dish it all up. We know what is going on underneath, but even ninety minutes seems too long in saying it.

Christopher Edwards, *The Spectator*, 8 Oct. 1988

In presenting the British premiere of this 'lost' play by Lorca, first produced in Spain only a couple of years ago, Stratford's Theatre Royal has come up with a highly original piece of programming. It's a complex, elusive, thoroughly surreal work in which a theatre director is assailed by figures who seem to represent different aspects of sexuality, especially homosexuality. Through all the sudden transformations of character and amid the striking, bizarre images, the main focus is his apparent reluctance to embrace his own urges and fashion a form of theatre which accepts the unconscious, as opposed to giving the public the anodyne entertainment it demands.

This description, however, conveys nothing of the dream-like world which Lorca creates. Four white horses invade the director's office at the start and reappear throughout the play; an ironic pastoral scene which involves a jangling figure covered with little bells and another dressed in vine leaves mines a dark vein of sexuality; Juliet is discovered in her tomb (Shakespeare's play was the director's latest triumph) and gets propositioned by the horses; the theatre is taken over by students while a Christ-like figure is tended by a male nurse.

Ultz, who both directs and designs, achieves some memorable visual effects and, more importantly, obtains performances of great sharpness and clarity from a huge cast of twenty-four. Clarity, though, in any conventional sense of the word, is the last quality you should expect from a piece which, many decades after Lorca wrote it, still looks as experimental as anything you'll find today.

Malcolm Hay, *Time Out*, 5 Oct. 1988

Comedy without Title

Written: 1936.

British production: Yorick Theatre Company, Edinburgh Festival, 1986; revived Young Vic Studio, London, 31 March 1987 (trans. Michael Batz and Isabel Hernandez; dir. Michael Batz).

The Author appears on stage and berates the audience for their refusal to accept art that portrays the 'truth'. He also objects to the appearance of an actress who lives out a theatrical fantasy. A debate takes place about A Midsummer Night's Dream *and its representation of 'truth'. The actress appears first as Titania and then as Lady Macbeth. Meanwhile revolution is breaking out in the streets and when a mother cries in fear for her children the actress criticizes her poor performance and shows her how to cry properly. The act ends with the theatre in flames and the Author declaring the success of the revolution.*

I am not going to raise the curtain in order to amuse the audience with plays on words, nor with a panorama showing a house where nothing goes on and where the theatre focuses its spotlight to entertain us and make us believe that life is really like that. . . . You attend the theatre with the sole idea of being entertained, and you have writers whom you pay to do that. . . . But today, the poet intends to take you prisoners because he wishes and aspires to move your hearts by showing you things you do not wish to see, by shouting out the truths that you do not wish to hear.

Lorca, opening speech for the character of the Author,
Comedy without Title, trans. Reed Anderson,
in *Federico Garcia Lorca*, 1984, p. 155

The first act (the only one we have) takes place in three distinct locations: first, on the stage proper, then among the audience in the theatre, and then, finally, outside the theatre altogether. Characters who appear on the stage and who have a major part in the play are the Author, a Servant, and the Actress, who, besides playing herself, takes the role of Queen Titania from *A Midsummer Night's Dream*, and Lady Macbeth. The minor speaking or walk-on parts are those of a Prompter, Nick Bottom from the Shakespeare play, a man dressed as a wolf, a Woodcutter, a Stagehand, and actors costumed as sylphs and fairies. In the audience are the First Spectator and his wife who appear at the beginning, and the Second Spectator and his wife who appear at the end of this act; there is a well-dressed Young Man in an orchestra seat, the theatre owner (A Man Dressed in Black), and a Worker seated high in the balcony. Finally, the action outside the theatre is represented by the sounds of gunshots, artillery, and a bombardment, as well as the voices of a throng of people in the streets.

Reed Anderson, *Federico Garcia Lorca*, 1984, p. 154-5

Lorca's *Comedy without Title* is a fascinating Pirandellian fragment uncompleted at the dramatist's death in 1936 and unperformed in Spain until 1978. It presents an author stepping out of a baroque proscenium arch and promising to banish the comforting lies of theatre to show us 'a little corner of reality'.

Members of the audience fulminate, an actress costumed as Titania protests. Then a *coup d'état* erupts in the streets outside and a noisy aerial bombardment takes place.

One of the spectators cries for her children and is shown by an actress how it should really be done. A dinner-jacketed bully, proclaiming his faith in God, takes charge and, producing a gun, shoots the author.

I am not sure the play needs the prelude and epilogue it has been given here, linking it to Lorca's own death at the hands of the Civil Government. It stands on its own both as a paradoxical piece that uses theatre to stress the medium's conventional unreality and as a poetic prophesy warning of imminent Fascism, the Guernica-like bombings of civilians, and of the Spanish preoccupation with what a spectator calls 'a pattern of death'.

But Michael Batz's production is a gripping piece of total theatre that shows a world of make-believe turned on its head first by the author's plea for true pain and then by the chaos of revolution. It also reminds us that Lorca was a deeply political writer, and gets a commanding performance from Jonathan Oliver as the Lorcaesque author.

Michael Billington, *The Guardian*, 2 April 1987

English productions have a habit of giving Lorca a Spanish Tourist Board feel. The Yorick company, indeed, has provided us with a torchlight Andalusian folk dance mingled with a depiction of the author's death by way of a prologue. This is accompanied by a semi-literate essay in the apology for a programme. In fact this is no less Spanish for being a dry, provocative piece wrapped round the idea of the theatre being capable both as a suppressor and as a revealer of truth. In a sense it's an anti-play — an assault on the proscenium arch tradition. The author figure (Jonathan Oliver in total command) calls out to allow the reality of daily life to invade the theatre. It does. As the civil war rages outside, bombs drop on the auditorium itself. Politically orientated, self-questioning, it invites obvious comparisons. It's an interesting fragment, but it is certainly no 'Kubla Khan'.

Robert Gore Langton, *Time Out*, 8 April 1987

Written and set in the beginnings of the Spanish Civil War, Lorca's last play, *Comedy without Title*, might have become the dramatic equivalent of Picasso's 'Guernica'. But Lorca was killed by the fascists before he had finished it — thus what could have been a great original piece fusing Brechtian and Pirandellian methods with his own unique abilities is left to us as a highly uneven play. Judging it is like reviewing a painting on the basis of a rudimentary collation of sketches or the early drafts of a novel. There are wonderful nuggets littered throughout — an actress tells a mother she is not crying out for her children in the correct dramatic way, and she cajoles the play's anti-hero writer not to go outside during a street battle: 'Don't risk it — don't endanger your talent.' The confusion is compounded by the adding of a well-intentioned but unnecessary prologue and epilogue by the company.

John Connor, *City Limits*, 9 April 1987

b: Adaptation

La Dama Boba

Adapted from the play *The Simple-Minded Lady*, by Lope de Vega , 1613.
Written: 1934.
First production: Teatro Espanol, Madrid, 1935 (dir. Margarita Xirgu).

3: Non-Dramatic Writing

a: Poems

The following collections of poems were published during Lorca's lifetime:

Book of Poems (1921)
Songs (1927)
Gypsy Ballads (1928)
Poem of Deep Song (1931)
First Songs (1936)

The following collections of poems are available in English:

Selected Poems, introduced and ed. J. L. Gili. Harmondsworth: Penguin, 1960.
The Selected Poems of Federico Garcia Lorca, ed. Francisco Garcia Lorca and Donald M. Allen. New York: New Directions, 1961.
The Gypsy Ballads of Federico Garcia Lorca, trans. Rolfe Humphries. Bloomington; London: Indiana University Press, fifth edition, 1969.
Poet in New York, introduced and ed. Christopher Maurer, trans. Greg Simon and Steven F. White. New York: Farrar Strauss Giroux, 1988. [Also includes a selection of letters and a translation of Lorca's lecture, 'A Poet in New York', first given in Madrid, March 1932.]

b: Prose

Few of Lorca's prose writings are available in English. A comprehensive Spanish collection can be found in

Obras Completas, ed. Arturo del Hoyo. Madrid: Aguilar.

Selections of prose available in English are:

Deep Song and Other Prose, ed. and trans. Christopher Maurer. London: Marion Boyars, 1980.
Selected Letters, ed. and trans. David Gershator. London: Marion Boyars, 1983.

c: Filmscripts

Trip to the Moon

Written: 1929.
Published: as *Trip to the Moon: a Filmscript*, trans. Bernice C. Duncan, introductory note by Richard Diers, in *New Directions*, XVIII (1964) p. 33-41; also in C. B. Morris, ed., *The Dream-House: Silent Films and Spanish Poets* (University of Hull Publications, 1977), p. 15-17.

It was something written by a dreamer, a visionary, which is what Lorca essentially was. It had the quality of all his writing. . . . The film was completely plastic, completely visual, and in it Lorca tried to describe parts of New York life as he saw it.

Emilio Amero, quoted by Richard Diers,
Introduction to *Trip to the Moon*, p. 35

It was in New York that Lorca wrote a screenplay, *Trip to the Moon* (*Viaje a la luna*), inspired by Bunuel's *Un Chien Andalou*, in which in seventy-eight scenes images of violence and extreme cruelty — a hand squeezing a fish, a background that fades into a male sex organ and then into a screaming mouth — pass before us in an unbroken sequence of transformations that defy all physical laws and suggest to us that things and people are never what they seem to be.

Gwynne Edwards, *The Theatre Beneath the Sand*, 1980. p. 65

On Fuente Vaqueros

It is built upon water. Everywhere the irrigation ditches sing and the poplars grow tall and the wind plays soft music in them in the summertime. At the heart of the village is a fountain that flows ceaselessly, and above the rooftops are the blue mountains of the Vega, aloof and distant, as though they did not want their stones to reach this place, where the soft fertile earth makes every sort of fruit tree flower. . . . The fact is that the people of this village are born with a feeling for art — a feeling for art and for happiness, which is to say a feeling for life. I have often observed how upon entering this village there is a clamour, a trembling that wells forth from the deepest, most intimate part of it — a clamour, a rhythm that is social yearning and human understanding.

Speech in honour of his birthplace,
In the Green Morning, trans. C. Maurer, p. 12-13

It was something like 1906. My homeland, a land of farmers, had always been tilled by those wooden ploughs that could scarcely scratch its surface. That year some of the ploughmen had got brand-new Brabante ploughs (the name sticks in my memory) which had won a prize in the Paris Exhibition of 1900. I was a curious little boy, and I followed that vigorous plough of ours all over the fields. I liked seeing how the huge steel prong could open incisions in the earth and draw forth roots instead of blood. On one occasion the plough hit something solid and stopped. The shiny steel blade was pulling up a Roman mosaic on which was inscribed . . . I can't remember, but for some reason I think of the shepherds Daphnis and Chloe. So that the first artistic wonder I ever felt was connected with the earth.

From an interview of 1934,
trans. Paul Binding, *The Gay Imagination*, p. 32

On Granada

Everyday I'm convinced more and more of how marvellous this country is. . . . A few days ago a purple-green moon came out over the bluish mist of the Sierra Nevada and in front of my door a woman sang a *berceuse* that was like a golden streamer entangling the whole countryside. Especially at twilight one lives in the fullest fantasy, a half-erased dream. . . .

There are times when everything evaporates and we're left in a desert of pearl grey, of rose and dead silver. I can't describe to you the vastness of this plain and this little white village in the midst of dark poplar groves.

At night our very flesh hurts from so many bright stars. . . .

Letter to Adolfo Salazar, 1921,
trans. Paul Binding, *The Gay Imagination*, p. 40

I love the land, all my emotions are linked to it and my earliest childhood memories have a taste of earth about them. The land and the countryside have played a large part in my life. Not many people can instinctively understand the ways of country people, animals and insects. But I can recapture these feelings with the same spontaneity as I did when I was a child. . . . That is why I have what the psychoanalysts would call an agrarian complex. Without this love of the land I could never have written *Blood Wedding*; nor could I have begun my next play, *Yerma*.

Obras Completas, Vol. III (Madrid: Aguilar, 1986), p. 599-60
trans. John Lyon, in Introduction to *Yerma*, 1987

I'm more interested in the people who inhabit the landscape than in the landscape itself. I can look at a mountain for a quarter of an hour; but then I immediately run and talk to the shepherd or woodcutter who lives on the mountain. Afterwards, when I'm writing, I recall these dialogues and up comes the authentic Andalusian expression. I've a huge storehouse of childhood recollections in which I can hear the people speaking. It's poetic memory and I trust it implicitly.

Obras Completas, Vol II (1980) p. 1041
trans. Ian Gibson, *Federico Garcia Lorca*, p. 341

On National Identity

I am totally Spanish, and it would be impossible for me to live outside my geographical boundaries. At the same time I hate anyone who is Spanish just because he was born a Spaniard. I am a brother to all men, and I detest the person who sacrifices himself for an abstract, nationalist ideal just because he loves his country with a blindfold over his eyes. A good Chinaman is closer to me than a bad Spaniard. I express Spain in my work and feel her in the very marrow of my bones; but first and foremost I'm cosmopolitan and a brother to all.

From an interview of 1936,
trans. Ian Gibson, *Federico Garcia Lorca*, p. 439

On His Vocation as a Playwright

There is no doubt at all that I really feel the theatre. A few days ago it occurred to me to write a play whose characters would be photographic enlargements: the people we see in the doorways of houses, newly-wed couples, sergeants, dead young people, the anonymous masses with their moustaches and wrinkles. It will be something awful. If I can get it all in focus, it will be deeply moving. In the midst of all these people, I will place an authentic fairy.

Letter to Melchor Fernandez Almagro, 1926,
In the Green Morning, trans. C. Maurer, p. 235

Otherwise, the beliefs, the aesthetic schools, do not worry me. I have not the slightest intention of pretending to be old or modern, I am only me, myself, quite naturally. I know perfectly well how the semi-intellectual drama is written, but that has no importance. In our time the poet must open his veins for the benefit of others.

From a Madrid newspaper interview,
trans. Rafael Martinez Nadal, *Lorca's The Public*, p. 222

The artist, and particularly the poet, is always an anarchist, and can only listen to the voices that rise up from within his own being, three imperious voices: the voice of Death, with all its presentiments; the voice of Love, and the voice of Art.

From an interview of 1933,
trans. Ian Gibson, *Federico Garcia Lorca*, p. 358

On Poetic Theatre

Theatre is poetry that rises up off the page and becomes human. And in so becoming, it speaks and shouts, it weeps and despairs. Theatre needs for its characters to come on stage dressed in the garb of poetry, and at the same time with their bones and their blood showing through.

Interview reprinted in *Obras Completas*, Vol. III (1986), p. 673,
trans. Reed Anderson, *Federico Garcia Lorca*, p. 19-20

The theatre that has always endured is theatre written by poets, and theatre has been great in proportion to the greatness of the poet. I am not talking about the lyric poet, of course, but the dramatic poet.

Interview reprinted in *Obras Completas*, Vol. III (1986), p. 628,
trans. Reed Anderson, *Federico Garcia Lorca*, p. 27

Distinguished ladies and gentlemen. . . . (*Pause.*) Or rather, ladies and gentlemen, which is not to say the writer doesn't think you are distinguished. In fact, the opposite. But the word contains the tiniest hint of fear, a kind of plea for the audience to be kind to the actors' performance and the writer's brilliance. The writer doesn't ask for kindness; just for attention once he's leapt that barbed and dreadful barrier of fear that writers have of writing for the theatre. Because of this, which is quite absurd, and because the theatre is often simply a business, poetry has disappeared from the stage in search of other places where audiences will not be shocked, for instance, when a tree becomes a puff of smoke, or three small fishes, obeying a command, become three million to satisfy the hunger of the multitude. This writer has chosen to express a dramatic concept in the lively rhythm of a lowly little shoemaker's wife. . . .

The Dramatist's opening speech
from the Prologue to *The Shoemaker's Wonderful Wife*,
trans. Gwynne Edwards, in Lorca, *Plays: Two*, 1990

On Puppet Theatre

The object of this letter is to invite you to the puppet show that [Manuel de] Falla and I are going to give in my house. It will be an extraordinary puppet show and we will produce something of pure art, which we need so badly. In *Cristobicas* we will perform a poem full of tenderness and grotesque turns that I've composed with music arranged by Falla for clarinet, viola, and piano. The poem is called *The Child who Waters the Pot of Basil and the Noisy Prince* and has a great Granadan flavour. We will also stage, with the same set-up as *Cristobicas*, the brief play by Cervantes, *The Talkers*, with music by Stravinsky. And to conclude we will perform, in a theatrical way, the old *Play of the Three Wise Men*, with fifteenth-century music and decorations copied from the codex of Albert the Great in our University. . . .

Letter to Melchor Fernandez Almagro, 1922,
in *Selected Letters*, trans. David Gershator (1983)

On Salvador Dali

Everyday I appreciate Dali's talent even more. He seems to me unique and he possesses a serenity and a clarity of judgement about whatever he's planning to do that is truly moving. He makes mistakes and it doesn't matter. He's alive. His denigrating intelligence unites with his disconcerting childishness, in such an unusual combination that it is absolutely captivating and original. What moves me most about him now is his fever of constructions (that is to say, creation), in which he tries to create out of nothing with such strenuous efforts and throws himself into the gales of creativity with so much faith and so much intensity that it seems incredible. . . . Dali inspires the same pure emotion (and may God Our Father forgive me) as that of the baby Jesus abandoned on the doorstep of Bethlehem, with the germ of the crucifixion already latent beneath the straws of the cradle.

Selected Letters, trans. David Gershator, p. 118

On Ritual

Theatre is an art, a great art, born with man, who carries it high in his soul. When he wants to express the deepest recesses of his history and of his own being he expresses it by representation, by repeating words, gestures, and movements. The Holy Office of Mass is still the most perfect theatrical performance that can be seen.

Public speech, Buenos Aires, 1933,
trans. Rafael Martinez Nadal, *Lorca's The Public*, p. 221

On Audiences

Personally I would rip out the boxes and stalls and bring the gods downstairs. We've got to get ordinary working people into the theatre. 'Are you wearing a nice silk dress, Madam? Yes? Then, get out.' An audience dressed in hemp shirts watching *Hamlet*, the works of Aeschylus, and all the other great plays, that's it.

From an interview of 1933, Buenos Aires,
trans. Ian Gibson, *Federico Garcia Lorca*, p. 366

The public in little villages always show a respect, a curiosity, and desire to understand not always matched by spectators in big cities.

Quoted by Rafael Martinez Nadal,
Lorca's The Public, p. 226

When they talk to me about the decadence of the theatre I think of the young dramatic authors who, because of the present organization, leave the world of their dreams and do something else, tired of fighting; when they talk to me about the decadence of the stage I think of the millions of men who in fields and in the poor quarters of towns wait to see with their own eyes, fresh with astonishment, that idyll with nightingale, *Romeo and Juliet*, Falstaff's belly full of wine, or the lament of our

Segismundo [the protagonist of Calderon de la Barca's famous play *Life is a Dream*], struggling face to face with Heaven. I do not believe in the decadence of the theatre, just as I do not believe in the decadence of painting or music.

Address to audience, Buenos Aires, 1934,
trans. Rafael Martinez Nadal, *Lorca's The Public*, p. 224

Human beings are afraid to see themselves reflected in the theatre. . . . I aspire to express the social drama of the period in which we're living and my aim is that audiences learn not to be frightened of situations and symbols. I want audiences to come to terms with those fantasies and ideas without which I cannot advance a step in the theatre.

Radio broadcast, Buenos Aires, 1935,
trans. Ian Gibson, *Federico Garcia Lorca*, p. 417

On Didactic Theatre

The idea of art for art's sake is something that would be cruel if it weren't, fortunately, so ridiculous. No decent person believes any longer in all that nonsense about pure art, art for art's sake.

At this dramatic moment in time, the artist should laugh and cry with his people. We must put down the bouquet of lilies and bury ourselves up to the waist in mud to help those who are looking for lilies. For myself, I have a genuine need to communicate with others. That's why I knocked at the door of the theatre and why I now devote all my talents to it.

From a newspaper interview, June 1936,
trans. Ian Gibson, *Federico Garcia Lorca*, p. 439

On Crisis in the Theatre

Tonight I do not speak as a playwright or a poet or a simple student of the rich panorama of human life, but as an ardent and passionate admirer of the theatre of social action. The theatre is one of the most expressive and useful instruments for the edification of a country and the barometer that measures its greatness or decline. A theatre that is sensitive and healthy in all its forms, from tragedy to vaudeville, can change people's sensibility in a few years; a decadent theatre in which hoofs have taken the place of wings can cheapen and deaden a whole nation.

The theatre is a school of tears and laughter and a free platform where people can test out traditional or questionable moral views and reveal the eternal truths of the heart and emotion of mankind with vivid examples.

A people which does not aid or promote its theatre is dying, if not dead. Similarly, a theatre which does not recognize the social and historical tempo, the drama of its people and the true colour of its landscape and spirit, with laughter and tears, does not have the right to call itself theatre. . . .

Every day, dear friends, I hear talk of the crisis in the theatre, and I always think that we never really see the problem directly. It's not the flower, the work of art itself, that is the problem; the root of the evil is the actual organization of the theatre.

So long as actors and playwrights are governed by commercial enterprise, devoid of literary or state control of any kind, ignorant of all criteria and without guarantee of any quality, actors, authors, and the whole theatre will sink further each day, without any prospect of salvation.

The delightful theatre of light revue, vaudeville, and low comedy, genres of which I am a passionate spectator, will be able to defend themselves and be saved. But verse drama, historical drama, and what we call Spanish light opera will suffer more setbacks every day, because they are forms that make great demands and are suitable for genuine innovation, and there is no impetus or spirit of sacrifice for making them known to a public which must be tamed by forcefulness and contradicted and attacked on many occasions. The theatre should influence the public, and not the public influence the theatre. To do this, playwrights and actors have to assume great authority, with blood (sweat and tears), because the theatrical public is like schoolchildren, who adore the grave and austere master, who demands and dispenses justice, but fill the chairs with cruel needles when they sense their teachers are the shy and cringing types, who are neither able to teach nor allowed to teach. The public can be taught (note that I say public and not people). Some years ago I saw Debussy and Ravel jeered, but they became acceptable, finally, as a result of higher and more authoritative criteria than current public taste. The same is true of Wedekind in Germany, Pirandello in Italy, and so many others.

It's necessary to do this for the good of the theatre and the glory and status of the performers. It's necessary to maintain a dignified attitude, with the security of being abundantly rewarded. The alternative is to shake with fear in the flying gallery and to kill the fantasies, the imagination, and the comic character of the theatre, which is always, always an art and always will be a sublime art, even though there has been a period during which everything and anything was called 'art', in order to lower the atmosphere, to destroy poetry, and to make the stage a haven for con artists.

Art above everything. Most noble art, and you, dear actors, artists above everything. . . . Enthusiasm and certainty dictate my words. I am not easily deceived. I have thought a good deal and with coolness. . . . I know that the one who knows the truth is not he who says, 'Today, today, today', while eating his bread close to the lamp, but rather the one who serenely admires the first distant dawn light of the countryside.

I know that the one who is right is not he who says, 'Now, now, now', with his eyes fixed on the small jaws of the box office, but rather the one who says, 'Tomorrow, tomorrow, tomorrow', and senses the arrival of a new life blossoming in the world.

Talk at Madrid National Theatre, 1935

On Commercialism

It is intolerable and shameful that a man, by the mere fact of having a few millions, should be able to set himself up as a censor of plays and arbiter of the theatre. It is a tyranny that, like all others, can lead only to disaster. . . .

From a newspaper interview of 1934,
trans. Gwynne Edwards, *The Theatre Beneath the Sand*, p. 22

On La Barraca

It is amazing the concentration, the intelligence and the unity with which these students are working. A professional company would be hard put to come up with the kind of results they are achieving . . . and with all of the rehearsals and experimentations, I feel that I am becoming trained as a director, a difficult and slow apprenticeship. I am stimulated to use this experience to go on to do many other things.

From an interview of 1934,
trans. Reed Anderson, *Federico Garcia Lorca*, p. 17

La Barraca will really be two barracas, one permanent, in Madrid, placed preferably in a public park, where plays will be presented while the students are at work in the winter time; the other, the wandering barraca, the caravan theatre, will go on wheels through the outskirts of Madrid and into La Mancha on weekends and holidays. And in the summer we will tour Spain. We will have an omnibus for the actors, and a truck with two tents, one for men and one for women. That will also carry the scenery. Students will do all the work — students in architecture will make the barracas and go along with us in the caravan to do the stage setting and the assembling, students in philosophy will collaborate with the group of poets on the executive committee. . . .

The theatre is specially adapted to educational purposes here in Spain. It used to be the most important means of popular instruction, popular exchange of ideas. In the days of Lope de Rueda it was just such a theatre on wheels as we are planning now. It went into all the villages, and gave all the famous old plays which foreigners find so marvellous, and which are so badly neglected in Spain. Outside of Madrid today, the theatre, which is in its very essence a part of the life of the people, is almost dead, and the people suffer accordingly, as they would if they had lost eyes or ears or sense of taste. We are going to give it back to them in the terms in which they used to know it, with the very plays they used to love. We are also going to give them plays, plays of today, done in the modern manner, explained ahead of time very simply, and presented with that extreme simplification which will be necessary for the success of our plan and which makes the experimental theatre so interesting.

We are going to try all sorts of things at first, and gradually work out the type and the technique that wins the best response. For instance, we want to put on the famous *El magico prodigioso* in two ways, on two succeeding nights — the first old-fashioned, realistic, the second simplified, stylized, as new as the latest experiment and as old as the most ancient technique of stage setting and gesture. We will watch to see which the audience prefers.

We plan to adjust prices to the audience, too, to hold invitation performances for the rich people of a town, and then the following nights charge little or nothing, so that the working people can come. You see we really are very much in earnest. We believe we can do our part toward the great ideal of educating the people of our beloved Republic by means of restoring to them their own theatre. We will take God and Evil, God and Faith into the towns of Spain again, stop our caravan, and set them to play their parts in the old Roman theatre in Merida, in the Alhambra, in those plazas all over Spain that are the centre of the people's life, those plazas that see markets and bullfights, that are marked by a lantern or a cross. We have had a dream for a long time, and now we are working to make it come true.

'The Theatre in the Spanish Republic', *Obras Completas*, Vol. III (1986), p. 506-8, trans. Mildred Adams

On New York

The two elements the traveller first captures in the big city are extra-human architecture and furious rhythm. Geometry and anguish. At first glance, the rhythm can seem to be gaiety, but when you look more closely at the mechanism of social life and the painful slavery of both men and machines you understand it as a typical, empty anguish that makes even crime and banditry forgivable means of evasion.

Willing neither clouds nor glory, the edges of the buildings rise to the sky. While Gothic edges rise from the hearts of the dead and buried, these ones climb coldly skyward with beauty that has no roots and no yearning, stupidly sure of themselves and utterly unable to conquer or transcend, as does spiritual architecture, the always inferior intentions of the architect. There is nothing more poetic and terrible than the skyscrapers' battle with the heavens that cover them. Snow, rain, and mist set off, wet, and hide the vast towers, but these towers, hostile to mystery, blind to any sort of play, shear off the rain's tresses and shine their three thousand swords through the soft swan of the mist.

It only takes a few days before you get the impression that that immense world has no roots. . . .

'A Poet in New York', *Deep Song and Other Prose*, 1929,
trans. Paul Binding, *The Gay Imagination*, p. 13

And then once again the frenetic rhythm of New York. But it no longer surprises me. I know the mechanism of the streets and talk to people and penetrate a bit deeper into social life. And I denounce it. Denounce it because I have come from the countryside and do not believe that man is the most important thing in the world.

'A Poet in New York', *Deep Song and Other Prose*, 1929
trans. Paul Binding, *The Gay Imagination*, p. 81

On Harlem

In one cabaret, Small's Paradise . . . I saw a naked dancer shaking convulsively under an invisible rain of fire. But while everyone shouted as though believing her possessed by the rhythm, I was able, for a second, to catch remoteness in her eyes — remoteness, reserve, the conviction that she was far away from that admiring audience of foreigners and Americans. All Harlem was like her.

'A Poet in New York', *Deep Song and Other Prose*, 1929,
trans. Paul Binding, *The Gay Imagination*, p. 125

The most important Black city in the world, where lewdness has an innocent accent that makes it disturbing and religious. A neighbourhood of rosy houses, full of pianolas and radios and cinemas, but with the mistrust that characterizes the race. . . . I wanted to make the poem of the Black race in North America and to emphasize the pain that Blacks feel to be Black in a contrary world. They are slaves of all the white man's inventions and machines. . . .

'A Poet in New York', *Deep Song and Other Prose*, 1929,
trans. Paul Binding, *The Gay Imagination*, p. 126

On 'Duende'

All that has dark sounds has *duende*. And there is no greater truth.

These 'dark sounds' are the mystery, the roots thrusting into the fertile loam known to all of us, ignored by all of us, but from which we get what is real in art. . . . Thus the *duende* is a power and not a behaviour, it is a struggle and not a concept. I have heard an old guitarist master say, 'The *duende* is not in the throat; the *duende* surges up from the soles of the feet.' Which means that it is not a matter of ability, but of real live form; of blood; of ancient culture; of creative action.

'Theory and Function of the *Duende*', *Selected Poems*, p. 127,
trans. Paul Binding, *The Gay Imagination*, p. 160-1

Spain is always moved by *duende*, being a country of ancient music and dance, where the *duende* squeezes lemons of daybreak, as well as being a nation of death, a nation open to death.

In every country death has finality. It arrives and the blinds are drawn. Not in Spain. In Spain they are lifted. Many Spaniards live between walls until the day they die, when they are taken out to the sun. A dead person in Spain is more alive when dead than is the case anywhere else — his profile cuts like the edge of a barber's razor.

'Theory and Function of the *Duende*', *Selected Poems*, p. 133,
trans. Paul Binding, *The Gay Imagination*, p. 163

On Islamic Influence

When our songs reach the very extremes of pain and love they become the expressive sisters of the magnificent verses of Arabian and Persian poets. The truth is that in the air of Cordoba and Granada one still finds gestures and lines of remote Arabia, and remembrances of lost cities still arise from the murky palimpsest of the Albaicin. . . .

But where the resemblance is most striking of all is in the sublime amorous *ghazals* [short lyric poems usually on an erotic theme] of Hafiz, the national poet of Persia, who sang of the wine, beautiful women, mysterious stones, and infinite blue night of Shiraz.

Deep Song and Other Prose,
trans. Christopher Maurer, p. 36-7

On Future Plans

My path in the theatre . . . is something that I see very clearly. I want to complete the trilogy of *Blood Wedding*, *Yerma*, and *The Tragedy of Lot's Daughters*. I still have to write the latter. Afterwards I want to do something different, including modern plays on the age we live in, and I want to put on the stage themes and problems that people are afraid to face.

From a newspaper interview of 1934,
trans. Gwynne Edwards, *The Theatre Beneath the Sand*, p. 26

'Tell me, Garcia Lorca, do you have the impression that your present literary form is, in fact, your definitive one?'

'No. That is nonsense. Every morning I forget what I have written. It is the secret of being modest and working courageously. . . . In fact, I am planning to write several plays of the human, social type. One of these plays will be against war. These works have a material that is very different from that of *Yerma* or *Blood Wedding*, for example, so that one must treat them with a different technique.'

From an interview of 1935,
In the Green Morning, trans. C. Maurer, p. 215

5: A Select Bibliography

a: Primary Sources in English

Plays

The Puppet Play of Don Cristobal, Dialogue of Amargo, The Scene of the Lieutenant Colonel of the Civil Guard, trans. E. Honig, *New Directions*, No. 8 (1944).

Three Tragedies, trans. James Graham-Lujan and Richard L. O'Connell, with Introduction by Francisco Garcia Lorca. New York: New Directions; London: Secker and Warburg, 1947; Harmondsworth: Penguin, 1961. [Includes *Blood Wedding*, *Yerma*, and *The House of Bernarda Alba*.]

Buster Keaton's Promenade, trans. T. Reynolds, *Accent*, XVII, No. 3 (1957).

Five Plays: Comedies and Tragicomedies, trans. James Graham-Lujan and Richard L. O'Connell, with Introduction by Francisco Garcia Lorca. New York: New Directions, 1963; London: Secker and Warburg, 1965; Harmondsworth: Penguin, 1970. [Includes *The Billy-Club Puppets*, *The Shoemaker's Prodigious Wife*, *The Love of Don Perlimplin*, *Dona Rosita the Spinster*, and *The Butterfly's Evil Spell*, and also scores of the original music for some of the plays.]

Collected Plays, trans. James Graham-Lujan and Richard L. O'Connell. London: Secker and Warburg, 1976. [Includes *The Butterfly's Evil Spell*, *The Billy-Club Puppets*, *The Shoemaker's Prodigious Wife*, *Don Perlimplin*, *Blood Wedding*, *Yerma*, *Dona Rosita the Spinster*, and *The House of Bernarda Alba*.]

Three Tragedies, trans. Sue Bradbury, illus. Peter Pendry. London: Folio Society, 1977. [Includes *Yerma*, *Blood Wedding*, and *The House of Bernarda Alba*.]

Play without a Title, trans. Carlos Bauer. New York: New Directions, 1983.

Three Plays, with introduction by Gwynne Edwards. London: Methuen, 1987; reissued as *Plays: One*, 1991. [Includes *Blood Wedding* and *Dona Rosita the Spinster*, trans. Gwynne Edwards, and *Yerma*, trans. Peter Luke.]

Yerma, trans. and with introduction and notes by Ian Macpherson and Jacqueline Minett, and a general introduction by John Lyon. Warminster: Aris and Phillips, 1987.

Mariana Pineda, trans. Robert G. Havard. Warminster: Aris and Phillips, 1987.
Plays: Two, trans. and introduced by Gwynne Edwards. London: Methuen, 1990. [Includes *The Shoemaker's Wonderful Wife*, *The Love of Don Perlimplin*, *The Puppet Play of Don Cristobal*, *The Butterfly's Evil Spell*, and *When Five Years Pass*.]
Plays: Three. Methuen, 1991. [Includes *Mariana Pineda*, *Play without Title*, and *The Public*.]

Filmscript

Trip to the Moon, trans. Bernice C. Duncan, with an introductory note by Richard Diers, *New Directions*, XVIII (1964), p. 33-41.

b: Secondary Sources in English

Full-Length Studies

Arturo Barea, *The Poet and His People*. London: Faber and Faber, 1944.
Manuel Duran, ed., *Lorca: a Collection of Critical Essays*. Englewood Cliffs, New Jersey: Prentice-Hall, 1962.
Robert Lima, *The Theater of Garcia Lorca*. New York: Las Americas, 1963.
Edwin Honig, *Federico Garcia Lorca*. London: Jonathan Cape, 1968.
Ian Gibson, *The Assassination of Federico Garcia Lorca*. London: W.H. Allen, 1973.
R. C. Allen, *Psyche and Symbol in the Theater of Federico Garcia Lorca*. Austin: University of Texas Press, 1974.
Rafael Martinez Nadal, *Lorca's The Public: a Study of His Unfinished Play (El Publico) and of Love and Death in the Work of Federico Garcia Lorca*. London: Calder and Boyars, 1974.
Suzanne Byrd, *'La Barraca' and the Spanish National Theatre*. New York: Ediciones Abra, 1975.
Virginia Higginbotham, *The Comic Spirit of Federico Garcia Lorca*. Austin; London: University of Texas Press, 1976.
Mildred Adams, *Garcia Lorca: the Playwright and Poet*. New York: Braziller, 1977.
Gwynne Edwards, *Lorca: the Theatre Beneath the Sand*. London: Marion Boyars, 1980.
Reed Anderson, *Federico Garcia Lorca*. London: Macmillan, 1984.

Paul Binding, *Lorca: the Gay Imagination.* London: Gay Men's Press, 1985.
Helen Oppenheimer, *Lorca, the Drawings: Their Relation to the Poet's Life and Work.* London: Herbert, 1986.
Francisco Garcia Lorca, trans. Christopher Maurer, *In The Green Morning: Memories of Federico.* London: Peter Owen, 1989.
Ian Gibson, *Federico Garcia Lorca: a Life.* London: Faber and Faber, 1989.

Articles and Chapters in Books

Eric Bentley, *In Search of Theater.* New York: Knopf, 1953. [In 'The Poet in Dublin' Bentley discusses his own Abbey Theatre production of *The House of Bernarda Alba* in 1950.]
Summer M. Greenfield, 'Poetry and Stagecraft in *La Casa de Bernarda Alba*', Hispania, XXXVIII (1955), p. 456-61.
Robert Barnes, 'The Fusion of Poetry and Drama in *Blood Wedding*', *Modern Drama,* II (1960), p. 395-402.
Calvin Cannon, 'The Imagery of Lorca's *Yerma*', *Modern Language Quarterly,* XXI (1960), p. 122-30.
Ronald J. Dickson, 'Archetypal Symbolism in Lorca's *Bodas de sangre (Blood Wedding)*', *Literature and Psychology,* X (1961), p. 76-9.
Thomas F. Sharp, 'The Mechanics of Lorca's Drama in *La Casa de Bernarda Alba*', *Hispania,* XLIV (1961), p. 230-3.
William I. Oliver, 'Lorca: the Puppets and the Artist', *Tulane Drama Review,* VII (1962), p. 76-96.
Warren Carrier, 'Poetry in the Drama of Lorca', *Drama Survey,* II (1963), p. 297-304.
Ronald Gaskell, 'Theme and Form: Lorca's *Blood Wedding*', *Modern Drama,* V (1963), p. 431-9.
Eva K. Touster, 'Thematic Patterns in Lorca's *Blood Wedding*', *Modern Drama,* VII (1964-65), p. 188-216.
Robert Lott, '*Yerma,* the Tragedy of Unjust Barrenness', *Modern Drama,* VIII (1965), p. 20-7.
Robert Skloot, 'Theme and Image in Lorca's *Yerma*', *Drama Survey,* V (1966), p. 151-61.
Julian Palley, 'Archetypal Symbols in *Bodas de sangre (Blood Wedding)*', Hispania, L (1967), p. 74-9.
C. Ll. Halliburton, 'Garcia Lorca, the Tragedian: an Aristotelian Analysis of *Bodas de sangre (Blood Wedding)*', *Revista de Estudios Hispanicos,* II (1968), p. 35-40.
Virginia Higginbotham, 'Bernarda Alba: a Comic Character?', *Drama Survey,* VI (1968), p. 258-65.

R. A. Zimbardo, 'The Mythic Pattern in Lorca's *Blood Wedding*', *Modern Drama*, X (1968), p. 364-71.

R. A. Young, 'Garcia Lorca's *Bernarda Alba*: a Microcosm of Spanish Culture', *Modern Languages*, L (1969), p. 66-72.

C. B. Morris, 'Lorca's Yerma: Wife without an Anchor', *Neophilologus*, LVI (1972), p. 285-97.

Virginia Higginbotham, 'Lorca and Twentieth-Century Spanish Theatre: Three Precursors', *Modern Drama*, XV (1972), p. 164-74.

Reed Anderson, 'The Idea of Tragedy in Garcia Lorca's *Bodas de sangre* (*Blood Wedding*)', *Revista Hispanica Moderna*, XXXVIII (1974-75), p. 174-88.

H. Ramsden, '*Bodas de Sangre*'. Manchester: Manchester University Press, 1980. [Spanish text of *Blood Wedding*, with a detailed commentary on the play in English.]

Gwynne Edwards, *Dramatists in Perspective: Spanish Theatre in the Twentieth Century*. Cardiff: University of Wales Press, 1985. [Useful introduction, and separate chapter on the plays of Lorca, p. 75-126).

Gwynne Edwards, 'Lorca on the English Stage: Problems of Production and Translation', *New Theatre Quarterly*, IV, No. 16 (Nov. 1988) p. 344-55.

Reference Sources

Francesca Colecchia, ed., *Garcia Lorca: a Selectively Annotated Bibliography of Criticism*. New York: Garland, 1979.

TUNISIA

Imprint

208 colour photographs
17 town plans, 9 situation plans, 10 ground-plans, 17 drawings, 7 general maps and 1 large map of Tunisia (list at end of book)

Text: Anja Schliebitz, with contributions from Vera Beck, Professor Wolfgang Hassenpflug, Dr Günther Ludwig, Dr Udo Moll and Andrea Petri

Editorial work: Baedeker-Redaktion (Anja Schliebitz)
English language edition: Alec Court

General direction: Dr Peter Baumgarten, Baedeker Stuttgart

Cartography: Franz Kaiser, Sindelfingen; Christoph Gallus, Hohberg-Niederschopfheim; Gert Oberländer, Munich; Hallwag AG (large map of Tunisia)

Source of Illustrations: Bäcker (3), Bildagentur Schuster (4), Histporia (4), Ludwig (1), Mahdaoui(1), Moll (6), Schliebitz-Schleicher (189)

English translation: James Hogarth

Following the tradition established by Karl Baedeker in 1844, sights of particular interest are distinguished by either one or two stars.

To make it easier to locate the various sights listed in the "A to Z" section of the Guide, their coordinates on the large map of Tunisia are shown in red at the head of each entry.

Only a selection of hotels and restaurants can be given: no reflection is implied, therefore, on establishments not included.

The symbol ⓘ on a town plan indicates the local tourist office from which further information can be obtained. The post-horn symbol indicates a post office.

In a time of rapid change it is difficult to ensure that all the information given is entirely accurate and up-to-date, and the possibility of error can never be entirely eliminated. Although the publishers can accept no responsibility for inaccuracies and omissions, they are always grateful for corrections and suggestions for improvement.

1st English edition 1992

US and Canadian edition
Prentice Hall Press

Distributed in the United Kingdom by the Publishing Division of the Automobile Association, Fanum House, Basingstoke, Hampshire RG21 2EA

Licensed user:
Mairs Geographischer Verlag GmbH & Co., Ostfildern-Kemnat bei Stuttgart

The name *Baedeker* is a registered trade mark
A CIP catalogue record of this book is available from the British Library

Printed in Italy by G. Canale & C.S.p.A – Borgaro T.se –Turin

ISBN UK 0 7495 0559 1
US and Canada 0–13–059551–9

Contents

The Principal Sights at a Glance

Preface

This guide to Tunisia is one of the new generation of Baedeker guides.

These guides, illustrated throughout in colour, are designed to meet the needs of the modern traveller. They are quick and easy to consult, with the principal places of interest described in alphabetical order, and the information is presented in a format that is both attractive and easy to follow.

This guide is in three parts. The first part gives a general account of Tunisia, its topography, climate, flora and fauna, population, religion, educational system, government and administration, economy, history, famous people, art and culture. A selection of quotations about Tunisia and a number of suggested routes provide a transition to the second part, in which places and features of tourist interest – towns and villages, regions, excavation sites – are described. The third part contains a variety of practical information. Both the sights and the practical information are listed in alphabetical order.

The new Baedeker guides are noted for their concentration on essentials and their convenience of use. They contain numerous specially drawn plans and colour illustrations; and at the end of the book is a large map making it easy to locate the various places described in the "A to Z" section of the guide with the help of the coordinates given at the head of each entry.

Facts and Figures

With its beautiful beaches extending endlessly along the Mediterranean and its guaranteed sunshine, Tunisia is an ideal holiday land. But in addition to sand, sea and sunshine it has much more to offer: the fertile country in the north, the lonely hill and desert regions, the picturesque towns and villages of the interior, and in addition to all this the traces of a long and eventful past. Tunisia's geographical situation laid it open from time immemorial to influences from other lands, and in the course of three thousand years it saw the passage of Phoenicians, Romans, Vandals, Byzantines, Arabs, Turks, Spaniards and finally the French, all of them leaving evidence of their presence; and in our own day Tunisia is still a bridge between the Western, the African and the Islamic worlds – a country to whose wide range of interest and beauty this guide offers an introduction.

General

Situation

Tunisia is the most northerly country in Africa, facing towards Europe, from which it is separated only by the 140 kilometres/90 miles of sea between Cap Bon and the western tip of Sicily.

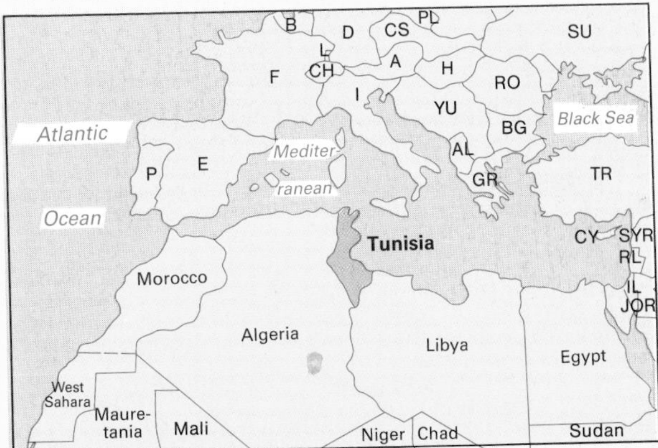

Maghreb

It occupies the eastern part of the Maghreb, the area in north-western Africa which includes Morocco, Algeria and Tunisia together with Libya and Mauretania. The name Maghreb means "the land where the sun sets in front of the ocean". Together with the Makhrek to the east, which begins in the desert between Libya and Egypt, it forms the Arab world. Tunisia is called Maghreb el Edna, the "Near West", Algeria Maghreb el Awsat, the "Middle West", and Morocco Maghreb el Aqsa, the "Far West".

Area

Tunisia is the smallest of the Maghreb countries, with an area of some 164,150sq.km/63,380sq.miles, or about two-thirds the size of the United Kingdom. (The figure may vary slightly, since there are disputes between Tunisia and Libya over the demarcation of the frontier).

◀ *Spring blossom in the High Tell, south of Le Kef*

General

The greatest extent of the country from north to south is 897km/557 miles (between Cap Blanc and the frontier post at Bordj el Khadra), from east to west 330km/205 miles (between the island of Djerba and Nefta).

Frontiers

Tunisia is bounded on the north and east by the Mediterranean, on the west by Algeria and on the south-east, in the northern Sahara, by Libya.

Topography

Tunisia has been likened to a sea horse with its head in green country, its belly in water and its rear in sand. Bordered on the north by the Mediterranean but reaching into the Sahara in the south, Tunisia – like its neighbours Morocco, Algeria and Libya – covers a wide climatic range, from the Mediterranean climate with its rainy winters in the north to the desertic climate of the Sahara in the south, and shows a corresponding variety of topography, influenced not only by climatic factors but also by geological differences.

Four main landscape forms can be distinguished: the northern Tunisian uplands with their cliff-fringed coast and Mediterranean climate; the Sahel and the long flat east coast to the south of Cap Bon with its wide sandy beaches; the central Tunisian steppe, to the south of the uplands and west of the Sahel; and the Sahara in the desertic south.

Northern Tunisian uplands

The predominant feature in the topography of north-western Tunisia is the Tell-Atlas, the foothills of the mighty Atlas Mountains which extend from east to west along the whole length of the Maghreb for a distance of some 2200km/1366 miles, though within Tunisia they are substantially lower than in the neighbouring countries. Running parallel to the rocky north coast of Tunisia from the Algerian coast in the west to the lagoon of Bizerte in the east is the Kroumirie range, continued north-eastward by the Mogod hills, which fall down to the seat at Cap Blanc. The Kroumirie range reaches heights of 700–800m/2300–2625ft, the Mogod hills only 300–400m/985–1300ft

Kroumirie and Mogod uplands

The hills, largely forest-covered, consist of soft Tertiary limestones overlaid by beds of sandstone, much folded and eroded by the heavy rainfall in this area.

Oued Medjerda

To the south of the hills, sheltered from the wind, is the basin of the Oued Medjerda, the largest perennial river in the country, and its tributaries. Its upper course, near the Algerian frontier, is flanked by the thinly populated hills of the Tell, an outlier of the Saharan Atlas of Algeria. Its lower course is one of Tunisia's most important agricultural regions.

Dorsale

The range of hills known as the Dorsale ("Backbone"), which runs from north-east to south-west for some 220km/137 miles, marks the climatic boundary between the Mediterranean north of the country and the dry steppeland of central Tunisia. Isolated limestone massifs rise out of the lower country round them like towers; to the south-west, near the Algerian frontier, are Tunisia's highest hills: Djebel Chambi (1544m/5066ft), Djebel Mdilla (1378m/4521ft) and Djebel Semmama (1314m/4311ft).

The Dorsale falls gradually away towards the coast, with a height of 576m/1890ft in Djebel Bou Kornine, to end in the Cap Bon peninsula. Between the northern slopes of the Dorsale and the chains of hills bounding it on the south are extensive plateaus, sometimes called the High Tell. This is the most important cereal-growing area in Tunisia after the Oued Medjerda basin.

Rainfall

The Kroumirie hills are the rainiest part of Tunisia, with over 1500mm/59in of rain a year. The wettest month is usually November, the driest July – a rainfall pattern characteristic of the Mediterranean climatic zone of northern Tunisia. In the lower Mogod hills the annual rainfall is still around

The fertile uplands of northern Tunisia

600mm/24in. Towards the Oued Medjerda, in the shelter of the outliers of the Tell, the figure falls to around 400mm/16in. These differences are reflected in the vegetation: while the Kroumirie range is covered with dense forests of cork-oaks, the Mogod hills have a dense growth of macchia (see Flora and Fauna).

The high rainfall of the Kroumirie hills makes an important contribution to the water supply of northern Tunisia. The rainwater is stored in a series of reservoirs on the southern fringes of the hills and channelled into the Medjerda basin.

In the Dorsale rainfall increases again to around 600mm/24in, and the northern slopes are covered by sparse forests of Aleppo pines intespersed with holm-oaks. The chains of hills which bound the Dorsale on the south and east form a transition between the semi-humid Mediterranean climatic zone in the north and the semi-arid steppeland of inland central Tunisia.

Sahel

The coastal area to the east of the Dorsale, round Sousse and Sfax, is known as the Sahel ("coast", "border"). This area was intensively cultivated from very early times, when techniques were developed for making the best use of the scanty water supply. In our own day a distinction can be observed between the more humid Sousse region in the north with its endless groves of olives and the drier country round Sfax to the south with its steppe vegetation of esparto grass and artemisia (though in recent years large plantations of olives have also been established here).

Much of the rain is brought by moisture-bearing east winds.

Central steppeland

To the south of the Dorsale, from the Algerian frontier in the west to the Sahel in the east, steppe country predominates – semi-arid upland steppe in the west, reaching heights of 600–800m/1970–2625ft, lowland steppe in the Kairouan basin.

In the southern part of the steppe area are the deposits of phosphates which make such an important contribution to the Tunisian economy.

Geographical Regions

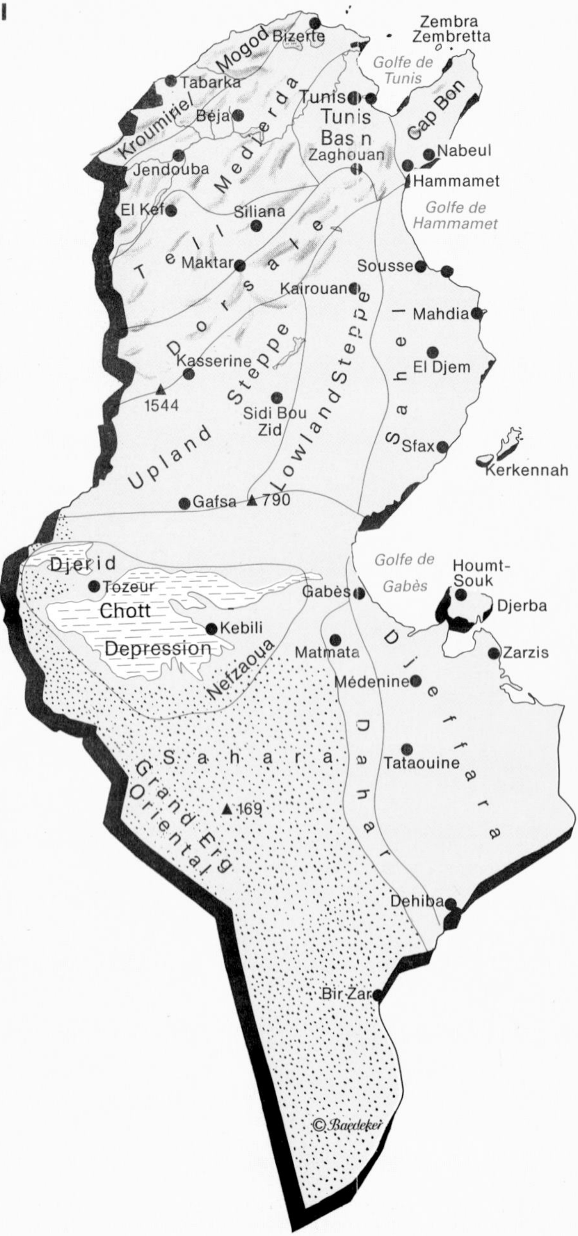

Bizerte
Zembra
Zembretta
Golfe de Tunis
Mogod
Tabarka
Kroumirie/
Medjerda
Tunis
Tunis Basin
Cap Bon
Béja
Nabeul
Jendouba
Zaghouan
Hammamet
Golfe de Hammamet
El Kef
Siliana
Tell
Dorsale
Maktar
Sousse
Kairouan
Mahdia
Kasserine
El Djem
1544
Upland Steppe
Lowland Steppe
Sidi Bou Zid
Sahel
Sfax
Kerkennah
Gafsa
790
Djerid
Tozeur
Chott
Depression
Kebili
Nefzaoua
Golfe de Gabès
Gabès
Houmt-Souk
Djerba
Matmata
Zarzis
Médenine
Djeffara
Sahara
Tataouine
Dahar
Grand Erg Oriental
169
Dehiba
Bir Zar
© Baedeker

A barren landscape on the edge of the Chott

Sahara

South of Tamerza, Gafsa and Meknassy begins the region of desertic steppe, which beyond the great depression occupied by the *chotts* – the large salt lakes (Chott el Rharsa, Chott el Djerid, Chott el Fedjadj) which divide the country into two roughly equal halves – gives place to the real desert, the Sahara (Arabic = "waterless sea").

Oases

On the fringes of the desert the existence of natural reserves of water or the creation of irrigation systems has given rise to oases – described by the Romans as "dark spots on the leopard's skin".

Grand Erg

To the south of the *chotts* are the ranges of dunes of the Grand Erg Oriental.

Djeffara plain

Along the Mediterranean coast extends the steep Djeffara plain, made up of clays and sandstones, with the island of Djerba lying offshore.

Dahar uplands

Between this and the Grand Erg Oriental are the Dahar uplands, a long narrow plateau of Cretaceous limestones rising to a height of 600m/2000ft, the home of the Berbers

Coast

Tunisia has some 1300km/807 miles of coastline on the Mediterranean. This consists predominantly of spacious open sandy beaches, which in the past offered easy access for foreign conquerors.

On the east coast are three large bays: the Gulf of Tunis, the Gulf of Hammamet and the Gulf of Gabès. The Gulfs of Hammamet and Gabès are the country's most popular holiday and tourist areas.

Rocky shores are found mainly on the north coast, round Tabarka. Other rocky coasts with sandy beaches extend to the east of this by way of Cap Négro, Sidi Mechrig and Cap Serrat to the little town of Bechateur. On the east coast there are rocky stretches at Hergla (north of Sousse), at the tip of Cap Bon (though on the west and east coasts of the peninsula there are long, beautiful sandy beaches) and on the offshore islands of Zembra and Zembretta just to the west of the cape.

Islands

Off the coasts of Tunisia lie a number of islands. Off the north coast is the La Galite group, only one of which is inhabited; another is a nature reserve.

On the west coast of Cap Bon

The islands of Zembra and Zembretta, off Cap Bon, were designated a National Park in 1974. At the south end of the Gulf of Hammamet, opposite Monastir, are the Iles Kuriate, and farther south, off Sfax, the Iles Kerkennah, two islands linked by a causeway and surrounded by a ring of smaller islets. At the south end of the Gulf of Gabès is Djerba, Tunisia's largest island.

Rivers

In northern Tunisia is the only river in the country that flows throughout the year and discharges into the Mediterranean, the Medjerda. Rising in eastern Algeria, it flows through Tunisia for 361km/224 miles to reach the sea in the Gulf of Tunis.

To the south of the Dorsale are many deeply indented valleys (*oueds* or *wadis),* which are almost always dry, though after heavy rain they turn into raging torrents. Most of them flow into basins near the coast, where the high evaporation rate leads to the formation of salt-marshes (*sebkhas*).

Climate

Tunisia's topography and its climate are closely linked: on the one hand the climate, in particular the rainfall, shapes the topographical pattern, while on the other the climate is influenced by the nature of the country.

Two climatic zones

In Tunisia the Mediterranean and Saharan climates come up against one another, while the barrier of the hills leads to a differentiation between north and south and the influence of the sea produces a variation from east to west. The influence of the Mediterranean declines steadily from east to west, while rainfall decreases from north to south but slightly increases from west to east.

Climatic differences

Four different types of climate can thus be distinguished:

– the north of the country, with wet winters and dry summers;

A fertile oasis

A deeply indented oued

– the central steppe country, with a changeable climate, hot summers, cold winters and lower rainfall;
– the Mediterranean coast, influenced by the sea, with much smaller climatic variations; and
– the desertic climate to the south of the *chotts*.

Rainfall

Throughout Tunisia the rain falls almost exclusively during the winter months. It is usually brought by offshoots of depressions in the region of west winds farther north, whose paths move far enough south to influence the climate of Tunisia only in the colder months of the year. During the summer the whole country lies within the subtropical high-pressure zone, which is extremely stable and diverts the areas of low pressure from the west-wind zone round the north of the Mediterranean. Nevertheless there are exceptions which prove the rule, for in Tunisia as in other countries holidaymakers may be caught unawares by showers of rain in summer. The likelihood of such an occurrence falls rapidly from north to south, particularly beyond the Dorsale in central Tunisia, whose peaks may bring down rain from stray areas of low pressure; but even in the steppe country to the south, and indeed also in the Saharan *chott* depression, there can be devastating rainstorms leading to dangerous floods. Within a few minutes the normally dry wadis can turn into raging torrents which sweep away anything in their track and make important roads impassable.

Temperatures

The climatic range from Mediterranean to Saharan is also reflected in variations in temperature. With increasing distance from the sea maritime influences decline and the climate becomes continental, with increasing differences in temperature between day and night and between summer and winter. Near the coast, with warm summers and mild winters, temperatures are equable, but in the Saharan climatic zone temperature variations of over 20°C/68°F between summer and winter are quite normal. The extremes in the Sahara are between summer temperatures of 50°C/122°F and ground frosts in winter.

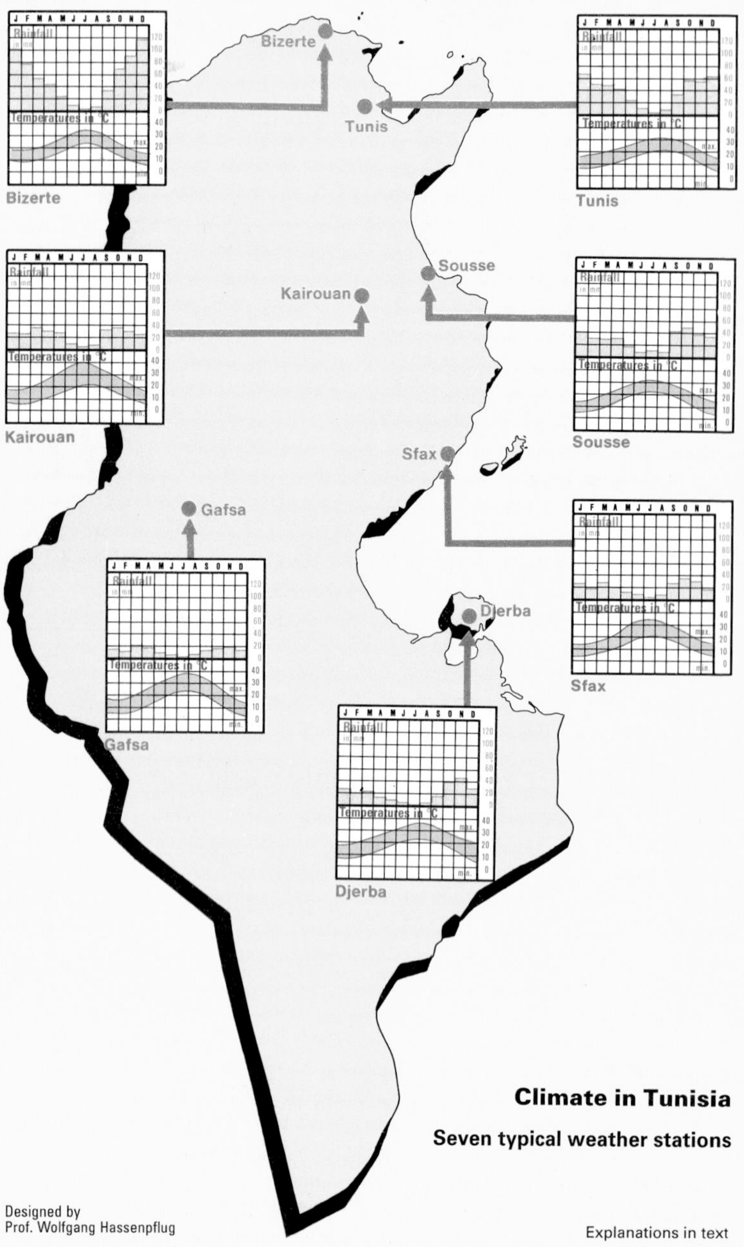

Climate in Tunisia

Seven typical weather stations

Designed by
Prof. Wolfgang Hassenpflug

Explanations in text

Coastal areas

Holidaymakers on the Tunisian coast can be sure of high summer temperatures both during the day and at night. Thanks to the moderating influence of the sea, wide temperature variations such as are found in the interior of the country do not occur on the coasts.
It can become intolerably hot only when the dry sirocco known in Tunisia as the *chehili* blows in from the Sahara. Disagreeable, too, can be the *chergui,* which occasionally blows inland from the Mediterranean, bringing with it masses of moist air and an increasing sultriness.

Climatic diagrams

The climatic characteristics of different parts of Tunisia are reflected in the diagrams of temperature and rainfall on page 16. The blue columns show annual rainfall in millimetres month by month in accordance with the blue scale on the right. The temperatures are shown in the red band, the upper edge of which shows average maximum day temperatures and the lower edge average minimum night temperatures in accordance with the red scale on the right.
There is less variation in the length of day and night in Tunisia than in more northerly latitudes. On average the sun rises in summer an hour later and sets an hour earlier than in northern Europe, and twilight lasts only half as long; while in winter the day is correspondingly longer. During the intermediate seasons day and night are of equal length.

Northern climatic zone

The hilly northern part of Tunisia has a Mediterranean climate, with dry, hot summers and relatively wet, mild winters. This results from the fact that the weather pattern is determined in summer by the subtropical high-pressure and drought zone and in winter by the extra-tropical west-wind zone of the temperate latitudes.
As a result of Tunisia's situation on the southern edge of the Mediterranean climatic zone subtropical influences are stronger than in the Mediterranean countries of Europe.
During the winter humid air masses move into Tunisia from the northwestern Mediterranean and discharge their moisture, usually in the form of violent showers, on the hills of the Dorsale. The wettest part of the country is around Ain Draham (alt. 739m/2425ft; annual rainfall 1537mm/61in). Rainfall decreases markedly towards the coast at lower levels, in areas farther from the coast to the south and on the east coast (Bizerte 653mm/26in, Tunis 44mm/1¾in).

Thanks to the heat stored in the Mediterranean average minimum night temperatures on the coast never fall below 8°C/46°F in winter, and even the absolute minimum winter temperatures scarcely fall below freezing point, whereas in the desertic interior of southern Tunisia they may fall as low as -4°C/+25°F. Maximum day temperatures in winter are around 15°C/59°F. At higher levels, however, there may be up to 40 days with snow.
In summer there are some 40 hot days (with maxima above 30°C/86°F) on the north coast (Bizerte); at Tunis there are 76; otherwise maxima remain below 30°C. Minimum night temperatures, at 20°C/68°F, are some 4°C/7°F below the temperature of the sea.
The hill regions have lower temperatures even in summer, and were much favoured by the French as summer retreats.

Central climatic zone

In a narrow transitional zone to the south of the Dorsale the climate changes to that of the desertic steppe, in which the rainfall and the number of days with rain decrease towards the south and the number of hot days increases. The fully desertic zone begins about the latitude of the Chott el Djerid and the Matmata uplands.

In Tunisia, as in other countries on the edge of the drought zone, actual levels of rainfall diverge widely from the average: in the wet winter of 1958–59, for example, rainfall was twice the average, while in the dry winter of 1960-61 it was only half the average. An annual rainfall of 400mm/16in is necessary to permit agriculture without artificial irrigation;

The zone of transition between the Djeffara plain and the Dahar uplands

and in dry years the boundary of the area with sufficient rainfall lies in the north of the transitional zone, while in wet years it moves south.

When there is rain this frequently takes the form of violent deluges, during which twice as much rain can fall in 24 hours as in a normal month. Most of the water drains rapidly away and only a small proportion seeps into the ground and is of benefit to agriculture.

In a narrow coastal strip the sea has a moderating influence on temperatures and promotes rainfall. Sousse has an annual rainfall of 331mm/13in, falling on 69 days in the year (7 of them between June and August); in Hammamet, to the north, the figures are rather higher; Sfax, to the south, has only 203mm/8in, falling on 43 days (4 of them between June and August). Summer temperatures in Sousse are barely 1°C/1.8°F higher than on the north coast (Bizerte), but with less cloud cover and lower rainfall there are more hours of sunshine than on the north coast.

The inland country to the west is distinctly drier than the regions to the east and north. It is too far from the Mediterranean in the east, and on the north it is sheltered by the hills, which cause the air masses coming in from the sea to rise and discharge their rain before falling again on the lee side of the hills, where the clouds disperse. In winter the fall winds (*djebili*) are cold, dry and stormy, causing damage to vegetation.

Kairouan, in north-eastern Tunisia, has only 298mm/12in of rain, falling on 53 days in the year (6 of them between June and August).

The lower humidity of the air leads to considerable variations in temperature over the day and over the year (reflected in a broader and more highly arched temperature band in the diagram). Maximum day temperatures at Kairouan in July and August are above 37°C/99°F, or 7°C/12.6°F higher than on the north coast. Kairouan has the greatest number of hot days (121) of all the weather stations. In the dry air, however, temperatures of this order are still relatively tolerable.

Southern climatic zone

The climate in the south is increasingly influenced, particularly in spring and summer, by southerly and south-westerly winds, which, as the sirocco (Tunisian *chehili)*, bring in the dry heat of the Sahara and may lead to a rise in temperature of around 10°C/18°F and a fall in the humidity of the air of 10–15%. Kairouan has 31 days of sirocco, Sousse 3–4, Tunis about half a day.
Masses of humid sea air are carried in from the east by the *chergui*, which is the main bringer of rain to Djerba, the Sahel and the Matmata area and may also bring an oppressive sultriness. At Gabès the chergui blows up to 125 days in the year. When there is rain it is a fine, long-lasting rain, which seeps into the soil and is beneficial to agriculture, particularly in spring.
The island of Djerba falls within the central Tunisian transitional zone, with rather higher rainfall than on the mainland (209mm/8¼in on 40 days in the year). Temperatures are 2–3°C/3½–5½°F higher than in the north, so that summers are hotter and winters milder.

On the mainland a coastal strip some 100km/60 miles wide has low annual rainfalls of between 200mm/8in and 100mm/4in (Gabès 180mm/7in, on 34 days in the year); only the Matmata upland region has rather more rain. Farther inland the climate tends towards a fully desertic character. In the Chott el Djerid region and the Grand Erg Oriental annual rainfall is below 100mm/4in. At Tozeur the annual rainfall is only 94mm/3¾in, while 1618mm/64in can be lost by evaporation. The number of hot days (with temperatures over 30°C/86°F) rises between Gabès and Gafsa from 71 to 114. Here, in the dry air, the ranges of temperature variation over the day and over the year are the highest in Tunisia. At Gafsa the average January temperatures are over 14°C/57°F at noon and 4°C/39°F at night; in July the corresponding figures are 38°C/100°F and 21°C/70°F.
Rarely recorded extreme values have been over 50°C/122°F at midday in summer and under -5°C/+23°F in winter. At Gafsa the average night temperature in winter falls below freezing point six times in the course of a year.

Farther south, in the desert regions not visited by tourists, variations in temperature are even greater. In the extreme south the average maximum day temperature in summer is around 43°C/109°F, falling to 22°C/72°F at night. In January the variation in temperature over the day ranges between 3°C/5½°F and 18°C/32°F. Rainfall also decreases sharply: in the extreme south it falls to 27mm/1in, spread over 7 days. The average duration of sunshine rises to 3382 hours (about 141 days).
The extreme conditions of the desert climate call for special precautions in dress (protection against the sun and against cold) and in supplies of water. Even without feeling thirsty visitors may lose so much water by evaporation in the dry air and high temperatures as to bring on collapse.

Flora and Fauna

Natural vegetation

The flora and fauna of Tunisia, conditioned by geographical situation and climate (particularly rainfall), reflect the transition from Mediterranean to Saharan vegetation. Almost half of Tunisia is Mediterranean, with plants and animals of familiar southern European types; the desert, however, forms an impassable barrier between European and African vegetation.
Human bones and rock engravings dating from prehistoric times found in the Hoggar and Tassili hills (and now to be seen in the Bardo Museum in Tunis) show that in Palaeolithic and Mesolithic times, between 500,000 and 7000 years ago, the Sahara was a fertile region, the home of buffaloes, elephants, rhinoceroses and giraffes.

Flora

The original vegetation cover of Tunisia, with its cool, humid climate, was dense primeval forest, but the pattern has been radically changed over the many thousands of years during which man has brought the land into cultivation and destroyed the natural vegetation. Of the plants cultivated in earlier days there still remain the fig, the vine and the carob-tree. The olive (see below) was introduced by the Phoenicians, while the prickly pear, now very common, was brought in from Central America by the Spaniards as recently as the 16th century.

The clearance of forest for cultivation, the felling of timber and over-grazing by stock have left very little of the once dense forest cover of northern Tunisia. Perhaps the only exception is the Kroumirie area, the western part of the coastal Tell. In this rainiest region of Tunisia there are still extensive forests of holm-oaks, cork-oaks and Aleppo pines; but in the Mogod hills, immediately east, the picture is very different. Large-scale clearance of the forests began in Roman and Punic times, and the vegetation now consists of the low-growing garrigue familiar throughout the Mediterranean area (mainly aromatic plants such as thyme, lavender and mint) and the macchia, a higher-growing scrub (2–4m/6½–13ft high) of sclerophyllous (hard-leaved) evergreens interspersed with myrtles, wild olives, cistus, arbutus and tree heaths. Even on Cap Bon, famous in ancient times as a source of timber for ship-building, this is the predominant vegetation pattern.

To the north of Tunis, around the mouth of the Oued Medjerda and on the southern shores of Lake Ichkeul, are extensive areas of marshland.

In the steppe country of central Tunisia the vegetation consists solely of plants which can withstand heat, drought and cold nights – mainly esparto grass (a raw material used in papermaking which is one of Tunisia's exports), both cultivated and wild; acacia bushes and trees; and various species of palms and cactuses, the commonest of which is the prickly pear (often used to make hedges).

In the wide steppe-like plain around Kairouan esparto grass is a monocultural crop. In the coastal strip between Hammamet in the north and Sfax in the south the fields of esparto give place to groves of olive-trees.

The olive

The olive-tree ranks after the date-palm as Tunisia's most important crop (some 30 million trees). It was brought in by Phoenician merchants about 500 B.C., and it is still cultivated in accordance with the rules laid down by the Carthaginian agricultural writer Mago. The trees are planted in a regular grid at a distance of 22m/72ft from one another. After twenty years a tree 8–10m/26–33ft high can yield between 8 and 10 kilograms of oil, depending on its age and the quantity of rain. The olives are picked with the aid of ladders in November and are exported either as oil or as preserves. The stones are processed to provide fodder, fertiliser or soap.

The desert

The desert covers about a quarter (45,000sq.km/17,374sq.miles) of the area of Tunisia. Its vegetation consists of plants which can stand drought, the scorching sun and the high salt content of the soil in some areas – agaves, thistles, cactuses and various thorny shrubs. Along the wadis, which can store moisture, grow tamarisks, oleanders and date-palms, which drive their roots deep into the ground. With the help of artificial irrigation the oases have been transformed into luxuriant gardens. Here, in a system of "tiered" cultivation, the main crop is dates; below the date-palms are fruit-trees (apricots, pears, pomegranates, bananas, figs, citrus fruits, olives); and under these again are vegetables, tobacco and cereals. Increasing shortage of ground-water and erosion, however, are leading to the steady encroachment of the desert on the oases. Efforts are being made to stem this development by afforestation, the construction of barriers of dunes and the extension of artificial irrigation.

The date

The date-palm (*Phoenix dactylifera*), which originally came from Persia and Arabia, is now grown by the million in southern as well as northern Tunisia. The palms, which can be up to 200 years old, are of separate sexes, and the female palms must be pollinated by hand. This is done by removing the small yellow fruits of the male palms and tying them to the clusters

An olive grove near Sfax

of fruit on the female palms. By this means some 200 female palms can be fertilised by one male palm.

A date-palm, depending on variety, can yield between 30 and 100 kilograms of dates a year. The dates are both a staple food and a cash crop. The only kind of date exported is the top-quality Deglat en Nour ("Finger of Light"). In addition the stones are used to make coffee substitute and fodder for stock, the palm-stems to make furniture, roof-beams, etc., the fibres to make rope. The long palm-leaves are bound together to form palisades to protect the oases from the encroaching desert.

A popular Tunisian drink is palm wine, made from the sap of the palm-tree by a process of fermentation which takes only 24 hours. Visitors should be wary of its intoxicating power and its effect on their digestion.

Fauna

Like its vegetation, Tunisia's fauna has been drastically reduced since ancient times. As a result of the extension of human settlement, deforestation and climatic changes the lions, leopards, elephants, ostriches and bears which once lived in northern Africa have long since disappeared. They were ruthlessly hunted by the Carthaginians and even more so by the Romans, and the last survivors were exterminated during the French protectorate. Species that are now almost extinct are the ostrich, the panther, the water buffalo, the Atlas or Berber deer, the moufflon, the forest fox, the fennec fox, the striped hyena, the mountain gazelle, the bustard, the monk seal and the desert monitor. The disappearance of animal species, however, is a symptom of the destruction of the earth which is now a concern of all its inhabitants. Accordingly the Tunisian government has sought since the country achieved independence in 1957 to protect the threatened environment by introducing new laws and by establishing nature reserves (see Practical Information, National Parks).

Mimosa

Prickly pear

In the marshy country around Lake Ichkeul there are believed to be a few surviving specimens (at present about twenty) of Tunisia's largest mammal, the water buffalo, which stands some 1.80m/6ft high and weighs well over a ton. In the wooded north-west of the country, between Tabarka and Ghardimaou, the shy Atlas deer can occasionally be seen; and in this area there are large herds of wild pigs, whose young provide a welcome prey for jackals. In the higher hill regions there are genets, red foxes, in the Medjerda valley otters, porcupines and Tunisia's smallest mammal, the 4cm/1½in long pigmy shrew. In the Djebel Chambi area there are a few isolated specimens of the moufflon (now a protected species), a distant relative of the goat, with heavy outward-curling horns and a mane which falls down from its chin over its breast.

Farther south the jerboa – looking very much like a miniature edition of a kangaroo when it stands up on its long hind legs, supporting itself on its tail – can sometimes be encountered at night. Prized as a delicacy by both humans and animals, it lives a very retired life. In the esparto steppe country the striped hyena lives in caves, feeding on Kabyl dogs and on goats and donkeys which have lost their way in the hills. On the fringes of the Sahara the big-eared fennec fox may occasionally be seen; previously hunted for the sake of its skin, it is now a protected species.
The gazelles which were formerly common in Tunisia are now rare. The Dorcas gazelle and the addax are occasionally met with in the southern Sahara.
Two important refuges for endangered species are the La Galite islands off the north coast and the islands of Zembra and Zembretta off Cap Bon, with the last surviving colonies of monk seals in the whole of the Mediterranean.

Dromedary

The dromedary, though now rarer than it was, still ranks with goats, sheep, donkeys and mules as one of the characteristic domesticated animals of Tunisia.

The ubiquitous donkey

Stork's nest in north-western Tunisia

The dromedary, which is distinguished from the camel by having only one hump and is found throughout North Africa and south-western Asia, has been for many centuries the very basis of life and survival for the nomads of the Sahara, having been brought in from Arabia some 2000 years ago. These undemanding animals, standing some 2.20m/7¼ft high at the shoulder, with a length of around 3m/10ft, can go without water for up to two weeks, after which they will drink 150 litres/33 gallons in one go. A herbivore, the dromedary can survive the winter on the barest thorny scrub and then make up for its abstinence in the brief green period in the Sahel. It has a distinctive amble, with the two legs on each side moving together.
The dromedary was for centuries the nomads' beast of burden, and to some extent still is. It can carry loads of up to 250kg/5cwt for distances of up to 40km/25 miles in a day, and only the coming of the lorry has offered it any serious competition.

Birds

Every year millions of migrant birds spend the winter in Tunisia. The inland lakes and salt-flats (*sebkhas*) and Cap Bon are the home of numerous species of songbirds and of long-eared owls, buzzards, falcons and sparrowhawks. In north-western Tunisia there are large numbers of storks, and nowhere in North Africa are so many greylag geese to be seen as on Lake Ichkeul. In spring countless flamingoes nest on salt lakes throughout Tunisia.

Snakes

Of the 22 species of snakes in Tunisia only five are poisonous. In the northern hills can be found the Levant viper; in central Tunisia the African forest or black-and-white cobra, the longest of the genus (2.5m/8¼ft); in the hot south the horned viper and sand viper. They live mainly on the ground; some of them bury themselves in the sand. The horned viper is identified by the two "horns" above its eyes. Vipers in general have a zigzag pattern along their back. The harmless viperine snake, found in many parts of the country, is often taken for a poisonous viper because of its markings.

Sheep grazing in the central Tunisian steppe

Scorpions

Scorpions, which belong to the class Arachnida, have their head fused with their thorax and a segmented abdomen. The tail, which consists of a number of separate joints, terminates in a poisonous sting which arches back towards the head. On the ten known species of scorpion in Tunisia two are particularly venomous.

Scorpions like to live in the vicinity of human settlements. They are nocturnal in habit, hiding during the day under stones or dry refuse, emerging at night to look for food (insects, particularly spiders) and in the process often entering houses. They are particularly active between June and the end of September. They do not attack unless they feel threatened.

The most dangerous scorpion is *Androctonus australis,* which grows to a length of 10cm/4in. Greyish yellow in colour, it has a darker under side and long pincers which are almost black. It is found mainly in the area between Foum Tataouine in the south, Gafsa in the west and Kairouan and Sousse in the north. *Buthus occitanus* is more delicately formed and reaches a length of only 7.5cm/2½in. Its pincers and body are straw-coloured, becoming darker towards the rear. Its sting is also extremely dangerous. It is commoner than *Androctonus australis* in the area between Hammamet and Le Kef in the north and the Sahara in the south.

Action if stung

For the immediate action to take if stung by a scorpion, see Practical Information, Health.

Population

Tunisia has a population of some 8.1 million. This figure, for the end of 1989, is an estimate: the last census was in 1984 when the figure was 7 million.

Particularly in the north of the country and in the larger towns many women wear European dress; but in general the street pattern is set by women wearing the traditional *sifsari*, a white cloak reaching down to the ground and half covering the face. The red felt skull-caps (*chechias*) worn by men, once so common, are now more rarely seen, but there is still a street in the Medina of Tunis named after them, the Souk el Chechia, where there are numerous shops specialising in their manufacture and sale.

Density and distribution

The average density of population in Tunisia is 47.7 to the square kilometre (123.5 to the square mile). By European standards this seems extraordinarily low; but the population is not evenly distributed and there are wide regional differences. On the one hand there is a distinct downward gradient from north to south; on the other there is a traditional contrast between town and country.
In the Mediterranean north, with its sufficiency of rain, roughly 50% of the total population live on 20% of the country's area. Another 20% live in the Sahel around Sousse and Sfax on 10% of the area. The rest of the population are distributed over the remaining 70%, with a sharp decline in density from north to south. The extreme south of the Sahara is almost completely unpopulated. The Tunis area has a population density of around 850 to the square kilometre (2200 to the square mile); in the Sahel the figure is 90 to the square kilometre (233 to the square mile).

Flight from the land

Around the middle of the 19th century only about 10% of the Tunisian population lived in towns; 75% were sedentary peasants and the remaining 15% were nomads. With the coming of Europeans, however, the situation changed: the old system of growing food only for domestic consumption gave place to a more modern agricultural pattern aimed at the marketing and export of produce. Large farming estates came into being, increasingly using the most modern machinery. The result of this new labour-saving technology was to leave the majority of the working population in rural areas – which in any case had grown considerably – without employment. Thereupon the dispossessed workers flooded into the towns, burdening the labour market there. Between 1966 and 1985 the proportion of the population living in towns rose from 40.1% to 56.8%. In spite of the government's efforts to stem the flight from the land by the development of rural areas (health, education and social services) the trend still continues.

Towns

With a few exceptions all the towns are in the coastal areas. The largest town is Tunis, with a population of around a million (2 million in the conurbation of Greater Tunis); the second largest is Sfax (pop. 232,000), followed by Sousse (100,000), Bizerte (94,000), Gabès (92,000), Menzel Bourguiba (90,000), Kairouan (75,000), Gafsa (65,000), Kasserine (50,000), Béja (50,000) and Nabeul (40,000). The towns of Le Kef, Monastir and Mahdia each have a population of around 35,000. (All these figures are estimates made in 1985.)

Population growth

The annual rate of population growth, based on the average for the years 1973–83, is about 2.5%. The birth rate over this period was 33 per 1000, the death rate only 9 per 1000. The infantile mortality rate is 83 per thousand, expectation of life 62 years.

In 1870 the estimated population of Tunisia was 1.5 million. By 1906 the figure had risen to 2 million; it now exceeds 8 million. The causes of this population explosion are the same as in most other developing countries: rapid improvements in public health and medical care as a result of the influence, direct or indirect, of the industrialised countries (in the case of Tunisia the influence of France after the establishment of the protectorate in 1881). In the developing countries, however – in contrast to the industrial countries – economic development (that is, industrialisation) could not keep pace with the growth in population. And in Tunisia it was the protecting power, France, that hindered the industrialisation of the country.

Tunisia was seen by France as primarily a supplier of raw materials, and accordingly the agricultural sector continued for too long to be the principal element in the country's economy. The contrast between the population explosion on the one hand and economic stagnation on the other grew steadily sharper, and Tunisia was classed as an under-developed country. The influence of Islam, which regards a large family as a blessing, was also significant in this respect. In spite of this, however, the government has devoted considerable effort to the regulation of births and family planning.

Unemployment

Unemployment is one of the greatest problems of the Tunisian economy. The unemployment rate in 1988 was given as 15%, but other estimates put it at 25%; the problem is particularly serious among young people and in rural areas. The difficulties are aggravated by the unfavourable economic situation in the countries of the West and by the conflicts with Libya, since in the past many Tunisians found work in western Europe and Libya.

Until 1979 most of the working population were employed in agriculture, forestry and fishing. Since 1984, however, the flight from the land and other factors have altered the situation, and 56% of the working population are now employed in industry, with the construction industries showing the highest rates of growth.

Ethnic Composition

Apart from small French, Italian and Maltese minorities, the population of Tunisia consists almost exclusively (95%) of Arabs and Arabised Berbers. In spite of appearances, however, Tunisia is by no means uniformly Arab, and the faces of people in the street show that Tunisians come from many different ethnic origins.

The original inhabitants of Tunisia were Berbers. Now, however, they constitute only a small minority of the population, having been overlaid in the course of many centuries by a variety of foreign peoples. Around 1000 B.C. the Phoenicians, a Semitic people, came to Tunisia. They were conquered by the Romans, who in turn gave place to the Vandals. Then from the 7th century onwards Arab conquerors thrust into the country from the east, and the Arabisation of Tunisia began. Between the 13th and the 17th centuries many Andalusians, including large numbers of Jews, fled to Tunisia from Spain during the reconquest of that country by the Christian armies.

In later centuries Tunisia was ruled by Turks, Spaniards and the French, each in turn influencing the composition of the population. The active slave trade with Black Africa also contributed to the population mix.

Berbers

Origins

The origins and history of the Berbers, the original inhabitants of Tunisia, are still obscure. All that is known is that they were settled in North Africa, reaching far south into the Sahara, 3000 years before the Phoenicians and that the Numidians, the Garamantes and the ancient Libyans were their ancestors. According to Egyptian sources of around 3000 B.C. they had occupied northern Africa as far as the Canary Islands and the Sahara. The Berbers themselves, who call themselves Imazhighen (Noble Ones), have a legend that in the time of Moses, or perhaps rather earlier, a king named Afriqus, of the race of the Himyarites and the Sabaeans, came to North Africa from the southern Yemen, conquered it and settled some of his Himyarite troops in the country. The incomers mingled with the peoples of

North Africa and gave rise to the three great Berber tribes, the Masmuda, the Sanhadja and the Zenata. The Berbers of southern Tunisia belong to the Zenata tribe.

The Berber language belongs to the Hamito-Semitic family of languages, to which the ancient Egyptian language, the Semitic languages of the Arabs, Hebrew, some languages in Cameroun, Chad and Nigeria and the Kushite languages spoken in parts of Somalia and Ethiopia also belong. The name of the Berbers is derived from the Greek *barbaroi* (Latin *barbari*, the "foreigners", the "bearded men") by way of the Arabic name Berbri. The Berbers have no written script of their own.

Tribal organisation

The Berber tribes were, and to some extent still are, organised in the same type of social structure. A tribe (*kabila* or *taqbilt*) consists of a number (up to 15) of sections, each of which in turn is made up of several kinship groups or extended families (clans). The head of each group is its eldest member. All the elders of a family form a family assembly (*djemaa*), with an elected head man. The clans belonging to each section have a similar assembly with an elected head man, as do the sections of each tribe. The sections meet regularly, the tribes only in cases of emergency or the event of war. All the male members of a clan or section are of equal status in the *djemaa*. There is thus a completely democratic form of organisation within the tribes and the clans, at any rate so far as men are concerned.

Position of women

Berber women have more rights and liberties than Arab women. Although the Berbers, like the Arabs, are Muslims, more Berber women appear in public unveiled, and within the family and the clan they have greater economic and social rights.

Way of life

Originally few Berbers led a settled life. They were nomads, moving with their flocks of sheep and goats and their herds of camels from grazing-place to grazing-place, building temporary accommodation of stone or living in caves hewn from tufa or chalk, huts constructed of branches or tents woven from camels' wool.
That the Berbers were not a unified people but were descended from different tribes is shown by the differences in their way of life, their ceremonies and their dialects. Common to them all, however – in addition to their language – was their leaning towards particularism, which hindered the development of any political unity and made it easier for foreign conquerors to overcome their resistance. They frequently rebelled, however, against their foreign masters, and as a result their Roman, Arab and Turkish conquerors used their military superiority to drive the Berbers into ever remoter areas in the south of the country. From A.D. 600 the Dahar hills, where native Berbers still survive, became their last retreat.
After bloody conflicts in the early stages of the Arab conquest the Arabisation and Islamisation of the country was achieved in the 7th century. It is estimated that only 2% of the population are now of pure Berber race, living mainly on the island of Djerba and in the southern Dahar hills.
Even after Tunisia became independent in 1957 there was no return to the old nomadic culture, and much of the ancient Berber tradition is now lost. There still remain Matmata, a village of troglodytic dwellings of the Achèche Berbers, the *ghorfas* (honeycomb-like groups of cells, several storeys high, with vaulted roofs) of the Djeffara nomads around Médenine and the rock-cut houses of Chenini. It is to be feared, however, that these typically Berber dwellings will within the foreseeable future be converted into holiday apartments for tourists and that the Berbers will preserve their cultural identity only in folk performances for visitors.

Arabs

The first Arabs came to Tunisia in the 7th century, and their campaigns of conquest in the name of Islam carried them as far west as Spain. There was a second wave of Arabs in the 11th century, when the nomads of the Beni Hilal tribe moved in, bringing with them a patriarchal tribal structure and the Sunnite version of Islam. With the beginning of the Reconquista in the 13th century large numbers of Islamic refugees fled from Spain to North Africa. Most of these Andalusians or Moors, as they were known, settled in Morocco, but many of them came to Tunisia. As they mostly belonged to the upper classes of society and were well educated many of them were employed in government, reinforcing Arab influence on the language, culture and attitudes of the North Africans. In the early 17th century there was a further large influx of Andalusians, most of whom settled on the land, giving a considerable boost to Tunisian agriculture.

Jews

The Jews are one of Tunisia's oldest minorities, contributing to the development and finally the assimilation of the original Berber population from the 1st century A.D. onwards. In the course of the centuries two groups of Jews established themselves in Carthage and on the island of Djerba, which still has fifteen synagogues, including the famous one at La Ghriba. As a result of the Arab-Israeli conflict, however, many of them have left the country. There are now variously estimated to be between 3000 and 10,000 Jews in Tunisia.

History

The first Jews left Jerusalem in 588 B.C., when Nebuchadnezzar captured the city, and a second group left after the destruction of Jerusalem by the Emperor Titus. Coming to Tunisia, they joined various Berber tribes which had previously been converted to Judaism. The largest group, however, was formed by the Jews from Spain, who moved into North Africa in successive waves in the 13th/14th, 16th and early 17th centuries. This last wave, in which the Jews were accompanied by Spanish Muslims, was the result of a decree by the Spanish king expelling all non-Christians from Spain.
There were Jewish communities around Tunis and on the island of Djerba from a very early stage. In the 11th century they were assigned a quarter of their own in Tunis (Hara); but they were required to wear a distinctive form of dress, were prohibited from owning land and had to pay a special tax. Since they were excluded from certain professions and trades they were obliged to confine their activity to those fields which were not permitted to Muslims or were held in low regard: moneylending (the charging of interest being banned by Islam), goldsmith's work (since Muslims were forbidden to work in metals which were credited with mysterious powers), trade and medicine. These various trades brought them prosperity, but this, combined with their religion, excited envy and suspicion – leading, over the centuries, to recurrent restrictions, attacks and pogroms. The situation improved only, under French pressure, in 1857, when the non-Islamic population of Tunisia were granted some degree of equal rights. In 1881, with the establishment of the French protectorate, Jews were permitted to have organisations of their own, for example for the building of schools. In 1956, when Tunisia became independent, there were some 85,000 Jews in the country. The foundation of the state of Israel in 1948 and the Arab-Israeli Six Days War in 1967, however, led large numbers of Jews to leave.

Town Life

Ancient times

Towns played an important part in Tunisian life from a very early stage. In Punic times the government of the country and its economic and cultural life were centred on the over-mighty city of Carthage, and the surrounding areas were of importance only as suppliers of raw materials and food to the capital. This sharp contrast between town and country was aggravated under Roman rule. The city of Carthage was still further developed, and in the rest of the country economic and social life was centred on the new towns established by the Romans, including Thysdrus (El Djem) and Sufetula (Sbeitla). Only the inhabitants of towns could enjoy the privilege of Roman citizenship.

Under the Arabs

The over-emphasis on urban life continued after the Arab invasion of Tunisia. The peasants in the country areas around the towns were still regarded merely as suppliers of raw materials and food, and political, religious and cultural life was confined to the towns. All that the rural population gained in return was military protection in the event of enemy attack, since the towns depended for their survival on the preservation of their rural hinterland.

The Medina

Islamic culture produced a distinctive type of town, still easily recognised in the old towns of Tunisia. The pattern of Muslim life was set by the prescriptions of the Koran and the regulations of the secular authorities, and this was reflected in the layout of the medina, as the Arabs called their towns. The medina was originally a fortified military camp, into which the civilian population later moved in peaceful times. In the centre stood the principal mosque, reflecting the position of the Koran in the centre of Muslim life. Also within the town walls was the Kasbah, the fortress which was the visible symbol of secular authority; but its battlemented walls and towers were always on the edge of the town, at an appropriate and symbolic distance from the mosque.

The residences of the rulers were always outside the town walls, as at Tunis (Bardo) and Kairouan (Reqqada).

Immediately surrounding the mosque, in the souk quarter, were the shops and workshops of the merchants who enjoyed the highest social standing in the community, the spice-dealers, perfume-dealers, booksellers and jewellery-dealers. Around this inner ring were the establishments of other tradesmen and suppliers such as cloth-dealers, tailors, smiths, saddlers and potters. Finally came the dwellings of the ordinary townspeople: blocks of houses closely huddled round blind alleys opening off the main streets and presenting blank faces to the outside world. Each quarter of the town had its own small mosque with its forecourt and various social amenities such as baths (hammams), fountains, coffee-houses and shops. Outside the town gates were the fondouks, the warehouses and hostelries of the large dealers and merchants.

The first departures from this traditional structure came during the colonial period, when the authorities of the French protectorate established their new towns around the medina, which now became known as the old town. As a result the social and economic divergence between town and country became even wider, particularly in the Tunis area, on which the whole of the country's economic life was still centred. After full freedom of movement was introduced the impoverished rural population swarmed into the towns, the populations of which increased at a disproportionate rate. The traditional structures were thus completely overwhelmed.

After the departure of the French the old-established inhabitants of the medina moved into the modern houses vacated in the new towns, while the new arrivals from the country settled in the old towns. The medinas thus developed into regular ghettoes occupied by the impoverished classes of the population and fell into a state of dilapidation. In the last twenty years or so, however, the situation has changed again. With the development of the tourist trade the old town centres have been rediscovered. The walled medinas with their irregular streets and lanes have acquired a new attraction and have been lovingly restored. As a result housing costs have become so high that rents in the medina are beyond the reach of ordinary people and the old town centres are increasingly becoming tourist areas occupied by enterprising shopkeepers and souvenir-sellers.

Social Order

The radical processes of change to which Tunisia has been exposed since the colonial period have not completely destroyed the traditional social order, but there have been signs of the dissolution of old-established structures and traditions. It is true that Islamic standards of conduct, the bonds of the extended family, respect for the older generation and the strict separation between the "public world" of men and the "private world" of women still shape the thoughts and actions of many Tunisians. It is also the case, however, that at least the more prosperous Tunisians are now largely Europeanised; and even in the middle ranges of the population there are clear signs that the attachment to traditional ways of life and thought is now much looser. This process of change has also begun to affect the rural population. The younger generation in particular – now in a majority as a result of the excess of births over deaths – tends to prefer European clothing and, particularly in the tourist centres, adopts European patterns of behaviour. The situation of women has also changed. Their equality of status is now guaranteed by the law, polygamy is prohibited and legal divorce is permitted. Some 40% of all schoolchildren are now girls.

Religion

Since 1956 the state religion of Tunisia has been Islam in its orthodox Sunnite form, to which some 98% of the population belong. An exception to the general rule is the population of Djerba, more than half of whom are Ibadites (a puritanical sect which split off from the Shiites). In addition there are a minority of around 15,000 Catholics, an even smaller group of Protestants and between 3000 and 10,000 Jews, living mainly on the island of Djerba.

Islam

General
Although Tunisia is an Islamic country the government has been concerned to reduce religious influence on public life. Thus in 1957 polygamy was prohibited; in 1964 the marriageable age for girls was increased from 12 to 17; and the practice of wearing veils and Islamic legal jurisdiction have been abolished. There is now, however, a movement throughout North Africa aimed at "re-Islamisation", and Islamic fundamentalists ("integrists") are seeking to strengthen the influence of Islam on political life and on society.

Origins

Islam, the youngest of the monotheistic world religions, was founded by Mohammed ibn Abdallah, later known as the Prophet Mohammed. Born in Mecca about A.D. 570, he belonged to an impoverished branch of the Quraysh tribe. He became a merchant and travelled widely through much of Arabia and probably also of Syria. With his profound religious interest, he developed a wide knowledge of the religions of the countries through which he travelled, and the doctrine which he proclaimed contained ideas taken from Judaism, Christianity, the religion of Persia and the religions of the various Arab tribes. His monotheistic view of the world, showing the influence of Judaism and Christianity, brought him into conflict with the polytheistic world in which he lived, and he was compelled to flee from Mecca to Medina, where he founded the first Muslim community. The Islamisation of the Maghreb began only fifteen years after Mohammed's death, when Arab horsemen thrust westward from Egypt and at Sufetula (Sbeitla) defeated a Byzantine army which had sought to halt their advance.

Monotheism

The central message of Islam is the doctrine of the unity and uniqueness of God (Allah), as opposed to polytheism, the belief in numbers of gods. A man's fate (*mektoub, kismet*) lies in the hands of this powerful, all-knowing creator God; it is predetermined by Allah and cannot be changed by man. This leads to a kind of fatalism, found in Tunisia as in other Muslim countries. The phrase "Inshallah" ("If Allah wills") is frequently heard in conversation. This belief is enshrined in the very name of Islam, which means complete submission to God and to God's will.

Prophets

The second fundamental principle of Islam is the doctrine of the transmission of God's directions and laws through prophets to whom He has revealed Himself. Islam regards as prophets both figures from the Old Testament (Abraham, Isaac, Moses) and the New Testament (Jesus, John the Baptist). But here there is an important difference from Christianity, for Islam does not recognise the divine nature of Jesus. Mohammed is the latest and the most important of the prophets.

Mohammed preached his new doctrine in Mecca from about 607. This brought him into conflict with members of his tribe, who were polytheists worshipping several important town gods, and finally in 622 he was compelled to flee from Mecca. Along with his supporters he sought refuge in the town of Yathrib, which thereafter became known as Medinet en Nabi ("Town of the Prophet"), or Medina for short. The year of Mohammed's flight from Mecca to Medina, the Hegira, marks the establishment of Islam and the starting-point of Islamic chronology.

Koran

The sacred book of Islam is the Koran, whoch is supplemented by the Sunna (see below). The Koran contains God's revelations to the Prophet Mohammed, transmitted to him through the angel Gabriel as the Word of God. It consists of 114 chapters or suras, which are arranged not according to their content but in order of length, so that suras in praise of God, depictions of hell and paradise and rules and commands on behaviour in everyday life alternate unsystematically.

Although it is recorded in tradition that Mohammed dictated the revelations to his secretaries there was no complete collection of them in existence at his death. Originally they were handed down orally: it was only in the time of the third Caliph ("Successor" to Mohammed), Othman (644–656), that they were brought together in their present form. The Koran is written in Arabic, and only in this form is it regarded as absolutely valid and holy, since the revelations by God were made in that language. The first translation of the Koran into the Berber language was made by Ibn Toumert at the beginning of the 12th century.

Sunna

The Arabic word *sunna* means "custom", "practice", the "way that is followed". The Islamic Sunna is a large collection of accounts of the *sunna* of the Prophet Mohammed, in which his life (and to some extent the lives of his companions), his conduct and his pronouncements are described so that they may serve as guidance for the life of a Muslim. Like the Koran, the Sunna was originally transmitted orally and was first recorded in writing in the 9th century.

Sunnites

Muslims who accept the Sunna as well as the Koran are known as Sunnites, in contrast to the Shiites, who do not recognise the Sunna. All Muslims in Tunisia are Sunnites of the orthodox Malikite school. Since the 17th century the Malikite school has been in dissension with the Ottoman Hanafite school. Since the Koran and the Sunna do not provide answers to all the questions that arise in life, and in some cases make contradictory statements, these points had to be interpreted by religious scholars, the Ulema. These interpretations, however, diverged from one another in a number of fundamental respects, thus giving rise to a number of different schools.

Sharia

The interpretations of the Sunna were collected and, together with the Koran and the Sunna itself, form the Sharia, the code of Islamic law. The Koran, the Sunna and its interpretations lay down rules for the whole public and private life of Muslims, regulating even the simplest daily activities (eating and drinking, personal hygiene, dress, etc.).

Shiites

The Shiites are the other main branch of orthodox Islam. The Shiite schism began with Ali, Mohammed's cousin and son-in-law, who became fourth Caliph (Successor of the Prophet) in 656, and it was finally sealed by the murder of Ali in 661 and the flight of his supporters. Ali laid down that only blood relatives of the Prophet could be his successors. Accordingly he and his adherents, the Shiites (Shiat Ali, the Party of Ali) did not recognise his three predecessors, Abu Bakr (632–634), Omar (d. 644) and Othman (d. 656) as Caliphs, holding that he himself was the first legitimate successor of the Prophet. The Shiites also refuse to recognise all Caliphs after Ali who were not related to him, and they reject the Sunna, which contains the *sunna* of Mohammed's successors as well as that of the Prophet himself.

The Shiites venerate the first Imams (Leaders) descended from Ali and look forward to the coming of the Mahdi, the last Imam, who shall establish a final kingdom of justice on earth. Most Shiites (the "Twelvers") recognise the Mahdi as the twelfth true successor to Mohammed; a minority (the "Seveners"; Ismailis) see him as the seventh successor. The Imams are revered as holy men – the Shiites having a more mystical conception of religion than the Sunnites.

Kharijites

The Kharijites split off from the Shiites in 657, since they regarded Ali as too ready to compromise with his opponents. They also believed that the decisive qualification for the office of Caliph was not blood relationship but religious merit. The members of this ascetic sect were ready from the outset to achieve their aims by force – they were responsible for the murder of Ali – and found adherents particularly among the Berbers, who in spite of their conversion to Islam felt themselves to be disadvantaged.

After their military defeat in the 10th century the Kharijites withdrew into particular areas and developed independently. The moderate Ibadites on the island of Djerba and the Mzab of Algeria are offshoots of the Kharijites.

The Laws of Islam

The five pillars of Islam

The five main duties of believers, known as the five pillars of Islam, are derived from the Koran and the Sunna. They are the confession of faith (*shahada),* prayer (*salat),* the giving of alms (*zakat),* fasting (*sawm*) and the pilgrimage to Mecca (*hajj*).

Shahada

The *shahada,* the confession of faith, is in the simple form: "There is no god but Allah, and Mohammed is his prophet." It must be spoken in the Arabic language and is repeated by believing Muslims many times in the course of a day. It is proclaimed to the faithful by the muezzin from the minaret five times a day (now usually a recording broadcast through loudspeakers). It is "a lullaby, a funeral hymn, a watchword, a recognition sign, a war cry and a cry of delight, all in one".

To become a convert to Islam it is only necessary to repeat the *shahada* in the presence of Muslim witnesses.

Salat

Salat is the Muslim's duty to pray five times daily. He is summoned to prayer by the muezzin's call (*adhat*) in the early morning, at midday, in the afternoon (3pm), immediately after sunset and two hours after sunset.

In preparation for prayer the believer must cleanse his face, mouth, hands and feet; he must stand on clean ground (on a carpet, a blanket or, if nothing else is available, an item of clothing); and he must silently declare that he desires to pray. There is always a fountain in the courtyard of a mosque for the ritual ablutions; where no water is available the cleansing may be symbolic (for example, with sand).

When praying the believer faces in the direction of Mecca. The actions and postures of prayer are strictly prescribed:

1. He stands erect with his hands raised to head height, his open palms facing forward, and recites the "Allahu akbar" ("God is great").
2. Still standing erect, with his arms hanging by his sides or with his right hand over his left in front of his body, he says the first sura of the Koran (the *fatiha),* followed by other suras or verses.

3. He makes a deep bow, with his hands on his knees, and pronounces prayers in praise of Allah.
4. He prostrates himself, with his forehead touching the ground, and pronounces further invocations in praise of Allah.
5. After every two parts of the prayer and after the last part he repeats the confession of faith, kneeling, with the index finger of his right hand extended on his knee.
6. At the conclusion of his prayer, again kneeling, he looks back over his right and then his left shoulder, offering a greeting to the guardian angels and his fellow-worshippers.

Muslims are required to attend a mosque only for the midday prayer on Fridays. In a mosque the direction of Mecca (*qibla*) is indicated by the *mihrab* (prayer niche). Elsewhere believers must judge the direction of Mecca from the position of the sun.

Islamic prayers contain neither requests nor wishes.

Zakat

Zakat, the giving of alms, is the most important duty of Muslims after the confession of faith and prayer. Mohammed himself prescribed the duty in Medina in the form of an alms tax. Originally this was the only tax payable by Muslims, designed for the benefit of the whole community (*umma),* in accordance with sura 9, verse 60, of the Koran:
"The income of the state [from the alms tax] is intended for the poor and needy; for those who are concerned with the tax [particularly the officials who collected the tax and received a certain proportion of it and the Caliphs, their successors, relatives and representatives who administered it]; for those who must be won over to the cause of Islam; for the ransoming of slaves [of the Muslim faith]; for debtors; for the holy war [against unbelievers]; and for travellers. So God ordains! God is all-knowing, all-wise!"
The rate of tax was set at 10% of the value of crops and of livestock and 2.5% of savings, of gold, silver and coins, of a merchant's goods and of earnings. Nowadays, with state taxation, the alms tax is of much less significance than in the past.

Sawm

Mohammed took the idea of the *sawm,* the month's fast during Ramadan, from Judaism. It is prescribed as an obligation in the second sura of the Koran, and is set in the ninth month of the Islamic calendar, since it was in that month that the angel Gabriel was believed to have appeared to Mohammed. The duty to fast applies only between sunrise and sunset, and extends not only to food and drink but also to smoking and sexual intercourse. Exempt from the duty are children (boys under seven who have not been circumcised and girls who have not menstruated), the old, the sick, pregnant women, travellers and heavy labourers.

Hajj

The obligation to make the pilgrimage to Mecca, the *hajj,* derives from ancient Arab, pre-Islamic, rites connected with the veneration of a large

black meteorite, the *hajjar,* which is preserved in the Kaaba, the sacred shrine in the inner courtyard of the Great Mosque in Mecca. The Kaaba is believed by Muslims to have been built by Abraham and Ishmael. The pilgrimage takes place in the twelfth month of the Islamic year (Dhu-l-Hijjah). All Muslims are required to make the pilgrimage once in the course of their life if their health and financial circumstances permit, and those who do so are entitled to bear the honorific style of El Hajj.
Five pilgrimages to the Tunisian holy city of Kairouan are equivalent to one pilgrimage to Mecca, but the style of El Hajj is reserved for pilgrims to Mecca.

Other prescriptions

Other important religious prescriptions affecting public and private life are the bans on the use of alcohol, the eating of pork, meat that has not been ritually slaughtered, blood and food containing blood, gambling and lending money at interest.

Holy war

Islam also enjoins the propagation of the faith. In earlier days this was pursued by violent means and was described as a holy war (*jihad*). The holy war is now understood only as a duty in the case of defence against an enemy of another faith. Some Islamic theologians, indeed, interpret it merely as a requirement to "bestir oneself on the way to Allah", that is, as a duty to combat one's own inner inadequacy.

Relations between men and women

The Koran and the Sunna also regulate relationships between the sexes. There is no equality between men and women in the Koran: the wife is subordinate to her husband (suras 4, 33, etc.), though the husband must protect and feed his wife and must not maltreat her. Suras 4,4 and 4,25–27 allow a man to have four wives and an unlimited number of concubines and slave-girls, provided that his legitimate wives are not thereby disadvantaged either materially or sexually.
Nowadays most Muslims cannot in any event afford to have several wives, and in modern Tunisia, as in Morocco, polygamy is now prohibited. Under the Tunisian constitution, too, all citizens have equal rights irrespective of sex; and since even the industrial countries of the world have difficulty in putting this principle into practice it is not surprising that Tunisia is likely to take some time to realise it. The first steps have, however, been taken. In the 1980s the percentage of girls attending school rose sharply, and although the number of women with university degrees is still small it too has shown a significant increase. The scene is changing, though the end is not yet in sight.
The Koranic requirement (sura 33,54) that women should wear veils has long been the subject of controversy. It is well established that in Mohammed's time women were not veiled. The practice arose after his death, under the influence of foreign peoples such as the Persians: free women wore veils to distinguish them from the unveiled slave-girls. In our own day, with the increasing influence of the Islamic fundamentalists, the wearing of head-scarves and also of veils has again become common.

Unity of religion and state

The relationship of Muslims with Allah does not require mediation by a priesthood. In Islam the observance of the rules and obligations of the faith is supervised by the religious community itself. The practice of religion is not institutionalised as in the Christian church: from the beginning state and religion in Islam formed an inseparable unity, the political leaders of which, legitimised by descent from Mohammed, combined in their own person all secular and spiritual authority. The legislature, executive and judiciary were frequently in the hands of judges (*qadis*), who, like many high government officials, were well educated scholars, members of the Ulema, who had studied both the law and the theology of Islam. The office of judge was thus always an organ of Islam as well.
In contrast to the political leaders, who in later periods were largely confined to a figurehead role, the Ulema increased in importance, since they were continually reinterpreting the Koran and the Sunna and could thus influence both religious and secular life.

Fundamentalism

In Tunisia, as elsewhere in North Africa, Islamic fundamentalists ("integrists") are increasing in strength and influence. In the first parliamentary election after the deposition of Bourguiba (1987), held in April 1989, fundamentalists gained 14% of the votes on the list of independent candidates, and the attempted coup against the Tunisian government in May 1991 is attributed to members of the Islamic Nahda movement. This development is similar to the situation in neighbouring Algeria, where the integrists have attained a degree of influence which a few years ago would have seemed unthinkable. And there are those who believe that the trend has not yet reached its peak.
The fundamentalists' opposition to the opening up of the country to the West and the consequent erosion of Islamic principles and their anti-capitalism seem to appeal particularly to the young and the poor. Perhaps, too, fundamentalism offers a firm basis with which people can identify in a time of rapid change when the objective or end-point of the development is still very far from clear.
The result of this trend, so far as it has gone, has been to produce a stronger Islamic consciousness and an increased emphasis on Islamic identity. A symptom of this is the appearance of young women in entirely European dress but wearing head-scarves. Even the state television service has joined the movement to the extent of interrupting its programmes for the daily prayers.

The question of Tunisia's future and the further development of fundamentalism, however, is closely bound up with the solution of the country's economic and social problems. It remains to be seen how far the 1300-year-old principles of Islam can show a way forward or perhaps offer alternatives to the western pattern of development.

Unorthodox Beliefs

Islam knows only one God, Allah. Popular belief, however, admits other supernatural elements – angels, a Devil (Shaytan) and spirits (djinns). The spirits are mostly malevolent beings. Just as the orthodox believer needs no priests, so man does not require the help and mediation of good spirits and angels to gain the benevolence and the blessing of Allah and to reach Paradise: all that he needs to do is to comply with God's laws and prescriptions as revealed in the Koran. The influence of the Devil or of evil spirits may hamper his efforts and may thus be harmful to him. Orthodox Sunnite Islam firmly rejects these "deviations" and recognises only the Koran in its scholarly interpretation as the sole way to God.

Sufism

From the 13th century onwards in particular mystical elements in Islam were widely diffused in many Arab countries. Their adherents founded religious orders and brotherhoods (*zaouias),* which frequently developed into influential sects.
Islamic mysticism (Tasawwuf) is represented by the Sufis, who took their name from the *suf,* the simple woollen garment worn by the early ascetics. The aim of the Sufis was to extend the scope of orthodox Islam, with its dogmatic approach, and to achieve a mystical union with Allah by spiritual practices. Accordingly they developed particular ways of promoting spiritual contemplation (ascetic practices, penance, fasting, mortification of the flesh) and also fanatical religious beliefs.

Veneration of holy men

Veneration is accorded to a variety of holy men – dead members of a family or tribe who were notable for their exemplary life and various legendary figures, particularly the founders and well-known representatives of "holy schools", orders and brotherhoods, known in Arabic as *marabouts,* in Berber as *igourramen.* These holy men are credited with miraculous powers and deeds, and are seen as a way towards Allah and as divine forces (*baraka*).

Holy men are venerated at their tombs (*marabouts* or *koubbas),* which are visited by large numbers of pious pilgrims on particular festivals or memorial days (*moussems),* and also at other times throughout the year, particularly during the month of pilgrimage. They remember the dead man, celebrate his virtues and seek through his mediation the fulfilment of their desires (health, fruitfulness, children, a good harvest and so on) as well as participation in his divine redeeming power.

Baraka

The belief in *baraka* is another central idea of Islamic mysticism. This divine redeeming power is possessed not only by the holy men themselves – including of course Mohammed and his descendants – but also by a variety of objects which were owned and touched by the holy men, by the places where they lived or merely stayed in passing, and by their tombs. When the believer visits these places or touches the objects something of the *baraka* passes to him. Even certain plants, springs or other objects possess *baraka,* which believers can acquire by carrying or touching them. *Baraka* not only protects its possessor from misfortune, the evil eye (*l'ain*) and other evil sorcery but brings him good luck.

Amulets

Amulets are objects which possess *baraka.* Silver, for example, has *baraka;* gold has not, and indeed brings misfortune. Berber women, therefore, wear only silver jewellery. A common piece of jewellery worn as an amulet is the "hand of Fatima" (after the Prophet's daughter, who is of course credited with a particularly strong *baraka);* the hand, with its fingers extended, is also known as the *khamsa* ("five").

Henna

Baraka is also attributed to the henna plant. It is used to produce a dye with which Berber women stain their hands and feet, finger- and toenails and hair. Mixed with lime-water, it forms a coloured paste which is applied to the face, arms and legs and protects its wearer from all misfortune, particularly from the evil eye.

The mystical ideas of Sufism are difficult to reconcile with orthodox Sunnite beliefs, and in the past the Ulema repeatedly sought to suppress them, but without success. The current trend towards "re-Islamisation" has brought them once again to the forefront of theological discussion; for in popular belief the veneration of holy men and the belief in *baraka* are still very much alive.

Islamic Calendar

See Practical Information, Calendars

Christianity

The history of Christianity in Tunisia goes back to the establishment of the church in Carthage. In the time of the early Christian writer Tertullian (*c.* A.D. 160–220; see Famous People) the Christian community already had a well developed organisation. The bishop of Carthage was a metropolitan: that is, he was the head of the church in the province of Africa Proconsularis. The Vandal conquest (439 onwards) largely destroyed the church in North Africa, and it was not until 1884 that Carthage again became a Roman Catholic archdiocese.

In 1964 the boundaries of the diocese were redefined to coincide with the territory of the Republic of Tunisia, and it became a territorial prelacy (directly subject to the Pope). Whereas before independence there were some 280,000 Catholics (mainly French) in Tunisia, there are now only 15,000. There are also a number of even smaller Christian denominations which cooperate with the Catholics on an ecumenical basis in the Association for Rural Development and Education (ASDEAR), an organisation entirely independent of the government.

Education

After Tunisia became independent considerable progress was made in the field of education, which still accounts for a third of the national budget. Whereas in 1958 only 23% of children between 6 and 11 had started school the figure had risen to 89% by 1985. The number of students in higher education doubled between 1975–76 and 1986–87 to reach 40,800. Unfortunately, however, neither the school-leaving certificate nor a university degree guarantees a job.
School attendance is compulsory between the ages of 6 and 14, and education is free. Visitors to Tunisia will encounter swarms of schoolchildren wherever they go.

Illiteracy

Although the illiteracy rate has fallen sharply it is still very high among women and in the rural population. While in 1980 54% of the Tunisian population over the age of 14 were illiterate the figure in rural areas was 62% and for women was 68%.

Schools

The school system is based on the French model. Primary education begins at the age of six and normally lasts for six years. Secondary education starts at the age of twelve and lasts for seven years.
In 1975–76 Tunisia had 2319 primary schools and 171 junior and senior secondary schools; in 1986–87 the numbers were 3358 and 420 – an increase of 52%.

Language

In the 1970s only Arabic was spoken in the first three years of primary school. Since 1986–87 French is used from the second primary year onwards, and higher education is almost exclusively in French.

Universities

There are universities in Tunis (founded 1960) and in Sfax and Sousse (founded 1986). Higher educational facilities, however, are still inadequate, so that over 10,000 Tunisian students have to study abroad, mainly in France, followed by the United States, Morocco, Belgium and Algeria.

Government and Administration

On March 20th 1956 the French protectorate established in 1881 came to an end. With the deposition of the last Husseinite Bey on July 25th 1957 Tunisia became a Republic.

Constitution

Tunisia, El Djumhuriya el Tunisiya in Arabic, République Tunisienne in French, has been since 1959 a democratic presidential republic. On the French model, the President has far-reaching powers: he is head of state and of the government, appoints the Council of State and the prime minister, determines national policy and has the right to reject proposed legislation. He is supreme commander of the armed forces and has power to declare a state of emergency.
Parliament has a single chamber of 125 members, elected every five years. Islam is the national religion. The religious (Sharia) courts were abolished in 1956 and replaced by a new judicial system on the French model. In 1957 polygamy was prohibited and the husband's right to reject his wife abolished; and finally the new constitution adopted on June 1st 1959 declared that male and female citizens of Tunisia enjoyed equal rights.

Coat of arms

The national coat of arms, introduced on May 30th 1963, consists of a shield bearing a Carthaginian galley, with the motto "Order, Freedom, Justice" and, above, the symbols of the scales (for justice) and the lion (for order). Over the shield is the Islamic emblem of the crescent moon and star which has featured on the Tunisian flag since 1835.

Flag

Language

The national language is Arabic, the spoken language Tunisian, a western Arabic dialect. The language of business and education is French.

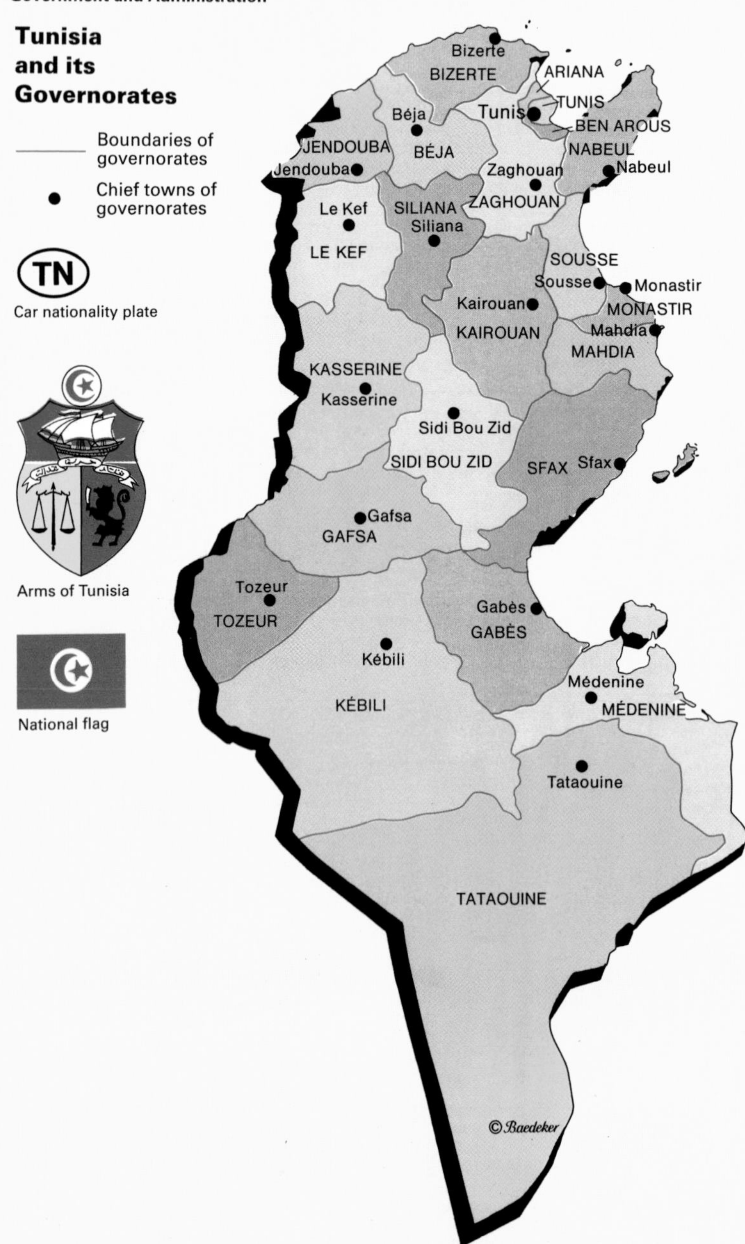
Tunisia
and its
Governorates
Boundaries of
governorates
Chief towns of
governorates
TN
Car nationality plate
Arms of Tunisia
National flag
Bizerte
BIZERTE
ARIANA
TUNIS
Tunis
BEN AROUS
Béja
BÉJA
JENDOUBA
Jendouba
NABEUL
Nabeul
Zaghouan
ZAGHOUAN
Le Kef
LE KEF
SILIANA
Siliana
SOUSSE
Sousse
Monastir
MONASTIR
Kairouan
KAIROUAN
Mahdia
MAHDIA
KASSERINE
Kasserine
Sidi Bou Zid
SIDI BOU ZID
SFAX
Sfax
Gafsa
GAFSA
Tozeur
TOZEUR
Gabès
GABÈS
Kébili
KÉBILI
Médenine
MÉDENINE
Tataouine
TATAOUINE
© Baedeker

Administration (see map, p. 38)

Tunisia is a centralised state with Tunis as its capital. It is divided into 23 governorates (Arabic *wilayas*). The governorates are divided into 136 delegations (Arabic *mutamadias*), which in turn are subdivided into some 1113 municipalities (*shaykhats*).

Governorate	Area in sq.km (sq.miles)	Population (1986)	Population density /sq.km (sq.mile)
Tunis City	346 (134)	815,600	2357.2 (6105)
Tunis Ariana	1,558 (602)	415,800	266.9 (692)
Tunis Ben Arous	761 (294)	271,600	356.9 (924)
Nabeul	2,788 (1,076)	489,600	175.6 (456)
Zaghouan	2,768 (1,069)	126,400	45.7 (119)
Bizerte	3,685 (1,423)	412,700	112.0 (290)
Béja	3,558 (1,374)	286,000	80.4 (207)
Jendouba	3,102 (1,198)	379,800	122.4 (316)
Le Kef	4,965 (1,917)	256,000	51.6 (135)
Siliana	4,631 (1,788)	232,700	50.2 (130)
Kairouan	6,712 (2,592)	451,000	67.2 (174)
Kasserine	8,066 (3,114)	322,700	40.0 (104)
Sidi Bou Zid	6,994 (2,700)	314,500	45.0 (117)
Sousse	2,621 (1,012)	346,000	132.0 (342)
Monastir	1,019 (393)	297,700	292.1 (756)
Mahdia	2,966 (1,145)	290,400	97.9 (254)
Sfax	7,545 (2,913)	627,000	83.1 (215)
Gafsa	8,990 (3,471)	253,300	28.2 (73)
Tozeur	4,719 (1,822)	73,900	15.7 (41)
Kebili	22,084 (8,527)	104,200	4.7 (13)
Gabès	7,175 (2,770)	264,000	37.8 (98)
Médenine	8,588 (3,316)	324,400	37.8 (98)
Tataouine	38,889 (15,015)	109,600	2.8 (8)

Parties

The party which has formed the government since 1964 is the socialist Destour party (Parti Socialiste Destourien, PSD) founded by Habib Bourguiba, which in 1988 changed its name to Rassemblement Constitutionnel Démocratique (RCD). In the last parliamentary election in 1989 it received 80% of the votes.

Among the opposition parties, which have been permitted to exist only since 1988, are the left-wing Mouvement d'Unité Populaire (MUP), originally founded by Ahmed Ben Salah in 1973, the Mouvement des Démocrates Socialistes (MDS), the Parti Communiste Tunisien (PCT), the Parti d'Unité Populaire (PUP) and the fundamentalist Mouvement de Tendance Islamique (MTI) led by Rachid Ghannouchi, which has changed its name to Nahda, the Party of Rebirth. In mid 1991 a moderate wing of MTI split off under the leadership of a lawyer named Mourou.

Trade unions

The Union Génerale Tunisienne du Travail (UGTT) is a confederation of 23 trade unions with a total of some 400,000 members. In 1983 the Union Générale des Travailleurs (UNTT) split off from the UGTT. Another important union is the women's organisation, the Union Nationale de Femmes de Tunisie (UNFT), with some 45,000 members.

International organisations

Tunisia is a member of the United Nations, the Organisation of African Unity (OAU) and the Arab League. Like Morocco and Algeria, it is an associate member of the European Community. It also belongs to the Organisation of Arab Petroleum-Exporting Countries (OAPEC), an Algerian-Moroccan-Tunisian Economic Commission and, since 1989, to the Maghreb Union, which also includes Morocco, Algeria, Libya and Mauretania.

Foreign policy

Tunisia sees itself as a mediator between Western Europe and Africa. In political crises such as the Gulf crisis this position involves a delicate

Parliament Building, Bardo

balancing act which calls for sacrifices from Tunisia itself and in the end leaves none of the parties concerned entirely satisfied.

Through its relations with both Morocco and socialist Algeria Tunisia seeks to act as a mediator within the Arab League. In 1982 it offered asylum to the PLO after it was driven out of Lebanon, but it also advocates negotiations with Israel. It maintains close economic and cultural relations with France, as well as with the United States, Italy and Germany.

Tunisia's relations with its eastern neighbour, Libya, have been the subject of some tension. In 1985, after the collapse in the price of oil, Libya expelled 40,000 Tunisian workers, whereupon relations between the two countries were broken off and the frontier between them was closed. Since then, however, the conflict has been settled, the frontier has been reopened and Tunisian workers are again welcome in Libya. Even a dispute with Libya over ownership of the continental shelf has been amicably settled.

Economy

Tunisian economic policy has taken three different directions since the country became independent. A socialist phase in the 1960s was followed in 1970 by a very liberal phase, which produced a certain prosperity but favoured its unequal distribution. The third phase, which sought to achieve a compromise between these two extremes, ended in the "bread" or "couscous riots" of January 1984, when the repercussions of the world economic crisis reached Tunisia. Since then there has been a degree of stability, and efforts are being made to develop a distinctive Tunisian economic policy. On the criteria of the International Monetary Fund Tunisia is a "threshold country", a state which in economic terms stands between

the poor Third World and the rich industrial nations. This may be true, so far as the figures go, in the capital, Tunis, and the other industrialised Tunisian towns.
With a gross domestic product of around 1230 US dollars per head in 1988, Tunisia ranks as the fifth wealthiest country in Africa, after Libya ($7170, thanks to its oil), Gabon ($3080), Algeria ($2590) and South Africa ($1850). Within a period of thirty years the GDP rose from 230 million dinars to 4.5 billion. Over the same period the population doubled and annual investment increased from 23 million dinars (10% of GDP) to 15 billion (just under 30% of GDP). In spite of this progress Tunisia is still faced with problems typical of developing countries: the uneven distribution of the country's modest prosperity (5% of the population have 22% of the national income, and the trend is still upward), high unemployment, sharp differences between north and south and between town and country, a high illiteracy rate, particularly in rural areas, unequal access to education, high infantile mortality and heavy foreign debts.

Agriculture

Since the earliest times Tunisia has been an agricultural country, and agriculture is still the most important element in the economy, in spite of the drive towards industrialisation in the last few decades. Although agriculture's contribution to the gross domestic product fell from 21% to 15% between 1976 and 1988 more than a quarter of the population are still employed in agriculture and, if account is taken of fishing and the processing of agricultural produce, around half the total population are dependent on it for their subsistence.
Roughly half the area of Tunisia is given up to agriculture and forestry. Arable land takes first place, with some 3.5 million hectares/8.75 million acres, 3% of which are artificially irrigated. Pastureland occupies 3 million

A farm in northern Tunisia

A modern power station, Sousse

hectares/7.5 million acres and permanent crops (mainly date-palms and olive-trees) 1.5 million hectares/3.75 million acres.

Agricultural zones

The main cereal-growing areas of Tunisia, which was known in antiquity as the "granary of Rome", are in the northern coastal strip and the Medjerda valley, well watered by a perennially flowing river and by storage reservoirs. Here too cork is harvested and there are numbers of stock farms. Most of the country's large farms are in these areas.

In the eastern coastal area olives, citrus fruits, vines, fruit and early vegetables are grown. Here too there are stock farms.

The central savanna region produces cereals in the north and esparto grass (used in the production of cellulose and paper, as fodder and in basketwork) in the centre and south.

The main centre of olive-growing is the coastal region round Sousse and Sfax.

In stock farming cattle increasingly give place to sheep towards the south.

Oases

The oases are among the most intensively cultivated areas in Tunisia, as they are in other desert regions. In these areas, which are green throughout the year, palm-trees flourish; and where adequate irrigation is available the "three-tier" system of cultivation is adopted, with fruit-trees (figs, apricots, peaches, pomegranates), grapes and bananas under the palms, and under these again ground-covering vegetables, cereals and fodder plants.

The oases, growing crops mainly for local consumption, were formerly important economic centres on the Saharan trade routes. Under French colonial rule, however, there were great changes. With the increasing importance of towns and new industrial centres and the development of the coastal towns the Saharan trade declined and the oases were increasingly neglected. The emigration of many of the inhabitants, the abandonment of the labour-intensive three-tier system of cultivation, the impoverishment of the peasants, many of whom were compelled to sell their water rights and then their land in order to pay their debts: these were only a few of the many problems.

The recent development of tourism in the oases holds out promising prospects for the future but has also created new problems – not least the increasing pressure on the scanty water supplies.

Irrigation

The problem of water supply is one that concerns not only the oases but the whole of Tunisia, as is evidenced by the reservoirs, aqueducts, complicated water distribution systems, wells and other means of raising water to be seen all over the country. As a longer-term project, hills and hillsides in northern and central Tunisia are being reafforested to enable the soil to retain more of the rainwater that falls in these regions.

In southern Tunisia twelve wells between 2000 and 2500m/6500 and 8000ft deep have been drilled within the last few years, old water channels have been relaid underground and old irrigation systems have been renovated. The efforts to improve agriculture in the oases, however, are still at a very early stage.

Foggaras

The foggaras are underground tunnels which convey water from rainy hill regions or underground reserves to the oases, often running for many miles at a gentle gradient. Their construction, usually by slaves, involved hard and dangerous manual labour: a series of vertical shafts were dug

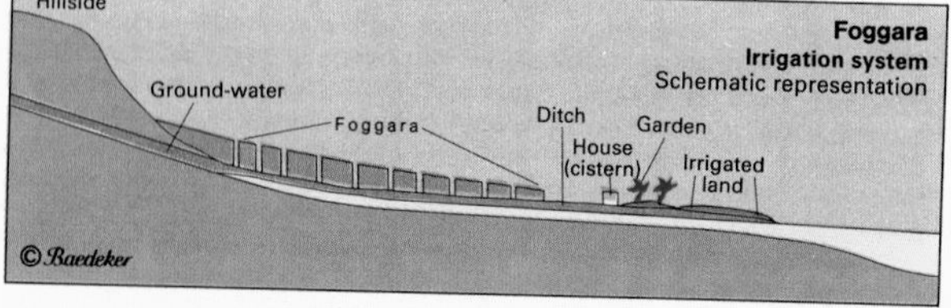

down to the appropriate depth, the tunnel was excavated and the excavated material was removed through the shafts. The advantage of these tunnels over open water channels was that there was much less evaporation.
The maintenance of the tunnels is also laborious and dangerous. Foggaras still in use can be seen in the Nefzaoua oasis and at El Guettar, near Gafsa.

Agricultural produce

The most important agricultural product is olive oil. In the area around Sousse and Sfax there are some 30 million olive-trees, which yield an annual 100,000 tons of oil for export. Tunisia is the world's largest exporter of olive oil after Greece.
Cereals are grown for domestic consumption rather than for export; but owing to the unreliable rainfall yields are relatively low.
The main crop in the oases is dates. There are some 3 million date-palms, yielding an annual crop of around 50,000 tons of dates. The only type of date exported is the Deglat en Nour ("Finger of Light").
The forests of cork-oaks in the Kroumirie range (north-western Tunisia) produce an annual 7000 tons of cork.

Future prospects

After several successive years of drought Tunisian agriculture is faced with severe problems. Particular attention is therefore being given to agriculture in the government's economic policy, partly because of its importance in providing employment but also to reduce the costs involved in importing agricultural produce (which accounts for 12% of total imports).
Since Tunisia became independent the number employed in agriculture and the annual cereal crop have remained static. Radical reform is hampered, however, by the pattern of land ownership. Much of the most fertile land is in large holdings and state farms (35% of the arable land being occupied by 5% of the total number of farms). At the other extreme are large numbers of small holdings (83% of farms having less than 20 hectares/50 acres) which lack the financial resources to introduce modern methods of cultivation.
Efforts are being made to reduce the growing social pressures (flight from the land, unemployment), which to some extent have contributed to the support for the fundamentalists, by constructing reservoirs and irrigation systems to increase the country's water resources, developing stock farming, decentralising agricultural administration and providing credits on favourable terms, especially for smallholders. It is also planned to bring farms expropriated by the state, mainly in the mid sixties, back into intensive cultivation.

Minerals

Mining plays an important part in the economy of Tunisia, which has reserves of natural gas and phosphates as well as iron, lead and zinc.
The principal earners of foreign currency are oil and phosphates. 20% of Tunisia's income from exports comes from oil (5.1 million tons a year). The oilfields at El Borma and Kasserine, however, are now almost exhausted, so that Tunisia is faced with the prospect of having to import oil again within the foreseeable future. The hope of finding large offshore oilfields on the continental shelf, around the Kerkennah Islands, has not been fulfilled.
Natural gas is extracted on the Cap Bon peninsula, in the Sfax area, in the Gulf of Gabès and at El Borma. La Skhira (between Sfax and Gabès), situated at the end of a pipeline from the Algerian oilfields, has developed into Tunisia's oil-exporting port.
The country's most important mineral resource, however, is still its phosphates, worked in six mines, the most important of which are at Metlaoui and Kalaat. The annual output is around 6 million tons, giving Tunisia fifth place among the world's producers. It supplies 4.4% of total world consumption of phosphates and earns 15% of its income from exports from this source.

Industry

The industrialisation of Tunisia has made great strides in the last ten years. Whereas in the late seventies manufacturing industry accounted for only 25% of the gross domestic product, by 1984 the proportion had risen to 40%. The leading sectors are textiles and the clothing industry; the processing of domestic agricultural produce and raw materials has declined in importance, largely because of the low yield of Tunisian agriculture.
Industrial plants are predominantly small and medium-sized; there are few large concerns. The most important installations are the Peugeot assembly works at Sousse, sugar refineries at Béja and Bou Salem, factories producing building materials at Tunis, Bizerte and El Hamma du Gabès, a steelworks at Menzel Bourguiba, phosphate processing plants at Gabès and Sfax and oil refineries at Bizerte and Gabès.
A variety of tax concessions are offered as inducements to both Tunisian and foreign investors.

Income from exports and tourism: a comparison (figures for 1989, in million dinars):

Oil and oil derivates	855.2
Olive oil	81.5
Phosphates	32.5
Phosphoric acid	159.3
Textiles	816.0
Dates and citrus fruits	47.4
Tourism	855.2
Total	2847.1

A colourful pottery market

A fishing fleet in harbour

Crafts

In Tunisia, as in all Arab countries, the traditional crafts continue to be of great economic importance. Among the various crafts the making of carpets and blankets takes pride of place.

Carpet-making

The technique of knotting carpets originated in Asia but was already established in North Africa by the 13th century. Carpets are made in many Tunisian towns, but the main centre of production is the Kairouan area, where the carpets are made either in people's homes or in special workshops. Three types of carpets are distinguished: the knotted carpet (*zerbiya*), the woven and embroidered carpet (*mergoum*) and the woven wall carpet or tapestry (*kilim*), which was originally made by the bedouin of the Gafsa and Sfax region and is now manufactured at Oudref, near Gabès.

Pottery

Pottery is made at Guellala on Djerba and increasingly also at Nabeul on the north coast. From there the whole country is supplied with wall tiles, tableware, vases, candlesticks, flower-pots, etc.

The craftsmen of Djerba make beautiful jewellery and ornaments based on ancient models.

Brass and copperware are now produced all over Tunisia. The brassware from the south of the country in particular is made solely for tourists, but the copperware of Gabès and Médenine has a long tradition behind it.

Basketware (mats, shopping bags) made from esparto grass is found all over the country.

At Gabès chairs and small tables are made from reeds, in the *chott* region and at Tozeur and Nefta from the wood of date-palms, at Tabarka from oleander wood.

Fisheries

In spite of Tunisia's 1300km/807 mile long coastline its fisheries are still relatively undeveloped. Traditional methods are still predominant, and since the boats are mostly small they can fish only close inshore. In recent years increased efforts have been made – by the improvement of fishing harbours, the enlargement and modernisation of the coastal fishing fleet and the building up of a seagoing fleet – to exploit the riches of the sea more effectively. The main exports are tunny (caught off Cap Bon and Sidi Daoud), mackerel and sardines. Sponge-fishing, once important, has declined sharply.

Transport

The French protectorate left Tunisia with an excellent network of roads. There are now some 150,000 registered private cars.
Communications are particularly good in the north of the country, and there are good road and rail connections with Algeria. Towards the south and inland from the coast the road network is less dense. Altogether Tunisia has 26,700km/16,580 miles of roads (1986), 14,900km/9253 miles of them properly made up, and 2192km/1362 miles of railway lines. A motorway from Tunis via Hammamet to Sousse is under construction; the Tunis-Hammamet section is already completed.
Tunisia's principal ports are Tunis-La Goulette, Bizerte, Sfax, Sousse, Gabès and the oil port of La Skhira, which handles not only Tunisian oil but also oil from Edjeleh in Algeria. There are 22 smaller ports of merely local or regional importance.
Tunisia has five international airports – Tunis-Carthage (2 million passengers a year), Tunis-Al Aoumina, Djerba, Monastir-Skanès and Tozeur – and another, at Tabarba, north-west of Tunis, due to come into service in 1992. There are also airports at Sfax and Gabès.

Tourism

Since the beginning of the 1960s tourism has developed into one of the most important elements in the Tunisian economy. In 1989 it contributed just under 5% of the gross domestic product, accounted for 20% of the country's earnings of foreign currency and covered 70% of its trade deficit. It provides employment for 44,000 people in the hotel and travel trade and, indirectly, for another 200,000 (service trades, building, etc.). The country has a total of some 111,750 beds available for visitors. Tourism in the Sahara is being intensively developed, and a new tourist centre is under construction at Montazah Tabarka in north-western Tunisia.
All the larger towns have hotel training schools, with 1640 training places – at Sidi Dhrif (Tunis), Nabeul, Hammamet, Monastir and Sousse and on Djerba.
In 1990 3.2 million foreign visitors came to Tunisia. Following a sharp decline in the number of visitors in 1989 – a feature common to other Mediterranean countries – efforts are being made to get rid of the idea of Tunisia as merely a cheap seaside holiday area and to cater for visitors interested in the culture and natural attractions of the country. Thus it is planned to increase bed capacity in the Sahara region, to promote "health tourism" and to attract visitors to parts of the country which have been less developed for tourism in order to reduce the pressure on the east coast resorts. Facilities for water sports, shooting and golf are to be improved, and attention is to be given to protecting the environment of the traditional seaside resorts. Measures planned include the provision of more parks and gardens in the towns, new sewage disposal schemes, new National Parks and afforestation programmes.
The Gulf war led in Tunisia as in other Arab countries to a fall in the number of holiday visitors and showed how vulnerable is an economy which has become so dependent on the tourist trade.

Environment

The dangers resulting from rapid industrialisation and an increasing tourist trade have become evident in Tunisia, and the government is making some

effort to deal with them. Here as in other countries there is a direct relationship between the wellbeing of a nation and its willingness to spend money on the endangered environment. This is recognised in Tunisia, and the first necessary steps have been taken. In the very year in which the country became independent the government showed its interest in the problem by promulgating a comprehensive programme for the protection of nature. Through stricter controls on shooting and the establishment of National Parks it is hoped to guarantee the survival of threatened species of animals, and reafforestation programmes, irrigation systems and the erection of barriers of dunes are designed to halt the encroachment of the desert on cultivated land.
The construction of new sewage and purification plants will prevent the emission into the Mediterranean of untreated sewage from holiday resorts and industrial effluents, and visitors are being invited to play their part in avoiding pollution of Tunisia's water supplies and coastal waters.

The Future

Maghreb Union

Like the other Maghreb countries, Morocco and Algeria, Tunisia is concerned to establish industrial relations with Europe and to solve the problems of unemployment and poverty. The foundation of the Maghreb Union (Tunisia, Morocco, Algeria, Libya and Mauretania) in 1989 was an important step forward, and the establishment of the Algerian-Moroccan-Tunisian Economic Commission is a serious attempt to promote economic cooperation between these three countries. Hitherto the trade between the Maghreb countries has accounted for under 5% of their total volume of trade. Since Morocco, Algeria and Tunisia have complementary economies – Morocco is mainly an agricultural producer, Algeria has well developed heavy industry and Tunisia has good service trades – there is room for profitable trade and cooperation between them.
Tunisia is seeking to prepare itself for the "post-oil" period. Its main objectives in this respect are the development of tourism (as an earner of foreign currency) and of agriculture, mainly because of its importance in providing employment but also with the aim of limiting expenditure on imports of agricultural produce (at present 12% of total imports), which with the fall in oil revenues must be reduced.
It is planned also to promote the development of backward areas and involve them in the national economy, and thus reduce the concentration of 65% of the country's industry in the Tunis area, produce a more even distribution of incomes and obviate one of the causes of the flight from the land.
The urgently necessary modernisation of small agricultural holdings and craft industries is to be promoted by the granting of credits on favourable terms, the road system is to be improved and new sources of energy are to be developed. Other priority areas are professional and vocational training and the creation of urgently needed new jobs in industry and the tourist trade, on the development of which the future of the Tunisian economy depends.
At present the Tunisian economy is still suffering from the effects of the Gulf war (see History). The tourist trade collapsed completely in 1991, with losses said to be around 350 million dollars. Remittances from Tunisians working in the Arab states in the Gulf ceased. Tunisia's exports suffered from the embargo on trade with Iraq, involving a loss estimated by the Ministry of Finance at 463 million dollars. American aid was reduced, and no money was received from the Kuwaiti and Arab Funds for Economic Development. The deficit on the balance of trade rose from 1.5 to 2 billion dollars, and tax revenue in 1991 was estimated to be 242 million dollars less than in the previous year. The total cost of the war is estimated at well over a billion dollars.
This crisis hit the Tunisian economy at a time when the liberalisation initiated in 1987 after the deposition of Bourguiba (see History) had begun

to bear fruit. The budget deficit, which in 1986 had still amounted to 8% of the domestic product, had largely been eliminated. The government had begun to abolish numerous restrictions on imports, abandon price controls and promote investment.

Tunisia will probably be unable to solve its pressing problems without outside help. Hitherto the European Community has devoted only 3% of its aid budget to the developing countries of the Mediterranean area – although two-thirds of Tunisia's foreign trade is with Community countries.

Only by a programme of agricultural development which offers work and prosperity to the people of the Maghreb countries can such problems as illegal immigration into European Community countries and the increasing radicalisation of the mass of the people be prevented.

History

The history of Tunisia can be divided into the following periods:
prehistory and the early historical period;
the Phoenicians and Carthaginians (12th c. B.C. to 146 B.C.);
the Romans (146 B.C. to A.D. 439);
the Arab conquests (647 to the present day)
Aghlabids (800–909)
Fatimids and Zirids (909–1159)
Almohads and Hafsids (1159–1547);
the Normans (1148–59);
the Turks (1574–1705) and Husseinites (1705–1956);
the French protectorate (1881–1956); and
the Republic (1956 to the present day).

Prehistory and the Early Historical Period

The beginnings of human settlement in North Africa are estimated to go back a million years. The earliest evidence dates from the Early Palaeolithic (500,000 B.C.), the period known in Africa as Acheulian. At this time the Sahara was a green and fertile savanna, the home of a variety of animals still found in the savannas of Africa.
The big game of the period (antelopes, rhinoceroses, elephants, hippopotamuses) provided food for small, non-sedentary groups of hunters of the human type known as Homo erectus.

There were several alternations between humid and dry periods associated with the European ice ages.

The first evidence of human settlement dates from the Middle Palaeolithic (Mousterian period), in the form of human bones of Neanderthal type (Homo sapiens neandertalensis). *c.* 80,000 B.C.

Aterian culture of the Late Palaeolithic, attested by shafted stone implements from Cap Blanc and Monastir. *c.* 40,000 B.C.

Two large cultural groups now came to the fore. In the northern coastal region the Ibero-Maurusian culture is found from about 12,000 B.C. Skeletal remains have shown that the people of this culture were of Cromagnon type, known from the place where they were found as the people of Mechta el Arbi. In middens up to 100m/330ft long have been found ashes, bones, snail- and sea-shells, a variety of implements, including flint flakes of triangular, trapezoid or circular section set in wooden or bone shafts, and burials. 13,000 to 5000 B.C.

Better known is the Capsian culture, which takes its name from the ancient city of Capsa (now Gafsa in southern Tunisia). Later than the Ibero-Maurusian, it dates from the middle of the 8th millennium B.C. to the end of the 4th and is found in a relatively small area between the northern edge of the Chott and the Tebessa region. 8000–4000 B.C.
The people of this culture, who are believed to have been of negroid type, were hunters and gatherers, who left behind the large mounds of debris known as kitchen middens, up to 40m/130ft long and 25m/80ft across, containing huge numbers of bones of buffaloes, gazelles, antelopes, a species of zebra, beasts of prey and birds, as well as wood ashes, innumerable seashells and stone implements.
The mounds were also used as places of burial. The dead were sprinkled with red chalk or ochre and buried in a recumbent or crouching position.

Ornaments, carved figures of animals and decorated ostrich eggs give evidence of a desire to embellish the human environment.
Whether and to what extent these people were related to the first true Berbers, who appear in North Africa at the beginning of the historical period, is not known.

c. 5000–1300 B.C.

Along the coast the Ibero-Maurusian culture was gradually displaced by the Capsian culture. From 5000 B.C., however, the Neolithic came to North Africa, rather later than in Europe. Finds like obsidian points from Italy and evidence of the megalithic culture show that before the coming of the Phoenicians there was seafaring activity and contact with Europe. This brought a new, lighter-skinned and slenderer human type to the coastal regions. At the same time tribes from the central Sahara moved northward, probably fleeing from a period of drought. They were later known to the Greeks as Libyans, Garamantes, Numidians, Nubians, Gaetulians and Nasamones. From this mingling of peoples came the Berbers.

Finds of pottery provide evidence that arable farming and stock-rearing had begun and that the first permanent settlements had been established, and deposits of ash show that whole forests were burned down to provide more land for cultivation. The long process of destruction of the landscape, therefore, began before the coming of the Carthaginians.
There is no evidence, however, of urban culture.

Phoenicians and Carthaginians

c. 1100–146 B.C.

Around 3000 B.C. the Phoenicians (from Greek *phoinos,* "purple", after the colour of their garments), a Semitic people from the Persian Gulf, settled on the Syrian coast, and when in the 12th century B.C. Egypt, Crete and Mesopotamia lost their dominant role, they became the new Mediterranean commercial power. Their best-known cities were Byblos, Sidon and Tyre. Their voyages took them to to Sicily, southern Spain, West Africa and Britain, and they built up a far-reaching network of trading connections. Their trading posts grew in size and developed into independent city states. As early as the 12th century B.C. the town of Utica was founded on the north side of the Gulf of Tunis, near the mouth of the river known in antiquity as Bagradas (Medjerda), and in 814 B.C. Carthage was founded by Phoenicians from Tyre.

Carthage

According to the foundation myth the foundress of Carthage was Elissa, daughter of the king of Tyre, who was known to Virgil as Dido. The legend had it that after a dispute over the succession to the throne with her brother, who had her husband, a wealthy priest, murdered for the sake of his money, Elissa fled to Cyprus and from there sailed to the North African coast with the high priest of Astarte and 80 hierodules (female temple servants), who were to become the mothers of the tribe. An unsuspecting Numidian prince granted her request for a piece of land the size of a cow-hide: whereupon she cut the hide into narrow strips with which she encompassed the whole of the peninsula later known as Carthage (Qart Hadasht, the "new capital"). When the Numidian prince asked for her hand she at first agreed, but asked that she should be allowed to make a burnt offering to her first husband; and when this request was granted she threw herself into the burning pyre.
Carthage developed rapidly, overtook the older foundation of Utica and soon outshone its mother city of Tyre. In the 5th century it gained control of its Numidian hinterland, and, with a population of some 400,000, became the largest and probably the wealthiest city in the Mediterranean.

Although neither the Phoenicians nor the Carthaginians have left any written records, it is known that Carthage had an aristocratic constitution and had worshipped as its principal god Baal-Ammon, the sun god. Baal-

View of Carthage from the Byrsa Hill

Ammon was increasingly displaced by his consort Tanit, a moon and fertility goddess. Other deities were Eshmun, the god of healing, and Melkart, son of Baal and Tanit, and there were also various divinities worshipped locally or taken over from the Egyptians or Greeks.

Among the achievements of the Phoenicians, further developed by the Carthaginians, were the first alphabetic script (Ugarit, in what is now Syria), major innovations in agriculture (including the growing of olives and vines), shipbuilding and navigation.

From the 6th century Carthage increasingly came into conflict with Greece, which had also become a great power. The Greeks prevented Carthage from gaining control of the coasts of France and Spain and the island of Sicily. Carthage therefore entered into an alliance with Rome with the object of driving back the Greeks in Sicily. After achieving victory, however, the two ambitious allies became enemies. Their fight for supremacy in the three Punic Wars ended in the destruction of Carthage in 146 B.C.

In the First Punic War (264–241 B.C.) Carthage suffered a heavy defeat. In the Second Punic War (218–201 B.C.) Hannibal crossed the river Ebro with 50,000 foot-soldiers, 12,000 horsemen and 37 elephants, advanced through southern France and made his way over the Alps at the cost of heavy losses. With the help of Gallic mercenaries he inflicted heavy defeats on the Romans and in 211 B.C. laid siege to Rome itself. Meanwhile Scipio Africanus had conquered the whole of the Spanish coast, and in the spring of 204 he landed in Africa, at Ghar el Melh; then, having entered into an alliance with a Numidian prince, Masinissa, he marched on Carthage. Returning to Africa after an absence of fifteen years, Hannibal encountered the Romans at Zama (202 B.C.) and was defeated. Carthage now lost all its possessions outside Africa, its fleet and its war elephants and was compelled to pay heavy reparations; and it was prohibited from waging war, even a defensive war, without Roman permission.

Carthage's independence in its reduced state, however, did not last long. Rome's ally Masinissa gradually conquered the Numidian hinterland and

Hannibal crossing the Alps

established a kingdom which included large areas of Tunisia and present-day Algeria. This brought it into competition with Carthage, and when Carthage, without Rome's permission, took up arms against an attack by Masinissa the Third Punic War (149–146 B.C.) broke out. Rome sent an army against Carthage, which at once surrendered and gave up all its arms. In spite of this Rome insisted that the Carthaginians should themselves destroy their city and abandon it. When the Carthaginians refused the war resumed, ending in the complete annihilation of Carthage.
Those Carthaginians who survived and were not enslaved by the Romans sought refuge in other coastal towns or in the interior, where they preserved their language and customs for many years, in spite of Roman influence, developing a "neo-Punic" culture which was a mingling of Carthaginian, Numidian and Roman elements.

Numidians

The Numidians – their name is a Latinised form of the Greek word for "nomads" – were a native North African people known to the Greeks as Libyans. They belonged to a number of large tribal confederations: in the western coastal region the Mauri, on the edge of the desert the Gaetuli, in present-day Algeria, extending into Tunisia, the Masaesyli and Massyli. Their script has been preserved by a Berber group, the Tuaregs, their language in the Berber dialects. Masinissa (b. 240 B.C.; see Famous People) established the first large Berber kingdom, which originally was tributary to the Carthaginians. Victorious in the fight against Hannibal, it rose rapidly thereafter, both politically and economically, until Masinissa controlled an area extending from the present Moroccan-Algerian frontier to Carthage. After defeating Carthage Rome established control over the fertile region around the old Carthaginian capital, which became part of the Roman province of Africa, with Utica as the new capital. The adjoining territory to the west was left to Masinissa, whose sphere of influence now extended into the regions of present-day Algeria and Morocco.
Under Masinissa's successors his kingdom was divided up. His ambitious grandson Jugurtha came into conflict with Rome when he sought to establish a large new Numidian kingdom, and after his execution in Rome in

104 B.C. his kingdom passed to King Bocchus of Mauretania and became part of the most westerly region in North Africa.
After Caesar's defeat of Pompey and his Numidian allies in the Civil War he reorganised the administration of North Africa, forming the western Numidian kingdom into the province of Africa Nova alongside the old province of Africa Vetus. Then in 23 B.C. Augustus combined the two in the province of Africa Proconsularis. Mauretania was governed by Juba II (see Famous People), a Berber king who had been brought up in Rome and who now fostered trade, industry and learning. His son and successor, however, was murdered in A.D. 40 on the orders of the Emperor Caligula. After the defeat of a Berber rising Mauretania was divided into the provinces of Mauretania Caesariensis (Algeria) and Mauretania Tingitana (Morocco), bringing to an end the last of the Numidian and Mauretanian kingdoms.

Roman Rule

146 B.C.–A.D. 439

As early as 123 B.C. the Gracchi had made plans to develop the economy of North Africa. Some decades later Roman veterans were settled in North Africa, but the planned colonisation of Africa Proconsularis began only in the reign of Augustus. In the south of the province a fortified frontier zone, the Limes Tripolitanus, was established in order to protect the territory from nomad raids. Many new towns were founded, a number of Carthaginian settlements were taken over and given limited rights, and Carthage itself was rebuilt. The settlements of veterans in particular promoted linguistic and cultural Romanisation. The poor rural population, however, continued to speak Libyan/Berber dialects, which are still to some extent preserved in the modern Berber dialects and in folksongs.
Africa Proconsularis developed into the granary of Rome, and at times three-quarters of the capital's supplies of wheat came from North Africa. This led to the exhaustion of the soil and to a consequent switch from corn to olives, wine and fruit. In A.D. 212 all free inhabitants of the Empire were granted Roman citizenship. The province was now one of the richest in the Roman Empire, and magnificent and richly decorated public buildings were erected in the larger towns. The majority of the population (roughly five-sixths), however, lived very modestly as merchants, craftsmen and slaves – though there were fewer and fewer slaves, their place being taken by new settlers, peasant farmers who were granted plots of land on condition that they provided certain services.
The effects of the crisis in the Roman Empire in the 3rd century A.D. were felt in Africa Proconsularis as in the rest of the Empire, and there were risings against sharp increases in taxation. The Berber tribes, resentful at being driven back into barren desert regions, took advantage of these disturbances to make trouble on their own account and raided the Roman province.
The slow decline in the Roman Empire had begun, and it continued in spite of the fact that Africa Proconsularis was now divided into the three new provinces of Zeugitana in the north, Byzacena in central Tunisia and Tripolitana in the south and that further reforms were carried out.

Christianity

Christian missionaries appeared in Africa in the late 1st century. The first community is recorded in 180, the first bishop, Tertullian (see Famous People), in 197. In spite of persecutions the spread of Christianity could no longer be halted. In the early 4th century there was a schism in the church. The Donatists, a group led by their bishop Donatus who rejected Roman authority and were strongly attached to the cult of martyrs, soon attracted support from the majority of the impoverished Numidian rural population. They called for a strictly egalitarian society and a way of life closely modelled on Christian ideals. In the 4th century their radical wing became involved in risings against the civil authorities and in plundering expeditions: whereupon the Donatists were outlawed. In 411 an attempt at mediation by Augustine (see Famous People), an Algerian Berber, was unsuccessful.

Roman Tunisia

Africa Proconsularis

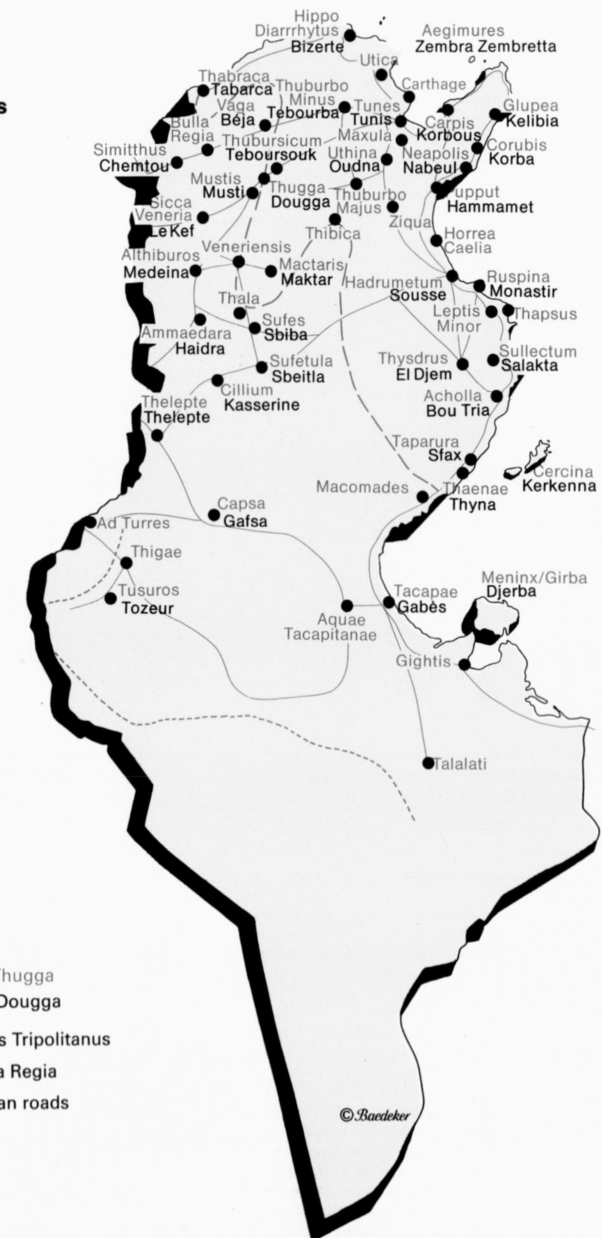

Roman Name: Thugga
Present Name: Dougga

- - - - - - - - Limes Tripolitanus
— — — — Fossa Regia
——— Roman roads

Thereafter the Donatists were repressed by force and ruthlessly persecuted as heretics.
This dissension within the Christian church was no doubt one of the reasons for the rapid success of Islam among the native population of North Africa in the 7th century.
The division of the Roman Empire in 395 into a Western (Catholic) and an Eastern (Byzantine; Orthodox) Empire marked the beginning of the end of Roman rule in North Africa.

Vandals and Byzantines

439–533

The Vandals, a Germanic people led by Genseric or Gaiseric, found their way into North Africa by way of Silesia, Hungary, Gaul and Spain. In 429 they took Tangier, in 439 the province of Africa. They were Arian Christians, opposed – like the Donatists, from whom they gained recruits – to the Catholic church.
For a brief period this Germanic state was the leading power in the western Mediterranean. Sicily, Corsica, Sardinia, Malta and the Balearics were conquered. Soon after Genseric's death, however, the Vandal kingdom fell into decline, weakened from within by Berber and peasant risings and from outside by invasions. In 533 the East Roman general Belisarius landed in North Africa with an army of 5000 men and in a short campaign destroyed the Vandal state. Its legacy can still be seen in small numbers of fair-haired North African Berbers.

533–647

Carthage now became an exarchate province of the Eastern Empire, and many new churches were built. The attempt by the Byzantines to establish a new world empire lasted no more than a century; its influence was confined to the coastal regions, and in spite of elaborate fortifications the Berber tribes in the hinterland were a constantly increasing threat.

The Arab Conquest

The first thrusts in the great expansion of Islam which was to extend over North Africa, much of the Iberian peninsula, southern France and the Mediterranean islands began in 647, only fifteen years after Mohammed's death, when Arab forces advanced westward through Egypt, plundering Sufetula (Sbeitla). At first Byzantine and Berber forces successfully resisted their progress and then secured their withdrawal by buying them off. From 670 onwards, however, the Roman province was conquered by Oqba ibn Nafi, a general in the service of the Omayyad Caliph Muawiya. The starting-point for further advance was the new capital (founded 671) of the country which the Arabs called Ifriqiya, Kairouan, now the fourth holy city of Islam. The Byzantines could do little to stop the invaders, but the Berbers put up a fierce resistance, first under the leadership of their chief Kasila and later under the legendary prophetess known as El Kahina (see Famous People). After her death resistance collapsed, and the process of Arabisation of the country began.
Between the 8th and 11th centuries dissensions within Islam led to its division into three schools, the Sunnites, the Shiites and the Kharijites (see Religion). The Berber tribes who had resisted Arabisation sided with the Kharijites out of opposition to the ruling Shiites, and the country was racked by risings and rebellions.

Abbasids

After the violent end of the Omayyad dynasty at the hands of the Abbasid Caliphs the province of Ifriqiya was administered from Baghdad. Since the risings in the province still continued Ibrahim ibn el-Aghlab, a learned and militarily experienced follower of the Abbasids, was given the task of suppressing them, and as a reward for his success was made Emir (Governor) of Ifriqiya. Then, in recognition of his further services and in exchange for payments of tribute, his post was made hereditary.

Aghlabids

Ibrahim ibn el-Aghlab founded the Aghlabid dynasty, which ruled from 800 to 909. He chose Kairouan as the new capital of the now independent state, whose territory covered present-day Tunisia, the coastal region of Tripolitania as far as Barka and eastern Algeria, and established his residence at Al Abbasiya, to the south of Kairouan. In 876 the ruler's residence was transferred to the new town of Reqqada, south-west of Kairouan.
The successful assimilation between the numerically superior native population and the Arab conquerors now began, and the country's economy and culture developed. Irrigation systems which had been abandoned since the Vandal invasions were brought back into use and there was much new building. Expeditions of conquest were launched against Sicily, Malta, southern Italy and Sardinia, and their success contributed to the internal stabilisation of the country.

Fatimids

At the beginning of the 10th century Kairouan was captured by a Shiite clan, the Fatimids, led by Mahdi Obeid Allah, a relative of the Prophet Mohammed. They put an end to the Aghlabid dynasty and founded their own Fatimid dynasty, which ruled from 909 to 973. The new capital was Mahdia, a strongly fortified coastal town. Under Fatimid rule, in spite of bloody Kharijite risings, trade and industry (glass, pottery, textiles) flourished. In their missionary zeal the Fatimids conquered Egypt in 969 and finally, in 973, moved their capital to Cairo.

Zirids

The Fatimids handed over control of Ifriqiya to the Zirids, a Berber family who founded their own dynasty (973–1159). In 1048 the Zirid ruler ceased payment of tribute to Cairo, and by way of reprisal the Fatimids sent the Beni Hilal, a warlike tribe from Upper Egypt, into Tunisia. These nomads, known as the "Huns of Islam", ranged through the country, plundering and destroying; fields were devastated, towns razed to the ground. Thereafter the country declined to the level of a nomadic economy. Local dynasties established themselves in the interior, foreign conquerors occupied coastal towns, and in the mid 12th century Roger II, the Norman king of Naples and Sicily, gained control of a large area along the coast.

Almohads and Hafsids

In 1160 an army of the Almohads (rulers of Morocco), under the leadership of Abd el Moumin, conquered the devastated land of Ifriqiya, and under the Almohad dynasty the Maghreb was for the first time in its history united under a single ruler. From their capital at Marrakech the Almohads ruled a kingdom which extended from Spain to Tripolitania, maintaining their authority with the help of Berber, Turkish and even Christian auxiliaries. The country's economy and culture again flourished. When unrest broke out in their kingdom in the 13th century the Almohads appointed as governor a member of the Hafsid family, who made Tunis his capital. The Hafsid regime was so successful that the country soon became independent under a Hafsid dynasty which ruled from 1229 to 1574.
Tunis now became the capital and focal point of the Islamic world. During the Hafsid period the covered souks (streets of shops) around the Great Mosque were built, the Kasbah became a citadel and the ruler's palace was rebuilt. When the Reconquista began in Spain many Muslim and Jewish refugees settled in the city and contributed to its economic and cultural development.
In 1270 Tunis repelled attacks by King Louis IX of France and by tribes from the desert. The 14th century was a time of unrest, but thereafter Tunis enjoyed a period of stability. Raids on Christian shipping by corsairs (the most popular of whom was Dragut: see Famous People) brought great wealth to the town.
In the 16th century disputes over the succession and discontent with the Hafsid administration led to risings and to a further period of decline.

Turks and Husseinites

In 1534 Turkish corsairs captured Tunis, and in despair the Hafsid ruler appealed to the Emperor Charles V for help. In the following year the Turks were expelled by Spanish troops, and for a brief period Tunisia fell within the Spanish sphere of influence.

In 1574, however, Tunis was again taken by the Turks, and for the next 300 years the country was a province of the Ottoman empire, administered by a governor, the Pasha, appointed by Istanbul, who was supported by the Dey, the commander of the armed forces, and the Bey, a civilian official responsible for the collection of taxes.

In 1587 the Janissaries, an elite Turkish military force, rebelled and appointed their elected commander, the Dey, to head the administration. The country, whose main sources of revenue were the highly profitable trade of piracy, ransoms for prisoners and a growing volume of trade, was now governed by a kind of military aristocracy with the support of the janissaries and the Turkish corsairs. This regime brought a degree of prosperity, mainly to some of the coastal towns, which was increased by a further wave of refugees from Andalusia, who brought with them new farming methods and new industries such as silk-weaving.

A period of grave political unrest, aggravated by an outbreak of plague, saw the rise to power of Bey Hussein ben Ali, who in 1705 succeeded in converting his elective office into a hereditary one, establishing the Husseinite dynasty which ruled, at any rate nominally, until 1957.

Thereafter Tunisia became practically independent of Turkey; but disputes over the succession, frontier conflicts with Algeria, risings in the interior of the country, the transfer of international trade routes from the Mediterranean to the Atlantic and the end of piracy weakened the country economically, militarily and politically. With the increasing industrialisation of western Europe Tunisia, like the other North African countries, was flooded with cheap mass-produced foreign products. Around 1815 it got into increasing difficulty and became deeply indebted to French and British banks. This led to a steady increase in European influence in Tunisia: in 1857 foreigners were granted equal rights in the acquisition of land and the exercise of professions, in 1861 the jurisdiction of the religious courts was abolished and in 1869 Tunisian financial affairs were put in the hands of an international commission.

French Protectorate

In 1830 Algeria had been occupied by the French, and at the Congress of Berlin in 1878 France was given a free hand in eastern North Africa in return for concessions in other parts of the world. A pretext was soon found for intervening in Tunisia, now fully independent but torn by dissension and unrest, and in April 1881 32,000 French troops marched into the country from Algeria. In the following month the Bey signed the treaty of Bardo establishing a French protectorate, and this was followed in June 1883 by the treaty of La Marsa, which confirmed French sovereignty. In 1884 the first Resident-General, the supreme representative of the colonial power, was appointed. He was responsible for finance, the armed forces and foreign policy, while the Bey remained formally head of state, with responsibility for domestic policy. "Non-registered" land (that is, land occupied by nomadic tribes) was expropriated and converted first into state-owned and then into private estates, and French and Italian settlers (*colons*) were encouraged to come to Tunisia. To promote the country's economic development new roads, railways and ports were built.

In the First World War Tunisia fought on the Allied side, and after the war attached great hopes to the right of national self-determination enshrined in President Woodrow Wilson's Fourteen Points. Nothing came of this, however, and the process of colonisation continued. The number of foreigners living in Tunisia, mostly engaged in farming, increased further. The Tunisian economy centred on the fertile regions in the north of the country

with their monocultures; stock-farming and mining played only subordinate roles; and there was very little in the way of industry, craft production or food-processing factories.
The development of the country on this basis brought an economic upswing but also grave social problems. The European *colons* forced the native rural population and the nomadic tribes into inhospitable marginal areas; the practice of monoculture led to the exhaustion of the land; and the mass import of cheap industrial products led to the decline of the country's traditional trade and crafts. There was an influx of impoverished and now rootless peasants from the country areas into the few towns.

Resistance was at first on a small scale. In 1907 young Tunisian intellectuals formed the Young Tunisians group, which set out to secure reforms within the system. In 1920 intellectuals and representative of the upper classes of the population founded the Destour (Constitution) Party, which also sought to secure reforms.
1925 saw the establishment of the CGTT, a trade union which rapidly increased its membership. In 1934 Habib Bourguiba, a law graduate of the Sorbonne, founded the Neo-Destour Party, the radical wing of the Destour Party, and the newspaper "L'Action Tunisienne". The new party attracted large numbers of supporters and became the leader of the independence movement. The response of the colonial authorities was to ban both the party and the trade union; and in 1938 Bourguiba was arrested and deported to France.
During the Second World War part of Tunisia was occupied by the German Africa Corps, following an appeal for aid from the Italians, who had in the meantime occupied Libya. There was fierce fighting along the Mareth Line to the south of Gabès, but in 1943 the Germans were finally driven out by British forces.
After the end of the war the national movement in Tunisia was given increased impetus by the devastation caused by the war and the famine resulting from two catastrophic years of drought (1945 and 1947). Negotiations with the French foundered on the uncompromising attitude of the *colons*. The murder of a nationalist trade union leader, Farhat Hached, by a French extremist group, the Main Rouge (Red Hand), led to the outbreak of civil war (1952–54), during which Bourguiba was again imprisoned by the French.
France's defeat in Indochina and the outbreak of the Algerian war, however, compelled the French to make concessions. On June 1st 1955 Bourguiba arrived in La Goulette, and two days later Tunisia was granted domestic self-government. Finally a treaty signed on March 20th 1956 put an end to the French protectorate.

Independent Tunisia

With the deposition of the last Husseinite Bey on July 25th 1957 the 250-year-old dynasty came to an end, and for the second time in its almost three thousand years of history Tunisia was declared a republic (the first republic having been destroyed by the Romans in 146 B.C.). In the country's first free election in April 1956 the Neo-Destour Party won an overwhelming victory. Habib Bourguiba became prime minister and, after the deposition of the Bey, President of the Republic.
Bourguiba's first reforms included the abolition of the jurisdiction of religious courts, the promulgation of the Code of Personal Status (which banned polygamy and removed the husband's right to reject his wife), the granting of equal rights to women, the establishment of secular schools and the introduction of compulsory school attendance, new laws on health and safety at work and new social legislation, the closure of Islamic faculties and the opening of a new University.
These policies encountered some resistance. The Islamic clergy and orthodox Muslims criticised the process of secularisation, the trade unions claimed that the reforms did not go far enough and Destour supporters objected to the pro-Western foreign policy. The Bourguiba government responded to the protests with arrests, a ban on strikes, the deportation of

leading critics (including Salah ben Youssef, who was murdered in Frankfurt in 1961), the dismissal of the trade union leader Ben Salah (who later became a member of the government) and the establishment of re-education camps for young trouble-makers. Nevertheless Bourguiba consolidated his position, and in a presidential election in November 1959 he received 95.5% of the votes.
In foreign policy there were conflicts with France, which accused Bourguiba of supporting the Algerian rebels. Economic aid was cut off, and in April 1958 the French army attacked the frontier village of Sakiet Sidi Youssef. In 1961 there was a Tunisian attack on the French garrison which was still maintained in the naval port of Bizerte.
The country's most pressing problems, however, were economic – problems which were aggravated by the influx of 120,000 refugees from Algeria.

Socialist experiments 1962–69

The country's first ten-year plan was based on the coexistence of trade unions and the public and private sectors. The priorities were declared to be agriculture, afforestation, the expansion of cultivation in the Medjerda valley, the Sahel and the steppe country, education, health services and housing.
Land reform was carried out in 1964. Hitherto only French-owned estates and large farms had been expropriated: now all the remaining *colons,* still numbering some 110,000, were dispossessed. The result was a mass emigration of *colons,* which in turn led to a shortage of skilled workers and a deterioration of Franco-Tunisian relations.
The large Tunisian-owned estates were not affected by the reform. A plan by Ben Salah to convert large and medium-sized holdings into co-operatives was frustrated by their resistance, and in 1969 he was arrested and removed from his post. With left-wing critics silenced, the way was clear to dismantle the socialist experiment. By now some 60% of the economy was under state control.

Liberalisation 1970–79

The second ten-year plan concentrated on industry and tourism. Tax concessions were introduced to attract foreign capital, and most of the new hotels were built with foreign money.
In the mid seventies an economic recession brought unrest and strikes. At the height of the crisis the police shot down a strike in Tunis called by the UGTT (Union Générale Tunisienne du Travail) and a state of emergency was declared (1978).
In 1979 Tunis became the headquarters of the Arab League.

1980

In 1980 country-wide strikes and student unrest culminated in an armed attack on the Gafsa garrison. Bourguiba reacted on the one hand with death sentences on the ringleaders and on the other with cautious reforms.

End of the Bourguiba regime

In an election in November 1981 Bourguiba's National Front received 94.6% of the votes and won all the parliamentary seats. The leading opposition parties, however, had been excluded from the election, and anti-government candidates had been hampered by the threat of repression. After the suppression and exclusion of all political opposition there remained only the Islamic fundamentalist groups, which now gained a huge increase in membership.
In 1984 the "bread" or "couscous riots" broke out, with country-wide unrest following increases in the price of bread and millet (the staple foods of the poor). Action by the police and army led to many deaths. Calm was restored only when the price increases were cancelled.
In August 1985 Tunisia broke off relations with Libya. After the fall in the price of oil Libya had expelled almost 600,000 foreign workers, including some 35,000 of the 80,000 Tunisians working in Libya. Following the breaking off of diplomatic relations the frontier between the two countries was closed.
On October 1st 1985 six Israeli fighter aircraft attacked the headquarters of the Palestine Liberation Organisation at Bordj Cedria (in Hammam-Lif, a suburb of Tunis). More than 70 people were killed, most of them civilians.

"Jasmine Revolution"

On November 7th 1987 the 85-year-old President of the Republic, Habib Bourguiba – who had made himself President for life by an amendment to the constitution in 1976 – was deposed on the ground of "infirmity". The leader of this bloodless "Jasmine Revolution" and Bourguiba's successor was Zine el Abidine ben Ali, who as head of the military secret service could rely on the support of the army.

Ben Ali now dissolved the Destour Party, replacing it by the Rassemblement Constitutionnel Démocratique (RCD), with a new leadership. Opposition movements were given more freedom, a multi-party system was promised and trade unionists, members of the opposition and fundamentalists who had been arrested were released. This liberalisation awakened hopes of further democratisation.

In April 1989 Ben Ali's suggestion to the opposition parties that in order to avoid an open electoral battle in the first parliamentary election to be held since Bourguiba's deposition the parties should not put forward separate lists of candidates but should form a joint list with the government party gave rise to dissension. The Social Democrats (MDS) rejected the proposal. The Islamic fundamentalist movement (MTI), now renamed Al Nahda, the Party of Rebirth, was not accepted as a party, under the law prohibiting political organisations based on religion, and entered its candidates on the list of Independents. Other party groups put up candidates in only six of the twenty-five constituencies.

The preparations for the election brought further restrictions, and the government party (RCD) was also favoured by the first-past-the-post system and the demarcation of constituencies, which enabled them to win seats even with a simple majority. About a quarter of the electorate of 3.6 million, mainly younger voters, did not receive voters' cards, well-known opposition figures were excluded from the lists of candidates, and speakers were allowed to address the voters only in closed halls – to mention only a few of the obstacles.

In the parliamentary and presidential elections the government party received 80% of the votes: which, as a result of the first-past-the-post system, gave them 141 parliamentary seats. The Islamic fundamentalists (Al Nahda), standing as Independents, made striking gains, receiving 14% of the votes.

1989

Foundation of the Maghreb Union (Tunisia, Morocco, Algeria, Libya and Mauretania: see Economy, The Future).

In local government elections in June 1990 RCD again won almost all the 3774 seats, with only 34 going to independent candidates, including 12 in Monastir (though there were independent candidates in only 19 of the 246 constituencies). The government party was again accused of influencing and rigging the poll.

In May 1991 the fundamentalists launched an unsuccessful coup. Al Nahda still enjoys much support, but the exact number of its supporters cannot be established since it is still banned as a party.

The Gulf war

Tunisia's economic and social problems were aggravated in 1991 by the Gulf war. Until then it had maintained good relations with both Kuwait and Iraq, and it was linked with the West by economic interests. Tunisia condemned Iraq's invasion of Kuwait, but did not attend the meeting of the Arab League in Cairo at which a decision was taken to send Arab forces to defend Saudi Arabia against a threatened attack. President Ben Ali criticised the sending in of Western forces as an outside intrusion into the conflict, but nevertheless observed the embargo on dealings with Iraq.

This balancing act did not pay off. Tunisia suffered severe damage to its economy, and the total cost of the war is estimated at well over a billion dollars (see Economy).

The unification of the Maghreb on the basis of the Maghreb Union of 1989 is still a long way ahead. Tunisia is more than ever dependent on foreign capital, particularly on the International Monetary Fund. The country's future depends also on the solution of the problems which have been outlined in this section.

Famous People

This section contains brief biographies of notable people who were born, lived and worked in Tunisia or who died there.

Apuleius (b. about A.D. 125)

Perhaps the best known work written in the heyday of Latin literature in North Africa is the "Golden Ass" (also known as the "Metamorphoses"), a satirical novel by Lucius Apuleius, a much travelled writer who was born at Madaura in Numidia, was brought up in Carthage and studied in Athens. The book describes the fantastic adventures of a Greek named Loukios (Lucius) who has been transformed into an ass. The story takes the hero through a variety of adventures and ends in his release by the goddess Isis. The poetic tale of "Amor and Psyche" forms an episode in the story.

Augustine (354–430)

It is not always remembered that St Augustine, one of the greatest of Christian teachers and thinkers, was a North African. Although he was born outside the bounds of present-day Tunisia, in the Numidian frontier territory of north-eastern Algeria, he studied in Carthage and taught there for many years before going to Rome and Milan to teach rhetoric.
Aurelius Augustinus came from a Romanised middle-class family in Thagaste (now Souk Ahras): hence his European-sounding name. His father was a Roman official and a believer in the old gods, his mother a Christian. Altogether Augustine published 232 works, the best known of which are his "Confessions", the first large-scale autobiography in world literature, and the "City of God", from which many European creeds have drawn inspiration.
Augustine died in Hippo Regius (now Annaba/Bone in Algeria), of which he was bishop.

Zine el Abidine ben Ali (b. 1936)

Born in Hammam-Sousse in 1936, Ben Ali was one of the principal agents in the deposition of President Habib Bourguiba in the bloodless "Jasmine Revolution" of November 1987.
From 1958 to 1974 Ben Ali was head of the security police and later Commissioner for National Security. In 1984 Bourguiba appointed him prime minister, but he soon found himself at odds with the President over the solution of pressing domestic problems and anticipated his dismissal by organising the bloodless coup to which many Tunisians had been looking forward. Since then the country's hopes of more democracy and of progress hinge on him.

Habib Bourguiba (b. 1903)

The name of Habib Bourguiba is inseparable from the foundation and development of present-day Tunisia. Born in Monastir, he studied law in Paris and in 1934 founded the Neo-Destour Party, whose object was to secure the release of Tunisia from the French protectorate. It was to be another 22 years before Bourguiba achieved his object, almost without bloodshed, with the signature of the treaty giving Tunisia independence. During these years his resistance to the French brought him several times into prison.
At last, in 1957, as the first President of the new state of Tunisia, Bourguiba was able to begin his far-reaching programme of reform. Though never breaking completely with Islam, he introduced legislation giving women equal rights with men, developed the country's health services, made school attendance compulsory and promulgated a progressive code of family law.
His economic policies, however, failed to overcome the great social contrasts within Tunisia. His systematic repression and neutralisation of opposition over many years aroused criticism both within Tunisia and abroad; and although in 1978 his party, then running a single-party state, pro-

Augustine Bourguiba Hannibal

claimed its intention of moving towards a multi-party system, press censorship and the repression of critics of the government remained the order of the day. Finally on November 7th 1987 Bourguiba was deposed after 31 years as President.

Muhammad el Rachid ben Hussayn ben Ali Bey (d. 1759)

Tunisia has an extensive musical heritage from Andalusia, comprising thirteen different styles. El Rachid Bey, a progressive Tunisian ruler, was the first to draw up rules for organising a concert with these various styles, and these rules still govern the Nawba, the classic Tunisian concert programme. The El Rachidiya Institute of Arab Music in Tunis, founded in 1935, is named after him and carries on his work.

Dragut (*c.* 1485–1565)

Dorghout Rais or Dragut was born in Anatolia, the son of poor peasants. He went to sea and soon made a name for himself, following in the footsteps of the much-dreaded pirate Khair ed-Din Barbarossa. From his base on Djerba he made the waters round Malta, Sardinia, Sicily and Corsica unsafe for shipping. In 1540 he fell into the hands of the Genoese and spent three years as a galley slave before being ransomed by the Turkish Sultan.
In 1551 the people of Djerba enabled Dragut to escape from a siege by secretly digging a channel through which he and his ships could leave. In 1560 he attacked a Spanish fleet off Houmt-Souk; after his victory he had the surviving Spaniards beheaded and built a "tower of skulls" which remained as a memorial of the occasion until in 1846, under pressure from the French consul, it was replaced by an obelisk. Dragut died during a siege of Malta.

Hannibal (247/246 to 183 B.C.)

During the Second Punic War (218–201 B.C.) the Carthaginian general Hannibal, son of Hamilcar Barca, crossed the Ebro with 50,000 men, 12,000 horsemen and 37 elephants, thrust through southern France and crossed the Alps. With the support of Gallic forces he inflicted a series of defeats on the Romans. In 211 B.C. the cry went up in Rome: "Hannibal ante portas" ("Hannibal is at the gates of the city"). He lacked the necessary reinforcements from North Africa to take Rome itself, however, since in the meantime Scipio Africanus had conquered the whole coast of Spain.
Hannibal was not only the greatest general of his time after Scipio Africanus, who finally defeated him in 202 B.C., but a man of outstanding quality. In 196 B.C. he was elected suffete (supreme judge) by the Carthaginians, and in that capacity carried out a democratic reform of the Council of One Hundred, making membership elective for a year at a time instead of hereditary as it had previously been.
Under pressure from the Romans and the native nobility Hannibal was compelled to seek refuge at Libyssa in Bithynia (Asia Minor), where he committed suicide by taking poison in order to escape being handed over

to the Romans. He is believed to have been buried near the Turkish town of Gebze on the Gulf of Izmit (Sea of Marmara).

Ibn Khaldun (1332–1406)

Wali ed Din Abd er Rahman ben Mohammed ben Abu Bakr Mohammed ben el Hasan, or Ibn Khaldun for short, born in Tunis to a wealthy family of Sevillian origin, is the greatest and most celebrated Islamic historian and philosopher of the Middle Ages. After studying Islamic theology and law, logic and mathematics at the Kairaouine University in Fez he wrote various mathematical treatises and other books. At the age of 20 he gained his first important position at the Sultan's court. Then, to complete his education, he visited the best universities of the time in Andalusia (Granada), Algeria (Algiers), Tunisia (Kairouan), Egypt (Cairo) and Syria (Damascus). In the writings on logic which he then published he became the first Islamic thinker to see reason as an independent force and not merely the handmaiden of theology. Thereafter he taught at the Kairaouine University and at the same time, from 1353 to 1375, was attached to the court of the Merinid rulers of Morocco in various capacities (as court poet, judge, secretary, chancellor, diplomat). In a period when there were frequent changes of ruler he fell victim to court intrigues, being several times dismissed from his office and then reinstated, and on one occasion spending two years in prison.

Ibn Khaldun finally concentrated on the writing of history, seeking to deduce general laws from the vicissitudes of history in his time, much of which he had himself experienced. In 1375 he withdrew to the fortress of Ibn Salama in Algeria and there, in solitude, wrote the "Muqaddima", the first modern, rationalist work of history. In this book he describes the history of the Berbers and explains the recurring dynastic crises in the Maghreb as the result of the constant struggle for power between two different types of society, on the one hand the nomads and on the other Arab urban culture. On this theory the old dynasties which have become decadent in the urban setting are overthrown by the young and vital nomadic tribes. They come to power, flourish for a time, and then grow soft and are displaced by new nomadic tribes. The social differences between the ordinary people (including the strongly religious tribes) as the "base" and the increasingly decadent ruling dynasties as the "superstructure" of society give rise to the national crises which occur with remarkable regularity in the Maghreb.

After finishing the "Muqaddima" Ibn Khaldun went to the Cairo court, where he taught Malikite law at the University and also worked as a government official and diplomat. Here he wrote a three-volume universal history, the first rationalist work of the kind, in which he extrapolated the alternation between the winning of power and the loss of power in the Maghreb to the whole course of human history. In the long preface to his "Qitab al Ibar" ("Book of World History") he expounds views worthy of an Adam Smith, a Ricardo or a Karl Marx on the philosophy of history and on the most modern sociology. His main thesis is that the social groupings within a state and their relationships with one another essentially depend on the differences between their patterns of economic life.

Ibn Khaldun died in Cairo and is buried in the Sufi cemetery there.

El Idrisi (11th–12th c.)

Abu Abd Allah Mohammed ben Mohammed ben Abd Allah ben Idris el Ali Bi Amra Allah, also known as El Sherif el Idrisi, or El Idrisi for short, was one of the greatest and best known geographers of his time. He had an extraordinary life. It is known that, for reasons that are not clear, he went to the court of the Norman, Christian king of Sicily, Roger II, and that while there he wrote his most important work, the "Book of Roger", in praise of the king. Little else is known about his life. The Islamic historians regarded him as a renegade and ignored him completely. It is believed, however, that he was born in Ceuta about 1099–1100 and that he studied in Córdoba. He himself tells us that he has travelled widely in Spain and North Africa. He is thought to have died in 1164–65, but nothing is known about his later years or his death.

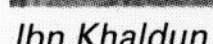

Ibn Khaldun

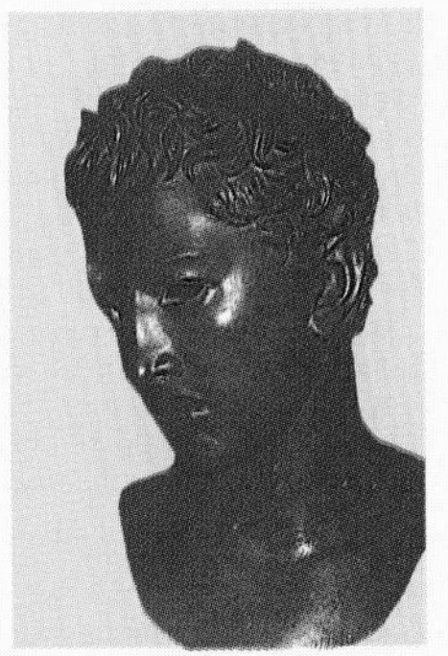

Juba II

Masinissa

El Idrisi made for Roger II a celestial sphere showing the sun, moon, stars and the earth, a round silver map of the earth and his famous atlas, with commentaries, depicting the whole world as it was then known. Particularly valuable are his maps of the seven climatic zones which he defined and his map of the world.

Juba II
(*c.* 50 B.C. to c. 23–24 B.C.)

The life of King Juba II of Numidia reflects the surprisingly close association of this Berber ruler with the culture of Rome. He was the son of Juba I, who fought on Pompey's side in the Civil War with Caesar and committed suicide when he was defeated at Thapsus in 46 B.C. and his kingdom became a Roman province. Caesar took his four-year-old son prisoner and had him brought up in Rome, where he is believed to have married Cleopatra Selene, daughter of Mark Antony and Cleopatra. Augustus granted Juba Roman citizenship and sent him back to North Africa in 26–25 B.C. as king of Mauretania, with his residence at Iol, renamed Caesarea (now the Algerian port of Cherchell). There Juba reigned for almost 50 years, dying in A.D. 23–24.

Juba was a highly cultivated and learned man who had completely assimilated Hellenistic and Roman culture. He built temples, palaces and public baths in his capital and assembled a collection of antique sculpture and other works of art.

His scholarly interests found expression in numerous writings – preserved only in a fragmentary state – on history, philology and geography. Among them is a description of the euphorbia, a plant discovered in the Atlas Mountains and named after his personal physician. The great Roman writer Pliny the Elder, author of the "Natural History", made use of Juba's accounts of the geography, geology, flora and fauna of Africa.

El Kahina
(6th–7th c. A.D.)

El Kahina, one of the few women in Berber history of whom we have any knowledge, belonged to the Christianised Djerawa tribe, a branch of the great Zenata tribe. Her exact origins are unclear: she is said to have been born of a Greek/Berber intermarriage and herself to have married a Greek. One of her two sons is said to have had a Greek father, the other a Berber. She had a reputation as a prophetess, who when inspiration came over her fell into a state of wild excitement, loosing her hair and beating her breast before receiving a revelation. Her status among the Berbers was undoubtedly due to her prophetic gift. The name of El Kahina, the Sorceress, was given to her by her enemies, the Arabs; her original name is said to have been Dihya.

She came into her own as a leader of the Berber resistance to the Arabs as a widow at an advanced age. Under her leadership the Berbers combined for a period of six years in the fight against the Arab conquerors. About the year 692 an Arab force led by Hassan Ben el Nouman attacked the Aurès

area (in present-day Algeria), the principal stronghold of the Berber resistance and the residence of El Kahina, the "queen of the Aurès". Her military tactics were ruthless, but for years they brought success. She razed to the ground her family seat, Baghaya, to prevent it from falling into Hassan's hands. How much fertile land was devastated by this "scorched earth" policy is the subject of controversy, but so much land was destroyed that some Berbers at least welcomed Hassan as a saviour.
About 697-698 Hassan returned with reinforcements, and this time – probably with the help of large numbers of Berbers – he succeeded in overcoming El Kahina's resistance. Shortly before she met her death, together with a small band of trusty supporters, she had agreed with the Arab victors that the majority of her followers should go unpunished on condition that the Berber tribes gave hostages and supplied auxiliary forces under Arab command.

Jugurtha
(160–104 B.C.)

The Numidian king Jugurtha came very close to being the founder of the Tunisian state, until the Romans put an end to his continuing guerrilla activity. Unlike his famous grandfather Masinissa, he was opposed to the Roman overlordship in North Africa. He was ready to use any means to gain power, and his two cousins were merely the first victims of his ruthless ambition. In his skirmishes with Roman legionaries his light guerrilla forces were able to outmanoeuvre the more heavily armed Romans and inflict severe losses on them. Finally, however, Jugurtha was run to earth in his hiding-place, handed over to the Romans and executed in 104 B.C.

Isabelle Eberhardt
(1877–1904)

Isabelle Eberhardt, the illegitimate daughter of a Russian general's widow, was brought up in Switzerland, in a house which was the meeting-place of Russian anarchists, Polish revolutionaries and Turkish nationalists. She may have derived her individuality and eccentricity from her father, a former Orthodox priest. She began writing at an early age, and at the age of twenty went to Algeria and became a convert to Islam. Dressed as a man, she travelled widely through the Algerian desert and the Tunisian Sahel. She died in a storm in the desert in 1904 and is buried near the Algerian town of Ain Sefra. She left a record of her experiences and reflections in a number of unfinished novels, diaries and travel notes.

El Bachir Khrayef
(b. 1917)

The literature of Tunisia reflects the country's striving towards independence. One of the leading representatives of the realist school, which seeks to depict the everyday life of the people and the social contrasts within the country, is El Bachir Khrayef. He wrote his first story at the age of nineteen, but his talent is mainly displayed in his later novels. He won a literary prize with his historical novel "Barq el Lail" (1961), the love story of a black slave set against the background of 16th century Tunis.

Nja Mahdaoui
(b. 1937)

The work of the Tunisian artist Nja Mahdaoui, particularly his ink drawings on parchment or animal skin (see illustration, page 82), have something of the character of calligraphy. Mahdaoui draws inspiration from the extraordinary richness of form of Arab calligraphy (see Art and Culture, Islamic Art and Architecture), but frees them from any religious significance. A knowledge of the Arabic language and script does not in itself lead to understanding of Mahdaoui's "messages". His characters cannot be "translated" like the characters of an alphabet: they do not convey meaning, but rather a sense of form.
After attending Koranic and secondary schools Nja Mahdaoui studied art history and drawing at a private art school in Tunis. In the sixties and seventies he lived for some years in Italy and then in France, where he studied painting and philosophy. He also began to work intensively in the various techniques of calligraphy. In 1977 he returned to Tunisia, and since then has lived near Tunis.
Mahdaoui is indefatigable in devising new compositions, and thus makes his own personal contribution to a period during which Arab culture is striving to reach a new understanding of itself.

Masinissa (240–148 B.C.)

The Numidian king Masinissa was a less famous contemporary of Hannibal and Scipio Africanus. While Rome and Carthage were fighting for predominance in the Mediterranean, Masinissa, king of Eastern Numidia, and Syphax, king of Western Numidia, were engaged in a similar conflict for predominance in North Africa: a contest in which Masinissa, allying himself with Rome, was victorious. Subsequently he wrested some 70 towns and fortresses from Carthage, defeated in the Second Punic War and reduced to impotence by a harsh peace treaty, and founded the first large Berber kingdom, extending from the Libyan coast to Morocco.
But Masinissa was not merely a successful warrior who was able to defeat and outmanoeuvre rival Berber chieftains: he had a progressive agricultural policy, inducing the nomadic tribes to take up a settled life, promoted Mediterranean trade and invited Greek artists to Numidia. After his death – under some pressure from Rome – his country was divided up between his sons and thus weakened.

Sidi Mahrez (d. 1022)

Sidi Mahrez is known as Sultan el Medina, the patron saint of Tunis. He is famed not only for his theological writings but for his social concern. After the destruction caused in Tunis by various risings, plunderings and sieges he cared for the poor, had the town walls rebuilt and gave the Jews, for the first time, a district of their own in Tunis, the Hara. (Previously they had been compelled to live outside the walls and were allowed into the town only during the day.) Sidi Mahrez himself lived a strictly ascetic life, earning the name of El Abid (the Ascetic).

Tertullian (*c.* 160–220 A.D.)

Tertullian (Quintus Septimius Florens Tertullianus), born in Carthage, the son of a Roman captain, was the first Christian theologian to write in Greek and Latin. Legally trained, he combined the precision of a lawyer with great polemical vigour. He created the basic concepts of Western theology, although the church sometimes condemned his interpretations and made his work accessible to posterity only in the form of extracts.
Tertullian, who is believed to have lived for some time in Rome, died in his native city of Carthage.

Yahia Turki (1900–60)

Yahia Turki was an artist who dared to do what for strict Muslims is unthinkable: he painted representational pictures, ignoring a taboo imposed by Islam on believers. He made it his life's work to develop a pictorial language for a country in which the only recognised form of artistic expression was ornament. His style was influenced by Matisse, Bonnard and Marquet, but his subjects were taken from everyday life in Tunisia.

Art and Culture

Tunisian Art and Architecture

Prehistory

Very few remains dating from before the Phoenician colonisation have been found. Items displayed in the Bardo National Museum in Tunis (see entry) include simple stone and, from the 4th millennium B.C. onwards, bronze implements, small receptacles and amulets made from bone, pierced sea-shells and snail shells and decorated ostrich eggs. There are no rock engravings in Tunisia of the type found in Morocco.

Phoenicians and Carthaginians

In antiquity the Phoenicians, the ancestors of the Carthaginians, were not highly rated. Greek and Roman writers including Cicero, Livy, Plutarch and Appian describe them as cunning, mendacious, treacherous and cruel. Although this picture – disseminated by their enemies and competitors – has since been questioned and corrected, a similarly negative view of their art prevailed into the 18th and 19th centuries, and indeed until the mid 20th century. The question at issue – whether the cultures of the ancient world reached maturity as a result of mediation by the Phoenicians or whether the Phoenicians merely copied Egyptian and Greek models – has not yet been definitely resolved.

The Phoenicians (*c.* 1100–800 B.C.) and the Carthaginians (until 146 B.C.) were known mainly as outstanding seamen and shipbuilders rather than as great artists. Nevertheless their fine fabrics, ivory carvings, metalwork, gold and silver jewellery, vessels of coloured glass, richly decorated tableware and dainty toilet utensils were much prized at princely courts throughout the Mediterranean world from the 8th century B.C. onwards. There are also a number of important cultural inventions which are ascribed alternately to the Phoenicians and the Egyptians – the manufacture of glass and glass paste, the technique of niello decoration (in which silver is inlaid with engraved designs in a dark-coloured alloy), the goldsmith's technique of granulation (forming tiny spheres of gold on a gold base) and the monopoly of the purple dye from which the Phoenicians took their name, to say nothing of the devising of an alphabetic script.

Among the objects which have survived are tiny heads of glass paste with round staring eyes which were worn as amulets and deposited in tombs. There are also hollow-eyed clay masks of rather Oriental aspect, far removed from any ideal type familiar to the Egyptians, Greeks or Romans, which are thought to have been designed to ward off demons.

Since the Semitic ban on the representation of figures is thought to have remained in force until the end of Carthaginian history, the sculptural representation of gods was not permitted. Thus Tanit, consort of Baal and the principal goddess of Carthage, who is attested from the 5th century B.C., appears only in the form of a symbol: an isosceles triangle with a bar across the top terminating in raised curving ends. The head is represented by a circle, frequently topped by a crescent; eyes, a mouth and a nose are added at a much later stage. This symbol of a goddess with her arms raised in blessing is found on narrow, tapering stone pillars, on the stelae set up over graves, in pavement mosaics and incised on gold signet-rings.

Tanit Symbol

◀ *Numidian mausoleum, Dougga*

Punic glass head, Carthage

Stele with symbol of Tanit and solar disc

On stelae found in the Tophet (sacred precinct) of Carthage are inscriptions referring to the Carthaginian custom of offering sacrifices of children (*molek*) to the divine couple Baal and Tanit in times of crisis. The children are believed to have been ceremonially burned in a hollow bronze statue and then buried one above the other in several layers.

Since the Romans frequently built their towns on the ruins of destroyed Carthaginian towns little Carthaginian architecture has survived. Some remains, mainly showing Greek influence, can be seen at Carthage, Utica and Kerkouane.

Numidian royal architecture

Examples of Numidian royal architecture – always situated on carefully selected commanding sites – are the remains of two hilltop sanctuaries at Chemtou and Kbor Klit and the tower mausoleum at Dougga. This tall square monument, the principle of which was taken over by the Romans and disseminated far beyond the bounds of North Africa, bears witness to the enduring quality of Numidian architecture.

Roman Period

After the destruction of Carthage in 146 B.C. the Romans conquered the whole of North Africa and erected their buildings – originally influenced by Etruscan and later by Greek architecture – all over the new province.

Of the 200 or so towns that the Romans are so far known to have founded impressive remains survive: at Dougga, Sufetula/Sbeitla, Bulla Regia, Maktar, Thuburbo Majus and Thysdrus/El Djem with its amphitheatre, to mention only a few of the most important sites.

Roman architecture

Since many Roman towns were built on the ruins of their irregularly laid out Carthaginian predecessors, they did not always show the usual regular Roman plan. The central feature of a Roman town was the forum, a large

Roman theatre, Dougga

paved area surrounded by numerous public buildings. At one end was the Capitol, a temple dedicated to Jupiter, Juno and Minerva, and closely adjoining this was the Basilica, an aisled hall which served as a court-room and later provided a model for the first Christian churches. The two main streets of the town, the cardo maximus running north-south and the decumanus maximus running east-west, intersected in the forum and divided the town into four quarters, in which the streets were laid out at right angles to one another. At Sbeitla (ancient Sufetula) this regular layout can be clearly seen.

The use of new building materials and the adoption of features from the clay-brick architecture of the East allowed the Romans to develop their preference for arches rather than rectangular openings and to replace the flat roof borne on columns by vaulting. At the height of their power they began to set quite new standards, and their colonial cities were equipped with numbers of magnificently decorated public buildings (temples, basilicas, curias, etc.). Viaducts, amphitheatres, sumptuous villas, sometimes containing underground rooms, and grandiose public baths still bear witness to the singlemindedness with which the Romans used architecture and art to project the image and the prestige of their empire.

The Roman writer Apuleius (see Famous People) gives a vivid description of a luxurious villa in North Africa in his "Golden Ass":

"The ceiling is finely vaulted, inlaid with ivory and lemon-wood and borne on golden columns. The walls are covered with beaten silver... The floor is laid with the most precious stones, cut small and of many colours, and so skilfully put together that they make the most beautiful pictures. Oh, twice and many times happy are those who are permitted to tread on the gold and the precious stones!"

Roman sculpture

The interiors of the houses were decorated with bronze and marble sculpture, mosaic pavements and wall paintings. The sculpture found in Tunisia consists of Greek originals (mainly gods, ephebes and maenads), Roman

The villa of a landowner named Julius (Bardo Museum, Tunis)

copies of famous Greek works of sculpture, portraits of Roman emperors, procurators and generals, memorial stones with relief decoration, votive altars and stelae, and relief decoration on triumphal arches, the façades of buildings, columns and roof-ridges.

Mosaics

As early as the 3rd millennium B.C. walls and pillars were being decorated in the East by the insertion of coloured clay pegs into the plaster facing. The oldest mosaic pavement in the Mediterranean area (5th–4th c. B.C.), made of black and white pebbles, was found at Olynthus in northern Greece. In Hellenistic times this technique was further developed, using small pieces of cut stone (tesserae) or glass (smalt), fitted together to produce designs and pictures for the decoration of walls and floors.

The technique of mosaic-work was known to the Carthaginians, as finds in Kerkouane and Carthage have shown. The great flowering of mosaic art, however, was in the time of the Romans. In no other country have so many floor mosaics been found as in Tunisia, and the museums of Tunis, Sousse, El Djem and Sfax have the world's finest collections of mosaics.

The simple forms of mosaics, with the stones arranged in no particular pattern, developed in the course of time into elaborate picture mosaics. At first the artists merely copied existing models, but soon they began to follow their own ideas or those of their patron. Thus at first the mosaics depict mythological scenes, but then they begin to show scenes from everyday life, farming, merchants and craftsmen, sports and games. Particularly popular are fishing scenes, lake scenery and seascapes. They give a lively picture of the life of the upper classes of the Roman population, showing them in their homes, at work and enjoying their leisure, and are often of considerable documentary value.

From the 4th century onwards mosaics were mainly used for the decoration of tombs. Christian symbols such as fish, birds and grape-vines, as well as figures of the dead person, increasingly feature on gravestones,

Triumph of Bacchus (Bardo Museum, Tunis)

and whole scenes from the Old Testament point to the enhanced influence of Christianity in the Roman world.

Transitional Period

Towards the end of the 3rd century A.D. Roman power and wealth began to decline, and art and architecture became simpler. The Vandals, who established a kingdom in Tunisia in 439, left few traces of their presence, and the influence of the Byzantines, who conquered North Africa from 530 onwards, was comparatively limited. They built fortresses (Ksar Lemsa, ancient Limisa; Ain Tounga, ancient Thignica; Haidra, ancient Ammaedara) and basilicas with three aisles separated by columns, frequently built into old Roman buildings. Their mosaics were composed of larger pieces of stone, most commonly in simple geometric designs. The interior walls of their churches were frequently faced with terracotta slabs.

Berber Art

The abstract geometric ornament of the Berbers has long played an important part in Tunisian architecture, art, applied art and pottery, and even modern artists such as Njib Belkodja, a pioneer of abstract painting in Tunisia, show its influence.

Architecture

The particular geographical and climatic conditions of southern Tunisia, with its hot summers, cold winters and lack of fuel for heating, together with the centuries-old practice of living in extended family groups, led to the development of very distinctive types of architecture. The troglodytic dwellings and fortified granaries of the Berbers demonstrate their ability to adapt to the natural conditions. Some of these old structures have been preserved and can be visited. In the eyes of the Tunisian authorities, however, they are survivals from the past which no longer meet modern requirements. Most of the old troglodytic dwellings and fortified granaries have been demolished and their occupants rehoused in modern housing schemes; others had already been abandoned and left to fall into decay. The need to restore them was overlooked for many years, and considerations of expense precluded any idea of constructing new troglodytic dwellings. A few examples have been preserved as tourist attractions and converted into museums or hotels.

Troglodytic dwellings

Two types of troglodytic dwellings can be distinguished, the pit type and the hillside type. For the construction of either type the right rock formations are essential, with alternating strata of soft and easily worked marl, clay or sandstone and harder layers of limestone. The only tools required are picks, crowbars and spades.

Pit type

The pit type of troglodytic dwelling is found in gently rolling upland regions. The dwellings are laid out around a square pit measuring between 10 and 20m/33 and 66ft each way and between 6 and 12m/20 and 40ft deep. Off this central courtyard, which is common to the whole extended family, open the underground dwellings occupied by individual families, some of them of two storeys. Each family has its own cooking-place. If the extended family increases in size another dwelling is hewn from the rock. From the courtyard a tunnel runs up to the surface, with store-rooms and stalls for animals opening off it.

Examples of this type can be seen in the Matmata uplands.

Hillside type

On hills and hillsides a different type of troglodytic dwelling is found. Depending on the nature of the rock, the individual dwellings may be hewn out side by side or one on top of the other. Each of them has direct access to a common courtyard, which is usually closed by a high wall or by buildings of one or more storeys containing store-rooms, kitchens and stalls for animals.

Examples of this type can be found in the southern Dahar uplands, at Chenini, Douirat and Guermessa.

Fortified granaries (*ksar/ksour*)

The semi-nomadic way of life produced another distinctive type of building, the fortified granary or *ksar* (plural *ksour*).

The *ksar* is a complex of *ghorfas,* barrel-vaulted cells 8–10m/26–33ft long and 3m/10ft wide, store-rooms (sometimes also used as dwellings) in which a family's reserves of food could be kept in safety during their periodic wanderings. The *ghorfas,* sometimes rising to a height of eight

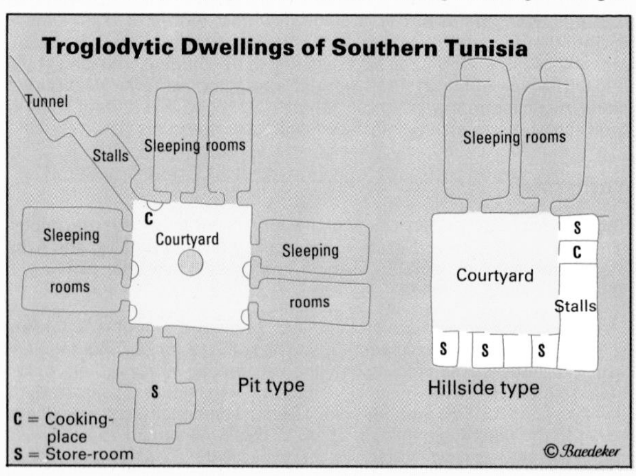

storeys, were laid out round an enclosed courtyard, and above the whole complex there might be a protective fortress (*kalaa*).
Examples are to be found mainly in the southern Dahar uplands, at Metameur (restored for the benefit of tourists), Médenine, where a few examples have escaped the bulldozer, and Ksar Haddada.

Islamic Art

From the 7th century onwards Islam thrust westward as far as Spain and eastward into Pakistan. On their campaigns of conquest the Arabs came into contact with foreign cultures, and from this interaction with other peoples developed Islamic/Arab culture.
Islamic art finds expression principally in calligraphy, ornament and architecture, both sacred (mosques, ribats, mausoleums, medersas, etc.) and secular (palaces, hammams, kasbahs, town walls, merchants' houses, etc.).

Classical Islamic/Arab art came into being under the Omayyads (7th–8th c.), establishing a tradition which influenced later centuries. In the West the tradition was continued in Moorish art under a series of Berber dynasties, the Almoravids, Almohads and Nasrids (11th–15th c.), and through their interrelationships Moorish art travelled from Spain to North Africa, where, given fresh impulsions by successive waves of refugees from Andalusia, it enjoyed a great flowering.

Ban on figural representation

In accordance with an edict by Caliph Yazid II in 721 Islamic art expressly excludes any representation of human beings or animals in painting or sculpture. The ban is usually justified on the basis of the prescriptions of the Koran, under which the imitation of nature is regarded as blasphemous. There must, however, have been other reasons, for representations of living creatures are quite common in early mosques and other Islamic buildings. It may be that representations of the wealthy founders of sacred buildings became too frequent and came to be seen as symbols of wealth and luxury; and it was also realised that Islamic art could not compete with the richness of form and expressive power of Byzantine painting. The principle of avoiding figural representation thus became established. Strictly speaking, the ban applied only to religious art, and even in that there were exceptions. In Persia and India figural art developed in miniature painting, mainly in court circles.

Geometric designs

The ban on the representation of figures led to a great flowering of non-figural representation, as Islamic artists turned to calligraphy and ornament and developed a great range of geometric, stylised and abstract forms. The relative shortage of themes meant that they were continually repeated. They feature, in a great variety of colours, in the patterns of wall and floor tiles, carved wood ornament on doors and ceilings, window grilles, silversmiths' work and incised metal ornament.

Ornament

"God's Web"

The basic elements of Arab ornament are calligraphy, arabesques, stalactitic vaulting and geometric patterns built up from polygons (usually octagons and hexagons) linked by straight lines.

"God's web"

The most important of these patterns is "God's web", a system of lines forming stars with from eight to sixteen points, in which each line runs from the centre of one star to the centre of another. Since this kind of ornament called for exceedingly delicate work it was possible only with suitable material. Accordingly wood and plaster became the favourite materials and stucco ornament the characteristic feature of interior decoration.

Calligraphy

In creating bands of inscriptions Arab artists followed the model of Greek and Persian inscriptions, replacing the text of the inscriptions by verses from the Koran or the name of Allah. This gave rise to the specifically Arab art form of calligraphy, using the stylised Arabic script as ornament. There are two types of script, the angular Kufic script and the Naskhi script which originated in the 11th century, a rounded cursive form with a wider range of variations than Kufic.

Arabesques

Another very typical Arab form of decoration is the arabesque, which is frequently combined with calligraphic ornament. The arabesque, a type developed from Persian and Greco-Byzantine models (acanthus, palmette, etc.), is built up from stylised plant elements (stems, tendrils, leaves, flowers) closely intertwined with one another and was used in borders and friezes and in association with calligraphy.

Stalactitic vaulting (*muqarnas*)

The stalactitic vaulting characteristic of Muslim architecture was developed out of the Persian type of squinch vaulting. The multiplication, horizontally and vertically, of small concave segments in honeycomb formation produced magnificently patterned vaulting, used in porches, doorways and ceilings.

Islamic Architecture

As a nomadic people of the desert the Arabs originally had no large buildings, either public or private. It was only after they had come into contact with other cultures during their campaigns of conquest that they developed a characteristic architectural style influenced by Hellenistic and Roman, Sassanid (Persian) and Christian (in western Islam specifically Visigothic) architecture, combining the Greek basilica with the Persian columned hall and taking over the horseshoe arch from the Visigoths. The apses and chapel niches of Christian churches provided models for the mihrab, church towers for minarets.

Moorish style

The main characteristics of Moorish architecture are:
– the increased breadth of buildings (in contrast to the upward movement of Gothic architecture). The predominant form in mosques is a T-shaped plan, with a transept in front of the qibla wall (facing Mecca); emphasis is given to the central aisle by its greater width and its domes; and the aisles are separated by a forest of elegant columns, tapering towards the top so that the roof appears to be floating in space;
– the absence of decoration on the outer walls and the restrained pattern of doors and windows;
– the use of the typical (Visigothic) horseshoe arch on doors and windows and between the columns;

Types of arch

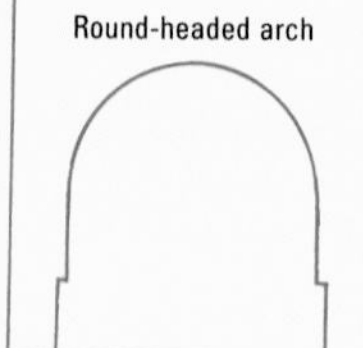

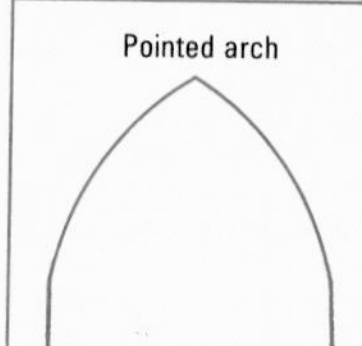

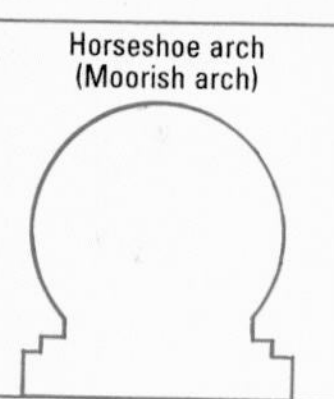

- stalactitic vaulting of wood or plaster; and
- rich interior decoration, with faience tiles, marble pavement mosaics, elaborately carved window screens, intarsia work and carved woodwork.

All these features are found in both sacred and secular public buildings, and for many centuries preserved a remarkable uniformity.

Sacred Buildings

N.B.

Since 1972 non-Muslims have been prohibited from entering mosques in Tunisia. They may, however, enter the courtyards during the morning. Further information about admission to mosques is given in the "Tunisia from A to Z" section of this guide or can be obtained from local tourist information offices.

The mosque

The most important Islamic sacred building is the mosque. The Arabic name for the ordinary district mosque is *masjid* (the "place of prostration" in prayer); the large congregational or Friday mosque is *djemaa* ("place of assembly").

Unlike a Christian church, a mosque is not a sacred place in the strict sense: between the times of prayer it used to serve as a court-house, a theological college, a place for conducting business or a home for the poor or travellers with no other accommodation. This also finds expression in its ground-plan.

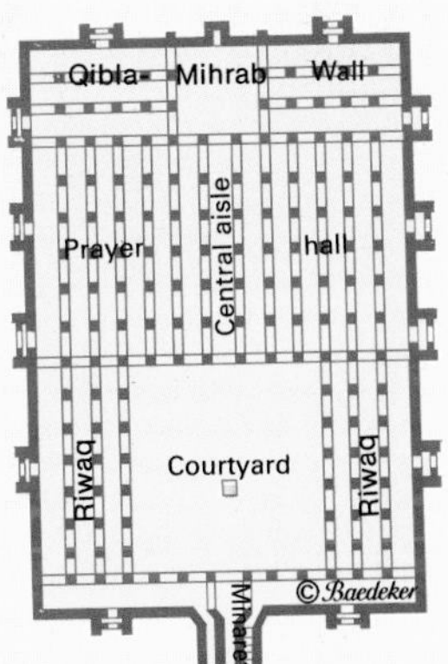

Ground-plan of a mosque

The original model for a mosque was Mohammed's house in Medina, built about A.D. 622, the courtyard of which, with roofs along the sides to provide shade, was the first meeting-place of the Muslim community. The place where the Prophet had stood in prayer was marked by a niche, later to become the mihrab; and the small platform on which he sat while instructing the believers became the model for the minbar, the high pulpit near the mihrab from which the imam gives his Friday address.

The second model was the former temple precinct (temenos) of Damascus with its enclosing walls and four corner towers, which around A.D. 706 became an annex to a prayer hall of basilican type. The central part of the area was surrounded on three sides by arcades and became the courtyard of the mosque.

From these two models developed the early Omayyad type of hall-mosque, which in turn became the model for subsequent centuries.

Types of arch

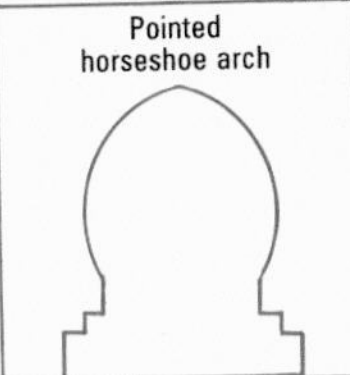

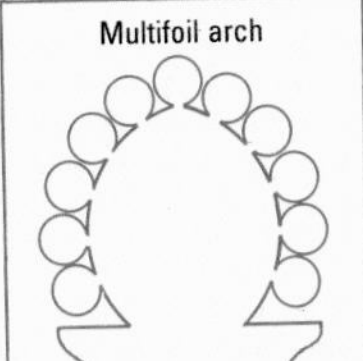

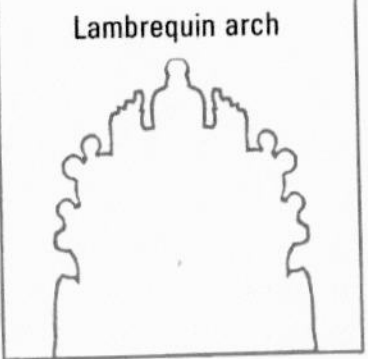

Doorway of Barber's Mosque, Kairouan

Mosque, Bardo Palace

In Iran, Syria and Egypt there developed from the 10th century onwards a type of mosque derived from Sassanid palaces in which the central courtyard was surrounded on all four sides by arcaded halls. In Istanbul the Ottoman type of domed mosque developed from the 16th century onwards, following the model of the church of Hagia Sophia.
In the Maghreb the pattern of the Omayyad mosque was followed.

Both the Christian church and the Islamic mosque originally derived from the ancient basilica. The Christian liturgy led to the main emphasis being placed on the central longitudinal axis: in the mosque, however, the main hall was usually set at right angles to the longitudinal axis and gradually developed into a broad prayer hall which could be extended to whatever size was required and was of the same height over its whole area.

Minbar

The typical Maghrebine mosque has the classic T-shaped ground-plan of the Omayyad mosques. The prayer hall is divided by rows of columns into numerous aisles, with a wider central aisle, running at right angles to the qibla wall (prayer wall), in front of which is a transverse aisle. The main central aisle and the qibla aisle produce the typical T-shaped ground-plan of the mosque.

The central aisle and the qibla aisle intersect in front of the mihrab, the richly decorated niche which marks the direction of prayer (until 624 towards Jerusalem, thereafter towards Mecca). Over this "crossing" is a dome. Beside the mihrab, usually standing at right angles to the qibla wall, is the minbar, a high pulpit with a steep flight of steps. Adjoining this again is the *maqsura*, an enclosed place of prayer for the Caliph, in which he could take part in the prayer without being seen by his people.

The mosque has nothing corresponding to the icons and representations of scenes from Biblical history which are found in Christian churches. The decoration comes from the rich variety of forms offered by calligraphy, geometric ornament and arabesques.

In the forecourt of the prayer hall, which is also full of worshippers on days of festival, there are usually open fountains or fountain-houses at which the ritual ablutions necessary before prayer are performed.

Minarets

At one corner of the outer walls or of the side galleries stands the minaret – a feature of the mosque since Omayyad times – from which the muezzin calls the faithful to prayer five times a day. (Nowadays, however, the call to prayer is usually recorded and broadcast by loudspeaker.) In North Africa and Spain the minaret is usually a richly decorated square tower of three or four successively smaller storeys topped by a dome, above which are up to three shimmering gold balls (the number of balls depending on the importance of the mosque). The Kasbah Mosque in Tunis, as the principal town mosque, has four balls.
There is also a slender octagonal minaret, known as the Hanafite type, which was brought to Tunisia by the Turks.
In the eastern Islamic world the predominant type of minaret was circular or sometimes polygonal, and usually pencil-slim. The prototype is thought to have been the minaret of the Great Mosque at Samarra in Iraq (846–852), which is surrounded by a broad spiral ramp.

Medersas

Another important sacred building is the medrese (Maghrebine form medersa), a term derived from Arabic *darasa* (study). This is a college of theology and Islamic law (occasionally also of medicine and science) with living accommodation for the students and a mosque-like prayer hall. The most important of the Tunisian medersas are in Tunis and Kairouan.
The medersa is built round a rectangular courtyard (with a fountain), at one end of which is the prayer hall. On the ground floor of the two- or three-storey buildings round the courtyard are the lecture rooms, the library and the college offices; on the upper floor are the students' rooms, often small and cell-like. The entrance doorway of the medersa and the walls of the courtyard are frequently decorated with tiles, carved woodwork, stalactitic vaulting and delicate stucco ornament.

Ribats

A ribat is a fortified monastery. During the 8th century a large number of ribats were built along the North African coast as part of a system of coastal observation and defence. In times of peace the monks devoted themselves to propagating and consolidating the faith of Islam in the country, but in time of danger the local people found shelter and protection within the fortress and the warlike monks were ready to defend the faith by military means. It was said of the ribat in Monastir that three days on garrison duty there opened the gates of Paradise.
The layout of the ribat was simple: a square structure surrounding an inner courtyard, round which were the monks' cells, store-rooms and offices. The only communal room was the mosque.

Types of minaret

Sidi Oqba
Kairouan

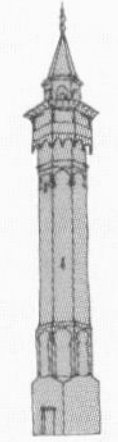
Hammouda Pacha
Tunis

Great Mosque
Samarra

Selimiye
Edirne

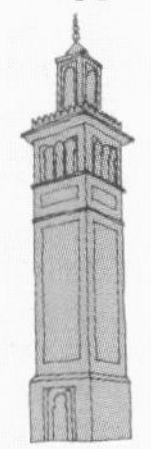
Almohad
Tunis

Ibn Tulun
Cairo

Ribat, Sousse

Koubba, Nefta

The best preserved examples of ribats are to be seen at Sousse and Monastir.

Koubbas

Among the most characteristic sacred buildings in the western Maghreb are the koubbas or marabouts, the small cube-shaped domed buildings which house the tombs of holy men (the word marabout means "holy man" as well as "tomb"). Gleaming in the sunlight in their coat of whitewash, frequently renewed, the koubbas are prominent features of the landscape, visible from a long way off.

Zaouias

A zaouia is the headquarters of a religious brotherhood, which in addition to living quarters includes the tombs of the principal holy men of the brotherhood, often in the form of mausoleums, and a mosque. A good example is the zaouia of Sidi Sahab at Kairouan.

Secular Architecture

Palaces

The most imposing secular buildings in Tunisia were the palaces of the country's rulers, but of these few remains have survived – the Bardo Palace in Tunis, Al Abbasiya and Reqqada near Kairouan and scanty remains at Mahdia. The palaces consisted of a variety of individual buildings, erected over the years without any unified plan. Frequently they formed a bizarre complex of walls, buildings, towers, open squares, inner courtyards, parks and gardens with ponds and fountains. Four main types of buildings, however, can be distinguished:

Mechouar

the mechouar, a large courtyard for audiences, assemblies, court hearings or parades of troops;

Divan

the divan, containing the main state apartments, including the throne-room for important acts of state and various council chambers;

Harem

the harem, the ruler's private apartments, with the women's quarters; and,

Subsidiary buildings

surrounding the palace proper, various domestic offices, kitchens, accommodation for servants and the barracks of the ruler's bodyguard.

Fortifications

Many Tunisian towns have preserved old fortifications, town walls and gates. Particularly impressive are those to be seen at Tunis, Kairouan, Sousse, Sfax, Mahdia, Monastir and Bizerte.
Purely functional structures, they are usually undecorated. This does not, however, apply to certain monumental gateways, usually the entrances to the ruler's residence or the kasbah or the gates outside which court hearings were held: these are often sumptuously decorated with tiles, bearing witness to the wealth, power and artistic sense of their builders.

Hammams

Like other Islamic countries, Tunisia has numerous public and private bath-houses (hammams), in line with the Muslim obligation to perform ablutions before prayer.
On the model of the baths of antiquity, the hammams, which are separate for men and women, consist of a sequence of rooms – a cold bath, a warm bath, a sweat bath and a rest room.
The entrance to the hammam, like the inner courtyard of a Moorish house, leads round a number of corners, so that passers-by cannot see into the interior, which is usually faced with faience tiles. There is a bath-master responsible for maintaining order and decency.
The hammam also has a fountain (often of marble) and lavatories.

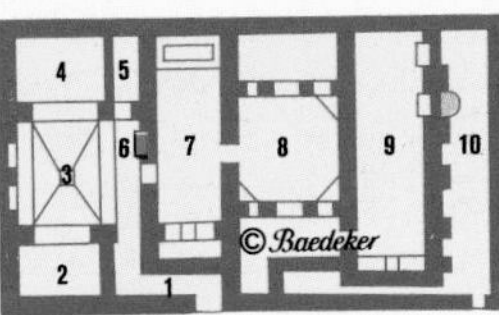

Layout of a hammam

1 Entrance
2 Bath-master's room
3 Courtyard
4 Rest room
5 Lavatory
6 Fountain
7 Cold room
8 Warm room
9 Hot room
10 Stove and boiler room

Fountains

Notable features of Tunisian towns are the numerous public fountains, many of them still in use. The most attractive examples are in Moorish style, often richly decorated, with stalactitic vaulting of stucco or wood; sometimes they have a domed roof borne on elegant columns.

Fondouks

Fondouks (Arabic *funduq),* inns which provided accommodation for travelling merchants and the animals of their caravan, are now rarely to be seen. They are buildings of several storeys surrounding a rectangular courtyard, with a single entrance closed by a heavy door. On the ground floor were warehouses and stalls for the animals; on the upper floors, looking on to the courtyard and reached by means of external staircases and galleries, were the lodgings for travellers.
Some of the surviving fondouks are now occupied by craftsmen or used for storage.

Present-Day Art and Culture

Present-day Tunisian culture bears the imprint of its Arab heritage and of African, Mediterranean and European (particularly French) influences. While in the 1950s there was widespread enthusiasm for all manner of international, and especially European, ideas and fashions, there has in recent years been an increased interest in the country's own native traditions and cultural history.

Art

Tunisia now has a whole range of artists whose reputation extends beyond the country's boundaries – men such as Hatim el Mekki (b. 1917), Mahmoud Sehili, Ali Bellagha, Abdelazy Gorgi and Nja Mahdaoui (b. 1937). The work of Nja Mahdaoui (see Famous People) shows how enriching a return

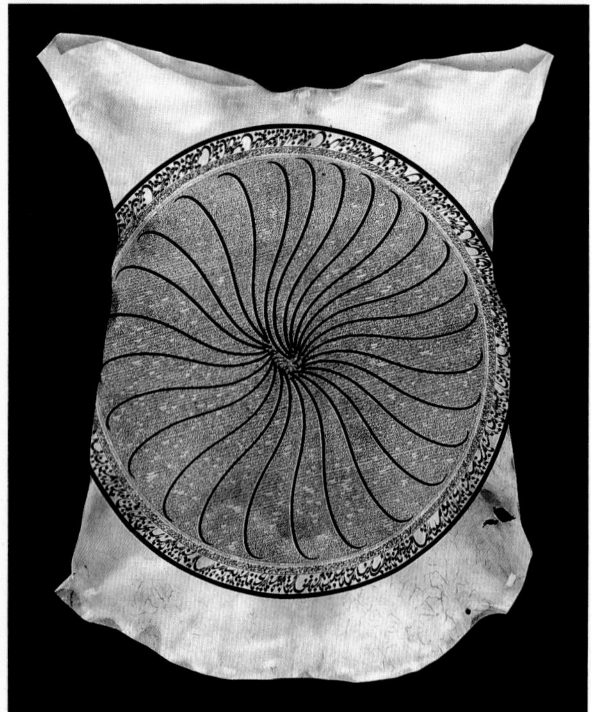

Nja Mahdaoui, "Untitled" (ink on a parchment-like animal skin)

to native traditions can be when combined with the ideas and techniques of modern painting: a discovery made, in the reverse direction, by many western artists travelling in the east (Paul Klee, August Macke, Matisse, etc.).

Music

Music, both instrumental and vocal, is an essential element in Tunisian life. In addition to the more familiar light music, showing western influence, visitors will hear much classical Arab music which at first will seem very alien.

The type of urban music known as *malouf* originally came from Arabia, travelling under the Omayyads by way of Baghdad and Damascus to Andalusia in southern Spain – hence its other name of "Andalusian music" – and then returning to Tunisia with the Muslim refugees from Andalusia. Its characteristics are chromatic sequences and an alternation between instrumental and vocal passages. The commonest instruments are stringed instruments (lutes, mandolines, harps, zithers), followed by flutes, drums and tambourines.

Many contributions by Tunisian musicians and dancers at regional, national and international festivals (see Practical Information, Events) bear witness to the popularity of this form of entertainment. The belly dance, however, came to Tunisia only in the time of the Ottomans.

Literature and the theatre

An independent Tunisian literature began to develop in the second half of the 19th century, and after the Second World War a number of newspapers and literary journals were founded which served as focal points for groups of writers. Two main trends can be distinguished: those writers who were strongly influenced by European ideas and those who feared that European influence would destroy Islamic values. The two most important representatives of the former school were Abul Qacin Chabbi (1909–34) and Tahar Haddad (also writing in the first quarter of the 20th century); the latter wrote in favour of women's right to education and against polygamy.

With the emergence of the independence movement a distinctive Tunisian literary scene developed, though always in the shadow of French censorship. Tunisian journalists, writers and musicians sought to promote the development of their native culture, at first on a small scale and later in increasing numbers. Light plays and the classics of foreign literatures were translated, and plays dealing with the Arab past, frequently containing concealed criticisms of the present-day situation, appealed to a wide public.

The achievement of independence in 1956 marked the beginning of a new phase in Tunisian literature, promoted by the establishment of numerous periodicals which provided a forum both for the discussion of social questions of all kinds and for narrative writings. The 1960s saw the rise of a new "committed" theatre, in which Aly ben Ayed played a major part until his death in 1970.

Cinema

The origins of Tunisian cinema go back to the period before independence, but this gave a great boost to its development – though it has never reached the position of the cinema in Egypt, which has established itself as the Hollywood of the East. It has had to cope with a variety of difficulties, including the absence of government aid, censorship, chronic shortage of finance and the lack of interest of commercial distributors.

The Arab/African film festival known as the Journées Cinématographiques de Carthage, held in alternate years at Ouagadougou (Burkina Faso), now has a reputation extending well beyond the bounds of Tunisia.

The films produced in Tunisia in the 1970s were largely on political themes. French colonisation and the struggle for independence provided the subject of a number of films: "Au Pays de Tararani" ("In the Land of Tararani"), by Hamouda ben Halima, Ferid Boughedir and Hedi ben Khelifat, 1970; "Sejnane", by Abdellatif ben Ammar, 1974; "L'Aube" ("Dawn"), by Omar Khlifi, 1966; and "Les Fellages" ("The Fellahin"), also by Omar Khlifi, 1972.

Other films were concerned with the theme of the family, in particular the role of women in Islamic society: "Om Abbès" ("The Mother of Abbès"), by Ali Abdelwahab, 1970; "Omi Traki", by Abderrazak Hammami, 1973; "Fatma 75" (1978), by Selma Baccar, one of the few women film-makers in Tunisia; and "La Trace" ("The Trail", 1982), by Nejia ben Mabrouk, the first long feature film by a Tunisian woman director.

The impoverishment of the rural population, the flight from the land and emigration were the theme of films such as "L'Ombre de la Terre" ("Shadow of the Earth", 1982) by Taieb Louichi and "Les Ambassadeurs" ("The Ambassadors", 1975) by Nacer Ktari.

"Le Soleil des Hyènes" ("Sun of the Hyenas", 1977, by Ridha Behi) was directed against the escalating development of tourism.

More recently Tunisian films have tended to turn inward, frequently reflecting the director's own life and experiences. The most successful film-makers at present are Nouri Bouzid and Ferid Boughedir, with their films "Les Sabots en Or" ("Clogs of Gold") and "Halfaouine" (the name of a district in Tunis), both produced with financial support from European television corporations. This, combined with the fact that two Tunisian films ("Automne 86" by Radid Ferchiou and "Chichkhan" by Mahmoud ben Mahmoud and Fadhel Jaibi) were shown at the Cannes Film Festival in 1991, suggests that there is now an increasing interest in Arab cinema.

Glossary

Abacus The upper part of the capital of a Doric column, a square slab above the echinus (see drawing, page 96).

Abaton, Adyton The innermost sanctuary of a temple, to which only priests were admitted.

Abu, Bou Father, owner of . . .

Acanthus A spiny-leaved plant used in the decoration of Corinthian and Byzantine (Justinianic) capitals.

Acropolis The highest part of a Greek city, the citadel, usually with a temple precinct.

Acroterion A figure or ornament on a roof ridge or the top of a pediment. See drawing, page 96.

Adhan The call to prayer.

Adyton See Abaton.

Aedicula Niche in a wall, with columns supporting a pediment; a small chapel-like structure.

Agora The market-place of a Greek city, the main centre of public life.

Aid Festival. Aid es Seghir, a small festival at the end of Ramadan; Aid el Kebir, the Great Festival (commemorating Abraham's sacrifice of a lamb).

Ain (plural *aioun*) Spring; often part of a place-name.

Allah God.

Allahu Akbar "God is greatest" (a formula used in prayer).

Amphiprostyle (Temple) with columned portico at both ends (see drawing, page 94).

Amphitheatre An elliptical arena for fights between animals and gladiators, surrounded by tiers of seats for spectators.

Amphora A two-handled jar of bulbous form.

Annulus A ring round the shaft of a Doric column below the echinus.

Anta A pillar-like projection at the end of the side wall of a temple. Temple in antis, a temple with columns between antae at the front end. Double anta temple, a temple with antae at both ends (see drawing, page 94).

Apodyterium The changing room in Roman baths.

Apotheosis The deification of a human being.

Apse A recess, usually semicircular, at the east end of a church.

Aqueduct A conduit for water at some height above the ground.

Arabesque A curvilinear form of ornament with intertwining plant or geometric designs.

Archaic art Greek art of the 7th and 6th centuries B.C.

Architrave A horizontal stone lintel resting on the columns of a temple.

Artesian water Ground-water which is forced upward by underground pressure.

Asr Afternoon; the afternoon prayer.

Aterian A Palaeolithic culture of North Africa, named after the type site at Bir el Ater.

Atlas figure A figure of Atlas supporting an architrave; also known as a Telamon.

Atrium 1. The principal room in a Roman house.
2. The forecourt of an Early Christian basilica.

Attic A low wall above the cornice of a classical façade.

Baal The principal Phoenician god, corresponding to the Greek Zeus and Roman Jupiter. (Semitic *baal* = "lord").

Bab (plural *biban*) Gate, entrance.

Baetyl A sacred stone or pillar.

Bahr Sea, lake.

Balnea Private bath in a Roman house.

Baptistery An Early Christian baptismal chapel.

Baraka A beneficent power granted by God (see page 36).

Barga A large dune.

Basileus King.

Basilica 1. Originally a royal hall, usually divided into aisles, used for commercial or judicial purposes.
2. The standard form of Christian church developed in the 4th century, with three or five aisles, the central aisle or nave being higher than the lateral aisles, and a semicircular apse.

Baths Roman baths (thermae) consisted of a changing room (apodyterium), a cold bath (frigidarium), a warm room (tepidarium), a hot bath (caldarium), a sweat bath (sudarium) and other rooms for rest and recreation, with heating by a hypocaust.

Bema 1. A platform used by orators.
2. The sanctuary of a Christian church.

Ben Son of . . .

Bent Daughter of . . .

Bey The title of the head of the Turkish administration.

Bir Fountain.

Bled, blad Country area.

Blind arcade Arches with the purely decorative function of relieving a wall surface.

Bordj Fort, fortress.

Bou See Abu.

Burnous A long cloak with an attached hood.

Glossary

Caldarium The hot room in Roman baths.

Caliph Successor to the Prophet Mohammed; the title of the supreme secular ruler until the abolition of the Caliphate by Atatürk in 1924.

Capital The moulded or carved top of a column or pillar, supporting the entablature (see drawing, page 96).

Capitol The main temple in a Roman town (after the Capitoline temple in Rome).

Capsian A Mesolithic culture of North Africa, named after the site at Gafsa (ancient Capsa).

Cardo The north-south axis of a Roman camp or town, at right angles to the decumanus.

Caryatid A female figure supporting an entablature.

Catacomb An underground burial-place (after the place named Ad Catacumbas on the Via Appia in Rome).

Cathedra Bishop's throne.

Cavea The semicircular banks of seats in a Roman theatre; Greek *koilon*.

Cella The inner chamber of a temple; Greek *naos*.

Cenotaph A funerary monument not containing a body.

Chechia A red felt hat.

Chicha Water-pipe, hookah

Choir The area between the nave or transepts and the main apse of a Christian church.

Choir arch The arch separating the nave and transepts from the choir.

hott Salt lake.

hthonian Of the earth (applying to divinities such as Persephone).

ippus A cylindrical or cube-shaped boundary stone or gravestone.

olon A French settler.

olossal order Columns or pilasters several storeys high.

olumbarium A Roman tomb with wall niches for funerary urns. (Latin *columbarium* = "dovecot").

omposite capital See page 97.

onch The half-dome of an apse.

rinthian order See pages 96, 97.

epidoma The three-stepped platform of a temple (see drawing, page 000).

omagnon An early type of Homo sapiens, named after the site in south-western France, in which it was discovered.

ossing The area at the intersection of the nave and transepts of a church.

Crypt Underground chamber beneath a church; lower church.

Curia The "town hall" of a Roman town.

Cyclopean (Walls) of large irregular blocks, ascribed in antiquity to the Cyclopes.

Dahar A ridge of hills.

Dar House.

Decumanus The east-west axis of a Roman camp or town, at right angles to the cardo.

Destrictarium The room for the removal of bodily hair in Roman baths.

Dey Turkish commander.

Diakonikon A room in the right-hand lateral apse of a Byzantine church.

Diazoma The horizontal gangway between tiers of seats in a theatre.

Dijebba Woollen cloak (burnous).

Dipteral (Temple) surrounded by a double row of columns (see drawing, page 94).

Djebel Hill, mountain.

Djebeli Hill-dweller.

Djellaba Cloak.

Djemaa Friday; congregation, assembly; Friday mosque.

Djerbi Inhabitant of the island of Djerba.

Djinn Spirit.

Domed cruciform church A type of Byzantine church with a central dome over the intersection of the four arms of a Greek cross.

Doric order See pages 95, 96.

Echinus A convex moulding under the abacus of a Doric capital (see drawing, page 96).

El, al The Arabic article, common to all three genders, singular and plural; often assimilated to the first consonant of the following word (ed, er, es, esh, et, ez).

Elaeothesium The room in Roman baths in which bathers anointed themselves with oil.

Entasis A swelling in the lower part of a column.

Epiphany Appearance, manifestation of a divinity.

Epistyle Another name for an architrave (see drawing, page 96).

Erg Sandy desert.

Eskhara An altar for burnt offerings.

Esonarthex The inner narthex or porch of a church.

Esparto grass A very tough steppe grass (Stipa tenacissima), used in the making of ships' cables and in basketwork.

Euthynteria — A levelling course between the foundations and the superstructure of a temple.

Exedra — A recess, usually semicircular, containing benches.

Exonarthex — The outer narthex or porch of a church.

Faience — Ornamental or painted pottery.

Fantasia — A horsemen's festival or cavalcade.

Fish — A symbol of good fortune.

Fluting — Vertical grooves on a column or pillar (see drawing, page 96).

Foggara — An underground water channel (see drawing, page 42).

Fondouk — Warehouse, inn, rest-house, caravanserai.

Forum — The main square of a Roman town, the centre of political life.

Foum — Gorge; opening; mouth.

Frieze — The decorative band above the architrave of a temple; in the Doric order made up of metopes and triglyphs, in the Ionic order plain or with continuous carved decoration (see drawing, page 96).

Frigidarium — The cold room in Roman baths.

Geison — The cornice of a temple (see drawing, page 96).

Ghorfa — A barrel-vaulted Berber store-room or granary.

Gigantomachia — A fight between gods and giants.

Greek cross — A cross with four arms of equal length.

Gourbi — Straw hut.

Guttae — Stone pegs on the underside of the geison or cornice to help in the drip of rainwater.

Gymnasion — A school for physical training and general education, consisting of a square or rectangular courtyard surrounded by colonnades and rooms of varying size and function.

Hadith — Orally transmitted sayings of the Prophet Mohammed and his companions.

Hajj — The pilgrimage to Mecca.

Hammam (plural *hammamat*) — A Moorish hot bath.

Hanafiya — Ablution fountain in a mosque.

Hanafites — A school of Islamic law founded by Abu Hanifa (d. 855).

Hara — Ghetto, Jewish quarter.

Harem — The private apartments in the palace of an Ottoman ruler.

Hellenistic period — The period from Alexander the Great to Augustus (330–30 B.C.).

Peasant farm, small estate.	**Henchir**
A shrub which yields a reddish dye used by women to stain their hair, feet and hands.	**Henna**
A square pillar with the head of Hermes and his genitals; later with a portrait head.	**Herm**
The layout of a town with a regular grid of streets intersecting at right angles (named after Hippodamus of Miletus, 5th c. B.C.).	**Hippodamian layout**
An elliptical course for horse and chariot races.	**Hippodrome**
Quarter, district.	**Houmt**
A heating system for baths and houses, with ducts carrying hot air under the floors and in the walls.	**Hypocaust**
An underground burial vault or cult chamber.	**Hypogeum**
A Neolithic culture of North Africa.	**Iberomaurusian**
A screen in a Byzantine church between the sanctuary and the main part of the church, bearing tiers of icons.	**Iconostasis**
The leader, especially the leader in prayer, of an Islamic community; for the Shiites a title borne by Caliph Ali and his successors.	**Imam**
The upper course of masonry on which an arch rests.	**Impost**
The facing of a wall with precious material (particularly marble).	**Incrustation**
A block of houses in a Roman town, bounded by streets intersecting at right angles.	**Insula**
The spacing of, or distance between, columns.	**Intercolumniation**
See page 96.	**Ionic order**
Horizontally coursed (masonry).	**Isodomic**
The elite forces of the Ottoman Sultans.	**Janissaries**
See Djebel.	**Jebel**
The principal Muslim shrine in Mecca.	**Kaaba**
Fortress.	**Kalaa**
A garment of rich fabric worn by women.	**Kaftan**
A soft flannel-like material used in making cloaks and other articles of clothing.	**Kasha**
A tenant who must give up four-fifths of his crops to the landowner, retaining a fifth for himself; from *khamsa,* "five".	**Khammes**
See Qibla.	**Kibla**
The sacred book of Islam.	**Koran**
Maiden; statue of a girl; the designation of Persephone, the Maiden.	**Kore**

Glossary

Kothon A Phoenician harbour linked with the sea by a canal.

Koubba Mausoleum, usually domed.

Kouros Statue of a naked youth.

Ksar (plural *ksour*) Fortified village, hamlet or granary.

Laconicum The sweat bath in a Roman bath-house.

Lalla Holy woman.

Lantern A small tower on top of a dome which admits light to the building.

Latin cross A cross with one long arm and three short arms.

Lunette A semicircular panel over a door or window.

Maenad A woman who took part in the ecstatic rites of Dionysus; a bacchante. Usually depicted on Greek vases, less commonly in sculpture.

Maghreb Sunset; the sunset prayer; the western part of the Arab/Muslim world.

Mahdi One sent by God.

Malikites A school of Islamic law founded by Melik ibn Anas (d. 795).

Malouf Classical Andalusian music.

Maqsura Enclosure in a mosque for the Caliph.

Marabout An Islamic holy man; his tomb.

Meander An ornamental pattern of wavy lines (from the name of the river Maeander, now Menderes, in Asia Minor).

Medersa, medrese Koranic college.

Medina (plural *medoun*) An Arab town; now usually applied to the old part of a town.

Medjez Ford.

Menzel (plural *manzel*) Settlement.

Metope A rectangular panel between the triglyphs in the frieze of a Doric temple, either plain or with relief decoration. See drawing, page 96.

Microlith A small Mesolithic flint tool.

Midha A place for ritual purification.

Mihrab Prayer niche in a mosque indicating the direction of Mecca (qibla).

Minaret The tower of a mosque. See drawing, page 79.

Minbar The high pulpit in a mosque.

Molek Sacrifice (a Hebrew word).

Monopteral (Temple) without a naos, usually circular. See drawing, page 94.

Mosque The Muslim house of prayer.

The official in a mosque who calls the faithful to prayer.	**Muezzin**
Legal scholar.	**Mufti**
A native community in the Roman Empire with restricted rights of citizenship.	**Municipium**
Stalactitic vaulting.	**Muqarnas**
A tower, usually round, in a Muslim fortress.	**Nador**
Temple; the inner room in a Greek temple in which the divine image was housed (Latin *cella*).	**Naos**
The porch or entrance hall of a Byzantine church.	**Narthex**
An open-air swimming pool in a Roman bathing establishment.	**Natatio**
Cemetery; the "city of the dead".	**Necropolis**
A water-wheel with buckets for raising water.	**Noria**
A precinct dedicated to the nymphs; a fountain-house.	**Nymphaeum**
A hall (usually roofed) for musical performances, recitations, etc.	**Odeon**
Reception room in a Roman house.	**Oecus**
A chamber at the rear end of a temple.	**Opisthodomos**
A type of masonry used by the Phoenicians in which monolithic piers were set up at intervals and the gaps filled in with undressed stone or other material.	**Opus africanum**
Roman concrete made from lime and volcanic ash (pozzolana).	**Opus caementicium**
Mosaic work (also known as opus alexandrinum).	**Opus musivum**
Masonry with small stones set in a net-like pattern.	**Opus reticulatum**
A mosaic of marble slabs.	**Opus sectile**
A mosaic of small pieces of marble; also called pavimentum punicum.	**Opus signinum**
Masonry laid in a herringbone pattern.	**Opus spicatum**
Pictorial mosaic.	**Opus vermiculatum**
A circular or semicircular area between the stage and the auditorium of a theatre in which the chorus danced.	**Orchestra**
The classical orders are the different types of column (Doric, Ionic and Corinthian) used in Greek and Roman architecture (see pages 96, 97).	**Orders**
A large slab of stone, set vertically, in the lower part of a temple wall.	**Orthostat**
A steep-sided dry valley, with a flow of water only after heavy rain.	**Oued, wadi** (plural *oudiane*)
A group of natives living in a Roman town.	**Pagus**
A training school for physical exercises (wrestling, etc.); often associated with baths.	**Palaestra**

Glossary

Pantocrator	Christ as "Ruler of All"
Parodos	Side entrance to the orchestra of a theatre.
Pasha	Ottoman title for a senior official or officer.
Pendentive	A triangular section of vaulting forming the transition from a square base to a circular dome.
Peribolos	The enclosure wall of a sacred precinct.
Peripteral	(Temple) surrounded by a peristyle (see drawing, page 94).
Peristasis	Another term for peristyle.
Peristyle	A rectangular court lined by a colonnade; a colonnade round a building.
Pilaster	A pillar engaged in a wall.
Pinax	A painted wooden, clay or stone panel.
Piscina	Swimming pool in a Roman bath-house.
Pliocene	The final stage of the Tertiary.
Pluvial	A period of high rainfall and low temperatures, the counterpart of a glacial period in more northern latitudes.
Podium	A raised substructure.
Poros	A soft, coarse limestone; the commonest Greek building stone.
Portico	A colonnade or colonnaded porch.
Praefurnium	The stove of a hypocaust.
Proconsul	A former consul acting as governor of a Roman province.
Proedria	The bench of honour in a stadium or theatre.
Pronaos	A vestibule at the entrance to a temple, usually surrounded by columns.
Propylaia (plural)	A monumental form of propylon.
Propylon	Gateway of a cult precinct or palace.
Proscaenium, proskenion	Fore-stage.
Prostyle	(Temple) with columned portico in front (see drawing, page 94).
Prothesis	A room in the left-hand lateral apse of a Byzantine church.
Protome	The upper part of a human body or forepart of an animal, used as a decoration on buildings or vases.
Pulpitum	The platform from which an orator spoke; a wall between the stage and orchestra of a theatre.
Qadi	Judge.
Qibla	The direction of prayer (towards Mecca).
Quaternary	The most recent period of geological time.

Ramadan The Islamic month of fasting.

Ras Head; cape; summit.

Reg An expanse of small stones and gravel in the desert.

Riad Inner courtyard.

Ribat Fortified monastery, occupied by Islamic monks organised on a military basis.

Rostrum The platform from which an orator spoke.

Sahel The fringe area of the Sahara; in Tunisia a fertile region between the desert and the coast.

Salam Arab greeting.

Salat The prayers prescribed by Islam to be performed five times daily.

Scenae frons The rear wall of the stage in a Roman theatre, several storeys high and usually richly decorated.

Schola A meeting-place for teaching and discussion.

Sebkha Salt-flats.

Sefsari A veil worn by women.

Seguia Irrigation channel.

Serual White trousers worn by men.

Sharia The code of Islamic law.

Shaykh Teacher; dignitary; head of a tribe or organisation.

Shiites One of the two main branches of orthodox Islam, the other being the Sunnites (see page 32).

Sidi Master, lord; usually part of the name of an Islamic holy man.

Sima The gutter of a temple, with lion's-head water-spouts (see drawing, page 96).

Skene The stage building of a Greek theatre.

Souk Market, market street.

Spira The curving base of a column or temple wall.

Spolia Re-used fragments of an earlier building.

Squinch A small arch built obliquely across the angles of a square tower in order to support a circular dome.

Stadion
1. A measure of length, 600 feet; a stade.
2. A running track 600ft long.
3. A stadium, with a running track and embankments or benches for spectators.

Stele An upright stone slab (often a tombstone), usually with an inscription and frequently with relief carving.

Types of temple

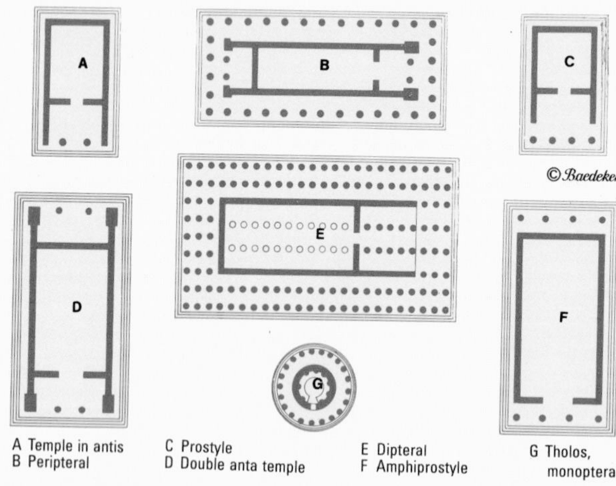

A Temple in antis
B Peripteral
C Prostyle
D Double anta temple
E Dipteral
F Amphiprostyle
G Tholos, monopteral

Stoa A portico; a hall with columns along the front.

Stylobate The uppermost step of a temple platform (see drawing, page 96).

Sudatorium The sweat bath in a Roman bath-house.

Suffete The highest official of the Carthaginian government, appointed for a one-year term.

Sufism Islamic mysticism (see page 35).

Sunna A collection of the Prophet Mohammed's saying and actions, traditionally handed down (see page 31).

Sunnites The main school of orthodox Islam (see page 31).

Sura A chapter of the Koran (which contains 114 suras, arranged in order of length).

Tafsir Commentaries on the Koran.

Talent An ancient unit of weight and currency.

Tanit A Phoenician goddess of North African origin.

Temenos Sacred precinct.

Tepidarium The warm bath in a Roman bath-house.

Tertiary The third great division of geological time, preceding the Quaternary.

Terma The finishing-point in a stadium.

Theatre 1. The Greek theatre consisted of the stage building (skene), the stage (proskenion), the circular or semicircular orchestra for the chorus and the

cavea, the tiers of benches for the spectators, extending round the orchestra in rather more than a semicircle. The theatre was usually constructed in a natural hollow on a hillside.
2. The Roman theatre had the same general form, but the rear wall of the stage (scenae frons) was carried up to the same height as the top of the cavea, creating an enclosed (though roofless) space. In the later period the stage was raised on a podium. The orchestra was semicircular, and the cavea (under the front ends of which were entrances for the chorus) was also strictly semicircular. The cavea was usually built up on substructures, within which were passages and staircases giving access to the seats.

Thermae See Baths.

Thesauros Treasury.

Tholos A circular building, rotunda (monopteral) (see drawing, page 94).

Thyrsos A staff entwined by ivy and vines; an attribute of Bacchus.

Tophet A cult site and place of sacrifice.

Triassic A geological formation of the Mesozoic era.

Triclinium Dining-room in a Roman house.

Triglyph A projecting member, with two vertical channels, between the metopes of the Doric order (see drawing, page 96).

Triumphal arch 1. A monumental Roman gateway.
2. The choir arch of a Christian basilica.

Tympanon, tympanum 1. The triangular pediment of a Greek temple (see drawing, page 96).
2. The space bounded by the arch and lintel of a church doorway.

Ulema A body of Muslim scholars; a member of it.

Villa A Roman country house with a garden.

Volute The spiral element of an Ionic capital.

Wadi See Oued.

Zakat The Islamic duty to give alms.

Zaouia The seat of a religious brotherhood.

Zitouna Olive; olive-tree.

The Classical Orders

Doric Order

In the Doric order the shaft of the column, which tapers towards the top and has between 16 and 20 flutings, stands directly, without a base, on the stylobate above the three-stepped substructure. A characteristic feature is the entasis (swelling) of the columns, which along with the frequently applied curvature of the steps of the substructure relieves the austerity of the building.
The capital consists of the echinus, curving up from the shaft, and the square abacus. It carries the architrave with its frieze of triglyphs and metopes, which may be either plain or with relief ornament. Between and

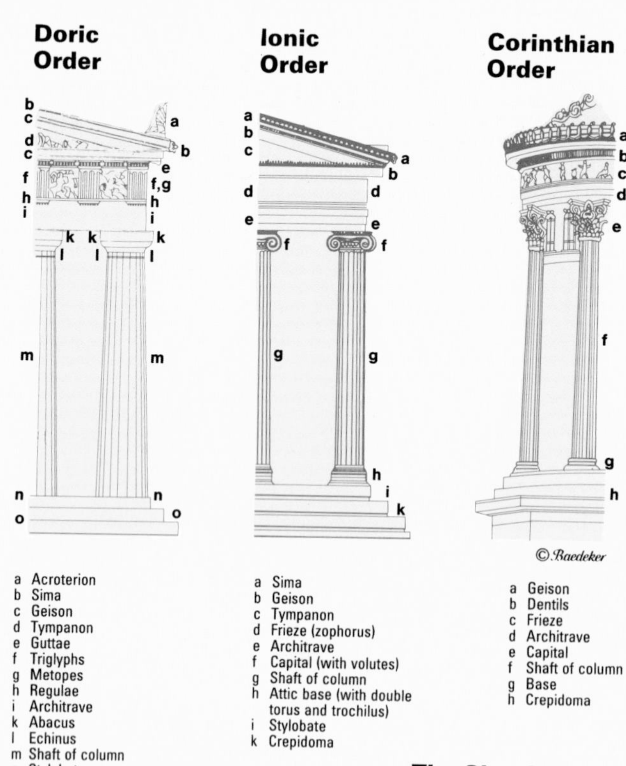

The Classical Orders

below the triglyphs are the drop-like guttae. The tympanon is enclosed by the horizontal cornice (geison) and the sloping cornices which form an angle with it, and usually contains the pediment figures. The sculptured decoration normally consists of the carving on the metopes and the pediment figures, but may extend also to the front of the pronaos.

Where limestone and not marble was used it was faced with a coat of stucco. The surface was not left in its natural colour but was painted, the dominant colours being blue, red and white.

Ionic Order

The Ionic order has more slender and gentler forms than the Doric, the "male" order. The flutings of the columns are separated by narrow ridges. The column stands on a base, which may be either of the Anatolian type (with several concave mouldings) or the Attic type (with an alternation between the convex torus and the concave trochilus).

The characteristic feature of the capital is the spiral volute on either side. The architrave is not straight-sided, but is made up of three sections, each projecting over the one below. The frieze is continuous, without triglyphs to divide it up.

Corinthian Order

The Corinthian order is similar to the Ionic except in the form of the capital. The characteristic feature of this is the acanthus leaves which enclose the circular body of the capital, with tendrils reaching up to the concave architrave.

The Corinthian order was particularly popular under the Roman Empire, which also evolved the "composite" capital out of a marriage of the Ionic and Corinthian forms and developed ever more elaborate decorative schemes.

Quotations

Marcus Porcius Cato Censorius (234–149 B.C. Roman statesman

Ceterum censeo Carthaginem esse delendam
(I believe that Carthage must be destroyed).

Diodorus Siculus (1st c. B.C.) Greek historian

Cap Bon:
It consisted of nothing but vegetable and fruit gardens, with every conceivable variety of fruit, and the whole area was irrigated by canalised watercourses. Everywhere were sumptuous country houses faced with stucco, bearing witness to the wealth of their owners.
The storehouses were bursting with all the things necessary for a luxurious life, for during a long period of peace the population had been able to accumulate an abundance of supplies.

From Diodorus's world history, the "Library".

Virgil (70–19 B.C.) Roman poet

Ancient was the city of Carthage, established by Tyrians,
Facing the land of Italy, far from the Tiber's mouth,
Great in power and hardened by constant war.

"Aeneid", Book I, verses 12–14.

Apuleius (2nd c. A.D.) Roman writer

What title of honour is splendid enough and adequate to laud Carthage, a city where I encounter only cultivated men who love all forms of learning! . . .
Carthage is the venerable school of our province; Carthage is the divine muse of Africa; Carthage is the mother of all those who wear the toga.

Appian (2nd c. A.D.) Hellenistic historian

All the streets leading from the Forum to the Byrsa were lined by six-storey houses, from which the defenders poured down a hail of fire on the Romans. When the attackers forced their way into the houses fighting continued on the roofs and on the beams which had been laid over the gaps between adjoining houses. Many men were hurled down to the ground or on to the weapons and fighters in the streets below. Then Scipio ordered his men to set fire to the whole district and clear away the rubble so that his troops could pass through. When this was done there fell down along with the walls the bodies of many of the defenders who had hidden in the upper floors and had been burned alive, together with many who were still alive but had been wounded or severely burned. Scipio kept a body of legionaries ready to clear the streets for the advancing Romans. The dead and the living alike were thrown into pits, and it frequently happened that those who were still alive were trampled by the horses of the cavalry – not deliberately, but in the heat of the battle.

From Appian's "Romaïka". He based his description of the destruction of Carthage in 146 B.C. on an account by the Greek historian Polybius (*c.* 200 to after 120 B.C.), who had fought in Scipio's army.

Koran Sura 22, verse 6

And thou seest the earth without life; but when We send down water upon it, then it stirs and swells and puts forth species of all kinds which delight the eye.

Ibn Khaldun (1332–1406) Arab historian

The course of history:
You must know that in the course of its history a ruling dynasty passes through various phases and that the situations in which it may find itself are ever subject to change. . .
In general, five stages can be distinguished:
First comes the phase of success. A dynasty has defeated the enemies who previously held sway, repelled their attacks and seized power from them. . .

In the second phase the ruler concentrates all authority in his own person and wields monarchic power without regard for the fellow-members of his tribe. . .
The third phase is a period of pacification and consolidation of the regime. The rulers seek to establish order in the finances of their country, erect magnificent buildings and shower benefits on their subjects. . .
The fourth phase is one of satisfaction with what has been achieved and of comparison with the achievements of earlier regimes. The rulers seek to live in peace with their peers. . .
The fifth phase is a period of extravagance. The sovereign gives in to the immoderate demands of those round him and makes himself increasingly dependent on vassals. . . And thus the structure built up by his predecessors collapses. . . And finally, after a last desperate flurry, the dynasty comes to an end. . .
This is a fated and inevitable development.

From the "Muqaddima" (1375–79), a collection of sociological and economic writings by the Arab historian Abd er Rahman ibn Khaldun (see Famous People).

Popular tales

In the evening a large table was laid for Ali with every imaginable delicacy: meat soup and meat of various kinds, stuffed peppers and salads, couscous, apples of paradise and other fruits, small cakes and sweetmeats of every imaginable kind – in short, everything from the savoury first course to the sweet last course. . .
Now a lamb was selected from the flock, slaughtered and cooked. The father of the maiden invited the vizier to sit down to his meal, but he replied: "I can neither eat nor drink." When he was asked why, he replied: "The Sultan's son, to whom throughout my life I have never done any harm, has put a question to me that Satan himself could not answer. Or can you tell me what the water says when you put it on the fire and it boils?" The bedouin called his daughter and asked her to explain the riddle. The maiden said: "I cry with pain: I flowed down from heaven, I lay in the ground, and the wood to which I gave life is now burning me."

From the Tunisian fairytale "Prince Ali".

Once upon a time there was a shrewd and cunning bedouin named Shann who swore an oath that he would travel the world until he found a woman who was his equal, and that when he found her he would marry her.
During his travels he met a man, and the two travelled on together. Then Shann suddenly asked his companion: "Will you carry me, or shall I carry you?"
The man replied: "I am riding, and you too are on horseback. How can you carry me or I carry you?"
And so they continued on their way until they came to a village where they encountered a funeral procession. Then Shann asked: "What do you think? Is the man on the bier dead or alive?" The other said: "You see a funeral and you ask whether the corpse is dead or alive?" Shann made no reply, and considered whether he should separate himself from his companion. But the man would not have it, and insisted on accompanying Shann until they reached his house.
The man had a daughter named Tabaka; and when they reached his house and entered it the daughter asked her father whom he had brought with him. He said at once: "I have never come across a greater simpleton," and told her what Shann had said. "My dear father," said the girl, "I do not think that he is a simpleton, for all his questions have a meaning. When he says 'Will you carry me or shall I carry you?' he means 'Will you entertain me or shall I entertain you?' When he asked about the dead man he meant 'Has he left descendants who will keep his memory alive or has he not?'" Then the man went to Shann and said: "Would you like me to explain what you meant by your questions during our journey?" Shann said "Yes", and the

man gave the explanation. Then Shann said: "You did not think of that yourself! Who told you?", and the man answered that his daughter had told him.
Then Shann asked for the hand of his daughter, and the man gave him Tabaka to wife. Since then people say, when they see a well-matched couple: "They are like Shann and Tabaka."

From a collection of Arab fairytales published in 1984.

Lady Mary Wortley Montague (1689–1762)

I went very early yesterday morning (after one night's repose) to see the ruins of Carthage. – I was, however, half broiled in the sun, and overjoyed to be led into one of the subterranean apartments, which they call the stables of the elephants, but which I cannot believe were ever designed for that use. I found in many of them broken pieces of columns of fine marble, and some of porphyry. I cannot think anybody would take the insignificant pains of carrying them thither, and I cannot imagine such fine pillars were designed for the ornament of a stable. I am apt to believe they were summer apartments under their palaces, which the heat of the climate rendered necessary. They are now used as granaries by the country people. While I sat here, from the town of Tents, not far off, many of the women flocked to see me, and we were equally entertained with viewing one another.

Letter, July 1718.

Heinrich Barth (1821–65) German traveller in Africa

We began at once to fit ourselves out with clothing; for Tunis is a little Paris and far ahead of Tripoli in the craft of tailoring.

Gustave Flaubert (1821–80) French novelist

The preparations for the sacrifice had already begun. Part of the wall of the temple of Moloch had been pulled down so that the brazen image of the god might be brought out... Now a fire of aloes, cedarwood and laurel was burning between the legs of the colossus. . . The oils with which he had been anointed flowed over his brazen limbs like sweat. Children shrouded in black veils formed a motionless circle round the stone on which he stood, and his disproportionately long arms stretched down as if to seize this garland and carry it up to heaven. The rich citizens, the elders, the women, the whole multitude thronged behind the priests and on the terraces of the houses... Many fainted; others, in their ecstasy, remained motionless, as if turned to stone. All were filled with an immense anguish. Gradually the last cries died away, and the people of Carthage panted in expectation of the horror to come. . . The temple servants, using a long hook, opened the seven compartments, one above the other, in the body of Baal. Flour was put in the uppermost compartment, two turtledoves in the second, a monkey in the third, a ram in the fourth, a ewe in the fifth. Since there were no oxen for the sixth compartment, a tanned skin brought from the sanctuary was thrown into it instead. The seventh compartment remained open and empty. . . The children were gradually brought closer. . . None of them moved; they were tied hand and foot, and the dark veils prevented them from seeing anything and prevented them from being recognised. . .
The bronze arms were now working faster... Each time that a child was put in them the priests touched it with their hand to charge it with the sins of the people, crying "They are not human beings, they are oxen!", and the people repeated "Oxen! Oxen!"...
Scarcely had the victims reached the edge of the opening in the god's body than they disappeared, like drops of water on a red-hot plate, and a plume of white smoke rose in the air... The god's appetite was still unsatisfied; he demanded ever more... All this lasted a long, an infinitely long time until evening. . . Clouds gathered over Baal. The fire, no longer burning, was now a pyramid of embers reaching up to the god's knees.

From Flaubert's novel "Salammbo" (1863).

Heinrich von Maltzan (1826–74) German travel writer

The coffee-seller is an important figure in Arab street life. Although he usually has a small booth where he dispenses the fragrant beverage the travelling coffee-house offers him greater profits and better customers. The travelling coffee-house is carried on his back, in the form of a charcoal brazier, jars, cups and numbers of tiny coffee-pots.

R. Bosworth Smith English travel writer

To the south and east, almost beneath one's feet, is the broad and beautiful Gulf of Tunis, stretching away to the open Mediterranean between the far-famed Promontories of Mercury and Apollo. Beyond the gulf is the Peninsula of the Dakhla, whose majestic mountains – Hammam-el-Enf, the most commanding among them – by their shape, their silence and their barrenness, recall what one had read of the "Alps unclothed", as they have been well described, of the Peninsula of Mount Sinai. . .

To the west and north is a sandy plain, flanked by the Lake of Tunis, with its flamingo-haunted waters, and by the ancient city, whose glaring houses and whitened roof-tops recall the name of "the white", given to Tunis by Diodorus Siculus eighteen centuries ago. The plain is dotted here and there with houses of the wealthy Tunisians, with olive plantations, with one or two solitary palm trees, and with huge hedges of the Barbary fig, whose sharp fleshy leaves afford sure protection against every animal except the camel. . . Trees are cut down, but new ones are never planted. Even the olive plantations seem to be dying away from want of tending or renewal. There is nothing therefore to help the thirsty soil to retain even that modicum of rain from heaven which falls upon it, while scientific irrigation with the help of the rivers, which was carried to such a wonderful pitch in ancient times by the Phoenicians and by the Romans, is now entirely neglected.

Wandering over the pasture lands may be seen the flocks and herds of the Arabs, and the long lines of their camels. Here and there are their black tents, which may be shifted at convenience. But some of the natives, passing gradually from the nomadic to the agricultural stage, have found a more permanent, if not a more congenial abode in the numerous subterranean magazines or cisterns, which the forethought of their more civilised predecessors constructed; and the domestic animals of the Arabs are found stabling in the very buildings which may once, perhaps, have sheltered the Carthaginian elephants.

Stretching right across the plain, "like the bleached vertebrae of some gigantic serpent", as they have been well described by Sir Grenville Temple, may be seen great blocks of the noble Roman aqueduct, which brought from the mountains of Zaghouan (Mons Zeugitanus) and Djebel Djougar (Mons Zuccharus) – from a distance, that is, of over sixty miles – those perennial streams of fresh water which not only supplied the inhabitants of the city, but sufficed to irrigate its suburbs and its gardens, and made much even of the surrounding country to smile as the Garden of the Lord. It was the handiwork of that Roman emperor [Hadrian] who has left behind him traces of his truly imperial passion for building and for travelling in every province of his vast empire.

From "Carthage and the Carthaginians" (1878).

Guy de Maupassant (1850–93) French writer

The most interesting part of the Arab town is the souk quarter. This is an area of long streets covered by flat or arched wooden roofs, through the cracks in which the sun sends sharp shafts of light, seeming to stab the strollers, the passers-by and the street dealers. In galleries opening off the streets in all directions is the bazaar, with the merchants sitting or squatting by their wares in small covered booths, shouting to attract customers or remaining quiet and motionless in their little niches, hung with carpets, brightly coloured fabrics, leather goods, reins, saddles and horse trappings decorated with gold, or with strings of yellow and red slippers.

Each type of ware has its own street, and you can see craftsmen in the same trade working in adjoining galleries and performing the same movements. The general hurly-burly, the rich colours and the gaiety of these eastern markets is almost beyond description; for how can one describe at the

same time the delight for the eyes, the noise and the movement of the whole scene?
One of these souks is so grotesque that the memory of it remains with me like a remembered dream. This is the souk of the fragrant smells.
On both sides of the long and rather dark gallery, in a series of identical huts, so small that they seem like the cells of a honeycomb, men of transparent complexion, almost all young and dressed in light-coloured garments, sit like Buddhas. They draw one's attention by their rigid pose and their setting of long wax candles hanging from the ceiling and forming a strange regular pattern round their heads and shoulders. The shorter candles hang in a ring above their turban, the longer ones reach down to their shoulders and the longest of all hang beside their arms. The symmetrical form of this unusual form of decoration varies slightly from booth to booth. The merchants themselves – pale-faced, motionless, silent – seem like wax figures in their chapels of wax. Round their knees and feet – within easy reach if a customer should come along – are spices and aromatic substances in unimaginable variety, packed in tiny boxes, bottles and bags. The souk is filled with aromas and fragrances which begin to intoxicate the senses.

From "La Vie errante" (1890).

Baedeker

Tunisia, the eastern part of the Maghreb, an area of some 129,000 square kilometres, has a population, according to unreliable estimates, of between half a million and 2 millions, including in addition to the Mohammedans (Berbers, Arabs, Moors, Koulouglis and negroes), some 60,000 Jews (Arabic *Ihûdi,* plural *Ihûd*), both Spanish and the so-called Livornese Jews, 81,000 Italians (with 20 private schools and a hospital in Tunis), 35,000 French, 10,000 Maltese and 2400 other Europeans. The coastline, some 1000 kilometres long, extends from Cap Roux to Râs Adjir. . .
Visitors can move about the country without difficulty and without a guide, but should be careful not to offend the sensibilities of the Mohammedans and not to enter their cemeteries or the tombs of their holy men. Christians (but not Jews!) may enter mosques and zaouias only in Le Kef, Kairouan, Gafsa and Tozeur.
First-class hotels are to be found only in Tunis. The inns in other towns have similar facilities to those in Algeria, but are almost all even simpler and, with a few praiseworthy exceptions, are not up to modern standards of amenity. In the steppe country and the Sahara travellers will frequently have to look to the fortified caravanserais or the native authorities for accommodation.

From the first edition of Baedeker's Handbook for Travellers to the Mediterranean (1909).

Paul Klee
(1879–1940)
Swiss painter

When you come to Hammamet it is still a little way into the town. What a day it is! In all the hedges birds are singing. We look into a garden where a dromedary is working at the cistern. It is a very Biblical scene; and the mechanism has certainly not changed. One could watch for hours as the camel, guided by a girl, paces grumblingly to and fro, providing power for lowering the hose, drawing the water, pulling it up and emptying it out.

From his diary of a journey to Tunis, 1914.

Habib Bourguiba
(b. 1903)
Former President
of Tunisia

If your wives go about the streets muffled up, you won't be able to recognise them if they are in the company of another man!

Max-Pol Fouchet
(1913–80)
French poet

Consider the water-pipe: its curving tube is already a sign. An unmistakable sign that here you must not look for the shortest distance between two points and the busy trunk roads here give place to the winding paths of private dreams, full of surprises and enchantments.

Rightly considered, the water-pipe reveals what it is: an anchor which we throw out in order to spend time at some peaceful place. The tube of the pipe ties the smoker as closely to his resting-place as the anchor chain ties a vessel to its moorings.

Tunis (AP). On Thursday afternoon, in the former Throne Room of the Bardo Palace in Tunis, the Constitutional Assembly of Tunisia proclaimed the deposition of Bey Mohammad Lamin I, resolved to declare a Republic and elected Prime Minister Habib Bourguiba as first President of the new Republic.

Press report (1957)

Tourism makes us blind. Western civilisation is being brought to us – and by what bearers! They are wealthy. . . they delude us into dreaming. Since achieving independence the Arab world in general and Tunisia in particular have not taken time to reflect on their roots and their own values. We have allowed ourselves to be driven. Amid this cultural uncertainty tourism has come upon us and has caused great confusion. . . Take carpets, for example. The Kairouan wool market has been ruined by the national craft centre established in the town, which has monopolised the field. The tourists have imposed their taste, and the traditional carpets have now become prohibitively expensive. When we get married we must buy the same carpets as the tourists: we ourselves are becoming tourists.

Ridha Behi
Tunisian
film director

From "Understanding Tunisia" (1984).

In the name of gracious and forgiving God we, Zine el Abidine ben Ali, prime minister of the Republic of Tunisia, make the following declaration: Citizens and citizenesses, the extraordinary achievements and sacrifices of our leader Habib Bourguiba and his comrades-in-arms in the liberation of Tunisia and its development are indisputable. . . His age and state of health, however, have so far deteriorated that he must be declared unfit to perform the duties of his office. . . With the help of the Almighty, therefore, we hereby take over, in accordance with Article 57 of the constitution, the presidency of the Republic and the supreme command of the armed forces. In exercising our responsibilities we rely on the contribution of all the children of our beloved fatherland. . . The independence of our country, the integrity of our territory and the progress of our people are the concern of all Tunisians. Love of the fatherland, its protection and all that contributes to its prosperity are a sacred duty of all citizens.

Government
declaration
(1987)

From a television declaration by Ben Ali, November 7th 1987.

Suggested Routes

To see all the sights of Tunisia in a single trip is clearly out of the question for the ordinary visitor, if only on grounds of time. If, nevertheless, the first of the routes suggested in this section amounts to just such a "grand tour", this is merely to set out the possibilities so that individual travellers can select what they want to see. This route and the two others can be varied, extended in certain directions or combined according to individual preference and to the time available.

The second route concentrates on Roman and Carthaginian Tunisia, mainly in the north of the country.

The third route covers southern Tunisia.

The routes are designed to take in the main places of interest; but there are other sights which lie at some distance from the main routes and are best seen on detours from some of the main centres. Suggestions for excursions and detours are contained in the individual entries in the "Tunisia from A to Z" section of this guide.

The suggested routes can be followed on the map of Tunisia at the end of the book, which will help in detailed route planning.

Places which are the subject of a separate entry in the "A to Z" section are shown in **bold** type. Descriptions of other places can be found by reference to the Index.

The distances shown in brackets in the heading of each route refer to the direct route, without allowing for detours.

1. Grand Tour of Tunisia (*c.* 4500km/2800 miles)

The starting-point of the tour is the country's capital, **Tunis**. Tunis is a good base from which to visit a number of places within easy reach of the city, including **Carthage**, **Sidi Bou Said**, **Utica** and **Thuburbo Majus**. The tour of **Cap Bon** (see entry) can also be undertaken from Tunis.

From Tunis the main route runs north via **Carthage**, **Sidi Bou Said** and **Utica** to **Bizerte**, near which is the attractive Lake Ichkeul (nature reserve).

Then on to Téboursouk, from which the Roman site of **Dougga** can be visited.

From Téboursouk the route continues south-west, passing the site of ancient Mustis, to **Le Kef** and from there south-east to the two large Roman sites of **Maktar** (Mactaris) and **Sbeitla** (Sufetula).

The route then turns south-east via **Kasserine** and continues to **Gafsa**, the first oasis town on the route.

From the phosphate town of **Metlaoui** a detour can be made (in the nostalgic "Lézard Rouge" train) to the magnificent Seldja Gorge. The route continues by way of the Tamerza, Midès and Chebika oases, near the Algerian frontier, to **Tozeur**. From here the little oasis town of Nefta, 27km/17 miles west, can be visited.

◀ *The Capitol seen through the Arch of Antoninus Pius, Sbeitla*

From Tozeur a good asphalted road crosses the **Chott el Djerid** and runs via **Kebili** to the town of **Gabès**, on the Gulf of Gabès.

From Gabès the troglodytic village of Matmata can be visited. (The alternative route to Matmata from Médenine, to the south, is not to be recommended, since the road is in very poor condition.)

The next place on the route, after a detour to the excavation site of Gightis, is the island of **Djerba**, which can be reached on the ferry from Djorf to Adjim.

The route then continues via Zarzis to **Médenine** and Tataouine, from which the *ksar* villages of Douirat, Chenini, Guermessa and Ghoumrassen can be visited.

The route now turns north on the coast road to **Sfax**. Off the coast lie the **Kerkennah Islands**.

From Sfax the route runs inland to **El Djem** and then returns to the coast, continuing via **Mahdia** and **Monastir** to **Sousse**. Sousse is a good base for a visit to **Kairouan**, the fourth holy city of Islam.

From Kairouan the route continues north, passing the site of **Thuburbo Majus**, to **Hammamet** and **Nabeul**, the principal towns on the **Cap Bon** peninsula. Those who have already visited Thuburbo Majus from Tunis can take the direct road to the coast and from there to Hammamet and Nabeul.

From Hammamet and Nabeul it is possible either to return direct to Tunis or to make the attractive trip round **Cap Bon**.

2. Carthaginian and Roman Tunisia (*c.* 1300km/807 miles)

The starting-point of this tour is again **Tunis**, with the many places of interest in the surrounding area (see above).

After visiting **Carthage** and **Utica** the route continues via Testour, Ain Tounga and Téboursouk to the Roman site of **Dougga**. From Téboursouk the sites of **Chemtou** and **Bulla Regia**, to the north-west, can also be visited.

Then via the site of Mustis and the town of **Le Kef** (with a possible detour to the site of **Haidra**) to **Maktar** and **Sbeitla** (Roman Sufetula).

From Sbeitla the route continues through the steppe country of central Tunisia to **Kairouan**; then, after a visit to **El Djem**, the most southerly town on this route, north-eastward to the coastal town of **Mahdia**, from there along the coast to Monastir and Sousse, inland to **Thuburbo Majus**, then back to the coast and on to **Hammamet** and **Nabeul**, on **Cap Bon**.

From Hammamet and Nabeul it is possible either to return direct to Tunis or to make the attractive trip round **Cap Bon**.

3. Southern Tunisia (*c.* 1200km/745 miles)

The starting-point of this tour is the island of **Djerba**. From there, by way of Zarzis and **Médenine**, the route runs south to Tataouine, from which excursions can be made to Douirat, Chenini and Guermessa. Then on a secondary road north-west to Ghoumrassen and Beni Kheddache, and so back to Médenine. From there the route continues to **Gabès**, from which a detour can be made to the troglodytic village of Matmata.

From Gabès the route runs west through the central Tunisian steppe country to **Gafsa** and **Metlaoui**; then follows, after a trip in the "Lézard Rouge" train to the Seldja Gorge, a tour of the hill oases of Tamerza, Midès and Chebika. From Metlaoui the route continues south-west to the oasis of **Nefta**, bypassing the oasis town of **Tozeur**, which is visited on the return route. Alternatively Tozeur could be taken as the base for a trip to Nefta.

From Tozeur, after crossing the **Chott el Djerid**, the route continues on a good road to Kebili and Gabès, and then, after a possible detour to Gightis, returns to Djerba (ferry from Djorf to Adjim).

Tunisia from A to Z

Spelling of Tunisian names

There is no generally accepted method of transcribing Tunisian Arabic into English, and even in Tunisian sources there are many variations. Place-names are given in their French spellings, which are used on maps and road signs throughout the country. Personal names are also generally given in their French form, except where there is an accepted English form. The Glossary on pages 84–97 will be found helpful in interpreting some place-names.

Abbreviations

GP (followed by a number) = Grand parcours: a main road, asphalted
MC (followed by a number) = Moyenne communication: a secondary road, frequently asphalted but sometimes a sand or stone track consolidated by traffic.
ONAT = Organisation Nationale de l'Artisanat Tunisien (Tunisian National Handicrafts Organisation)
ONTT = Office National du Tourisme Tunisien (Tunisian National Tourist Office)

Ain Draham

See Tabarka, Surroundings

Béja B 5

Chief town of the governorate of Béja
Altitude: 250m/820ft
Population: 50,000

Access

Béja lies 109km/68 miles west of Tunis on GP 6 (Tunis–Jendouba). There are regular rail connections with Tunis, Jendouba and Tabarka.

Situation and characteristics

The flourishing agricultural centre of Béja, chief town of the governorate of that name, lies in the fertile Medjerda valley, in the foothills of Djebel Acheul. The town owed its prosperity in the past to the growing of grain, but this has now given place to sugar-cane. The crop is processed in a sugar refinery in the town.

History

The site, known in antiquity as Vaga, is believed to have been occupied since the 6th century B.C. In 146 B.C. it became part of Masinissa's kingdom, and in 109 B.C. was conquered by Metellus. Situated in the centre of the province of Ifriqiya, the granary of Rome, it developed into an important market for corn. Sallust (85–35 B.C.), who was governor of the province of Africa Nova for some years, refers to a sanctuary of Ceres/Demeter and to a lively festival in honour of Ceres. In A.D. 448 the town was destroyed by the Vandals, but it was later rebuilt and fortified by Justinian. A raid by Beni Hilal nomads in the 11th century laid waste the surrounding countryside, and the town recovered only during the French occupation. It is now the principal market town and communications centre of the Medjerda area.

Sights

Kasbah

The Kasbah which rises above the town goes back to the time of Justinian, when the town was named Theodoriana in honour of the Emperor's wife.

◀ *In the Ribat, Monastir*

At one time it had twenty towers and three gates. A steep stepped lane leads up to it. From the top there are fine views of the town and surrounding area.
There are only scanty remains of the old fortress, including a keep with two round towers (in military occupation; not open to the public).

Old town

The old town with its numerous mosques and bustling streets lined by shops is well worth a visit.
The former church is now a House of the People. In front of it can be seen the little mausoleum of Sidi Bou Arbaa. At the end of Rue Kheireddine, near the remains of an ancient gate (Bab el Ain), is an ancient fountain.
In the western district of Mzara are cave dwellings.

Surroundings of Béja

Pont de Trajan

13km/8 miles south, spanning the Oued Béja, is the Pont de Trajan (Trajan's Bridge). It is reached on MC 76, which runs broadly parallel to the railway; part of the road is in poor condition.
The bridge, excellently preserved, is 70m/77yds long, with three arches. It is believed to have been built in A.D. 29 to carry the road from Carthage to Bulla Regia.

Other Roman sites

At Henchir Rhiria (9km/6 miles west) and Fej Geddour (13km/8 miles west) are remains of Roman buildings, including a basilica (not yet excavated) and a large gateway.

Henchir el Fouar

At Henchir el Fouar (8km/5 miles north-east on the road to Mateur), ancient Belalia Major, excavations begun in the 1960s have brought to light a small forum, baths and two Christian basilicas. A Muslim fort was later built on the foundations of the larger of the two basilicas.

Bizerte

A 6

Chief town of the governorate of Bizerte
Altitude: 0–5m/0–16ft
Population: 94,000

Access

Bizerte lies 65km/40 miles north of Tunis on GP 8 (Tunis–Bizerte). There are regular bus connections with Tunis, Menzel Bourguiba, Mateur and Tabarka and rail connections with Tunis and Tabarka (via Mateur).

Situation and characteristics

Bizerte (Arabic Benzert) lies at the outflow of the Lac de Bizerte, which is linked with the Mediterranean by a canal. Until 1963 it was a French naval port.
The picturesque old Arab town with its fishing harbour extends along the canal, with the modern European quarter at the point where the canal enters the lake.
Bizerte, chief town of the governorate of the same name, is one of the country's leading commercial ports, exporting oil, iron ore, cereals, cork, cement and other bulk goods. The principal imports are timber, building materials and coal (mostly used in the Menzel Bourguiba steelworks on the south side of the lake). Also of economic importance are the cement industry, a tyre-manufacturing plant, a porcelain factory and an oil refinery.
In recent years Bizerte has developed into a popular seaside resort. Along the Corniche (coast road) are extensive dunes and beautiful uncrowded beaches.

History

Bizerte was originally the Phoenician trading station of Hippo Diarrhytus, founded in the 9th century B.C., soon after Carthage. The Phoenicians built the first canal linking the lake with the sea. In 310 B.C. the town was captured

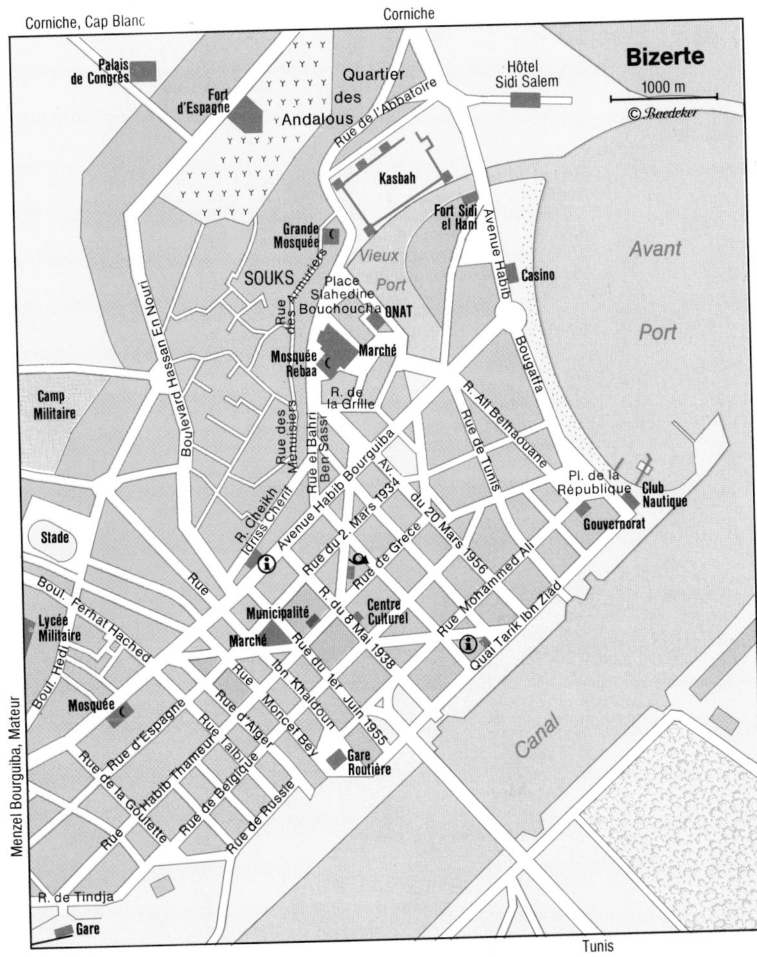

by Agathocles, tyrant of Syracuse. In Roman times it had a military garrison and exported corn to Rome. In A.D. 661 it was taken by the Arabs and renamed Benzert.

In the 13th century the Arab town enjoyed a first period of prosperity as the residence of the Hafsid ruler El Mostansir Bihillah. In the 15th and 16th centuries Moors expelled from Spain built the Andalusian quarter to the north of the old town and established an important trading centre. In 1535 the town was captured by Spanish forces. In 1572 it was taken by the Turks, under whose rule it became notorious as a pirates' lair. Under the French protectorate Bizerte became a naval base (1881). During the Second World War it was occupied by the Germans and suffered heavy damage in air attacks.

After the war Bizerte remained an important French military base, which was evacuated only on October 15th 1963 (seven years after Tunisia officially became independent), following violent rioting and heavy loss of life. October 15th is now celebrated as the Fête de l'Evacuation.

Sights

Medina

Round the picturesque Vieux Port (Old Harbour) is the Medina, the old Arab town. With its labyrinth of tortuous streets and covered souks, it has a very Oriental atmosphere. The streets are named after the various craftsmen who live and work in them – the smiths in the Rue des Forgerons, the armourers in the Rue des Armuriers, the carpenters in the Rue des Menuisiers, the butchers in the Rue des Bouchers, and so on.

*Vieux Port

The Vieux Port (Old Harbour) is now used only by fishing boats. It is linked by a canal with the large outer harbour (Avant-Port).

Kasbah

On the north side of the Vieux Port rise the old walls of the 17th century Kasbah. From the top of the walls (which are open to the public) there is a fine view of the Vieux Port. The interior of the Kasbah is now occupied by houses, and contains a 17th century Hanafite mosque.

Fort Sidi el Hani

On the south side of the Vieux Port, opposite the Kasbah, stands the little fort of Sidi el Hani, which also dates from the 17th century. It has recently been restored and now houses a small oceanographic museum (Musée Océanographique).
From the terrace of the fort there are fine views of the Vieux Port, the Kasbah and the town.

Rebaa Mosque

Between the souks of the old town and the harbour is Place Slahedine Bouchoucha, with the 17th century Rebaa Mosque, whose octagonal mina-

Old Harbour, Bizerte

ret with its gallery shows Turkish influence. Adjoining is a covered market (mainly fish).

Bey Youssef fountain

Farther along the street, where it comes to the Vieux Port, can be seen the elegant Moorish/Andalusian fountain of Bey Youssef (1642), roofed with green glazed tiles. Now dry, it was once famed for the quality of its water, as an inscription in Turkish and Arabic attests: "Drink of the spring of Paradise and you will be the better of it".

Fort d'Espagne

On a hill north-east of the Kasbah stands the massive Fort d'Espagne, flanked by an old cemetery. The fort was built by a Turkish pirate named Eudj Ali in 1570–73 as a protection against attacks by the Spanish, who frequently responded to his raids on their shipping by attacking Bizerte. From the terrace of the fort there are superb views of the old town, with the modern harbour beyond it.
In summer there are theatrical and musical performances in the fort.

Quartier des Andalous

Between the Kasbah and the fort lies the Quartier des Andalous (Andalusian Quarter), established in the 15th and 16th centuries by Moors expelled from Spain. Only a few of the picturesque old lanes with their characteristic blue wrought-iron window grilles and doors have been preserved.

Corniche

On the north side of the town, beyond the Vieux Port and the Kasbah, the coast road known as the Corniche runs north, skirting the town's long sandy beaches and lined by hotels, restaurants, holiday apartments and elegant villas. In the past Bizerte was less famed as a seaside resort than Hammamet, Sousse and Djerba, but in recent years many European tour operators have discovered the attractions of its mile-long beaches of fine sand.

Other sights

From the town centre Avenue Habib Bourguiba runs west past the Military Academy (Lycée Militaire), above which is the old European cemetery, with French and Italian mausoleums. Beyond this is the Martyrs' Memorial, a column with relief decoration commemorating the liberation of the town and those who died in the struggle.

Surroundings of Bizerte

Cap Blanc

An attractive trip from Bizerte is to Cap Blanc (10km/6 miles north). Leave the town by way of Boulevard Habib Bougatfa and continue on the Corniche, passing numbers of hotels and idyllic little coves (bathing). 2km/1¼ miles beyond Cap Bizerte (lighthouse) a little side road branches off on the right to Cap Blanc, the most northerly point in Africa, with cliffs falling steeply down to the sea. The crystal-clear water is a happy hunting-ground for divers.

Djebel Nador

1.5km/1 mile farther on a difficult track branches off on the right to Djebel Nador (260m/850ft), on the summit of which is a radio signal station; fine views of Cap Blanc below and Bizerte in the distance.

Menzel Bourguiba

24km/15 miles south is the town of Menzel Bourguiba (pop. 30,000; with surrounding area 90,000), originally founded by the French under the name of Ferryville. This former arsenal town has developed since 1963 into an important industrial centre (steelworks, metalworking, textiles). It has a large harbour, with a direct connection to the Mediterranean by way of the Bizerte canal.

*Lake Ichkeul

35km/22 miles south-west of Bizerte on GP 11 (the Mateur road) lies Lake Ichkeul (area 110sq.km/42sq.miles), a lake well stocked with fish which is fed by streams flowing down from the Mogod uplands and is linked with the Lac de Bizerte by the Oued Tindja. It is unusual in having water which is partly fresh and partly salt. When there is heavy rain the proportion of fresh

Lake Ichkeul, with Djebell Ichkeul in the background

water rises, while during the dry summer months the proportion of salt water increases. On the south side of the lake is a large nature reserve, dominated by the bulk of Djebel Ichkeul (511m/1677ft). On its most northerly foothill is the recently opened Museum of Ecology (information about the National Park).

This oasis of marshland is the home of many interesting plants, including pink and pale purple garlic, occasional fritillaries with bell-shaped flowers ranging in colour from crimson to yellowish-green, various species of rushes, bog asphodels, irises, reeds and waterlilies. It is also the haunt of countless waterfowl and small numbers of water buffaloes, Tunisia's largest mammals (1.80m/6ft high, weighing well over a ton), now an endangered species.

During the winter months, when heavy rainfall makes the lake flood its shores and the marshland flora begins to bloom, hundreds of thousands of migrant birds from Europe settle here for the winter.

Only experienced motorists should try to drive round Djebel Ichkeul, for the track is difficult to negotiate. For a trip of any length it is advisable to take a local guide. Information and advice can be obtained from the tourist information office in Bizerte.

The unstable ecological balance of Lake Ichkeul is now being threatened by the dams that have recently been constructed. Excessive quantities of water are being drained away to meet the needs of the tourist centres and the lake is threatening to dry up. There is a conflict of interests here calling urgently for a solution, which will not be easy to find.

R'Mel
Ras el Djebel
Raf-Raf

South and south-east of Bizerte are the beaches of R'Mel (south), Ras el Djebel, Raf-Raf and Sidi Ali el Mekki (south-east), which are among the most beautiful stretches of coast in the area.

Utica

35km/22 miles south-east is Utica (see entry).

Bulla Regia

B 5

Governorate: Jendouba

Access

Bulla Regia, 60km/37 miles south of Tabarka, is reached by way of GP 17 (Tabarka–Jendouba). 6km/4 miles before Jendouba MC 59, signposted to Bou Salem, goes off on the left. The site lies on the left of this road, 7km/4½ miles north-east of Jendouba.

Situation and characteristics

Bulla Regia lies at the foot of Djebel Rebia (617m/2024ft), in country which slopes gradually down to the Medjerda valley. It is one of the most important Roman sites in Tunisia, with the remains of baths, cisterns, temples, a theatre, a forum and a series of handsome villas. To provide protection from the summer heat the houses were built with underground rooms – a method of construction which had proved itself in the troglodytic dwellings of southern Tunisia.

Some of the finest mosaics from Bulla Regia are now in the Bardo Museum in Tunis (see entry); a few, however, have been left in situ.

History

The Phoenician town on this site was apparently captured by Masinissa about 150 B.C. After his death – as the "Regia" in its name indicates – it became the capital of one of the three Numidian kingdoms created by Rome. The process of Romanisation began in A.D. 50, and in the reign of Hadrian (117/118) Bulla Regia was raised to the status of a Roman colony. Thereafter its trade in olives and in corn made it one of the wealthiest towns in Roman Africa.

Roman street in Bulla Regia

In 339 Augustine spent some time in the town, which had become the see of a bishop in 380, and inveighed against the townspeople's passion for the theatre.
Two basilicas, of which remains survive, were built during the Byzantine period.
The decline of Bulla Regia began with the Arab invasion in the 7th century, and the town was finally abandoned in the late 12th century.
The first excavations were carried out by L. Carton at the beginning of the 20th century. Excavation of the site, by the Institut National d'Archéologie de Tunis and the Ecole Française de Rome, is continuing, and has brought to light further remains of both the Roman and the medieval periods.

**The Site

The site is open from 8am to 6pm (admission charge). Tickets are issued in the little Antiquarium opposite the entrance to the site.
The interesting underground rooms of the villas are frequently closed: it is advisable, therefore, to borrow the keys from the custodian or to ask him to act as a guide.

Tour of site

The tour begins at the Baths of Julia Memmia. From there it goes north, passing the two Byzantine basilicas and various dwelling-houses, to the House of Amphitrite, from which it turns south, passing the forum, the temples and the theatre, to return to the starting-point.
Just inside the site, to left and right, are cisterns (restored). Also on the right can be seen an enigmatic structure of the 1st century A.D., known from its type of masonry merely as Opus Reticulatium; the interior is divided into three aisles by rows of pillars.

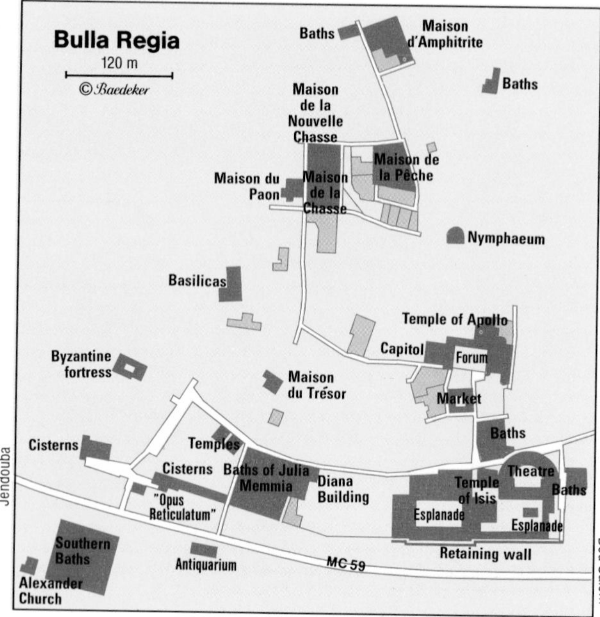

Baths of . . .

. . . Julia Memmia

Baths of Julia Memmia

Following the ancient street, which runs north-east, we pass the foundations of an arch and, farther west (left) the remains of a Byzantine fortress. To the right, past two temples, are the Baths of Julia Memmia, a fine example of a town bathing establishment, built by a wealthy citizen named Julia Memmia about A.D.189. On the side facing the street, standing higher than the rest of the building, is a portico, off which open a number of small rooms, probably shops.

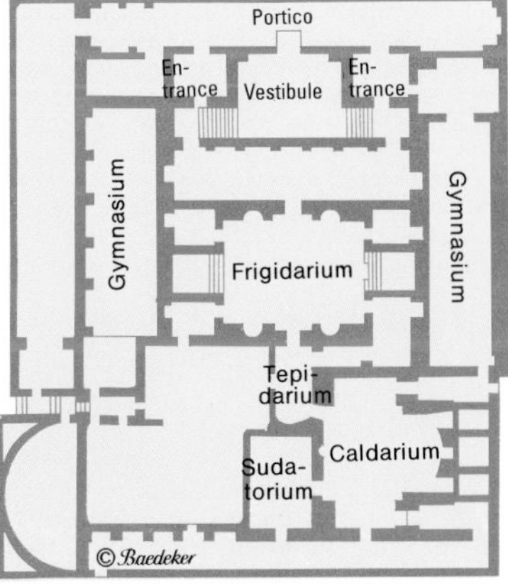

From the portico the entrance leads into a vestibule, beyond which, on a lower level, are the baths, laid out on the usual symmetrical plan. The changing room (apodyterium, vestiarium) is followed by the cold bath (frigidarium), with two pools of cold water and a pavement mosaic depicting the Cretan Labyrinth. On either side are long rooms, probably gymnasia. Farther south are the warm room (tepidarium), hot bath (caldarium) and a steam bath (sudatorium), the latter two being surrounded by boiler rooms and a service passage. At the south-west corner of the building is a semicircular apartment, probably a latrine.

On the east side of the baths are remains of a dwelling-house, the Diana Building, with a vaulted octagonal room.
Crossing the street, which is paved with stone slabs, we continue the tour in a north-westerly direction.

Villas

The houses (3rd and 4th c. A.D.) belonging to wealthy citizens of the town, some of which are excellently preserved, are named after the mosaics found in them. They are laid out on an unusual plan (some older houses having evidently been altered to conform with the plan). The rooms lay round a colonnaded courtyard, as was normal in Roman houses, but the main residential apartments were in the basement and, protected from direct sunlight, were pleasantly cool. In the commonest type of plan an underground passage gave access to three rooms, which were sometimes linked with one another and were supplied with indirect light and air by shafts to the rear (seen, for example, in the House of the Treasure). A more elaborate plan is seen in the House of the Hunt and the House of the Fishing Scene, whose underground rooms surround a colonnaded courtyard.
The best preserved of these houses are described below.

Maison du Trésor

To the left is the Maison du Trésor (House of the Treasure), named after a Byzantine hoard of silver found in it. In the basement is a well preserved geometric mosaic.

Basilicas

To the north are two well preserved 6th century Christian basilicas, linked with one another. The older and larger of the two preserves a few marble columns, a font and a mosaic of fishes and birds.

Viewpoint

From a low hill in the centre of the site there is a good general view of the excavations.

Maison de la Chasse

The large Maison de la Chasse (House of the Hunt), which takes its name from a mosaic, now almost effaced, in the basement, evidently belonged to a wealthy citizen. It was constructed by combining and altering a number of small existing houses. The upper floor is badly ruined, but the basement, lying some 5m/16ft below ground level, is well preserved. The rooms, laid out round a courtyard lined with Corinthian columns. include bedrooms (identified by the small mosaic-decorated platforms for the beds) and a large dining room (triclinium), also with a pavement mosaic. The bedrooms have an interesting air supply and ventilation system, with pipes built into the walls which communicate with an air shaft surrounding the rooms.
The layout on the ground floor is similar, with two colonnaded courtyards, dining and living rooms, bedrooms and a small bath-house.

Maison de la Nouvelle Chasse

Adjoining the Maison de la Chasse on the north is the Maison de la Nouvelle Chasse (House of the New Hunt), excavated in 1972. In the dining room (triclinium) can be seen the mosaic from which the house takes its name. Like some of the other villas, the Maison de la Nouvelle Chasse was later used as a place of burial.

Vaulting technique

The villas of Bulla Regia show an unusual method of constructing vaults which is found on many other Roman sites in Tunisia. It seems to have evolved in the 2nd century and to have been used until the Arab conquest. A number of terracotta tubes were fitted into one another to form a dome shape and the joints were filled in; a number of such arches were set up next to one another to form a vault, and the under surface was then faced with plaster.

Maison de la Pêche

A little way east is the Maison de la Pêche (House of the Fishing Scene), one of the best preserved houses in Bulla Regia. The basement in particular is well preserved. Round the colonnaded inner courtyard runs a vaulted gallery with a number of rooms opening off it. The mosaic depicts a sea swarming with fish, with cupids and ducks angling for them.

Maison d'Amphitrite

The finest and best preserved mosaics are in the Maison d'Amphitrite (House of Amphitrite), a little way north-east of the Maison de la Pêche. The building which bears this name was probably in fact a temple of Neptune. An underground passage leads into a large room with a mosaic of Venus Marina (formerly confused with the sea-nymph Amphitrite) and Neptune on a marine centaur. On the ground floor of this building was a large mosaic of the freeing of Andromeda, now in the Bardo Museum in Tunis.

Other sights

From the Maison d'Amphitrite we return south, passing the Maison de la Pêche and then, to the left, a nymphaeum. The fountain is still running, though it has been disfigured by a modern installation.

Forum
Capitol

Just to the south is the Forum, a large paved square in a poor state of preservation. Little is left of the buildings which surrounded it. Only the foundations of the Capitol survive.

Temple of Apollo

The temple of Apollo, to the north, consisted of a forecourt and a cella, a typically African plan. Marble statues of the divine triad of Apollo, Ceres and Aesculapius which were found here are now in the Bardo Museum in Tunis.

Market

From the Forum a street runs south to the Market, a large paved square surrounded by a colonnade, with small shops along the north and south sides.

Theatre

The street continues south, passing baths and dwelling-houses, to end at the theatre (restored). Originally built in the 2nd century, it dates in its present form from the 4th.
Of the auditorium, which has a diameter of 60m/200ft, there survives the lowest tier of seats. The floor of the orchestra has a mosaic depicting bears. On the south side of the theatre is a portico, beyond which is a large open

Basement courtyard, House of the Hunt

Venus Marina (mosaic in House of Amphitrite)

square or esplanade, with colonnades, a pool, a fountain and a temple. Immediately west of the theatre are the remains of a temple of Isis.
Farther west is another esplanade, laid out round a garden and surrounded by public buildings.
On the south side of the whole complex is a retaining wall. From here we turn west to return to the entrance, passing the Baths of Julia Memmia.

Southern Baths
Alexander Church

On the south side of the road (MC 59) are the remains of the large Southern Baths (Thermes du Sud; 60m/200ft by 55m/180ft) and the little Alexander Church (Eglise d'Alexandre), a rectangular building with two rows of stone troughs. The function of the building, which was destroyed by fire, is not clear: it may originally have been used for the collection and distribution of agricultural produce, for the material recovered by excavation included a hundred jars and amphoras for the storage of corn, wine and oil.

Cap Blanc

See Bizerte, Surroundings

Cap Bon

A/B 7/8

Governorate: Nabeul
Population: 450,000

Access

Cap Bon is reached on GP 1 from Tunis (Tunis–Soliman, 38km/24 miles) or from Sousse (Sousse–Hammamet, 120km/75 miles). The stretch of motorway between Tunis and Hammamet is at present being extended.

Situation and
*characteristics

The Cap Bon peninsula, 70km/44 miles long and up to 40km/25 miles wide, occupies the extreme north-eastern tip of Tunisia, extending into the Mediterranean like a finger and separating the Gulf of Tunis to the north from the Gulf of Hammamet to the south. The cliffs at the end of the peninsula fall steeply down to the Sicilian Channel, which at this point is only 140km/87 miles wide. With its variety of scenery, this "garden of Tunisia", as it is called, is one of the most attractive areas in the country.

Events

There is a full programme of events throughout the year on the Cap Bon peninsula. Among the most important are the following:
March/April: Orange Festival at Menzel Bou Zelfa;
April/May: Spring Festival in Nabeul;
June: Sparrow-Hawk Festival at El Haouaria;
May/June: Matanza (tunny-killing) at Sidi Daoud (only with special permission);
June: Musical and Folk Festival in Nabeul;
July: Agricultural Show at Menzel Temime;
July/August: International Cultural Festival in Hammamet;
August: Amateur Film Festival at Kelibia (alternate years);
August: Drama Festival at Korba (alternate years);
September; Wine Festival at Grombalia and Bou Arkoub.
Numerous events in Nabeul and Hammamet during the main holiday season.

Topography

Geologically the Cap Bon peninsula is an outlier of the Atlas Mountains which traverse the whole of the Maghreb. The Dorsale, the southern border of the range, extends north-eastward to the base of the peninsula but is separated from it by a depression. The backbone of the peninsula is Djebel Sidi Abd er Rahmane, a ridge of hills rising to a height of up to 600m/2000ft and ending in Djebel Sidi Abiod (393m/1289ft), which falls steeply down to the Mediterranean.

The northern tip of Cap Bon

Between the two ranges of hills is the Grombalia plain, which towards the end of the last ice age was covered by the waters of the Gulf of Tunis, then extending considerably farther south than it does today. Thereafter the plain was formed by geologically recent upthrusts and by the deposit of silt. Cap Bon is now one of the most intensively cultivated agricultural regions in Tunisia, thanks to its fertile alluvial soil and to the relatively high rainfall which, particularly in the north-west of the peninsula, promotes a luxuriant growth of Mediterranean vegetation.
The landscape as well as the structure of the peninsula is determined by geology. In the Grombalia plain to the south-west vegetable-growing and vines predominate; the north-west and north coasts are cliff-fringed, with many small rocky coves and inlets; the interior of the peninsula is a region of cornfields and pastureland; the east coast has endless beaches of white sand; and in the south-eastern coastal strip vegetable-growing again predominates. Apart from Hammamet/Nabeul, the country's second largest tourist centre, there are no major hotel complexes along the coasts of the peninsula.

History

The history of the peninsula has been influenced since ancient times by its nearness to Sicily (only 140km/90 miles away) and thus to Europe. Even the name of the peninsula – which originally applied only to the rocky cape at its northern tip – comes from Italian.
As early as the 7th century B.C. the Carthaginians had recognised the agricultural possibilities of the peninsula. They grew mainly corn and olives, together with wine, figs and pomegranates. The Romans continued this agricultural tradition, but in course of time gave preference to the growing of olives, then a more profitable crop.
Extensive raiding by the Beni Hilal nomads almost completely destroyed the agriculture of the peninsula in the 11th century. It revived only 600 years later, when Muslim refugees from Andalusia settled here, bringing with them more advanced agricultural techniques and new crops. Thanks to

Inland landscape, Cap Bon

elaborate water supply systems (wells worked by animal power, norias), the introduction of the Spanish plough and the cultivation of a greater variety of crops, agriculture prospered as never before. Soon the peninsula was producing all the various Mediterranean species of fruit and vegetables, as well as tobacco, maize, pepper and tomatoes, and had again become the garden of Tunisia. Agriculture continued to flourish under the French protectorate, but it was now mainly settlers from Italy who grew vines, citrus fruits and vegetables in the peninsula. The most favoured region was the Grombalia plain, which soon developed into a major wine-producing area.

Well over 80% of the population still depend on agriculture for their subsistence. The peninsula now has 45% of Tunisia's total vine-growing area and produces 70% of the country's output of citrus fruits.

The supply of water for this intensive cultivation is now a major problem. The large-scale withdrawal of water by deep wells has led to a disturbing fall in the water table, and it has become necessary to bring in water by pipeline from the hills of northern Tunisia.

Tour of the Peninsula

The route suggested in this section takes in the main features of interest on the peninsula (total distance about 250km/155 miles).

Soliman

The little country town of Soliman (pop. 14,000) lies on the north-western edge of the Grombalia plain. Thanks to this situation it rapidly developed during the colonial period into a local market centre, surrounded by an extensive agricultural area producing potatoes, tomatoes, olives and fruit. The town was founded in the early 17th century. It provided a home for many refugees from Andalusia, and its architecture still shows Andalusian features. It suffered heavy destruction in 1943.

The main features of interest in the picturesque old part of the town are the 17th century Malikite mosque, roofed with semicircular tiles, and the Hanafite mosque with its octagonal minaret.
The coastal resort of Soliman Plage is a popular weekend retreat with the inhabitants of Tunis.

*Cote du Soleil

8km/5 miles north of Soliman MC 128 branches off MC 26 on the left and runs along the cliff-fringed coast of Djebel Bou Korbous, here known as the Cote du Soleil (Sunshine Coast). This 12km/7½ mile long stretch is one of the most beautiful roads in Tunisia. On the right are steeply scarped hills, rising to 419m/1375ft, on the left sheer cliffs falling down to the sea. From various viewpoints along the road there are magnificent distant views, extending as far west as Carthage.

Korbous

A few kilometres beyond the little fishing village of Sidi Rais, the Roman settlement of Carpi, the road comes to Korbous, Tunisia's leading spa.
The town huddles in a narrow valley opening on to the sea. Its hot springs (44–60°C/111–140°F) were already frequented in Roman times, when the place was known as Aquae Calidae Carpitanae. They were rediscovered in 1801 by Ahmed Bey, who established the spa, which was further developed by the French. The town is now concerned not only to cater for visitors who come to take the cure but also to develop the wider holiday and tourist trade. It is planned to turn this quiet and idyllic little resort into a seawater therapy centre with a luxury hotel and a yachting harbour and to increase its bed capacity to 5000. The water, containing calcium, sulphur and sulphates, is recommended for the treatment of skin conditions, affections of the respiratory passages, rheumatism and arthritis. The Etablissement Thermal (Spa Establishment) occupies the former Bey's Palace.

Zerziha Rock

Below the Presidential Palace is the Zerziha Rock, which is believed to cure infertility and has been worn smooth by generations of women sliding down it.

Côte du Soleil

Etablissement Thermal, Korbous

Grottes Romaines

View from Djebel Abiod

Hamma el Atrous

2km/1¼ miles north, by the roadside, is the Hamma el Atrous, a hot spring (50°C/122°F) which cascades into the sea. It is a hive of activity at weekends, when people from Tunis and the surrounding area swarm round the hot pool on the beach or stand in the sea under the waterfall.

MC 23 now leaves the coast and runs through a fertile region, with the ridge of Djebel Sidi Abd er Rahman running parallel to the road on the right.

Sidi Daoud

Near the northern tip of Cap Bon, reached by a 3km/2 mile long sand road going off MC 26 on the left, is Sidi Daoud, a little fishing port at which about half the total Tunisian catch of tunny is landed. The now controversial method of killing the tunny known as the Matanza (originally of Sicilian origin) is still practised. It takes place during the spawning season, between the end of April and the beginning of July. As soon as the nets are drawn out of the water the fishermen set about killing the fish with cudgels, harpoons or long knives. The authorities try to keep visitors away from the bloody spectacle, which can be seen only with special permission from the Office National des Pêches (26 Avenue de Paris, Tunis). On the harbour is a canning factory in which the fish are at once processed.

Zembra Zembretta

Far out at sea can be seen the outlines of two rocky islands, Zembra and Zembretta, known to the Romans as the Aegimuri.
The islands are now a marine nature reserve, in which the oldest species of seal known to man, the monk seal, is now again gradually increasing in numbers. In spring thousands of shearwaters nest here and millions of migrant birds pause on their way to Europe.
The smaller of the two islands, Zembretta, has a lighthouse but is otherwise uninhabited. The larger one, Zembra (area 5sq.km/2sq.miles; alt. 432m/1417ft), was formerly a quarantine station for pilgrims to Mecca. It now has a diving centre (established 1963) and a yachting harbour (diving and sailing schools). Accommodation is in modest huts and comfortable chalets. There is an irregular boat service from Sidi Daoud to Zembra.

Punic settlement, Kerkouane

El Haouaria

El Haouaria, a few kilometres beyond Sidi Daoud at the northern tip of the peninsula, is also a fishing village (tunny). It is famed for the falcons which call in here every spring on their way to Europe. In February and March some of them are caught with nets and trained to hunt quail. The hunting season ends on the last day in May, and the falcons are then released in the course of a great falconry festival.

*Roman Caves

A few kilometres north-east, on the coast, are the Roman Caves (French Grottes Romaines, Arabic Ghar el Kebir), hewn out of the sandstone cliffs which fall steeply down to the sea.

The caves were formed by the quarrying of the rock by the Carthaginians and later by the Romans, and the marks of their tools can still be seen. Shafts up to 30m/100ft long were driven into the rock by slaves, and the blocks they extracted were hauled up by ropes and loaded into ships which took them direct to Carthage.

The road to the caves is easy to find. An asphalted road runs through El Haouaria, passes the marabout of the local holy man and soon afterwards degenerates into a sand track, which ends in the car park of a small café near the caves.

***Djebel Abiod**

It is well worth climbing Djebel Abiod (*c.* 400m/1300ft) for the sake of the views it offers; the path leaves just outside El Haouaria. From the top there is a magnificent prospect of the west coast and the offshore islands of Zembra and Zembretta, the tip of Cape Bon with its lighthouse, and the north-eastern coast of the peninsula, with the pumping station near Kelibia for the submarine pipeline carrying natural gas from Algeria to Sicily.

Kerkouane

12km/7½ miles farther on a road goes off on the left to Kerkouane (signposted). The excavations here are among the most important in the whole of North Africa, bringing to light the remains of the only large Punic town so far discovered. The site is open daily except Monday from 9am to noon and 2 to 5pm.

Fortress, Kelibia

History

Kerkouane is believed to have been a Phoenician port of call long before the foundation of Carthage. At least as early as the 6th century B.C. this developed into a small village of fishermen and dyers, the name of which is unknown. In the 2nd century B.C. the town was taken by Scipio, and in the Third Punic War it was razed to the ground by the Romans. Unlike Carthage, it was never rebuilt, so that the layout of the Punic town has been preserved intact.

*Excavations

The site was discovered only in 1952, and excavation began in 1966. The town, laid out in the shape of a horseshoe, is bounded on the east by the sea. It was enclosed by a double ring of walls with two gates.
The excavations have revealed mainly the foundations of buildings and the network of streets. The houses had marble floors with red and white mosaic decoration, many of which have been preserved. In many houses the rooms were laid out round a central courtyard with a fountain. It is notable that almost every house had its own bathroom, and at many points can be seen the trough-shaped baths which were filled from small water channels. There are also drainage channels which show that the town had a highly developed drainage system.
Also of interest are the remains of a dye factory, with tubs hewn from the rock in which the shellfish (murex) used to make the purple dye were collected. Piles of discarded shells were also discovered. The Phoenicians had a monopoly of the production of the dye, the most prized dye of ancient times (almost 5000 shellfish being required to produce a gram of the dye).

Museum

Outside the town a necropolis was discovered. Adjoining the site can be found a small museum which illustrates the history of Kerkouane and of the excavations.

Kelibia

Kelibia (pop. 20,000), 13km/8 miles south of Kerkouane, is now an important fishing port and the agricultural market centre for the northern part of the peninsula. It is noted for the Kelibia muscatel wine produced in the area.

This was probably also a Punic foundation. In 309 B.C. it was taken by Agathocles of Syracuse and renamed Aspis (the "Shield"). In 255 B.C., during the First Punic War, it was captured by the Roman consul, Regulus, and 110 years later, during the Third Punic War, it was razed to the ground. Later the town was rebuilt by the Romans under the name of Clupea.

***Fortress**

The town's only tourist sight is the fortress which crowns a 150m/500ft high crag. Originally Byzantine, it was enlarged and strengthened under the Hafsids (1229–1574). A steep drive leads up to the gateway of the fortress, the massive walls of which are excellently preserved. Extensive excavation and restoration work is being carried out in the interior, part of which is still inhabited.

There are magnificent views from the bastions, extending in clear weather as far as Sicily. In summer there is a hydrofoil service to Pantelleria and Trapani (Sicily).

From Menzel Temime, 12km/7½ miles south of Kelibia, a road passes through the varied scenery of the interior of the peninsula by way of Menzel Bou Zelfa and Soliman to the starting-point of the tour.

MC 27, the coast road, runs south via Korba to Nabeul and Hammamet.

Nabeul

See entry

Beni Khiar

See Nabeul, Surroundings

Dar Chaabane

See Nabeul, Surroundings

Hammamet

See entry

Carthage

A 7

Governorate: Tunis Nord
Altitude: 0–70m/0–230ft

View of modern Carthage and the Punic naval harbour

Carthage

Access

20km/12½ miles east of Tunis on the road to La Goulette. Regular bus services; suburban railway (TGM, Tunis–Carthage) from the station at the east end of Avenue Habib Bourguiba, Tunis (either Salammbo or Hannibal stop).

Situation and *characteristics

Carthage lies on a peninsula reaching out into the Bay of Tunis which is protected on the landward side by two shallow lakes. With its avenues lined by palms and eucalyptus trees, its villas and gardens full of red hibiscus blossom and purple bougainvilleas, Carthage is Tunis's most attractive suburb. But of ancient Carthage, once the greatest city in North Africa, and its thousand years of history there are only scanty and scattered remains, and visitors who have seen Dougga, Bulla Regia, Sbeitla or Maktar may be disappointed. These other cities, however, have the advantage of not having been wilfully destroyed and used for more than a thousand years as a quarry of building stone; nor have they been built over in the 19th and 20th centuries as Carthage has. Nevertheless the remains of this ancient city are still worth a visit for the sake of the structures, mainly of the Roman period, which have survived.

History

The foundation of Carthage goes back to a distant legendary past. According to legend a Phoenician princess named Elissa, daughter of the king of Tyre, fled from Tyre following a dispute over succession to the throne and landed on the coast of Tunisia, with a few faithful followers, in 814 B.C. A Numidian prince agreed to her request for a piece of land the size of a cow-hide: whereupon Elissa cut the hide into thin strips and with them enclosed an area of land on which the town of Qart Hadasht (known to the Romans as Carthago) was built. The truth of the legend cannot be checked, but at any rate there is evidence of the existence of Carthage as early as 750 B.C., and the first Carthaginian settlement was built on the hill known as Byrsa, the "Cow-Hide".

In antiquity the Sebkha Ariana (salt lake) was still linked with the sea, so that Carthage lay at the end of an easily defensible peninsula linked with the mainland only at its east end. It was enclosed by a wall over 40km/25 miles long, 10m/33ft thick and up to 13m/43ft high, reinforced by towers, ditches and earthworks, which protected the city and the surrounding agricultural area from enemy attack. The city was defended by 20,000 infantry, 4000 cavalry and 300 elephants. Under the Magonid dynasty (Hamilcar, Hasdrubal, Hannibal) Carthage became the leading commercial power in the western Mediterranean; its seamen sailed round the whole of Africa and discovered the coasts of Britain. The conflict between Carthage and the other Mediterranean power, Rome, led to the three Punic Wars, which ended in the complete destruction of Carthage in 146 B.C. The city was plundered, burned down, razed to the ground and ploughed over; and the whole area was sprinkled with salt so that even the soil should be made infertile.

Something over a hundred years later the area was resettled by the Romans: in the reign of Augustus the Colonia Julia Carthago was founded, and soon afterwards it became the seat of the provincial government. Thereafter it grew and flourished, and by the early 2nd century A.D. it was the third largest city in the Roman Empire, with a population of around 300,000. Magnificent public buildings were erected during this period, second only to those in Rome itself. As in Punic times, the central feature of the city was the hill of Byrsa, with the Capitol and the forum, and the Romans largely preserved the general layout of the Punic town.

By the beginning of the 4th century Carthage had become the leading city in Christian Africa and the see of a bishop. Under Byzantine rule it retained its predominance in North Africa, until in 692 the Arabs arrived and once again utterly destroyed the city. Thereafter Carthage fell into an oblivion which ended only under the French protectorate, when the Catholic Mission, honouring the city's early Christian tradition, established its African headquarters in Carthage.

Excavations

Excavation of the site began in 1857 and is still continuing. In 1974 UNESCO initiated a programme, backed by substantial resources, for saving a site of such outstanding importance in human history, and since then excavation work has been steadily expanded. Fourteen countries are now involved in the project.

So far three main phases in the city's development have been identified: an early settlement of small mud-brick houses, all aligned in the same direction; then a densely populated city with streets laid out at right angles to one another, cisterns and a triple ring of walls; and a final phase, from the city's heyday to its destruction.

Sights

The ancient remains are open in summer from 9am to 7pm, in winter from 9am to 5pm. They are scattered over the whole area of the town, and the principal sights can most conveniently be seen on foot. Alternatively it is possible to hire a horse-drawn carriage or a taxi. The drivers know their

way around and can take visitors wherever they want. In order to avoid misunderstandings it is advisable to agree the fare in advance.
The suburban railway (TGM) can also be a help in getting to the various sites.

Punic Carthage

The main remains of Punic Carthage are on the Byrsa Hill and in the Carthage-Salammbo district, between the main road (La Goulette–Sidi Bou Said) and the sea. The most important features are the National Museum and Quartier Punique (excavations of a Punic residential quarter), the Tophet (sacred precinct), the Punic harbour (Kothon) and the Quartier Magon.

Roman Carthage

If time permits, the tour of the site should begin with a visit to the National Museum and the Quartier Punique, both on the Byrsa Hill, and continue with the Tophet, the Kothon and the Quartier Magon. Close by are the Baths of Antoninus Pius, which provide a transition to the Roman period in Carthage, and the tour then ends with visits to the theatre, the Roman villas and the Christian churches.

Byrsa Hill

On the inland side of the main road (Avenue Habib Bourguiba), near the TGM station Carthage-Hannibal, rises the Byrsa Hill (originally 70m/230ft high), crowned by the conspicuous Cathedral of Saint-Louis. From the top of the hill there are fine views of modern Carthage, the Punic harbour, La Goulette, Tunis, the Mediterranean and the finely formed Djebel Bou Kornine.
The hill was the central feature of the Punic settlement. The Romans sliced some 6m/20ft off the summit in order to make a broader platform for imperial buildings. (There is a model of the Roman Capitol in the Museum).

Cathedral of St-Louis

The Cathedral, in Moorish/Byzantine style, was built in 1890 and is dedicated to St Louis of France (King Louis IX), who died here in 1270 during the siege of Tunis. The largest church in North Africa, it was until 1965 the seat of the Archbishop of Carthage and Primate of Africa. It belonged to the monastery of the Pères Blancs (White Fathers), a missionary order founded by Cardinal Lavigerie whose declared aim was the reconquest of North Africa for Christianity. The White Fathers had established themselves on the Byrsa Hill in 1881, and in addition to their missionary work had begun to collect antiquities. The Cathedral and conventual buildings – which now house the National Archaeological Museum – became state property in 1964.

*National Archaeological Museum

The National Archaeological Museum (Musée National de Carthage), still in course of development, has a very interesting collection of material, including information about the course of the excavations, a model of Punic Carthage, Punic and Early Christian antiquities, jewellery and ornaments, everyday objects, clay masks, little heads in coloured glass paste with large staring eyes, funerary stelae, sarcophagi, mosaics and models of the Tophet and the Capitol built by the Romans on the ruins of Punic Carthage.
The museum gardens are also worth visiting. Amid the greenery are a variety of ancient remains and a 3m/10ft high marble statue commemorating Louis IX (though in fact the statue is a likeness of the Emperor Charles V).

*Quartier Punique

To the south of the Museum is the Quartier Punique (Punic Quarter). Excavation has shown that in the earliest period the hill was used as a burial-ground. In the 5th century the Carthaginians built workshops here, which later gave place to houses. After the destruction of Carthage the hill remained unoccupied. It was only in the reign of Augustus (30 B.C.–A.D. 14) that the summit of the hill was levelled off – involving the destruction of the Punic remains, including a temple of Eshmun (Asklepios) which stood here – and work began on the construction of a huge forum and Capitol. This was the starting-point of the two main axes of Roman Carthage, the decu-

Cathedral of St Louis

Cenotaph of Louis IX (St Louis)

manus running from east to west and the cardo from north to south. During excavations under the church and the monastery various Roman remains were found: the foundations of temples, mosaics and the altar of the Gens Augusta which is now in the Bardo Museum in Tunis. Visitors' eyes will be caught first by the two rows of piers running at an angle to the Punic street pattern – the foundations of a platform on which the Capitol was to stand. Two sections of the Punic town have now been excavated, giving an excellent impression of the layout of the houses. Usually of two storeys, they had round underground cisterns, with fountains on the floor above to provide a water supply for the house.

Baths of Gargilius

North of the Byrsa Hill, to the left, are the remains of the Baths of Gargilius, which are believed to have been the meeting-place of the Council of Carthage in 411.

*Tophet

The Tophet is reached by taking the street which runs east towards the sea from the TGM station Carthage-Salammbo and turning left into Rue Hannibal.

History

The name Tophet, which is found in the Old Testament ("in the valley of the children of Hinnom"), was the sacred place where human sacrifices (*molek*) were offered to the gods. The principal gods of Carthage were the sun god Baal-Ammon (the equivalent of the Greek Kronos and Roman Saturn) and the moon goddess Tanit (the "Face of Baal"; the equivalent of the Phoenician Astarte, Greek Hera and Roman Juno Caelestis).

The Tophet, a sanctuary enclosed by walls, is believed to have been built on the spot where the legendary foundress of Carthage, Elissa, landed in Tunisia.

The excavations have shown that the custom of sacrificing first-born children, particularly boys, which was common in earlier times in the Near East, was also practised in the early days of Carthage. Although the heyday

Quartier Punique on the Byrsa Hill

of the cult was from the 6th to the 3rd centuries B.C., the Tophet continued in use as a cult site into the early Christian period.

Gustave Flaubert gives a vivid account of the sacrifice of children in Carthage in his novel "Salammbo" (see Quotations).

The ashes of the victims were deposited in the sacred precinct, originally in urns surrounded by vertical slabs of stone; later the urns were buried in the ground and each grave was marked by a stele between 30 and 90cm (1 and 3ft) high. Many of these stones have inscriptions in Punic (Libyan) script, magical signs and stylised representation of the gods. When the Tophet was full the place of sacrifice was covered with earth and a new layer began to be built up.

At the lowest level of all the excavators discovered a small niche, the Chapel of Cintas, which may possibly have been the burial chapel of Elissa herself.

The Carthaginians hoped by these human sacrifices to win the favour of the gods in a time of need. Estimates of the number of victims put the figure as high as 7000. Some evidence was provided by the numbers of stelae and pottery urns found during the excavations, many of which are displayed in the museums of Tunis and Carthage. Since most of the sacred precinct, which covers an area of 2 hectares/5 acres, has been built over, it has been possible so far to excavate only a very small part of it. The site is a maze of burial shafts and remains of foundations, with numerous stelae, some of them bearing inscriptions and symbols.

On the offer of a small tip the custodian will open a shed containing numerous stelae, most of them with inscriptions, and pottery urns, still said to contain the ashes of the unfortunate victims.

Kothon (Punic harbour)

A little way north of the Tophet along Rue Hannibal lies the Kothon, the old Punic harbour, with two basins in which the mightiest fleet in the Mediterranean once lay at anchor.

Punic tophet

Punic urn and funerary stele

According to the ancient sources the commercial harbour was in the shape of a rectangle measuring 456m/500yds by 356m/390yds, linked with the sea by a channel 20m/65ft wide. The entrance to the harbour could be closed by a chain.

The naval harbour to the north, which was surrounded by a high wall, had a diameter of 325m/355yds. A channel giving it direct access to the sea was constructed only during the Third Punic War. In the centre of the harbour is a small island, on which the palace of the commander of the fleet once stood. The naval harbour alone had moorings for some 220 vessels, both along the landward side and round the island.

Oceanographic Museum

Between the two harbours can be found the Oceanographic Museum, with a small museum of marine biology. Open: Tue.–Sat., April–June 3–6pm, July–Sept. 4–7pm, winter months 2–5pm; Sun., 10am–noon, June-Sept. 9–11am; closed Mon.

The displays include specimens of Mediterranean fishes, a collection of sea-shells, Tunisian fishing boats, Tunisian birds and a sea-water aquarium.

Quartier Magon

The Quartier Magon excavation site is in a small park (entrance on the sea front, between the Kothon and the Archaeological Park). The site gives some impression of the development of the town in Punic times. Immediately behind the sea wall (5th c. B.C.), which just before the Third Punic War was 13m/43ft high, was the craftsmen's quarter; beyond this were larger houses, and beyond these again luxurious villas with richly patterned terrazzo floors.

There is a small museum with models of the Punic town walls, houses and streets, pavement mosaics of the Punic period and a model of the ancient quarries at El Haouaria (see Cap Bon).

*Baths of Antoninus Pius

The most important remains of Roman Carthage are the Baths of Antoninus Pius and the adjoining Archaeological Park, which lie between Avenue

Model of Tophet (National Museum, Carthage)

Habib Bourguiba and the sea. A reproduction of a capital from the Baths marks the intersection of the town's two principal streets, Avenue Reine Didon and Avenue Habib Bourguiba, from which Avenue des Thermes d'Antonin runs down towards the sea, with the entrance to the Baths at the end of it.

The massive remains of the Baths of Antoninus Pius, which were the largest in the Roman world outside Rome, occupy an area of 1.8 hectares/4½ acres. Built between A.D. 146 and 162, in the reign of the Emperor Antoninus Pius, they were extensively restored in 389 but subsequently collapsed, presumably as a result of a structural defect, and thereafter were used for centuries as a quarry of building stone. As a result all that remains is the walls of the basement storey, which owing to the nearness of the baths to the coast had particularly deep foundations, and a stretch of masonry on the west side extending up both storeys.

On the ground floor – and not, as was the normal arrangement, in the basement – were the heating and water supply systems, together with rest rooms and rooms for the staff of the baths. The baths proper were on the upper floors, with a grand staircase (of which nothing remains) leading down from them to the sea.

The ground-plan of the baths was strictly symmetrical; one wing may have been used by men, the other by women. Eight colossal columns of grey granite (each 1.60m/5¼ft in diameter, weighing 50 tons, with Corinthian capitals of white marble, 1.8m/6ft high and weighing over 4 tons) supported the vaulting of the central chamber, the frigidarium, which was 50m/165ft long by 20m/65ft wide. One of the eight columns has been restored and re-erected.

A visit to the baths followed a fairly regular sequence. After undressing in the apodyterium the bather had the choice between the warm pool and physical exercise in the palaestra or the covered gymnasium. Then he could warm himself in the warm room (tepidarium), attend to his personal hygiene in the destrictarium, have a good sweat in the laconicum, followed

Baths of Antoninus Pius

by a hot bath in the caldarium, cool down gradually in the tepidarium and finally have a cold bath in one of the four basins in the frigidarium, the central feature of the whole establishment.
On the seaward side of the baths was a sunbathing terrace with an open-air swimming pool (natatio), on the landward side two semicircular communal latrines.

Archaeological Park

The Archaeological Park (Parc Archéologique) behind the baths was laid out in 1953. The rectangular grid of streets shows the layout of this residential quarter of the Roman town. The park reflects the long history of Carthage, with Punic graves of the 6th and 5th centuries B.C., the five-aisled Basilica of Douimès, dating from the 6th century A.D., and an underground burial chapel (the Chapelle Sainte-Monique) of the 7th century for one Asterius, moved here from its original site. In one of the numerous apses of the Schola (a kind of club or meeting-place) is a well preserved Late Roman mosaic depicting preparations for some imperial ceremony. All over the site are the remains of Roman cisterns, and under a tree are numbers of limestone "cannonballs", projectiles from Carthaginian arsenals.

North-east of the Archaeological Park, on a site formerly occupied by a 19th century Bey's Palace, stands the well guarded Presidential Palace.

Roman and Early Christian Museum

Along Avenue Habib Bourguiba to the south is the Roman and Early Christian Museum (Musée Romain et Paléo-Chrétien), with material of the 4th–7th centuries A.D. and plans of the excavations.

Theatre

Avenue Reine Didon runs east to the Roman theatre (2nd C. A.D.), built into a hillside facing the sea, with seating for 5000 spectators. The stage, slightly raised, is backed by a *scenae frons* (stage wall). After much earlier alteration and destruction the theatre has now been almost completely restored, and is used for open-air performances in July and August and for the Film Festival.

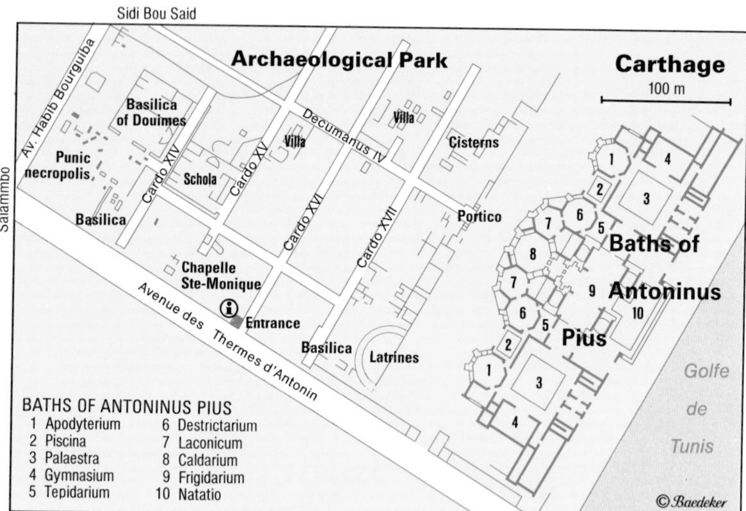

Roman villas

Immediately adjoining the theatre is the Park of the Roman Villas (Parc des Villas Romaines). Once a Punic cemetery (in which a number of shaft graves are still to be seen), the site was later occupied by the peristyle villas of wealthy Romans. One 3rd century house, the Villa des Volières, has been restored and now contains a small Antiquarium; fine pavement mosaics.

View

From the terrace, on which there are a number of fragments of sculpture, there is a fine view of Carthage, with the Presidential Palace below, the Gulf of Tunis and beyond this Cap Bon.

Odeon

On the top of the hill are the remains of the Odeon, a small covered hall built in A.D. 207.

Amphitheatre

1km/¾ mile north-west of the Byrsa Hill, on the left of the road to Tunis (and opposite the La Malga cisterns), can be found the 2nd century Roman amphitheatre, a five-storey structure with seating for some 50,000 spectators – i.e. about the same as the theatre of El Djem (see entry). The arena could be flooded for naumachias (mock naval battles). Apart from its massive foundations and a few underground rooms, however, the whole structure has been destroyed.
During the persecution of Christians, on March 17th 202, St Perpetua, her slave-girl Felicitas and others were martyred here by being trampled to death by a wild cow. They are commemorated by a marble column erected by the Pères Blancs.
St Cyprian was beheaded here in 258, the first African bishop to be martyred, and St Augustine (see Famous People) lectured in the arena.

Circus

To the south is the Circus, now identified only by a long depression in the ground.

Cisterns

On the opposite side of the street from the amphitheatre a footpath leads to the La Malga cisterns, built by the Romans to store water brought from the Zaghouan hills in an aqueduct 132km/82 miles long (see Tunis, Surroundings). Only 15 of the original 24 cisterns are now left, each 95m/312ft long, 12.5m/41ft wide and 11.50m/38ft high.

Stucco ceiling and . . .

. . . capital from the Baths

Roman mosaic in Archaeological Park

View from terrace of Villa des Volières

Hill of Juno

To the north of the Byrsa Hill is the Hill of Juno, with a former Carmelite convent. On the north-western slopes is a building with twin columns, the function of which is unknown.

Christian churches

Outside the ancient town, on the west side of the main road to Sidi Bou Said (TGM station Carthage-Présidence), are the remains of the basilica of Damous el Karita (from *domus caritatis),* the largest Early Christian church in Tunisia. Of this great nine-aisled building nothing is left but a forest of broken columns and pillars. Adjoining is the cemetery of the Pères Blancs. To the east of the main road are the basilica of St Cyprian and the convent of St Monica (Augustine's mother), with a church (originally seven-aisled). Farther north is the Basilica Majorum, of which only the outlines can be distinguished. In a chapel in this church SS. Perpetua, Felicitas and their companions were buried.

Surroundings of Carthage

Sidi Bou Said

7km/4½ miles north: see entry

La Goulette

See Tunis, Surroundings

La Marsa

See Tunis, Surroundings

Gammarth

See Tunis, Surroundings

Utica

57km/35 miles north: see entry

Chemtou

B 5

Governorate: Jendouba

Access

Chemtou, 28km/17 miles north-west of Jendouba, is reached by way of GP 17 (Tabarka–Jendouba) and MC 59, which branches off it on the west, signposted to Chemtou. (In the opposite direction MC 59 runs east to Bulla Regia). Then continue as below.
Coming from the opposite direction, take GP 6 (Béja–Jendouba), turn off into GP 17, signposted to Tabarka, and in 10km/6 miles take MC 59 to Chemtou.
In 11km/7 miles MC 59 degenerates into a gravel track and in another 5km/3 miles comes to the excavation site.

Situation and characteristics

The site of ancient Simitthus lies in a beautiful setting on the flanks of Djebel Chemtou. From the earliest times the Medjerda plain was one of the granaries of North Africa, and the wide valley is still mainly devoted to the growing of grain. The Medjerda (ancient Bagradas), Tunisia's largest river, which flows throughout the year, rises beyond the Algerian frontier, which is only a short distance away. The ancient city of Simitthus (now Chemtou) lay at the intersection of two important roads, between Carthage and Hippo Regius (Annaba, in Algeria) and between Sicca Veneria (Le Kef) and Thabraca (Tabarka).

Marmor numidicus

In this area are the quarries, worked from Numidian times in the 2nd century B.C. to Byzantine times in the 6th century A.D., which yielded the famous *marmor numidicus,* in colours ranging from a uniform dark yellow to light pink and creamy white, used in the construction of imperial buildings throughout the Mediterranean area. This Numidian marble, now known as giallo antico, ranked after Egyptian porphyry and the green

Landscape round Chemtou

serpentine of Sparta as the most precious stone of antiquity, and its quarrying was an imperial monopoly.

Work camp

Air photography has revealed a work camp, lying outside the town, built to house the quarrymen, slaves and forced labourers, many of them Christians, who worked in the largest quarry in North Africa. Nearby was a factory in which luxury marble articles were produced.
Excavation of the site by Tunisian and German archaeologists began in 1970. So far only a small part of the area has been explored, but it is already clear that the Chemtou work camp is the largest and most complete installation of the kind known in the whole Roman world. It is now possible, for the first time, to follow the whole process of production and gain valuable information about methods of quarrying and processing the stone.

History

The site of Chemtou, on a narrow ridge of hill projecting into the Medjerda/Bagradas valley at a ford in the river, safe from the danger of flooding, is thought to have been occupied by an earlier Numidian settlement. In the mid 2nd century B.C. the Numidian king Masinissa (see Famous People) had captured the fertile corn-growing areas in the upper Bagradas valley and around Dougga from the Carthaginians and had thus pushed the frontiers of his kingdom far to the east. A few decades later Masinissa or his son and successor Micipsa founded a hilltop sanctuary on the summit of Djebel Chemtou, 20km/12½ miles from the royal capital of Bulla Regia. In the course of constructing the sanctuary the Numidians came upon the yellow Numidian marble which forms the whole of the western half of Djebel Chemtou. The systematic working of the marble, using highly developed quarrying techniques, however, began only in Roman times, when the settlement of Colonia Augusta Numidica Simitthus was founded (27 B.C.).

Transport and use

The blocks of marble were either transported by boat down the river to Carthage or on a new road built for the purpose to Thabraca (Tabarka), and

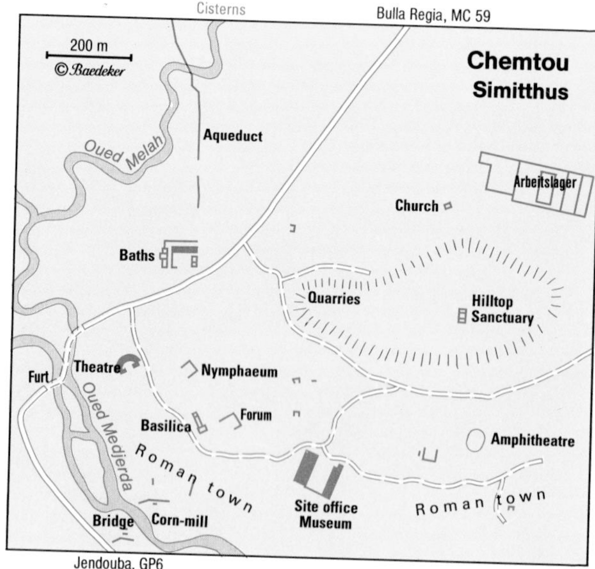

from there conveyed to the remotest corners of the Roman Empire. Augustus used the stone in the construction of his Forum, Domitian for his Domus Flavia, Trajan for his Forum and Hadrian for his villa at Tivoli. The quarries continued to be worked until the Arab conquest. In the 19th century an attempt was made to reopen them, but this was soon abandoned. During the war of Algerian liberation the Algerian army established an important base here.

*Excavations

The site lies on the east side of the access road. Our description begins at the Baths, just beside the road.

Simitthus

The site of ancient Simitthus (a name of Berber origin), on which so far little excavation has been carried out, lies at the foot of the hill. Situated as it was at an important road intersection, it developed rapidly; its real importance, however, lay in the surrounding marble quarries.

The Baths, like the rest of the city, were supplied with water by an aqueduct which conveyed it from a spring 30km/20 miles away. 2km/1¼ miles north is a cistern with a capacity of 15,000 litres/3300 gallons.

On the east side of the town is the amphitheatre, north-west of which is another cistern.

To the south of the town, lying partly in the river Medjerda and partly on its banks, are the massive remains of a Roman bridge which collapsed during a flood in the 4th century. Immediately adjoining the bridge are the remains of a water-driven corn-mill, into which the water was directed through narrow channels. There is a model of the mill in the site museum.

Museum

Near the bridge, in the site office, is an interesting small museum (not always open) with finds from the site, plans of the excavations and a reconstruction of the corn-mill.

Remains of the theatre of Simitthus

Hilltop sanctuary, Chemtou

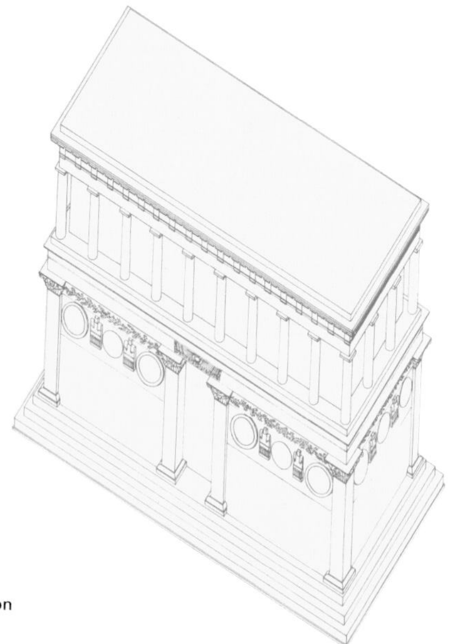

Isometric reconstruction on scale 1:100

Theatre

To the north of the bridge are the remains of the theatre, which like the one at Bulla Regia (see entry), was free-standing. Part of the cavea has been preserved but nothing is left of the stage wall. Nearby are the remains of the forum, with a basilica and a nymphaeum.

Hilltop sanctuary

The hilltop sanctuary of the 2nd century B.C. on the summit of Djebel Chemtou (85m/280ft) was dedicated to the Punic god Baal-Ammon. There are only scanty remains of the monumental marble altar, a two-storied structure over 10m/33ft high; the base, measuring 12.15m/40ft by 5.64m/18½ft, survives.

Handsome architectural elements from the sanctuary, which was richly decorated, were found during the excavations and can now be seen in the museum. They include marble blocks with relief decoration, 1.20m/4ft high, from the base of the building and a 1.9m/6¼ft long architrave from a false door, with Egyptian-style decoration (a band of lotus-flower decoration surmounted by a solar disc with stylised rays which is flanked by two crowned uraeuses).

In the second century A.D. the Romans enlarged the sanctuary and converted it into a temple of Saturn. In the 4th century it was replaced by a small three-aisled church, which was later embellished with pavement mosaics.

It is planned to re-erect the sanctuary, with casts of the original features.

View

From the hill there is a view of the work camp to the north.

Work camp

The work camp was identified in 1961 in air photographs taken after a period of heavy rain. Built in A.D. 154 at some distance from the town, it covered an area of some 4 hectares/10 acres (of which about a fifth has been excavated) and was enclosed, like a prison, by high walls. Round a series of large courtyards were laid out the living quarters, workshops, offices and stores, together with baths and temples for both workers and officials of the huge quarries. The camps accommodated large numbers of slaves and workers condemned to forced labour in the quarries (*ad metalla*), including many Christians.

Marble factory

The most important building within the camp was the factory (*fabrica*), with six long workshops, also surrounded by walls, in which a variety of articles designed for export – marble slabs, dishes, pestles and mortars, plates with relief decoration, etc. – were turned out in a highly developed system of mass production based on the division of labour. A series of specialised work-benches have been identified in a kind of ancient assembly line at the end of which the finished articles emerged at the north end of the factory ready for despatch.

Quarries

In the quarries themselves rock faces up to 20m/65ft high show the marks of Roman quarrying. Numbers of blocks left in the quarries bear inscriptions with the name of an Emperor, a consul or a quarry official and an indication of the section of the quarry from which they came.

Rock-cut reliefs

On the south-west, west and north sides of the temple hill a long series of reliefs carved on the rock (more than 200 in number) were discovered. They range in height between 20 and 55cm/8 and 21in and in width between 30 and 35cm/12 and 14in, but can be seen only when the sun is in certain positions, and then only for a few minutes. Crudely carved, they depict mainly sacrifices in honour of Saturn (successor to the Punic god Baal-Ammon) and are of great cultic interest.

Chenini

See Médenine, Surroundings

Chott el Djerid

F/G 4–7

Governorates: Tozeur, Kebili, Gabès (part)
Altitude: 17–25m/56–82ft

Situation and *characteristics

Tunisia is divided into two almost equal parts by a series of salt lakes (*chotts*), the largest of which is the Chott el Djerid. The boundary runs to the south of a line from Tamerza (near the Algerian frontier) by way of Gafsa to Maknassy and from there to the Gulf of Gabès. To the north is the steppe country of southern Tunisia, which becomes increasingly barren towards the south and beyond the *chotts* gives place to the desert.
Within Tunisia the string of *chotts* begins in the west with the Chott el Rharsa and is continued by the Chott el Djerid (110km/68 miles long by 70km/43 miles wide) and its eastern offshoot the Chott el Fedjadj (90km/56 miles long by up to 20km/12½ miles wide), which together form the largest salt lake in the Sahara (7700sq.km/2975sq.miles).
Within this region are the two largest areas of oases in Tunisia: to the north the Bled el Djerid around Tozeur, Nefta, El Oudiane and El Hamma, to the south-east the Nefzaoua oases round Kebili and Douz. In this region there are more than 3 million date palms: hence the name of Bled el Djerid, the Land of Palms (*djerid* = "palm").
These charming oases, set amid an alien landscape, are now popular tourist attractions, and there are numerous ambitious projects for the planned development of the tourist trade.

Origins

The scenically very impressive depression occupied by the lakes, part of which is below sea level, was formed by tectonic movements in the late Tertiary era, some 1.5 million years ago. The depression is believed to have been flooded by the sea at one time and then dried out. In spring and autumn heavy rain and underground springs of water coming from the

In the Chott el Djerid

Close-up view of the salt crust

hills to the north lead to the formation of great expanses of shallow pools and salt marshes. The rain, however, soon evaporates (the evaporation rate being five times higher than the rainfall), leaving the salt washed out of the rock on the surface. Great areas are covered with a shimmering bluish-white crust of salt, which crystallises in huge and bizarrely shaped masses. Under the salt lakes are huge fossil reserves of water, which irrigate the surrounding oases and frequently emerge on the surface as fresh-water springs (*aioun,* singular *ain*). It is highly dangerous to leave the proper track (see below) and try to cross the *chotts,* since in many places the salt crust does not rest on solid ground and may collapse.
In spring the Chott el Rharsa and Chott el Fedjadj are a favoured breeding ground for flamingoes, who fly in from northern Tunisia, build their nests, produce and rear their young and then fly off again at the beginning of July. Deposits of coloured salt crystals, mirages (optical illusions produced by the refraction of light in unevenly warmed layers of air) and the occasional dust-storms on exceptionally hot afternoons are among the unusual experiences that visitors may encounter in this strange landscape.

Crossing the Chott el Djerid

There is no difficulty about crossing the Chott at any time of year on the causeway which carries GP 16 from Kriz (near Tozeur) to Bechri (near Kebili), except perhaps after heavy rain, when part of the road may be under water. During the hot summer months there will certainly be no problem (see Practical Information, Sahara Tourism).
From Tozeur the road at first runs through steppe country, mostly flat; then all at once the salt crust of the Chott comes into view, stretching endlessly into the distance, interrupted here and there by pools of water. To the south can be seen dunes planted with palms, marking the Nefzaoua oases. Along the road are occasional souvenir stalls offering sand roses ("roses du Sahara"). A signpost points to a sand-surfing school, where visitors can learn the art of surfing on polyester boards fitted with rollers.

The oases on the fringes of the Chott, in the region known as the Bled el Djerid, or Djerid for short, are densely populated: see Nefta, Tozeur and Gabès.

Oases in the Djerid

To the north-west, in delightful hill scenery, are the upland oases of Midès, Tamerza and Chebika (see Tozeur, Surroundings).

Upland oases

On the south-eastern edge of the Chott are the numerous widely scattered Nefzaoua oases, the chief places in which are Kebili and Douz (see Kebili).

Nefzaoua

Djerba

F 8

Governorate: Médenine
Altitude: 30–54m/98–177ft
Population: 90,000

Access
By air

The Djerba-Mellita international airport lies 10km/6 miles west of Houmt-Souk, the chief place on the island. There are regular flights by Tunis Air from London, as well as from Tunis, Monastir and Tozeur, and by Tunisavia from Sfax; regular flights by Tunis Air and Air France from Brussels, Frankfurt, Geneva, Lyons, Marseilles, Paris and Zurich; and numerous charter flights from European airports.

By bus

There are bus services to Djerba from Tunis, Sousse, Sfax, Gabès, Médenine, Zarzis and Ben Gardane. The bus station (Gare Routière) in Houmt-Souk is in Avenue Habib Bourguiba.

On the island itself there are bus services between the tourist hotels and Midoun, Adjim, Guellala, Sedouikech, Er Riadh (also called Hara Seghira), Qualegh, Houmt-Souk and Mellita (airport).

By car and ferry

GP 1 (Gabès–Médenine). Turn off just south of Mareth into MC 116, which runs north-east and comes in 50km/30 miles to Djorf, from which there is a car ferry to Adjim on Djerba.

By causeway

Alternatively turn off GP 1 15km/9 miles north-west of Médenine into MC 118, which runs north-east to Zarzis. From there it is 20km/12½ miles to the 6.4km/4 mile long causeway leading to El Kantara on Djerba.

Situation and *characteristics

The island of Djerba lies 5km/3 miles off the southern coast of Tunisia in the Gulf of Gabès, known in antiquity as Syrtis Minor. Thanks to its long and for the most part gently sloping sandy beaches, particularly on the north-east and south-east coasts, and its unchanging Mediterranean climate Djerba ranks with Sousse/Monastir and Hammamet/Nabeul as one of the three most popular tourist centres in Tunisia.

In addition to the chief town, Houmt-Souk, there are many other places of interest, which are described below in the form of a tour of the island. Another rewarding possibility is a trip into the interior on a dromedary – an attraction which many dromedary boys will be ready to offer. Information can usually be obtained from your hotel.

With an area of 514sq.km/198sq.miles, measuring some 30km/20 miles from north to south and from east to west, Djerba is the largest island off the North African coast.

Geologically it belongs to the mainland, but when the level of the Mediterranean rose after the Ice Age it was cut off from the coastal plain. The little Gulf of Bou Grara, which separates Djerba from the mainland, is still shallow and lagoon-like.

The island is linked with the mainland by a 6.4km/4 mile long causeway. The chief place is Houmt-Souk, on the north coast.

Vegetation and water supply

Djerba is built up of Tertiary deposits, partly covered by a layer of chalk. Apart from a low hill (54m/177ft) in the south-east of the island it is flat.

Djerba's problem since time immemorial has been its water supply, for with its low rainfall (an annual 200m/8lin.) and lack of hills it has no

Inselkarte

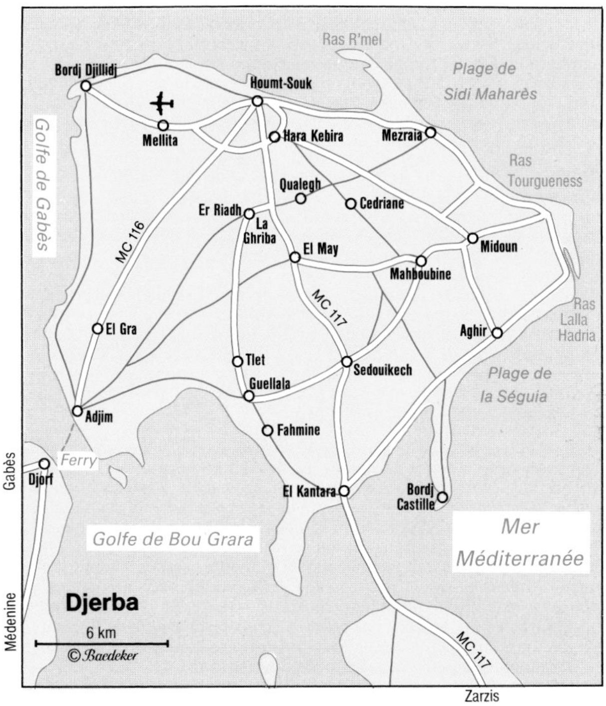

above-ground water resources. Apart from the tourist areas on the north coast, which are supplied with water by pipeline from the mainland, Djerba is dependent on some 4000 wells and 2000 cisterns, the water in which is slightly saline. The quality of the water farther inland is rather better than on the coast.

The shortage of water influences the structure of the island's agriculture. In the coastal areas the pattern is set by large numbers of date-palms (1.2 million in all), in the shadow of which figs, corn and wine are grown; farther inland are olive-groves (some 600,000 trees); and in the centre of the island are extensive areas given up to irrigated horticulture (fruit-trees).

Economy

Apart from agriculture major contributions are made to the economy by the traditional crafts of pottery and hand weaving. Djerba is famed for the pottery of Guellala, the fabrics woven from wool spun from sheepskins imported from the mainland and the work of its goldsmiths and silversmiths.

Fishing and sponge-diving are also traditional activities. The waters around Djerba are well stocked with fish, the commonest species being horse mackerel, barbel, tunny, bass, bream, prawns and shrimps. Cuttle-fish are caught by putting out long lines with large numbers of small clay jars in which the fish take shelter.

After the Second World War the island's traditional sources of income were supplemented by the development of tourism along the north coast, with

◀ *View over Djerba*

its dry, sunny and, thanks to the moderating influence of the Mediterranean, equable climate, which combined with its long sandy beaches to make Djerba, together with the mainland oasis of Zarzis, the largest resort area in southern Tunisia. On the north-east coast round Sidi Mahrez and La Seguia there are now some 20 hotels offering European standards of amenity, with a total of around 10,000 beds. The airport at Mellita, only 20–35km/12–22 miles away, provides a convenient link with the European countries from which most of the holidaymakers come.

Population

Characteristic of Djerba is a scattered pattern of settlement. This does not, however, imply a low density of population: on the contrary, the population density of Djerba, at 156 to the square kilometre (404 to the square mile), is very high by Tunisian standards. The pattern of settlement seems rather to reflect the predominance of smallholdings on Djerba, in contrast to the rest of Tunisia.

A quarter of the inhabitants, known as Djerbi, still speak Berber dialects. In the past many people left the island because its agriculture could not produce enough to feed the rapidly growing population. Only a few of them found work in the large tourist centres, since many hotel employees came in from other parts of the country; while in all the larger Tunisian towns incomers from Djerba are found working as skilled craftsmen and tradesmen.

Jews

Formerly there were large numbers of Jews on Djerba, but in recent years there has been a sharp decline in the Jewish population as a result of emigration. The two villages of Hara Kebira and Hara Seghira (now Er Riadh) were founded by Jewish incomers (see below). Every year, 33 days after Easter, Jewish pilgrims from all over North Africa make their way to the famous synagogue of La Ghriba.

As noted above, most of the inhabitants of Djerba live in scattered settlements (*menzel*) – walled farmsteads with enough accommodation to house the extended family. Characteristic features of the landscape are the impenetrable hedges of prickly pears which enclose the fields. Typical of Djerba, too, are the numerous little mosques scattered over the island, most of them used only by a few neighbouring families.

The Berber people of Djerba belong to two different schools of Islamic belief, the Ibadites and the Malikites (the sect to which a majority of Tunisians belong). The Ibadites split off from the mainstream of Islamic belief in the 7th century under the name of Kharijites ("Seceders") and found many adherents among the Berbers. Fleeing from their orthodox fellow-Muslims, they found a refuge on the island of Djerba, where they established a new home and began to call themselves Ibadites. Now adherents of their version of the faith are found only on Djerba (mainly in the west of the island), in Algeria (where they are called Mozabites) and in Oman. It appears nowadays that adherence to one or other belief has lost its divisive function.

Altogether there are some 250 small mosques on Djerba – plain and simple buildings in line with the worshippers' religious beliefs. Ibadite mosques have either a square minaret or none at all; Malikite ones have slender tapering minarets.

History

Djerba is claimed by some to be the island of the lotus-eaters on which Odysseus landed during his wanderings. Historical knowledge of the island goes back to the 9th century B.C., when the Phoenicians established trading posts on what was known in antiquity as the island of Meninx. It seems likely, on the evidence of the great quantities of murex shells (the shellfish which yielded a precious purple dye) found on the island, that they also operated a dye factory. Under Roman rule Djerba prospered, since it was from here that the slaves and other wares brought from the Sahara and central Africa by the merchants' caravans were shipped to Rome. There were four cities on the island – Haribus, Tipasa, Meninx and Girba (from which the name of Djerba is probably derived). To improve access to the island the Romans built a causeway (possibly on even earlier foundations) over a stretch of water ranging between 4m/12ft and 25m/80ft in depth; its remains are now incorporated in the foundations of the present causeway between El Kantara (ancient Meninx) and the mainland.

The fall of Rome meant for Djerba the beginning of a long decline. The raids by the Vandals in A.D. 410 were followed by the Byzantines, the Arab conquest in the 7th century and the devastation wrought by the Beni Hilal nomads in the 11th century. The fight for dominance in the Mediterranean opened up a new period in the history of Djerba. In 1135 it was captured by Normans from Sicily, from whom it was recovered only twenty years later by the Almohads. The Spaniards gained control of the island in 1284, but were driven out by a bloody rising in 1334. In the second half of the 15th century, under the Hafsids, Djerba enjoyed a further period of prosperity, when it became notorious as a pirates' lair. A questionable fame was enjoyed by the great corsair Dragut (see Famous People), who had the full support of the Ottoman Sultan. Around 1550 he strengthened the fortress of Houmt-Souk for protection against Spanish reprisals. Ten years later Spain sent a force of 30 ships and 30,000 men against Houmt-Souk and took the fortress; but the returning Spanish fleet was attacked by Dragut and some 18,000 Spanish and Maltese lost their lives. Finally Dragut laid siege to the fortress, whose garrison of 5000 men were compelled to surrender and were forthwith beheaded. As a further deterrent Dragut had their skulls built up into a pyramid, which stood outside the fortress for almost 300 years, before being removed in 1848. There is now a monument commemorating the inglorious history of the fortress.

Later Djerba came under Turkish rule and in 1881 under French rule, against which there were several rebellions.

Houmt-Souk

Situation and characteristics

Houmt-Souk (pop. 20,000), chief town and administrative centre of Djerba, lies on the north coast of the island. The name ("market quarter") points to

Pottery market, Houmt-Souk

A potter at work

a long tradition as a trading town. The Romans, recognising the advantages of this situation on the open sea, founded a settlement here to which they gave the name of Girba, and this rapidly developed into a busy trading centre.

*Old town

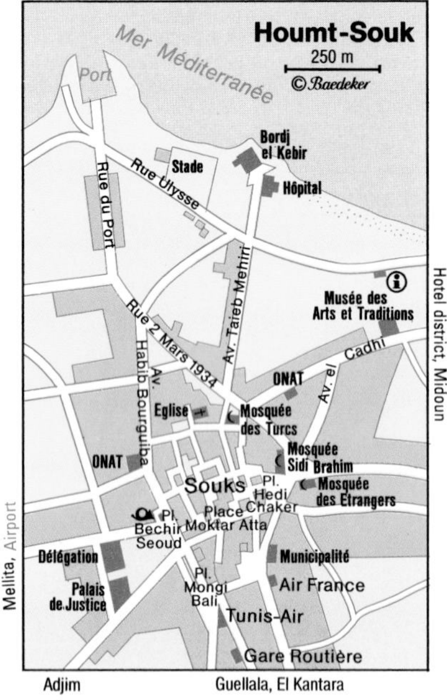

Houmt-Souk has a small fishing harbour, an attractive old town and a picturesque and labyrinthine souk in which there are markets on Mondays and Thursdays.

The displays of goods in the souk, now mainly designed to cater for tourists, include jewellery, clothes for the whole family, shoes, silk, brass and silverware and leather goods. Locally made woollen blankets, usually red, in traditional geometric patterns, are also popular souvenirs.

Fondouks

In the souk quarter are a number of old fondouks or caravanserais – combined warehouses and inns, several storeys high, built round an arcaded courtyard. In the past the fondouks provided accommodation for travelling merchants and safe keeping for their wares. Some of them are now modest hotels or restaurants.

Strangers' Mosque

On the east side of the old town can be seen the Strangers' Mosque (Mosquée des Etrangers, Djemaa el Ghorba). Its square minaret has a frieze of inscriptions round the top.

Diagonally opposite is the Zaouia of Sidi Brahim (1674). From here Avenue Habib Thameur runs north for some 200m/220yds to the 17th century Mosque of the Turks (Mosquée des Turcs, Djemaa Tourk). With its seven domes and circular minaret it is regarded as Houmt-Souk's finest mosque. A market is held in the square in front of the mosque on Mondays and Thursdays.

*Folk Museum

From the Zaouia of Sidi Brahim Avenue Abdel Hamid el Khadi runs northeast. 500m/550yds along this street, on the left (just before the Hotel School), is an interesting little folk museum, the Musée des Arts et Traditions Populaires (Musée ATP for short), which has been housed since 1968 in the 18th century Zaouia of Sidi Zitouni. The museum is open daily, except Monday, from 9am to noon and 3 to 6pm.

The former prayer hall now contains a colourful display of traditional costumes. Other exhibits include beautiful old jewellery, a potter's workshop, fine pottery, kitchen equipment and old marriage chests. One small room is devoted to old editions of the Koran. The zaouia has very beautiful stalactitic ceilings.

Bordj el Kebir

The main axis of Houmt-Souk is the Avenue Habib Bourguiba, which bisects the new town from north to south. Its northward continuation, Rue

Strangers' Mosque

Mosque of the Turks

du Port, leads to the harbour. Just before it reaches the harbour Rue Ulysse goes off on the right, leading by way of a street on the left to the Bordj el Kebir or Bordj Ghazi Mustafa. A fort was built here in the 13th century and strengthened in the 15th; then between 1560 and 1570 the notorious corsair Dragut built the massive fortress which we see today. Extensive restoration has been carried out since 1968, and it is planned to instal a museum in the restored building.
Between the fort and the harbour can be seen a small obelisk commemorating the pyramid of skulls which Dragut erected here.

Tour of the Island

Er Riadh (Hara Seghira)

8km/5 miles from Houmt-Souk is Er Riadh, formerly known as Hara Seghira (the "Little Ghetto"), the island's second Jewish community. (The first was Hara Kebira, the "Great Ghetto", on the south-eastern outskirts of Houmt-Souk.)

History

It is known that numbers of Jews came to Djerba after the destruction of Jerusalem in A.D. 70, though according to other sources the first Jews arrived at a much earlier date – in the 6th century B.C., following the destruction of Jerusalem by Nebuchadnezzar. In the 16th and 17th centuries there was a large influx of refugees from Andalusia, who were able to live in peace on the island, for the people of Djerba were very tolerant of other religions. A hundred years ago Jews accounted for 10% of the island's population, but the establishment of the state of Israel after the Second World War led to large-scale emigration, and there are now no more than 1000–2000 Jews on Djerba.

*La Ghriba Synagogue

The most notable Jewish building on Djerba is the La Ghriba ("Wonder-working") Synagogue 1km/¾ mile east of Er Riadh (closed on Saturdays).

Bordj el Kebir

A fisherman's family

In its present form this modest-looking building dates only from the 1920s, but its origins go much further back. There are many legends about its foundation: one story is that the site was chosen when a "holy stone" (perhaps a meteorite) fell to earth here.

The interior has fine panelling, old candlesticks, valuable Torah scrolls and other cult objects. The rabbis, who live in the pilgrim hostel opposite the synagogue, ensure that all visitors take off their shoes and wear a head covering (which can be hired for a modest sum at the entrance).

Every year, 33 days after Easter, La Ghriba is the scene of a great pilgrimage of Jews from all over the Maghreb.

El May

3km/2 miles south-east of La Ghriba is El May (pop. 5000), with the picturesque 16th century Ibadite mosque of Umm et Turkiya (non-Muslims not admitted).

From here a minor country road runs west to join a larger road to Guellala.

Guellala

11km/7 miles south of Er Riadh, near the south coast, lies the village of Guellala, the pottery centre of the island.

Ancient Haribus (a name derived from *heres,* a jar) was famed for its pottery, which was despatched all over the Sahara; and the main street of the present-day village is still lined with potters' shops offering their wares to tourists. There are said to be some 450 potters in this scattered village, and it is well worth visiting at least one of their workshops.

The traditional products of the Guellala potters are unglazed storage jars modelled on the ancient amphora. These can still be seen, but the main output now consists of items designed to appeal to tourists, with a predominance of painted pottery.

The clay used by the potters is excavated from shafts up to 80m/260ft deep, dried out for two or three days and then broken up and mixed with water (fresh water for red pottery, salt water for white). The pottery is left to dry for 60 days and is then fired for four days in semi-underground kilns, in which it remains for another ten days to cool gradually.

Potter's workshop . . .

. . . and kiln, Guellala

Sedouikech

6km/4 miles east of Guellala is Sedouikech (pop. 4000; market on Tuesdays), another potters' village.

El Kantara

At the south end of the island is El Kantara. Little trace is left of the once important Roman town of Meninx which occupied the site. In the remains of a large Christian basilica was found a cruciform font, now in the Bardo Museum in Tunis.
El Kantara lies at the end of the causeway (6.4km/4 miles long, 10m/33ft wide) linking Djerba with the mainland, which rests on Roman and perhaps even older foundations. Parallel with it runs the pipeline which supplies the hotels in the north-east of the island with water from the mainland.

Bordj Castille

From El Kantara the coast road leads east to a long narrow peninsula, at the southern tip of which is the Bordj Castille, a fort originally built in the 13th century and enlarged in the 15th.

Séguia

Between Aghir and Ras Lalla Hadria is the Plage de la Séguia, a 5km/3 mile long stretch of sandy beach interrupted here and there by rocks, with many hotels. There are regular bus services to and from Houmt-Souk and Midoun.

Midoun

5km/3 miles inland is Midoun, surrounded by gardens, fruit orchards and groves of date-palms. It is the largest market town on Djerba, with a population of 7000 (market on Friday). The market square, now lined with souvenir shops, is the central point of the picturesque old Medina. The population includes many descendants of slaves brought here from the Sudan. During the main holiday season there is a "fantasia" every Tuesday, with a representation of a traditional wedding celebration (complete with dromedary, folk dancing and equestrian games but without a bride).

Mahboubine

4km/2½ miles south-west of Midoun is Mahboubine, with the El Katib Mosque (1903), a small-scale copy of the Haghia Sophia.

Plage Sidi Maharès

9km/6 miles east of Houmt-Souk is the Plage Sidi Maharès, the oldest and best developed resort area on the island, extending for some 13km/8 miles to Ras Tourgueness with its 54m/177ft high lighthouse. Regular bus services to and from Houmt-Souk and Midoun.

Bordj Djillidj

From Houmt-Souk a road runs west to Mellita Airport and, 3km/2 miles beyond this, the most north-westerly point on the island, with an old fortress of 1745 now containing a lighthouse.
From here a narrow and little used road goes down the coast to Adjim.

Adjim

From Houmt-Souk MC 116 runs south-west through a thinly populated region of olive-trees and later palm-groves, coming in 22km/14 miles to Adjim, on the site of ancient Tipasa (of which there are few remains). It is now a sponge-fishing centre. There is a regular car ferry service between Adjim and the mainland (Djorf).

Surroundings of Djerba

Gightis
Access

Gightis lies on MC 108 (Djorf–Médenine), just south of the turn-off for Bou Grara.

Situation and characteristics

Some 20km/12½ miles south of Djorf and 27km/17 miles north of Médenine is the Roman site of Gightis. Although it is not quite so impressive as the Roman towns of northern Tunisia, it makes an attractive trip from Djerba.

History

A trading post was established here in the 6th century B.C. by Phoenicians from Tyre. Thanks to its situation on the Gulf of Bou Grara it soon devel-

El Katib Mosque, Mohboubine

oped into an important port where the caravans discharged their wares. In A.D. 48 the Romans captured the town and developed it further. It survived the fall of the Roman Empire and in the 4th century became a Christian stronghold in southern Tunisia, but thereafter was destroyed by the Vandals.

*Excavations

Gightis's active trading relations led to cultural exchanges, and Greek, Egyptian and Punic influences left their mark on the town, particularly in the architecture. The remains now visible date mainly from the 2nd century A.D. Coming from Djorf, we first encounter the remains of Roman baths, a rectangular complex with a circular palaestra. To the east was the forum, surrounded by the principal public buildings. On the north side was the temple of Apollo, Concord and Hercules, on the east side a temple of Dionysus (Liber Pater) and on the west side the Capitoline temple (probably dedicated to the Egyptian divinities Isis and Serapis), of which there remain only the steps leading up to the podium and six stumps of columns.

To the south of the forum were the market and the residential areas of the town, lying beyond the little river Chabel el Hassian, with a view of the sea. In the south-west of the town are the remains of an early 3rd century temple of Mercury.

Finds from the site and a model of the town can be seen in the Bardo National Museum in Tunis.

On the north side of the site can be seen a Byzantine fortress.

Zarzis

Access

From the mainland end of the causeway from El Kantara MC 117 runs south-east to Zarzis (20km/12½ miles). The "Route Touristique" (Route des Hotels), which also starts at the end of the dam, follows the coast and leads direct, via Hassi, to the hotel zone on the sea.

Situation and characteristics

The second major tourist centre of southern Tunisia is the oasis of Zarzis, 20km/12½ miles south-east of Djerba on the Akkara peninsula. Geographically belonging to the Djeffara plain, this coastal oasis was developed by the French in the late 19th century. The landscape pattern is set by olive plantations (700,000 trees), groves of date-palms (110,000 trees; the dates are used only for animal fodder) and market gardens. The town of Zarzis (pop. 11,000) is strongly marked by the tourist trade.

The hotel zone extends for some 8km/5 miles along the coast, ending 4km/2½ miles from the town, with which it is connected by regular bus services.

Other sights

Djerba is a good base from which to visit places of interest on the mainland: in particular Chott el Djerid, Gabès, Gafsa, Tozeur, Nefta, Kebili and Médenine (see entries).

Dougga

B 5/6

Governorate: Siliana
Altitude: 520–600m/1710–1970ft

Access

GP 5 (Tunis–Béja). At Medjez el Bab, 60km/37 miles from Tunis, GP 5 branches off on the left and runs south-west via Testour and Téboursouk to Le Kef. Some 50km/31 miles down this road, soon after the turning for Téboursouk, a narrow road on the right (signposted) runs 7km/4½ miles north to the site of Dougga (ancient Thugga).

Situation and characteristics

Thugga is the best preserved Roman city in Africa. In a setting of great scenic beauty, surrounded by pastureland and olive-groves, the remains are prominently situated on a plateau on the edge of the Monts de Téboursouk, steeply scarped on the north side but sloping gently down on the south side to the valley of the Oued Khalled. Nearby is the spring of Ain Mizeh, which is still in use.

Dougga, dominated by its Capitol

The town, which in Roman times was not walled, occupied an area of some 25 hectares/62½ acres. It was not laid out on any definite plan, and – in contrast to most Roman towns with their regular street grid – was a labyrinth of paved streets suitable only for pedestrians.
A theatrical festival is held here annually in June.

History

The choice of site, on a steeply sloping hillside (hence the town's name, from *tukka,* a sheer rock), suggests that this, like Sicca Veneria (see Le Kef) and Bulla Regia (see entry), was a Numidian foundation. In the 2nd century B.C. the settlement was enlarged by the Numidian king Masinissa to form a royal residence. The remains of megalithic walls, a temple of Baal, dolmen tombs and a Numidian mausoleum date from this period.
Around 105 B.C. the first Romans settled round the town, which according to the Greek historian Diodorus Siculus (1st c. B.C.) was already "large and handsome".
In 46 B.C. Caesar incorporated the town in the province of Africa Nova. The Numidian settlement on the hill remained, while the Romans settled in the plain below. In the course of time the two settlements amalgamated, and in A.D. 205 the town was raised to the status of a *municipium* and all its free citizens were granted Roman citizenship. In 261, when Thugga was renamed Colonia Licinia, the city was at the peak of its development. From this period date most of its magnificent public buildings, financed by wealthy Roman landowners, as well as the many private houses of which remains survive.
Decline set in at the end of the 3rd century. Under Byzantine rule the town was fortified, using stone from ancient buildings. At some later period it was abandoned. Later still refugees from Andalusia settled in the area and re-established the cultivation of olives.
The site was rediscovered in the 17th century. Excavation began in 1899 and is still continuing.

**Excavations

The access road ends at the entrance to the site, where visitors buy their tickets and are offered the services of a guide. In engaging a guide care should be taken to agree the fee in advance.
The following description takes the form of a tour of the site, which can be undertaken without a guide.

Theatre

The Theatre, built into the hillside in the usual Roman fashion, was erected in A.D. 168/169 at the expense of a wealthy citizen of the town. It has a diameter of 120m/395ft. The three tiers of seating in the semicircular cavea, with 19 rows in each, rise to a height of 15m/50ft, with an arched corridor running round the top, and could accommodate 3500 spectators. At the foot of the cavea were seats for guests of honour. A low wall, the *pulpitum),*

GP5, Téboursouk

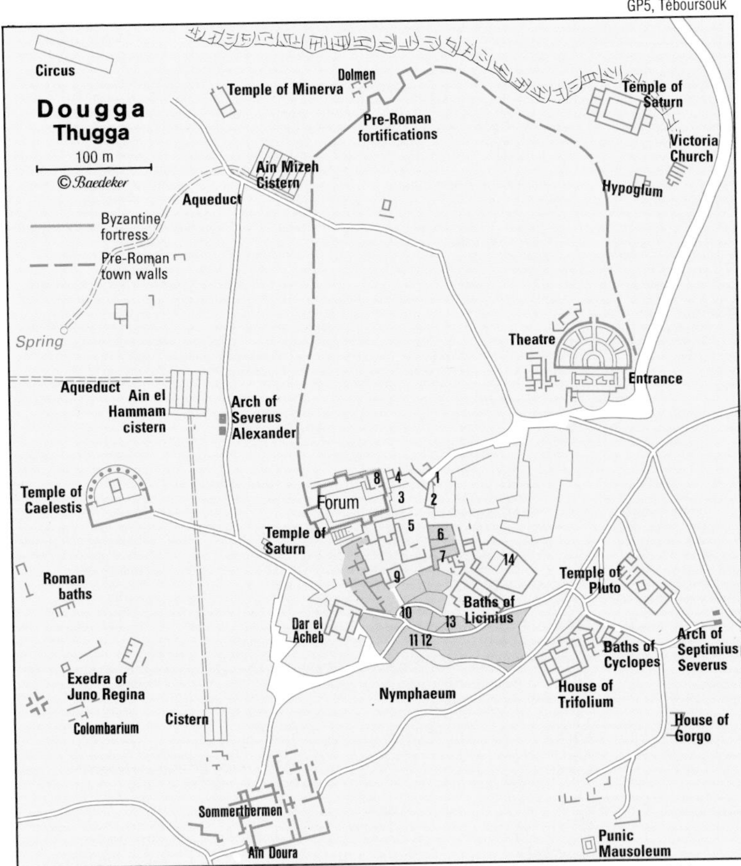

1 Temple of Pietas Augusta
2 Temple of Fortuna
3 Place de la Rose des Vents
4 Temple of Mercury
5 Macellum
6 House of the Cupbearer
7 House of the Steps
8 Capitol
9 Temple of Tellus
10 "Omnia tibi felicia"
11 House of Dionysus and Odysseus
12 House of the Labyrinth
13 House of the Three Masks
14 Temples of Concord, Frugifer and Liber Pater

with numerous niches for marble statues separated the auditorium from the stage.

The fine view into the valley, over the whole area of the ancient city and down to the Numidian mausoleum (see below), which present-day visitors enjoy from the top rows of seating was originally closed off by a high stage wall, now represented only by a few columns; originally it consisted of three superimposed rows of columns with a flight of steps in front of them. The theatre was used for performances of comedies and pantomimes.

A doorway on the stage leads into a hall with Corinthian columns, the foyer of the theatre. Here there is an inscription naming the generous founder of the theatre and describing its amenities.

In the basement of the stage building were property stores and other store-rooms.

Above the theatre, to the north, are the Temple of Saturn (the columns of which are a landmark visible from the access road), the Victoria Church and a pagan cemetery.

Temple of Saturn

The magnificently situated Temple of Saturn was built in A.D. 195 on the site of a pre-Roman temple of Baal (a few ash-urns and funerary stelae from which were found by the excavators). At the east end is a vestibule with four Corinthian columns; the inner courtyard is surrounded on three sides by a Corinthian portico; and at the west end are three cellae. In a cistern under the courtyard was found the head of the cult statue of Saturn, which presumably stood in the central cella (it is now in the Bardo National Museum in Tunis). The cella on the south side has preserved part of its stucco-covered vaulting.

Below the temple is a hypogeum, an underground burial-place entered by a flight of seven steps, originally in a pagan cemetery.

Victoria Church

Immediately east is the Victoria Church, a small aisled building with remains of mosaics. In a crypt below the raised presbytery was found a sarcophagus bearing the inscription "Victoria". This little church with its irregular ground-plan was built in the 5th century A.D. with stone from the Temple of Saturn.

Temple of Pietas Augusta

Returning to the Theatre, we follow a paved street running south-west, lined by the remains of shops and houses. Rainwater was carried off by gutters in the middle of the street connecting with underground drains. The street leads to the little semicircular temple of Pietas Augusta (2nd c. A.D.), of which there remain two columns with Corinthian capitals. Beyond this are the substructure of a temple of Fortuna and a small mosque.

Place de la Rose des Vents

Just beyond this lies the Place de la Rose des Vents, a square with a semicircular east end, paved with limestone slabs and surrounded by colonnades, which was built around A.D. 190 as an extension to the forum. It takes its name from the "rose of the winds" incised in the paving in the 3rd century, with the names of the twelve winds (Septentrio, Aquilo, Euraquilo, Vulturnus, Eurus, Leuconotus, Auster, Libonotus, Africus, Favonius, Argestes and Circius).

Temple of Mercury

On the north side of the square is the Temple of Mercury, dedicated to the god of trade. A ten-columned portico leads into the sanctuary, with three cellae – perhaps pointing to the worship of an African trinity of gods.

Market

On the south side of the square is the Market (Macellum), probably built in the 1st century A.D. and converted into a meat market at the end of the 2nd century. It was largely destroyed during the construction of the Byzantine fortress in the 6th century.

On the east side of the square are two dwelling-houses, the House of the Cupbearers (named after a mosaic found in the basement and now in the Bardo Museum in Tunis) and the House of the Steps.

Temple of Saturn

Arch of Severus Alexander

Capitol

Between the Place de la Rose des Vents and the Forum, on a high base, stands the Capitol, a temple dedicated to the Capitoline triad of Jupiter, Juno and Minerva. Built in A.D. 166 or 167, it is one of the finest and best preserved Roman temples in North Africa.

A monumental staircase leads up to the portico in front of the cella. All but one of the six Corinthian columns of the portico (four in front and two on the sides) are limestone monoliths. An inscription on the architrave gives the names of the donors of the temple and contains a dedication to the Emperors Marcus Aurelius and Lucius Verus. The badly weathered carving on the pediment depicts a man being carried upward by an eagle, perhaps symbolising the deification of the Emperor Antoninus Pius.

In the rear wall of the cella, which is almost square (13m/43ft by 14m/46ft), are three niches for statues of gods – a semicircular one in the middle for Jupiter, flanked by square niches for Juno and Minerva.

In the basement of the temple was an aisled crypt, which may have been used as a church. Here the excavators found the white marble head of the cult statue of Jupiter.

Forum

To the west of the temple is the Forum, laid out between A.D. 14 and 37, which is of modest size (38.5m/126ft long by 24m/79ft wide). It was originally surrounded on three sides by porticoes of red-veined marble columns with Corinthian capitals of white marble. Opening off it were a number of public buildings.

In the 6th century the Forum, the Capitol and the Temple of Saturn were all incorporated in a Byzantine fortress with two added towers, built with stone taken from surrounding buildings.

Arch of Severus Alexander

North-west of the Forum is the Arch of Severus Alexander, known in Arabic as Bab er Roumia (Gate of the Christian Woman). It was erected about 223–235, probably to celebrate the granting of further privileges to the city.

Temple of Caelestis

Cisterns

Beyond this can be seen the Ain el Hammam cistern, with five basins, each 33m/108ft long by 5m/16ft high, with a total capacity of 6000 cubic metres/1.3 million gallons of water.

150m/165yds north is the Ain Mizeh cistern, with seven basins and a total capacity of 9000 cubic metres/2 million gallons. From here water – brought in an aqueduct from a spring 12km/7½ miles west of the town – was distributed to the town's baths and fountains and to some private houses.

Temple of Minerva

Little is left of the Temple of Minerva, built between A.D. 138 and 161, or of the nearby pre-Roman town walls. Also in this area are a number of Roman tombs and prehistoric dolmens.

Circus

Beyond the Temple of Minerva is the 170m/185yd long Circus, constructed in A.D. 204 in a natural hollow in the ground. Although it has been excavated, there is little to see.

Temple of Juno Caelestis

On the way back to the starting-point of the tour we pass the Temple of Juno Caelestis, the Roman equivalent of the Punic goddess Tanit. Its semicircular layout recalls the crescent moon which was the commonest symbol for Tanit.

Built between 222 and 235 by Julius Gabinius and his wife Julia Gabinia Venusta, the peripteral temple is surrounded by a semicircular portico which itself is enclosed by a semicircular wall. The basin for ritual purification lay between the ring wall and a subsidiary building to the east of the temple precinct.

On the north side of the temple is an apse, constructed when it was converted into a church.

Below the temple are the Exedra of Juno Regina, a small oratory and the Columbarium of the Remii, a Roman family tomb of the 2nd/3rd century A.D.

◀ *Capitoline temple, Dougga*

Summer Baths

At the south-west corner of the site, near the Ain Doura spring, are the so-called Summer Baths.

Temple of Tellus

Below the Forum is a temple (probably built in A.D. 261) dedicated to Tellus, a fertility goddess. In three niches in the cella wall can be seen statues of Tellus, Pluto and Ceres.

Dar el Acheb

South-west of this is a building known as Dar el Acheb, thought to be a temple built in A.D. 164–166, with a rectangular doorway leading into a walled courtyard.

Villas

On the paved road running east are a number of villas, once sumptuously appointed, which are named after the mosaics found in them (now in the Bardo National Museum in Tunis). Built in the mid 3rd century A.D., they were laid out on a plan commonly found in North Africa. A doorway in the windowless wall facing the street led into a vestibule, beyond which were the main rooms in the house, preceded by porticoes. In large houses the rooms looked out into a garden; in smaller ones they were built round an inner courtyard or patio (peristyle). In summer the cooler rooms in the basement were used, in winter the upper floors. This method of construction, found also in Bulla Regia (see entry), was particularly well suited to the sloping site of Dougga.

The house known from its inscription as "Omnia tibi felicia" ("May all good fortune be yours"), with rooms laid out round a small peristyle, may have been the municipal brothel. Opposite it is the House of Dionysus and Odysseus, one of the best preserved villas in Dougga.

Beyond this are the House of the Labyrinth and the House of the Three Masks. Farther south is the House of the Trifolium (so called from its clover-leaf plan), thought to have been the largest private house in the town, of which only the lower rooms survive.

Baths of the Cyclopes

Adjoining the House of the Trifolium is the complex of buildings known as the Baths of the Cyclopes, with vaulted rooms in the basement. On the

Latrines

Baths of Licinius

south side of the complex are the baths proper, in the frigidarium of which was a mosaic of the Cyclopes (now, like the others, in the Bardo National Museum).
A feature of the baths is the well preserved public latrine (entered from a side street), with twelve seats on a horseshoe-shaped bench and a drainage system feeding into the town's main drain.

Arch of Septimius Severus

The Arch of Septimius Severus (5m/16ft wide) was erected in A.D. 205 to mark the town's promotion to the status of *municipium,* which carried with it the right to its own constitution, administration and civic law. The arch leads into the road from Carthage to Theveste (Tébessa).

Mausoleum of Ateban

The Mausoleum of Ateban, in the valley, is the only surviving Numidian/Punic structure in Tunisia. (Another was recently discovered at Sabratha in Libya.) The monument was almost completely destroyed in 1842, when the British consul in Tunis extracted from it a bilingual inscription on the façade. It was rebuilt by a French archaeologist in 1910.
The three-storey monument, 21m/69ft high, was built about the middle of the 2nd century A.D. for Ateban, a contemporary of Masinissa, son of Jepmatath and grandson of Palu. The bilingual inscription in Punic and Numidian (now in the British Museum) made it possible to decipher the Libyan script devised by the Numidians – an early form of the Tifinagh script which is still used by the Touareg of the Sahara.
The form of the monument with its relief decoration shows Hellenistic and Egyptian influences. A six-stepped substructure supports a square plinth with pilasters topped by Aeolic capitals at the corners. The tomb chamber was entered through two windows which were closed by stone panels. Above this are three steps bearing the second storey, which is articulated by fluted Ionic semi-columns. A further three steps lead up to the third storey, at the corners of which stood equestrian statues. The final stage is a pyramidal roof.
From here a road runs past the House of Gorgo to the Baths of Licinius.

Baths of Licinius

The Baths of Licinius, or Winter Baths, were built about 260 and rebuilt in the 4th century. So far as the sloping site permitted they were laid out on the usual symmetrical plan. On the north side was the almost exactly square entrance hall, surrounded by a colonnade of twelve columns supporting a "tube vault" of the kind found at Bulla Regia (see entry). The walls were faced with marble and the floor was decorated with a mosaic.
A small vestibule led into the richly decorated frigidarium (cold room) in the centre of the complex. Diametrically opposite the entrance hall was the palaestra, also surrounded by a colonnade. From the frigidarium the bather entered the tepidarium (warm bath) to the north and beyond this the caldarium (hot bath), heated by an under-floor hypocaust. Other rooms included a latrine and the sudatorium (sweat bath).

Temple of Concord

Beyond the main entrance to the baths are the temples of Concord, Frugifer (Pluto) and Liber Pater (Dionysus/Bacchus), built between A.D. 128 and 138 by wealthy citizens of the town.
At the south-east corner can be seen a small theatre, originally roofed, which was unfortunately obstructed by a later town wall.

Surroundings of Dougga

Mustis

Mustis lies 12km/7½ miles south-west of Dougga on GP 5 (Medjez el Bab to Le Kef). Marius is believed to have settled native veterans here at the end of the 2nd century B.C., after his victory over Jugurtha. Lying on the trade route between Carthage and Theveste (Tébessa), the town prospered and was raised (probably by Caesar) to the status of a *municipium.* There were triumphal arches at both ends of the town; the one at the east end is well preserved.

The tour of the site begins at the remains of a temple of Apollo, adjoining which is a temple of Ceres. A paved road leads to the scanty remains of a Roman house. Beyond this is an oil press, and to the east the remains of a temple of Pluto. Opposite the foundations of a three-aisled Byzantine basilica are the ruins of a Byzantine fortress, built with stones from Roman structures.

Le Kef

30km/20 miles south-west: see entry

Ain Tounga

See Testour, Surroundings

Testour

22km/14 miles north-east: see entry

Douz

See Kebili, Surroundings

El Djem

D 7/8

Governorate: Mahdia
Altitude: 110m/360ft
Population: 12,000

Access

El Djem lies on GP 1, half way between Sousse (63km/39 miles) and Sfax (64km/40 miles), some 210km/130 miles south of Tunis. Daily rail connections with Sousse/Tunis and Sfax and with Gabès and Gafsa–Metlaoui–Tozeur; regular bus services to and from Sousse, Mahdia and Sfax.

Situation and characteristics

The little market town of El Djem lies in the Tunisian Sahel between Sousse in the north and Sfax in the south. The town's great landmark is the amphitheatre, the largest Roman building in North Africa, whose walls rise high above the surrounding houses. From whatever direction you approach El Djem, the amphitheatre is the first thing that catches your eye. There is a busy market here every Monday. During the summer musical performances are given in the amphitheatre.

History

There was a Punic settlement here in the 3rd century B.C., but it became a place of some importance only when Caesar, after landing at Ruspina (now Monastir), founded the Roman town of Thysdrus on the site in 46 B.C. The town lay on an important road and in the centre of a large olive-growing region; and since olive oil was in great demand in Rome at that period – both as a foodstuff and as fuel and in the manufacture of soap and cooking essences – the town rapidly prospered. In the reign of Hadrian (2nd c. A.D.) it was the leading olive-growing centre in the whole of North Africa, and its olive-trees were famed both for their above-average yield and the high quality of the olives. With a population of between 20,000 and 30,000, the town accumulated enormous wealth, much of which – as in other Roman towns – was spent on the erection of both public buildings and private houses.

The amphitheatre, begun at the end of the 2nd century A.D., was designed to be a symbol of this prosperity; but while it was still under construction the decline of Thysdrus set in. The occasion for this decline was the reintroduction of the tax on olive oil in A.D. 238, sparking off a rebellion which spread throughout Tunisia. A group of large landowners, with the help of the *juvenes* (a kind of officers' training corps or militia), murdered the imperial procurator, the chief financial official in the province, and proclaimed an 80-year-old proconsul, Gordian, as Emperor. The rising was repressed and the town sacked. Thysdrus never recovered from this blow, and predominance passed to Sufetula (Sbeitla). Later the amphitheatre

Amphitheatre, El Djem

was converted into a fortress, and in 699 it served as a refuge for the Berber leader El Kahina (see Famous People) during her fight against the Arab invaders. After their victory the town was abandoned, and the site was reoccupied only during the French colonial period.

Sights

**Amphitheatre

The Amphitheatre, in the centre of the town, is known as the African Colosseum – and with some reason, for it is the fourth largest amphitheatre in the Roman world, coming after the Colosseum in Rome, the amphitheatre at Pozzuoli, near Naples, and the one at Carthage, of which little now survives.

Oval in form, the amphitheatre is 149m/486ft long by 122m/400ft across (compared with the Colosseum's measurements of 188m/617ft by 156m/512ft). It is also of impressive height (40m/130ft) – a height which would be still further increased by the canvas sails (*vela*) which protected the audience from the sun. It provided seating for over 30,000 (according to some estimates 60,000) spectators of the sporting events, bloody gladiatorial contests and slaughters of criminals by wild animals which were staged in the arena. It was thus too big for a town the size of Thysdrus, and was evidently intended as a demonstration of the city's power and prosperity. Although the amphitheatre was used for centuries as a quarry of building stone it is better preserved than the Colosseum in Rome. Restoration work was carried out in the 1970s, and has recently been resumed.

Only two-thirds of the circuit of walls with their three storeys of arcades have survived. The north-west side was blown up in 1695 on the orders of the Turkish Bey, Mohammed, to prevent it from being used as a stronghold by Berber rebels, who had frequently entrenched themselves within its walls.

Each of the three storeys originally had 30 arches, of which there remain a total of 68.

Roman mosaics in the Museum, El Djem

Little is left of the tiers of seating in the interior, but under the arena (which measures 65m/213ft by 37m/121ft) can be seen the two intersecting underground passages (excavated in 1908) through which the wild animals and their victims entered the arena. On either side of the passages were cages for the animals and cells for the prisoners.
At the entrance is a flight of steps leading to the upper tiers of arcades, from which there are good general views of the amphitheatre and of the town.

*Archaeological Museum

Outside the town centre, on the road to Sfax (past the post office, on right), is the interesting Archaeological Museum (Musée Archéologique), which is open daily, except Monday, from 8.30am to noon and 2 to 5.30pm.
Round a colonnaded courtyard are fragments of sculpture and terracotta panels with relief decoration from the walls of Christian churches. Within the museum itself are displays of small Roman objects (terracottas, oil lamps, coins, etc.) and a number of very fine mosaics with geometric, plant and animal decoration from the villas of wealthy landowners. Among them are two lions tearing a wild boar to pieces and a tiger attacking two wild asses (both 2nd c.). Numbers of fine mosaics from El Djem are now in the Bardo National Museum in Tunis.

Other excavations

Immediately beyond the museum is the excavation site. The best of the mosaics found here are now in the museum, but some have been left in situ, for example in the House of the Peacock (Maison du Paon), a huge villa with shops along the front, and the House of Sollertiana.
On the opposite side of the street, beyond the railway, are a small amphitheatre of the 1st century B.C. and another which has not yet been excavated.
Adjoining the amphitheatres are other remains of ancient Thysdrus, including residential quarters on the west side of the town, a circus measuring 500m/550yds by 100m/110yds (located by air photography but not yet excavated), 2nd century baths and the remains of sumptuous Roman villas.

These sites are, however, open only to visitors with a special archaeological interest.

Ellès

See Maktar, Surroundings

Foum Tataouine

See Médenine, Surroundings

Gabès

F 7

Chief town of the governorate of Gabès
Altitude: 0–40m/0–130ft
Population: 65,000

Access

Gabès is on GP 1 (Sfax–Médenine), 405km/252 miles south of Tunis. Rail connections with Sfax, Sousse and Tunis; station in Rue Mongi Slim. Bus services to and from Sfax, Sousse, Tunis, Kairouan, Médenine/Foum Tataouine, Gafsa, Tozeur, Kebili/Douz, Matmata, Djorf/Djerba and Ben Gardane/Tripoli; bus station (Gare Routière) on the norh-west side of the town (Sfax road).

Situation and characteristics

Gabès (Arabic Kabis), the "gateway to the South", lies on the Gulf of Gabès, known in antiquity as Syrtis Minor. To the north are the fringes of the fertile Sahel, to the south lies the coastal zone known as the Littoral, merging on the landward side into the semi-desertic Djeffara plain which extends to the Libyan frontier.
Gabès, an amalgamation of the two old villages of Djara to the north and Menzel to the south, is the chief town of a long coastal oasis in which there are nine other settlements. Within the oasis are more than half a million date palms and extensive plantations of fruit-trees (apricots, figs, olives, pomegranates). Its water comes from the oued which rises 10km/6 miles away and from artesian wells.
The town's economy depends not only on agriculture and fisheries but also increasingly on the large industrial plants established in recent years round the New Harbour to the north of the town (phosphate works, oil refinery, cement factory). The principal exports from the Old Harbour are local agricultural products. Other important sources of income are the traditional crafts of carpet-making, basketwork and jewellery.
Thanks to the town's mild climate, even in winter, and to the attractions offered by the oasis and the magnificent sandy beaches there has been a considerable development of the tourist trade in recent years. There are musical and folk festivals in July and August, and the local holy man, Sidi Boulbaba, is commemorated at the end of Ramadan, the month of fasting.

History

The Phoenicians established a trading post on this site between the steppe country, the desert and the sea, with a source of fresh water nearby. Thanks to its situation at the intersection of the caravan routes from the Sahara and the coastal road to the north the settlement rapidly prospered. Under the Romans it became the Colonia Tacapae. Soon, however, its situation turned from an advantage into a disadvantage, when successive conquerors passed through the area on their way to North Africa. Peace returned only in the 7th century under Arab rule, when Sidi Boulbaba, Mohammed's barber, settled in the town.
During the Middle Ages Gabès enjoyed a second period of prosperity as a trading centre for caravans from the interior of the continent. Under the

A spice stall in the souk

Fishing harbour, Gabès

French protectorate it was overshadowed by the more northerly towns of Sfax and Sousse.

In the Second World War Gabès, lying between the German and Allied fronts (the Mareth Line), suffered frequent bombing and heavy destruction. Its economy recovered with the development of industrialisation, and Gabès is now the leading industrial centre in southern Tunisia.

Sights

The town

Gabès is predominantly a modern town. After a stroll along Avenue Habib Bourguiba, the main shopping and business street, and a visit to the Grande Jara, the souk quarter around the Great Mosque, it is worth looking in at the showrooms of ONAT (Organisation Nationale de l'Artisanat Tunisien), with its demonstration of carpet-making and its display of craft products for sale.

To the north of the oued lies the old quarter known as Petite Jara, with the 11th century Mosque of Sidi Driss (restored 1972) and the camping site.

From Avenue Habib Bourguiba its continuation, Avenue Habib Thameur, descends to the harbour.

Mosque of Sidi Boulbaba

Gabès's principal sight is the Mosque of Sidi Boulbaba, situated on a hill to the left of the Matmata road, on the south-western outskirts of the town. Here too is the tomb of Sidi Boulbaba, the Prophet Mohammed's barber, who retired to Gabès in the 7th century. The walls of the courtyard (which visitors may enter) are decorated with beautiful tiles and bands of inscriptions.

Immediately adjoining is the former Koranic school (medersa), which now houses a small folk museum.

Museum

The museum (Musée des Arts et Traditions Populaires), open daily from 9am to noon and 2 to 5pm, has an interesting collection which includes everyday objects, traditional woven fabrics, local costumes and a bride's dress, jewellery and trousseau, as well as Punic, Roman and Byzantine antiquities.

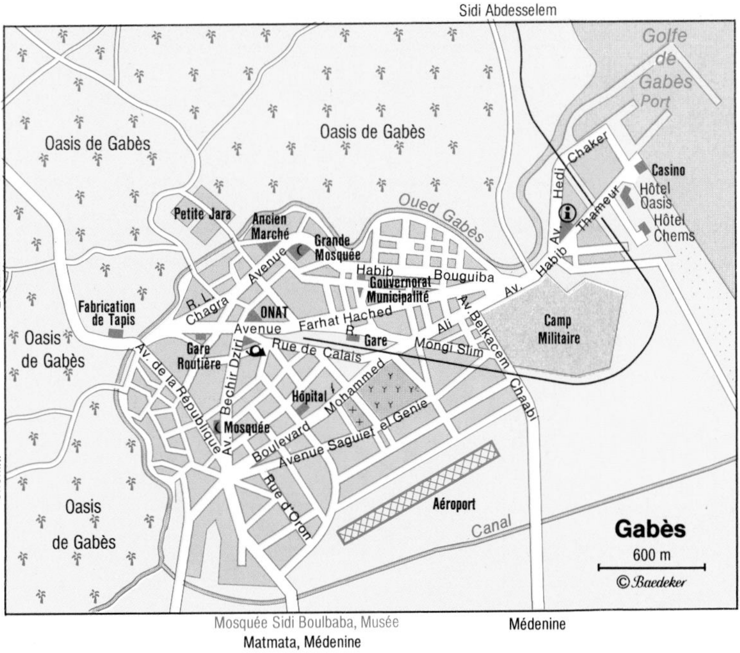

*The Oasis

Every visitor should drive through the extensive oasis to the north and west of the town, in which there are a number of small settlements.

The trip can be done by car, but a more leisurely form of transport is a horse-drawn carriage (*calèche),* which can be hired at the entrance to the town, near the bus station. To avoid any misunderstanding the fare should be agreed before setting out.

The water supply for the oasis, which covers an area of some 2000 hectares/5000 acres, comes from the Oued Gabès and numerous artesian wells. Serious difficulties have arisen, however, as a result of the low rainfall of recent years and the heavy consumption of water by industry. The water table has fallen markedly and it has been necessary to draw water from a depth of several hundred metres.

This is the only oasis in North Africa lying directly on the sea. The resultant high humidity of the air reduces the yield of the date-palms (the sap of which is fermented to produce a palm-wine known as *laghmi*) and the quality of the dates, and accordingly the economy of the oasis depends mainly on its market gardens and fruit orchards. This was also the case in Roman times, as Pliny the Elder reports in his "Natural History":

Sidi Boulbaba Mosque

"When you reach the Syrtes and Leptis Magna you come to an African city called Tacapae. . . In the shadow of the tall palms grows the olive, under the olive the fig-tree, below this the pomegranate and the vine, and under the vines corn and vegetables; one plant grows in the shade of another, and all bear fruit in the same year."

The picture is still basically the same as in Roman times. The market gardens and fruit orchards are mostly in the centre of the oasis, while the date-palms are concentrated mainly on the fringes. The principal horticultural crops are vegetables, tobacco, pepper, grapes, indigo, pumpkins, bananas and melons; the main types of fruit are peaches, apricots, pomegranates, olives and citrus fruits.

Chenini du Gabès

The most visited of the oasis villages is Chenini du Gabès (4km/2½ miles west of Gabès), which is famed for its beautiful basketwork. It is reached by leaving Gabès on the Sfax road, turning left just before the bridge over the Oued Gabès and thereafter following the signposts.

On the outskirts of Chenini we come to the so-called Barrage Romain, a storage reservoir which regulates the flow of the Oued Gabès. There is believed to have been a dam here in Roman times, and this may have yielded the large blocks of dressed stone used in the present dam. Here too is a small zoo of desert animals, including gazelles, crocodiles and various species of birds.

Above the reservoir, easily reached on foot, is the Chela Club Hotel, with a fine view from the plateau over the treetops of the oasis.

Surroundings of Gabès

El Hamma du Gabès

27km/17 miles west of Gabès is the oasis of El Hamma du Gabès, with a number of villages. The hot sulphurous springs (46°C/115°F) were already frequented in Roman times, when the "spa" of Aquae Tacapitanae was founded. There are remains of Roman basins. Market day is Wednesday.

Cave dwellings, Matmata

*Matmata

45km/28 miles south of Gabès is Matmata, the best known and most visited troglodytic village in Tunisia. It is reached on MC 107, which runs via Matmata Nouvelle to the site of the underground dwellings.

The little town (pop. 3000) lies on the eastern slopes of the Dahar uplands (see Médenine) at a height of 650m/2130ft. Matmata Nouvelle, founded only in the 1960s, is now the centre of the region, with shops, a school, a post office and a petrol station.

15km/9 miles beyond Matmata Nouvelle is the cratered landscape of the old troglodytic village, most of which is now uninhabited. The inhabitants of the village sought shelter from the sun by constructing their curious underground cave dwellings (see sketch on page 81). They first excavated a circular pit some 12m/40ft in diameter and between 6 and 12m (20 and 40ft) deep, round which living quarters (usually two-storied), store-rooms, granaries and stalls for animals were hewn from the rock. In this central courtyard, which was entered through a sloping tunnel and was used in common by the members of the extended family, was the oven (*tabouna*) for baking bread. Some of these underground dwellings have been converted into simple hotels; others now house small museums.

The population live by agriculture. Rainwater is collected in ponds formed by the damming of depressions in the ground and distributed in small channels to the surrounding plantations of olives, dates, figs and corn. There is a good general view of the area from the hill to the west.

Warning

Visitors should not attempt to drive on their own to Douz (100km/60 miles south-west). Long stretches of sand interrupted by oueds makes this a difficult and potentially dangerous journey.

The hill road to Médenine (61km/38 miles) is recommended only for experienced drivers with all-terrain vehicles.

Médenine and Foum Tataouine are good bases for further excursions (see Médenine).

Tamezret

10km/6 miles west, commandingly situated on a hill, is the Berber village of Tamezret.

Médenine

73km/45 miles south: see entry

Gafsa

E 5

Chief town of the governorate of Gafsa
Altitude: 325m/1065ft
Population: 61,000

Access

Gafsa lies at the intersection of a number of important roads: GP 15 from Kasserine; GP 3, coming from Kairouane and continuing to Tozeur; GP 14 from Sfax; and GP 15 from Gabès. It is 146km/91 miles north-west of Gabès, 106km/66 miles south of Kasserine and 93km/58 miles north-east of Tozeur.
Rail connections with Metlaoui/Tozeur, Gabès and Sfax/Sousse/Tunis; station (Gafsa-Gare) 3km/2 miles south-east on the Gabès road.
Bus services to and from Metlaoui, Tozeur, Nefta, Kairouan/Tunis, Sfax and Gabès; bus station (Gare Routière) in the town centre.

Situation and characteristics

Gafsa, situated on the border between the steppe country and the desert, is the principal commercial and communications centre of south-western Tunisia. It lies in a large upland oasis with some 300,000 date-palms, huge plantations of olive-trees and artificially irrigated fruit orchards and vineyards.
Nearby are large deposits of phosphates and iron ore.
The town's economy is centred on the marketing of agricultural produce and the production of woven fabrics in traditional designs. Many families live by making and selling fine carpets and white-and-red striped woollen blankets, and many men find employment in the phosphate mines at Metlaoui (see entry), 42km/26 miles east. There is a large market on Tuesdays.

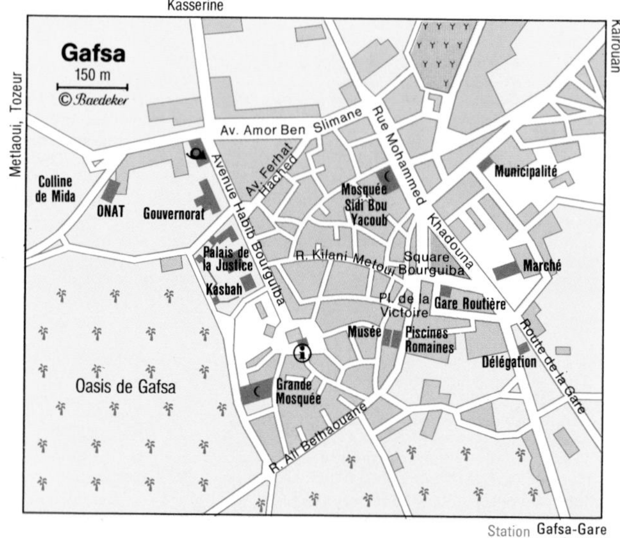

Roman pool

History

The Gafsa area was already settled by man in the 8th millennium B.C. The culture of that period is known as Capsian (from Capsa, the Latin name for Gafsa), after the type site on Djebel Assalah (3km/2 miles from the town). In the 2nd century B.C. there was a Numidian settlement here, which was conquered and destroyed by Marius in 106 B.C. The town was refounded under the Roman Empire and developed into an important garrison town and spa. In the reign of Trajan it was given the status of a *colonia*. In 540 it was fortified by the Byzantines and renamed Justiniania. It was again destroyed by the Arabs in 680 and thereafter was slow to recover. The old Kasbah, built by the Hafsids in 1434, was captured by the Turkish corsair Dragut (see Famous People) in 1556.

The discovery of phosphate deposits in the early 20th century brought a rapid economic upswing. The phosphates are now processed in Gafsa, Sfax and Gabès to produce artificial fertilisers, fluorine and phosphoric acid.

In the Second World War the town suffered severe destruction during fighting between German and Allied forces. In 1980 it was the target of a guerrilla attack, allegedly supported by Libya, in an attempted coup d'état.

Sights

After the destruction it suffered during the Second World War Gafsa was rebuilt with wide avenues and spacious squares and is now a town of mainly modern aspect, with few remains of the Roman period.

Square Bourguiba

The focal point of Gafsa is Square Bourguiba on the east side of the town, with numerous shops and cafés flanking the gardens in the centre. On the north-east side of the square (which is actually triangular) runs Rue Mohammed Khadouna, and on the west side is the smaller Place de la Victoire, the hub of the busy old town. Parallel to Rue Mohammed Khadouna on the west side of the town is Avenue Habib Bourguiba, lined with government offices and public buildings.

Kasbah

In Avenue Habib Bourguiba is the Kasbah, built in 1434 by the Hafsid ruler Abou Abdallah Mohammed on the foundations of a Byzantine fortress. It was badly damaged in 1943 when a German ammunition depot exploded, but it has now been restored to its original appearance. Incorporated in it is a new building housing the Law Courts (Palais de Justice).

*Roman Pools

At the south-east end of Avenue Habib Bourguiba can be found Gafsa's principal tourist sight, the Roman Pools (Piscines Romaines). There are two 4m/13ft deep pools linked by a small tunnel and fed by thermal springs at a temperature of 25°C/77°F. The massive blocks of dressed stone of which the pools are constructed date from the Roman period, and some of them bear inscriptions. When there are any tourists about the local children jump into the pools from the top of the walls or from the surrounding palm-trees in the expectation of a suitable reward. In the water live blue-lipped mouth-breeders (cichlids), a species of fish which incubate their eggs in their mouths.

Beside the larger of the two pools stands the old Turkish Bey's Palace, with arcading borne on columns with antique capitals.

Museum

Adjoining the Roman Pools is a small museum displaying Roman mosaics, partly originals and partly large-scale reproductions of mosaics in the museums of Sousse and Tunis (see entries).

Great Mosque

A short distance south-west of the Roman Pools through the narrow streets of the rebuilt old town is the Great Mosque (Grande Mosquée), its minaret a prominent landmark. Originally dating from the 14th century, it was rebuilt in the 1960s. The ground-plan, with 19 aisles, each of five bays, is reminiscent of the Sidi Oqba Mosque in Kairouan. The prayer hall has numerous antique columns, blue tile decoration and a beautifully carved minbar (pulpit).

From the minaret there are fine views of the town, the oasis and the hills to the north.

ONAT

On the west side of the town, just off the Tozeur road, is the ONAT (Organisation Nationale de l'Artisanat Tunisien) shop, with demonstrations of weaving.

Surroundings of Gafsa

Oasis

The Gafsa oasis, consisting of three large groves of date-palms, encircles the town on the south, east and west. Because of the local climate the dates are of inferior quality and are used only as animal fodder. The more important crops are fruit (apricots, oranges, lemons), figs, vines and vegetables.

Lalla

The Lalla oasis, 7km/4½ miles south-east, is scenically the most attractive. It is reached by leaving Gafsa on the Gabès road and taking a road on the left immediately after crossing the railway. Above the Oued Melah is a small café from which there is a fine view of the oasis.

Mida Hill

The best view of the town and the oasis is from the Mida Hill, which is reached from the Tozeur road.

El Guettar

El Guettar is a small oasis village 18km/11 miles south of Gafsa on the Chott el Guettar. The palm-groves here, which yield high-quality dates, are still

Crystal-clear water in the Roman pool

Great Mosque

irrigated by the traditional *foggaras*, otherwise found only in the Nefzaoua oases on the south-east side of the Chott el Djerid (see drawing, page 42). The water flows through underground channels, the line of which is marked by a series of vertical shafts, with a built-up mound of earth at the point where the channel emerges from underground. The advantage of this system is the reduction in the amount of water lost by evaporation. Many of the underground channels, however, are now blocked.

Sidi Ahmed Zarrouk

6km/4 miles north-west, off the Tozeur road, is the little oasis of Sidi Ahmed Zarrouk, with thermal baths (sulphurous water) and a hotel.

Seldja Gorge

50km/30 miles west: see Metlaoui, Surroundings

Upland oases

Gafsa is a good base from which to visit the upland oases of Chebika, Tamerza and Midès (see Tozeur, Surroundings).

Tozeur

93km/58 miles south-west: see entry

Nefta

113km/70 miles south-west: see entry

Sbeitla

144km/89 miles north is the site of Roman Sufetula: see Sbeitla.

Gightis

See Djerba, Surroundings

Haidra

C 5

Governorate: Kasserine
Altitude: 900m/2950ft

Haidra

Access

GP 17 (Le Kef–Kasserine). Turn off at the mining town of Kalaa Khasba (formerly called Kalaa Djerda) into GP 4, which leads west towards the Algerian frontier and in 18km/11 miles comes to Haidra.
Kalaa Khasba is the terminus of a railway line from Tunis; irregular bus services from there to Haidra.

Situation and characteristics

The site of ancient Ammaedara lies at a height of 900m/2950ft near the Algerian frontier. The present frontier village of Haidra dates only from the end of the Second World War.

History

The Berber settlement of Ammaedara, strategically situated on the main roads between Carthage and Hadrumetum (Sousse) on the one hand and between Carthage and Theveste (Tébessa) on the other, was taken over by the Romans, who established a military camp here, later to develop into a considerable town.
From the time of Augustus the famous Third Legion Augusta was stationed here to protect the frontiers of the province of Africa. In the reign of Vespasian the troops were moved farther west to Theveste, and Ammaedara became a colony of veterans under the style of Colonia Flavia Augusta Emerita Ammaedara.
Ammaedara is recorded in Byzantine times as the see of a bishop, and the town was involved in the conflict with the Donatists (see Religion). Around 540 a powerful Byzantine fortress was built. The reasons for the town's later decline are unknown. Because of its frontier situation there were recurrent plans to rebuild the fortress, and in 1840 the north wall was re-erected. Excavation of the site began in 1883 and has not yet been completed.

* Excavations

The road from Kalaa Khasba to Tébessa (in Algeria) cuts across the site. Parallel to it is the decumanus, running from east to west. The cardo runs at right angles to it from north to south, crosses the Oued Haidra and continues in the direction of Thelepte (see Kasserine, Surroundings).
The tour of the site described below starts at its east end.

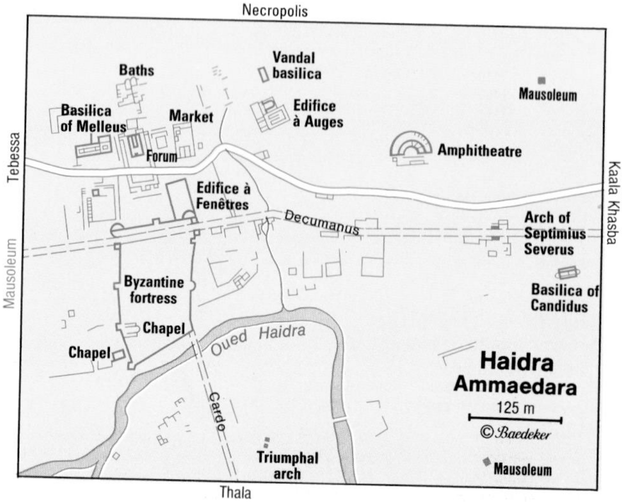

Arch of Septimius Severus

Basilica of Candidus

To the south of the decumanus is a three-aisled Christian basilica (4th–7th c.) known as the Basilica of Candidus or the Martyrs' Basilica, built over an earlier burial-ground. The outer walls, in *opus africanum* (see Glossary), were later reinforced by an additional inner wall. The delicate pavement mosaics from this church are now in the Bardo Museum in Tunis.

Arch of Septimius Severus

North-west of the basilica is the Arch of Septimius Severus (A.D. 195), which was later incorporated in the Byzantine fortress and as a result is well preserved. It stood on the decumanus, traces of which can be seen on the inner (west) side of the arch.
On the other side of the road are the scanty remains of a free-standing theatre (A.D. 299).
North-east of the theatre stands a two-storey mausoleum with a square base bearing a temple-like structure which has Corinthian pilasters on the corners.

Edifice à Auges

North-west of the theatre is the Edifice à Auges (Building of the Troughs). The ground-plan is similar to that of a basilica; the troughs suggest that it may have been a collecting-point for foodstuffs or possibly a posting station.

Immediately north of this building is a three-aisled Vandal basilica measuring 21m/70ft by 9m/30ft.

Byzantine fortress

On the south side of the road can be seen the remains of a once mighty Byzantine fortress built in the time of Justinian (527–565). The ground-plan was in the form of a parallelogram (200m/650ft by 110m/360ft), with four towers on the west side and one on the east side.

The north side was rebuilt in 1840; the south side was swept away by the Oued Haidra in a flash flood some years ago. The Roman road from Carthage to Theveste ran along the north side of the fortress; on the south side was a bridge over the river carrying the road to Thala and Thelepte.

East side of the Byzantine fortress

Within the fortress are the remains of a small chapel with a raised apse, and at its north-east corner the remains of a building with windows, the Edifice à Fenêtres.

Basilica of Melleus

North of the fortress, beyond the modern road, can be found the principal church of Ammaedara, the Basilica of Melleus (late 4th c.), the largest in the town (60m/200ft by 30m/100ft). Within the church the excavators found numerous tombs, including that of Bishop Melleus from whom it takes its name.

Immediately east of the basilica is the Roman forum, and beyond this is a barely traceable building which may possibly have been a market.

Surroundings of Haidra

Thala

GP 17, which runs south to Kasserine (see entry) through steppe country covered with esparto grass, passes the little town of Thala (pop. 4000), situated at an altitude of 1017m/3337ft.
At the entrance to the town, on both sides of the road, are scattered remains which may mark the site of Thala, mentioned by Sallust in his "Jugurthine War".

Hammamet B 7

Governorate: Nabeul
Altitude: 0–50m/0–165ft
Population: 20,000

Access

Hammamet, 63km/39 miles south-east of Tunis (70km/43 miles from the Tunis-Carthage international airport), is linked with the capital by motorway and by GP 1.

Rail connections with Tunis, Nabeul and Bir Bou Rekba (from which there are connections with Sousse and Sfax); the station is 1km/¾mile outside the town.
Bus services to and from Tunis, Nabeul, Sousse, Monastir, Mahdia, Kelibia and Kairouan.

Situation and *characteristics

Hammamet, picturesquely situated in its bay on the Cap Bon peninsula (see entry), is the original nucleus and the main centre of the Tunisian tourist trade. Together with Nabeul (see entry), 10km/6 miles north-east, this former fishing village now forms the largest seaside resort in the country. Its great attractions are its magnificent sandy beaches, with groves of oranges and lemons lying just inland, and its sheltered situation in the wind shadow of the long range of hills known as the Dorsale, an offshoot of which forms the backbone of the Cap Bon peninsula.
In summer there are dramatic performances and other cultural events.

The town

The old town, the Medina, lies on a rocky promontory jutting out into the Mediterranean, dominated by the high walls of the Kasbah which once protected the little fishing harbour. In spite of the influx of tourists it has managed to preserve its picturesque character and its charm.
North and south of the Medina are beautiful sandy beaches, fringed by well laid out parks and gardens in which are set the hotels built since the late sixties, now with a total of well over 16,000 beds. In spite of this rapid development, which is still continuing, the new buildings have taken account of traditional architectural styles and fit harmoniously into the landscape.

History

Hammamet occupies the site of a small Roman settlement named Pupput (Put Put), of which only scanty remains have survived. Although a fortress was built here in the 13th century, the town began to develop only two centuries later. In its early days it was a pirates' lair, but soon afterwards it fell into the hands of the Spaniards, who hunted down the pirates.
Thereafter Hammamet fell into oblivion, from which it emerged only in the late 19th and early 20th century, when the picturesque little fishing village was discovered by writers and artists, including Paul Klee, Gustave Flaub-

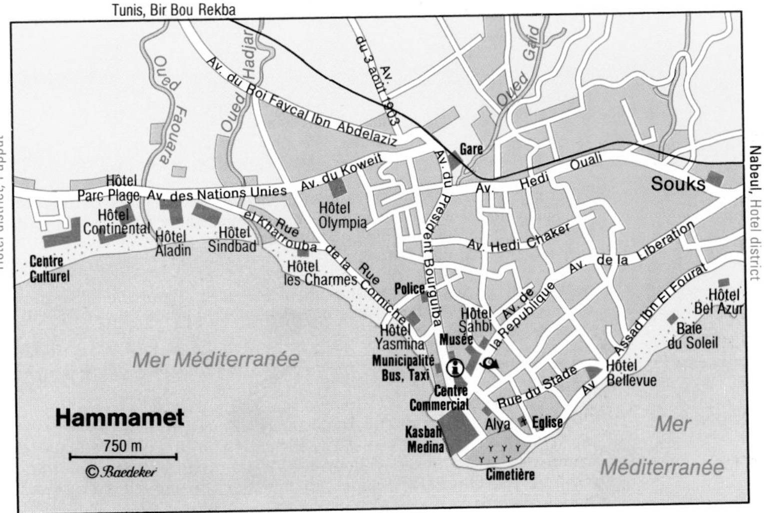

Fishing harbour, Hammamet

ert, August Macke, Guy de Maupassant, Oscar Wilde and André Gide. They were followed after the First World War by wealthy British, American and French visitors, who built themselves luxurious villas in Hammamet. Then the real boom began in the late sixties, when mass tourism came to Tunisia. Hammamet is now Tunisia's principal seaside resort, which during the main holiday season has almost as many visitors as native inhabitants.

Sights

*Medina

The little Medina, surrounded by 15th century walls, is a maze of narrow and sometimes covered lanes. The wares displayed in the souks are all designed to appeal to the tourists. The most popular articles, unfortunately rather over-priced, are embroidery, pottery, leather goods and carpets.

Great Mosque

Along side streets in the souks are the town's two mosques. The Great Mosque, with its old rectangular minaret, dates from the 15th century; it was restored in 1972. Adjoining is the Sidi Abdel Kader Mosque (1798), now used as a Koranic school.

Kasbah

The Kasbah is worth a visit for the sake of its small but interesting museum and above all for its fine views of the Medina, the new town and the picturesque fishing harbour.

Cemeteries

On the east side of the Medina are an old French cemetery and an Islamic cemetery.

Other sights

West and north of the Medina is the centre of modern Hammamet, from which the town's two main business and shopping streets, Avenue Habib Bourguiba and Avenue de la République, run north and east. At the junction of the two streets is the new shopping centre (Centre Commercial) opened in 1979.

View over the roofs of the Medina

Cultural Centre

In the southern hotel zone, beyond the Hotel Continental, is the International Cultural Centre (Centre Culturel International), housed in the sumptuous villa built in the 1920s by a wealthy Romanian named George Sebastian, the first millionaire to settle in Hammamet.
In July and August the beautiful grounds of the villa are the setting of an international festival of music and drama. The theatre, based on Greek and Roman models, was built in 1964 for the purposes of the festival.

Farther out, between the Samira Club and Tanfous Hotels, are the excavations of the Roman settlement of Pupput.

Surroundings of Hammamet

Hammamet is an excellent base for excursions in the surrounding area.

Cap Bon

A tour of the Cap Bon peninsula is strongly recommended (see Cap Bon).

Tunis

63km/39 miles north-west: see entry.

Thuburbo Majus

The magnificent Roman site of Thuburbo Majus (see entry) lies 80km/50 miles west of Hammamet.

Zaghouan

On the way to Thuburbo Majus it is worth stopping at Zaghouan (38km/24 miles west) to see the Roman nymphaeum (see Tunis, Surroundings).

Nabeul

10km/6 miles north-east of Hammamet is the neighbouring resort of Nabeul (see entry), with a small but interesting museum.

Dar Chaabane

See Nabeul, Surroundings

Beni Khiar

See Nabeul, Surroundings

Houmt-Souk

See Djerba

Lake Ichkeul

See Bizerte, Surroundings

Kairouan

C 7

Chief town of the governorate of Kairouan
Altitude: 60m/200ft
Population: 75,000

Access

Kairouan lies at the intersection of a number of main roads, 155km/96 miles south-west of Tunis (GP 3, Tunis–Kairouan), 97km/60 miles south-west of Hammamet (GP 1, Hammamet–Sousse; at Enfidaville GP 2 to Kairouan), 53km/33 miles west of Sousse (GP 12, Sousse–Kairouan) and 159km/99 miles north of Gabès (42km/26 miles on GP 1, Gabès–Sfax, then at La Skhira GP 2 to Kairouan).
No rail connections (goods station only).
Bus services to and from Tunis, Sousse, Maktar, Sbeitla, Gafsa, Gabès, Tozeur/Nefta and Le Kef; bus station (Gare Routière) on Sousse road.

Situation and **characteristics

Kairouan, the fourth holy city of Islam (after Mecca, Medina and Jerusalem), situated in desolate steppe country on the western edge of the Sahel, has preserved its purely Arab and Muslim aspect intact into modern times, and the walled Medina with its great mosques and other sacred buildings is one of the finest and most visited sights in the whole of the Maghreb. There is a busy market on Mondays.

Economy

As the chief Islamic centre in North Africa Kairouan draws millions of pilgrims and is one of Tunisia's leading tourist centres. The fifth largest town in Tunisia, it is famed for the woven and knotted carpets made here, mainly by women and children (see Practical Information, Carpets) and for a variety of other crafts (wood articles, brass and copperware, leather goods). Visitors can see and purchase a wide range of craft products in the showrooms of the government handicrafts organisation ONAT (Organisation Nationale de l'Artisanat Tunisien).

Kairouan itself has little water, and since its foundation supplies have had to be brought to the town from great distances. The surrounding plain, on the other hand, has a very high rainfall, mainly in winter. Dams have been built to the south-west of the town and on the Oued Zeroud, near Sidi Saad, and the water thus stored is used to irrigate the steppe country and meet the needs of agriculture, which takes the form of sheep-farming (there is a daily livestock market in Kairouan) and the growing of grain and fruit. The agricultural produce of the area is processed in a number of small factories.

Fantasia

A Fantasia (equestrian festival) is held annually in September at Sidi Ali ben Nasrallah.

History

In A.D. 671 Oqba ibn Nafi, commander of the Arab army which was thrusting into North Africa and since 670 governor of Ifriqiya, established his headquarters here in the middle of the steppe country. The site was chosen

Minaret of the Sidi Oqba Mosque ▶

on strategic grounds, for there was neither a Roman nor any earlier settle ment in this waterless area. It lay half way between Cap Bon and the Chott; the hills to the west provided protection from Berber raids, and the wide plain to the east offered security against surprise attacks by the Byzantines, who still controlled the coastal region.

Kairouan then became the base from which the victorious Islamic forces advanced westward through North Africa and into Spain. Its great days were in the 9th century, when the Aghlabids made it their capital; but this heyday did not last long, for the leading role in North Africa passed to Mahdia after its foundation in 916 and to Cairo after its conquest by the

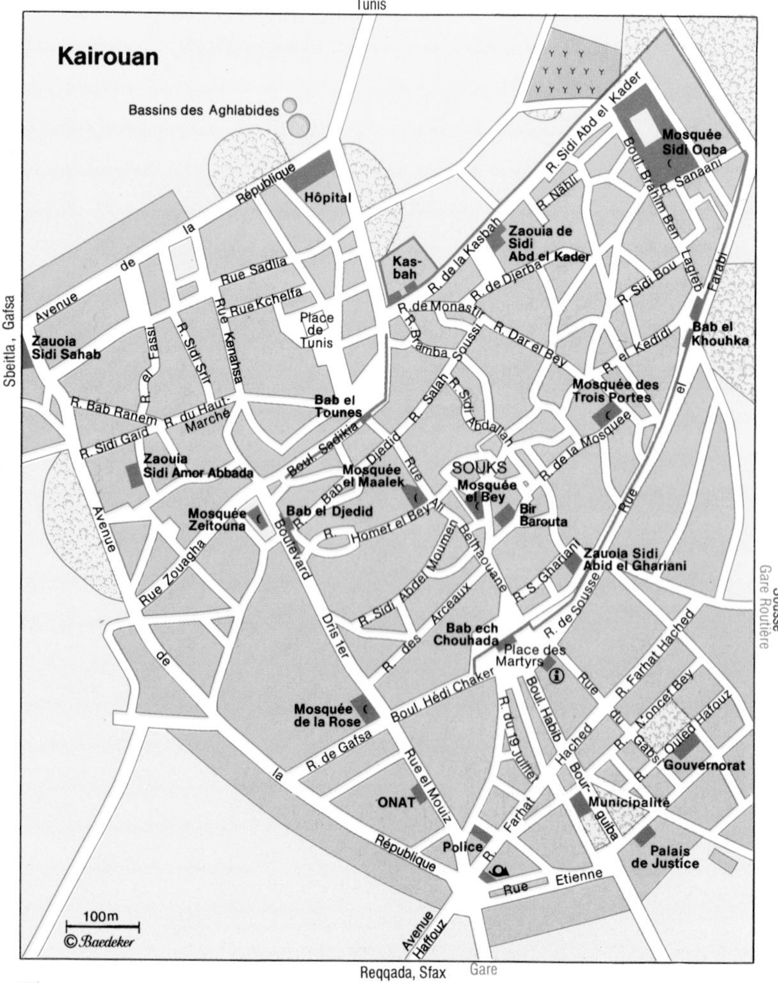

Fatimids in 973. Its final decline began with a raid by the Beni Hilal nomads, who sacked and destroyed Kairouan in 1057, though sparing the religious buildings.
In the 14th century the town was rebuilt by the Hafsids, and in the early 18th century it was extended by the Husseinites. Although Tunis was now the uncontested political capital of Tunisia, Kairouan retained its religious importance for the Muslims of North Africa; and seven pilgrimages to Kairouan are regarded as equivalent to the prescribed pilgrimage to Mecca.

The town

Kairouan's Medina (old town) is the best preserved in Tunisia. Some 1000m/1100yds long by 500m/550yds across, it is surrounded by a 3.5km/2 mile long circuit of brick walls 10m/33ft high, reinforced by numerous towers (wall-walk open for part of the way). The present walls were built by the Husseinites in 1706–12 on the foundations of earlier walls dating from 1052, and have been frequently restored since then. On the north and west sides of the Medina are a number of old-established outer districts (Gueblia, Djeblia, Zlass); the new town lies to the south.

Sights

New town

The main axis of the newer part of the town, which is smaller than in other Tunisian towns, is the Boulevard Habib Bourguiba, a busy pedestrian street lined by coffee-houses and souvenir shops which leads in a straight line to Bab ech Chouhada (Porte des Martyrs; 1772), originally called Bab el Jalladin, the Gate of the Leather-Dealers, which leads into the Medina; stones from ancient buildings can be seen built into the inner side of the gateway. In front of the gate is the Place Mohammed el Bejaoui or Place des Martyrs, on the near side of which, to the right, can be found the tourist information office (ONTT).

**Medina

This is the best starting-point for a tour of the Medina. Here visitors must obtain tickets for admission to the principal sights including the Zaouia of Sidi Abid el Ghariani, the Sidi Oqba Mosque, the Aghlabid Basins and the Zaouia of Sidi Sahab. Although (as in other mosques in Tunisia) non-Moslems are not allowed to enter the prayer hall of the Sidi Oqba Mosque visitors should make a point of going into the beautiful inner courtyard (open daily, except Friday afternoon and public holidays, 8am–12.30pm and 4.30–5.30pm, in winter 8am–12.30pm and 2.45–4.30pm). Other religious buildings are open daily 9am–6pm.
Tickets covering visits to all the main sights must be obtained from the ONTT office; no tickets are issued at the individual buildings. When buying tickets visitors are required to sign a declaration (the "annexe touristique") undertaking to respect the sacred buildings (to be suitably dressed, to avoid unnecessary noise or disturbance, not to smoke, not to enter the prayer hall in a mosque, etc.).

Zaouia of Sidi Abid el Ghariani

From Bab ech Chouhada the main street of the Medina, Rue Ali Belhaouane, runs straight ahead. A few yards along the second street on the right (Rue Sidi Ghariani) is the Zaouia of Sidi Abid el Ghariani, with the tomb of a holy man who lived in Kairouan in the 14th century. Notable features are the fine wood and stucco ceiling, the sumptuously decorated dome of the tomb and the inner courtyard with its beautiful arcades. This is due to become the headquarters of the Association de Sauvegarde de la Médina, which is concerned with the preservation and restoration of the old town. It is also planned to establish a museum of Arabic calligraphy, with a collection of inscribed gravestones of the 9th–11th centuries.

Another 100 yards along the main street of the souk, at the old-established Café Halfaouine, Rue des Cuirs goes off on the right. A few yards along this

In the Medina, Kairouan

Bir Barouta

street is the blue entrance door of the Bir Barouta, a 17th century draw-well on the upper floor of the building. Here a dromedary, its eyes bound, provides the motive power for a water-wheel which raises water in pottery jars. Originally the water was collected here and distributed in conduits to houses in the town. According to legend the well is connected by an underground channel with the Zemzem spring in Mecca. This is now a rather unhappy spectacle laid on for the benefit of tourists in quest of Oriental atmosphere.

Mosque of the Three Doors

Beyond Bir Barouta is Rue de la Mosquée, which runs north to the Mosque of the Three Doors (Mosquée des Trois Portes, Djemaa Tleta Bibane), one of the oldest buildings in Kairouan, founded by a learned man from Andalusia in 866. Its most notable feature is the façade, with the three doorways from which it takes its name and two friezes of Kufic inscriptions, the lower of which is dated to 1440. The minaret also dates from 1440.

Souks

Rue Ali Belhaouane continues through the souk quarter of the old town, built mainly in the 17th and 18th centuries and still occupied by practitioners of traditional crafts. After passing the El Bey Mosque (on the right) and the El Maalek Mosque (on the left) it comes to Bab el Tounès (1771), the Tunis Gate.

The other sights of old Kairouan are all within easy reach of Bab el Tounès. To the right, along the town walls, is the Kasbah (not open to the public). From here a street continues north along the inner side of the walls to the Sidi Oqba Mosque.

Sidi Oqba Mosque

The Sidi Oqba Mosque, or Great Mosque, stands at the north-east corner of the Medina, its massive minaret incorporated in the town walls. The oldest and most important Islamic building in North Africa and the model for all later Moorish sacred architecture, it was originally built by Oqba ibn Nafi, the Arab commander who founded Kairouan, in 672. After being pulled

Courtyard of Zaouia Ghariani

Mosque of the Three Doors

down, rebuilt, altered and enlarged on various occasions it was given its present form about 836, in the reign of the Aghlabid ruler Ziyadet Allah. Since then it has been frequently renovated, notably in 1025, 1294, 1618 and 1968–73. It originally stood in the centre of the town, but, as can be seen from the town plan, this has moved steadily south-westward.

The mosque covers an area 135m/443ft long by 80m/262ft wide. The entrance, on the west side, with the *midha* (room for ablutions), leads into the inner courtyard, off which open a number of doorways. In the form of a slightly irregular rectangle, it is surrounded on three sides by double-aisled colonnades of antique columns. Under the marble-paved courtyard, which slopes down gradually towards the centre, are cisterns for the storage of rainwater. At the north end is the minaret, at the south end the magnificent façade of the prayer hall. The vestibule, two bays deep, with a ribbed dome, dates from the 9th century.

Seventeen carved wooden doors give admission to the seventeen-aisled prayer hall. The central aisle, which is wider than the others, leads straight to the mihrab (prayer niche) on the qibla wall, along which extends a wide aisle. The bay in front of the mihrab is crowned by a dome, one of the oldest stone-built domes in North Africa. The prayer hall, measuring 80m/260ft by 40m/130ft, is a forest of columns with beautiful shafts and capitals from ancient buildings, some from as far afield as Carthage and Hadrumetum (Sousse). Including those in the courtyard, the mosque contains a total of 414 columns.

The mihrab marking the direction of Mecca (though later measurements have shown that it is 30° off the true line) is faced with fine faience tiles, given a metallic sheen by the addition of metal oxides to the glaze – a process not known in the west when the tiles were imported from Baghdad in 862. The rear wall is clad with 28 decorated marble slabs measuring 60cm/2ft by 45cm/18in. The round-headed arch over the mihrab is borne on marble columns. To the right of the mihrab is the wooden minbar (pulpit), decorated with the finest intarsia work, which also dates from the 9th

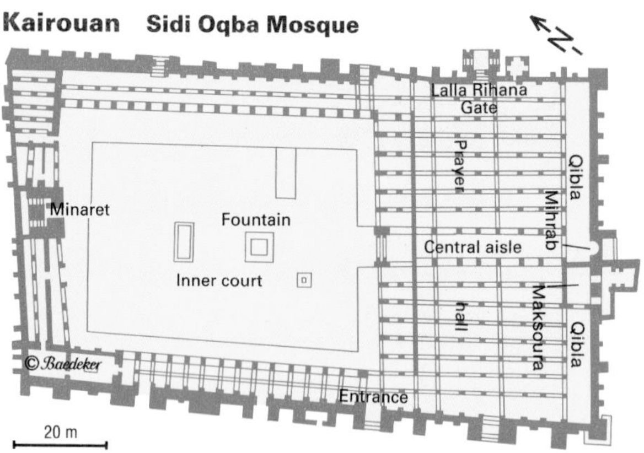

century and is thus the oldest surviving minbar in the whole Islamic world. (There are a reproduction and photographs of it in the Islamic Museum: see below.) The maqsura (the screen behind which the ruler could participate in worship) is a masterpiece of carving (1022).

Although non-Muslims have since 1972 been banned from entering the prayer hall, it may be possible to get a glimpse of the interior through an open door.

Minaret

The 35m/115ft high minaret was built in 724–728, and is thus not only the oldest part of the building but the oldest minaret in North Africa. Its three successively smaller sections are decorated with crenellations, blind arcades and open arches. The third section carries the ribbed dome added in the 13th century, which to mark the importance of the mosque is topped by three copper spheres. A staircase of 128 steps leads up to the top; some of the steps are formed of early Christian gravestones, symbolising the triumph of Islam over Christianity.

Lalla Rihana Gate

On the east side of the mosque, leading directly into the prayer hall, is the Lalla Rihana Gate (named after a local holy woman), a square structure in Hispano-Mauresque style (1294) projecting from the massive mosque walls.

There is a good view of the mosque and the Medina from the town walls opposite the minaret.

200m/220yds north of the Sidi Oqba Mosque, outside the town walls, is a large cemetery.

Aghlabid Basins

To the north of the Kasbah, beyond the Avenue de la République, are the Aghlabid Basins (restored 1969). These two pools (originally there were more) stored water for the Aghlabid palace which occupied the site of the present-day cemetery.

The water was brought by an aqueduct from Djebel Cherichera, 36km/22 miles away. The smaller basin (17-sided, 37m/121ft in diameter) was a settling tank, from which the water flowed into the larger one (48-sided, 128m/420ft in diameter, 10m/33ft deep), which had a capacity of 50,000cu.m/11 million gallons.

In the centre of the larger pool is the base of a pavilion in which the Aghlabid rulers used to relax.

Another pool has been discovered farther to the west.

Courtyard of Sidi Oqba Mosque

Zaouia Sidi Sahab (Barber's Mosque)

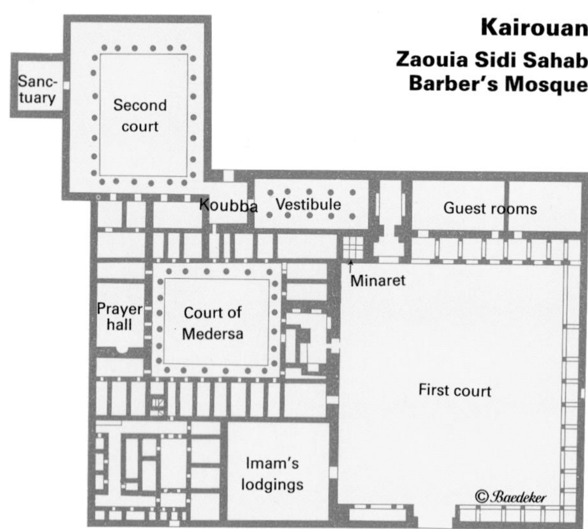

Zaouia of Sidi Sahab (Barber's Mosque)

Going west along Avenue de la République, we come in some 800m/½ mile to the Zaouia of Sidi Sahab, also known as the Barber's Mosque, a complex including a mausoleum and a medersa which was built between 1629 and 1692 over the tomb of one of Mohammed's companions who died in 685. According to legend Sidi Sahab, out of reverence for the Prophet, always carried a few hairs from his beard: hence the name of the Barber's Mosque. (Sidi Sahab was not Mohammed's barber, who is buried in Gabès).

The zaouia is notable for its magnificent decoration, much of which dates only from the 19th century. It is entered through a forecourt, on the left of which are the imam's lodgings, guest-rooms and ablution fountains. Opposite the entrance is the minaret. The forecourt also gives access to the medersa, laid out round a small courtyard, the prayer hall beyond it and (by way of a passage adjoining the minaret) another colonnaded courtyard, off which opens the tomb of Sidi Sahab (whose original name was Abu Djama el Balani). The tomb (not open to the public) has beautiful tiled decoration and a dome with stucco ornament.

Zaouia of Sidi Amor Abbada (Mosque of the Sabres)

Going south along Avenue Zama el Balaoui, turning left into Rue Sidi Gaid and in 150m/165yds taking a street on the right, we reach the Zaouia of Sidi Amor Abbada or Mosque of the Sabres (1860), the tomb of a local smith who is revered as a holy man. With its five ribbed domes, the zaouia is one of the principal pilgrim shrines in Kairouan. Round the tomb are examples of the craftsman's skill – sabres, stirrups, anchors, chests – together with his tobacco-pipe and wooden tablets inscribed with his prophecies.

Surroundings of Kairouan

Reqqada

10km/6 miles south-west of Kairouan, on the Sfax road (GP 2), is Reqqada, once the residence of the Aghlabid ruler Ibrahim II (875–902). There are only scanty remains of his palace (a large basin, a smaller one, foundation walls).

*Islamic Museum

The interesting Museum of Islamic Art (Musée National d'Art Islamique) is housed in a presidential palace built in 1970, set in a beautiful park. It is open daily, except Monday, 9am–noon and 2.30–5.30pm. The exhibits include finds from Kairouan, the Aghlabid residences at Reqqada and Al Abbasiya and other towns in the region. A special exhibition is devoted to the excavations at Sabra Mansourya, 6km/4 miles away (a circular palace built by Caliph El Mansour in the middle of the 10th century).

In the entrance hall are a model of the Sidi Oqba Mosque and a reproduction of its mihrab. In other rooms are old prints with views of local towns, coins of the various dynasties (Aghlabids, Fatimids, Zirids), old Koranic inscriptions (including one on a gazelle skin dyed blue), a variety of pottery and funerary stelae with inscriptions.

The museum is still being built up, so that a complete description is not yet possible. Moreover the exhibits are labelled only in Arabic. However, even in its present state the museum is well worth a visit.

Sidi Ben Nasrallah

In this village north-west of Kairouan semi-nomadic Zlass tribesmen breed thoroughbred Arab horses. In summer they organise "fantasias" (equestrian games).

Kasserine

D 5

Chief town of the governorate of Kasserine
Altitude: 570m/1870ft
Population: 24,000

Access

Kasserine lies on both GP 17, coming from Le Kef, and GP 3, coming from Kairouan; it is 120km/75 miles south of Le Kef and 155km/96 miles south-west of Kairouan.

No rail connections (goods station only). Bus services to and from Gafsa, Kairouan, Le Kef, Sbeitla, Sfax, Thala and Maktar; bus station (Gare Routière) in town centre.

Situation and characteristics

Kasserine lies on the Oued el Habeb in the upland steppe country of central Tunisia, surrounded by the country's highest hill, Djebel Chambi (1544m/5066ft), to the north-east, Djebel Semmama (1314m/4311ft) to the north-west and Djebel Selloum (1373m/4505ft) to the south-east. Thanks to its situation it is an important traffic junction and market town (market on Tuesdays); but it is now mainly an industrial centre. In the largest industrial plant in central Tunisia, established in 1963, the esparto grass which grows in the surrounding steppe is used in the manufacture of cellulose and paper.

History

The town was founded by the Romans, probably in the 2nd century A.D., under the name of Cellium, and in the 3rd century was raised to the status of a *colonia*. With the fall of the Roman Empire it declined in importance, and until the colonial period remained no more than a small market centre for the surrounding villages. The French built a railway station and settled European *colons* on the land.

Sights

New town

During the period of French colonial rule a modern town was built around the old centre. The town is traversed by its 4km/2½ mile long main street, Avenue Habib Bourguiba, in the eastern section of which (towards Kairouan) is the modern town centre, with the railway station, bus station and numerous shops. The ancient remains are at the other end of the street, in the direction of Gafsa.

Mausoleum

At the west end of the town, opposite the barracks, can be seen the scanty remains (the base and fragments of two walls) of a tower-like mausoleum.

A barren steppe landscape

Mausoleum of Flavius

Some 600m/660yds farther west (200m/220yds beyond the bridge over the Oued Derb), opposite the Governor's Office, is another tower-mausoleum, in an excellent state of preservation, of similar type to the Numidian mausoleum at Dougga (see entry). It is of three storeys, with a 110-line inscription on the base lauding the virtues of its founder, Flavius Secundus, buried here with his family. The middle section of the tomb is decorated with half-columns; there is a niche on the third section which once contained a statue of Flavius; and the whole structure was originally crowned by a pyramidal roof.

Cillium

Outside the town, on the road to Gafsa (soon after GP 17 goes off on the right to Thala, some 200m/220yds beyond the Hotel Cillium), is the site of ancient Cillium. The remains lie on the left of the road.

Only a small area of the site has been excavated. The best preserved structure is a triumphal arch with a decorative frieze and an inscription; like most of the remains, it dates from the 3rd century. Nearby are the foundations of a Christian basilica and a small Byzantine fortress. Farther away, on the slopes of a hill, is the theatre, which lacks the stage wall.

Surroundings of Kasserine

Djebel Chambi

Djebel Chambi, Tunisia's highest hill (1544m/5066ft), was declared a National Park in 1981. The hill is covered with dense forests of Aleppo pines, interrupted here and there by clearings overgrown with esparto grass, and is now again the habitat of species which had become rare – mountain gazelles, moufflons, hyenas, eagles, vultures and peregrine falcons.

At the foot of the hill, in the middle of the forest, is the National Park information office, with a small natural history museum.

Access

Leave Kasserine on GP 17, signposted to Thala, which in 5km/3 miles turns north-west. In another 4km/2½ miles take a track on the left which runs south to the village of Chambi. This is negotiable by an all-terrain vehicle to a height of 1300m/4265ft, where there is a radio transmitter and the small lead mine of Kef. From here it is a 2-hour climb to the summit, which is crowned by a crescent; extensive panoramic views. For information about the condition of the track consult the Arrondissement Forestier in Kasserine.

Thélepte

30km/19 miles south-west of Kasserine, 700m/770yds beyond the village of Thélepte, is the site of Roman and Byzantine Thamesmida, an extensive scatter of remains on both sides of the road and the railway line which is likely to be of interest only to archaeological enthusiasts.
To reach the site, leave Kasserine on the Gafsa road (GP 17), and when it joins G 15 turn right.

Feriana

The little market town of Feriana (pop. 4000) lies 4km/2½ miles farther south on the Gafsa road (GP 15).

Haidra

60km/37 miles north-west: see entry.

Sbeitla

The remains of ancient Sufetula lie 38km/24 miles north-east of Kasserine on the road to Kairouan (GP 13): see Sbeitla.

Kebili

F 5/6

Chief town of the governorate of Kebili
Population: 6000

Access

Kebili lies on GP 16 (Gabès–Tozeur), 122km/76 miles west of Gabès and 89km/55 miles south-east of Tozeur.
There are regular bus services to and from Gabès and Tozeur.

Situation and characteristics

Kebili, the administrative centre and market town (market on Tuesdays) of the Nefzaoua oases, lies below Djebel Tebaga on a tongue of land between the Chott el Fedjadj to the north-east and the Chott el Djerid to the south-west. To the south extends the sandy desert of the Grand Erg Oriental.
Until the prohibition of the slave trade in the mid 19th century Kebili was an important slave market, and its population includes many descendants of slaves, known as Haratin.
During the French protectorate Kebili was a garrison town, to which Habib Bourguiba was exiled in 1934. An old French fort, the Fort des Autruches (Fort of the Ostriches), is now a hotel.
The town has no features of outstanding interest. On the road to Douz (see below) is a reservoir which offers the possibility of refreshment. Kebili is now mainly of interest to visitors as a base from which to visit the Nefzaoua and Djerid oases and to cross the Chott el Djerid (see entry).

Nefzaoua oases

Between the foothills of Djebel Tebaga to the north-east and the Chotts to the north-west lie the Nefzaoua oases: the two main oases of Kebili and Douz and numerous smaller ones including Bechri, Menchia, Blidet, Nouail, Zaafrane, Es Sabria and Bazma.
Like the Djerid oases (see Tozeur and Nefta) they owe their existence to artesian wells. The water is distributed by the *foggara* system (see drawing, page 42), otherwise found only at El Guettar (see Gafsa).

Douz

Some 30km/20 miles south of Kebili (bus services from Gafsa and Tozeur) is the oasis of Douz, home of the Mherazig Berbers. Most of them have been settled in the oasis for several generations; only some twenty families still live a nomadic life all year round between the oasis of Ksar Ghilane in the

Herd of dromedaries in the desert

south-east and and Regim Maâtoug on the Algerian frontier. Four groups of dwellings lie round the centre of the village, with the oasis extending to the north, south and west. The village has no tourist sights in the ordinary sense. Thursday is a busy market day, and at the end of December there is a Saharan festival, with dromedary and horse races, a representation of a traditional wedding ceremony and performances of music and dancing.

Tourism

Hitherto Douz has been little affected by the tourist trade, but a huge new tourist complex covering an area of 45 hectares/110 acres, with between 5000 and 7000 beds, is now in course of construction.
In addition to the positive results in the way of providing employment and bringing in foreign currency which are expected from a development of this kind there are likely also to be negative consequences – particularly conflicts over the distribution of the precious water supply and damage to the environment. A foreign visitor, consuming an average of 300 litres/65 gallons of water a day, uses as much water in 26 days as an inhabitant of one of the towns on the coast needs in a year, and that water is lost to agriculture. To make good the deficiency existing wells must be driven deeper and new ones sunk. As a result the water table falls, and still deeper wells must be sunk. And in addition the new developments encroach on the land of the oases and threaten the environment.

El Hofra

4km/2½ miles south of Douz, near the Zaafrane road (MC 206), is the great El Hofra dune, from the top of which there are wide views of the seemingly endless sandy desert of the Grand Erg Oriental.
A large hotel complex is at present under construction below the dune – a development which worries those concerned with the protection of the environment.

Kerkennah Islands · Iles Kerkennah

D/E 8

Governorate: Sfax
Altitude: 0–13m/0–43ft
Population: 15,000

Boat services

From Sfax (see entry) there are, depending on the season, between two and five car ferries daily to Sidi Youssef, at the south-western tip of the island of Gharbi; the crossing takes 75 minutes. From Sidi Youssef there are several buses daily to places in the interior of the island.

Situation and characteristics

The attractive Kerkennah Islands lie off the Tunisian coast between 20 and 40km (12½ and 25 miles) east of Sfax. The archipelago consists of seven islands with a total area of some 180sq.km/70sq.miles. Only the two principal islands, Gharbi and Chergui, are inhabited. They are linked by a 1km/¾ mile long causeway built in 1961 on Roman foundations.

Landscape

The islands are predominantly flat (highest point 13m/43ft) and sandy. There is little farming, for rainfall is low (200mm/8in. a year) and the ground-water is of poor quality. As a result of the high humidity of the air the extensive palm-groves seen on the road from Sidi Youssef at the southern tip of Gharbi and El Attaia in the north-east of Chergui bear practically no fruit. The most useful part of the palms is the leaves, which are used in the construction of the V-shaped fish-traps to be seen in shallow water all round the islands.

Economy

The inhabitants of the islands' thirteen villages live mainly by fishing, sponge-diving and the sale of their craft products. Recently the tourist trade has established a foothold on Chergui, with a new holiday complex at Sidi Fredj, west of the village of Ouled Kacem on the south-west coast of the island. The sandy beaches, most of them still almost unfrequented, offer excellent conditions for diving.

Chergui

Chergui, also known as Grand Kerkennah, is 22km/14 miles long and up to 10km/6 miles wide at its northern end.

Gharbi

The smaller island of Gharbi (chief place Mellita) measures only 14km/8½ miles by 6km/4 miles.

History

The Kerkennah Islands were known to the Greeks as Kyrannis and to the Romans as Cercina. It is established that they were already occupied in Punic times, for Hannibal chose them as his place of banishment after his defeat in the battle of Zama in 202 B.C.
In Roman times Sallust made the islands his base during Caesar's conflict with Pompey. In later centuries they became involved in the conflicts between Arabs and Christians, and later still suffered during Spanish punitive expeditions against the corsairs who infested the North African coasts. The villages were destroyed and finally abandoned because it was no longer safe to live in them.
The ancestors of the present population came to the islands from the mainland only in the 17th and 18th centuries. They emerged into the light of history again during the Tunisian struggle for independence. The future trade union leader Farhat Hached was born here, and in 1945 Habib Bourguiba escaped from French custody on Chergui and took refuge in Libya.

Tour of the islands

The Kerkennah Islands have no features of great historical or artistic interest, but they are worth a visit for the sake of the peace and relaxation they offer.

Mellita

From Sidi Youssef a good road runs the length of Gharbi and Chergui. At Mellita are the ruins of a Turkish defensive tower. The road then continues to Remla (petrol station, bank, shops), El Kellabine, El Abassia and the village of Ech Chergui, from which Bourguiba escaped to Libya. Visitors can see the hut in which he spent the night and the boat which he used. The road is signposted "Résidence du Salut du Président Bourguiba".

El Attaia

At the north-east corner of Chergui is El Attaia, the chief place on the Kerkennah Islands.

Kerkouane

See Cap Bon, Tour of the Peninsula

Korbous

See Cap Bon, Tour of the Peninsula

La Marsa

See Tunis, Surroundings

Le Kef

C 5

Chief town of the governorate of Le Kef
Altitude: 700–850m/2300–2800ft
Population: 29,000

Access

Le Kef lies on GP 5, 170km/106 miles south-west of Tunis and 42km/26 miles east of the Algerian frontier.
Regular bus services to and from Tunis, Tabarka, Maktar, Kairouan and Kasserine; bus station (Gare Routière) in the lower town.

Situation and characteristics

The old town of Le Kef (*kef* = "rock"), known in Arabic as Chikka Benar, is picturesquely situated on the slopes of Dir el Kef, an outlier of the High Tell. It is the market centre of the surrounding upland region, with a busy market on Thursdays.
The upper town, crowned by the Kasbah, has so far been little affected by tourism, though there are plans to develop its tourist potentialities. If this should come about Le Kef will make a good base from which to visit some of Tunisia's most important ancient sites lying within easy reach, including Dougga, Bulla Regia and Maktar (see entries).

History

Nothing is left of a settlement established by the Numidians on this commanding site. The place came under the influence of Carthage at an early stage. At the end of the First Punic War (241 B.C.) Carthage resettled here numbers of mercenaries who had mutinied in Sicily – a move which sparked off the bloody Mercenary War of 240–237 B.C. Among them were Elymians from the Sicilian city of Eryx, who brought with them their cult of the goddess Sicca Veneria, and the town, now renamed Sicca Veneria, became an important centre of the cult.
The goddess worshipped as Sicca Veneria was identified with the Carthaginian Astarte, the Greek Aphrodite and the Roman Venus. Temple prostitution featured prominently in the cult; but although Elissa, the legendary founder of Carthage (see History), is said to have brought the cult with her, along with eighty hierodules (female temple servants), Le Kef is the only place in Punic Africa where traces of the cult have been found; and the town's Arabic name of Chikka Benar or Chakbenaria still recalls the ancient Sicca Veneria.

View of Le Kef

The Romans took over the town, preserving its Punic name of Sicca Veneria. In the reign of Augustus it was raised to the status of a *colonia,* and during the 2nd and 3rd centuries it achieved great prosperity. As early as 256 it was the see of a bishop.
After the Vandal raids the town lost much of its population, and after the Arab conquest it was abandoned, to be refounded only in the 16th century under the name of Le Kef. As a frontier town it was long disputed between Algiers and Tunis. Its massive Kasbah was built by the Algerians towards the end of the 17th century, but Tunisian control was finally established in the 18th century. During the Second World War the town was for a time the seat of the government of the French protectorate.

Sights

The town

The old town of Le Kef, on the slopes of the hill, is dominated by the massive bulk of the Kasbah, from which remains of the old town walls run east to the former Presidential Palace. At the foot of the old town is the lower town, built during the French protectorate, with the railway and bus stations.
Le Kef's main street, Avenue Habib Bourguiba, bisects the two parts of the town, half way up the hill. From its east end (where it turns south-west towards the new town) Rue de la Source leads to a mosque beyond which is a small excavation site. Here too begins the old town, a maze of tortuous streets and stepped lanes.

Dar el Kous

In Rue Farhat Hached, which leads east from Avenue Habib Bourguiba, is a three-aisled early Christian church dedicated to St Peter and now known as the Dar el Kous (restored). Until Tunisia became independent services were still held in the vaulted narthex of the church. Over the lintel of the doorway, on the right-hand outer wall, are Christian symbols. The raised apse, excellently preserved, is similar to that of the fortified church at Haidra (see entry).

Mausoleum

Higher up, opposite a long abandoned synagogue, is the 17th century mausoleum of Husain ben Ali, father of the first Husseinite ruler.

Zaouia Qadriya

On the east side of the town, south of the walled Presidential Palace (Habib Bourguiba's first wife came from Le Kef), is the Zaouia Qadriya or Zaouia Sidi Mizouni (1834), with a large dome surrounded by four smaller ones. Fine view.

Folk Museum

To the north of the former Presidential Palace is the Zaouia of Sidi ben Aissa (1784), now occupied by the Folk Museum (Musée Régional des Arts et Traditions Populaires; open daily, except Mondays, 9.30am–4.30pm).
The exhibits include traditional costumes, brides' dresses and jewellery, a nomad tent, everyday objects, domestic pottery, woven fabrics and horse trappings.

Kasbah

From here the street continues to the Turkish Kasbah, built by Mohammed Bey of Algiers in 1679 on Byzantine foundations, using stone from ancient buildings. Much altered in subsequent centuries, it was used until recently as a barracks. It is now being restored to house a cultural centre and an archaeological museum.
There is a fine view from the tower, and even more extensive views of the town and the surrounding plain from a bastion higher up to the north-east.

Djemaa el Kebir

In front of the Kasbah is the former Great Mosque, Djemaa el Kebir (restored), built in the 8th century on the site of an earlier building. It is now used for social and public occasions. In the gardens and inside the building are fragments of stone, remains of mosaics and stelae.

Mosque of Sidi Bou Makhlouf

Below the Kasbah are the beautiful Mosque and Zaouia of Sidi Bou Makhlouf, with two ribbed domes and an octagonal minaret (16th c.). The interior has delicate stucco ornament and attractive tile decoration; the dome of the three-aisled prayer hall is borne on antique columns.

Cisterns

To the north of the town are eleven Roman cisterns, each measuring 11m/36ft by 6m/20ft.

Surroundings of Le Kef

Mustis

See Dougga, Surroundings

Dougga

80km/50 miles north-east: see entry

Chemtou

83km/52 miles north: see entry

Bulla Regia

70km/43 miles north: see entry

Kalaat es Senan (Table de Jugurtha)

To the south of Le Kef is a prominent tabular hill, Kalaat es Senan, known as the Table de Jugurtha, in the form of a truncated cone flanked by rock walls rising vertically to a height of 70m/230ft. A path leads to a flight of steps hewn from the rock which goes up to the plateau. Half way up is a Byzantine arched gateway. At a height of 1271m/4170ft are the remains of a Byzantine fortress, a number of cave dwellings and the marabout of Sidi Abd el Jouad. From here there are magnificent wide-ranging views.

Access

GP 5, then GP 17, signposted to Kasserine. Beyond Tadjerouine take a road on the right which heads towards the Algerian frontier. Just after the mosque in the village of Kalaat es Senan (pop. 2000) a road runs up to Ain Senan; then a narrow road on the left leading to a hamlet from which the footpath runs up to the plateau (2 hours' climb).

Maktar

70km/43 miles south-east: see entry

Haidra

80km/50 miles south: see entry

Medeina

38km/24 miles south, between the Oued Ain Oum el Abid and the Oued Medeina, is the site of ancient Althiburos, only a small part of which has been excavated.

Access

Leave Le Kef on the Tunis road (GP 5) and in 3km/2 miles turn into MC 71, which leads south-east to Dahmani (formerly Ebba Ksour). From Dahmani take MC 72, going west. 7km/4½ miles along this road, at a small hamlet, follow a narrow track which runs south and in 500m/550yds crosses a small ford. Just beyond this a track on the right leads to the site; the road to the left leads back to Dahmani.

History

There was probably a Numidian settlement on the site, which, like Le Kef, lay outside the Roman province and received an influx of refugees from Carthage after the Third Punic War. Romanisation proceeded very slowly here, and it was not until the reign of Hadrian (A.D.117–138) that the town achieved the status of a *municipium*. Thereafter, thanks to its strategic situation on the road from Carthage to Theveste (Tébessa in Algeria), the fertile surrounding country and the nearby quarries, the town prospered. In the 4th century it was the see of a bishop. It was ruined by the Vandal raids and the Arab invasion.

Excavations

The layout of the paved forum (44.60m/146ft by 37.15m/122ft) can be clearly identified; of the portico there remain only a few Corinthian capitals. Between the forum and the Capitol, which lay on its south-east side, extends a paved street. To the north-west are the remains of a triumphal arch (A.D. 128) dedicated to Hadrian. At the other end of the street can be seen a well preserved fountain.

To the south is the amphitheatre, of which a few arches remain. Farther east is a mausoleum.

North-west of the forum is the Maison de la Pêche, named after a mosaic of a fishing scene which is now in the Bardo National Museum in Tunis. On the other side of the river are two other Roman houses, the Maison des Muses and the Edifice des Asclepeia (much altered in the 3rd and 4th centuries); the mosaics from these houses are also in the Bardo National Museum.

Mactaris

See Maktar

Mahdia

C 8

Chief town of the governorate of Mahdia
Population: 27,000

Access

Mahdia lies on MC 82, 68km/42 miles south-east of Sousse and 20km/12½ miles north-east of El Djem. It is easily reached by car, and there are good Metro and bus connections with Monastir and Sousse.

Situation and characteristics

Mahdia lies in a sheltered situation on a small rocky peninsula, 1.5km/1 mile long and barely 500m/550yds across, which is linked with the mainland only by a narrow isthmus. It is the economic centre of the southern Sahel and in recent years has developed into Tunisia's largest fishing port. About a third of the country's total catch is landed here and processed in numerous canning factories.

There is an annual festival here in July or August, the "Nuits de Mahdia", with performances of classical and folk dancing and illuminated fishing boats in the bay.

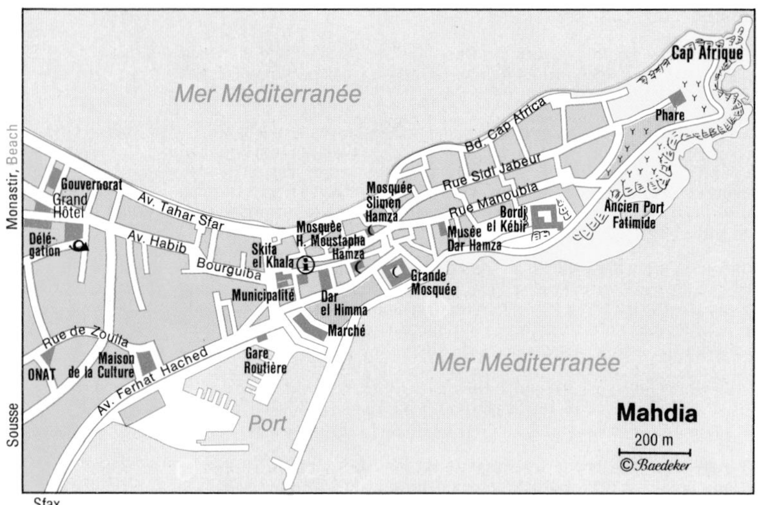

Mahdia has a picturesque Medina and a beautiful sandy beach to the north of the town. So far, however, tourism has made little headway. The Friday market is held in Place Farhat Hached, on the harbour.

History

The strategic advantages of this site on its tongue of land were realised by the Phoenicians, who built a rectangular harbour, the Kothon, with watch-towers to defend it. The harbour, on the north side of the peninsula, is still in use.

There are no traces worth mentioning of the Punic settlement or the Roman town which succeeded it. In 1907, however, sponge-divers found a Roman vessel with a cargo from Greece which had sunk off the coast in 86 B.C. (see below).

During the Arab conquest the town was utterly destroyed. It was refounded in 913 by the Fatimid Caliph Obaid Allah el Mahdi – who saw that possession of this site on Cap Afrique (Ifriqiya) would give him control over coastal shipping – and named after him. A large settlement was laid out on the peninsula, protected by an 11m/36ft thick wall with four bastions and a single gateway with six portcullises, and a harbour was built. Parts of the walls and fortifications can still be seen. After the completion of this almost impregnable stronghold, in 921, the Caliph moved his capital to Mahdia from his former seat at Reqqada (see Kairouan, Surroundings). This was the base from which the Fatimids set out on the conquest of Egypt; then, having achieved this, they transferred the capital to Cairo in 973 and Mahdia fell into oblivion.

The stronghold of Mahdia was taken twice, once by the Normans in the 12th century and later by the Spaniards, who laid siege to the town during their punitive campaigns against the great corsair Dragut (see Famous People). When they left the town in 1554 they blew up all the bastions, which were never rebuilt, and thereafter Mahdia sank into insignificance.

Sights

Medina

In the centre of Mahdia, on the narrow rocky peninsula, is the Medina. The new town extends to the west and south; to the north-west is a beautiful sandy beach.

*Skifa el Kahla

The entrance to the old town is through the town gate, the Skifa el Kahla (Black Gate) or Bab Zouila. The gatehouse with its 44m/144ft long entrance passage was formerly incorporated in the 11m/36ft thick wall, 175m/190yds long, which crossed the peninsula. The present gate is not the original Fatimid structure but was rebuilt in 1554 after the destruction of Mahdia by the Spaniards, using stone from the Fatimid fortress. Of the original round towers, on polygonal bases, which stood at the north and south ends of the wall there remain only stumps at the north end. The residential quarter of Zouila lay to the west of the fortress. Here too were the souks, of which no trace now remains.

Skifa el Kahla

Views

From the roof of the gatehouse there are fine views of the Medina, extending to the tip of the peninsula, the modern harbour and, to the south-west, the new town. The steps leading up to the roof are on the inner side of the gate, to the rear of the Town Hall (Municipalité).

The gate leads into Rue Obaid Allah el Mahdi, on the left-hand side of which is a small covered souk.
On the opposite side of the street is the entrance to Dar el Himma, a small Silk Museum (at present closed for renovation).

*Great Mosque

Farther along the street are Place du Caire and Place El Kadhi Noamene, on the right of which, directly on the sea, stands the Great Mosque. Built in 921 by the founder of the town, Obaid Allah el Mahdi, it was the first Fatimid mosque modelled on the Sidi Oqba Mosque in Kairouan. It was connected on two sides with the town walls, and when these were blown up by the

View over the Medina of Mahdia

Doorway of Great Mosque

Old Harbour

Spaniards the mosque too was destroyed with the exception of the north front. A temporary building was erected to replace it, but when this was found to be in danger of collapse and was pulled down in the 1960s the Great Mosque was carefully rebuilt on its old site in accordance with the original plans.

The mosque is entered through a monumental doorway which was originally used only by the Caliph. Over the doorway is a large horseshoe arch, and on either side are tall niches, shallow on ground level and deeper on the upper level.

The inner courtyard, 42m/138ft by 50m/164ft, is surrounded on three sides by a colonnade with horseshoe arches.

The nine-aisled prayer hall, three bays deep, has the same ground-plan as its prototype in Kairouan. The central aisle leading to the mihrab is wider than the other eight. The bay in front of the mihrab is crowned by a dome.

Bordj el Kebir

From the Great Mosque it is a short distance along the seafront to the Bordj el Kebir. This massive square fortress, built in 1595, is commandingly situated on the highest point on the peninsula. Of the palace built by Obaid Allah el Mahdi in the 10th century nothing is left but a few fragments of masonry from the entrance.

In the courtyard of the fortress is a small mosque. In the masonry of the tower at the south-west corner are two reliefs which are believed to have come from an earlier building.

The main attraction of the Bordj el Kebir is the magnificent view from the battlements over the town, the Old Harbour (see below) and Cap Afrique. The fortress is open daily, except Sundays and public holidays, 9am–noon and 3–4pm.

Between the Bordj el Kebir and the lighthouse (Phare) at the end of the peninsula lies a cemetery. Near the lighthouse are a number of 10th century Shiite tombs and remains of cisterns.

Bordj el Kebir

On the south coast of the peninsula is the Old Harbour (Ancien Port Fatimide), measuring 126m/138yds by 57m/62yds, probably the old Punic *kothon* which was later used by the Romans. The narrow entrance channel, 15m/16yds long, was protected by two Fatimid watch-towers which were incorporated in the town walls and were later linked by an arch. The *kothon* is very similar to the one at Carthage (see entry).

The Mahdia wreck

The existence of a harbour at least in Roman times seems to be evidenced by the discovery by sponge-divers off Cap Afrique in 1907 of a Roman sailing ship which had sunk in a storm in 86 B.C. Its cargo, which included dedicatory reliefs from Piraeus and large numbers of marble columns, showed that the ship came from Piraeus. The ship is now in the Bardo Museum in Tunis.

Surroundings of Mahdia

El Djem

42km/26 miles south-west: see entry

Monastir

45km/28 miles north: see entry

Sousse

62km/39 miles north: see entry

Archaeological tour

For visitors interested in archaeology a trip down the coast by way of Salakta and La Chebba to Ras Bou Tria (59km/37 miles) can be recommended.

Salakta

14km/8½ miles from Mahdia, beyond the little town of Ksour Essaf, is Salakta, with the modest remains of ancient Sullectum. This was probably the port to which lions for the gladiatorial contests in the amphitheatre at El Djem were shipped.

La Chebba

23km/14 miles beyond this is La Chebba, near which, on the headland of Ras Kaboudia, are the remains of the ribat of Bordj Kjadidja, built on Byzantine foundations. This was one of a chain of similar forts built by the Abbasids along the coasts of the Sahel in the 8th century (see also Sousse and Monastir). The ancient settlement on this site was known as Caput Vada; the Byzantine general Belisarius landed here in 533 and went on to inflict a devastating defeat on the Vandals.

Ras Bou Tria

Acholla

15km/9 miles south of La Chebba is the promontory of Ras Bou Tria (reached on a side road which goes off on the left 8km/5 miles beyond Mellouleche), with the remains of ancient Acholla. Excavations here have brought to light the foundations of Roman houses and remains of an amphitheatre and baths.

Moknine, Ksar Hellal

See Monastir, Surroundings

Maktar

C 6

Governorate: Siliana
Altitude: 950m/3115ft
Population: 6000

Access

Maktar lies on GP 12 (Le Kef–Kairouan), 114km/71 miles north-west of Kairouan and 69km/43 miles south-east of Le Kef, and on GP 4 (which branches off GP 3 at El Fahs), 156km/97 miles south-west of Tunis.
Bus services to and from Tunis, Téboursouk/Tunis, Le Kef, Sbeitla/Kasserine and Kairouan; bus station (Gare Routière) in the market square.

Situation and characteristics

The little market town of Maktar, founded only in 1887, is commandingly situated on a high plateau in the High Tell, the hills of central Tunisia. The surrounding countryside is Tunisia's largest corn-growing area after the Medjerda valley, and in spite of the altitude olives also flourish here.
Situated between the uplands and the steppe, Maktar is an important market centre (market on Mondays).
The principal attraction of Maktar, in a beautiful setting, is the site of Roman Mactaris, which ranks with Dougga and Bulla Regia (see entries) as one of the most important archaeological sites in Tunisia.

History

A Numidian settlement was established here in the 2nd century B.C., in a commanding situation which offered safety from attack and enabled it to control the routes between the uplands and the steppe; and the abundant summer rainfall guaranteed a water supply for the adjoining valley.
After the destruction of Carthage in 146 B.C. many Punic refugees came to Maktar, since the town, by now fortified, lay outside the Roman province of Africa (until 46 B.C., when it was incorporated in the new province of Africa Nova). The remains of a tophet and numerous funerary stelae and Punic inscriptions are evidence of an enduring Libyan/Punic influence. As in other towns, the two communities – the old-established Libyan/Punic *civitas* and the Roman *pagus* – lived in harmony side by side. It took almost 200 years until the Romanisation of Mactaris (as the Romans called the town) was complete. In the reign of Trajan, at the beginning of the 2nd century A.D., it was given the status of a *municipium;* and in 180, in the reign of Marcus Aurelius, it became a *colonia* and its inhabitants were given Roman citizenship. Maktaris now controlled some 60 villages in the surrounding area and became one of the wealthiest cities in the province. Its trade in corn, olives, livestock and textiles flourished as never before, and this promoted much new building.
In the first half of the 3rd century Mactaris took part in the revolt headed by Gordian against the reintroduction of the tax on olive oil; but – unlike El Djem, then the most prosperous city in the Sahel, which was ruined – it managed to recover after the repression of the rising. It also survived the Vandal raids (439–534) and thereafter was fortified by the Byzantines.

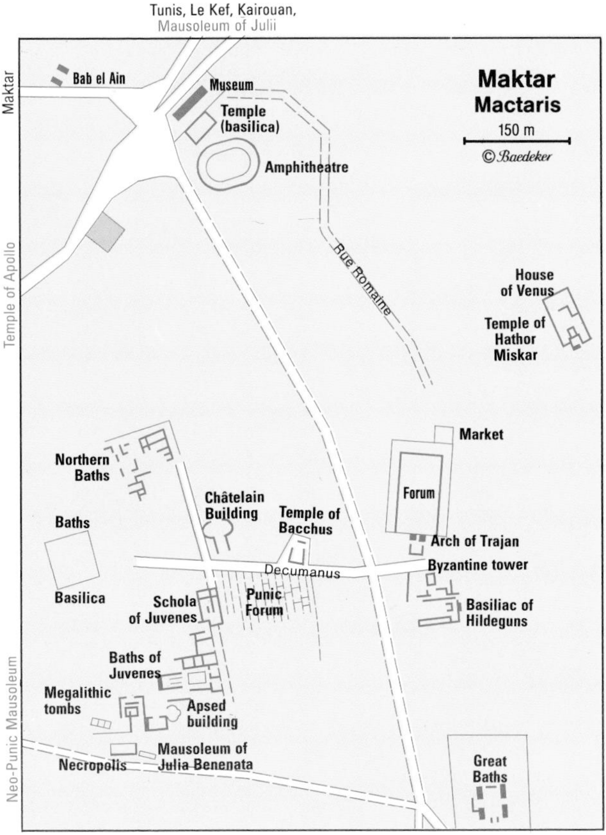

After the Arab invasion the city's decline set in, and was finally consummated by the raids of the Beni Hilal nomads (1050).

The town was re-founded by the French colonial authorities in 1887 as an administrative and market centre. Excavation of the ancient site began in 1914, but so far only a third of the very extensive area of Roman Mactaris has been brought to light.

**Excavations

The entrance to the site is through the gardens of the Museum, on the main Kairouan–Le Kef road. It is open daily 9am–noon and 2.30–6.30pm, in winter 2–5.30pm.

Bab el Ain

At the far end of the town, outside the excavation site, is Bab el Ain, one of the old town gates (restored). Here, near the stream, was the Punic tophet dedicated to Baal-Ammon.

Museum

On the opposite side of the road is the small but interesting Museum of Maktar.

The Museum has a fine collection of gravestones and stelae of the 1st century B.C.–3rd century A.D., some of them with Punic inscriptions and symbols (crescents, pigeons, peacocks, grapes, pomegranates, fishes, etc.). The Roman period is represented by sculpture and fragments of architecture, the Byzantine period by bronzes, oil lamps and a 6th century pavement mosaic with figures of animals and an inscription.

Behind the museum are the remains of an ancient temple which was later converted into a basilica.

A paved Roman road runs past an amphitheatre, the arena of which has been preserved, to an eminence from which can be seen, some distance away, the well preserved Arch of Trajan (see below).

Temple of Hathor Miskar

On the east (left) side of the Roman road is the little temple of Hathor Miskar (a love goddess of Egyptian origin), a Punic shrine, probably of the 1st century B.C., which was rebuilt in the 2nd century A.D. and converted into a Christian church in the 4th century. The ground-plan consists of a walled forecourt, a vestibule and the cella. An inscription gives the names of three suffetes (Punic municipal officials). The apse was presumably added in the 4th century. Under the cella was a chamber in which the temple treasure was kept.

House of Venus

Immediately adjoining is a Roman house, the Maison de Vénus, in which was found a well preserved mosaic depicting Venus taking off her sandals, with birds and fishes (2nd/3rd c.).

Forum

Beyond this, at the intersection of the cardo and the decumanus, lies the rectangular Forum, paved with marble, which was probably laid out in the early 2nd century, when Mactaris became a *municipium*. Nothing is left of the colonnades and buildings which stood round it. At the north-east corner is a small market.

Arch of Trajan

At the south end of the forum stands the magnificently preserved Arch of Trajan, erected in A.D. 116 in honour of the town's promotion to the status of *municipium*. An inscription dedicates it to "the Emperor Caesar Nerva Trajanus Augustus, the best of all Emperors, conqueror of the Germans, the Armenians and the Parthians, in his 21st year as a tribune". In Byzantine times the gateway was walled up and incorporated in the fortifications of the town.

Basilica of Hildeguns

Beyond the Arch of Trajan are the remains of a three-aisled basilica, much altered and rebuilt, with a baptistery flanked by four columns and the tomb of a Vandal prince named Hildeguns.

Great Baths

Farther south are the imposing remains of the Great Baths (Grands Thermes), built at the end of the 2nd century, which are among the best preserved Roman baths in Africa. The lower floor is completely preserved. The walls of the central hall (*cella media*) and the adjoining frigidarium (cold bath) and caldarium (warm bath) stand to a height of 12–15m/40–50ft, as far as the springing of the vaulting. The floors are paved with fine mosaics. Amid the plant ornament of the capitals appear various fabulous animals, showing that the Libyan/Punic cultural heritage was still very much alive in Roman times.

Punic Forum
Temple of Bacchus

Along the paved decumanus to the west is the old Punic Forum used by the Libyan/Punic population of the town. Just north of this is the Temple of Bacchus (Liber Pater), of which little remains apart from a double crypt; the present masonry belongs to a later building.

Arch of Trajan

To the west of the Punic Forum is a street intersection. To the right are the remains of the Châtelain Building, named after the French archaeologist who discovered it, and the Northern Baths, which have fine pavement mosaics. The street on the left along the side of the Punic Forum leads to the numerous remains in the south-western corner of the site, beginning with the Schola of the Juvenes.

Schola of Juvenes

The Schola of the Juvenes was a kind of clubhouse and training school for young men – found also in other Roman cities under the name of Collegia Juvenum – in which, in addition to being trained in various sports and the military art, they were given instruction in politics, taxation law and commerce. They were then employed not only in the collection of taxes but also in the defence of the wealthy city of Mactaris against raids by plundering nomadic tribesmen.
The building of the Schola began in A.D. 88, on the evidence of an inscription found on the site giving the name of 70 members of the school, but it was completed only towards the end of the 2nd century. By the early 3rd century the Schola had become an extremely powerful organisation, as is shown by its participation in the Gordian rising in A.D. 238. After the rising, however, it was dissolved and the buildings were destroyed. Later, in the reign of Diocletian, they were rebuilt. Particularly well preserved is the palaestra, built at the expense of a wealthy citizen named Julius Piso, with an inner courtyard surrounded by Corinthian columns and a small

lecture hall adjoining. The assembly hall (basilica) of A.D. 88, later converted into a Christian church (with a Punic sarcophagus serving as altar), can also be readily identified.
In the palaestra is a memorial to the munificent donor and his daughter Julia, with a beautifully decorated column for the daughter.
To the south of the Schola are the Baths of the Juvenes, the early Christian mausoleum of Julia Benenata (4th c.) and the Edifice à Auges, a building with four apses (three of them added in the 4th century).

Necropolis

Immediately beyond this is a necropolis which was in use for burial from the foundation of the Roman town until the 4th century, together with a number of megalithic tombs of the Numidian period.

Neo-Punic mausoleum

Some 300m/330yds west can be found a two-storey mausoleum with a pyramidal roof, a Roman version of the Numidian and Punic tower tombs, the best preserved example of which is the mausoleum at Dougga (see entry).

Other sights

To the north-west are the remains of a temple of Apollo (2nd c.), probably built on the site of an earlier shrine of Baal-Ammon, and fragments of an aqueduct.
Outside the excavation site, north-east of the Museum, is the half-ruined Mausoleum of the Julii.

Surroundings of Maktar

Hammam Zouakra

Around Maktar are numerous other excavation sites of lesser importance. At Hammam Zouakra (19km/12 miles north-west) are the remains of an

Megalithic tombs, Ellès

ancient settlement, with a triumphal arch, a megalithic monument and a number of mausoleums.

Ellès

At Ellès (ancient Thigibba), north-west of Maktar, can be seen over 40 megalithic tombs of the Punic period (2nd c. B.C.). The tomb chambers and the passages leading to them are roofed with huge stone slabs weighing several tons, up to 12 sq.m/130 sq.ft in size and 50cm/20in thick.

Access

27km/17 miles from Maktar on the Le Kef road (GP 12), take a road on the left which runs south to Ellès (12km/7½ miles).

Kbor Klit

At Kbor Klit are the scanty remains (a few courses of masonry) of a victory monument erected after Caesar's defeat of Juba in 46 B.C.

Access

Leave Maktar on the Le Kef road (GP 12) and in 22km/14 miles turn right into GP 4, signposted to Siliana; then in 8km/5 miles take a road on the left which comes in 1km/¾mile to the site.

Ksar Touar

On the far side of the hill, in the middle of a field, is a Roman mausoleum, originally three-storied.

Matmata

See Gabès, Surroundings

Medeina

See Le Kef, Surroundings

Médenine F/G 7/8

Chief town of the governorate of Médenine
Population: 18,000

Access

Médenine lies on GP 1 (Gabès–Ben Gardane), 73km/45 miles south of Gabès, 77km/48 miles north-west of Ben Gardane and 62km/39 miles west of Zarzis.

Regular bus services to and from Tataouine, Djorf, Zarzis and Ben Gardane; bus station (Gare Routière) on Tataouine road.

Situation and characteristics

The little administrative and market town of Médenine is – like Tataouine (see below) – a good centre from which to visit the hill villages in the surrounding area.

Originally Médenine was an important staging point on the caravan route from the interior of Africa. During the French protectorate it was a garrison town and the administrative centre of southern Tunisia.

The town originally consisted of an assemblage of numerous *ksour* (fortified storehouses), with a total of over 6000 *ghorfas*. In these *ksour* (singular *ksar*) the semi-nomadic families kept their possessions while they went on their wanderings, each family having its own *ghorfa* (store-room, granary). These little barrel-vaulted cells were built side by side and one over the other in honeycomb-like blocks up to six storeys high. During the 1960s most of them were pulled down, and Médenine is now a predominantly modern town. On the road to Djorf there are still a few two-storey *ghorfas*, now occupied by souvenir shops.

There are large markets in Médenine on Mondays and Thursdays.

Ghorfas, Médenine

Surroundings of Médenine

Djeffara plain

Between Gabès to the north and the Libyan frontier to the south extends the desertic steppe country of the Djeffara plain, which has been since the 7th century the home of Arab and Arabised semi-nomads, whose tents can still occasionally be seen. Numbers of deserted *ghorfas* show, however, that the centuries-old way of life of the nomads belongs to the past. The *ghorfas* are now falling into ruin or, here and there, being restored and refurbished for the benefit of tourists.

Dahar Hills

On the inland side of the Djeffara plain are the Dahar Hills, a narrow ridge (*dahar*) of upland country rising to 600m/2000ft which falls down to the plain in a series of steps. The Dahar Hills are the home of the Djebalia, a Berber tribe who were driven back into the hills by the raiding Beni Hilal in the 11th century. Their five villages with their *ghorfas* and *ksour* are now tourist attractions.

Metameur

6km/4 miles north of Médenine is Metameur, with a large complex of *ghorfas* part of which has been converted into a hotel. In recent years most of the town's *ghorfas* have been pulled down; a few have been restored for the tourist trade.

From Metameur there is an easily negotiable track (MC 104) to Toujane (see below). The hill road from there to Matmata, however, is only to be recommended for experienced drivers with an all-terrain vehicle. Matmata is best visited from Gabès (see entry).

Chenini

Toujane

The hill village of Toujane, picturesquely situated on the slopes of Kef Toujane (632m/2074ft), is famed for its woven fabrics and its excellent honey.

Matmata

See Gabès, Surroundings

Tamezret

See Gabès, Surroundings

Ben Gardane

80km/50 miles east of Médenine is Ben Gardane (pop. 2500; market on Fridays), a little town founded by the French in 1892. From here it is only 33km/21 miles to the Libyan frontier.

Tataouine

49km/30 miles south of Médenine is Tataouine (or Foum Tataouine), a relatively young town (pop. 7000; market on Thursdays) which has grown out of a military camp. Like Médenine, it is a good base for visits to the hill villages.
This is the scene, annually in March/April, of the Ksar Festival (Festival des Ksours Sahariens), in which Berber tribesmen from all over southern Tunisia take part. The programme of this five-day event includes equestrian games and sports, representations of Berber weddings, camel races, etc.

Beni Barka

8km/5 miles south of Tataouine, prominently situated on a hill, is the village of Beni Barka, with a ruined *ksar*. The origins of the village go back to the 14th century.

*Ksar Soltane

10km/6 miles south-east of Tataouine (leave on Beni Barka road, then turn off into a road signposted to Maztouria and Tamellest) is Ksar Soltane, part of which is well preserved, with groups of *ghorfas* built round two inner courtyards. The oldest date from the 15th century, the youngest from the 19th.

*Douirat

The village of Douirat (pop. 1000), 13km/8 miles south-west of Tataouine, is reached by taking the road to Remada (MC 112) and in 9km/6 miles turning off into a track running west.
On top of the hill is a *ksar,* and lower down are abandoned cave dwellings, the former inhabitants of which now live in new houses at the foot of the hill.

Other hill villages

To the west of Médenine and Tataouine are numbers of picturesque old hill villages, some of which, however, are difficult of access.

*Chenini

One of the finest and most visited of these villages is Chenini, 18km/11 miles west of Tataouine. A whitewashed mosque stands out prominently against the earth-coloured and partly ruined *ghorfas* clinging to the slopes of the hill. Near the cemetery, between two hills, is the rock-cut Mosque of the Seven Giants, with seven long tombs.
20km/12½ miles south is Douirat (see above).

Excursion

An attractive excursion from Médenine is by way of Ksar Djouama (view), Beni Kheddache, El Hallouf oasis (detour from Beni Kheddache), Ksar Haddada (part of which is now a small hotel), Ghoumrassen (with the marabout of Sidi Arfa, a local holy man) and Huermessa to Tataouine.

Djerba

80km/50 miles north-east: see entry

Zarzis

62km/39 miles north-east: see Djerba, Surroundings

Gabès

73km/45 miles north: see entry

Chott el Djerid

See entry

Menzel Bourguiba

See Bizerte, Surroundings

Metameur

See Médenine, Surroundings

Mustis

See Dougga, Surroundings

Metlaoui

E 5

Governorate: Gafsa
Population: 18,000

Access

Metlaoui lies 2km/1¼ miles north of the Gafsa–Tozeur road (GP 3), 42km/26 miles south-west of Gafsa and 51km/32 miles north of Tozeur.
There are daily rail services from Metlaoui to Gafsa, Sfax, Tunis, Tozeur and Redeyef, but departures are mostly at inconvenient times. Evening departures are suitable only for long-distance journeys, since local trains do not run during the night but stop overnight at minor stations. (For trips to the Seldja Gorge in the "Lézard Rouge" see below.)

From the bus station (Gare Routière) in the market square there are services several times daily to Tozeur, Gafsa and Redeyef and once daily to the upland oases of Tamerza, Chebika and Midès.

Trips in the "Lézard Rouge"

Daily during the main holiday season and three times weekly (on Monday, Tuesday and Friday) at other times of year there are rail trips through the Seldja Gorge in the old-world "Lézard Rouge" ("Red Lizard"). Departures from Metlaoui are at 10.15am, the return from the gorge at 12.30pm.
The "Lézard Rouge" was originally presented to the Bey of Tunisia, Mohamed Naceur Pacha, by the French government in 1910 and was used by the Bey and his successors until 1945. In 1984 it was renovated and put into service again for the benefit of tourists.

Situation and characteristics

The mining and industrial town of Metlaoui, Tunisia's main phosphate-mining centre (with the head office of the Phosphate Company) and the administrative and market centre of the whole phosphate region of south-western Tunisia, lies on the southern edge of the Gafsa uplands, the foothills of the Tell-Atlas. It has a number of modern plants which process phosphates from a wide surrounding area, and these, along with the associated industries and power stations which have also been established, set the pattern of the town and its townscape.
Round a residential district of European aspect, built by the French around the turn of the century for engineers and administrators and now occupied by senior staff of the state-owned Phosphate Company, are the housing schemes in which the work force live, divided according to their country of origin (Tunisia, Morocco, Algeria, Libya). The mining area itself is a landscape of craters.
The population also includes numbers of peasant farmers growing vegetables, fruit and esparto grass. The Chaal agricultural estate, with an area of some 2600 hectares/6500 acres and over 170,000 olive-trees, belongs to the Phosphate Company.

Slag heaps and . . .

. . . narrow-gauge railway, Metlaoui

Olive grove

The "Lezard Rouge"

Phosphates

Metlaoui owes its existence to the massive deposits of phosphates in the surrounding area, which now account for 90% of total Tunisian phosphate production. Phosphates are an important raw material of the chemical industry, used in the manufacture of fertilisers, washing powders and rust-proofing substances, and are therefore in great demand in the world market. For many years Tunisia was the world's leading producer of phosphates, but it has now fallen to sixth place. The difficulty is that in Tunisia the deposits of phosphates lie 5–8m/16–26ft below the surface and must be worked by underground mining methods and then transported on the Phosphate Company's own narrow-gauge railway all the way to Sfax and Gabès, on the coast, for onward shipment. In other phosphate-producing countries the deposits lie nearer the coast and can be worked by opencast methods. On top of this there is now an increasing demand for phosphate-free detergents.

History

The deposits of phosphates in this region were discovered by Philippe Thomas, a veterinary officer in the French army and an amateur palaeontologist, who in 1886 came upon phosphate-bearing strata at Ras el Aioun, near Metlaoui. Mining rights were acquired by the Compagnie des Phosphats et du Chemin de Fer du Gafsa, which began to work the phosphates in 1896. A narrow-gauge railway to Sfax was opened in 1899. Soon afterwards further deposits were discovered at Redeyef and Moularès, and in 1904 and 1905 these places were linked by rail with Metlaoui and so with Sfax. In 1909 they were given their own railway line to Sousse by way of Kasserine and Sbeitla. Until 1945 the phosphates were shipped from Sousse; thereafter from Sfax.

In 1913 new deposits were discovered on Djebel Mdilla, south of Gafsa, and these too were linked up with the Gafsa–Sfax railway.

Metlaoui, a totally insignificant hamlet until the discovery of the phosphates, thereafter developed rapidly into the centre of the largest mining area in Tunisia. The workings now extend from Metlaoui and Djebel Mdilla to Midès on the Algerian frontier, producing an annual 3.5 million tons of phosphates. Although the main output now comes from the more westerly mining areas around Redeyef and Moularès, Metlaoui is still the headquarters of the now state-owned mining company, Phosphates de Gafsa, the largest industrial concern in Tunisia, with some 15,000 mining workers and office staff. It is now the most important town in the whole phosphate region, with schools, hospitals, local government offices and a railway station belonging to the company. The mines on Djebel Mdilla are worked by another company, the Compagnie Tunisienne du Phosphat du Djebel Mdilla, with a work force of 2000.

Natural History Museum

In the centre of the town is a small Natural History Museum (open daily 9am–noon and 2–5.30pm), with an interesting display of fossils, some of them discovered by Philippe Thomas, as well as prehistoric and Roman antiquities (including a beautiful mosaic from a Roman villa) from the surrounding area.

Zoo

In the Municipal Park is a small Zoo, with animals of the Tunisian steppe and desert regions, including hyenas, jackals and Dorcas gazelles.

Surroundings of Metlaoui

*Seldja Gorge

The wild gorge of the Oued Seldja, ranging in depth between 150 and 200m (500 and 650ft), lies 10km/6 miles west of Metlaoui. It extends for a total distance of 15km/9 miles; the finest part, with limestone walls falling vertically down on either side, is 8km/5 miles long.
The narrowest part of the gorge, known as the Coup du Sabre ("Sabre Stroke"), is particularly picturesque. According to the legend it was hewn out by a Berber prince named Al Mansour while fleeing with his beloved,

Seldja Gorge

Leila. In the rock walls can be seen traces of a Roman dam which spanned the gorge at this point.
The gorge begins as a narrow defile and then opens out into a small basin. Beyond this is the Coup du Sabre, after which the valley becomes wider again, forming a beautiful verdant basin which for many visitors is the finest part of the gorge. At the end of the gorge is another narrow passage, at the end of which is the spring of Ras el Aioun, where Philippe Thomas discovered the first deposits of phosphates.

Access

The Seldja Gorge is most easily seen by taking the mining company's tourist train, the "Lézard Rouge".
It can also be reached by car. From Metlaoui take the Tozeur road (GP 3) and in 5km/3 miles, at the Thilja road sign, turn right into a track which heads towards the hills. At a fork bear right into a track leading to the gorge, and continue through the gorge on foot.

Warning

Particularly during the hot summer months visitors may encounter poisonous snakes (the African cobra): stout footwear, therefore, is essential. For part of the way it is necessary to walk along the railway track: be sure to check the times of trains.

Gafsa

42km/26 miles north-east: see entry

Tozeur

51km/32 miles south: see entry

Midès, Tamerza and Chebika oases

See Tozeur, Surroundings
Here we describe only the road from Metlaoui. Leave on MC 122, which runs north to join MC 201, coming from Gafsa. To the east of the road is a large salt lake, the Garaet el Douza, a port of call for huge numbers of migrant birds in autumn and winter. At the junction with MC 201 turn left (signposted Moularès). 500m/550yds beyond the junction, beside the road, are the foundations of a Roman villa; a mosaic found here is now in the museum in Metlaoui.
37km/23 miles from Metlaoui is Moularès. The road runs through a desolate lunar landscape, cratered by mining and dotted with slag heaps. The rock faces show a succession of strata in variegated colours.
From Moularès there is a good asphalted road to Redeyef (18km/11 miles) and Tamerza (23km/14 miles).
The first section of the road which runs west from Tamerza to Midès is asphalted. 5km/3 miles along this road, which continues to the Algerian frontier (customs post), a poorer track goes off to Midès.
From Tamerza a bad road runs south-west and south, through beautiful scenery, to Chebika. From the road there are fine views of the Chott el Rharsa to the south (see Chott el Djerid). A side track winds its way in steep hairpin bends through a 150m/500ft deep gorge on the Oued Khanga.

Monastir C 8

Chief town of the governorate of Monastir
Population: 28,000

Access

Monastir lies 22km/14 miles south-east of Sousse (MC 82) and 165km/103 miles from Tunis (motorway from Tunis to Hammamet, then GP 1 to Sousse and from there MC 82 to Hammamet).
The international airport of Monastir-Skanès is 7km/4½ miles from the town centre on the road to Sousse. There are scheduled services to and from Tunis and Djerba and all European capitals, and daily charter flights during the summer.
On the west side of the Medina is the station of the Métro du Sahel, from which there are regular services to the airport, Sousse (hourly), Tunis and

View of Monastir

Gabès. From the bus station (Gare Routière) at Bab el Gharbi, on the south-west side of the Medina, there are regular services to Tunis, Sousse, Mahdia, Sfax and other places in the Sahel.

Situation and characteristics

Monastir, capital of its governorate and a university town, lies at the tip of a small rocky peninsula at the south end of the Gulf of Hammamet. It has a small walled Medina and an imposing old Ribat, which stood within sight of the one in Sousse (see entry).

Monastir, the birthplace in 1903 of ex-President Bourguiba, has developed within the last twenty years into one of the most popular seaside resorts in Tunisia. Around the town, particularly to the north at Dkhila and Skanès, are extensive hotel complexes with miles of broad beaches of fine sand.

In addition to the tourist trade the processing of olive oil and the extraction of salt make important contributions to the town's economy. There is a small fishing harbour, but the fisheries are of little economic importance. During the summer there are *son et lumière* shows in the Ribat.

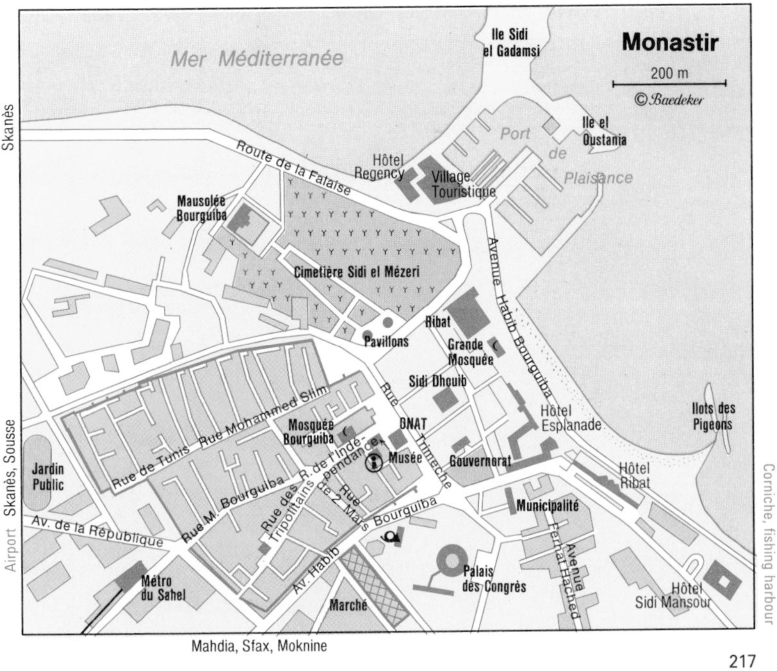

History

The Phoenicians established a trading station named Rous Penna on this strategic site, and under the Romans this became the town of Ruspina. During the civil war with Pompey (49–46 B.C.) Caesar made this his headquarters in North Africa and surrounded it with a triple ring of walls.

When the Arabs established a chain of fortified monasteries along the North African coast in the 8th century they recognised the strategic value of this site at the tip of the peninsula and built the Ribat from which the town takes its name (Greek *monasterion*). From here the soldier-monks launched a series of campaigns against the Christian island of Sicily. After the decline of Kairouan Monastir for a time took over its role as the holiest Islamic town in Tunisia.

The Ribat retained its military importance into the Turkish period, when the Beys made it a powerful stronghold. During the French protectorate, however, Monastir degenerated into an unimportant fishing and market town, which began to revive only after Tunisia achieved independence. It owes its present prosperity mainly to the development of mass tourism over the last twenty years. It now has some 20 hotels with a total of 9000 beds.

Sights

Medina

The Medina is surrounded by a battlemented wall built in the 18th century. Recently restored in the interests of the tourist trade, it now looks very smart and well cared for – perhaps, indeed, a little too much so. As in other tourist centres, the wares offered in the souk are designed to appeal to visitors, and the prices are correspondingly high.

Bourguiba Mosque

Notable features in the old town are the birthplace of Habib Bourguiba in Rue Trabelsia, with the Musée du Mouvement National (devoted to the history of Tunisia's struggle for independence), and the Bourguiba Mosque in the Rue de l'Indépendance, with an octagonal minaret, 41m/135ft high, which is a prominent landmark. The mosque, modelled on the Hammouda

Ribat, Monastir

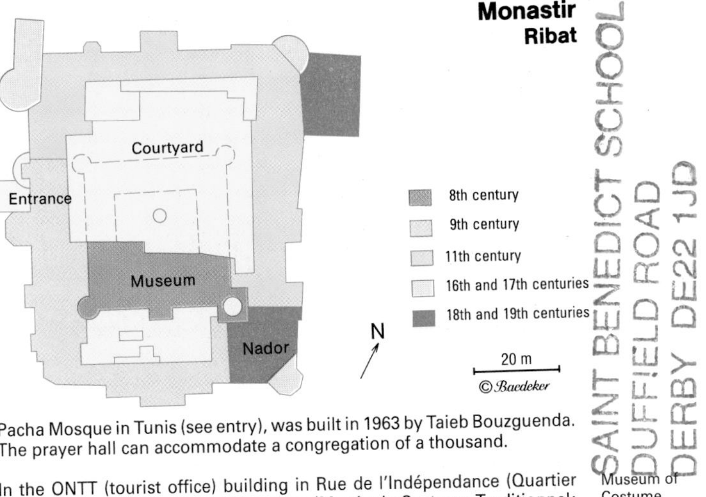

Pacha Mosque in Tunis (see entry), was built in 1963 by Taieb Bouzguenda. The prayer hall can accommodate a congregation of a thousand.

Museum of Costume

In the ONTT (tourist office) building in Rue de l'Indépendance (Quartier Chraga) is a small Museum of Costume (Musée du Costume Traditionnel; open 9am–noon and 3–6pm), with a display of wedding costumes from all over Tunisia.

**Ribat

Just off the harbour is Monastir's famous Ribat, built by Harthama ben Ayan in 796, which ranks with the Ribat of Sousse as one of the oldest Arab fortresses in North Africa; but while the Ribat in Monastir was further strengthened the one in Sousse soon lost its military importance to the later Kasbah. As a result the similarities between the two buildings are not at first sight evident.

In Monastir the Kasbah was built in the 9th and 11th centuries round the Ribat, which thus retained its dominant position in the Medina. Further buildings were added in the 16th/17th and 18th/19th centuries. Extensive renovation was carried out in the 1960s.

Basically the Ribat is similar in plan to the one in Sousse. Originally it was only 32.80m/108ft square and lacked the semicircular towers half way along the sides of the Ribat of Sousse. On the south-east side is the three-storey Nador tower, from the top of which there are fine views of the yachting harbour, the large cemetery containing the Bourguiba Mausoleum, the Great Mosque and the roofs of the Medina.

An imposing gateway on the west side of the Ribat leads into the inner courtyard, surrounded on three sides by buildings several storeys high containing the monks' cells, store-rooms and casemates. The monks' quarters were separated by another gateway from other buildings (perhaps women's quarters) probably added in the 9th century.

Islamic Museum

The former prayer hall on the upper floor is now occupied by the Islamic Museum, with an interesting collection of coins (10th–11th c.), Koranic inscriptions (8th–12th c.), fabrics (Coptic linen from Egypt, fine silks), glassware, bronze articles, pottery, jewellery and an astrolabe of 927 from Córdoba.

The Ribat is open daily, except Mondays and public holidays, 9.30am–4.30pm.

In and around the Ribat are film sets and studios. Franco Zeffirelli shot scenes from his film "Jesus of Nazareth" here in 1976.

Great Mosque

Great Mosque

To the south of the Ribat is the Great Mosque, built in the 9th century and enlarged by the Zirids in the 11th.

Saida Mosque

Opposite the Esplanade Hotel can be seen the remains of the Saida Mosque, a burial mosque which originally stood within another ribat.

Sidi Dhouib Ribat

Between the Great Mosque and the Medina is a third, rather smaller ribat, the Sidi Dhouib Ribat, the ground floor of which has been rebuilt.

Cemetery

Immediately north-west of the Ribat lies a large cemetery with a number of beautiful old marabouts, some of them decorated with bands of Kufic inscriptions and faience tiles. Particularly notable is the 12th century tomb of Sidi el Mazeri. The large size of the cemetery reflects the desire of many Muslims to be buried close to the Ribat, regarded as a sacred shrine.

Bourguiba Mausoleum

Conspicuously situated at the north end of the cemetery, on the axis of the two modern octagonal pavilions at its entrance, is the golden-domed Bourguiba Mausoleum, built in 1963 as the burial mosque of ex-President Habib Bourguiba and his family.
The two slender minarets, 25m/82ft high, are of Italian marble. To the right is the little marabout of Sidi Bou Zid.

Other sights

South-east of the Medina is the business and shopping district of the new town, with the modern Congress Centre, Theatre and Library.

Harbour

The seafront promenade (Corniche) leads to the yachting harbour (Port de plaisance), with a new holiday complex (Village touristique).

Islands

Off the coast, linked with the mainland by a causeway, are the two little islands of Sidi el Gadamsi and El Oustania.

Ilots des Pigeons

Between the coast road (Avenue Habib Bourguiba), lined by hotels, and the sea is a small sandy beach, with two tiny islets, the Ilots des Pigeons, lying

Bourguiba Mausoleum

just offshore. At the south-east end of the beach is the modern fishing harbour.

Skanès

On the north side of Monastir is the Route de la Falaise, which leads to the suburb of Skanès with its villas and hotels. The road passes the former Presidential Palace, enclosed by high walls with a large wrought-iron gate. From Skanès the Route Touristique de la Dkhila continues along the coast, edged by salt-pans, to shortly before Sousse.

Surroundings of Monastir

Moknine

15km/9 miles south of Monastir, on the shores of a salt lake, is Moknine, a little town noted for its craft products (jewellery, pottery). The former mosque of Sidi Babana is now occupied by a small Folk Museum (open daily, except Mondays and public holidays, 9am–noon and 2.30–6pm, in winter 9am–noon and 2–5.30pm).
This offers an interesting example of the type of "tube vaulting" found at Bulla Regia (see entry).

Ksar Hellal

This little industrial town (textiles) has now almost joined up with Moknine. The founding congress of the Neo-Destour party was held here in 1934.

Sousse

22km/14 miles north-west: see entry

Kairouan

83km/52 miles west: see entry

Mahdia

22km/14 miles south: see entry

El Djem

84km/52 miles south-west: see entry

Nabeul

B 7

Chief town of the governorate of Nabeul
Population: 40,000

Access

Nabeul, 70km/43 miles south-east of Tunis and the international airport of Tunis-Carthage, can be reached on either the motorway or GP 1 to Hammamet and MC 28 from there.

From the station in Avenue Habib Bourguiba there are rail services to Tunis and Hammamet/Bir Bou Rekba, with connections to Sousse and Sfax. From the bus station (Gare Routière) on the Hammamet road there are services to Tunis, Hammamet, Korbous, El Haouaria, Soliman, Kairouan, Zaghouan, Sousse and the international airport of Tunis-Carthage.

Situation and *characteristics

Nabeul, the largest town on Cap Bon (see entry), lies at the south-eastern end of the peninsula, near the long sandy beach which extends round the Gulf of Hammamet. Together with Hammamet (see entry), 10km/6 miles down the coast, Nabeul forms the second largest holiday centre in Tunisia, but still contrives to retain something of its original character. It is surrounded by an intensively cultivated agricultural region, producing fruit and vegetables whicb are sold in the town's important Friday market. Nabeul is also famed as the principal centre of Tunisian craft production, particularly for its traditional pottery trade (which has been given a considerable boost by tourism) and for the perfumes manufactured here. Much sought after, too, are Nabeul's plaited mats, stone-carving, embroidery and woven fabrics.

Most of the hotels are situated to the south of the town, in the direction of Hammamet, with one or two more exclusive establishments on the Kelibia road to the north. Altogether the town has some twelve hotel complexes with some 6000 beds.

History

Ancient Neapolis (Greek, the "new town"), situated directly on the coast, was originally a Carthaginian foundation of the 5th century B.C. During the Third Punic War it was occupied by the Romans. In the 2nd century A.D. it was given the status of a *colonia,* and in 256 it became the see of a bishop.

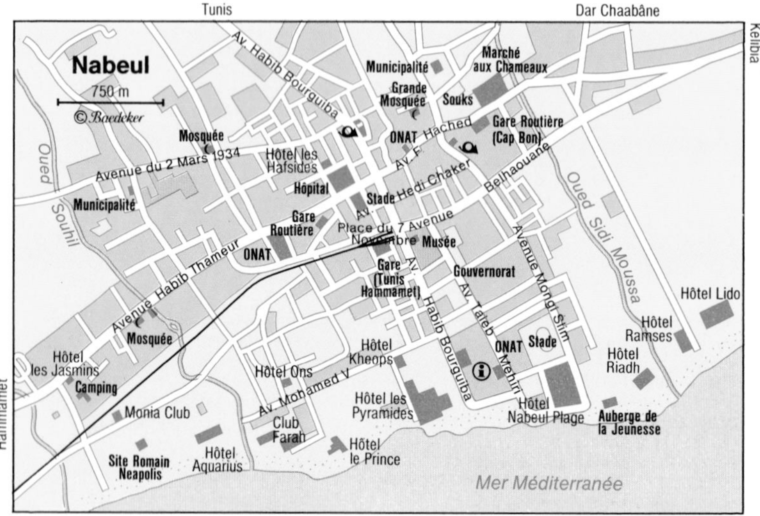

Tile-decorated façade, Nabeul

In the 16th and 17th centuries it provided a home for refugees from Andalusia, whose influence on the local crafts, particularly on the pottery, is still evident.

Sights

Neapolis

Nabeul is predominantly a modern town. A few scanty remains of ancient Neapolis were found during the construction of the Hotel Neapolis and near the Hotel Jasmin, including an establishment for the manufacture of garum, a sauce made from pickled fish which was much favoured by the Romans and remained popular throughout Europe into the Middle Ages.

Place du 7 Novembre

The hub of the town's life, with banks, restaurants and shops, is the Place du 7 Novembre, at the intersection of Avenue Habib Thameur, coming from Hammamet (with its continuation Avenue Farhat Hached), and Avenue Habib Bourguiba, which runs up from the coast. Here too is Nabeul's municipal emblem, the symbol of its old-established pottery trade – a huge painted pottery jar with a tree growing out of it.

Camel market

The once famous camel market held on Fridays is now a mere tourist attraction. It is less crowded in the early morning.

Crafts

A stroll through the souks, with their tempting displays of the products of the town's potters, stone-carvers and weavers, is recommended to all visitors.

The predominant colours of the pottery are green (a mixture of lead and copper oxides) and yellow (lead and antimony). The technique was originally introduced in the 17th century by a family from Djerba. The simple geometric designs go back to ancient models.

It is worth enquiring beforehand in the showrooms of ONAT (Organisation Nationale de l'Artisanat Tunisien) in Avenue Habib Thameur about the quality and prices of local products.

Marsyas and Apollo (Archaeological Museum, Nabeul)

Archaeological Museum

In Avenue Habib Bourguiba, diagonally opposite the railway station, is the small but very interesting Archaeological Museum (open daily, except Mondays, 9am–4.30pm).

In the entrance hall are a historical map of Cap Bon and a plan of ancient Neapolis.

Room I (to the left of the entrance hall) displays material of the Punic period (7th–4th c. B.C.), including pottery, oil lamps, jewellery and coins, mostly from excavations at Kerkouane (see Cap Bon, Tour of the Peninsula).

In the corridor are finds of Punic and Roman material from the Bir Bou Rekba area.

Also of interest are the clay statues of the Carthaginian deities Baal Hammon and Tanit, showing that the Punic religion lingered on even after the Roman conquest.

In the inner courtyard are a number of fine Roman mosaics, including examples from Kelibia (2nd/3rd c. A.D.) and Neapolis (4th c.); a collection of Roman stelae (4th c.); and fragments of statues.

Surroundings of Nabeul

Nabeul, like Hammamet, is a good base for excursions in the surrounding area.

Cap Bon

One very rewarding trip is a tour of the Cap Bon peninsula (see entry).

Dar Chaabane

The craftsmen's village of Dar Chaabane, 2km/1¼ miles north-east of Nabeul, is famed for its stone-carvers, whose work is found in doorways and windows all over Tunisia.

Beni Khiar

5km/3 miles north-east is the weavers' village of Beni Khiar, whose woollen blankets, articles of clothing and kelims find a ready market among foreign visitors.
Here too is Nabeul's fishing harbour.

Es Somaa

Es Somaa, 8.5km/5¼ miles from Nabeul, is noted for its plaited mats.

Korba

20km/12½ miles north-east is Korba, where the Festival of Young Theatre is held annually in August. Information from the ONTT office in Nabeul.

Kerkouane

75km/47 miles north: see Cap Bon.

Tunis

74km/46 miles north: see entry

Thuburbo Majus

90km/56 miles west: see entry

Zaghouan

On the way to Thuburbo Majus it is worth pausing in Zaghouan (48km/30 miles west; see Tunis, Surroundings) to see the Roman nymphaeum.

Hammamet

10km/6 miles south-west: see entry

Kairouan

110km/68 miles south-west: see entry

Nefta

F 4

Governorate: Tozeur
Population: 15,000

Access

Nefta lies on GP 3 (Gafsa-Nefta), 25km/16 miles south-west of Tozeur (airport; regular services to and from Tunis, Monastir and Djerba) and 113km/70 miles south-west of Gafsa.
From the bus station (Gare Routière) in Avenue Habib Bourguiba there are regular bus services to Tozeur and Gafsa and a once-daily service to Douz

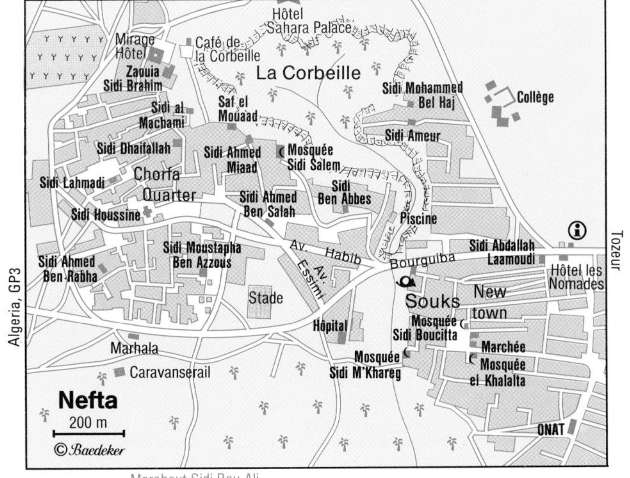

Marabout Sidi Bou Ali

and Hazaoua, the frontier post for the crossing into Algeria. The 4km/2½ miles from there to the frontier must be done either on foot or in a *louage* (communal taxi). From the Algerian frontier post there are buses to El Oued.

Situation and characteristics

The little town of Nefta lies in its oasis (area 1100 hectares/2750 acres) south-west of Tozeur, only 36km/22 miles from the Algerian frontier, on the western edge of the Chott el Djerid. It is the market centre of Tunisia's most westerly oasis, with a busy market on Wednesdays. Its inhabitants earn their living from oasis agriculture (over 400,000 date-palms, including 70,000 which produce the high quality *deglat en nour* or "finger of light" date), trade and craft productions. Nefta is famed for its carpet-makers, its silk weavers and its potters.

Tourism

In recent years tourism has come to Nefta. Here as in the oasis of Douz (see Kebili) the magic word "Sahara" has begun to attract large numbers of visitors. Many new hotels have been built or are under construction, and the town's bed capacity is to be still further increased in coming years. Apart from permanent sunshine the attractions offered to tourists include Landrover excursions into the desert, visits to other oases including Tozeur (see entry) and the Nefzaoua oases (see Kebili) and trips across the Chott el Djerid (see entry) or through the Seldja Gorge (see Metlaoui).

Events

Nefta is a pilgrimage centre to which pilgrims travel throughout the year. There is a Folk Festival in April and a Date Festival in November/December.

Nefta as a religious centre

Nefta is the religious centre of the Bled el Djerid, the "Land of Palms", with more than 24 mosques and 100 marabouts. The marabouts still attract pilgrims from all over southern Tunisia and even from Algeria. This great veneration of the marabouts reflects the continuing vigour of Sufism, the movement which grew up in the 12th century around the learned Sufi Abu Madian (d. 1197). The name of the Sufis came from the simple woollen garment (*suf*) they wore. They believed that the adherents of Islam, a religion of the desert, should show particular modesty of behaviour and asceticism, and were much given to mysticism, the veneration of holy men, spiritual contemplation and meditation. Sufism is also marked by religious forms taken over from the pre-Islamic, animistic religions of the Berber population which orthodox Islam seeks to repress – belief in spirits, witchcraft, fortune-telling, the efficacy of amulets, etc.

Regional variants of Sufism were propagated by holy men, who frequently founded their own brotherhoods, with centres for the teaching of disciples. They are credited with numerous miracles and revered for their holiness, and their tombs (marabouts) are places of pilgrimage, attracting varying numbers of pilgrims according to their reputation. In the past these holy men were also appealed to as judges in the conflicts which frequently occurred between the nomadic tribes and the settled population of the oases.

Nefta is the last stronghold of this Sufism, and is sometimes called, not without justification, the "Kairouan of the South". The marabouts venerated here are scattered about throughout the old town of Nefta and the oasis.

The town

The town is divided into two parts by a small oued and a depression at its northern end. To the east of the oued is the new town, with the old souk quarter at its south-western corner; to the west, on the slopes of a hill, is the old town.

The main road from Tozeur runs through the new town as Avenue Habib Bourguiba, which then crosses the oued and skirts the old town. At its western end a street branches off on the right, ascends the hill, goes round the old town and the sand-bowl and returns to Avenue Habib Bourguiba.

Nefta is a town of cube-shaped, flat-roofed houses huddled closely together, with Tozeur-style decoration (see Tozeur). In some of the streets

View of the Corbeille

the upper storeys of the houses, borne on round-headed arches, project over the street, forming a kind of tunnel which offers protection from the sun.

It is planned to restore the old town in the very near future.

History

The history of the oases of the Djerid reaches far back into the past. They are believed to have been settled by Numidians, but only their Roman names have been preserved, such as Thusuros (Tozeur), Aggasel, Nepte (Nefta), Thigae (Kriz), Aquae (El Hamma) and Capsa (Gafsa). The Romans and later the Byzantines built forts in the oases to provide protection against raids by desert nomads. In Byzantine times Nefta and Tozeur were episcopal sees.

In the mid 7th century Nefta was conquered by the Arabs and, in spite of fierce resistance, converted to Islam. In subsequent centuries it prospered as an important staging-point for caravans (for a time the most important in Tunisia). Its decline began in the 15th century as a result of more frequent raids by the nomadic tribes and the general falling off in the caravan trade. With the coming of the French in 1881, however, it took on a fresh lease of life.

Sights

Before looking round the sights of Nefta it is a good idea to get a general view of the town and its surroundings. There are two fine viewpoints on the north side of the town, the Café de la Corbeille and the terrace of the Sahara Palace Hotel to the east, overlooking the whole of Nefta with the white domes of its marabouts, the Corbeille (see below), the oasis and the surrounding desert.

**Corbeille de Nefta

The Corbeille ("Basket") is the name given to the 30m/100ft deep depression at the head of the oued, filled with a closely planted grove of tall palms. Here two small streams fed by a number of springs at the north end of the gorge join to form the oued which waters the oasis.

The springs which feed the oued now have a much less abundant flow than in the past. In 1893 they supplied 1000 litres/220 gallons of water a second, but in 1982 the flow was only 300 litres/66 gallons a second. It has been necessary, therefore, to drive wells down to a depth of 600 to 1000m (2000 to 3300ft) to tap the ground-water far below.

There is a pleasant walk through the Corbeille, following the warm stream to a clearing in the palm-grove where the water has formed a pool.

The town

The old town of Nefta is a warren of picturesque streets and houses with decorated brick façades, interspersed with the domes and minarets of the mosques.

Zaouia of Sidi Brahim (Sidi Kadria)

Adjoining the Café de la Corbeille, immediately in front of the Hotel Mirage, is the Zaouia of Sidi Brahim (Sidi Kadria), with the tomb of the holy man and his sons. Visitors are admitted to the prayer hall and the teaching room. Sidi Brahim was an important Sufi, and the Zaouia is a much-visited centre of Sufism.

Mosque of Sidi Salem (Great Mosque)

A tortuous route through the old town leads to the 16th century Mosque of Sidi Salem or Great Mosque (Djemaa el Kebir), Nefta's oldest mosque. Situated on the western edge of the Corbeille, it offers a fine view of the palm-grove.

Market square

From the mosque a narrow lane on the right, partly roofed over, leads to the Place de l'Indépendance, the market square of the old town and in particu-

Sidi Salem Mosque

lar of the Chorfa quarter in its centre. The houses in the square have elaborately patterned mud-brick façades. Lower down is Avenue Habib Bourguiba, the town's main street, which runs south-east to the bridge over the oued, here emerging from the Corbeille, and continues into the new town, with its banks, petrol stations, modern shops, post office and tourist information office (ONTT).

Chorfa quarter

New town

At the post office a narrow street goes off on the right, leading through the picturesque little lanes of the souk quarter to the market square of this quarter, the Place de la Libération, with numerous shops and cafés and the market hall.

Souk quarter

The Oasis

To the south of this quarter the town comes to an end, giving place to the garden-like country of the oasis, traversed by sandy tracks and small irrigation channels which distribute water to the various holdings of land in accordance with traditional rules (see Tozeur).

The most important products of the oasis, in addition to corn, vegetables and citrus fruits, are the famous *deglat en nour* dates. Since the economic and social structure of Nefta, like that of Tozeur, is antiquated – with a small number (some 2% of the population) of large landowners owning over 1000 palms each and some hundreds of smallholdings of under 50 palms – productivity is much lower than in recently planted palm-groves such as those in the oasis of El Hamma (see Tozeur, Surroundings).

The most important marabout and place of pilgrimage in the oasis is the Marabout of Sidi Bou Ali, reached on a narrow road which branches off the main road to the frontier opposite Avenue Esslim (to the east of the Hotel Marhala) and runs south into the oasis. The marabout is dedicated to a Moroccan holy man who came to Nefta in the 13th century to settle a serious religious dispute which had almost led to a schism. He died in Nefta and was buried at the place where he had been teaching.
The tomb (not open to non-Muslims) has a beautifully decorated burial chamber and prayer hall with a plaster stalactitic ceiling. On the northern edge of the oasis, opposite the Mosque of Sidi M'Khareg, is a café.

Marabout of Sidi Bou Ali

Surroundings of Nefta

15km/9 miles west of Nefta the main road into Algeria (GP 3) runs through a large area of dunes, an offshoot of the Grand Erg Oriental.

Dunes

25km/16 miles east: see entry

Tozeur

See Tozeur, Surroundings

Oasis of El Oudiane

See Tozeur, Surroundings

Oases of Chebika, Tamerza and Midès

The road over the Chott el Djerid (see entry) from Kriz to Kebili begins 40km/25 miles north-east of Nefta.

Chott el Djerid

Nefzaoua

See Kebili

Port el Kantaoui

See Sousse, Surroundings

Reqqada

See Kairouan, Surroundings

Sbeitla

D 6

Governorate: Kasserine
Altitude: 537m/1762ft
Population: *c.* 8000

Access

Sbeitla lies near the junction of GP 3 (Kairouan–Kasserine) with GP 13 (Sfax–Kasserine), 40km/25 miles north-east of Kasserine, 117km/73 miles south-west of Kairouan and 165km/103 miles north-west of Sfax. There are bus services from the town centre to Maktar, Kairouan, Tunis, Kasserine, Gafsa and Tozeur.

Situation and characteristics

The little market town of Sbeitla lies in the zone of transition between the Dorsale and the central Tunisian steppe country. It is surrounded by irrigated agricultural land, and has a fruit- and olive-growing research station and a collection point for the esparto grass grown in the steppe country. The nearby site of Roman Sufetula ranks with Dougga, Bulla Regia and Maktar (see entries) as one of the finest ancient sites in Tunisia.

History

Little is known about the early history of Sufetula. Only a small part of the site has been excavated, and the archaeologists' work is hampered by the presence of Byzantine buildings overlying the earlier remains.
The town, situated near a river at the intersection of ancient roads, seems to have been founded by the Romans at the end of the 1st century A.D. Originally a *municipium,* it was later raised to the status of a *colonia.* Christianity came to the town in the 3rd century, and a number of churches dating from this period have been found. The town survived the Vandal invasion unscathed, and it became a Byzantine stronghold against the Arab advance. Sufetula featured briefly on the world stage in 647, when the Byzantine governor, Exarch Gregorius, had himself proclaimed Emperor here in opposition to Constantine II. In the same year, however, he was killed in the first battle with the advancing Arabs.
The Arabs plundered the town but left it largely undamaged. It finally fell into Arab hands after the conquest of Carthage in 698, and its new rulers founded a new town, present-day Sbeitla, to the south of Sufetula, which was now abandoned. Thereafter its fine buildings gradually fell into ruin or were used as a quarry of building stone.
The existence of the site became known in Europe only in the 18th century, and the first excavations began in 1907. Only about a third of the town – which is estimated to have had a population of around 10,000 – has so far been excavated.

** Excavations

The enclosed excavation site (open daily 9am–5pm) lies on the western outskirts of Sbeitla, to the south of the Hotel Sufetula. The entrance is on the Kasserine road (GP 13); opposite it is a small museum (see below).

The ancient city lies on a gently sloping plateau bounded on the east by the Oued Sbeitla. The regular grid of its streets, centred on the decumanus maximus, running east–west, and the cardo maximus (north–south), is clearly visible. At the intersection of the two principal streets is the Forum.

Arch of Diocletian

The south gate of the city was the Arch of Diocletian (3rd c. A.D.) This magnificently preserved triumphal arch can be seen a long way off when approaching the site.
Turning left from the entrance to the site, we pass a number of small Byzantine forts (7th c.) and the foundations of a 7th century church dedicated to SS. Gervasius, Protasius and Tryphon. Opposite this are the remains of ancient baths. Bearing right from here, we pass the remains of an oil-press and come to the Great Baths or Winter Baths. Adjoining are the ruined columns of a fountain. Lower down, on the banks of the river, is a small theatre.

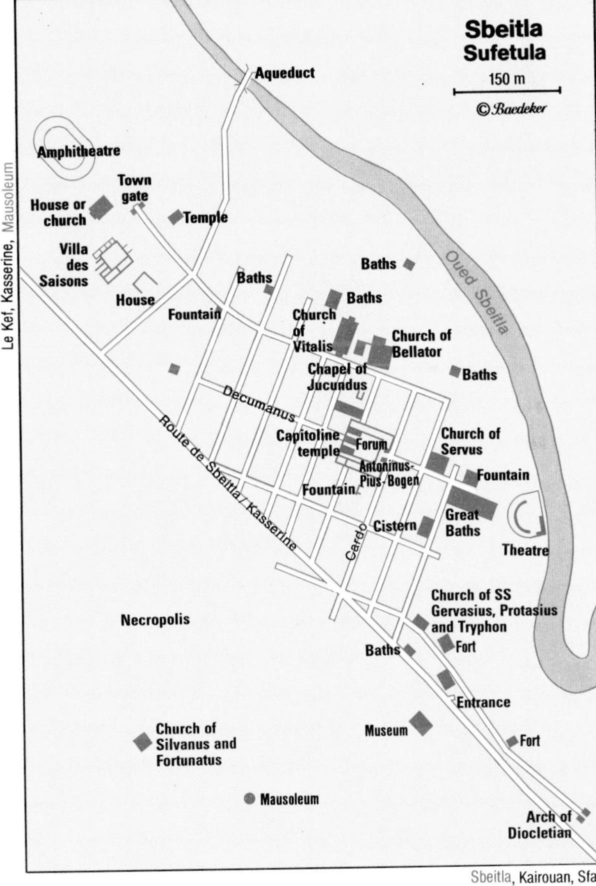

Arch of Diocletian

From the Great Baths the decumanus, lined with shops, runs past the 5th century Church of Servus, built in the peristyle of a temple, to end at a three-bayed arch, the entrance to the Forum.

Forum

Arch of Antoninus Pius

The Forum is outstandingly well preserved, the finest of its kind in the whole of North Africa. Measuring 34.75m/114ft by 37.20m/122ft and paved with stone slabs, it is entered through the Arch of Antoninus Pius. This is the only structure in Sufetula whose date can be certainly established (A.D. 139) It was evidently left unfinished, for the shafts of the four Corinthian columns on the façade have not been smoothed off.

The Forum, now enclosed by a 4m/13ft high Byzantine wall, was surrounded on three sides by slightly raised porticoes, behind which were shops and offices.

On the north-west side of the Forum are three temples dedicated to Jupiter, Juno and Minerva. These three deities were normally worshipped in a single Capitoline temple with three cellas, as at Dougga (see entry), and it is unusual to find them with three separate temples, as here (and also in the Roman town of Belo in southern Spain). Each temple is entered by a short flight of steps. In front of the central temple of Jupiter is the rostrum (the orators' tribune).

At the south-east corner of the Forum can be seen the remains of a 4th century fountain.

Early Christian Sufetula

Church of Bellator

Turning right (north-east) from the Forum, we follow a street which passes the foundations of a three-aisled church to the central feature of Early Christian Sufetula, the Church of Bellator. This was the city's first episcopal church, probably built in the 4th century on the site of an ancient temple but set at an angle to the Roman street grid. Originally a three-aisled basilica, it was later enlarged. In the apse (also a later addition) were found remains of an earlier mosaic.

Chapel of Jucundus

On the left of the church is the Chapel of Jucundus, commemorating Bishop Jucundus, who represented Sufetula at the Council of Carthage and is thought to have been martyred during the period of Vandal rule.

Church of Vitalis

Beyond this are the remains of the Church of Vitalis, built on the site of a large villa towards the end of the 5th century, when the Christian community had become too large for the church of Bellator. Sited in conformity with the Roman street grid, it had five aisles, separated by double columns, and measured 50m/164ft by 25m/82ft. The baptistery is particularly well preserved, with four columns which supported a canopy over the font.

A fragment of a mosaic from an earlier building (probably 3rd century) was found on the site.

Immediately behind the church are remains of baths of the Christian period.

Other sights

From the Church of Vitalis the Roman street continues north-west, roughly parallel to the modern road to Kasserine which can be seen on the left. In 350m/380yds it comes to the remains of other Roman buildings, which are likely to appeal only to those with a serious interest in archaeology. On the left are the remains of a fountain similar to those beside the Church of Servus and at the south end of the Forum. From here a track on the right runs north-east to a three-arched 2nd century bridge, frequently restored, carrying an aqueduct over the Oued Sbeitla.

The town of Sfax, 166km/103 miles away on the coast, gets its water from the source of the Oued Sbeitla.

The road continues to the remains of a small temple of unknown dedication and a town gate of the Severan period. Beyond this, on the left, are the

Forum, with the Capitoline temple of Juno, Jupiter and Minerva

remains of a 5th century house and/or church. 50m/55yds farther on a depression in the ground marks the site of the amphitheatre, which has not yet been excavated.

Returning towards the entrance, we pass the foundations of the large Villa des Saisons, named after a mosaic of the Seasons which is now in the Bardo Museum in Tunis.

Little excavation has been done south-west of the Kasserine road. So far only the remains of two mausoleums and a 4th century church dedicated to SS. Silvanus and Fortunatus have been found: evidently this area was used by both Romans and Christians for the burial of their dead.

Farther north is a mound which is believed to mark the site of a Punic tophet.

Museum

The little museum (opened 1988) displays in its three rooms a variety of finds from the site, including mosaics, pottery, coins and funerary stelae.

Surroundings of Sbeitla

Thelepte

67km/42 miles south-west of Sbeitla on the Gafsa road (GP 13) is the village of Thelepte, just beyond which, at kilometre-stone 208, a road goes off on the right to the scanty remains (for the archaeological enthusiast only) of the Roman and Byzantine settlement of Thamusmida.

Kasserine

There are more substantial remains at Kasserine (see entry), 38km/24 miles south-west of Sbeitla.

Sbiba

40km/25 miles north of Sbeitla on the road to Le Kef (MC 71) is the village of Sbiba, with the remains of the Roman town of Sufes, including a nymphaeum, a basilica and the walls of a Byzantine fortress. Here again the remains are so scanty as to be of interest only to dedicated enthusiasts.

Seldja Gorge

See Metlaoui, Surroundings

Sfax

D 8

Chief town of the governorate of Sfax
Population: 232,000 (with suburbs over 300,000)

Access

Sfax lies on GP 1 (Sousse-Gabès), 127km/79 miles south of Sousse and 137km/85 miles north of Gabés.
From the airport, 10km/6 miles west of the town on the Gafsa road (GP 14), there are flights to Tunis, Gabès, Djerba/Tripoli (Libya), Malta and France.
Rail services (station at seaward end of Avenue Habib Bourguiba) to Tunis, Sousse, Gabès and Gafsa/Metlaoui/Tozeur.
Bus services (from Gare Routière at west end of Avenue Habib Bourguiba) to Sousse/Tunis, Kairouan, Kasserine, Gafsa/Tozeur, Gabès/Médenine and Djerba.

Situation and characteristics

Sfax (Arabic Safakis) lies at the north end of the Gulf of Gabès, 155km/96 miles south-west of Tunis, in the most extensive olive-growing area in Tunisia. It is the country's largest city after Tunis and the economic centre of southern Tunisia.

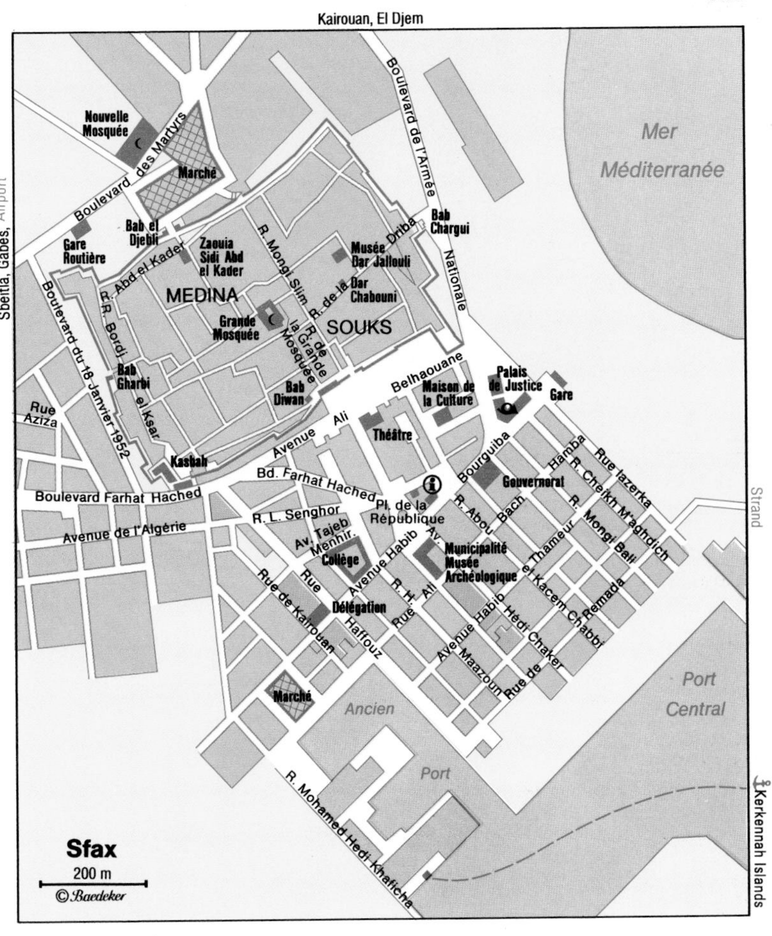

Tourism plays little part in the economy of Sfax, which lacks the attraction of the long sandy beaches possessed by other coastal towns (it has only a small beach, artificially built up). But it is well worth a visit for the sake of its Medina, one of the finest in the whole of Tunisia. It is also a good base for excursions to El Djem and the Kerkennah Islands (see entries).

Economy

Olives have been grown in the Sahel since ancient times, for the maritime climate, reaching far inland, allows the soil to retain its moisture and moderates the effects of the desert winds. Huge olive-groves extend endlessly around the town, with over 8 million trees reaching far into the steppe country. Some 20km/12½ miles from the town the picture changes, as olive-trees (many of them old and past their best) give place to almond-trees. A 4–8km/2½–5 mile wide belt of small gardens growing fruit, vegetables and flowers, with numbers of summer cottages, runs round the town, which is steadily extending farther into the surrounding countryside.

Place de la République

Olive-trees as far as the eye can see

The olives of the Sahel are processed in over 400 oil-mills in the town and sold in the Olive Exchange. Large quantities are exported from the commercial harbour.

Sfax also has important industries, including leatherworking, the manufacture of perfume and optical glass, the processing of olive residues to make soap, two phosphate works (also producing fertilisers) and a factory producing cellulose from esparto grass.

The major part of the port's turnover is accounted for by the export of phosphates from the Metlaoui (see entry) and Djebel Mdilla areas, which are transported by rail to Sfax. Other bulk goods shipped from here are corn, esparto grass, sponges and salt. Sfax also has an important fishing harbour, at which over a fifth of the total Tunisian catch is landed.

History

Sfax was founded at the beginning of the 9th century A.D. on the site of ancient Taparura. There are no remains worth mentioning of the Roman town, which was probably a place of no great consequence; its regular street grid may, however, be reflected in the rectangular layout of the Medina. Of greater importance in Roman times was Thaenae (see below), 12km/7½ miles south. Sfax's economic heyday began under Arab rule at the beginning of the 10th century, when the trade in olive oil prospered as never before. After the devastation wrought by the Beni Hilal nomads the town took a long time to recover. From 1148 Sfax, like most of the coastal towns, was occupied by the Normans, who were driven out by the Almohads in 1159. The town suffered heavy damage during the French conquest in 1881 and also in the Second World War, when it was occupied by the Axis powers and bombed by the Allies in 1942–43. Fortunately the Medina survived largely unscathed.

Sights

New town

Between the harbour to the south-east and the Medina to the north-west is the new town, laid out on a regular grid during the French protectorate. In the centre of the town, at the intersection of Avenue Habib Bourguiba, running east–west, and Avenue Hedi Chaker, which leads to the Medina, is the Place de la République, with a monument to Bourguiba. Only a few buildings of the colonial period have survived; among them is the Town Hall (Municipalité) on the south-east side of the square, a building in neo-Moorish style with a tall minaret-like tower. Most of Sfax's public buildings are in the new town, including the tourist information office (ONTT), banks, local government offices and the Head Post Office, with a façade decorated by the Tunisian artist Zubeir Turki.

Town Hall

*Archaeological Museum

On the ground floor of the Municipalité is the very interesting Archaeological Museum (open daily, except Mondays, 8.30am–1pm and 3–6pm). The exhibits include Punic, Roman and Byzantine antiquities and animal, hunting and marine mosaics from Thaenae, Taparura and La Skhira, including "Daniel in the lions' den" (5th/6th c.) and "Ennius surrounded by the Muses" (3rd c.).

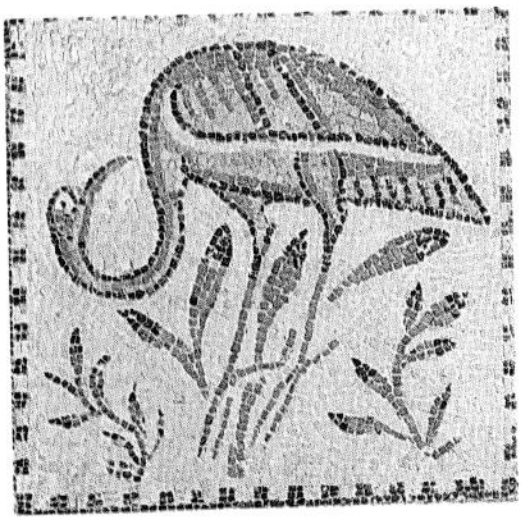

*Medina

Bab Diwan

Avenue Hedi Chaker runs north to the main gateway of the Medina, Bab Diwan, built in 1306 and subsequently much altered, almost totally destroyed by bombing in 1943 and rebuilt after the war in its original form. The Medina is relatively small, measuring only 400m/440yds by 500m/550yds, and is enclosed by a well preserved circuit of walls 2km/1¼ miles long. The walls, originally built in mud brick by the Aghlabids in

Minaret of the Great Mosque

Fish market

the 9th century, were later strongly fortified. The Kasbah at the south-west corner was built in the 17th century; the fortifications at the east end date from the 12th century.

Unusually, the streets of the Medina are mainly laid out on a rectangular plan, presumably inherited from the Roman town.

Rue Mongi Slim runs through the Medina from south to north. In Rue de la Driba, which goes off on the right, are a number of houses with handsome and imposing doorways; and in a side street opening off it on the left is the interesting Folk Museum.

*Folk Museum Dar Jellouli

The Folk Museum (Musée des Arts et Traditions Populaires, or Musée ATP for short) is housed in Dar Jellouli, a two-storey 18th century mansion which belonged to a wealthy Andalusian family, with a beautiful inner courtyard surrounded by horseshoe arches and delicately carved door and window framings of Gabès stone. The exhibits include a wide range of everyday objects, storage jars, kitchen equipment, a collection of spices, furniture and furnishings, traditional costumes and jewellery, glass paintings and Arab calligraphy.

Great Mosque

Rue de la Grande Mosquée, parallel to Rue Mongi Slim, leads to the Great Mosque, in the centre of the Medina. Founded in 849, it was rebuilt for the first time in the 10th/11th century and finally completed in 1759, under Turkish rule. Non-Muslims may enter only the inner courtyard (open daily, except Fridays, 9am–2pm). At the end of the rectangular courtyard is the nine-aisled, twelve-bayed prayer hall, its vaulting borne on antique columns. The graceful minaret, made up of three successively smaller sections and richly decorated with Kufic inscriptions and bands of ornament, is closely modelled on the one in Kairouan. Built into the wall on the east side of the mosque is a Byzantine inscription: "Grant us virtue and her companion, good fortune, that both may deck the house dedicated to Thee." The decoration of the façade dates from the Turkish period.

Other sights

Between the Great Mosque and Bab el Djebli, the north gate of the Medina, is the souk quarter. Near Bab el Djebli, at the end of Rue Abd el Kader, is the Zaouia of Sidi Abd el Kader. Outside the Medina walls lies the new Market (Marché), and beyond this the New Mosque (Nouvelle Mosquée). There are a number of other mosques in the Medina, their façades decorated with verses from the Koran and beautiful stucco ornament.
1.5km/1mile west of the town centre are a small park and the Stadium.

Harbour

Sfax's commercial harbour, the second largest in Tunisia, is linked with the Mediterranean by a short canal. Until the opening of the new fishing harbour 3km/2 miles south of the town the fishing fleet used the smaller of the two basins, on the south side of which is the departure point of the ferry to the Kerkennah Islands.
To the south-east is the town's small and not particularly attractive beach.

Surroundings of Sfax

El Djem

64km/40 miles north is the famous Roman amphitheatre of El Djem (see entry).

Kerkennah Islands

An attractive excursion from Sfax is a boat trip to the Kerkennah Islands (see entry).

Thyna

From Sfax GP 1, the Gabès road runs south-west, passing an Allied military cemetery and a phosphate processing plant. In 11km/7 miles it comes to the site of ancient Thaenae, lying to the east of the road, near the prominent lighthouse of Thyna. This was the most south-easterly outpost of Carthaginian territory.
Immediately south of the town began the Fossa Regia, constructed by the Romans in 146 B.C. to mark the frontier between the Roman province and the kingdom of Numidia, which ran north-west from here to Thabraca (Tabarka). In the reign of Hadrian (A.D. 117–138) the town was granted the status of *colonia*. Excavation has revealed the remains of various buildings of the 4th and 5th centuries, including baths (with mosaics), dwelling-houses and a Christian church. To the east of the site is a necropolis centred on an octagonal mausoleum.
To the north can be seen extensive salt-pans, frequented by large numbers of migrant birds in winter and spring. Information from the ONTT office in Sfax.

Plage de Chaffar

25km/16 miles south-west of Sfax is a beautiful beach, the Plage de Chaffar, which is much frequented by the population of Sfax.

Sidi Bou Said

A 7

Governorate: Tunis Nord
Altitude: 100m/330ft
Population: 5000

Access

Regular bus and TGM (suburban railway) services to and from Tunis (see entry), 16km/10 miles north-west.
The road from Tunis to La Goulette continues by way of Carthage to Sidi Bou Said, and GP 9 runs direct to Sidi Bou Said, passing the Lac de Tunis and the airport.

Note

Cars are banned in the village, and the little car park is permanently overcrowded during the summer. The best plan, therefore, is to take the TGM or a taxi from Tunis.

Situation and **townscape

The picturesque Andalusian-style village of Sidi Bou Said lies on the slopes of a rocky hill on Cap Carthage, which here falls 100m/330ft down to the

Sidi Bou Said

sea. It owes its fame in Europe to three young painters – Paul Klee, August Macke and Louis Moillet – who came here in 1914 and in a series of pictures which became widely famed recorded the beauty of this village of white-washed houses with blue doors and shutters and wrought-iron window grilles, with the Café des Mimosas and a minaret in the background. Sidi Bou Said is now one of the most popular resorts in Tunisia.
In August Sidi Bou Said is the scene of the Kharja religious festival, which attracts large numbers of believers from all over Tunisia.

History

The present-day lighthouse occupies the site of a ribat built in the 9th century, soon after the Arab conquest of Carthage. Here around 1207 the Sufi teacher Abu Said el Baji established himself and attracted many admirers, who settled in Sidi Bou Said. Later his cult gained many adherents among refugees from Andalusia, who after the end of Spanish rule (1535–74) also settled here as pirates, taking Abu Said el Baji as their patron saint and naming him "Lord of the Sea".
When members of the Husseinite dynasty took up residence here in the 18th century they brought with them many leading musicians and writers of the day, who laid the foundations of Sidi Bou Said's reputation as an artists' village. Thereafter it soon developed into an internationally known haunt of artists. Thanks to the efforts of the British banker and music-lover Baron Rudolphe d'Erlanger, author of a six-volume encyclopedia on Arab music, the village was given statutory protection in 1915 to ensure that it would be preserved in its original state.

Sights

Nowadays Sidi Bou Said is crowded with tourists during the summer: hence the numerous souvenir shops in and around the main square.

Café des Nattes

At the upper end of the square is the world-famed Café des Nattes, which features in August Macke's "View of a Mosque" (1914). Since Macke's time

Café des Nattes

Guineafowl on the cemetry wall

nothing essential has changed either in the exterior or interior of this typical Moorish coffee-house.

View

On the highest point in the village, below the lighthouse, is the zaouia (mausoleum) of Abu Said el Baji, with a minaret erected in Ottoman times. From here there are incomparable views of the Gulf of Tunis, Cap Bon, Djebel Zaghouan in the distance, Carthage, La Goulette and Tunis.

Surroundings of Sidi Bou Said

Tunis

See entry

La Marsa
Gammarth

See Tunis, Surroundings

Carthage

See entry

La Goulette

See Tunis, Surroundings

Sidi Daoud

See Cap Bon

Soliman

See Cap Bon

Sousse

C 7

Chief town of the governorate of Sousse
Altitude: 0–50m/0–165ft
Population: 100,000

Access

Sousse lies on GP 1 (Tunis–Sfax), 140km/87 miles south of Tunis and 127km/79 miles north of Sfax.
The airport of Skanès-Monastir (15km/9 miles south-east of the town on the Monastir road) is most conveniently reached on the Métro du Sahel or by bus (No. 52). From the airport there are flights to all the larger towns in Tunisia; and during the holiday season it is used by many charter flights from Europe.
Rail connections with Tunis, Sfax, Gabès, Gafsa/Metlaoui/Tozeur and Hammamet/Nabeul.
The Métro du Sahel, a new local express service, runs between Sousse and Monastir roughly every hour, with a halt at the airport.
Bus services from the Gare Routière in Avenue Léopold Senghor to Tunis, Kairouan, Sfax, Gabès, Gafsa, Le Kef and Kasserine.

Situation and characteristics

Sousse (Arabic Souza), the third largest city in Tunisia (after Tunis and Sfax) and capital of the Tunisian Sahel, lies at the south end of the Gulf of Hammamet, fringed by a beach of fine sand and surrounded by extensive olive plantations.
The old town, situated on a gently sloping hill and enclosed by walls, has many fine examples of Arab architecture and an interesting Archaeological Museum. The Medina, the beautiful sandy beaches and the many other places of interest within easy reach, including Kairouan, Monastir, Mahdia and El Djem, make Sousse a popular and attractive tourist and holiday centre.
Every Sunday there is a camel market near the Catacombs (see below).

Economy

Until the late sixties the economy of Sousse was almost exclusively centred on its harbour, which exported the agricultural produce (mainly olive oil and esparto grass) grown in the surrounding area and processed in the town as well as phosphates from the Metlaoui area. Fishing and fish-processing also made a contribution to the town's economy. Since then Sousse has developed into a considerable industrial town with a number of large factories, mostly to the south of the town. They include an assembly plant for goods vehicles, a large tannery, factories producing clothing for the European market, hardware, plastics and hothouses, and a large cement works opened in 1982.
The holiday and tourist trade has also flourished, and the Sousse area, including Monastir and Port El Kantaoui, is now one of Tunisia's leading tourist regions. The beaches are lined with new hotels in all categories, from expensive luxury establishments to modest guesthouses. To the north of the town is Port El Kantaoui, an ultra-modern tourist complex opened in 1979 (see below). This development has been promoted by the construction of the new Skanès-Monastir airport and the establishment of a hotel school.

History

In the 9th century B.C. the site of Sousse was occupied by an important Phoenician trading post, which in the 6th century came under the influence of Carthage. (A Punic tophet dating from that period has been discovered here.) During the Second Punic War this was Hannibal's base in his campaign against Scipio's Roman forces – a campaign which ended in his defeat at Zama in 202 B.C. In the Third Punic War the town, now known as Hadrumetum, went over to the Roman side and was rewarded with the grant of important privileges. These were lost, however, when Hadrumetum took Pompey's side in his conflict with Caesar. Thanks to its strategic

View over the Medina, Sousse ▶

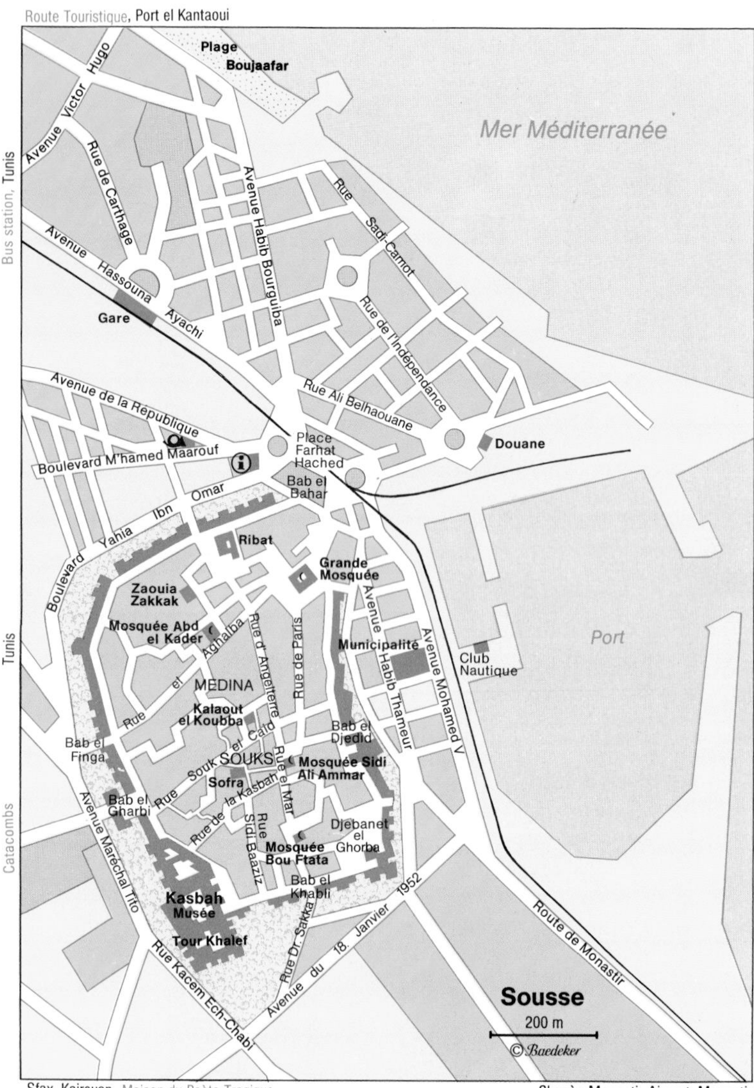

situation and its extensive olive groves it soon recovered, but it suffered a further setback after taking part in the Gordian rising in A.D. 238 (see El Djem).

In the reign of Diocletian (284–305) the town rose to some importance, and in Byzantine times became capital of the province of Byzacena. Later it was taken by the Vandals and renamed Hunericopolis; then recovered by the

Byzantines and given the new name of Justinianopolis. Towards the end of the 7th century it was conquered by Oqba ibn Nafi's Arab forces, after putting up a fierce resistance, and totally destroyed. As a result Sousse has few remains of Roman buildings apart from the catacombs of the 2nd/3rd century A.D.

Two hundred years later, under the Aghlabids, a new town was founded with the name of Susa to serve as the port for their inland capital of Kairouan. This was the period when the Ribat, the Great Mosque, the Kasbah and the town walls were built.

In the 12th century the Normans who then ruled Sicily captured Sousse, but were able to hold on to it for only eleven years. The town was in Turkish hands from the 16th century to 1881, when French troops entered it without a fight. During the Second World War, in 1942–43, Sousse suffered severe damage, which was rapidly made good after the war.

Sights

Place Farhat Hached

The hub of the town's traffic is Place Farhat Hached, immediately north-east of the Medina, from which the principal streets radiate. To the north is the new town, with Avenue Habib Bourguiba, lined with shops, banks and offices, and its continuation along the seafront, Boulevard Hedi Chaker. South-east of Place Farhat Hached lies the harbour.

At the south-west corner of Place Farhat Hached there formerly stood Bab el Bahr, the Sea Gate. This was originally the entrance to an inner harbour which silted up in the 16th century, or perhaps earlier. A fort was built on the site in the 18th century, but since the destruction caused during the Second World War there is a great gap in the walls of the Medina, through which it is now entered.

**Medina

The Medina, situated on rising ground above the harbour, is surrounded by a 2km/1¼mile circuit of walls built in 859 and renovated and strengthened in 874 and 1205. The massive blocks of dressed stone in the walls came from ancient Roman buildings. There were originally six gates, of which two survive: Bab el Khabli on the south side and Bab el Gharbi on the west. The gate on the east side, Bab el Djedid, dates only from 1864.

Measuring 700m/765yds by 500m/545yds, the Medina of Sousse is one of the finest examples of Arab architecture in Tunisia, preserved almost unchanged over the centuries.

Great Mosque

Just inside the Medina stands the fortress-like Great Mosque, built in 851, a few years after the re-foundation of the town by the Aghlabids, on the model of the Sidi Oqba Mosque in Kairouan. Following recent restoration work the exterior has recovered its original appearance.

As in other mosques in Tunisia, non-Muslims are allowed only into the inner courtyard, which is open daily, except Fridays, 8am–1pm. Admission tickets are issued by the ONTT office in Place Farhat Hached.

The mosque originally had two defensive towers which in earlier centuries guarded the harbour. The domes of the minarets were later additions. An unusual feature is the external staircase leading up from the courtyard to the minaret. The battlemented walls of the courtyard, which is surrounded on three sides by a colonnade of tall horseshoe arches borne on massive piers, are decorated with an elaborate Kufic frieze. The arcade in front of the thirteen-aisled prayer hall was added in 1675. The prayer hall originally consisted only of three barrel-vaulted bays, but by the 10th century it was found to be too small and was extended by the addition of three rather higher groin-vaulted bays on the side with the qibla wall. The beautifully decorated Aghlabid dome, now over the fourth bay, was originally over the bay in front of the mihrab.

Ribat

North-west of the Great Mosque rises the tower of the Ribat, a conspicuous landmark in the town and one of the finest examples of Islamic religious

Great Mosque

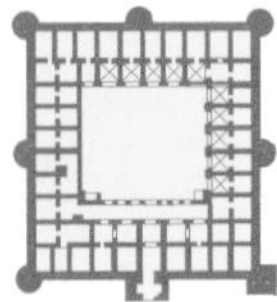

architecture in Tunisia. This was one of the chain of fortified monasteries built by the Aghlabids along the coasts of Tunisia around 800, only a few of which have been preserved. The ribats were occupied by warrior monks, fighters in the "holy war", who in times of peace devoted themselves to their religious duties and worked for the propagation of the faith in the interior of the country. In times of danger the ribats offered the population protection from enemy attack and served as bases for offensive and defensive action against the enemy. It has been suggested that these Muslim warrior monks provided a model which was followed in the later Christian knightly orders.

With the construction of the Kasbah at the south-west corner of the Medina the Ribat lost its military significance, and from the 11th century it gradually fell into a state of disrepair. Large-scale restoration work was carried out when it was converted into a medersa (Koranic school) in 1722. It was again thoroughly restored in the 1950s, and now ranks, with the Ribat of Monastir (see entry), as one of the best preserved in Tunisia.

The Ribat is believed to have been built about 787 on an almost exactly square ground-plan measuring 38m/125ft each way. Its 13.5m/44ft high outer walls are reinforced by four corner towers and three other towers along the sides.

View

At the south-east corner of the Ribat stands the Nador, a 27m/89ft high circular watch-tower, slightly tapering towards the top, which was added in 821. From the top there are fine views of the Medina and the harbour.

The only entrance to the Ribat, a rectangular gatehouse, is on the south side. The arched gateway is borne on two antique columns with Byzantine imposts. Originally there was a second gate with a portcullis, the grooves for which can be seen just before the entrance passage.

A vestibule roofed with early groined vaulting and flanked by two guardrooms leads into the inner courtyard, round which, on ground level, are the monks' cells, stables and store-rooms, preceded by a portico. A staircase

Nador Tower and . . . *. . . entrance to the Ribat*

leads up to the eleven-aisled prayer hall on the upper floor, the oldest in North Africa.

The Ribat is open daily, except Mondays, in summer 9am–noon and 3–6.30pm, in winter only 2–5.30pm. During the summer various cultural events are staged in the Ribat.

Zaouia Zakkak

100m/110yds west of the Ribat is the striking octagonal minaret, in a style almost reminiscent of Renaissance architecture, of the Zaouia Zakkak, which dates from the Turkish period. The complex includes a mosque, a medersa (Koranic school) and a mausoleum. A notable feature is the arcading, borne on antique columns, round the square inner courtyard.

Souk quarter

To the south of the Ribat is the picturesque Rue el Aghalba, which runs past the Great Mosque to the west side of the Medina. Off this street, on the left, opens Rue d'Angleterre, which leads south for some 250m/275yds to Souk el Reba (to the right). This is the beginning of the large souk quarter, partly roofed over, a scene of busy and colourful activity with all the atmosphere of the Orient. The most interesting parts are the side alleys, where the goods on display are not so evidently designed to appeal to tourists.

Kalaout el Koubba

In this area too is the Kalaout el Koubba, a domed building of the 11th century with zigzag ribbing on the façade, the original function of which is not known.

La Sofra

From Souk el Reba a side street runs south-west to the cisterns of La Sofra, entered through an iron gate. These huge underground cisterns, with a capacity of 3000cu.m/660,000 gallons, are presumably of Roman origin.

In Rue el Mar, the continuation of Rue d'Angleterre, are the mosques of Sidi Ali Ammar and Bou Ftata. The latter, which has an area of only 8sq.m/86sq.ft, is believed to have been built between 838 and 841 by the

Oceanus mosaic (Archaeological Museum, Sousse)

architect of the Great Mosque; its minaret, with tile decoration, is much later.

Kasbah

Along Souk el Reba and its continuation Souk el Caid is Bab el Gharbi, the west gate of the Medina. From here Boulevard Maréchal Tito (to the left) follows the outside of the Medina walls to the Kasbah, at its south-west corner.

The Kasbah was built in 859 on the site of an earlier Byzantine fortress. Its 30m/100ft high Khalef el Fata tower, named after its builder, is one of the oldest towers in the whole of North Africa. Its topmost platform is 50m/165ft above that of the Ribat and affords correspondingly more extensive views. Accordingly the Kasbah took over the military role of the Ribat, and the Khalef el Fata tower is still used as a lighthouse. Part of the Kasbah is occupied by the municipal prison.

It is well worth climbing the Khalef el Fata tower for the sake of the view. The entrance lies to the south of the entrance to the Museum.

**Archaeological Museum

The very interesting Archaeological Museum is on the ground floor of the Kasbah. It has the largest collection of antiquities in the country after the Bardo Museum in Tunis, including material of the Punic, Roman and Early Christian periods.

The Museum is open daily, except Mondays, 9am–noon and 3–6.30pm, in winter only 2–5.30pm. Visits to the Catacombs (see below) are also arranged through the Museum.

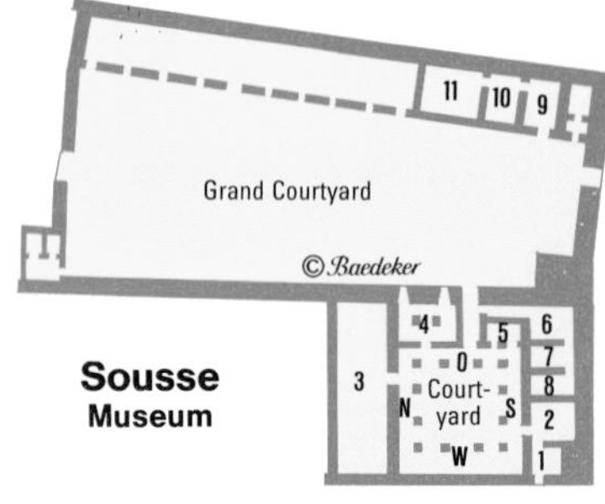

The exhibition rooms are laid out round a small courtyard garden.

Ganymede carried off by Zeus (Archaeological Museum, Sousse)

Room 2

Immediately beyond the entrance hall (1) is Room 2, with one of the finest items in the museum, a mosaic from the Roman baths with a central medallion containing a Medusa's head (2nd c.); round the walls are a head of Trajan, a statue of Apollo and a high relief of an Emperor in a triumphal chariot (3rd c.).

Courtyard

In the arcades round the courtyard are a variety of exhibits:
South side (S): mosaics with geometric designs (2nd c.); torsos, stucco fragments; mosaics depicting animals (fishes, peacocks, gazelles, wild beasts).
West side (W): stelae and gravestones, including some from the Catacombs; a fine mosaic of a bearded Oceanus (2nd c.) from the floor of a pool; a mosaic depicting the horses of Sorothus (3rd c.).
North side (N): funerary inscriptions, stelae; a relief of the Good Shepherd from the Catacombs; a mosaic of an anchor and a fish, used as a symbol and recognition sign during the persecutions of Christians (the initials of the Greek words "*I*esous *Ch*ristos *Th*eou *Y*ios *S*oter" ["Jesus Christ, Son of God, Saviour"] made up the word *ichthys,* "fish").
East side (E): sarcophagus of a woman named Theodora; Byzantine and Christian ceramic panels; funerary inscriptions.

Room 3

Room 3, which opens off the north side of the courtyard, contains a number of masterpieces of the mosaic-worker's art, including (in a clockwise direction) satyrs and bacchantes (3rd c.), a "Triumph of Bacchus" (3rd c., from Sousse; illustrated page 73), scenes of fishing and seafaring, centaurs and nereids (3rd c.), Zeus as an eagle carrying off Ganymede (3rd c.), Apollo and the Muses (3rd/4th c.).

Room 4

Room 4, off the east side of the courtyard, contains material (6th c. B.C.–1st c. A.D.) from the tophet found near the Great Mosque and the harbour (where the sacrifices of children practised in Carthage were gradually replaced by animal sacrifices). The exhibits include urns, stelae and lamps; of particular interest are the stelae with various symbols of Tanit.

Rooms 6–8

A passage decorated with mosaics leads to Rooms 6, 7 and 8, with finds from Punic, Roman and Early Christian tombs.

Grand courtyard

A narrow groin-vaulted passage runs from the east side of the small courtyard into the grand courtyard of the Kasbah, which is also laid out as a garden. Here are displayed a variety of torsos, sarcophagi, columns, capitals, gravestones, etc.

From the terrace roof there is a fine view of the Medina. On the far side of the grand courtyard are Rooms 9, 10 and 11, which contain a number of fine mosaics.

Room 9

In Room 9 are mosaics from the triclinium (dining room) of a house in El Djem depicting the Seasons and the Months (3rd c.) and the 2nd century mosaic of the Tragic Poet from a Roman house to the south of the museum (see below).

Room 10

Room 10 contains remains of frescoes on mythological themes (2nd–3rd c.).

Room 11

The mosaics in Room 11 include one from a triclinium depicting preparations for a fight between gladiators and animals (3rd c.).

House of the Tragic Poet

700m/770yds south of the Kasbah are the foundations of the "House of the Tragic Poet" (opening times as for Museum), named after the mosaic which is now to be seen in the Archaeological Museum.

Catacombs

On the western outskirts of Sousse is a large complex of Early Christian catacombs discovered in 1888. (To visit them, apply to the Museum).

This maze of underground passages and chambers was hewn from the soft local rock between the 2nd and 4th centuries, probably on the site of an earlier pagan necropolis. (The word catacomb comes from the name of an old Roman burial-place on the Via Appia outside Rome.) Of the four main shafts three have been excavated. Finds from the site are in the Museum. A total of some 15,000 people were buried, wrapped in shrouds, in niches in the walls of the catacombs, often hewn in tiers one above the other and closed by tiles or marble plaques. Only small sections of the catacombs – the roofs of which have to be supported on props because of the danger of collapse – are open to the public: the Catacombs of the Good Shepherd (Catacombes du Bon Pasteur; 1.6km/1mile long, with 6000 tombs; late 3rd c.), of Hermes (2500 tombs; 3rd c.) and Severus (5000 tombs; early 4th c.).

Access

Leave on Rue du 15 Octobre, opposite Bab el Gharbi, which runs west in the direction of Sfax and Kairouan; turn right off this street into Rue du 25 Juillet 1957; in 300m/330yds turn left into Rue Abou Hamed el Ghazali and in another 300m, at a mosque, left again. The entrance to the Catacombs is immediately before a tall radio aerial.

Sunday market

The Sunday market is held near the entrance to the Catacombs of the Good Shepherd.

Surroundings of Sousse

Port El Kantaoui

10km/6 miles north of Sousse is the modern holiday complex of Port El Kantaoui (the "Garden"), opened in 1979, a Moorish-style development modelled on the picturesque village of Sidi Bou Said (see entry), near Tunis.

Around a large marina with over 300 moorings are several luxury hotels, blocks of holiday apartments, restaurants, cafés, night clubs, a shopping centre and a wide range of sports facilities (tennis, golf, riding, sailing, etc.).

Hergla

35km/22 miles north of Sousse, on a rocky stretch of coast interrupted by sandy coves, is the little town of Hergla (pop. 6000), which is still relatively unspoiled by tourism. It occupies the site of ancient Horraca Caelia, which in the 2nd century A.D. lay on the boundary between the two provinces of Byzacena and Zeugitania. It was completely destroyed during the Arab invasion.

Hergla has a fine 18th century mosque, with a dome constructed in the "tube-vaulting" technique found at Bulla Regia (see entry). It was built over the tomb of a 10th century holy man named Sidi Bou Mendil, who according to his legend was able to turn his handkerchief into a flying carpet.

Enfida

43km/27 miles north is Enfida or Enfidaville (pop. 5000), the market centre of a large agricultural area. Before the French occupation the Beys had a large property here which was sold in 1880 to a French private company. The local peasants were forced to leave their land and a huge agricultural estate of over 100,000 hectares/250,000 acres was established on which olives, grain and vegetables were grown, using the most modern methods. When Tunisia became independent the estate was taken over by the government. Market on Sundays.

The former church now houses a small museum, with Early Christian mosaics from Uppenna and Sidi Abich (5km/3 miles and 3km/2 miles north) and Roman and Byzantine pottery.

*Takrouna

6km/4 miles west of Enfida, picturesquely situated on a rocky hill, is the old Berber village of Takrouna, now a popular tourist resort. In the centre of the village are a small mosque and the tomb of the local holy man Sidi Abd el Kader.

Kairouan

68km/42 miles west: see entry

El Djem

63km/39 miles south: see entry

Monastir

24km/15 miles south-east: see entry

Mahdia

62km/39 miles south-east: see entry

Sufetula

See Sbeitla

Tabarka

A 5

Governorate: Jendouba
Population: 8000

Access

Tabarka lies on GP 7 (Tunis–Tabarka), 175km/109 miles north-west of Tunis. Regular rail connections with Mateur and Tunis and bus connections with Tunis, Le Kef, Ain Draham and Bizerte.

Airport under construction 15km/9 miles east; due to come into operation in summer 1992.

Situation and *characteristics

Tabarka is a small fishing town at the north-western corner of Tunisia, near the Algerian frontier. It lies in a wide bay at the mouth of the Oued Kebir, between the foothills, clad with mimosas, cork-oaks and pines, of the Kroumirie range. Offshore is a small island connected with the mainland by a causeway originally constructed by the Carthaginians.

In the past the people of Tabarka gained their subsistence from agriculture, fishing, a coral factory and cork processing. More recently, however, the rocky coast with its sandy beaches, the crystal-clear water – a paradise for underwater anglers – and the beautiful country in the surrounding area have made this a popular tourist centre. Building is going on everywhere, and already more than 300 hectares/750 acres of the coastal forests, formerly a protected area, have been cleared to make way for the new developments. To the east of the old harbour the Montazah Tabarka holiday complex, with a marina and golf-course, is under construction, and there are even plans to build on the little island. It is to be hoped that the opponents of this project will be successful in preserving the landscape unspoiled.

In addition to its other attractions as a holiday centre Tabarka is a good base from which to visit such magnificent Roman sites as Bulla Regia, Chemtou and Dougga (see entries).

Coral fishing

Nowadays coral fishing plays only a minor part in the economy of Tabarka. During the fishing season (September to April) divers catch the pieces of coral by towing small nets suspended from a framework in the shape of a St Andrew's cross at depths of between 40m/130ft and 150m/490ft – a technique which dates from the 12th century.

Summer University

The Summer University (Université de l'Eté) is a festival during the months of July and August, when Tabarka becomes a huge holiday village and numbers of young people come to take part in a variety of sporting, craft and musical events.

History

In the 5th century B.C. the Phoenicians established a trading post here and built a causeway linking the island with the mainland. Later the Romans occupied the town, which they called Thabraca, using the harbour for the shipment of building timber, marble from Chemtou, minerals and agricultural produce (corn from the Béja plain, olive oil). Thabraca's merchants and shipowners prospered, and much of their wealth went to the embellishment of the town.

Christianity was also deeply rooted in the town. The famous "mosaics of the dead" in the Bardo National Museum in Tunis came from a church situated between the Bordj Messaoud and the Bordj el Djedid (see below).

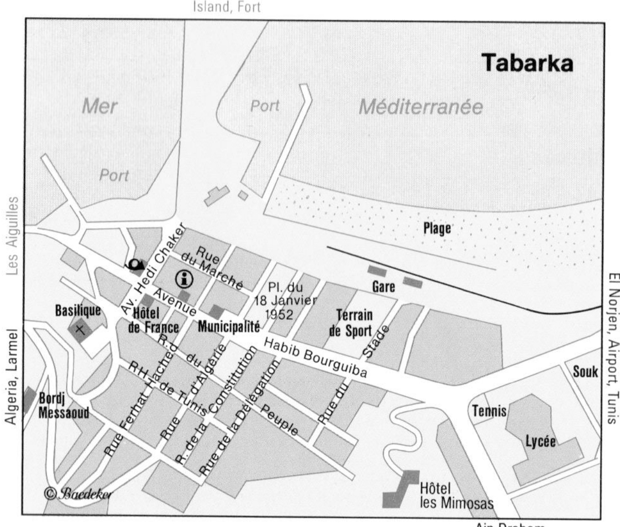

Genoese fort

When the notorious pirate Dragut (see Famous People) was captured by an Italian trading fleet in 1540 the island off Tabarka was handed over to the noble Genoese family of Lomellini in exchange for his freedom. The new owners then built a mighty fortress on the island, under the protection of which the fisheries and the coral trade were able to develop.
In 1741 the French, who already had a trading post on Cap Négro, offered to buy Tabarka from the Genoese: whereupon the Turkish Bey Ali Pacha sent troops to occupy the town and harbour and slight the fortress.
In 1881 Tabarka became an important French military base. In 1942–43 it was the scene of heavy fighting.

Sights

Hotel de France

The main street of the little town is Avenue Habib Bourguiba, lined with shops, cafés and restaurants. Opposite the tourist information office is the little Hotel de France, in which Habib Bourguiba, Mongi Slim and Habib Acour were interned in 1952. Mementoes of them are now displayed in the rooms they occupied.

Basilica

100m/110yds south-west of the hotel is the so-called Basilica – actually the remains of a Roman cistern of the 3rd or 4th century with a capacity of 2700cu.m/594,000 gallons which probably supplied public fountains and baths. The structure was later converted by the Pères Blancs (White Fathers: see Carthage) into a three-aisled church six bays long.
The building is used during the summer for small exhibitions, and the courtyard serves as an open-air theatre.

Bordj Messaoud

Farther south-west is the Bordj Messaoud, also originally a cistern which in the 12th century was converted by merchants from Marseilles and Padua into a fortress. In the 18th century this was enlarged and strengthened by the Turks.

Les Aiguilles

View of the rocky coast

Beyond this again is the Turkish fortress of Bordj el Djedid (viewing platform).

Island
Genoese fort

The island, measuring 400m/440yds by 600m/660yds, is linked with the mainland by a causeway 400m/440yds long. Although there are only scanty remains of the once mighty Genoese fort, it is worth visiting the island for the sake of the fine views of the town and the bay.

Les Aiguilles

To the west of the harbour are the Aiguilles (Needles), pinnacles of ochre-coloured rock, 20–25m/65–80ft high, worn into bizarre shapes by wind and water.

Beaches

To the west of the town, towards the Algerian frontier, are small shingle beaches; to the east are beautiful mile-long sandy beaches.

Surroundings of Tabarka

*Ain Draham

25km/16 miles south of Tabarka on the Jendouba road (GP 17) is the little hill resort of Ain Draham. Situated at an altitude of 823m/2700ft, surrounded by dense forests of cork-oak, it is a good centre for walks and climbs in the hills (waymarked footpaths).

Beni Mtir Lake

South-east of Ain Draham is the Beni Mtir reservoir, which supplies Tunis with water and electricity.

Hammam
Bourguiba

15km/9 miles west of Ain Draham, just on the Algerian frontier, is Hammam Bourguiba, a modern spa for the treatment of throat and kidney disorders.

La Galite

35km/22 miles off Cap Serrat, on the coast north-east of Tabarka, are the rocky La Galite islands, all uninhabited except the principal island from

Landscape round Ain Draham

Lake Sidi Salem

which the group takes its name. The Phoenicians had an anchorage on the island, which was known in classical times as Galathea. There are now no regular boat services to the islands, but a passage can usually be arranged in a fishing boat from Bizerte (100km/62 miles) or Tabarka (60km/37 miles). The islanders make a living by catching crayfish and growing wine. The highest point on the island, which is 5.3km/3¼ miles long by 2km/1¼ miles across, is the Montagne de la Garde (361m/1184ft). Scattered about in the plain are Punic tombs, Roman remains, abandoned quarries and caves.

Galiton

The little island of Galiton (lighthouse) is the home of a colony of monk seals, now a protected species. The waters around the islands are well stocked with fish and offer ideal conditions for diving.

Roman sites

Among the important Roman sites which can be visited from Tabarka are Bulla Regia (59km/37 miles south: see entry), Chemtou (64km/40 miles south: see entry), Dougga (155km/96 miles south-east: see entry) and Mustis (see Dougga, Surroundings).

Le Kef

121km/75 miles south: see entry

Bizerte

147km/91 miles north-east: see entry

Lake Ichkeul

See Bizerte, Surroundings

Tataouine

See Médenine, Surroundings

Testour

B 6

Governorate: Béja
Population: 8000

Access — Testour lies on GP 5 (Tunis–Le Kef), 80km/50 miles south-east of Tunis. There are regular bus services to and from Tunis.

Situation and characteristics — The pretty little farming town of Testour lies on the banks of the Oued Medjerda. It has a small but very busy market.

Events — The Malouf Festival of classical Andalusian music is held here annually in June.

History — In the 17th century Muslim refugees from Andalusia (Moriscos) settled on the banks of the Medjerda and founded a town on the site of ancient Tichilla. The town of Testour still has an Andalusian aspect.

Sights

Great Mosque — Spanish influence is also clearly recognisable in the Great Mosque. Its minaret, built of undressed stone and brick, has a square base and an octagonal upper section decorated with multi-coloured tiles (20th c.). The inner courtyard of the mosque is surrounded by arcades, borne (as are the arches in the nine-aisled prayer hall) on antique columns with Corinthian capitals.

Zaouia of Sidi Naceur — In the south of the town is the Zaouia of Sidi Nacer el Garouachi (1733), conspicuous with its beautiful green-tiled dome. It is now occupied by an elementary school (which can be visited).

Immediately adjoining is the tomb of a 16th century Jewish holy man named Es Saad Rebbi Fradji Chaoua who was born in Fez (Morocco) and died in Testour. There is an annual pilgrimage to his tomb.

Surroundings of Testour

Ain Tounga — South-west of Testour, just off GP 5, is Ain Tounga, with the remains of Roman Thignica, situated at the foot of Djebel Laouej (466m/1529ft). The Roman town lay on the important road from Carthage to Sicca Veneria (Le Kef). Higher up, dominating the road, is a 6th century Byzantine fortress built of stone taken from earlier Roman buildings. Trapezoid in shape, with five square corner towers, it is one of the best preserved Byzantine fortresses in Tunisia.

Beyond the citadel, on the slopes of the hill, are the remains of the ancient town, which was granted the status of *municipium* by Severus Alexander in the 3rd century. Among the features that can readily be identified are stretches of the town walls, a small triumphal arch, the remains of a temple of Mercury and of baths, a number of dwelling-houses and a small temple of Caelestis (the Roman name for the Punic goddess Tanit). Lower down is a small amphitheatre.

Lake Sidi Salem — 7km/4½ miles north-west of Testour, at the foot of Djebel Skhira, is the 34km/21 mile long artificial lake of Sidi Salem, which supplies water for the irrigation of extensive areas of agricultural land around Testour, on Cap Bon and in the Medjerda valley, as well as for Tunis, the towns on Cap Bon and Sousse. From the top of Djebel Skhira there are superb views.

Téboursouk — See Dougga, Surroundings

Dougga — 22km/14 miles west: see entry

Mustis — See Dougga, Surroundings

Le Kef — 100km/62 miles south-west: see entry

Thuburbo Majus — 57km/35 miles south-east: see entry

Capitol, Thuburbo Majus

Thuburbo Majus B 6

Governorate: Zaghouan

Access

Thuburbo Majus lies 1km/¾ mile west of GP 3 (Tunis–Kairouan), 63km/39 miles south of Tunis and 91km/57 miles north of Kairouan. Approach from Tunis: 62km/39 miles south of Tunis, 2km/1¼ miles before the village of El Fahs, turn off GP 3 into MC 28 (signposted to Medjez el Bab); 1km/¾ mile along this road is the entrance to the site (car park).

Situation and characteristics

Thuburbo Majus is the fifth of the great Roman sites in Tunisia, after Bulla Regia, Dougga, Maktar and Sbeitla (see entries). Thanks to its situation at the intersection of important trade routes from the interior to the cities of Hadrumetum (Sousse) and Carthage and to the fertile surrounding country the town prospered, and this prosperity found expression in much building activity, producing a series of splendid public buildings in the 2nd and early 3rd centuries.

An excursion to Thuburbo Majus, which lies in beautiful country, can be combined with visits to other places of interest on the way, such as La Mohammedia or Zaghouan (see Tunis, Surroundings).

Easter procession

There is an annual procession here at Easter in honour of St Perpetua – though the saint is now believed to have been born not at Thuburbo Majus but at Thuburbo Minus (Tébourba, west of Tunis).

History

There was a Punic town on this site, but there may well have been an earlier Berber settlement, since the name Thuburbo seems to be of Berber origin. In 27 B.C., during the reign of Augustus, a Roman settlement (*pagus*) was established alongside the Punic one (*civitas*). In A.D. 128 Hadrian promoted

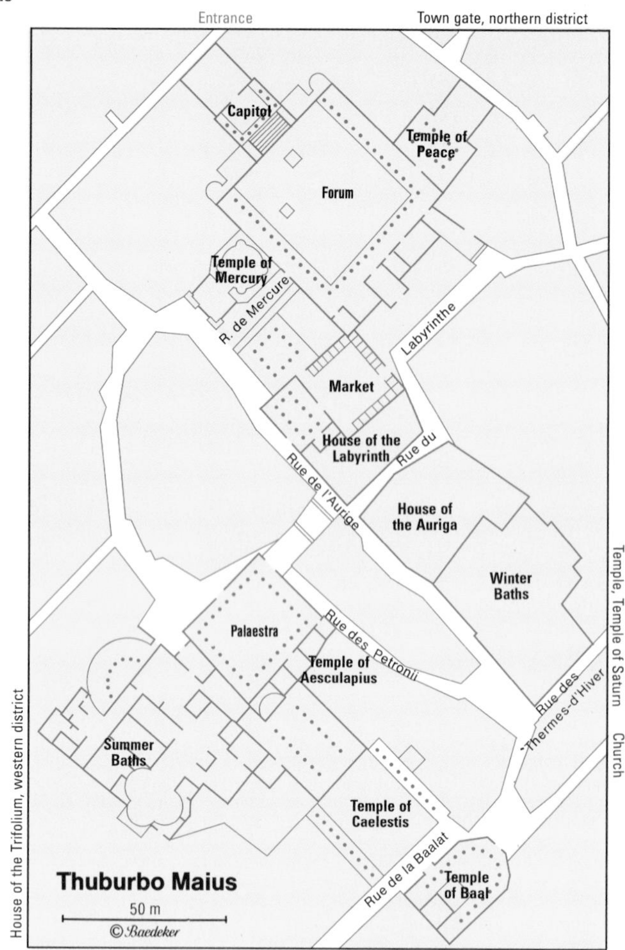

the town to the status of *municipium,* involving the grant of Roman citizenship. This marked the beginning of intensive Romanisation and the town's rise to prosperity. In 188 Commodus granted it the status of a *colonia* under the style of Colonia Julia Aurelia Commoda. Subsequent decades saw the erection of most of the town's splendid mosaic-decorated public buildings and private houses.

Decline set in towards the end of the 3rd century, interrupted by a brief upswing in the 4th century. During this period several buildings were restored and enlarged, and the town changed its name to Res Publica Felix Thuburbo Majus. Vandal raids, conflicts between Catholics and Donatists and finally the Arab invasion led to the final ruin of the town. One of the last signs of prosperity was a hoard of gold buried in the mid 7th century to save it from the Arabs.

The site was rediscovered in 1857, and since 1912 about a fifth of the total area has been excavated. It is estimated that the city, covering an area of some 40 hectares/99 acres, had a population of between 7000 and 12,000.

**Excavations

The site is open from sunrise to sunset (admission charge). The entrance is at the north end of the site. The following description takes the form of a tour of the site.

Opus africanum

The town had three gates but no walls, perhaps because of the absence of any suitable quarries in the area. This was certainly the reason for the type of masonry used in the buildings, the technique known as *opus africanum,* a method of constructing walls already practised by the Phoenicians in which monolithic slabs of stone were set up at intervals from one another and the gaps filled in with undressed stone, gravel or other material.

Forum

The Forum of Thuburbo Majus is square, measuring 49m/161ft each way – contrary to the views of the Roman architectural theorist Vitruvius, who held that a forum should be rectangular. The paved area was surrounded on three sides by a Corinthian portico, recorded by an inscription as having been built between 161 and 192 and restored in 376.

Capitol

The north-west side of the Forum is occupied by the Capitol, built in 168, which stands on a podium consisting of three courses of massive blocks of dressed stone. A broad flight of fifteen steps leads up to four (originally six) re-erected Corinthian columns of Carrara marble, 8.50m/28ft high. There is no trace of the cella which contained the cult statues of Jupiter, Juno and Minerva, but the excavators found the head of a statue of Jupiter which originally stood 7m/23ft high; it can now be seen in the Bardo Museum in Tunis.
The podium originally housed the temple treasury and was later occupied by an oil-press. From the Capitol there is a fine view over the ancient city.

Temple of Peace

At the north-east corner of the Forum is the Temple of Peace. This has a large square pillared courtyard preceding a smaller cella on the same level – a pattern commonly found in Africa.

Temple of Mercury

On the south-west side of the Forum, diagonally opposite the Temple of Peace, is the Temple of Mercury (built in 211), which has a similar plan. The square pillared courtyard has semicircular niches in the corners.

On the south-east side of the Forum, opposite the Capitol, was a smaller temple, on the right of which was the Curia, the administrative centre of the ancient city.

Market

At the south-west corner of the Forum, separated from the Temple of Mercury by a narrow street, is the Market, which consisted of two pillared courtyards and a third courtyard surrounded on three sides by shops. It was probably built in the late 2nd or early 3rd century.

West of the Temple of Mercury is a residential quarter which was occupied in turn by Romans, Vandals and finally Byzantines. The town is not laid out on the usual Roman regular plan but is highly irregular, presumably following an earlier Punic layout. In the neighbourhood of the west gate the streets are much more regular, probably because this area had not previously been built on.
Thuburbo Majus had an extensive water supply and drainage system serving both public buildings and private houses.

Palaestra of the Petronii

The Palaestra of the Petronii, with a square courtyard surrounded by a Corinthian portico, was built in 225 at the expense of Petronius Felix and his

Palaestra of the Petronii

sons. Part of the architrave, decorated with palmette and flower ornament, has been preserved. Letters carved in the paving at the south corner of the courtyard represent the "board" for the popular Roman game of the "36 letters". Here too was found a relief of three dancing Maenads which is now in the Bardo National Museum in Tunis.

Adjoining the Palaestra is the Temple of Aesculapius, the god of healing and protector of all places where sports were practised.

Summer Baths

Thuburbo Majus had two sets of baths, the Winter Baths (Thermes d'Hiver) and the Summer Baths (Thermes d'Eté). The Winter Baths, to the east of the Palaestra, were apparently much altered and rebuilt, and their layout is more difficult to follow. The Summer Baths, south-west of the Palaestra, covered an area of 2800sq.m/30,000sq.ft and – as the statues of Aesculapius, Hercules, Mercury and Venus and the fine mosaics now to be seen in the Bardo National Museum demonstrate – were sumptuously furnished. The entrance, on the side facing the Palaestra led into the apodyterium (changing room), frigidarium (cold bath, with three basins), tepidarium (warm room), sudatorium (sweat bath) and caldarium (hot room). On a stele is carved the town's coat of arms: an ear of corn, a bunch of grapes and a pine-cone. On the north-west side of the baths is a semicircular latrine 11m/36ft in diameter.

Temple of Baal

On the south side of the site is the Temple of Baal (Temple de la Baalat), the plan of which shows both Roman and Oriental influence. A semicircular porticoed courtyard of rather angular outline precedes a small prostyle temple standing on a podium.

Temple of Ceres

Farther east is the Temple of Ceres, later converted into a three-aisled church, the cella becoming the baptistery and the forecourt a cemetery.

Cistern
Amphitheatre

200m/220yds south, at the foot of a hill, are the remains of a huge cistern which supplied the town with water, and beyond this the badly ruined amphitheatre. From the hill there is a good view of the whole site.

Jupiter and . . .

. . . Aesculapius (Bardo Museum, Tunis)

Surroundings of Thuburbo Majus

El Fahs

2km/1¼ miles south of Thuburbo Majus on GP 3 is the little farming town of El Fahs (pop. 10,000), set in a fertile agricultural area.

Ksar Lemsa

42km/26 miles south is the Byzantine fortress of Ksar Lemsa, built between 560 and 600 on the site of an earlier Roman settlement. Square in plan, with four corner towers, it is the best preserved fortress of the period in Tunisia.

Access

Leave Thuburbo Majus on GP 3, going south, and at El Fahs take GP 4, which runs south-west towards Maktar; then, just beyond the artificial lake of Oued Kebir, turn left (south) into MC 46, the road to Ousseltia and Kairouan.

Mohammedia

See Tunis, Surroundings

Zaghouan

See Tunis, Surroundings

Hammamet

85km/53 miles north-east: see entry

Tozeur

F 4

Chief town of the governorate of Tozeur
Altitude: 60m/200ft
Population: 17,000

Access

Tozeur lies on the north-west side of the Chott el Djerid, 93km/58 miles south-west of Gafsa, 89km/55 miles west of Kebili, 23km/14 miles north-east of Nefta and only 58km/36 miles from the Algerian frontier.
From the airport, 6km/4 miles south-west on GP 3, there are weekly flights to Tunis and Paris. There are also charter flights to Tozeur during the holiday season.

Gaily coloured fabrics, Tozeur

The railway station, to the west of Avenue de la République (the road to Gafsa), is the terminus of the line from Tunis via Sousse and Sfax.
From the bus station, at the intersection of Avenue Habib Bourguiba and Rue de la Liberté, there are regular services to Tunis, Gafsa, Kebili, Nefta, Douz and Hazaoua, the most westerly town in Tunisia, situated on the frontier with Algeria.

Situation and characteristics

Tozeur is the chief town of the Bled el Djerid, the "Land of Palms", with a large and busy market on Tuesdays. The inhabitants earn their living from trade, farming and craft industry, the products of which are exchanged in the market for the products of the nomads of the surrounding area. Only the trade in dates is of more than local importance; the top quality *deglat en nour* ("fingers of light") dates in particular are mainly exported.
Typical local craft products are carpets, silk and woollen fabrics, clothing, leather articles and jewellery.
In recent years, as in other oases, there has been a considerable development of tourism. New hotels are being built and new roads laid out.

Oasis Festival

The Oasis Festival is held at the end of November and beginning of December, with a programme which includes parades, folk dances and camel races.

History

The history of Tozeur goes back a long way. Situated between the desert and the steppe country, it must have been from time immemorial an important staging-point on the caravan route from the Sahara to the north-eastern Mediterranean coast. The town is first mentioned in Roman times, together with other oases in the Djerid, under the name of Thusuros, as an important bastion in the defence of the southern frontier of the province of Africa. Other strong points on this line were Nepte (Nefta), Aquae (El Hamma) and Thigae (Kriz). In Christian times Thusuros became an important centre, the see of a bishop, as we know from a letter written by St

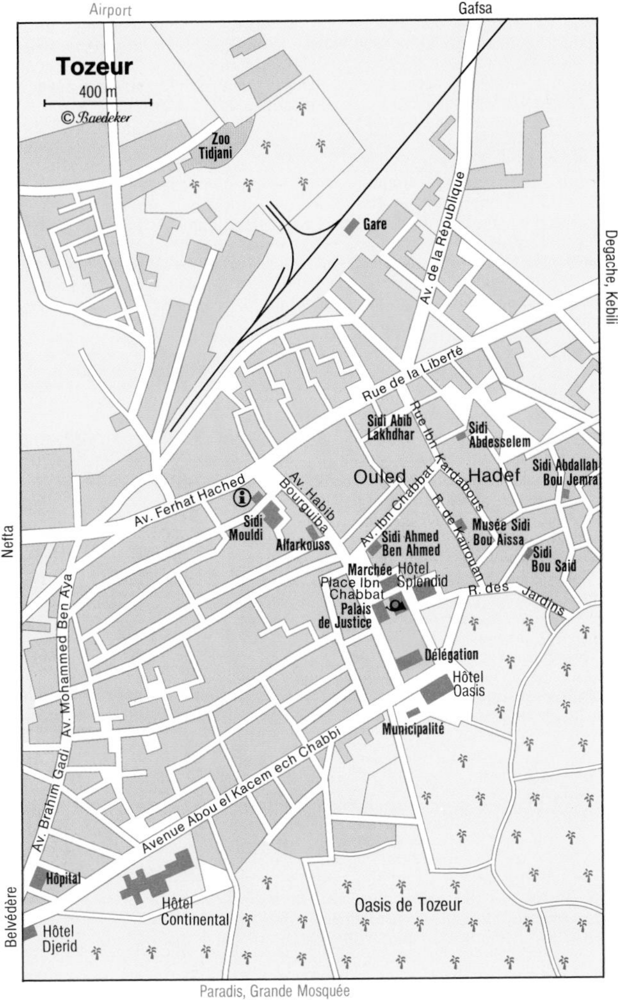

Augustine (see Famous People) to the bishop of Thusuros and other named bishops. There are, however, no remains of the Christian period in Tozeur. During the period of Vandal rule (5th c. onwards) many Christians were martyred here. The Byzantines, who gained control of the area in the 6th century after brief but violent encounters with the local Berber tribes, re-established the bishopric and, like the Romans before them, built a fortress to defend their southern frontier against the desert nomads.

In the middle of the 7th century the town was taken by the Arabs and after a long, hard struggle was Islamised. Under Arab rule Tozeur enjoyed a long period of peace during which, as the "gateway to the desert", it developed into an important staging-point on the caravan routes. The town prospered, and a number of well known Koranic schools (medersas) were established here. The caravans also brought many black slaves to Tozeur, which became an important slave market. Many of the town's present-day inhabitants are the descendants of black slaves (the Haratin).

The heyday of the town was in the 14th century, when it is believed to have had three times its present population. Its wealth, however, made it the target of increasingly frequent raids by the nomads and of oppressive taxation by the Ottoman authorities who now controlled Tunisia. As a result the economic decline of the town began in the 15th century, and in the following century it was visited by a devastating epidemic of cholera in which half the population died. Thus when Tozeur was taken by the French in 1881 without a fight it was an insignificant little oasis town. Thereafter it was developed on modern, European lines, though retaining its traditional style of brick architecture.

Sights

The town

Tozeur is famous for its brick architecture, exuberantly patterned in a variety of geometric designs formed from local kiln-fired clay or mud bricks measuring 25 by 10 by 4cm (10 by 4 by 1½ inches). This "Tozeur style" is found also in neighbouring towns such as Nefta (see entry).

Tozeur style

The division of the town into an old town (the Medina) and a new town is not so marked as in other Tunisian towns, since the buildings in the new town, apart from the large hotels, are mostly brick-built in the traditional style. Theold town (Oued Hadef) lies to the south of the Gafsa and Kebili roads and to the east of Avenue Habib Bourguiba and the market square, Place Ibn Chabbat.

Great Mosque

New town

The hub of the new town is Place Ibn Chabbat, named after the 13th century imam who laid down the water distribution system for the oases.

Flanking the square are the market hall built during the French protectorate, dominated by the minaret of the Great Mosque, the post office, banks, cafés and restaurants. In this area too are the larger hotels, mainly on Avenue Abou el Kacem ech Chabbi, along the south side of the new town.

*Old town Ouled Hadef

The old town of Tozeur (Ouled Hadef) lies between the Gafsa–Nefta road, Avenue Habib Bourguiba and Rue des Jardins. It is a maze of narrow and irregular lanes and handsome old houses with decorative brick façades in traditional style. The geometric patterns of the house-fronts are similar to the designs of many Berber carpets. Frequently the upper floors of the houses, borne in round-headed arches, extend over the street to touch the houses on the other side, forming tunnel-like passages which provide shelter from the sun.

Folk Museum

In Rue de Kairouan, housed in the Koubba of Sidi Bou Aissa, is the small Folk Museum (Musée des Arts et Traditions Populaires, or Musée ATP for short; open daily, except Monday, 9am–noon and 3–5.30pm). The exhibits, displayed in three small rooms and a courtyard, include Roman columns and fragments of statues from ancient Thusuros, local craft products both

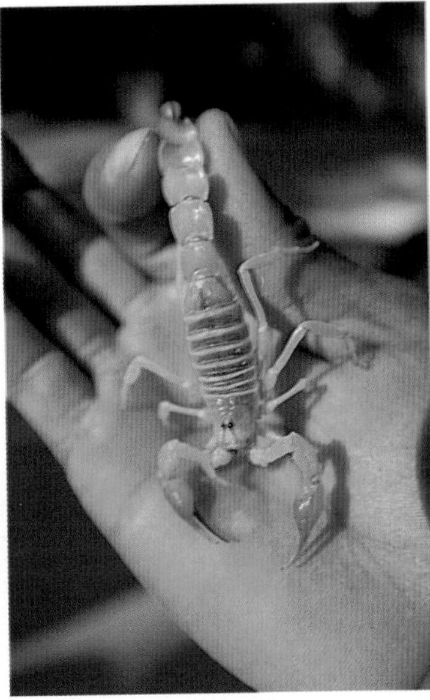

Monitors and . . . *. . . scorpion in the Desert Zoo*

ancient and modern, furniture and furnishings, coins, pottery, jewellery, wedding garments, everyday objects and old Koranic inscriptions.

Tidjani Zoo

In the northern outskirts of the town, beyond the railway, can be found the Desert Zoo (Zoo du Désert) of Si Tidjani, a citizen of Tozeur who was famed throughout Tunisia as a snake-catcher. In a series of cages, well kept but sometimes very small, are displayed various animals of the desert, now rarely or never met with in the wild. They include desert monitors, sand and horned vipers, scorpions, fennec foxes, jackals, birds of prey and a dromedary which drinks Coca Cola.

There is another, smaller zoo in the palm-grove to the south of the town (see below).

Belvédère

The best view of the oasis is to be had from the Belvédère, a viewpoint on the Ras el Aioun (alt. 20m/65ft), a pile of boulders 3km/2 miles west of the town on the edge of the oasis. At the foot are the numerous springs (*aioun*), including one at a temperature of 30°C/86°F, from which the rocks take their name. From the top there are fine views of the town, the oasis and the surrounding desert.

Access

Leave Tozeur on Avenue Abou el Kacem ech Chebbi, which runs southwest from the Hotel Oasis, passing the Hotel Continental, the Hotel Djerid and the tourist information office (ONTT). 200m/220yds beyond the ONTT office the road (asphalted) takes a sharp turn to the right. From here a sand track runs through the palm-grove along the right bank of the oued to its source at the foot of the Belvédère, where there are a small camping site and a café.

In the oasis, Tozeur

*The Oasis

There are various ways of exploring the oasis – in a horse-drawn carriage, on a dromedary or on a donkey. To avoid any possible misunderstanding the charge for the drive or the ride should be agreed in advance.

General

The oasis of Tozeur, an intensively cultivated area of some 1050 hectares/2600 acres, lies immediately south of the town. It contains some 400,000 date-palms, which provide shade for fruit trees (peaches, apricots, pomegranates, figs, citrus fruits and bananas). Ground crops such as vegetables, salad plants and corn, which consume a great deal of water, are only occasionally found.
The palms yield between 25,000 and 30,000 tons of dates annually, including only 1000 tons of the top quality *deglat en nour* dates – particularly aromatic, semi-sweet and not too soft – which grow only at the tips of palms in good soils well supplied with water.

Access

From Avenue Abou el Kacem ech Chabbi, on the south side of the town, a number of little streets run south into the oasis. There are six small hamlets in the oasis, the most important of which are Bled el Hader, Abbès and Sahraoui.

Irrigation

The oasis is supplied with water by some 200 springs and artesian wells with a total flow of 700 litres/154 gallons per second. Most of the springs are near the Belvédère, where they join to form the river which flows through the oasis and peters out at its end, on the edge of the Chott el Djerid. The water from the river and the artesian wells is channelled to the various land holdings within the oasis, in accordance with a complicated distribution system which still follows the ancient rules, through an intricate network of little open channels known as *seguias*.
The regulations on the distribution were originally laid down by Imam Ibn Chabbat (d. 1282 in Tozeur) in a book written in the middle of the 13th

century. Under this system each holding of land, depending on its situation, size and time of irrigation (morning, evening, etc.), is assigned a particular unit of time (*khaddous*), during which it is supplied with water through the seguias, all of which are of the same size. This close control over the distribution of water is necessitated by the scarcity of the supply. The artesian wells bring up water from depths of between 60 and 100m (200 and 330ft); but in recent years the water table has been slowly but steadily falling, so that the yield of the wells has been decreasing. They are now giving place to modern deep wells, which tap deposits of fossil water at a depth of 600m/2000ft – a supply dating from earlier geological periods which is not renewable.

Land ownership

Land ownership in Tozeur is still based on traditional and rather antiquated concepts and structures. Most of the land in the oasis belongs to no more than 60 families, who account for under 2% of the population, and the Zaouia Tidjaniya, a wealthy and influential religious brotherhood found throughout the Maghreb.

Only 8% of the land belongs to smallholders who work their own land and usually own no more than 50 palms. The large landowners – many of them merchants or nomads, who are traditionally disinclined to work on the land – and religious brotherhoods own more than 1000 palms apiece, and their land is worked by share-croppers (*khammes),* who retain between a tenth and a third (depending on the crop) of the harvest. The name *khammes* comes from *khamsa* ("five"), the croppers' average or traditional share being one-fifth.

This pattern of land ownership and employment developed over the centuries when the caravan routes fell out of use and oasis farming remained the only means of subsistence. The wealthier landowners bought up the impoverished smallholders' water rights, cut off their water supply and finally acquired their land, and the dispossessed peasants were then compelled to become their tenants. The share of the harvest they receive is sufficient only to meet the most basic requirements of subsistence.

Bled el Hader

Just before the Hotel Continental a track branches off Avenue Abou el Kacem ech Chabbi and runs south to the little hamlet of Bled el Hader, which is believed to occupy the site of ancient Thusuros. In the centre of the village is the mosque of Sidi Bou Ali. Of this five-aisled 11th century mosque there now remain only the ruin of a fine minaret and the mihrab of 1193, now incorporated in the new prayer hall adjoining. In the cemetery to the right of the minaret is the marabout (tomb) of Ibn Chabbat, creator of Tozeur's water distribution system (see above).

At the end of the village is an old zaouia, now occupied as a dwelling-house. There are also numbers of old houses with handsome brick façades in traditional style.

Abbès
Marabout of
Sidi Ali Bou Lifa

2km/1¼ miles south of Bled el Hader is the hamlet of Abbès, at the far end of which, on the left, is the marabout of a local holy man, Sidi Ali Bou Lifa, topped by a mighty dome. In front of the marabout, which attracts large numbers of pilgrims, is a large and much revered jujube tree, said to have been planted by the holy man himself.

Zoo du Désert
Paradis

400m/440yds from the marabout, outside the village, are the Zoo du Désert, another small desert zoo, and "Paradis", a small but interesting botanic garden. Here visitors can see desert animals and the plants of the oasis, including acacias, aloes, cactuses, henna, hibiscus and pomegranate trees. There is a small café which sells "rose wine" (wine with the addition of rose essence) and "teas" made from various kinds of flowers.

From here it is possible either to continue to the shores of the Chott el Djerid (see entry) or to return to Tozeur by way of the hamlet of Sahraoui.

Upland scenery near Tamerza and Chebika

Surroundings of Tozeur

Tozeur is a good base from which to visit a variety of other places of interest. Following are some suggestions:

Oases of the Djerid

The oases of Nefta (23km/14 miles west of Tozeur: see entry) and Gabès (see entry), on the Gulf of Gabès, are both densely populated. In these oases are grown the top quality *deglat en nour* dates, most of which are exported.

Chott el Djerid

See entry. The road across the Chott starts at Kriz, 14km/8½ miles north-east of Tozeur.

*Oases of Chebika, Tamerza and Midès

An attractive excursion from Tozeur, through beautiful scenery, is into the hills of Djebel en Negueb (900m/2950ft), an offshoot of the Atlas Mountains running from east to west. In this area, in which the Romans built a series of forts as the outworks of their defensive line, the Limes Tripolitanus, are the three little upland oases of Chebika, Tamerza and Midès.

These oases owe their fertility to the numerous little mountain streams whose water seeps into the ground and to the ground-water which is tapped by wells of varying depth. The water is conveyed through a system of underwater channels (*foggaras:* see drawing, page 42) at a gentle gradient to the cultivated land, water for private consumption being taken off on the way.

Here as in other oases the three-stage system of planting is followed, with palms providing shade for fruit-trees (apricots, peaches, pomegranates, bananas, citrus fruits and olives), under which in turn are vegetables, tobacco and corn.

Access

Leave Tozeur on the Gafsa road (GP 3), which traverses the oasis of El Hamma du Djerid (see below), and immediately beyond the oasis take a

road on the left which runs north-west, crosses the Chott el Rharsa and comes to Chebika, beyond which are Tamerza and Midès.
The road is an experience in itself. On the whole it presents no problems, though after a sandstorm stretches of the road may be blown away or interrupted by small sand-dunes.

Chebika

Chebika, on the site of a Roman military post called Ad Speculum, is a small village of stone and mud-brick houses, situated on the slopes of a hill above the palm-grove; the old village, now abandoned, is built into the hillside behind it. The springs which supply the oasis with water are in a picturesque deep gorge 500m/550yds beyond the village.
A road running along the foot of the hill passes the oasis of El Khanga and then winds its way steeply up for 10km/6 miles to enter the valley of the Oued Khanga.

Tamerza

The little oasis of Tamerza, the site of the Roman station Ad Turres, was the see of a bishop in the 6th century. The modern village has a population of some 1500; the old village of mud-brick huts lies on the other side of the river.

Midès

Directly on the Algerian frontier is the little oasis of Midès, on the site of the Roman frontier fort of Mades. It lies on the edge of two canyons 60m/200ft deep.

The return to Tozeur can be by way of Redeyef, Moularès and Metlaoui.

Gafsa

93km/58 miles north: see entry

Seldja Gorge

50km/30 miles north: see Metlaoui, Surroundings

El Hamma du Djerid

The oasis of El Hamma du Djerid lies on the south-eastern edge of the Chott el Rharsa, 9km/6 miles north of Tozeur on the Gafsa road (GP 3). There are four small villages – El Erg, Mhareb, Msaaba and Nemlet – with a total population of 3500. The oasis has an area of some 700 hectares/1750 acres and contains 110,000 palms, which are supplied with water by 20 springs. Among them are six hot springs (37–40°C/99–104°F) containing chlorine, sodium chloride and sulphur which were already being used by the Romans for medicinal purposes – there are remains of a Roman settlement 1km/¾ mile from Nemlet – and are still frequented by the local people for the treatment of skin complaints, neuralgia and arthritis. A "complexe touristique" (hotels, spa treatment facilities) is under construction at these springs.
In recent years a completely new plantation of date-palms, the Domaine de l'Oasis, has been established by a private company on the north side of the oasis. This has involved the sinking of deep wells to tap reservoirs of fossil ground-water at depths of between 600m/2000ft and 1000m/3300ft. Thanks to these wells, which operate much more effectively than those in Tozeur and Nefta (yielding a total flow, including both springs and wells, of 1900 litres/420 gallons per second), and to the adoption of modern methods of cultivation (e.g. looser planting at only 150 palms to the hectare, or 60 to the acre) yields are four times as high as at Tozeur, six times as high as in the rest of the oasis and ten times as high as at Nefta.

El Ouidane

9km/6 miles east of El Hamma is the oasis of El Ouidane, with several small villages, the most important of which are Degache and Kriz, respectively 16km/10 miles and 32km/20 miles from Tozeur. They can be reached either by way of GP 3, turning off at El Hamma, or directly on MC 106.
The oasis has a total population of 100,000, who grow dates (220,000 palms), citrus fruits, figs and olives (35,000 trees). All the villages are situated above the palm-groves on poor stony soil.
There are no sights of particular importance. In Ouled Majed, near Degache, there is an ancient little mud-brick mosque with a minaret built on Roman foundations.

Beyond Ouled Majed in the direction of Kriz can be found the marabout of Sidi Mohammed Krisane, and in Seddada the marabout of Sidi Bou Hilal, a well known place of pilgrimage.

Nefzaoua

On the south-eastern edge of the Chott el Djerid are the Nefzaoua oases. The chief places in this scatter of oases, widely separated from one another, are Kebili and Douz (see Kebili).

Tunis A/B 7

Capital of Tunisia and chief town of the governorate of Tunis City
Altitude: 0–88m/0–289ft
Population: 257,000 (with suburbs c. 1.4 million)

Air services

The international airport of Tunis-Carthage lies 8km/5 miles north-east of the city on GP 3 (the road to La Marsa). There are regular bus services to the airport from Avenue Habib Bourguiba/Rue de Rome (lines 27 and 41).

Rail services

From the railway station in Place Barcelone (separate entrances for local and long-distance services) there are regular connections with Sousse, Hammamet/Nabeul, El Djem/Sfax, Gabès, Tozeur, Bizerte, Algiers and Kalaat Khasba.

TGM

From the TGM (*T*unis–*G*oulette–*M*arsa: suburban railway) station at the east end of Avenue Habib Bourguiba, on the harbour, there are services to the north-western suburbs – La Goulette, Carthage, Sidi Bou Said, La Marsa, etc.

Métro

The Tunis Métro, a tram rather than a train, has a stop beside the TGM station. It runs to the railway station and to the southern suburb of Ben Arous.

Bus services
City buses

City bus services start from Place Barcelone, the Theatre (Avenue Habib Bourguiba) and the TGM station.

Long-distance services

Services to the south depart from the bus station (Gare Routière du Sud) at Bab Allouj. There are buses to Hammamet/Nabeul, Sousse, Monastir, Sfax, Gabès, Médenine, Djerba, Zarzis, Gafsa, Tozeur, Nefta, Kairouan, Le Kef, Maktar, Sbeitla, etc.
Services to the north depart from the Gare Routière du Nord near Bab Saadoun. Buses to Bizerte, Raf-Raf, Menzel Bourguiba, Mateur, Testour, Téboursouk, Le Kef, etc.

Boat services

There are ferry services to Europe (Marseilles, Genoa, Naples, Sardinia and Sicily) from La Goulette.

Head Post Office

The Head Post Office (PTT) is in Rue Charles de Gaulle, a little way west of the railway station. Poste restante mail can be collected at counter 8. The telephone office is in Rue Gamal Abdel Nasser (open 24 hours).

Situation and characteristics

Tunis, capital of the Tunisian Republic and the administrative, cultural, economic and communications centre of the country, lies on a hilly ridge of land some 3km/2 miles wide between the Lac de Tunis (Arabic El Bahira), a shallow brackish lagoon to the east and north-east, and the Sebkha es Sedjoumi, a shallow salt lake to the south-west. The city is sheltered on the north by the Belvédère hills, on the south by the Sidi Bel Hassen hills.
The Lake of Tunis is linked with the sea by a narrow canal, with the city's outer harbour in La Goulette, at its seaward end. In 1888–93 the French colonial authorities dredged out a channel 10km/6 miles long and 45m/150ft wide across the lake between the inner and outer harbours in order to enable vessels of greater draught to reach the inner harbour. The

excavated material was used in the construction of a causeway carrying a road and TGM line over the lake from the city centre to La Goulette.

As the country's cultural centre Tunis has numerous educational and cultural institutions of national importance. Of particular note are the University (founded 1960), the famous Islamic Zitouna University, with faculties of language, literature and Islamic law, and the world-famed Bardo National Museum; in addition there are several specialised higher educational establishments (technical colleges, etc.), the Institut Pasteur and the National Library. Tunis also offers a wide range of entertainments (cinemas, theatres, art galleries, sporting and cultural events).

With its well preserved Medina, numerous features of interest in its immediate surroundings and other major tourist sights within easy reach (Utica, Bizerte, Dougga, Thuburbo Majus, Cap Bon, etc.: see entries), Tunis justifies and will repay a stay of some length.

Topography

The historic centre of Tunis is the old Arab town, the Medina, which is bounded on the east by the harbour and on the north and south by the new town, a modern development of European aspect.

Around the main built-up area is a semicircular ring of suburbs, concentrated particularly in the coastal area. The outer limits of this Greater Tunis are marked by Gammarth on the north, Hammam-Lif at the southern tip of the Gulf of Tunis and La Manouba on the west.

The principal sights of Tunis are the Medina in the city centre, the new town to the east, the internationally famed Bardo National Museum in the western suburb of that name and, to the north-east, Carthage with its ancient remains and its museum and the pretty Moorish-style village of Sidi Bou Said. Carthage and Sidi Bou Said are linked with the city centre by the TGM (suburban railway).

Economy

Almost a quarter of Tunisia's population live in Tunis, which is the seat of government and the country's administrative centre, with the offices of

Roof terrace in the Medina

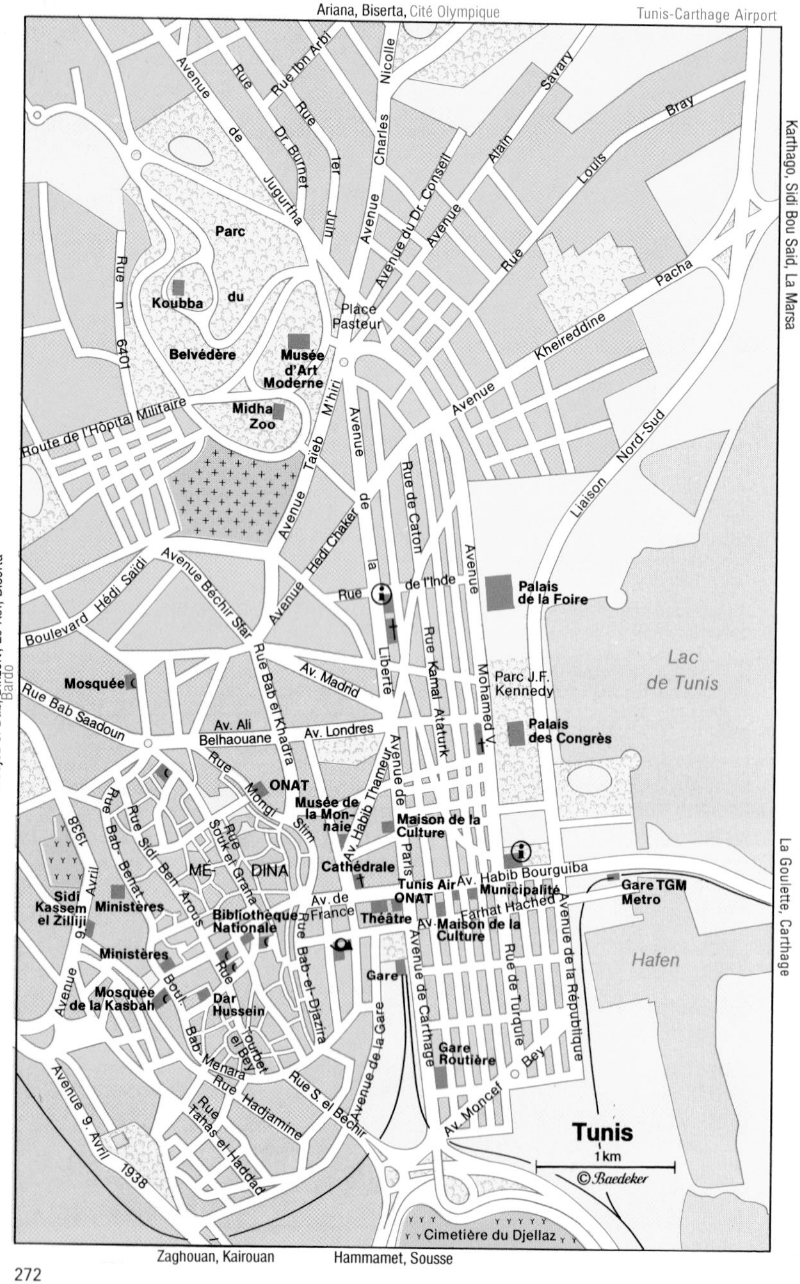

Ariana, Biserta, Cité Olympique

Tunis-Carthage Airport

Karthago, Sidi Bou Said, La Marsa

Medjez-el-Bab, Binzert, Le Kef, Biserta

Bardo

La Goulette, Carthage

Zaghouan, Kairouan

Hammamet, Sousse

Avenue de Jugurtha
Rue Dr. Burnet
Rue Ibn Arbi
Rue 1er Juin
Avenue Charles Nicolle
Avenue du Dr. Conseil
Avenue Alain Savary
Rue Louis Bray
Avenue Kheireddine Pacha
Rue n 6401
Parc du Belvédère
Koubba
Musée d'Art Moderne
Midha Zoo
Place Pasteur
Route de l'Hôpital Militaire
Avenue Taïeb M'hiri
Avenue de la Liberté
Rue de Caton
Avenue Mohamed V.
Liaison Nord-Sud
Avenue Hédi Chaker
Boulevard Hédi Saïdi
Avenue Béchir Sfar
Rue de l'Inde
Rue Kamal Atatürk
Palais de la Foire
Lac de Tunis
Parc J.F. Kennedy
Palais des Congrès
Mosquée
Rue Bab Saadoun
Rue Bab el Khadra
Av. Madrid
Av. Ali Belhaouane
Av. Londres
Rue Mongi Slim
ONAT
Musée de la Monnaie
Av. Habib Thameur
Avenue de Paris
Maison de la Culture
Rue Bab Benat
Rue Sidi Ben Arous
Rue Souk el Grana
MEDINA
Cathédrale
Avenue 9 Avril 1938
Av. Habib Bourguiba
Tunis Air
ONAT
Municipalité
Gare TGM Metro
Sidi Kassem el Zilliji
Ministères
Av. de France
Bibliothèque Nationale
Théâtre
Av. Farhat Hached
Maison de la Culture
Avenue de la République
Rue de Turquie
Hafen
Ministères
Rue Bab-el-Djazira
Gare
Avenue de Carthage
Mosquée de la Kasbah
Boul. Bab Menara
Dar Hussein
Rue Tourbet el Bey
Avenue de la Gare
Gare Routière
Rue Hadjamine
Rue S. el Béchir
Av. Moncef Bey
Rue Tahas el Haddad
Avenue 9. Avril 1938

Tunis
1 km
© Baedeker

Cimetière du Djellaz

Government office, Place du Gouvernement

Monument in Place de la Kasbah

almost all government departments and agencies and the headquarters of leading banks and large companies. The economic life of the city is centred on its industries (50% of all Tunisian industrial establishments are within the Tunis conurbation) and on the port. The most important industrial plants are to the south, west and north of the city, in Ben Arous, Radès, Djebel Djelloud, Bardo and Cherguia. The leading branches of industry are the chemical industry (large phosphate plant), the smelting of lead ore, cement works, the foodstuffs industries, engineering and papermaking. Most of the city's external trade (70%) is handled by the outer harbour at La Goulette, which has largely replaced the old inner harbour.

City transport

See Access, above

History

Thanks to its location on a wide, sheltered bay and to its fertile hinterland the site of ancient Tunes (present-day Tunis) was occupied by Numidians before the foundation of Carthage in 814 B.C. It thus ranks with Rome as one of the two oldest cities in the whole of the Mediterranean area.
In the 7th century B.C. the town came under Carthaginian control, was fortified by its new masters and thereafter shared the destinies of Carthage. During the three Punic Wars Tunes supported Carthage; in 246 B.C. it was taken by Regulus, and in 146 B.C., like Carthage, it was utterly destroyed. Later rebuilt by Caesar and Augustus, it continued to be overshadowed by its sister city Carthage.

The rise of Tunis began with the final destruction of Carthage by the Arabs in A.D. 698. The Lake of Tunis provided a natural harbour for the Muslim fleet. In 894 the Aghlabid ruler Ibrahim II transferred his capital from Kairouan to Tunis, and thereafter, particularly under the Hafsids (1228–1574), the town developed into the metropolis of North Africa, with a population of some 100,000, and one of the leading spiritual and intellectual centres of the Islamic world.

Sidi Youssef Mosque

Hammouda Pacha Mosque

In 1270 Tunis was besieged by a crusading army led by King Louis IX of France, who died in Carthage of the plague. The outbreak of war was prevented by the conclusion of a treaty with France granting equal rights to Christians.

In the 16th century Tunis's prosperity attracted the attentions of pirates, who captured and looted the town in 1534. In the following year they were driven out by the Emperor Charles V, and Tunis became Spanish, though the administration remained in the hands of the Hafsids. In 1569 the Spaniards were driven out by the Turks, who in turn were defeated by Don John of Austria. In 1574, however, Sinan Pasha won back the town for the Turks and it became the seat of an Ottoman governor.

In 1871 the Turkish Bey of Tunis, Hussein, declared himself independent of Constantinople. Thereafter the town developed rapidly and there was much new building. The new town which now came into being extended eastward from the old Medina.

The growth of Tunis accelerated from 1881 onwards, when the French made it the administrative centre of the protectorate. Most of the Medina's circuit of walls was pulled down, and the new town expanded farther towards the sea. Handsome public buildings were erected, new residential districts were developed for Europeans and a modern harbour was built.

From November 1942 to May 1943 the French protectorate was occupied by German forces. French rule finally ended on March 20th 1956, and in the following year Tunis became capital of the Tunisian Republic.

After the departure of most of the Europeans well-to-do Tunisians moved out of the Medina into the abandoned European districts, and less prosperous families occupied their houses in the old town. The Medina now has a population of around 200,000. The traditional craftsmen (smiths, saddlers, dyers, etc.), however, have now almost disappeared, their place increasingly being taken by souvenir-sellers.

Art Nouveau façade of the Theatre

Cathedral of St Vincent de Paul

In the outer districts of the city many overcrowded slum areas have been demolished and replaced by modern housing estates. Since the 1970s numbers of high-rise buildings occupied by luxury hotels, banks and insurance corporations have begun to dot the Tunis skyline. The Métro network is being actively developed in an attempt to alleviate the city's rush-hour traffic problems, and the Lake of Tunis is to be dredged and cleaned up.

Sights

Tunis has a great variety of historic buildings and other features of interest, reflecting its long and eventful history. At least two days should be allowed for seeing the sights, with an additional day for Carthage and Sidi Bou Said (see entries).

Excursions from Tunis

Tunis is a good base from which to visit other places of interest such as Cap Bon, Dougga, Utica and Thuburbo Majus (see entries).

New Town

Avenue Habib Bourguiba

The central axis of the new town between the Medina and the harbour which was developed during the period of French occupation is Avenue Habib Bourguiba. This magnificent avenue, planted with palms and eucalyptus trees, heads eastward in a dead straight line from Place de l'Indépendance, just outside the old town, towards the harbour, where it joins the expressway which crosses the Lake of Tunis on the causeway to La Goulette. On the harbour is the TGM station (services to the north-eastern suburbs of La Goulette, Carthage, Sidi Bou Said and La Marsa).

Place d'Afrique

Half way along Avenue Habib Bourguiba, at the intersection with the palm-shaded Avenue Mohammed V, which runs north to the Parc du

Belvédère, is Place d'Afrique, with a clock monument symbolising the "post-Bourguiba era" on a site previously occupied by an equestrian statue of President Bourguiba. This is a good starting-point for a tour of the town.

Hotel du Lac

On the right-hand side of the street (from Place d'Afrique) is the eye-catching ultra-modern Hotel du Lac, in the form of an inverted pyramid.

ONTT

Immediately in front of the hotel can be found the tourist information office (ONTT, Office National du Tourisme Tunisien).

Going east along Avenue Habib Bourguiba in the direction of the Medina, we pass the Ministry of the Interior (on left), readily recognisable by the barriers in front of the building and the strong police presence, and a series of shops, banks, cafés, travel agencies, restaurants, night spots and hotels, including the 21-storey tower block of the Hotel Africa (1967–70).

Avenue de Paris

At the next intersection Avenue Habib Bourguiba bisects Avenue de Paris, which runs north, lined by modern shops, into Avenue de la Liberté and so to the Parc du Belvédère, and Avenue de Carthage, which runs south, passing the railway station in Place Barcelone, to the Djellaz cemetery.

ONAT

On the far side of the intersection are the showrooms of ONAT (Organisation Nationale de l'Artisanat Tunisien), displaying a wide range of Tunisian craft products for sale.
Here too are three popular Tunis rendezvous, the Café de Paris, Café de Tunis and Brasserie Tunisia International.

Theatre

Just beyond this is the Municipal Theatre, with a striking Art Nouveau façade.

Cathedral

Avenue Habib Bourguiba now runs into Place de l'Indépendance, at the north end of which is the Cathedral of St-Vincent-de-Paul (1882), whose massive neo-Romanesque façade seems out of place at the gates of the Oriental old town. The Cathedral is the largest surviving building of the colonial period in Tunis. It contains the tomb of the Unknown Soldier.

French Embassy

Opposite the Cathedral is the French Embassy, formerly the seat of the French Resident-General.

Between these two relics of the French colonial presence in Tunisia can be seen a statue of Tunis's most celebrated citizen, Ibn Khaldun (1332–1406: see Famous People).

Bab el Bahr
Porte de France

On the far side of the square is the narrower Avenue de France, which ends at the entrance to the Medina, the Bab el Bahr (Sea Gate), formerly called the Porte de France, which has remained unchanged since its erection in 1848. The old town walls of the Hafsid period have disappeared.
Before entering the Medina it is worth while looking briefly along Rue Charles de Gaulle to the left.

Stamp Museum

In this street is the Head Post Office, an imposing colonial building, which also houses the Stamp Museum (Musée des Timbres), an interesting collection of stamps and postal equipment (entrance in Rue Gamal Abdel Nasser; same opening hours as the post office).

Fondouk el Ghalla

At the intersection with Rue d'Allemagne is the Fondouk el Ghalla, a large colonial-style market hall, where a lively and colourful foodstuffs market is held in the morning.

**Medina

The walls which once enclosed the Medina have long since disappeared, apart from a few town gates, and their place has been taken by a ring of

Bab el Bahr

streets around the old town, which is in the form of an oval measuring 1500m/1640yds from north to south by 800m/880yds from east to west. It is the largest Medina in Tunisia and the finest after the Medina of Kairouan. Originally going back to the 9th–11th centuries, it dates in its present form largely from the Hafsid (13th c.) and Turkish (17th–18th c.) periods. The French demolished its outer walls but left it otherwise unchanged.

ASMA

Systematic restoration and improvement work has been carried out in the Medina since 1974 under the direction of the Association for the Safeguard of the Medina (ASMA).
At first sight the Medina may seem a confusing and impenetrable labyrinth of narrow streets and lanes; but the names of the main streets are signposted in French as well as Arabic, and with the help of a town plan visitors should be able to find their way about without too much difficulty. If they lose their way they can get their direction from the position of the sun. They should beware of the narrowest lanes (*impasses*), which often turn out to be blind alleys.
On Fridays and increasingly on Sundays many shops in the souk quarter are closed. On other days the souk is a bustle of activity from the early morning.
Many buildings – medersas (Koranic schools), zaouias, mosques, mausoleums, palaces, etc. – are not open to the public, either because they are closed to non-Muslims (since 1972 non-Muslims are admitted to the inner courtyard of a mosque only during the morning and are prohibited from entering the prayer hall at any time) or because they are private property. On the guides who will frequently offer their services see Practical Information, Guides.

Rue Djemaa ez Zitouna

From Place de la Victoire, formerly the hub of the French quarter of Tunis, the Medina is entered through the Bab el Bahr. Straight ahead are the two main streets of the souk quarter, Rue Djemaa ez Zitouna to the left and Rue

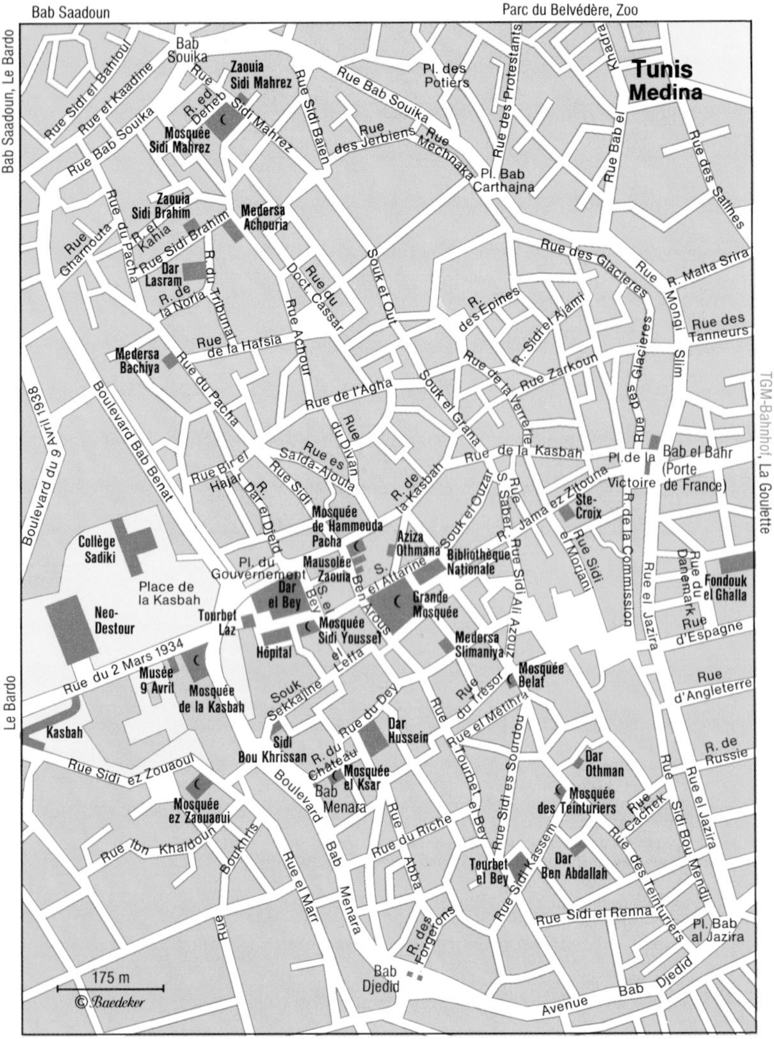

de la Kasbah to the right. The tour described in this section begins by going along Rue Djemaa ez Zitouna and ends by way of Rue de la Kasbah.
The shops in this quarter are exclusively targeted on tourists, and prices are correspondingly high. With a modicum of skill in haggling (see Practical Information, Shopping) it should be possible to bring them down to a more reasonable level.

Eglise de Ste-Croix

A few yards along Rue Djemaa ez Zitouna, on the left (No. 14), is the former Eglise de Ste-Croix (Holy Cross Church), founded in 1662 by a French chaplain named Jean Le Vacher, in the first fondouk (a warehouse and inn for European merchants) established in Tunis.

National Library

Farther along the street, on the right (No. 55), is the National Library (over 500,000 volumes), housed in the Sidi el Mordjani Barracks, erected by the Turks about 1813; the entrance is in Souk el Attarine.

Djemaa ez Zitouna (Olive-Tree Mosque)

The Great Mosque or Olive-Tree Mosque (Djemaa ez Zitouna) is the most important mosque in Tunisia after the Sidi Oqba Mosque in Kairouan. Even though non-Muslims may not enter the prayer hall it is well worth looking into the impressive inner courtyard (open daily, except Fridays, 8–11am). Admission tickets, which also cover a number of other sights, are issued immediately in front of the steps at the entrance.

The building of the mosque was begun by the Omayyads in 732. In 864 it was completely rebuilt by the Aghlabids, presumably because it was found to be too small, and in subsequent centuries it was repeatedly altered. The dome over the central bay was added in 991, the library in 1419. The vestibule was built by the Turks in 1637, the ceilings in the interior renewed in 1782. In the 19th century the minaret was increased in height by 44m/144ft; there is a magnificent view from the top over the roofs of the Medina.

The fifteen-aisled prayer hall is six bays deep. Beautiful horseshoe arches supporting the fine timber ceiling are borne on columns, most of them antique. The mihrab, under a beautiful dome of the Zirid period, is a masterpiece of Oriental carving. The floor is covered not with carpets but with esparto-grass mats. The large crystal chandeliers came from Murano (Italy).

Adjoining the mosque are the premises of its college of theology and Islamic law, which once ranked with the El Azhar Mosque in Cairo and the Kairaouine University in Fez as one of the leading centres of Islamic teaching. Since the foundation of the National University in 1960 it has declined in importance.

Souks

The mosque is surrounded on three sides by souks – a maze of streets and lanes, mostly roofed over, in which the shops are generally grouped by trades. A walk through the souks with their variety of exotic aromas and colours and their constant bustle of activity is part of the Tunisian experience for all visitors.

Roof terraces

It is well worth climbing to one of the roof terraces, paved with fine old tiles, over the carpet shops in the Souk el Leffa (for example the Palais d'Orient at No. 58) for the sake of the view over the Medina to the Great Mosque.

Souk el Attarine

On the north side of the mosque is the 13th century Souk el Attarine, the souk of the perfume-dealers, with the fine north doorway of the mosque, Bab el Bouhour (1081), borne on two columns. On the other side of the mosque (the qibla wall) is the Souk de la Laine, the souk of the woollen merchants, in which is the oldest doorway of the mosque (9th c.), framed in fragments of Roman friezes. From the Souk de la Laine Rue des Libraires runs south to the souk of the booksellers. At the far end of the street, on right, is the beautiful Medersa es Slimaniya, with a fine entrance and inner courtyard of 1754. On the west side of the mosque lies the 15th century Souk el Koumach, the souk of the cloth merchants.

The Souk el Attarine joins the Souk el Trouk, the old Turkish souk, in which is the old-established Café Mrabet. The Souk de la Laine leads into the Souk el Leffa (carpet and blanket dealers), from which the Souk el Berka runs north to the old slave market, in a square with a dome borne on striped red and green columns.

Lapidarium Sidi Bou Khrissan

The Souk el Leffa and its continuation Souk Sekkajine (the souk of the saddlers) lead south-west to the Lapidarium of Sidi Bou Khrissan, at the corner of Rue Ben Mahmoud.

Courtyard of the Olive-Tree Mosque

In an inner courtyard is the mausoleum of two Beni Khorasan emirs, dated by an inscription to 1093. Round the courtyard are numbers of inscribed funerary stelae of the 9th–19th centuries.

Dar Hussein

Rue Ben Mahmoud joins Rue Sidi Bou Khrissan, which leads to the little Place du Château. In this square is Dar Hussein, an 18th century Arab palace, much altered in the 19th century, with a beautiful inner courtyard, which now houses the National Institute of Archaeology and Art. Only the courtyard is open to the public.

El Ksar Mosque

Also in Place du Château is the El Ksar Mosque, which dates from 1106. It has a striking minaret in Hispano-Mauresque style (1647; restored 1978–79).

Kasbah Mosque

From the square Rue du Château leads to Boulevard Bab Menara, one of the ring of streets round the Medina. Along this street to the north (right) can be seen the square minaret (1235), with typical Andalusian/Moorish interlace decoration, of the Kasbah or Almohad Mosque. The minaret dates back to the 13th century Hafsid Kasbah, which was demolished soon after Tunisia became independent. The mosque is usually closed.

Neo-Destour House

In Place de la Kasbah are the massive headquarters of the Neo-Destour party and the Musée du 9 Avril (history of the Tunisian independence movement).

Mausoleum of Sidi Kassem el Zilliji

A short distance south-west, in Boulevard du 9 Avril, is the Mausoleum of Sidi Kassem el Zilliji (15th c., considerably enlarged in 18th c.), with a dome faced with green tiles, which now houses a small Ceramic Museum, together with an exhibition on the development of the Kufic script and a collection of funerary stelae.

Place du Gouvernement

Opposite the Kasbah Mosque is the Tourbet Laz, a small building with a tiled dome. Beyond it lies the Place du Gouvernement, in which are numerous government offices.

Ceramic tiles on a roof terrace

Mosque doorway with Roman friezes

Dar el Bey

Dar el Bey is a palace built about 1800 and altered in 1876, when it became the residence of the Bey of Tunis. It is now occupied by the Prime Minister's Office and the Foreign Ministry.

Sidi Youssef Mosque

South-east of Dar el Bey is the Sidi Youssef Mosque (1616), with a slender octagonal (Hanafite) minaret faced with green tiles (see Art and Culture, Islamic Architecture). Many of the 48 columns in the prayer hall have antique capitals. Over the mihrab is an octagonal dome. Associated with the mosque are the pyramid-roofed mausoleum of its founder, the Hafsid Bey Sidi Youssef, and a medersa (Koranic school) built in 1622.
At the end of Rue Sidi B. Ziad stands the Aziza Othman Hospital, the city's largest women's hospital, named after the daughter of Bey Othman, who is still revered (see below).

Souk des Chechias

On the east side of Dar el Bey is the Souk el Bey, off which opens the Souk des Chechias (Souk ech Chaouachiya), occupied since time immemorial by the makers of the woollen caps known as chechias. The craft was brought to Tunisia by Muslim refugees from Andalusia in the early 17th century.
The Souk des Chechias leads to Rue Sidi Ben Arous, named after the founder of a puritanical brotherhood who after his death in 1463 was buried in the zaouia at No. 23.

Mausoleum and Mosque of Hammouda Pacha

Farther down the street is the Mausoleum of Hammouda Pacha, a square building with a green-tiled pyramidal roof (1665). Adjoining is the Mosque of Hammouda Pacha (*c.* 1665), which has an octagonal minaret in Syrian style, one of the finest minarets in Tunis (illustration, page 291).

Mausoleum of Aziza Othman

Before returning to Bab el Bahr along Rue de la Kasbah it is worth while turning off that street into Rue el Jelloud to see, at the end of Impasse Echemmahia (No. 9), the Mausoleum of Aziza Othman. Aziza ("Beloved One"), daughter of Bey Othman, who died about 1643, was much loved by

Mausoleum in Sidi Bou Khrissan

Minaret of the Kasbah Mosque

the people of Tunis for her piety and her charitable works. The mausoleum, now in the forecourt of a private house, can be seen on payment of a small fee.

From here we can return by way of the Souk el Blaghija, the souk of the slipper-makers, to Rue de la Kasbah, which leads back to the starting-point of the tour at Bab el Bahr (Porte de France).

Tour of the northern Medina

Mosque of Sidi Mahrez

The starting-point of this tour of the northern Medina is Place Bab Souika, once the capital's place of execution and now the centre of a large new district of the town. In Rue Sidi Mahrez, which runs south-east from the square, is the Ottoman-style Mosque of Sidi Mahrez (*c.* 1675), with nine white domes. The 10th century marabout Mohammed Mahrez es Seddiki (the "Ascetic"), who is buried in the zaouia on the opposite side of the street, is the patron saint of Tunis. It is said that after the sacking of Tunis in 944 by the followers of the Kharijite leader Abou Yazid he encouraged his fellow-citizens to rebuild the town walls and develop trade and industry.

In Rue el Monastiri, which opens off Rue Sidi Mahrez, is Dar el Monastiri, an 18th century palace with a handsome doorway.

Medersa Achouria

At the corner of Rue Achour and Rue Sidi Brahim can be seen the Medersa Achouria, with a square minaret and a handsome doorway.

Zaouia Sidi Brahim

In Rue Sidi Brahim (No. 11) is the mid 19th century Zaouia Sidi Brahim, with a beautifully decorated interior, and in Rue du Tribunal, which goes off opposite it, stands Dar Lasram, an 18th century palace which now houses ASMA, the association for the preservation of the Medina.

Rue Sidi Brahim joins Rue du Pacha. The Turkish Pasha once resided in this street, and it became the main street of a select residential quarter (fine doorways). At No. 40 is the Medersa Bachiya (1756).

Rue du Pacha runs into Rue Sidi Ben Arous, which goes north to Rue Bab Souika and the starting-point of the tour and south to the Mausoleum of Hammouda Pacha.

View of modern Tunis from the Belvédère

Tour of the southern Medina

The starting-point for a tour of the southern Medina is Place Bab el Jazira.

Dyers' Mosque

Rue des Teinturiers leads north to the Dyers' Mosque (Mosquée des Teinturiers; known locally as the Djemaa el Djedid, the New Mosque), which with the associated medersa was built in 1715 by the founder of the Husseinite dynasty. It was modelled on the Sidi Youssef Mosque and, like it, has a slender octagonal minaret. The interior has beautiful carved woodwork.

Dar Othman

Opposite the Dyers' Mosque, in Rue el M'Bazaa, stands Dar Othman, a palace built about 1600 by Bey Othman, with a beautiful inner courtyard.

Dar Ben Abdallah

In Rue Sidi Kassem, which runs south-west off Rue des Teinturiers, is Dar Ben Abdallah, an 18th century palace which is now occupied by a folk museum, the Musée du Patrimoine Traditionnel de la Ville de Tunis (open daily, except Sunday, 9.30am–4.30pm). The exhibits include faience, stucco ornament, costumes and furniture.

Tourbet el Bey

At the intersection of Rue Sidi Kassem and Rue Tourbet rises the massive Tourbet el Bey (1758), crowned by a huge dome. This is the burial-place of almost all the rulers of the Husseinite dynasty (1705–1957). Open daily 8.30am–12.45pm and 3–5.45pm.
The house at No. 33 Rue Tourbet is said to have been the birthplace in 1332 of Ibn Khaldun (see Famous People).

Bab Djedid

From here Rue du Persan and Rue des Juges lead into Rue des Forgerons (Street of the Smiths), which runs south-west to Bab Djedid, Tunis's oldest town gate (1276).

Northern Tunis

Parc du Belvédère

In the north of the city is the Parc du Belvédère, laid out on the slopes of a hill (88m/289ft) and planted with Aleppo pines, carob-trees, olives, figs and palms. From the two summits of the hill, which are reached on well-kept paths, are fine views of the city and the Lake of Tunis, extending in clear weather to Carthage, the double peak of Bou Kornine and Cap Bon.

Zoo

Within the park is the Zoo (Parc Zoologique), which is of interest not only for its animals but also for its luxuriant subtropical vegetation (open daily 9am–7pm, in winter 9am–5pm).
Also in the park is a 17th century *midha* (ablutions fountain), formerly in the Souk el Trouk (Turks' Souk).

Koubba

On the Belvédère hill stands the Koubba, an elegant pavilion with shell vaulting and magnificent stucco decoration. This light and airy 17th century building, which originally belonged to a palace in La Manouba district, was re-erected here in 1901.

Museum of Modern Art

The former Casino, on the east side of the park, now houses the Museum of Modern Art, with pictures by modern Tunisian painters (open daily, except Mondays, 9.30am–noon and 3–6pm).

**Bardo National Museum

Le Bardo

4km/2½ miles west of Tunis is the suburb of Le Bardo, famed for the Bardo National Museum (Musée National du Bardo), which has the world's largest collection of Roman mosaics and ranks with the Egyptian Museum in Cairo as one of the two great museums of North Africa. (Other Tunisian museums with fine mosaics are those of Sousse, El Djem and Sfax: see entries.)

Access

The museum is easily reached from the city centre by public transport (bus No. 3 from the corner of Avenue Habib Bourguiba and Rue de Rome or No. 4 from Jardin Habib Thameur), by taxi or by car.
For those travelling by car the route is as follows: From Place Bab Souika, at the north end of the Medina, take Rue Bab Saadoun, which runs north-west to the roundabout at Bab Saadoun, one of the old town gates (restored), and from there follow Boulevard du 20 Mars 1956, passing the remains of a 13th century aqueduct (restored in the 17th century) which supplied Carthage with water. The Museum, set in a park, lies outside the town on the right of the road, concealed at first by the imposing 17th century palace occupied by the Tunisian National Assembly, its entrance flanked by two marble lions and guarded by men of the National Guard. Immediately beyond this is the National Museum (entrance by a gate in Rue Mongi Slim which leads to a large car park in front of a mosque). Much of the walled park around the museum is occupied by the army and closed to the public.

The Bardo Museum is open daily, except Mondays and public holidays, 9.30am–4.30pm. Admission tickets are issued at a kiosk in front of the entrance. A special ticket must be obtained for taking photographs; the use of flash and/or a tripod is banned.

History

The site, lying in fertile country immediately outside the gates of the capital, was occupied in the 13th century by a Hafsid palace. The origin of the name Bardo is disputed. Some hold that it is derived from the Spanish "Prado", others that it comes from the Moorish *berd* ("cold" – the suggestion being that it was not sufficiently insulated against the winter cold). The successors of the Hafsids appreciated the advantages of the situation, and each generation altered or added to the palace, creating over the centuries an extensive complex of buildings.

The National Museum itself is housed in the Little Palace, built in 1831–32, and the state apartments of the Great Palace. The mosque opposite the Museum dates from the 15th century (restored). The decision to establish a

Carthage room, seen from the gallery ▶

museum was taken in 1882, and six years later it was opened under the name of the Alaoui Museum (after the reigning Bey, Ali). After Tunisia became independent it was renamed the Bardo National Museum (Musée National du Bardo).

The collection

The Museum gives a comprehensive view of the prehistoric, Phoenician, Roman, Christian and Arab past of Tunisia. The collection is arranged chronologically and, within particular periods, by provenance.
On the history of mosaics in particular see Art and Culture in the introduction to this guide.

Continuing work on the renovation and alteration of the building, the closing of some rooms at certain times and rearrangement of exhibits – to say nothing of the labyrinthine ground-plan – make it impossible to give a detailed plan or description of the Museum. The following account seeks only, therefore, to direct attention to the main features of interest. In any event almost all the exhibits are labelled.

Ground floor
Room 1

Entrance; information; sale of guides and casts of statues and masks. Plaster model of Roman Gightis.

Room 2

Finds from the Tophet of Carthage, where children were sacrificed to Baal-Ammon (see Carthage). Urns, cippi and votive stelae of the 6th–2nd centuries B.C., showing the development of forms over the centuries. The oldest stelae have pyramidal roofs (6th c.), the later ones resemble Greek temples (3rd c.), while in the 2nd century they take the form of obelisks. Many stelae bear the symbol of the goddess Tanit (a triangle with a cross bar topped by a disc) or of Baal-Ammon (a solar disc) and inscriptions in Punic script.

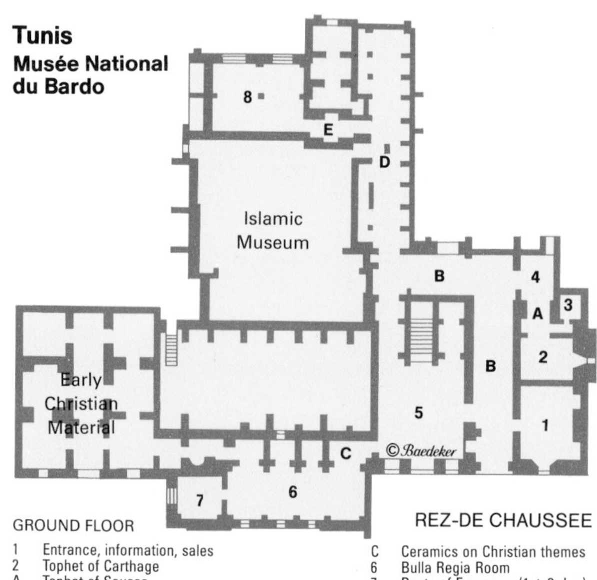

Behind protective glass is a stele with the incised figure of a priest holding a child ready for sacrifice (4th or early 3rd c. B.C.). A votive tablet dedicated to Baal-Ammon bears the earliest known Punic inscription (6th c. B.C.).

Corridor A

Finds from a tophet at Sousse (3rd–2nd c. B.C.). Two of the stelae show scenes of sacrifice.

Rooms 3 and 4

Bronze armour with a head of Minerva, originally from Campania, which was found in a cedarwood coffin at Ksour Essaf (see below). Punic grave goods (in cases). Of particular interest are the little heads (usually bearded) in coloured glass paste (5th and 4th c. B.C.) – amulets designed to ward off evil. Corinthian (7th–6th c. B.C.), Etruscan (6th c.) and Campanian (6th–2nd c. B.C.).

Egyptian influence can be seen in the clay masks intended either to ward off evil (grimacing heads) or to bring good fortune (smiling women).

Clay mask

Corridor B

Neo-Punic funerary stelae and clay statuettes of divinities (1st c. B.C.). The stelae, in the form of obelisks, have Punic inscriptions, likenesses of deities (Tanit or Baal-Ammon), figures of fishes and birds, crescents and fruit. They show that after the fall of Carthage in 146 B.C. Punic influence continued for a time (worship of Caelestis, identified with Tanit)

A richly decorated Roman sarcophagus

Perseus and Andromeda (Bardo Museum, Tunis)

but that Greco-Roman influence steadily increased (worship of Dionysus, Aphrodite, Zeus and Hermes). The material comes from Korba, Dougga, Maktar and Thuburbo Majus. Hellenistic influence can be seen to have reached the Numidians.
Also of interest are the cedarwood coffins from Punic tombs of the 3rd century B.C. at Gightis and Ksour Essaf. Just before the entrance to Corridor D is a fine Roman sarcophagus (3rd c.) with relief figures of the nine Muses, with a later (5th c.) sarcophagus above it.

Room 5

Early Christian material of the 4th–7th centuries from Carthage, Tabarka, Thuburbo Majus and Cap Bon. The mosaic grave-slabs depict the dead person, accompanied by Christian symbols (crosses, pigeons, fishes). Other mosaics depict Old Testament figures like Daniel and Jonah. They come from Early Christian and Byzantine churches and graves.
In the centre of the room is a cruciform marble immersion font (6th c.) from El Kantara (see Djerba). The mosaics come from Carthage, mostly from tombs. Some sarcophagi have inscriptions giving the name of the dead person.

Corridor C

On the walls are terracotta panels from Christian basilicas with relief decoration, mostly of Old Testament scenes.

Room 6 (Bulla Regia Room)

The mosaics in this room date from the heyday of Bulla Regia in the 2nd and 3rd centuries A.D. Opposite the entrance hangs the famous mosaic of Perseus and Andromeda from the dining room of a Roman villa (3rd or 4th c.). In niches along the opposite wall are statues of Apollo, Ceres and Aesculapius from the temple dedicated to this divine triad.

Room 7

This room originally contained material from the Punic necropolis at Thinissut (near Bir Bou Rekba, Cap Bon), now in the museum of Nabeul (see

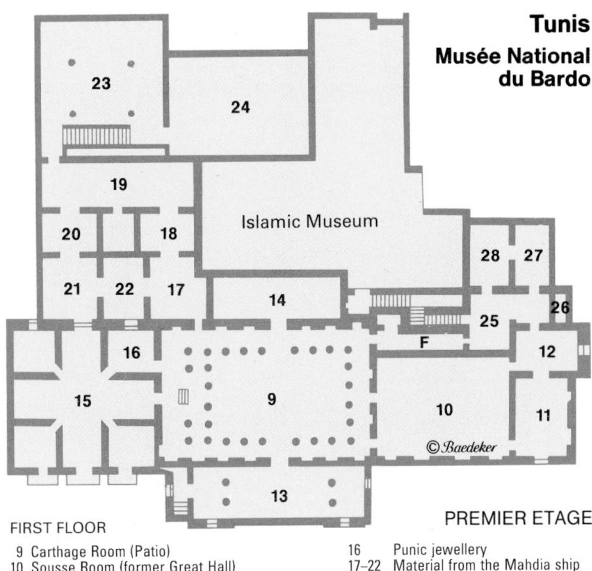

9 Carthage Room (Patio)
10 Sousse Room (former Great Hall)
11 Dougga Room
12 El Djem Room
13 Althiburos Room (former Music Room)
14 Oudna Room (former Dining Room)
15 Virgil Room (former Harem)
16 Punic jewellery
17–22 Material from the Mahdia ship
23 Marine mosaics
24 Roman mausoleum
F Mosaics
25–28 Mosaics

entry). The busts of Roman emperors now displayed here (including Hadrian, Caracalla, Lucius Verus, Marcus Aurelius, Vespasian, Gordian I, Trajan and Augustus) are from various Tunisian sites (1st–3rd c.).

Early Christian Rooms

The centrepiece of the Early Christian Rooms (Salles Paléo-Chrétiennes) is a mosaic-decorated immersion font in the shape of a Greek cross (6th c.) found in a church north of Kelibia (Cap Bon). Around it are displayed funerary mosaics from the same church, together with lamps, pottery and coins of the 4th–7th centuries.

Corridor D

Neo-Punic funerary stelae and richly decorated sarcophagi of the 2nd and 3rd centuries. Note particularly a sarcophagus at the near end of the corridor with symbols representing the wisdom of the dead man (from Carthage, early 4th c.).
Also notable (in a niche on the left) is an over-lifesize statue of an elderly man with an expressive face holding a sheaf of corn and poppies, indicating that he was a devotee of Ceres (late 3rd c.). On the floor are mosaics from Thuburbo Majus.

Islamic Museum

A doorway on the left of Corridor D leads into the Islamic Museum (see below).

Corridor E

Tablets with inscriptions and votive stelae.

Room 8 (Thuburbo Majus Room)

The mosaics and sculpture in this room come from private houses, public buildings and a temple (later converted into a church) in Thuburbo Majus (3rd and 4th c.).
The marble statue of Hercules has an inscription indicating that it was presented to the town by the guild of cloak-manufacturers (Sagarii, from *sagum,* "cloak", a garment originally introduced from Gaul).

Triumph of Neptune (Bardo Museum, Tunis)

First floor
(plan, p. 289)

From Room 5 a staircase (with Early Christian mosaics from Tabarka on the walls) leads to the upper floor.

Room 9
(Carthage Room)

In this colonnaded room with a ceiling decorated in Italian style, originally the Great Hall of the palace, are displayed finds from Roman Carthage. The best general view of the room is to be had from the gallery on the second floor.

In the centre of the room is an altar of the Gens Augusta, dating from around the beginning of the Christian era, which was found on the Byrsa Hill. It has fine relief decoration; on one side Aeneas is depicted fleeing from Troy with his father Anchises and his son Ascanius.

The two large mosaics on the floor come from the country house of a wealthy family of the 2nd century at Oudna (ancient Uthina). One of them depicts scenes of country life; the other shows King Ikarios of Attica learning the art of wine-making from Dionysus.

The statues and fragments of statues in the room (Hercules, Hermes, Venus, etc.) came from the Odeon and Theatre of Carthage (2nd and 3rd c. A.D.).

Room 10
(Sousse Room)

Material from Sousse (ancient Hadrumetum) is displayed in the former banqueting hall of the palace, which has a domed ceiling with delicate ornament by Tunisian craftsmen.

On the floor is a large mosaic (10.25m/34ft by 13.50m/44ft) depicting the "Triumph of Neptune" (late 2nd c.). In the centre is the sea god in his war chariot, surrounded by sirens, nereids, tritons and nymphs in circular and hexagonal medallions.

On the walls are other mosaics giving glimpses of everyday Roman life (4th–5th c.). Mosaics from Carthage and Tabarka depict various country houses; from Carthage and Gafsa come representations of chariot races and gladiatorial contests.

Virgil with Cleo and Melpomene (Bardo Museum, Tunis)

On the rear wall are the head and sandal-clad feet of a statue of Jupiter, originally 7m/23ft high, from the Capitol of Thuburbo Majus (3rd c.). In cases around the room are small finds, including pottery with relief decoration, vases, coins and oil lamps of the 2nd–5th centuries A.D.
The doorway to the right of the head of Jupiter leads into Room 11.

Room 11
(Dougga Room)

Most of the exhibits in this room come from Dougga (3rd and 4th c.). The mosaic of the Cyclopes (Brontes, Steropes and Pyracmon) forging thunderbolts comes from the frigidarium of the baths. There is also a fine representation of the victorious Eros in the Circus.
The fishing scene came from the baths in Carthage (2nd c.). The 2nd century mosaic of the "Triumph of Neptune" is from La Chebba, near Sfax (2nd c.). There are also statues of Saturn, Bacchus, Aesculapius, Jupiter and Venus and fine silver and goldsmiths' work, including a silver dish inlaid with gold from Bizerte (1st c.).
On the left of the doorway into Room 12 is part of a mosaic of Eros driving a chariot which gives the names of two horses, Amandus and Frunitus.
To right and left of the doorway are plaster models of the Capitol and theatre of Dougga.

Room 12
(El Djem Room)

This room is mainly devoted to material from El Djem (ancient Thysdrus). The mosaics mostly date from the 3rd century. Note particularly the "Triumph of Bacchus", a hunting scene depicted in three registers and a mosaic of the nine Muses.

Room 13
(Althiburos Room)

Room 13 takes its name from the large 3rd century mosaic from Althiburos (Medeina, near Le Kef). This depicts over twenty different types of ancient ships sailing in a sea teeming with fish, each type being labelled with its name in Greek and Latin. Other mosaics are from Carthage, El Djem, Radès, Bizerte and Béja.

This was originally the music room of the palace. It has an ornate painted ceiling in Italian style and two galleries. One of them, linked by a staircase with the harem of the palace, enabled the princesses of the Bey's family to attend concerts and other performances; the other, to the left of the entrance, was for the orchestra.
From the balcony opening off this room there is a view of the 15th century mosque in front of the Museum.
On the opposite side of the Great Hall is Room 14.

Room 14 (Oudna Room)

Room 14, the former dining room of the palace, which also has a painted ceiling in Italian style, contains mosaics of the 2nd and 3rd centuries from Oudna (ancient Uthina), 25km/15 miles south-west of Tunis. They include representations of Venus at her toilet and Orpheus surrounded by wild beasts. One mosaic is signed with the name of the artist, Masurus.

Room 15 (Virgil Room)

A short flight of steps at the lower end of the Great Hall leads into the Virgil Room. This was originally the centre of the harem, the Bey's private apartments, with the various rooms opening off it. Notable features are its cruciform plan and its decoration (19th c.). The central dome has rich stucco ornament, and the walls are clad with typical 19th century faience tiles.
The room contains a variety of statues (Demeter and Kore/Persephone, 1st c.) and portraits of Emperors. On the wall is a mosaic from Hadrumetum (Sousse) depicting Virgil with the Muses Clio (History) and Melpomene (Tragedy), who are inspiring him to write the "Aeneid". On the papyrus scroll in his lap can be read the words "Musa mihi causas memora, quo numine laeso, quidve . . ." ("Muse, tell me the reasons for which the offended divinity . . ."; "Aeneid", Book I, lines 8 and 9).
In the centre of the room is a hexagonal mosaic (3rd c.) from the Zaghouan area depicting the seven deities of the planets and the days of the week.

Room 16

Punic jewellery and ornaments (finely restored) of the 7th–3rd centuries B.C. Some of the items came from overseas.

Rooms 17–22

Rooms 17–22 display material recovered from the Roman ship which sank off the coast at Mahdia in 81 B.C. and was discovered by sponge-divers in 1906 lying at a depth of 39m/128ft. It was carrying a rich cargo from Greece, including statues, vases, bronzes and much else besides (3rd–2nd c. B.C.). Also on display are fragments of the wrecked vessel, which was around 40m/130ft long by 10m/35ft wide, and items of equipment.
Also in Room 19 are mosaics from Utica, El Djem and Thuburbo Majus.

Room 23

In Room 23, the Room of the Marine Mosaics, are a variety of mosaics, mainly from Carthage, Gightis, El Djem and Oudna.

Room 24

Room 24, the Room of the Mausoleum, contains a reconstruction of a 2nd century mausoleum from Carthage, all four sides of which are covered with fine bas-reliefs. Also in this room are mosaics from Carthage and Thuburbo Majus, including a representation of a stag-hunt and a large semicircular still life.

Corridor F

Mosaics from Carthage, Thuburbo Majus and El Djem.

Room 25

Mosaics, including a "Venus Pudica" (Carthage, late 3rd c.), "Bacchus and Ariadne" (Thuburbo Majus, 4th c.), a peacock displaying its tail (Bir Chana, 3rd c.) and "Diana the Huntress" (Oudna, 2nd/3rd c.).

Room 26

Floor mosaic from the baths in Thuburbo Majus (4th c.).

Room 27

Room 27 is called the Odysseus Room, after a mosaic from Dougga of which four fragments have been preserved; one of them shows Odysseus tied to the mast as he listens to the Sirens (3rd c.). A mosaic from El Djem

Virgil Room

Courtyard of Islamic Museum, Bardo

depicts the musical contest between Apollo and the satyr Marsyas (2nd c.), another the "Triumph of Venus" (Kasserine, 3rd c.).

Room 28

Mosaics from Ellès, Carthage and El Djem depicting mythological themes, hunting scenes and scenes in the circus.

Second floor
(no plan)

The mosaics on the walls of the staircase are from Kourba (2nd c.).

Room 29

The upper gallery of the Great Hall is lined with cases displaying small items from Roman tombs (terracotta statuettes, bronzes), vases, glass and pottery. From the gallery there is a good view of the Carthage Room below.

Rooms 30–32

Rooms 30–32 contain more mosaics, including representations of Theseus killing the Minotaur (Thuburbo Majus, 3rd/4th c.), Bacchus with a gecko on a leash, surrounded by wild animals (Room 30; El Djem, 4th c.), Diana the huntress (Utica, 2nd c.) and one from Thuburbo Majus (Room 31; 3rd/4th c.).

Room 33
(Acholla Room)

Mosaics from Acholla (present-day Ras Bou Tria, 40km/25 miles north of Sfax, near Djebeniana). Dating from the 2nd century, they are among the earliest mosaics found in Tunisia. Particularly fine is the "Triumph of Dionysus". In the centre of the room is a semicircular fountain.

Rooms 34 and 35

In spite of its name the Fresco Room mainly displays mosaics, including scenes in the circus (Dougga) and hunting scenes (El Djem), as well as remains of frescoes from Gightis.

Islamic Museum

The Museum of Islamic Art at Reqqada (see Kairouan, Surroundings) is still in course of development. Part of the Bardo collection has been and is being transferred there, and it is not therefore possible to say precisely what is still to be seen in the Bardo. In general, however, the exhibits are labelled, with an indication of provenance and date.

Ground floor

The Museum of Islamic Art, which is entered from Corridor D in the main Bardo Museum, is housed in the Hussein Palace (1824–35), which is linked with the main building.
In a room in the former harem, paved with beautiful glazed tiles, are a model of the Ribat of Sousse and a collection of rare ancient fabrics, some of them imported from Egypt.
The early Islamic gravestones have inscriptions in both Kufic and cursive script.
One room is devoted to Islamic Tunisia of the early medieval period, with examples – all exactly dated – of pottery, jewellery, coins of various ruling dynasties and beautifully illuminated pages from the Koran and Koran bindings.
Also of interest is a small astrolabe of the 13th or 14th century.

First floor

A pretty little inner courtyard gives access to other rooms. In a recess at the entrance are two thrones presented to the Bey by Napoleon III.
In a series of small rooms opening off the courtyard are 16th and 17th century prints with views of the town and a variety of other prints; a reception room furnished in traditional style (late 19th century); a collection of Jewish cult objects; and a small kitchen in which the Bey's morning coffee was made, with domestic equipment, including copper plates and jugs.
In other rooms are finely carved chests, traditional musical instruments with mother-of-pearl intarsia decoration, a collection of richly decorated weapons, beautiful jewellery and garments in traditional style.

Surroundings of Tunis

La Goulette

North-east of Tunis, at the end of the causeway over the Lake of Tunis, is La Goulette, the port suburb of the capital (pop. 50,000). It is reached by bus or TGM from Tunis, or by car over the causeway.
The name is derived from Arabic *halk el oued* ("river mouth") – referring to the natural channel through the strip of land bounding the Lake of Tunis, which has been open since ancient times. As a result La Goulette has been from time immemorial a place of strategic importance, controlling the entrance to Tunis's harbour. In the reign of the Emperor Charles V it was the most important Spanish possession in the eastern Maghreb; and from 1574 onwards the Turks enlarged and strengthened the fortress built by Spain.
La Goulette became a port only during the French colonial period, when the Lake of Tunis silted up and could no longer take ships of any size. Between 1888 and 1893 a shipping channel 10km/6 miles long and 45m/150ft wide was dredged out across the lake. Thereafter the harbour of La Goulette was greatly enlarged in 1905 and again in 1964–71, and the old harbour of Tunis steadily declined in importance. In addition to shipping bulk goods including phosphates, mineral ores and olives, La Goulette imports machinery and maintains ferry services with Europe. It also has a coal-fired power station and a variety of industry.
The main features of tourist interest in La Goulette are the Spanish and Turkish fort and the gateway of the old Arsenal on the Tunis road. The Avenue Franklin Roosevelt is a pleasant promenade in summer. There are innumerable restaurants offering tasty fish dishes as well as mutton sausages, cutlets and chicken. Beyond the harbour is a long sandy beach which attracts many visitors from Tunis.

Carthage

17km/10½ miles east of Tunis (regular bus and TGM services) is Carthage (see entry).

Landscape south-west of Tunis

Sidi Bou Said

20km/12½ miles north-east of Tunis (regular bus and TGM services) is Sidi Bou Said (see entry).

La Marsa Gammarth

22km/14 miles north-east of Tunis and 6km/4 miles north of La Goulette are the select residential towns and seaside resorts of La Marsa and Gammarth, much frequented by the people of Tunis.

Access

TGM Tunis–La Goulette–La Marsa, or by car on GP 9 (the road to the airport).

The name of La Marsa comes from its medieval designation of Marsa Roum ("Port of the Christians") – referring to the many Copts who came here from Egypt. In the 10th century Sidi Mahrez, Tunis's patron saint, lived and died here.

During the 19th century the Beys and their senior officials built summer palaces here, and thereafter the upper classes of the population began to patronise the resort. The President of Tunisia also has a residence here.

The main feature of interest in La Marsa is the market square, with its buildings of the Hafsid period. At the right-hand end of the square is the entrance to the Café Saf-Saf, built round a Hafsid fountain.

Gammarth

Below the market square of La Marsa is the palm-shaded Avenue de la Corniche, which runs along the coast to Gammarth. Just before the town is a French military cemetery, from the highest point of which there are beautiful views over the Gulf of Tunis, extending in clear weather to Cap Bon.

Raouad

North-west of Cap Gammarth is the endless-seeming beach of Raouad, another very popular resort for the people of Tunis in summer.

Utica

40km/25 miles north: see entry

Hammam-Lif

19km/12 miles south-east of Tunis on GP 1 is Hammam-Lif (pop. 30,000). Its beach, badly polluted though it is, and its popular Sunday market attract

Remains of the . . .

. . . Aqueduct of Hadrian

Zaghouan

large numbers of Tunis people at weekends. It has hot springs which were already being used for medicinal purposes in Roman times, though there are no traces of the Roman baths. From the 18th century this was the winter residence of the Beys of Tunis, and during the French colonial period the town became a fashionable bathing resort. The old bath-house of the Beys, now the Hotel des Thermes, is a reminder of past glories.
Hammam-Lif is a good starting-point for the ascent of the beautifully formed Djebel Bou Kornine, the "Horned Mountain", with two peaks respectively 576m/1890ft and 493m/1618ft high.

Bordj Cedria

2km/1¼ miles south of GP 1, to the west of Soliman Plage, is the Turkish fort of Bordj Cedria.

La Mohammedia

15km/9 miles south of Tunis on GP 3 is the village of La Mohammedia (reached by leaving Tunis on the motorway to Sousse and in 8km/5 miles turning off into GP 3, the Kairouan road; signposted).
Here can be seen the ruins of a palace built by Ahmed Bey (1842–47), who set out to create a Tunisian Versailles. The project, however, was brought to an untimely end by his early death.

*Aqueduct of Hadrian

2km/1¼ miles south of the village are the remains of the Aqueduct of Hadrian, which runs alongside the road for a distance of some 5km/3 miles. Built between 120 and 131 A.D. and borne on massive 20m/65ft high piers linked by arches, the aqueduct carried water to Carthage from Djebel Zaghouan (1295m/4249ft), the highest peak in the northern Dorsale, a distance of 90km/55 miles. After the fall of Rome the aqueduct continued to be used and kept in repair by the Byzantines, the Fatimids and the Hafsids, but from the 14th century onwards it gradually fell into ruin.

Zaghouan

The little agricultural town of Zaghouan (pop. 8000), at the foot of Djebel Zaghouan (1295m/4249ft), is reached from Tunis by way of GP 3 and MC 133.
This was the site of Roman Ziqua, of which nothing is left but an arched gateway (restored) at the foot of the main street. The town has an attractive old Medina with a maze of irregular streets dominated by two minarets, one Hanafite and the other Malikite (see Art and Culture, Islamic Architecture). At the upper end of the town is the green-tiled Zaouia of Sidi Ali Azouz, Zaghouan's patron saint.

*Nymphaeum

2km/1¼ miles from the town, higher up, is a Roman nymphaeum, known in Arabic as Ain el Kasbah and in French as the Temple des Eaux. The small square cella of the shrine was built over the principal spring (now dry). On either side of the cella was a semicircular portico enclosing a terrace open to the north-west. Here, opposite the cella, is a large basin in the form of a figure of eight, the starting-point of the 124km/74 mile long aqueduct carrying water to Carthage (see illustration, page 314).
From here a road runs up to a viewpoint at an altitude of 975m/3200ft), with radio and television aerials. In antiquity the hill was covered with forests of thuya; nowadays the slopes above 600m/2000ft bear a dense growth of macchia.
There are attractive trips from Zaghouan into the beautiful surrounding country.

Thuburbo Majus

63km/39 miles south: see entry

Cap Bon

See entry

Utica

A 6/7

Governorate: Bizerte

Access

Utica lies 37km/23 miles north of Tunis. It is reached by leaving the city on GP 3 and in 34km/21 miles, at Zhana (Zama), turning right into a road which comes in 3km/2 miles to the site (signposted).

Baths, Utica

Some 29km/18 miles from Tunis, to the right, is the seven-arched "Asses' Bridge" of Bey Hussein spanning the Oued Medjerda.

Situation and characteristics

The ancient Punic and Roman port of Utica now lies 15km/9 miles inland, near the mouth of the Oued Medjerda, Tunisia's largest perennial river. Most of the ancient town lies under a 5m/16ft deep layer of mud deposited by the river, the ancient name of which was Bagradas, and only a small part of the area has been excavated. It is, therefore, a less impressive site than Dougga, Sufetula, Bulla Regia or Maktar; but it is still well worth a visit by anyone with an interest in history or archaeology.

History

Utica is thought to have been founded about 1100 B.C. by Phoenicians from Tyre – the earliest Phoenician trading post in North Africa. Now 15km/9 miles from the sea, it originally lay directly on the coast and on a small offshore island, just north of the mouth of the Bagradas/Medjerda. The alluvial sands carried down by the river have moved its mouth steadily farther north-eastward.

Some 300 years later Carthage was founded, also by Phoenicians from Tyre. Until the 5th century B.C. Utica managed to preserve its independence, but thereafter fell increasingly under the influence of its powerful neighbour. During the Mercenary War of 240–237 B.C. Utica joined the rebellion against Carthage. In the Second Punic War (218–201 B.C.) it supported Carthage, but in 149 B.C., just before the outbreak of the Third Punic War, it again changed sides, and Scipio was able to use it as a base for his attack on Carthage.

After the destruction of Carthage Utica became capital of the Roman province of Africa, but during the reign of Augustus, in A.D. 14, it lost this role to Carthage, which had been re-founded by the Romans. During the civil war between Caesar and Pompey Utica was the headquarters of the Pompeians, commanded after Pompey's death by Cato the Younger. Foreseeing Caesar's victory, Cato committed suicide, and Utica was condemned to pay a large fine but was not destroyed.

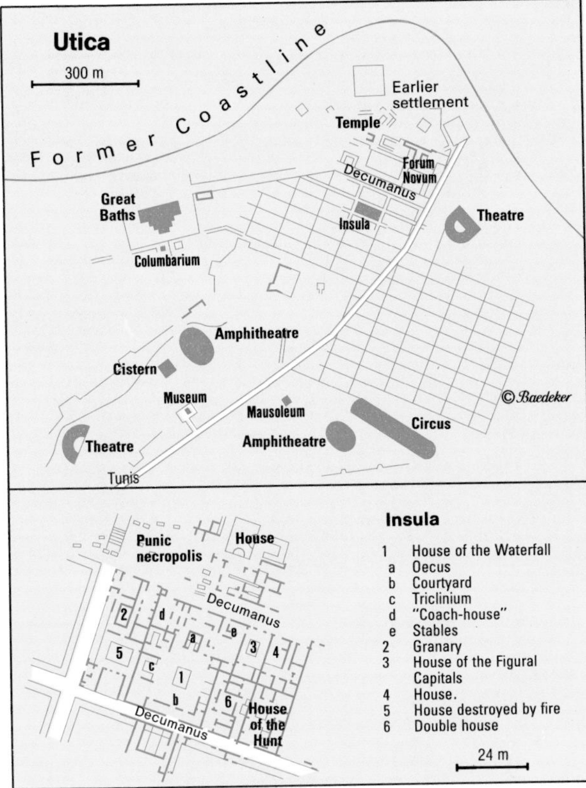

Thereafter Utica developed into a flourishing commercial centre, soon becoming the largest town in the province of Africa. Its heyday was in the 2nd century A.D., when it was the scene of great building activity.
In the 3rd century, however, the harbour began to silt up, and by the early medieval period it was completely buried under the deposits brought down by the Oued Medjerda. The town continued to exist during the period of Vandal rule, and from the 3rd to the 8th century it was the see of a bishop. It was unable, however, to recover from the destruction wrought by the advancing Arabs, and thereafter for many centuries was used as a quarry of building stone.

*Excavations

Exploration of the site began in the early 19th century, and much excavation was carried out between 1948 and 1958. So far, however, only a small part of the site has been brought to light, and most of it – in particular the lower town and harbour – is still covered by a thick layer of mud and in places, below the water table, by water or marshland.
There is a huge Punic cemetery, part of which was later built over. Of the Roman town, much of it built on Punic foundations, little survives after its use for so long as a quarry.

Mosaic in the House of the Waterfall

Museum

On the left of the road to the site, 800m/880yds before the entrance, is a small site museum (open daily, except Mondays, 8am–noon and 2–5.30pm).

The Phoenician, Carthaginian and Roman material displayed includes a wooden coffin of the Punic period, coins, lamps, pottery, jewellery, statuettes, vases, funerary stelae and a large mosaic of a marine scene.

The site

At the entrance to the site are the foundations of Roman baths, which originally lay directly on the coast. There are only scanty remains of public buildings of the Roman period; they include two theatres, the forum and a temple on its north-west side.

The excavated area includes a number of buildings, mainly dwelling-houses, contained within a large block (*insula,* "island"). Some of them contain mosaics which along with those displayed in the Bardo Museum in Tunis are among the oldest in Roman Africa. They are covered over for protection, but will be shown by the custodian of the site in consideration of a small gratuity.

House of the Waterfall

The best preserved dwelling-house is the House of the Waterfall (Maison de la Cascade), named after the mosaic found here. The entrance, on the north side, leads by way of a small living room (*oecus*) into a colonnaded courtyard, in the centre of which are a fountain with mosaic decoration and a (later) sundial. On the west side of the courtyard is a large triclinium (dining room) with a beautiful pavement mosaic. To the rear of the house are a "coach-house" and stables. On one side is a granary, apparently made out of an adjoining house. In this house was found a small hoard of coins: hence its name, the House of the Treasure (Maison du Trésor).

House of the Figural Capitals

The House of the Figural Capitals (Maison des Chapiteaux Historiés) is laid out round a two-storey colonnaded courtyard with richly decorated Corinthian capitals.

The House of the Hunt (Maison de la Chasse) takes its name from a mosaic found in it.

Punic cemetery

The Punic cemetery (6th c. B.C.) was partly covered by Roman buildings. From the higher Roman street level can be seen simple cavities hewn from the rock in which the dead were buried, a few sarcophagi hewn from single blocks of sandstone and tombs built up from bricks or stone. Grave goods found in the tombs can be seen in the museum (see above).

Zarzis

See Djerba, Surroundings

Practical Information

Accommodation

See Camping and Caravanning, Hotels, Youth Hostels

Airlines

The Tunisian national airline is Tunis Air (Société Tunisienne de l'Air). The smaller Tunisavia airline is also state-owned.

Tunis Air Office in the United Kingdom

Tunis Air
24 Sackville Street
London W1X 1DE
Tel. (071) 734 7644/5

Tunis Air Offices and Agents in Tunisia

Offices

8 rue Ibn el Jazzair
Tunis
Tel. (01) 28 81 00

48 Avenue Habib Bourguiba
Tunis
Tel. (01) 78 51 00
Reservations: tel. (01) 34 17 44 and 25 51 00

Aéroport International de Tunis-Carthage
Tel. (01) 23 50 00 and 23 60 00

Agents

76 Avenue Habib Bourguiba
Bizerte
Tel. (02) 3 22 01/02

Avenue Habib Bourguiba
Houmt-Souk (Djerba)
Tel. (05) 5 05 86 and 5 01 59

Aéroport International de Djerba-Zarzis
Mellita
Tel. (05) 5 02 33

Avenue Habib Bourguiba
Gabès
Tel. (05) 2 12 50 and 2 06 97

Avenue du 7 Novembre 1987
Kairouan
Tel. (07) 2 04 22 and 2 04 38

◄ *Dromedaries in the dunes of Djerba*

An aircraft of Tunis Air

Rue du 18 Janvier 1952
Médenine
Tel. (05) 87 01 42

Avenue de l'Indépendance, La Chagra
Monastir-Skanès
Tel. (03) 6 08 58 and 6 19 22

Aéroport International Habib Bourguiba de Monastir-Skanès
Tel. (03) 6 13 17/16/15/14

145 Avenue Habib Bourguiba
Nabeul
Tel. (02) 8 51 93 and 8 67 75

4 Avenue de l'Armée
Sfax
Tel. (04) 2 29 62, 2 86 28 and 2 80 28

Aéroport International de Sfax-Thyna
Tel. (04) 4 25 00, 4 17 40 and 4 08 79

5 Avenue Habib Bourguiba
Sousse
Tel. (03) 2 72 51, 2 72 52 and 2 79 55

Avenue Habib Bourguiba
Tozeur
Tel. (06) 5 00 38

Aéroport International de Tozeur-Nefta
Tel. (06) 5 03 88

Tunisavia Agents in Tunisia

Immeuble Saadi Spric
Tour C, 5e étage
L'Ariana
Tunis
Tel. (01) 23 15 55

Route de Sfax
Gabès
Tel. (05) 7 00 66 and 7 28 01

Agents of Western Airlines in Tunisia

British Airways

G.B. Airways
17 Avenue Habib Bourguiba
Tunis
Tel. (01) 24 442 61

Air France

1 rue d'Athènes
Tunis
Tel. (01) 25 45 22 (reservations)

Lufthansa

Boulevard Ouled Haffouz
Complexe Hotel El Mechtel, 1er étage
Tunis
Tel. (01) 89 44 11

Aéroport International de Tunis-Carthage
Tel. (01) 23 60 00 and 28 80 00

Swissair

45 Avenue Habib Bourguiba
Le Colisée
Tunis
Tel. (01) 34 27 44 (sales) and 34 01 22 (reservations)

Aéroport International de Tunis-Carthage
Tel. (01) 28 80 03

Further information

See Air Travel, Getting to Tunisia

Air Travel

International airports
Tunis

The most important international airport in Tunisia is the Aéroport International de Tunis-Carthage, 8km/5 miles north-east of the city.

Djerba, Mellita

Aéroport International de Djerba-Zarzis
Tel. (05) 5 02 33
8km/5 miles south-west of Houmt-Souk

Monastir-Skanès

Aéroport International Habib Bourguiba de Monastir-Skanès
Tel. (03) 6 13 17
8km/5 miles south-west of Monastir town centre

Sfax

Aéroport International de Sfax-Thyna
Tel. (04) 4 17 40 and 4 08 79
6km/4 miles south-west of Sfax

Tozeur-Nefta

Aéroport International de Tozeur-Nefta
Avenue Habib Bourguiba

Tel. (06) 5 03 88
A short distance north of Tozeur

Domestic services
(see map, p. 364)

Tunis Air flies from Tunis to Mellita/Djerba (flying time 45 minutes), Monastir and Tozeur.
Reservations: tel. (01) 25 51 00 and 34 17 44.

Tunisavia flies the following routes, among others:
Tunis–Djerba
Tunis–Monastir
Tunis–Sfax
Tunis–Tozeur
Tozeur–Djerba
Monastir–Djerba
Reservations: tel. (01) 25 42 38.

Charter flights

Tunisavia has small aircraft, seating from 9 to 50 passengers, available for charter.
Information and reservations: tel. (01) 25 42 39.

Transfers

Transfers between airport and hotel are usually arranged by the travel agency through which the booking is made. Other possibilities are taxis and hired cars (see Taxis, Car Rental).

Other information

See Airlines, Getting to Tunisia.

Banks

See Currency

Beaches

With a Mediterranean coastline of over 1000km/621 miles and more than 300 days of sunshine in the year, Tunisia offers ideal conditions for a holiday by the sea.

The following is merely a selection of popular bathing beaches.

North coast
Tabarka

The rocky coast to the north of Tabarka is a happy hunting ground for divers (diving centre: see Water Sports).

Cap Négro

The sandy beach, with rocks, at Cap Négro (28km/17 miles north-east of Tabarka) is particularly popular with snorkellers.

Sidi Mechrig

Farther north-east is the sandy beach, with rocks, of Sidi Mechrig.

Cap Serrat

South-west of Bizerte, reached by way of MC 51 (turning off just before Sedjenane in the direction of the coast), is Cap Serrat, with a sandy beach and rocks.

Bechateur

On the coast to the north of Bechateur, 15km/9 miles west of Bizerte (signposted), is a sandy beach with rocks and many little coves.

East coast
Bizerte

East of Bizerte (reached by way of GP 8) is the Plage de R'Mel, a long sandy beach, with beautiful country just inland.
Also to the east of Bizerte is the sandy beach of Ras Djebel, at the village of that name.

Cap Bon
Kelibia

At the northern tip of Cap Bon is the beautiful beach of Haouaria Plage.
Kelibia, 25km/15 miles south-east of Cap Bon, has a long beach which is sheltered by its harbour.
Hammamet and Nabeul: see below.

Djerba

On the north and south coasts of Djerba there are first-class sandy beaches sloping gently down to the sea. They are particularly suitable for children.

Gabès

Gabès has a large, clean sandy beach.

Hammamet

Hammamet attracts large numbers of holidaymakers with its mile-long sandy beach.

Kerkennah Islands

The Kerkennah Islands, north of Djerba, also offer good bathing, particularly at Sidi Fredj on the south-west coast of Chergui and at Kellabine on the east coast.

Monastir

The beach at Monastir is relatively small, but there are beautiful beaches at Skanès, north-west of the town (see below).

Nabeul

The beach at Nabeul is of similar quality to the one at Hammamet. It is an excellent resort for a quiet seaside holiday.

Sfax

Sfax has a bathing beach which in summer is usually overcrowded.

Skanès

Skanès, the villa suburb to the west of Monastir, has beautiful long beaches.

Soliman Plage

There is a long sandy beach fringed by dunes immediately west of the little resort of Soliman. (It is reached from Tunis on GP 1, turning left at Bordj Cedria into MC 26, the road to Soliman, and then taking a side road signposted to Soliman Plage).

Sousse
Port El Kantaoui

The long beach of fine sand at Sousse attracts large numbers of visitors, as does the beach at its villa suburb of Port El Kantaoui.

Further information

See Facts and Figures, Topography and Climate; individual entries in the "Tunisia from A to Z" section of this guide; and in this Practical information section Health, Naturism, Water Sports and When to Go.

Begging

Although begging is not unknown in the West, it has a very different significance in Islamic countries and calls for a different response. In Islam to beg is no disgrace, and the giving of alms (*zakat*) is one of the most sacred religious obligations (see Facts and Figures, Religion). Non-Muslims should regulate their practice accordingly, occasionally giving something to the beggars they will encounter – usually women, the old, the sick and the handicapped. They should not, however, give anything to children, since this will only encourage the neglect and abandonment from which such children suffer.

Breakdown Assistance

See Motoring in Tunisia

Business Hours

General

The opening times given below are, in general, applicable to the capital, Tunis. In tourist centres and in the interior of the country they are liable to vary.

Banks

See Currency

Chemists	See entry
Cinemas	Summer (and Ramadan): Mon.–Sat. 4–8pm and 9pm–midnight. Winter: 3–8pm and 9pm–midnight.
Department stores	Summer: Mon.–Sat. 8am–noon and 4–7/8pm. Winter: 8.30am–noon and 3–7/7.30pm. Ramadan: 9am–4pm. Some department stores are closed on Mondays.
Exchange offices	See Currency
Food shops	Summer: Mon.–Sat. 6am–1pm and 4–9pm. Winter: 7am–1pm and 3–8pm. Some of the larger foodshops are closed on Mondays.
Government offices	Summer: Mon.–Thu. 7am–1pm. Winter: Mon.–Thu. 9am–1pm and 3–6pm. Ramadan: 8am–2pm.
Markets	See entry
Mosques	See entry
Museums	See entry
ONAT	The shops of ONAT (Organisation Nationale de l'Artisanat Tunisien: see Shopping) are usually open Mon.–Sat. 9am–12.30pm and 3–7pm.
ONTT	The tourist information offices of ONTT (Office National du Tourisme Tunisien) are usually open Mon.–Sat. 9am–noon and 3–5pm.
Post offices	See Post, Telephone, Telegrams
Public holidays	See entry
Shops	Daily except Sundays and public holidays 9am–noon and 2/3–6pm.
Souks	See Markets

Bus Services

Tunisia has a dense network of bus services. The largest bus company is the Société Nationale des Transports Interurbains (SNTRI), with its head office at 74 Avenue de Carthage, Tunis, tel. (01) 24 73 68. There are also numerous regional companies (*sociétés régionales*).

Fares

Fares on Tunisian buses are very low.

Timetables

Timetables are posted up at all bus stations (*gares routières*).

Airport service

There is an hourly shuttle service, 6am to midnight, between Tunis-Carthage International Airport and the main railway station in the centre of Tunis.

Distances and journey times

Tunis–Djerba	520km/323 miles	9 hours
Tunis–Hammamet	66km/41 miles	1½ hours
Tunis–Kairouan	160km/99 miles	3–4 hours
Tunis–Kelibia (Cap Bon)	133km/83 miles	3¼ hours
Tunis–Monastir	162km/101 miles	3 hours
Tunis–Nabeul	65km/40 miles	1¼ hours

Tunis–Nefta	492km/306 miles	8¼ hours
Tunis–Sousse	149km/93 miles	2¼ hours
Tunis–Tabarka	175km/109 miles	3¾ hours

Over the frontiers

There are also bus services to and from towns in Algeria and Libya.

For alternative means of transport see Taxis.

Further information

See Air Travel, Car Rental, Excursions, Railways, Taxis

Cafés

See Food and Drink

Calendars

Two very different calendars are in use in Tunisia: the Gregorian calendar introduced from Europe, which is used in administration and commerce, and the Islamic calendar which determines the dates of public holidays and festivals (see Public Holidays).
Islamic chronology begins with the year A.D. 622, the date of Mohammed's flight from Mecca to Medina, the Hegira, which is year one in the Islamic calendar. The years of the Islamic calendar cannot, however, be equated to those of the Gregorian calendar, since the Islamic calendar is related to the phases of the moon, while the Gregorian is a solar calendar. The Islamic month has either 29 or 30 days depending on the time of appearance of the new moon, and the twelve months of the Islamic year have only 354 or 355 days: that is, ten or eleven days less than the Gregorian year. Thus 34 lunar years are equivalent to 33 solar years, and 100 Islamic years equal approximately 97 Gregorian years. The difference between the two calendars is gradually decreasing.
Examples (A.H. is commonly used as an abbreviation for year of the Hegira): A.H. 1 = A.D. 622; A.H. 100 = A.D. 719; A.H. 200 = A.D. 816; A.H. 500 = A.D. 1107; A.H. 1000 = A.D. 1592; A.H. 1300 = A.D. 1883; A.H. 1400 = A.D. 1980; A.H. 1409 = A.D. 1988/1989.

The beginning of the Islamic year and the Islamic festivals do not fall at any particular season of the year but in relation to the Gregorian calendar advance by about ten days every year. Thus Ramadan, the month of fasting, moves round the entire solar year.

The Islamic year begins on the tenth day of the month of Muharram (Moharrem). Each month begins on the first day of the new moon. The Islamic day runs from sunset to sunset.

Further information

See Manners and Customs, Public Holidays

Camping and Caravanning

Tunisia has few official camping sites equipped with washing facilities (showers), electricity, restaurants and/or shops, and most of them are open only during the main holiday season.

"Wild" camping

"Wild" camping outside the officially recognised camping sites is not prohibited, but it is advisable to ask the owner of the land for permission and/or to inform the local municipal or police authorities. It is also recommended to camp only in the immediate vicinity of a village or town.

All rubbish should be collected and properly disposed of. Campers should be careful not to cause a fire, which is a particular hazard in the hot, dry climate of Tunisia.

Official Camping Sites

Hammam-Lif — Le Moulin Bleu, Hammamet-Plage, Hammam-Lif (20km/12½ miles south of Tunis)

Hammamet — L'Idéal Camping, tel. (02) 8 03 02; Camping Caravaning Samaris, tel. 8 03 53

Gabès — Camping Centre des Jeunes, tel. (05) 7 02 17

Djerba — Camping Sidi Ali, tel. (05) 5 70 21

Nabeul — L'Auberge des Jasmins (11km/7 miles north-east of Hammamet)
Noulel Camping Site, Noulel, 120 pitches.

Tozeur — Campement Zaafrane, tel. (06) 9 50 74; Campement Paradis; Campement Nowil, tel. 9 53 87.

Zarzis — Sonia Camping et Caravaning

There are other camping sites, usually with limited facilities, at Bizerte, Douz, El Haouaria, Nefta and Sbeitla and in the Kerkennah Islands. For information apply to the local tourist office (see Information).
During the main holiday season some hotels in the tourist centres have sites for caravans.

Car Ferries

Caravans — Owners of trailer and motor caravans should check with the shipping line or with a travel agent that their vehicle is within the permitted limits of size.

International Car Ferries to and from Tunisia

SERVICE	FREQUENCY/DURATION	COMPANY
France–Tunisia		
Marseilles–Tunis	Twice weekly/24hrs Twice weekly/24hrs	Cie Tunisienne, Tunis SNCM
Italy–Tunisia		
Genoa–Tunis	Twice weekly/24hrs	Cie Tunisienne, Tunis
Naples–Tunis	Weekly/24hrs	Tirrenia
Naples–Trapani–Tunis	Twice weekly/24hrs	Alimar
Sardinia–Tunisia		
Cagliari–Tunis	Twice weekly/20hrs	Tirrenia SNCM
Sicily–Tunisia		
Trapani–Tunis	Weekly/10hrs	Tirrenia
Palermo–Tunis	Weekly/12hrs	Tirrenia

Information in UK

Ferries from French ports:
Continental Shipping and Travel Ltd
French Railway House
179 Piccadilly, London W1V 9DB
Tel. (071) 491 4968

Ferries from Italian ports:
Serena Holidays
40–42 Kenway Road
London SW5 0RA
Tel. (071) 373 6548

Car Ferries within Tunisia

Between Sfax and the Kerkennah Islands there are 4 services daily in summer and 2 services daily in winter.
Information and reservations:
Sonvic
34 rue Alexandre Dumas
Sfax
Tel. (04) 2 22 16

The island of Djerba is connected with the mainland by a ferry service between Adjim and Djorf, roughly every half hour. If the winds are too high the ferry does not sail, and access to the island is then by the causeway (see Tunisia from A to Z, Djerba).

Ferry port, Adjim

Further information can be obtained from local travel agencies or from:

Compagnie Tunisienne de Navigation
122 rue de Yougoslavie
1001 Tunis
Tel. (01) 24 28 01

Navitour
8 rue d'Alger
1001 Tunis
Tel. (01) 24 95 00

Carpets

Carpet-weaving or -knotting is one of the oldest Tunisian crafts. Kairouan in particular is world-famed for its carpets.

ONAT

Visitors who are thinking of buying a carpet will do well to ask for advice about qualities and prices in one of the shops and showrooms of ONAT, the Tunisian National Handicrafts Organisation. The address in Tunis is:

Organisation Nationale de l'Artisanat Tunisien (ONAT)
Rue des Teinturiers
Tunis
Tel. (01) 22 04 22.

There are ONAT showrooms in all the larger Tunisian towns. Their situation is shown on the town plans in the descriptive section of this guide.
ONAT also has carpet museums in Kairouan and Gabès in which fine examples of different types of carpet can be seen. There are sales points for carpets in hotels run by the state hotel organisation, SHTT.

Colours

The colours of Tunisian carpets often reflect the colouring of the country. Purple, blue, green, black and white are found in both darker and lighter shades, frequently separated by a yellow which reproduces the colour of sand-dunes. The sought-after older carpets use vegetable dyes; the colouring of modern carpets comes from synthetic dyes. There are also natural-coloured carpets (Alloucha), using wool from black, white and brown sheep, often mixed to produce a variety of colour effects.
Dye-baths for particular shades are noted on the mark of quality (see below).

Types of Carpet

Knotted Pile Carpets

There are two type of knotted pile carpets. The Guétafi type is a Berber patterned carpet with a pile between 3 and 5cm (1.2 and 2in) deep. The Kairouan carpet is hand-knotted, with the Turkish or Ghiordes knot, in which short lengths of yarn (consisting of between three and six strands of wool) are looped round the warp threads to form a pile standing perpendicular to the warp; the pile is then shorn to a depth of between .5 and 2.5cm (.2 and 1in).

Smooth-Faced Carpets

Mergoum

The smooth-faced type of carpet is represented in Tunisia by the mergoum, a woven carpet in geometric designs of Berber origin in which the yarn hangs down on the underside. See Shopping and Souvenirs, Oudref.

Hybrid Knotted/Woven

Kilim

A combination of knotting and weaving, in the tapestry technique, produces the kilim, which can be bought on the island of Djerba, in Sbeitla and in Oudref.

Macramé

Macramé work – a combination of weaving, knotting and plaiting – has become popular as a wall hanging rather than as a carpet. When well done this technique produces relief effects and interesting patterns.

Standards of Fineness

The fineness of a carpet depends on the number of knots to the sq. metre. The range is between 10,000 and 500,000 knots to the sq. metre. To assess the fineness of a particular carpet, turn it over and count the number of knots in an area 10cm square, then multiply the result by 100 to get the number per sq. metre.

Normal weave

10,000 knots per sq.metre
12,000 knots per sq.metre
19,600 knots per sq.metre
40,000 knots per sq.metre

Fine weave

65,000 knots per sq.metre
90,000 knots per sq.metre

Extra-fine weave

160,000 knots per sq.metre
250,000 knots per sq.metre
500,000 knots per sq.metre

Silk carpets

Silk carpets normally have over 500,000 knots to the sq.metre.

Guarantee and Mark of Quality

Genuine carpets have two or three labels on the underside. One of these bears the seal of the Tunisian Republic and the name Tunisia, and there must always be a control number, with an indication of the artist's name and the place of production, date, measurements, area, weight, fineness of weave and quality standard of the carpet. There may also be a maker's label with the address of the factory, a serial number, etc.

Carpet-Making Areas

Bizerte

Carpets in flower patterns.

Cap Bon

Long-haired woven carpets can be found, for example, at Beni Khiar and Hammamet. At Maamoura there are both self-coloured and flower-patterned carpets.

Djerba

Beautiful bedspreads (farchia) are made on the island of Djerba.

Gabès

Mergoums and kilims.

Gafsa

Woven carpets in traditional patterns and modern carpets.

Kairouan

Carpets in classic style and mergoums.

Kasserine

Kasserine and Sbeitla produce Berber (Guétifa) carpets.

Sfax

Patterned carpets.

Tunis

Carpets of all kinds can be found in the capital.

See also Shopping and Souvenirs.

Car Rental

Cars can be rented in all tourist resorts, at airports and in the larger towns throughout the country.
A visitor who wishes to rent a car in Tunisia should go to one of the internationally known car rental firms, to be reasonably sure that the

vehicle is properly maintained and in good condition for driving. The international car rental companies such as Avis, Hertz and InterRent/Europcar are well represented in Tunisia, but there are also numerous local firms and garages offering cars for hire.
Some car rental firms will give a discount to members of a motoring organisation such as the AA. A credit card may dispense with the need for putting down a deposit in cash.
The hire of a car can be arranged before leaving home through one of the international rental companies.

Check personal insurance, taking out additional insurance if necessary to ensure comprehensive cover.

Avis

In Bizerte:
7 Rue d'Alger. Tel. (02) 33 07 6

In Gabès:
Rue Tahar Sfar. Tel. (05) 2 02 10

In Hammamet:
Avenue Dag Hammarskjoeld
Tel. (02) 8 03 03;
Avenue de la Gare. Tel. (02) 8 01 64

In Houmt-Souk (Djerba):
Avenue El Cadhi. Tel. (05) 5 01 51

In Monastir:
Aéroport International de Monastir-Skanès
Tel. (03) 6 13 14

In Sfax:
Rue Tahar Sfar. Tel. (04) 2 46 05

In Sousse:
Boulevard de la Corniche
Tel. (03) 2 09 01

In Tozeur:
Avenue Farhat Hached
Tel. (06) 5 05 47

In Tunis:
90 Avenue de la Liberté
Tel. (01) 28 25 08;
Hilton Hotel
Tel. (01) 28 20 00;
Hotel Africa
Tel. (01) 34 74 77;
Aéroport International de Tunis-Carthage
Tel. (01) 28 80 00/213

In Zarzis:
Avenue des Hotels. Tel. (05) 5 01 43

Hertz

In Bizerte:
Place des Martyrs. Tel. (02) 3 36 79

In Gabès:
30 rue Ibn el Jazzar. Tel. (05) 2 09 25

In Hammamet:
Avenue des Hotels. Tel. (02) 8 01 87

On Djerba:
Dar Jerba. Tel. (05) 5 71 91;
Aéroport International de Djerba-Zarzis
Mellita
Tel. (05) 5 02 33/8

In Monastir:
Avenue Habib Bourguiba. Tel. (03) 6 14 04

In Nabeul:
Avenue Habib Bourguiba
Tel. (02) 8 50 27 and 8 53 27

In Sousse:
Avenue Habib Bourguiba. Tel. (03) 2 14 28

In Tozeur:
Avenue Farhat Hached. Tel. (06) 5 02 14

In Tunis:
8 Route de la Charguia
Tel. (01) 23 22 11;
29 Avenue Habib Bourguiba
Tel. (01) 24 85 59;
Hotel Baie des Singes
Tel. (01) 27 15 67;
Aéroport International de Tunis-Carthage
Tel. (01) 28 80 00/227

In Zarzis:
Avenue des Hotels. Tel. (05) 8 02 84

InterRent/Europcar

In Gabès:
Rue Farhat Hached. Tel. (05) 2 28 29

In Hammamet:
Route des Hotels. Tel. (02) 8 01 46

In Houmt-Souk (Djerba):
Avenue El Cadhi
Tel. (05) 5 03 77

In Monastir:
Aeroport H. Bourgiba. Tel. (03) 6 13 14

In Sousse:
Route de la Corniche. Tel. (03) 2 21 52

In Tozeur:
Avenue Farhat Hached. Tel. (06) 5 01 19

In Tunis:
29 Avenue Khéreddine Pacha
Tel. (01) 28 74 02;
Aéroport International de Tunis-Carthage
Tel. (01) 28 80 00/221

Further information

See Breakdown Assistance, Motoring in Tunisia, Travel Documents

Casinos

The operation of casinos is now permitted in Tunisia, and the first casino has been opened in the El Hana Palace Hotel in Sousse. Others are to follow in Tabarka and Hammamet and on Djerba.

Chemists

There are chemists' shops (*pharmacies*) in all Tunisian towns of any size, selling both home-produced and foreign medicines. A limited range of toilet articles is sold by chemists and department stores in larger towns.

Opening times

Chemists' shops are usually open Monday to Saturday 9am–1pm and 3–7pm. Some chemists are closed on Saturday afternoons.

Night services

The addresses of chemists who are open at night (usually from around 9pm to 7.30am) are posted up at all chemists' shops and are given in the newspapers.

Vocabulary

I have . . .	J'ai . . .
a cold	un rhume
a cough	Une toux
diarrhoea	de la diarrhée
a headache	mal à la tête
a sore throat	un mal de gorge
a stomach upset	des maux d'estomac
a temperature	de la fièvre
toothache	mal aux dents
a touch of the sun	un coup de soleil
I am diabetic	J'ai du diabète
injury	blessure
Prenez les médicaments . . .	Take the medicine . . .
avant les repas	before meals
après les repas	after meals
trois fois par jour	three times a day
selon prescription du médecin	as prescribed by the doctor
aspirin	aspirine
bandage	bandage, bande
cream, ointment	crème
drops	gouttes
gauze bandage	gaze
laxative	purgatif
pill	pilule
powder	poudre
remedy, cure	remède
sedative	calmant
sticking plaster	sparadrap
tablet	comprimé

Further information

See Emergencies, Health, Medical Aid

Consulates

See Diplomatic and Consular Offices

Credit Cards

See Currency

Currency

The unit of currency is the Tunisian dinar, which is divided into 1000 millimes. There are banknotes for ½, 1, 5, 10 and 20 dinars and coins in denominations of 1, 2, 5, 10, 20, 50 and 100 millimes and ½ and 1 dinar.

Prices of small items are usually expressed in millimes (e.g. 1500 millimes = 1.5 dinars).

Exchange rates

Exchange rates are subject to fluctuation; current rates can be obtained from banks, bureaux de change and tourist offices.

Import/export of currency

The import and export of Tunisian currency are prohibited. There are no restrictions on the import or export of foreign currency; amounts equivalent to more than 500 dinars should, however, be declared on entry.

Changing back Tunisian currency

On leaving Tunisia visitors can change back into foreign currency up to 30% of the Tunisian currency they have acquired, subject to a maximum of 100 dinars. When changing money in Tunisia, therefore, the exchange receipt should be kept as evidence that Tunisian currency has been legitimately acquired.

Bank opening times

Beginning of July to mid September: Monday to Friday 7–11.30am.
Rest of year: Monday to Thursday 8–11.30am and 2–4.30pm, Friday 8–11am and 1.15–3pm.

Exchange offices

Some exchange offices (e.g. in large hotels and at airports, ports and frontier crossings) are also open on Saturdays, Sundays and public holidays.

Travellers' cheques

Travellers' cheques are accepted at most banks and many hotels. There may sometimes be difficulty in using them in the remoter parts of the country.

Eurocheques

Eurocheques are accepted at banks and a few major hotels. Up to 175 dinars can be cashed on each cheque at banks.

Credit cards

All major credit cards are accepted in shops, restaurants and hotels, at least in the tourist areas of the country. They cannot be used for withdrawing cash.

Tunisian currency

Currency

Loss of cards and cheques

If travellers' cheques, Eurocheques, Eurocheque cards or credit cards are lost the bank or other issuing authority should be informed immediately by telephone, with confirmation in writing.

Customs Regulations

Visitors may take into Tunisia, without payment of duty, personal effects and sporting equipment, binoculars, a portable radio, a portable typewriter, a tape-recorder, two cameras (which must be of different type or make) with 20 films, a video camera with 20 films and gifts up to a value of 10 dinars.

In addition persons over 18 may take in 1 litre of spirits (over 25% alcohol), 2 litres of wine or other alcoholic drinks under 25% alcohol, 400 cigarettes (or 100 cigars or 500 grams of tobacco), ¼ litre of perfume and 1 litre of toilet water.

Large items such as a video camera will be entered in the visitor's passport in order to check that they are re-exported.

Vehicles, trailers and boats can be taken into Tunisia without payment of duty. A permit authorising import for a period of up to three months will be issued by the customs authorities on entry.

Desert Safaris

See Motoring in Tunisia, Sahara Tourism

Diplomatic and Consular Offices

Tunisian Embassies

United Kingdom

29 Princes Gate
London SW7 1QG
Tel. (071) 823 7749

USA

1515 Massachusetts Avenue
NW Washington DC 20005
Tel. (202) 234 6644

3401 Sacramento Street
San Francisco CA
Tel. (415) 922 9222

Canada

515 O'Connor Street
Ottawa
Tel. (613) 237 0330

Embassies and Consulates in Tunisia

United Kingdom

Embassy:
5 Place de la Victoire
Tunis
Tel. (01) 24 51 00, 24 48 05, 24 53 24, 24 56 49
Consular Section:
141–143 Avenue de la Liberté

Tunis
Tel. (01) 79 33 22, 79 48 10, 79 40 05

Consulate:
Rue de Madagascar
3000 Bab el Bahr
Sfax
Tel. (04) 2 85 55

USA

Embassy:
144 Avenue de la Liberté
1002 Tunis Belvédère
Tel. (01) 28 25 66

Canada
(also handles
Australian affairs)

3 rue Didon
Tunis
Tel. (01) 28 65 77

Distances

The following table shows the distances (in kilometres) by the best route between selected places in Tunisia:

	Béja	Ben Gardane	Bizerte	Douz	Tataouine	Gabès	Gafsa	Ghdames	Houmt-Souk	Jendouba	Kairouan	Kasserine	El Kel	Mahdia	Médenine	Nabeul	Nefta	Remada	Sfax	Sidi Bou Zid	Siliana	Sousse	Tabarka	Tunis	Zaghouan	Zarzis
Béja		606	107	391	578	453	246	974	553	49	180	225	105	252	529	172	447	656	317	285	183	190	71	105	117	591
Ben Gardane	606		624	302	91	153	299	487	100	581	571	405	600	539	77	512	415	169	435	397	432	416	646	559	505	46
Bizerte	107	624		553	596	471	408	992	570	156	218	332	212	270	547	132	524	674	335	348	192	208	136	65	122	609
Douz	391	302	553		274	149	145	670	249	427	344	397	371	439	225	458	146	352	285	243	412	401	492	488	463	287
Tataouine	578	91	596	274		125	271	396	118	600	397	377	572	450	49	484	387	78	261	369	536	388	649	531	474	111
Gabès	453	153	471	149	125		146	521	100	428	212	252	447	240	76	359	241	203	136	244	411	263	493	406	352	138
Gafsa	246	299	408	145	271	146		667	331	282	199	106	226	294	222	313	116	324	190	98	267	256	347	343	318	284
Ghdames	974	487	992	670	396	521	667		514	996	793	673	968	846	445	880	783	474	657	896	832	784	1045	927	870	507
Houmt-Souk	553	100	570	249	118	100	331	514		575	372	352	547	340	69	459	362	196	236	344	511	363	623	506	497	52
Jendouba	49	581	156	427	600	428	282	996	575		203	176	56	322	551	221	398	678	339	236	134	260	65	154	166	613
Kairouan	180	571	218	344	397	212	199	793	372	203		145	175	119	348	114	315	258	136	130	139	57	251	153	119	410
Kasserine	225	405	332	397	377	252	106	673	352	176	145		120	264	328	259	222	455	192	87	167	202	241	198	264	390
El Kel	105	600	212	371	572	447	226	968	547	56	175	120		294	523	238	342	650	278	173	106	232	121	171	154	585
Mahdia	252	539	270	439	450	240	294	846	340	322	119	264	294		316	158	410	443	104	249	258	62	223	205	151	378
Médenine	529	77	547	225	49	76	222	445	69	551	348	328	523	316		435	338	127	212	218	355	339	569	482	428	62
Nabeul	172	512	132	458	484	359	313	880	459	221	114	259	238	158	435		429	562	223	244	192	96	242	67	66	497
Nefta	447	415	524	146	387	241	116	783	362	398	315	222	342	410	338	429		465	306	214	383	372	463	459	434	400
Remada	656	169	674	352	78	203	324	474	196	678	258	455	650	443	127	562	465		339	422	614	466	727	609	552	189
Sfax	317	435	335	285	261	136	190	657	236	339	136	192	278	104	212	223	306	339		121	275	127	387	270	216	274
Sidi Bou Zid	285	397	348	243	369	244	98	896	344	236	130	87	173	249	218	244	214	422	121		172	187	301	283	237	382
Siliana	183	432	192	412	536	411	267	832	311	134	139	167	106	258	355	192	383	614	275	172		196	160	127	70	417
Sousse	190	416	208	401	388	263	256	784	363	260	57	202	232	62	339	96	372	466	127	187	196		261	143	89	401
Tabarka	71	646	136	492	649	493	347	1045	623	65	251	241	121	223	569	242	463	727	387	301	160	261		175	188	631
Tunis	105	559	65	488	531	406	343	927	506	154	153	198	171	205	482	67	459	609	270	283	127	143	175		57	544
Zaghouan	117	505	122	463	474	352	318	870	497	166	119	264	154	151	428	66	434	552	216	237	70	89	188	57		490
Zarzis	591	46	609	287	111	138	284	507	52	613	410	390	585	378	62	497	400	189	274	382	417	401	631	544	490	

Diving

See Water Sports

Dress

In summer light cotton garments and comfortable shoes are the most suitable form of dress during the day. In the evening, when it can become cool, something warmer is required.
Bikinis, shorts and jogging outfits are acceptable only on the beach or in the hotel. Elsewhere they are frowned on and may give rise to unpleasantness.

In winter warm clothing is essential, particularly in the north but also in the south.
Rainwear is necessary only between November and March.

Further information

See Manners and Customs, Naturism

Drugs

There are heavy penalties, in the form of high fines and imprisonment, for the possession of drugs. Prison sentences on foreigners must be served in full, and those who have been imprisoned for a drug offence are banned for life from re-entering Tunisia.

Electricity

In the more modern hotels and houses in Tunisia the electricity supply is 220 volts AC; some older buildings still have 110 volts.
British and North American visitors (among others) should take adaptors for appliances such as electric razors and hair-dryers.

Emergencies

Emergency number country-wide

Throughout Tunisia dial 197

In Tunis

Fire: dial 198
Police: dial 197
Ambulance: dial 49 13 13

Hospital emergency services in Tunis

Hopital Charles Nicolle
Bab el Allouij
Boulevard du 9 Avril 1938
Tel. (01) 66 30 10

Hopital Aziza Othmana
Place du Gouvernement. Tel. (01) 66 36 55

Snake-bite

Special snake-bite clinic:

Institut Pasteur
Place du Gouvernement
Tunis. Tel. (01) 28 30 22

Breakdown assistance

See entry

Theft

Thefts should be reported to the local police station (*commissariat de police*).

Further information

See Chemists; Diplomatic and Consular Offices; Information; Medical Aid; Post, Telephone, Telegraph; Radio and Television

Events

Throughout the year, even in quite small villages, there are many religious and traditional festivals. The number of events of this kind is steadily increasing, so that only a small selection can be mentioned here.

February
Kalaa-Kebira

Festival de l'Olivier (Olive-Tree Festival)

April
Nabeul

Festival des Fleurs (Orange-Blossom Festival)

Nefta

Nefta Festival (processions, camel fights, camel races)

Tataouine

Festival des Ksour Sahariens (Ksar Festival)

Tunis

Medina Festival (during Ramadan)

Mid May
El Haouaria

Festival de l'Epervier (Sparrow-Hawk Festival: see Tunisia from A to Z, Cap Bon)

Tunis

Flower Show

Fantasia at Midoun (Djerba)

Meknassy	Festival of Arab Horses
May/June Sidi Daoud	Matanza (tunny-killing: see Tunisia from A to Z, Cap Bon)
June Dougga	Dougga Festival (performances of classical plays in Roman theatre)
Testour	International Malouf Festival (traditional Arab music)
El Djem	Musical Festival in Roman theatre
Beginning July Tabarka	Festival des Corails (Coral Festival)
July El Kantaoui	Festival d'El Kantaoui (Harbour Festival in boating harbour)
Beja	Summer Festival.
July 1st–August 15th Hammamet	Hammamet International Festival (music, drama, dancing; folk presentations in Cultural Centre)
Sousse	Festival of Aoussou (music, dancing; films; folk events in open-air theatre)
July 1st–August 31st Bizerte	Festival of Bizerte; International Festival of Mediterranean Music (every 2 years).
Tabarka	Tabarka International Festival (avantgarde music and drama; folk dancing; student theatre)
July and August Houmt-Souk (Djerba)	Festival d'Ulysse (re-enactment of Ulysses' arrival in the land of the lotus-eaters; folk singing and dancing)
Carthage	Carthage International Festival (drama, dancing and folk presentations in Roman amphitheatre; student theatre; *son et lumière*).
Mahdia	Les Nuits de Mahdia (street festival, with folk events, theatrical and other performances)
Mahrès	Festival des Arts Plastiques
August Beja	Wheat Festival
Kelibia	Amateur Film Festival (in alternate years: 1992, 1994, etc.)
Korba	Festival of the Young Theatre
Sidi Bou Said	Kharja Festival (a religious festival)
September Kairouan	Cavalry Festival (races, dancing)
Djerba	Régate de la Planche à Voile (wind-surfing races) Bulla Regia Festival
October Carthage	Journées Cinématographiques (Film Festival: see page 83)
October–June Tunis	Theatrical season
November Matmata	Matmata Festival (a colourful traditional festival)
Tozeur	Festival des Oasis (colourful floats, folk dancing, camel races, etc.)
December Douz	Douz Festival (a Saharan festival, with folk dancing, camel races, camel fights, hunting with greyhounds, etc.)

Excursions

Organised tours

Package tour operators usually offer a variety of optional excursions, and these can also be arranged through numerous local travel agents. They include trips into the desert, round oases and to ancient sites, with varying modes of transport (horse-drawn carriages, four-wheel-drive vehicles, camels, etc.).

Individual tours

In the more densely populated areas of Tunisia and in parts of the country that have been developed for tourism there is no difficulty about exploring alone, either by car or by public transport (see Bus Services. Railways). For trips into the desert, however, it is essential to be properly equipped and to be accompanied by a local guide.

Marine fauna

For visitors with a special interest in the marine fauna of Tunisia there are many possibilities – trips to watch the coral harvest at Tabarka, the squid fisheries of the Kerkennah Islands, the sponge-divers of Sfax, the tunny-killing at Sidi Daoud, and so on. Anglers can arrange to go out on a day trip with a Tunisian fisherman.
Information about the possibility of such trips can be obtained from local travel agencies, tourist offices and hotels.

On the Mainland

Excursions from Hammamet

Half-day trips to Kairouan; half- or whole-day trips to Tunis, with visits to the Bardo Museum, the remains of ancient Carthage and the Moorish village of Sidi Bou Said; whole-day trips to the Roman cities of Dougga and Thuburbo Majus; whole-day trips to Sousse and Monastir; two-day trips to Sfax, Gabès, Chenini and El Hamma; two- or three-day trips to the oasis towns of Nefta, Tozeur, Kebili and Douz.

From Kairouan

Day trips to Sousse, Monastir and Mahdia; day trips to the Roman site of Maktar, a Berber village and Sbeitla, with the remains of ancient Sufetula.

From Sousse or Port El Kantaoui

Half-day sightseeing tours of Sousse; half-day trips to Kairouan; half-day trips to Nabeul and Hammamet; half-day trips to Monastir and Moknine; day trips to Tunis, with visits to the Bardo Museum, the remains of ancient Carthage and the Moorish village of Sidi Bou Said; whole-day trips to the Roman cities of Dougga and Thuburbo Majus; day trips to Gabès and Matmata; day trips to Kairouan and El Djem; two- and three-day oasis tours; three-day trips into the desert.

From Tunis

Day trips to Carthage, Sidi Bou Said and Utica; one- and two-day trips to ancient sites in northern Tunisia; one- and two-day trips round the Cap Bon peninsula; etc., etc.

Djerba

Half-day trips round the island; excursions to the Berber villages of southern Tunisia; trips to the coastal oasis of Zarzis and the ancient site of Gightis; across the Chott el Djerid and to the oasis towns of Tozeur and Nefta.

Boat Trips

From Houmt-Souk

Boat trips from Houmt-Souk (Djerba).

From Sousse

Half-day trips to Hergla or Monastir.

From Monastir

Mini-cruises on "El Kahlia" to the Iles Kuriates. Information: SHTT Monastir, tel. (03) 6 01 56/633.

Trips on Camelback and Horseback and in Horse-drawn Carriages

On camelback

For adventurous visitors a two- or three-day ride into the desert on a dromedary will offer an unforgettable experience. This is a strenuous trip for which a high standard of fitness is required.

In the desert

Starting-points of such trips are Metameur and various oases in southern Tunisia (Es Sabria, El Faouar, Douz, Tozeur, Nefta).
For the less energetic there are also brief rides round the oases on dromedaries.
Information from local tourist offices.

On horseback

Most tourist centres also offer rides and treks on Arab horses.

Horse-drawn carriages

At Tozeur, Nefta and Gabès visitors can take trips round the oases in horse-drawn carriages (*calèches*).

"Lézard Rouge" train

See Tunisia from A to Z, Metlaoui

Further information

See Bus Services, Car Rental, Events, Motoring in Tunisia, Railways, Sahara Tourism, Sports, Taxis

Ferries

See Car Ferries

Fishing

See Sports

Food and Drink

Restaurants

The restaurants in the larger hotels usually offer European cuisine. It is well worth while, however, sampling some of the local dishes in an ordinary

Tunisian restaurant (for a selection, see Restaurants). Since the popular restaurants may be crowded, particularly at weekends, it is advisable to book a table: this can be done through your hotel.

Snack bars

In towns throughout Tunisia there are numerous snack bars serving cassecroûtes (see below) and other light snacks, either for eating on the premises or for taking away.

Cafés

As a rule Tunisian cafés are patronised only by men, but in the tourist centres there are now also cafés of European type, frequented by Tunisian families as well as by visitors, which serve coffee (espresso, café noir or café au lait), peppermint tea (thé à la menthe, well sweetened) or tea with pistachios.

Favourite spices

Aniseed, barat (a mixture of ground cinnamon and rosebuds: mild), caraway, cinnamon, coriander, harissa (a mixture of garlic, red peppers, tomato puree and olive oil: usually very hot), orange-blossom water, peppermint, rose-water, saffron, tabil (a mixture of coriander, caraway, garlic and dried red peppers: hot).

Tunisian specialities

Tunisian cuisine is a successful marriage between East and West, and a meal in a good Tunisian restaurant can be a rewarding experience.

Acida

Acida is a Kairouan speciality, served on the morning of the Mouled festival (see Public Holidays). There are two ways of preparing it: either from boiled semolina or flour with the addition of oil (sometimes butter) and honey, or (probably following a Turkish recipe) from pine-seeds covered with a thick layer of cream and garnished with walnuts, pine-kernels, pistachios and ground almonds.

Brik

Brik à l'oeuf is an egg wrapped in a thin pastry envelope and deep-fried, leaving the yolk soft.
Briks may also be stuffed with tunny, minced meat or various kinds of seafood.

Brochettes

Meat grilled on the spit.

Cassecroûte

A sandwich of white bread filled with chopped olives, pieces of tunny, capers and vegetables, with a dressing of oil and vinegar or harissa.

Chakchouka

A spicy stew of onions, tomatoes, pimentoes and other vegetables.

Chorba à l'agneau

A substantial and highly spiced soup of noodles, lamb and vegetables.

Complet poisson

Fish, grilled or fried, with salad, chips and other accompaniments.

Couscous

Steamed semolina grains, served with meat or poultry and vegetables.

Doulma

Courgettes with meat stuffing.

Felfel

Stuffed peppers.

Gnaouia

Lamb with a caper and pimento sauce.

Hargma

Boiled knuckle of veal with a spicy and slightly sharp sauce.

Kaftadji

Fried meat balls, served with chopped liver, paprika and courgettes.

Klaia

Kidneys in a sauce made from olive oil, finely chopped tomatoes, pepper and garlic.

Koucha

Roast lamb and potatoes.

Food and Drink

Lablabi	A highly spiced chick-pea soup with the addition of lemon-juice; served with white bread.
Makroudh	A semolina pastry stuffed with dates and soaked in honey.
Mechoui	Lamb chops grilled on the spit over an open fire.
Merguez	Small highly spiced sausages of mutton or beef.
Mirmiz	Mutton stewed with beans and tomatoes.
Mosli	Stew.
Objabilmergais	Hard spiced sausages in potato soup with tomato puree and garlic.
Slata mechouia	A salad of finely chopped tomatoes, paprika, peppers and onions with a dressing of garlic, lemon and plenty of olive oil.
Tajine	A kind of omelette stuffed with chopped meat, onions, beans or peas, sprinkled with grated cheese and baked in the oven.

Desserts Usually fruit in season, blancmange, ice-cream and a variety of *gâteaux tunisiens* (Tunisian cakes) – acida (see above), baklava (flaky pastry with a nut filling, soaked in honey), doigt de Fatima (flaky pastry with an almond filling) or makroudh (see above).

Drinks There is a wide variety of non-alcoholic drinks, including fruit juices, mineral water (Safia, Ain Okter, Ain Garci, etc.), cola and lemonade, coffee and tea. To be safe it is best to keep to bottled drinks.

Alcoholic drinks Although Muslims are not allowed to drink alcohol (Arabic *alkhaha),* alcoholic drinks are served in all tourist restaurants, bars and hotels in Tunisia. In addition to the usual imported drinks there are excellent and reasonably priced Tunisian wines (see page 330) and a locally brewed light beer (Celtia). Boukha is a popular fig brandy, Thibarine a liqueur. Laghmi (date brandy) is obtainable only in the oases in spring, when it is drunk fresh.

A French-English Glossary of Food and Drink

Food	abats	giblets
	abricots	apricots
	agneau	lamb
	ail	garlic
	aioli	garlic mayonnaise
	amandes	almonds
	anchois	anchovies
	ange de mer	angel-fish
	artichauts	artichokes
	asperges	asparagus
	baguette	a long thin loaf of white bread
	baudroie	angler-fish
	bécasse	woodcock
	beignet	fritter
	betterave	beetroot
	beurre	butter
	biscotte	rusk
	blette	spinach-beet
	boeuf	beef
	boulette	meat or fish ball
	brochette	(meat on the) spit
	caille	quail

calamar	squid
canard	duck
cannelle	cinnamon
câpres	capers
carottes	carrots
carré	loin
céleri	celery; celeriac
cèpes	boletus mushrooms
cervelle	brain
charcuterie	cold meats, delicatessen
châteaubriant	porterhouse steak
chou	cabbage
chou de Bruxelles	Brussels sprouts
chou rouge	red cabbage
choufleur	cauliflower
ciboulette	chives
cochon de lait	sucking pig
coeur	heart
coing	quince
concombre	cucumber
confit	candied (fruit)
consommé	clear soup
coq au vin	chicken cooked in red wine
coquillages	shellfish
cotelette	cutlet
courge	gourd
crêpe	pancake
crevettes	shrimps
cru	raw
crudités	raw vegetable hors d'oeuvres
cumin	caraway
dattes	dates
daurade	sea bream
déjeuner	lunch
dessert	dessert, sweet
dinde, dindon	turkey
échalote	shallot
entrecote	(rib) steak
épaule	shoulder
épices	spices
épinard	spinach
escargots	snails
farci	stuffed
fenouil	fennel
figues	figs
flan	baked custard
foie	liver
frais	fresh
fraises	strawberries
friture	fried food, fry
fromage	cheese
fromage blanc	cream cheese
fromage de chèvre	goat's-milk cheese
fruits de mer	seafood
fumé	smoked
garni	with vegetables or other accompaniments
gâteau	cake
gaufrettes	waffles
gibier	game
gigot	leg of mutton
gingembre	ginger

glace	ice
au gratin	(cooked) with breadcrumbs and grated cheese
grillade	grilled meat
grillé	grilled
groseilles (rouges)	red currants
haché	chopped, minced
haricots	beans
herbes	herbs
huítres	oysters
jambon	ham
jambon cru	raw ham
jarret	knuckle (veal), shin (beef)
laitue	lettuce
langouste	crayfish
langue	tongue
lapin	rabbit
lard	bacon
légume	vegetable
loup de mer	sea perch
maquereau	mackerel
mariné	marinaded
marjolaine	marjoram
melon	melon
menthe	(pepper)mint
merguez	small spiced sausage
mérou	grouper
miel	honey
mouton	mutton
navet	turnip
noisette	hazelnut
noix	walnut
nouilles	noodles
oeuf	egg
oeuf à la coque	soft-boiled egg
oeuf sur le plat	fried egg
oeufs brouillés	scrambled egg
oie	goose
oignon	onion
origan	origano
oseille	sorrel
pageot	sea bream
pain	bread
pain de seigle	rye bread
pastèque	water-melon
pâté	pâté
pâtes	pasta, noodles
pâtisserie	pastry, cake
pêche	peach
petits pois	peas
pied de veau	calf's foot
pistache	pistachio
plat du jour	"dish of the day" (on a menu)
poire	pear
poireau	leek
pois chiches	chick peas
poivre	pepper
poivron	pimento
pomme	apple
pommes de terre	potatoes
en robe de chambre	in their jackets
sautées	roast potatoes

porc	pork
pot au feu	boiled beef with vegetables
potage	soup
poulet	chicken
poulpe	octopus
prune	plum
raie	ray
raisin	grapes
râpé	grated
rascasse	hog-fish
repas	meal
riz	rice
rognons	kidneys
roti	roast
rouget	red mullet
saignant	lightly done, rare (meat)
salade	salad
sanglier	wild boar
sar	sea bream
sardine	sardine
saucisse	sausage
sauge	sage
sel	salt
semoule	semolina
sole	sole
sorbet	sorbet, water ice
sorgho	sorghum, Indian millet
soupe	soup
sucre	sugar
tarte	tart
terrine	pâté
tête	head
thon	tunny
thym	thyme
tranche	slice
tripes	tripe
truffes	truffles
turbot	turbot
tomates	tomatoes
veau	veal
velouté	thick cream soup
vermicelles	vermicelli
viande	meat
vinaigre	vinegar
vinaigrette	salad dressing (oil and vinegar)
volaille	poultry
yaourt	yoghourt

Drinks

alcools	spirits
bière	beer
boga	lemonade (a brand name)
bouteille	bottle
café	coffee
au lait	with milk
glacé	iced
noir	black
chocolat	chocolate
demi-litre	half a litre
digestif	brandy or liqueur
eau	water
eau gazeuse	aerated water
infusion	tea

de camomille	camomile tea
à la menthe	peppermint tea
de verveine	verbena tea
jus de fruits	fruit juice
de citron	lemon juice
d'orange	orange juice
de tomate	tomato juice
lait	milk
limonade	lemonade
orange pressée	freshly pressed orange juice
pastis	aniseed aperitif
quart	quarter
thé au citron	tea with lemon
thé au lait	tea with milk
thé nature	black tea
tisane	herb tea
verre	glass
vin	wine
vin blanc	white wine
vin rosé	rosé wine
vin rouge	red wine

Wine

Vine-growing in Tunisia dates back to the time of the Carthaginians. The improvement in the quality of Tunisian wines in modern times is mainly due to the French and the Italians. The most important wine-producing areas are on Cap Bon and around Tunis (Mornag), Bizerte and Thibar.
All wine-making establishments, whether privately run, state-owned or cooperative, are subject to control by the Office du Vin, under a system similar to the French *appellations controlées*.
The largest producer is the Union des Caves Coopératives Viticoles de Tunisie. Among the best independent producers are the Société Lomblot, Château Feriani, Tené Laveau and Tardi.

Red wines

Among the best known red wines are Magon, Kahena, Coteaux d'Utique, Royal Tardi, Domaine Karim, Coteaux de Carthage, Château Mornag, Château Thibar, Château Feriani, Sidi Salem and Château Khanguet.

Rosé wines

Château Mornag, Gris de Tunisie, Clairet de Bizerte and Sidi Rais (dry, with a slight flavour of muscatel).

White wines

Blanc de Blanc, Domaine de Karim, Haut Mornag – all smooth and fruity. Particularly good is the dry Muscat de Kelibia, with the typical muscatel taste.

Further information

Further information about Tunisian wines can be obtained from the Union des Caves Coopératives Viticoles de Tunisie, Route de Mornag, Djebel Djelloud, tel. (01) 24 79 95.

Getting to Tunisia

By air

There are direct scheduled flights from London to Tunis by GB Airways (twice weekly from Gatwick; booking through British Airways) and Tunis Air (twice weekly from Heathrow; see Airlines), as well as numerous charter flights during the holiday season from London and some other British airports, mostly to Monastir. The flight from London takes about 2¾ hours. There are much more frequent services to Tunis and other Tunisian airports from Paris.
There are no direct flights from North America to Tunisia. The best plan for visitors from the United States and Canada is to fly to London or Paris and take a connecting flight from there.

Vineyard, Djerba

Some Tunisian wines

See also Air Travel.

By private aircraft

Visitors flying to Tunisia by private aircraft must apply for permission to land, three days before arrival, to the Direction de l'Aviation Civile, 1 rue d'Athènes, Tunis, tel. (01) 24 54 92.
For detailed information about the regulations, apply to the Tunisian National Tourist Office.

By road

The long journey to Tunisia by road, using a car ferry from one of the French or Italian ports (see Car Ferries), is likely to be undertaken only by those who have plenty of time at their disposal and want to see something of France or Italy on the way.

By sea

The only permissible ports for entry to Tunisia are those which have police and customs clearance facilities: e.g. Adjim (Djerba), Bizerte, Gabès, Kelibia, La Goulette, Houmt-Souk (Djerba), Mahdia, Monastir, Port El Kantaoui, Sidi Bou Said, Sidi Daoud, Sfax, Sousse, Tabarka and Tunis.

From Algeria

The main frontier crossing points for entry into Tunisia from Algeria are (from north to south) just south-west of Tabarka; Babouche; Ghardimaou; Sakiet Sidi Youssef; Bou Chebka; and Hazoua (south-west of Nefta).
The Trans-Maghreb line (see Railways) provides a rail link between Morocco, Algeria and Tunisia.

From Libya

The points of entry from Libya are Ben Gardane and Dehibat. There are numerous bus connections between Libya and Tunisia.

Further information

See Air Travel, Bus Services, Customs Regulations, Motoring in Tunisia, Railways, Safety and Security, Sahara Tourism, Sports, Travel Documents, Water Sports.

Golf

See Sports

Guides

Unofficial guides

Visitors to Tunisia, particularly those travelling on their own, are likely to be pestered wherever they go by men, youths and sometimes children offering their services as guides. They begin in a friendly and ingratiating tone but are extremely persistent and if their services are refused may become abusive and aggressive. Any guiding they do will usually end up in some shop or other, where they will expect to receive commission from any purchases made. Although unofficial guiding of this kind is forbidden by police regulations and subject to significant penalties the number of young men who see this as a quick way of earning money in a time of rising unemployment is steadily increasing.

Although it is not too difficult for a stranger to find his way around Tunisian towns, medinas and excavation sites, there are advantages in having a guide; and if you are seen to have one the importuning by other would-be guides will stop. Before taking on an unofficial guide, however, ask to see his identity card and make a note of its number, and be sure to agree on a price before setting out. On no account rely on the prospective guide's offer, "Give me what you like!", since this inevitably leads to disputes over the proper rate. You should also tell the guide in advance what you want to see.

Official guides

There are also numbers of official guides, who are identifiable by a round badge and have an official pass issued by the Ministry of Tourism. They are sometimes to be found in or around large hotels, at the entrance to medinas or on excavation sites, but are usually engaged by telephone through the hotel reception desk or at the local ONTT tourist office. These guides have taken an intensive (and expensive) two-year course at the ONTT School of Tourism in Tunis and must speak at least two languages.

The fees for official guides, which vary somewhat from town to town, are laid down by the Ministry of Tourism; for information about the local rates apply to the ONTT office. The amount should, however, be confirmed with the guide himself before setting out.

Hammams

The hammams found throughout the Maghreb and the Near East are the public bath-houses, commonly known in English as Turkish baths, which in earlier times made up for the lack of private washing facilities and accordingly are situated in the oldest part of present-day towns, the medina.

The hammam (see plan, page 41) is equipped with baths of warm and cold water, showers and steam baths, and bathers can also have a massage. Towels can usually be hired. There may be separate baths for men and women or, more usually, different times of day for the two sexes.

Health

General

Hygienic conditions in Tunisian tourist resorts are comparable with those in other Mediterranean countries.

Inoculations

No inoculations are obligatory for entry to Tunisia except for visitors coming from countries infected with cholera or yellow fever. It is a wise precaution, however, to be inoculated against polio, tetanus and typhoid. In case of doubt a doctor should be consulted some weeks before leaving home.

First aid kit

A first aid kit should include remedies for diarrhoea, stomach and intestinal upsets, colds and chills, sunburn and insect bites; insect repellants, suntan oil with a high screening factor, sticking plaster and bandages.

Some precautions

Particular attention should be paid to health during the first few days of the holiday.
Proper protection from the sun is essential (head-covering, sun-glasses, sun creams).
In order to make up for the heavy loss of water from the body drink plenty of liquid. The water in the large hotels is safe; in the south of the country and in street restaurants drink only bottled water.
It may be safer also to avoid ice-cream and ice cubes in long drinks.
The best protection against infection is cleanliness.
If an insect bite is followed by a large swelling or other change, consult a doctor at once.

Snake and scorpion bites

When travelling in the south of the country stout footwear is recommended as a protection against snake bites. Do not turn over stones, which may harbour snakes seeking shelter from the sun.
If camping in a tent shake out clothes and shoes in the morning to dislodge any scorpions which may have been active during the night.
Scorpions can be removed by catching the extreme tip of the tail between the thumb and first finger; but this is a dangerous operation for the inexperienced.
A visitor who is bitten should see a doctor at once; but if this is not possible a deep cut should be made round the bite with a knife, or preferably a razor blade, so that the blood flows freely.

AIDS

The usual precautions against the transmission of AIDS (French SIDA) apply. Injections and the taking of blood samples should be done only with disposable syringes. If a blood transfusion is required it is better to avoid the use of blood from the local blood bank and to look for donors known to reliable doctors. Any surgical or dental procedures not immediately urgent should be postponed until the visitor returns home.
The main source of infection with AIDS is unprotected sexual intercourse, either homosexual or heterosexual. The risk of infection can be reduced by the use of condoms.

Further information

See Chemists, Emergencies, Medical Aid

Help for the Disabled

Information

In Britain the main sources of information and advice on travel by the disabled are the Royal Association for Disability and Rehabilitation (RADAR), 25 Mortimer Street, London W1N 8AB, tel. (071) 637 5400; the Spinal Injuries Association, 76 St James Lane, London N10 3RD, tel. (081) 444 2121; and Mobility International, 228 Borough High Street, London SE1 1TD, tel. (071) 403 5688.

Useful publications

"Holiday and Travel Abroad – A Guide for Disabled People", published by RADAR.

"The World Wheelchair Traveller", published by the AA for the Spinal Injuries Association.

"Low Cost Travel Tips for People Using Wheelchairs", published by Mobility International.

The AA also publishes a "Guide for the Disabled Traveller" (free to members).

Major sources of information in the United States are Louise Weiss's "Access to the World: A Travel Guide for the Handicapped" (available from Facts on File, 460 Park Avenue South, New York NY 10016) and the Society for the Advancement of Travel by the Handicapped, 26 Court Street, Penthouse Suite, Brooklyn NY 11242.

Hotels

The tourist areas of Tunisia are well equipped with hotels. All hotels are officially classified and their tariffs are controlled by the government. Hotels in the higher categories are fully up to European standards of comfort and amenity. There are also numerous middle-grade hotels and numbers of more modest establishments.

Hotels are classified into the following categories:
****L four-star luxury hotels
**** four-star hotels
*** three-star hotels
** two-star hotels
* one-star hotels

There are also apartment hotels and holiday villages (villages de vacances) and, in southern Tunisia, marhalas and ksars (traditional types of buildings which have been converted into hotels).

Abbreviations

AH apartment hotel
NC unclassified
PF guesthouse (pension de famille)
VV holiday village (village de vacances)

b. = number of beds; r. = number of rooms; SP = swimming pool; DC = telephone dialling code

The following is only a small selection of hotels. A full list can be obtained from the Tunisian National Tourist Office.

Ain Draham (DC: 08)

***Hammam Bourguiba, Hammam Bourguiba, tel. 4 72 27/4 71 06/4 73 00, 80 b.; **Les Chênes, tel. 4 72 11, 68 b., SP; **Rihana, tel. 4 73 91/4 73 92/3/4, 150 b.; Beau Séjour (NC), Avenue Habib Bourguiba, tel. 4 70 05, 32 b.

Béja (DC: 08)

**Vaga, Avenue Habib Bourguiba, tel. 5 08 18, 36 b.; Phénix (NC), Avenue de France, tel. 5 01 88, 25 b.

Bizerte (DC: 02)

***Corniche, tel. 3 18 44, 174 b., SP; ***Jalta, tel. 3 22 50, 200 b.; **Nador, tel. 3 18 48/3 38 17/3 93 09, 200 b., SP; **Petit Mousse, Route de la Corniche, tel. 3 21 85, 24 b., SP; Ain Mariem (AH), tel. 3 76 15/3 88 59, 126 b.

Borj Cedria

***Salwa, tel. (01) 29 08 30/29 02 33, 352 b., SP; **Dar Hotel, tel. (01) 29 01 88, 288 b., SP.

Bou Salem

Les Agriculteurs (NC), Avenue Habib Bourguiba, tel. (08) 4 92 39, 16 b.

Carthage (DC: 01)

***Reine Elyssa Didon, tel. 27 51 79, 44 b.; **Résidence Carthage, 16 rue Hannibal Salammbo, tel. 73 10 72, 23 b.

Djerba (DC: 05)

****Abou Nawas, tel. 5 77 00, 450 b., SP; ****El Menzel, tel. 5 70 71, 368 b., SP; ****Palm Beach, tel. 5 73 50, 402 b., SP; ***Dar Jerba (also **Dar Jerba), tel. 5 71 91/5 71 78, 2723 b., SP; **El Jazira, tel. 5 73 00, 340 b., SP; **Meninx, tel. 5 70 52, 366 b., SP; **Toumana Club (VV), tel. 5 71 09/5 74 09, 244 b., SP; **Yati, Midoun, tel. 5 70 16, 88 b., SP; **Dar Faiza, tel. 5 00 83,

24 b.; *Haji, Houmt-Souk, tel. 5 06 30, 92 b.; Touring Club (NC), Rue Moncef Bey, Houmt-Souk, tel. 5 01 46, 120 b.

Douz (DC: 05)

***Mehari, Grande Dune, tel. 9 51 49/9 50 88, 252 b.; Marhala (NC), tel. 9 53 15, 102 b., SP; Roses de Sable (NC), tel. 9 54 84/9 53 66, 200 b.; Saharien (NC), tel. 9 53 37, 235 b., SP; El Faouar (NC), El Faouar, tel. 9 50 85, 185 b., SP.

El Djem

*Relais Julius, tel. (03) 9 00 44, 30 b.

El Haouaria

**L'Epervier, tel. (02) 9 70 17, 26 b.

Ez Zahra

****Ez-Zahra, tel. (01) 45 27 88, 246 b.; La Siesta (PF), tel. (01) 48 09 59, 88 b.

Gabès (DC: 05)

***Oasis, tel. 7 03 81, 184 b.; ***Chems, tel. 7 04 36, 556 b., SP; **Nejib, tel. 7 15 47, 128 b.; **Tacapes, tel. 7 07 01, 56 b.; *Atlantic, Avenue Habib Bourguiba, tel. 7 04 42, 140 b.; Kilani (NC), 7 03 20, 40 b.; Medina (NC), tel. 7 12 71, 40 b.

Gafsa (DC: 06)

***Jugurtha, tel. 2 13 00, 152 b., SP; ***Maamoun, tel. 2 25 01/2 27 40/2 24 33, 138 b., SP; **Gafsa, tel. 2 24 68, 78 b.; *Lune, tel. 2 22 12, 18 b.; Ennour (NC), tel. 2 06 20, 36 b.

Gammarth (DC: 01)

****L Abou Nawas, Av. Taieb Mehiri, tel. 74 04 00, 446 b., SP; ***Cap Carthage, Chottel Ghaba, tel. 74 14 68/74 15 85, 324 b., SP; Tour Blanche, tel. 27 16 94, 160 b., SP; Dar Naouar (VV), tel. 74 10 00, 1064 b., SP.

Ghardimaou

Thubernic (NC), Gare Ferroviaire, tel. (08) 4 50 43, 26 b.

Hammamet (DC: 02)

****L El Manar, tel. 8 13 33, 708 b., SP; ****L Sindbad, tel. 8 01 22, 335 b., SP; ****Abou Nawas, tel. 8 10 96, 450 b., SP; ****Phénicia, tel. 8 03 36/8 05 33, 720 b., SP; ***Continental, tel. 8 04 56, 350 b., SP; ***El Fell, tel. 8 07 44, 556 b., SP; ***Les Charmes, tel. 8 00 10, 340 b., SP; **Cyprès, tel. 8 08 06, 78 b.; **El Bousten, tel. 8 04 44/8 01 26, 764 b., SP; **Club Méditerranée (VV), Diar Hammamet, tel. 8 19 39, 448 b., SP; **Omar Khayam, tel. 8 03 55, 484 b.

Hammam-Lif

Bon Repos (NC), 14 rue Belhassen Chedli, tel. 29 14 58, 24 b.; Hotel des Thermes (NC), , tel. 29 14 58/29 07 38, 22 b.

Jendouba

**Atlas, Rue du 1er Juin 1955, tel. (08) 3 05 66, 32 b.

Kairouan (DC: 07)

****Continental, tel. 2 11 35, 352 b., SP; ***Les Aghlabites, Rue de Fès, tel. 2 08 55, 124 b., SP; ***Splendid, Rue du 9 Avril, tel. 2 05 22, 83 b.; **Tunisia, tel. 2 18 55, 76 b.; Marhala (NC), 35 Souk el Belaghjia, tel. 2 07 36, 69 b.

Kasserine

***Cillium, tel. (07) 7 01 06, 72 b., SP.

Kebili

**Fort des Autruches, tel. (05) 9 02 33, 112 b.

Kelibia

*Florida, tel. (02) 9 62 48, 25 b.; El Mansourah (VV), tel. (02) 9 61 56, 232 b.

Kerkennah (DC: 04)

**Farhat, tel. 8 12 36, 308 b., SP; **Grand Hotel, tel. 8 12 66, 225 b., SP.

Korba

Club Méditerranée, tel. (02) 8 84 11, 1200 b., SP.

Korbous (DC: 02)

***Oktor, tel. 9 45 52, 52 b., SP; ***Les Sources, tel. 9 45 33, 103 b., SP; Chiraz (AH), Route de Korbous, tel. 9 32 30, 16 b.

Ksar Haddada (Ghoumrassen)

Ksar Haddada (NC), near Ghoumrassen, tel. (05) 6 96 05, 72 b.

La Marsa

Corniche Plaza (PF), tel. (01) 27 00 98, 28 b., SP.

Le Kef

La Source (NC), Place de la Source, tel. (08) 2 13 97, 18 b.

Hotels

Mahdia (DC: 03)	***Club Cap Mahdia, tel. 8 19 00, 508 b., SP; ***El Mehdi, tel. 8 14 37, 426 b., SP; *Sables d'Or, tel. 8 11 37, 202 b.
Mahrès	**Marzouk, tel. (04) 9 02 61, 40 b.; Yourga (NC), tel. (04) 9 03 34, 20 b.
Maktar	Mactaris (NC), Avenue Habib Bourguiba, tel. (08) 7 60 14, 24 b.
Matmata (DC: 05)	**Matmata Hotel, tel. 3 00 66, 67 b.; Les Berbères (NC), tel. 3 00 24, 80 b.; Marhala (NC), tel. 3 00 15, 100 b.; Sidi Driss (NC), tel. 3 00 05, 140 b.
Médenine	*Agil, tel. (05) 4 01 51, 26 b.
Menzel Bourguiba	*Younes, Guengla Plage, tel. (02) 6 16 06, 32 b.
Menzel Temime	**Temime, tel. (02) 9 86 73, 88 b.
Metameur	El Ghorfa, tel. (05) 4 02 94, 13 r.
Metlaoui	Ennacim (NC), tel. (06) 4 02 71, 36 b.; Mabrouk (NC), tel. (07) 8 52 02, 40 b.
Monastir (DC: 03)	****L Regency Monastir, tel. 6 00 33, 384 b., SP; ****Habib, tel. 6 29/941, 400 b., SP; ****Kuriat Palace, tel. 6 13 69/6 12 00, 476 b., SP; ***Ruspina, tel. 6 13 60, 500 b., SP; ***Sahara Beach, tel. 6 08 26/966/477, 2000 b., SP; **Les Palmiers, tel. 6 01 52, 126 b. In Monastir-Skanès: Club Méditerranée (VV), tel. 3 15 62, 1080 b., SP.
Nabeul (DC: 02)	***Al Diana Club, tel. 8 54 00, 440 b., SP; ***Lido, tel. 8 57 86, 972 b., SP; ***Nabeul Plage, tel. 8 62 63, 556 b., SP; **Neapolis, tel. 8 57 77; **Ramses Résidence, tel. 8 63 63, 548 b., SP; *Les Jasmins, tel. 8 53 43, 76 b.
Nefta (DC: 06)	****Sahara Palace, 5 70 48/5 71 38, 216 b., SP; ***Caravansérail Sunoa, tel. 5 73 55/5 74 16, 154 b., SP; Marhala Nefta (NC), tel. 5 70 27, 76 b.
Port El Kantaoui (DC: 03)	****L Hannibal Palace, tel. 4 15 77, 500 b., SP; ****L Diar El Andalous, tel. 3 17 99, 609 b., SP; ***Abou Sofiane, tel. 4 07 22, 600 b., SP; ***Bulla Regia, tel. 4 09 23/2; 104 b., SP; **Tergui, tel. 4 84 88, 486 b., SP.
Raf-Raf	Dalia (NC), Plage, tel. (02) 4 76 88, 22 b.
Sbeitla (DC: 07)	**Sufetula, tel. 6 50 74/6 53 11, 92 b., SP; **Bakini, tel. 6 52 44/330, 80 b., SP.
Sfax (DC: 04)	****L Sfax Centre, tel. 2 57 00/2 57 01, 260 b., SP; ****Syphax, tel. 4 33 33, 254 b.; ***Les Oliviers, tel. 2 51 89, 112 b., SP; **Le Colisée, tel. 2 78 00/2 78 06; 100 b.; *Alexander, Rue Alexandre Dumas, tel. 2 19 11, 72 b.
Sidi Bou Said (DC: 01)	****Sidi Bou Said, tel. 74 51 29, 64 b., SP; **Dar Said, tel. 27 07 92, 23 b.
Sidi Bou Zid	*Chems, tel. (06) 3 05 15, 18 b.
Soliman (DC: 02)	***Medi Sea, tel. 29 30 13, 220 b.; **Solymar, tel. 9 01 05, 400 b.
Sousse (DC: 03)	****Chems El Hana, tel. 2 81 90, 518 b., SP; ****El Hana, tel. 2 58 18, 262 b., SP; ****Marhaba Palace, tel. 4 36 33, 648 b.; ***El Hana Beach, tel. 2 69 00, 1300 b., SP; ***Shéhrasade, tel. 4 14 12, 416 b., SP; ***Sousse Palace, tel. 2 52 00, 456 b., SP; **Jawhara Club, tel. 2 56 11, 688 b., SP; **Salem, tel. 4 19 66, 474 b., SP.
Tabarka (DC: 08)	***Mimosas, tel. 4 45 00, 154 b.; ***Morjane, tel. 4 44 11, 320 b., SP.
Tamerza	Les Cascades (NC), tel. (06) 4 85 20, 150 b., SP.
Tataouine	**La Gazelle, tel. (05) 6 00 09/913, 46 b.

Hotel, Sidi Bou Said

Téboursouk

** Thugga, tel. (08) 6 57 13, 66 b.

Testour

Ibn Zeidoun (NC), Route du Kef, tel. (08) 6 80 33, 60 b.

Thala

Bouthelja, tel. (07) 8 00 57, 26 b.

Tozeur (DC: 06)

*** Continental, tel. 6 00 29, 300 b., SP; *** Ras El Ain, tel. 5 08 11/5 09 35/5 05 27, 120 b., SP; *** Hafsi, tel. 5 05 58/559, 129 b., SP; *** Oasis, tel. 5 04 34, 160 b., SP; *** Dar Cherait, tel. 5 11 00; ** Les Dunes, 162 b.; * El Jerid, tel. 5 05 54, 90 b., SP; * Splendid, tel. 5 00 53, 52 b., SP; * Aicha, tel. 5 09 73, 78 b.; Essaada (NC), tel. 5 00 97, 35 b.

Tunis (DC: 01)

**** L Abou Nawas Tunis, tel. 35 03 55 and 35 34 43, 650 r., 31 suites; **** L Africa Meridien, tel. 1 55 36 and 1 40 35, 328 b., SP; **** L Hilton, tel. 28 20 00 and 78 28 00, 467 b., SP; **** L International Tunisia, tel. 25 48 55, 456 b.; **** Le Belvédère, tel. 78 31 33, 118 b.; **** Le Diplomate, tel. 78 52 33, 286 b.; **** El Mechtel, tel. 78 32 00, 1010 b.; *** Les Ambassadeurs, tel. 28 80 11, 182 b.; *** Golf Royal, tel. 34 43 11, 108 b.; *** Ibn Khaldoun, tel. 89 22 11, 271 b.; *** Majestic, tel. 24 28 48 and 24 26 66, 184 b.; *** Le National, tel. 78 29 55, 156 b.; *** Hotel du Lac, tel. 25 83 22, 388 b.; ** Tunis Parc Hotel, 7 rue Damas, tel. 28 66 96, 72 b.; ** Maison Dorée, 6 bis rue de Hollande, tel. 24 62 54, 93 b.; ** Saint Georges, 16 rue de Cologne, tel. 28 29 37, 72 b.; ** Tej, 14 rue Lt Aziz Tej, tel. 34 48 99 and 34 26 66, 62 b.; ** Plaza Corniche, 22 rue du Maroc, La Marsa, tel. 27 00 98; * Salammbo, 6 rue de Grèce, tel. 24 42 52, 105 b.; * Transatlantique, 106 rue de Yougoslavie, tel. 24 06 80, 83 b.

Zaghouan (DC: 02)

*** Jebel el Oust, tel. 7 97 40/977, 98 b.; ** Les Nymphes, tel. 7 50 94, 80 b.

Zarzis (DC: 05)

*** Oamarit, tel. 8 05 65/8 06 85, 844 b., SP; *** Sangho, tel. 8 01 24, 722 b., SP; *** Zarzis, tel. 8 01 72, 594 b., SP; ** Zita, tel. 8 14 81/8 02 92, 1112 b., SP; Emira (NC), tel. 8 01 88, 22 b.

Information

Outside Tunisia

United Kingdom

Tunisian National Tourist Office
77A Wigmore Street
London W1H 9LJ
Tel. (071) 224 5561/98

USA

Embassy of Tunisia
1515 Massachusetts Avenue
NW Washington DC 20005
Tel. (202) 234 6644

Canada

Embassy of Tunisia
515 O'Connor Street
Ottawa
Tel. (613) 237 0330

In Tunisia

In all the larger towns and tourist resorts there are tourist information offices run by the Tunisian National Tourist Office (Office National du Tourisme Tunisien, ONTT). In many towns information can also be obtained from the local Syndicat d'Initiative or Bureau du Tourisme.

ONTT

The head office of the Tunisian National Tourist Office is:

Office National du Tourisme Tunisien (ONTT)
1 Avenue Mohamed V
1001 Tunis
Tel. (01) 34 10 77

There are also regional offices of ONTT in the following towns:

Bizerte

1 rue de Constantinople
7000 Bizerte
Tel. (02) 3 28 97

Houmt-Souk (Djerba)

Houmt-Souk
4180 Houmt-Souk/Djerba
Tel. (05) 5 00 16/518

Monastir

Rue de l'Indépéndence, Quartier Chraga
5000 Monastir
Tel. (03) 6 12 05

Nabeul

Avenue Taieb Mehiri
8000 Nabeul
Tel. (02) 8 67 37/800

Sousse

1 Avenue Habib Bourguiba
4000 Sousse
Tel. (03) 2 51 57/8

Tozeur

Avenue Aboul el Kacem Chebbi
2200 Tozeur
Tel. (06) 5 05 03 and 5 00 88

Tunis

29 rue de Palestine
1001 Tunis
Tel. (01) 28 94 03

Zarzis

Route du Port
4170 Zarzis
Tel. (05) 8 04 45

Further information

See Airlines, Breakdown Assistance, Car Ferries, Diplomatic and Consular Offices, Emergencies, Railways

Insurance

Visitors should ensure that they have adequate insurance cover (car insurance, health insurance, insurance against loss and theft of property).

See Motoring, Travel Documents

Language

The main language of Tunisia is Arabic in its Tunisian form, but French – a legacy of colonial times – is also widely spoken. In the larger towns and tourist centres many people, particularly those with whom visitors are likely to be in contact, also speak English.

Berber dialects, still spoken by many people in Morocco and Algeria, are now found in Tunisia only in isolated pockets, for example on the island of Djerba or in the Dahar Hills. On Djerba there is also a Hebrew-speaking Jewish minority.

Arabic

The official language of Tunisia is Arabic, one of the great world languages, spoken by almost 200 million people in Africa and the Near East. The written language is standard throughout the Arab world, but there are considerable regional differences in the spoken language, and the colloquial Arabic of Tunisia is markedly different, for example, from the language of Egypt.

Arabic is fundamentally different from the Indo-European languages, not only in grammatical structure but also in the script it uses. The Arabic script, which runs from right to left, is essentially concerned with the consonantal structure of words, which determines their semantic content. Since the numerous dialects of Arabic differ mainly in the form of their vowels, a consonantal script of this kind is more widely applicable than a fully developed phonetic alphabet would be.

The 28 characters of the Arabic alphabet vary considerably in form according to whether they occur at the beginning, middle or end of a word (initial, medial and final positions) or stand by themselves (independent position). No generally agreed system of transcription into the Latin alphabet has yet been devised; and since Arabic has some sounds which have no equivalent in that alphabet a word will appear in different forms in an English, a French or a German transcription.

The transcription of place-names and other Arabic terms in this guide generally follows the French transliteration which appears on maps and road signs.

The English pronunciation of the letters and groups of letters used in the French transcription is as follows:

Arabic Alphabet

Name	Independent	Final	Medial	Initial	Tran-scription	Pronunciation
alif	ا	ـا	—	—	ā	glottal stop
ba	ب	ـب	ـبـ	بـ	b	b
ta	ت	ـت	ـتـ	تـ	t	t
tha	ث	ـث	ـثـ	ثـ	ṯ	th (as in 'thing')
gim	ج	ـج	ـجـ	جـ	ǧ	g (hard)
ha	ح	ـح	ـحـ	حـ	ḥ	h (guttural)
kha	خ	ـخ	ـخـ	خـ	ḫ	ch (as in 'loch')
dal	د	ـد	—	—	d	d
dhal	ذ	ـذ	—	—	ḏ	th (as in 'the')
ra	ر	ـر	—	—	r	r (rolled)
za	ز	ـز	—	—	z	z
sin	س	ـس	ـسـ	سـ	s	s
shin	ش	ـش	ـشـ	شـ	š	sh
ṣad	ص	ـص	ـصـ	صـ	ṣ	s (emphatic)
ḍad	ض	ـض	ـضـ	ضـ	ḍ	d (emphatic)
ṭa	ط	ـط	ـطـ	طـ	ṭ	t (emphatic)
ẓa	ظ	ـظ	ـظـ	ظـ	ẓ	z (emphatic)
'ain	ع	ـع	ـعـ	عـ	'	(a harsh guttural sound)
ghain	غ	ـغ	ـغـ	غـ	ġ	gh (guttural)
fa	ف	ـف	ـفـ	فـ	f	f
ḳaf	ق	ـق	ـقـ	قـ	q	k, q (velar)
kaf	ك	ـك	ـكـ	كـ	k	k (palatal)
lam	ل	ـل	ـلـ	لـ	l	l
mim	م	ـم	ـمـ	مـ	m	m
nun	ن	ـن	ـنـ	نـ	n	n
ha	ه	ـه	ـهـ	هـ	h	h
waw	و	ـو	—	—	w(ū)	w
ya	ى	ـى	ـيـ	يـ	y(ē, ī)	y

French	English
ch	=sh
kh	=ch as in Scottish "loch"
dh	=th in "the"
gh	=a uvular r
h	=h
gue, gui	=like "gay" and "ghee" (with a hard g)
j	=zh
dj	=j
r	=rolled r
s	=s
z	=z
ou	=w
w	=w
e	=not pronounced when it occurs at the end of a word
eu	=as in French "peur"
q	=a guttural k
y	=consonantal y

The following pages contain a select vocabulary of Arabic words, in an English transcription indicating the approximate pronunciation.

Arabic alphabet

The Arabic alphabet (see table on page 340) consists of 28 characters. With the exception of the three long vowels alif, waw and ya they are all consonants; other vowels are not written.

Numbers

Arabic numbers, unlike the Arabic script, are written from left to right.

Cardinal numbers

0	sifr
1	wahed
2	tneen, soosh
3	tlata
4	rabraa
5	khamsa
6	setta
7	sebaa
8	tmenya
9	tsaa
10	ashra
11	hedash
12	tnash
13	tlatash
14	rabatash
15	khamstash
16	sarrash
17	sabatash
18	tmantash
19	tsatash
20	ashreen
21	wahed we ashreen
22	tneem we ashreen
30	tleteen

Arabic Figures
(read from left to right)

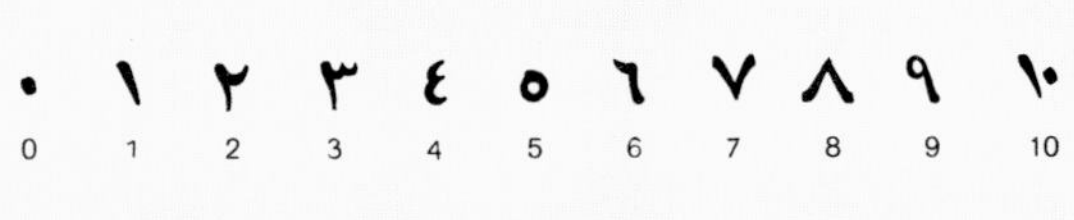

40	rabaeen
50	khamseen
60	serreen
70	sabaeen
80	tmaneen
90	taseen
100	meea
101	meeawahed
200	meeateen
300	talatmeea
400	rabameea
500	khamsameea
600	settameea
700	sebameea
800	temnemeea
900	tessameea
1000	alf
2000	alfaeen
3000	tlatalaf
4000	rabalaf
5000	khamstalaf
10,000	ashralaf
100,000	meetalf
1,000,000	malyon

Banks, hotels, restaurants, filling stations, etc., in Tunisia almost always use European ("Arabic") figures in bills.

After the numbers 2–10 the plural form of the following noun is used; after 2 the dual form is correct and is normally used at least by educated Tunisians (*kalben,* two dogs). After numbers from 11 onwards the singular is used (*tleteen kalb,* thirty dogs, but *tlata kilab,* three dogs).

Ordinals	1st	el auwal (*m.*) el auwala, el oola (*f.*)
	2nd	tanee (*m.*), taneeya (*f.*)
	3rd	taleet (*m.*), talta (*f.*)
	4th	rabee (*m.*), raba (*f.*)
	5th	khamees (*m.*), khamsa (*f.*)
	6th	sadees (*m.*), sadsa (*f.*)
	7th	sabee (*m.*), saba (*f.*)
	8th	tameen (*m.*), tamna (*f.*)
	9th	tasee (*m.*), tasa (*f.*)
	10th	asheer (*m.*), ashra (*f.*)
Fractions	½	noos
	⅓	toolt
	¼	rubaa
	¾	talat rubaa
	⅒	oshr
Islamic calendar	See Calendars	
Months	January	yenayeer
	February	febrayeer
	March	mars
	April	abreel
	May	mayo
	June	yoonioo
	July	yoolioo
	August	aghostos
	September	sebtember

English	Arabic	
October	oktober	
November	nofember	
December	desember	
1st month	moharrem	Months of Islamic calendar
2nd month	safar	
3rd month	rebeea el wel	
4th month	rebeea et tanee	
5th month	joomad el wel	
6th month	joomad et tanee	
7th month	rejjeb	
8th month	shaban	
9th month	ramadan	
10th month	shooel	
11th month	dool kada	
12th month	dool hijja	
Sunday	el had	Days of week
Monday	et tneen	
Tuesday	et tlata	
Wednesday	el arba	
Thursday	el khemees	
Friday	el jemaa	
Saturday	es sebt	
year	sanna	Time
month	shahr	
week	oosboo (simana)	
day	n'har	
evening	asheea	
morning	sbah	
night	leel	
hour	sa'a	
today	el yoom	
yesterday	elbarah (during the day) yamess (evening)	
tomorrow	ghedda, bookra	
now	daba, debba	
later	minbad	
at once	biserba	
the day after tomorrow	baad bookra	
house	dar	Accommodation
hotel (modest)	fondook	
hotel (better quality)	hotel	
luggage	hwejj	
room	beet	
bath	hammam	
bed	fraash	
restaurant	mahtaam	Food and drink
breakfast	ftoor	
lunch	ghda	
dinner	laasha	
bill, please!	habeet khalas	
thirst	atash	
I am thirsty	ranee achan(a)	
soup	shorba	
meat and vegetable stew	tasheen	
potatoes	batata	
bread	khobs	
butter	sebda	

	meat	leham
	fish	hoota
	mutton	kebsh
	chicken	jajja
	salt	melh
	coffee	kava
	tea	shay, thé
	water	elma
	milk	haleeb
	egg	beeda
	sugar	sokkar
	oil	zeet
	onion	bsel
	garlic	tooma
	orange	cheena
	grapes	eneb
	dates	tmar
	spoon	m'allqa
	knife	moohs
	plate	tobsee
	glass	kess
Travelling	car	tomobeel, seeara
	bus	tobus, trolee
	petrol station	makhdar petrol (essence)
	workshop (garage)	mahal mekhanik
	road	treeq
	street (small)	derb
	street (larger)	shareea, avenue (French)
	square	seha
	tyre	pneu (French)
	tyre change	bad'dal pneu
	sparking plug	shemaa, bougie (French)
	oil	seet
	oil change	bad'dal seet
	water (for radiator)	mah el seeara
	engine	mootoor
	police	shoorda, police (French)
	where . . .	ween
	. . . is the road to . . .?	hadee trek . . .
	here	hena
	there	l'heh
	far	ba'eed
	right	leemeen
	left	lesar
	straight ahead	neeshel
	big	kebeer
	small	segheer (srheer)
	passport	paspor
	railway	sekka
	train	keitar
	station	khetar
	ticket-office	geesheh
	ticket	karta safar
	information	steekbaal
	1st class	darakha al auwala
	2nd class	darakha taneea
	non-smoker, smoker	mamnooa tajeen, masmooa tajeen
	sleeping-car	couchette (French)
	luggage	hwejj
	left luggage office	sandook hwejj
	ship	basheera, babor

ferry	maslahad assiyarad di al basheera
harbour	marsa
departure	dahab
arrival	al oosol
sea	bahar

Greetings

Between Muslims:	
Peace be upon you!	As-salam aleikum!
Response:	
And upon you be peace!	Aleikum as-salam!
To non-Muslims:	
May your day be happy!	Nahark sa'id!
Meeting someone on a journey:	
Welcome, good day!	Marhaba, ahlen!
Response:	
Twice welcome!	Marhaben!
To someone setting out on a journey:	
In safety!	Ma' as-salama!
Response:	
May God preserve you in safety!	Allah yisallimak!
On visiting or meeting someone:	
How is your health?	Kef halik?
Response:	
Well, thank God!	Halu labas, Allah yibarik fik!
On leaving:	
In God's care!	Alallah!
or: Let us go!	Yalla!
Exclamation of surprise:	
What God wills (happens)!	Mashallah!
As God wills!	Inshallah!
To strengthen an assertion:	
By God!	Wallah, Wallahi!
Before eating, working, etc.:	
In the name of God!	Bismallah!
Response:	
May you enjoy it!	Bil-hana! Bisaha!
On completion of something:	
Praise be to God!	El-hamd lilla!
Good morning, good day!	Sabah el-khir! Sabahkum el-khir!
Response:	
God grant you a good morning!	Allah sabah aleikum el-khir!
Good evening!	Misa el-khir! Mesikum el-khir!
Response:	
God grant you a good evening!	M'sakum Allah el-khir!
Good night!	Lila mebruka!
Goodbye!	Besslama!

Useful words and phrases

Sir (*addressing a man*)	sidi
Madam (*addressing a woman*)	lalla
Give me . . .	ateenee
Have you . . .?	aandeek . . .?
I have not	ma'andeesh
What? I beg your pardon?	neshnoo
I am called . . .	ana ismee . . .
I am . . .	ana . . .
(*There is no verb "to be" in Arabic*)	
Britain	ingiltira
I am British	ana inglizi

Do you speak . . .	tkalam anta (anti) . . .
English?	l'ingliziya?
French?	faranziya?
Arabic?	arabiya?
I do not understand	ana ma afhamsch
Excuse me!	smehlee
I beg your pardon	samahni
I should like . . .	min fadlak
Thank you	khukran, saha
(*more formally*)	barak, Allahu fik (Allah bless you!)
Listen!	afak, asma
Look here	shof, shofoo (*plural*)
yes	naham
no	la
Certainly not!	makash, mafish
Watch out!	balek, balkum (*plural*)
good	nakha
beautiful	mezian
bad	duni, khaib
Where can I . . .?	fen mumkin ana . . .
Where is there . . .?	fen . . .
It doesn't matter	malesh
I don't care	kif-kif
How much?	ash-hal
That is too dear	rhalee b'seff
much, a lot	ktir, besehf
too much	bezzaid
little	shoo'ia
enough	ikfi
money	floos
I have no money	makash floos
Come here!	ayee lahna
Go away	seer, seeroo
Off you go!	mshi
Get out! (*coarse*)	barra
Leave me alone!	khalini fhali
Bring me . . .	jeeb, jeeboo (*plural*)
Take it away!	eddi, eddin (*plural*)
Take it	hak

French

French is fairly generally understood throughout Tunisia, particularly in the towns. Visitors who have at least some knowledge of French, therefore, should have no difficulty in getting about.

Pronunciation

Characteristic features are the placing of the stress towards the end of the word and the frequent nasalisation of vowels.

Vowels (always pronounced without the diphthongisation found in English): *ai* like English *ay*; *ais* an open *e* as in "bed"; *é* like *ay*; *è* and *ê* an open *e*; *an, en, em* at the end of a syllable like a nasalised *on* (not quite *ong*); *un, im, in, ein* at the end of a syllable like a nasalised *un* (not quite *ung*); *eu* a little like the *u* in "fur"; *oi, oy* like *wa*; *ou* like *oo*; *u* a sound obtained by pronouncing *ee* with rounded lips.

Consonants: *c* before *e, i* or *y* and *ç* before other vowels, like *s*; *c* before *a, o* or *u* like *k*; *j*, and *g* before *e, i* or *y*, like *zh*; *g* before *a, o* or *u* like a hard English *g*; *ch* like *sh*; *gn* usually like *ny* in "canyon"; *h* always silent; *ll* between vowels often palatalised to a consonantal *y* sound, but sometimes a light *l* (e.g. in *elle*); *q, qu* like *k*.

The following letters are usually silent at the end of a word (and often also at the end of a syllable): *d, e, r* (only after *e*), *s, t, x, z*.

Numbers

0 zéro	22 vingt-deux
1 un, une	30 trente
2 deux	40 quarante
3 trois	50 cinquante
4 quatre	60 soixante
5 cinq	70 soixante-dix
6 six	71 soixante et onze
7 sept	80 quatre-vingt(s)
8 huit	81 quatre-vingt-un
9 neuf	90 quatre-vingt-dix
10 dix	91 quatre-vingt-onze
11 onze	100 cent
12 douze	101 cent un
13 treize	153 cent cinquante trois
14 quatorze	200 deux cent(s)
15 quinze	300 trois cent(s)
16 seize	400 quatre cent(s)
17 dix-sept	500 cinq cent(s)
18 dix-huit	1000 mille
19 dix-neuf	1001 mille un
20 vingt	2000 deux mille
21 vingt et un	1,000,000 un million

Ordinals

1st premier, première	7th septième
2nd deuxième, second(e)	8th huitième
3rd troisième	9th neuvième
4th quatrième	10th dixième
5th cinquième	11th onzième
6th sixième	12th douzième
	100th centième

Fractions

Half	demi(e)
Third	tiers
Quarter	quart
Three-quarters	trois quarts

Useful Expressions

When addressing anyone it is usual to add the polite *Monsieur, Madame* or *Mademoiselle,* and any request or enquiry should be accompanied by *s'il vous plaít* ("please").

Good morning, good day!	Bonjour!
Good evening!	Bonsoir!
Good night!	Bonne nuit!
Goodbye	Au revoir
Do you speak English?	Parlez-vous anglais?
I do not understand	Je ne comprends pas
Yes	Oui
No	Non
Please	S'il vous plaít
Thank you	Merci
Yesterday	Hier
Today	Aujourd'hui
Tomorrow	Demain
Help!	Au secours!
Have you a single room?	Avez-vous une chambre à un lit?
Have you a double room?	Avez-vous une chambre à deux lits?
Have you a room with private bath?	Avez-vous une chambre avec bain?
How much does it cost?	Combien (est-ce que) ça coûte? Quel est le prix de . . .?
Please wake me at 6	Veuillez me réveiller à six heures
Where is the lavatory?	Où sont les toilettes?
Where is the chemist's?	Où est la pharmacie?

	Where is the post office?	Où est la poste?
	Where is there a doctor?	Où y a-t-il un médecin?
	Where is there a dentist?	Où y a-t-il un dentiste?
	Is this the way to the station?	Est-ce le chemin de la gare?
Months	January	Janvier
	February	Février
	March	Mars
	April	Avril
	May	Mai
	June	Juin
	July	Juillet
	August	Août
	September	Septembre
	October	Octobre
	November	Novembre
	December	Décembre
Days of the week	Sunday	Dimanche
	Monday	Lundi
	Tuesday	Mardi
	Wednesday	Mercredi
	Thursday	Jeudi
	Friday	Vendredi
	Saturday	Samedi
	Day	Jour, journée
	Public holiday	Jour de fête
Festivals	New Year	Nouvel An
	Easter	Pâques
	Ascension	Ascension
	Whitsun	Pentecote
	Corpus Christi	Fête-Dieu
	Assumption	Assomption
	All Saints	Toussaint
	Christmas	Noël
	New Year's Eve	La Saint-Sylvestre
Food and drink	See entry	
Road and traffic signs	See Motoring in Tunisia	
Rail and air travel	Airport	Aéroport
	All aboard!	En voiture!
	Arrival	Arrivée
	Baggage	Bagages
	Baggage check	Bulletin de bagages
	Bus station	Gare routière
	Couchette	Couchette
	Departure	Départ
	Flight	Vol
	Halt	Arrêt
	Information	Information, renseignements
	Lavatory	Toilette(s)
	Left luggage office	Consigne
	Line (railway)	Voie
	Luggage	Bagages
	Non-smoking	Non-fumeurs
	Platform	Quai
	Porter	Porteur
	Restaurant-car	Wagon-restaurant
	Sleeping-car	Wagon-lit

Smoking	Fumeurs
Station	Gare
Stewardess	Hotesse (de l'air)
Stop	Arrêt
Ticket	Billet, ticket
Ticket collector	Controleur
Ticket window	Guichet
Timetable	Horaire
Train	Train
Waiting room	Salle d'attente
Window seat	Coin fenêtre

At the post office

Address	Adresse
Express	Exprès
Letter	Lettre
Letter-box	Boíte à lettres
Parcel	Paquet, colis
Postcard	Carte postale
Poste restante	Poste restante
Postman	Facteur
Registered	Recommandé
Small packet	Petit paquet
Stamp	Timbre(-poste)
Telegram	Télégramme
Telephone	Téléphone
Telex	Télex

Topographical terms

Abbaye	Abbey
Aiguille	Pinnacle, crag
Anse	Bay
Archipel	Archipelago
Arène	Amphitheatre
Autoroute	Motorway
Avenue	Avenue
Bac	Ferry
Baie	Bay
Bain	Bath(s)
Barrage	Dam; reservoir, artificial lake
Bassin	Dock; ornamental lake, pond
Belvédère	Viewpoint
Bibliothèque	Library
Bois	Wood
Boulevard	Boulevard, avenue
Bourse	(Stock) exchange
Butte	Low hill, bluff
Cabane	Hut
Cabinets	Lavatory, toilet
Campagne	Countryside
Camping	Camping site
Capitainerie	Harbourmaster's office
Carrefour	Road intersection
Carrière	Quarry
Cascade	Waterfall
Cathédrale	Cathedral
Cave	Cellar
Caverne	Cave
Chaíne	Chain, range (of hills)
Chalet	Chalet; mountain hut
Champ	Field

Chapelle	Chapel
Château	Castle, country house, manor-house
Chemin	Road, track
Chemin de fer	Railway
Cime	Peak, summit
Cimetière	Cemetery
Citadelle	Citadel
Cloítre	Cloister
Clos	Enclosure, field, vineyard
Col	Pass
Collégiale	Collegiate church
Colline	Hill
Colonne	Column
Corniche	Corniche road (along side of hill)
Cote	Coast; slope (of hill)
Coté	Side
Cour	Courtyard
Cours	Avenue
Cours d'eau	River, watercourse
Couvent	Convent, religious house
Crête	Crest, ridge (of hill)
Défilé	Defile, gorge
Dent	Crag, pinnacle (of mountain)
Dome	Dome; rounded hill
Donjon	Keep
Ecluse	Lock (on canal)
Ecole	School
Escalier	Staircase
Est	East
Estuaire	Estuary
Etablissement thermal	Spa establishment
Etang	Pond, lake
Fleuve	River (flowing into sea)
Fontaine	Fountain
Forêt	Forest
Fort	Fort
Forteresse	Fortress
Fosse	Pit; grave
Fossé	Ditch; moat
Gare	Railway station
Gare routière	Bus station
Golf	Golf-course
Golfe	Gulf, bay
Gorge	Gorge
Grotte	Cave
Hauteur	Height, hill
Hopital	Hospital
Hotel	Hotel; aristocratic mansion
Hotel de ville	Town hall
Ile	Island
Ilot	Islet
Impasse	Cul-de-sac
Jardin	Garden
Jardin des plantes	Botanic garden
Lac	Lake
Lagune	Lagoon
Maison	House
Maquis	Scrub(land)
Marais	Marsh, bog
Marché	Market
Marécage	Marsh, bog
Mer	Sea

Mont	Mount(ain)
Montagne	Mountain
Municipalité	Local authority, municipality; town hall
Mur, muraille	Wall
Musée	Museum
Nez	Nose, cape
Nord	North
Ouest	West
Palais de justice	Law courts
Parc	Park
Pays	Country
Phare	Lighthouse
Pic	Peak
Piscine	Swimming pool
Place	Square
Plage	Beach
Plaine	Plain
Plâteau	Plateau
Pointe	Cape, point; peak (of hill)
Pont	Bridge
Porche	Porch
Port	Port, harbour
Portail	Doorway
Porte	Door
Poste	Post office
Presqu'íle	Peninsula
Promontoire	Promontory
PTT	Post office
Puits	Well
Quai	Quay; embankment
Quartier	Quarter, district (of a town)
Rade	Anchorage, roadsteads
Refuge	Traffic island; mountain hut
Remparts	Ramparts
Rivière	River (not flowing into sea)
Roc, roche, rocher	Rock
Route	Road
Rue	Street
Sable	Sand
Saline	Salt-pan
Salle	Hall, room
Saut	Waterfall
Source	Spring; source of river
Square	Public square with gardens
Stade	Stadium
Station	Resort; station
Station thermale	Spa, health resort
Sud	South
Téléférique	Cableway
Thermes	Baths
Tombe, tombeau	Tomb
Torrent	Mountain stream
Tour	Tower
Trésor	Treasure, treasury
Trottoir	Pavement
Trou	Hole
Tunnel	Tunnel
Université	University
Val, vallée, vallon	Valley
Village	Village
Ville	Town

Lost Property

There are no lost property offices in Tunisia. Articles found in Tunisian towns are usually handed in to the police, so that if anything is lost enquiry should be made at the local police office (*commissariat de police*).

Louages

See Taxis

Manners and Customs

Visitors to Tunisia should always remember that they are in an Islamic country whose way of life, customs and attitudes are very different from those of the West. All too often, through ignorance or indifference, this is forgotten, resulting in misunderstanding and unpleasantness.
A few hints on behaviour may help to avoid difficulties.
Public displays of affection between the sexes and unduly light clothing, particularly in the case of women, are regarded as breaches of good manners.
It hardly needs saying that visitors should respect religious customs and practices which are strange to them. Particular tact is called for during Ramadan, the month of fasting, when visitors should so far as possible avoid eating, drinking or smoking in public. See Facts and Figures, Religion.
In Islamic society great importance is attached to the obligations of acquaintanceship and friendship. If invited to someone's house it is regarded as impolite not to accept the invitation except for some compelling reason. The whole house is then at the guest's disposal. And of course in the event of a return visit to the visitor's home the same courtesy will be expected.
It is usual for the visitor to offer a small gift to his host or hostess.
Strict Muslims drink no alcohol and eat no pork.

Further information — See Food and Drink, Public Holidays

Maps

A selection of maps of Tunisia on different scales:

1:1,000,000 — Kümmerly & Frey: Tunisia
Ravenstein: Tunisia
Michelin: Algeria and Tunisia
Hallwag: Tunisia and Algeria

1:900,000 — Hildebrand: Tunisia

1:800,000 — GeoCenter International: Tunisia
Freytag & Berndt: Tunisia (with town plans of Tunis and Sousse, site plan of Carthage and inset map of Djerba)

1:500,000 — Official road map of Tunisia, with tourist sights and information (also Tunis area at 1:150,000 and Southern Tunisia at 1:1,000,000)
Official map of Tunisia in four sheets (Tunis, Sfax, Gabès, Ghadamès)

Markets · Souks

The term *souk,* also spelt *souq* or *suq* ("market, market street"), applies both to the weekly market in a country village and the square in which it is held and to the central market areas, often roofed over, of the medinas, with their shops and craftsmen's workshops – the equivalent of the bazaar in the eastern Arab countries and Iran.

In towns

The souks in the medinas are the old shopping and trading centres of the towns. They consist of a maze of narrow and irregularly laid out streets and side alleys, with the various trades concentrated in particular streets and quarters of their own. They are permanently operating markets, open daily except Friday afternoons and Sundays (and in tourist centres often open on Sunday as well), with permanent shops catering for the needs of the urban population. They sell agricultural produce, craft products and modern industrial products. Shops selling artistic and craft products actually made on the premises are becoming increasingly rare, replaced by shops selling mass-produced articles and souvenirs designed for the tourist market. The owners of the shops are now dealers, often wholesalers, rather than craftsmen.

In the country

In the country, on the other hand, the souks have retained their role as the weekly market for the surrounding area. A visit to a village market is an experience not to be missed.
The market is usually held only once a week on the same day in the week. The wares on offer cover all the requirements of everyday life – foodstuffs, spices, clothing, crockery and cutlery, hardware, baskets and other plaited articles, leather goods, carpets, jewellery and ornaments, modern household equipment, plastic articles, electrical appliances. Often part of the square is set aside for a livestock market, in which sheep and goats and occasionally also mules and donkeys are bought and sold.
In contrast to the town souks, the stallholders in the village market are still mainly selling their own agricultural produce or craft products, though here too the numbers of professional dealers are increasing.

The following is a selection of weekly markets in villages and towns throughout Tunisia.

Monday

Ain Draham, Grombalia, Houmt-Souk (Djerba), Kairouan, Kelibia, La Chebba, Mahrès, Maktar, Tataouine.

Tuesday

Béja, El Hajeb, Hafouz, Kasserine, Le Krib, Menzel Temime, Sedouikech (Djerba).

Wednesday

Adjim (Djerba), Jendouba, Sers, Sbeitla.
Nefta has one of the finest markets of all the oasis towns.

Thursday

Boussalem, Gafsa, Hammamet, Houmt-Souk (Djerba), Menzel Bouzelfa, Siliana, Téboursouk.
The market (which includes a camel market) at Douz, south-west of the Chott el Djerid, is frequented by many nomads from the surrounding area.

Friday

Djebeniana, Djemmal (camel market), Ksour Essaf, Mateur, Midoun (Djerba), Queslatia, Sfax, Tabarka, Testour, Thala, Zaghouan, Zarzis.
In Monastir there is a Friday fruit and vegetable market, the Souk el Jomâa, in Rue Salem B'Chir. (The town's central market is in Avenue Habib Bourguiba.)
Of particular interest to visitors is the Friday market in Nabeul, which attracts large numbers of country people, including many from the far south, in their colourful costumes, and almost takes on the aspect of a fair. In addition to livestock (chickens, camels, cattle, sheep, goats) the wares offered for sale include domestic equipment and souvenirs of all kinds. A special section of the market is devoted to an endless range of spices.

Saturday

Ben Gardane, El Fahs, El Mai (Djerba), Thibar.
There is also a Saturday market in Monastir (Place Guedir El Foul, Rue Salem B'Chir), offering a wide range of goods, including carpets (which are given the seal of quality at the point of sale).

Sunday

El Djem, Enfida, Fernana, Hammam-Lif, Korba, Ksar Hellal.
The Sunday market of Sfax is held on the south side of the town, on the road to Sfax.

Medical Care

In the larger towns and in tourist areas standards of medical care are good; in the country, which is less well provided with doctors, care may not be so readily available.
In case of emergency the hotel reception desk or local police will be able to help.
Advice on minor health problems can also be obtained from chemists, who supply a wide range of medicines, including some available in western countries only on prescription.
In the event of accident or illness requiring hospital treatment it is preferable to be flown home for treatment.
Doctors and chemists will normally speak French; some may also speak some English.

Insurance

It is essential before leaving home to take out short-term insurance covering health care. Britain has no reciprocal arrangements with Tunisia, and medical treatment must be paid for. (The receipts should of course be kept for presentation to the insurance company.)

Military Cemeteries

Information about British and Commonwealth military cemeteries of the Second World War in Tunisia can be obtained from the Commonwealth War Graves Commission, 2 Marlow Road, Maidenhead, Berkshire SL6 7DX, tel. (0628) 34221. The Commission will be glad to help trace the graves of individual casualties.

Mosques

Since 1972 non-Muslims have been banned from entering the prayer hall of a mosque. As a rule, however, they are allowed to enter the courtyard (mornings only, except Fridays).
Further information is given in the descriptive section of this guide, or can be obtained from the local tourist office.

Further information

See Facts and Figures, Art and Culture, Islamic Architecture; Calendars; Manners and Customs

Motoring in Tunisia

General

Tunisia has a well developed road system (see Facts and Figures, Transport); but it is desirable to avoid travelling any great distance after dark. The roads are narrow and unlighted, and it is quite conmmon, particularly in the south of the country, to encounter oncoming vehicles with inadequate lights or none at all. Horse- or donkey-drawn traffic crossing the road may also be difficult or impossible to distinguish.

Seat-belts

Seat-belts must be worn by the driver of the vehicle and by passengers in both the front and back seats.

Breakdown Assistance

There are no organised breakdown assistance services in Tunisia. In the event of a breakdown, therefore, it is necessary to wait for some helpful car-

or lorry-driver to turn up, who may be able to solve the problem or convey a message to the nearest garage. Motorists can also apply for help to the police (Garde Nationale) who operate throughout the whole country and have frequent traffic patrols, or to the nearest police station (*poste de police*).
The Tunisian motoring organisations do not operate road patrols.

Repair garages

In towns and villages of any size there is no shortage of garages equipped to carry out repairs, and many petrol stations will also do minor repair jobs. Anyone intending to travel in southern Tunisia must ensure that the vehicle is in first-rate condition and spare parts should be carried.

Accidents in Tunisia

However carefully a car is driven, accidents can happen. If involved in an accident, the first rules are: whatever the provocation, do not get angry; be polite; and keep calm. Then take the following action:

1. Warn oncoming traffic by switching on the car's warning lights and setting a warning triangle (and, if possible, a flashing light) some distance before the scene of the accident.

2. Look after anyone who has been injured, calling an ambulance if necessary.

3. Inform the police.

4. Record full particulars of the accident. These should include:
a names and addresses of witnesses (independent witnesses are particularly important);
b damage to the vehicles involved;
c name and address of the other driver, and of the owner if different;
d name and address of the other party's insurance company and, if possible, the number of the insurance certificate;
e registration number of the other vehicle;
f damage or injury to yourself or other persons;
g number of police officer or address of police station if involved;
h date, time and location of the accident;
i speed of the vehicles involved;
j width of the road, any road signs and the condition of the road surface;
k any marks on the road relevant to the accident;
l the weather and the manner of the other driver's driving.

5. Draw a sketch of the accident, showing the layout of the road, the direction in which the vehicles were travelling and their position at the time of impact, any road signs and the names of streets or roads. If a camera is available, take photographs of the scene.

Make no admission of responsibility for the accident, and above all do not sign any document in a language not understood.

On return home report the accident to your insurance company and give them the full particulars.

Car papers

See Travel Documents

Motoring organisations

National Automobile Club de Tunisie
28 Avenue Habib Bourguiba

1001 Tunis
Tel. (01) 24 39 21

Touring Club de Tunisie
15 rue d'Allemagne
1001 Tunis
Tel. (01) 24 31 82 and 24 31 14

The motoring organisations have a purely advisory function (particularly on trips into the desert), and can also supply maps.

Maps

See entry

Road markings and road signs

Trunk roads (grands parcours, GP) are marked by red kilometre stones, secondary roads (moyennes communications, MC) by green ones. Some sand tracks negotiable by an ordinary car are also included in the latter category.

Road signs throughout the country, with a very few exceptions, have legends in French as well as in Arabic.

Rule of the road

Vehicles travel on the right, with overtaking on the left. At intersections and roundabouts traffic on the right has priority.
In built-up areas with adequate lighting cars may drive using only sidelights.
Motorcyclists and moped riders must wear a helmet.

Alcohol

Driving is prohibited after drinking even the smallest quantity of alcohol.

Toutes directions

As in France, the sign "Toutes directions" in a town of any size is designed to guide transit traffic through the town.

Autres directions

At a street intersection in a town with road signs pointing to particular destinations the sign "Autres directions" indicates the direction for other traffic.

Centre Ville
Ville Nouvelle

In large towns these signs indicate the way to the new part of the town.

Medina
Ville Ancienne

These signs indicate the way to the old town.

Road warning signs

Allure modérée	Slow
Arrêt	Stop
Arrêt interdit	Stopping prohibited
Attention!	Caution
Au pas!	Dead slow
Avertissez	Sound horn
Bouchon	Tailback
Brouillard	Fog
Centre ville	To town centre
Chantier	Road works
Croisement	Intersection
Danger (de mort)	Danger (of death)
Déviation	Diversion
Douane	Customs
Fin de limitation de vitesse	End of speed restriction
Frontière	Frontier
Garage	Parking; passing place
Gravier, gravillons	Loose stones, gravel
Halte!	Stop
Impasse	No through road; cul-de-sac
Limitation de vitesse	Speed restriction
Passage à niveau	Level crossing

Passage interdit!	No entry, no thoroughfare
Passage protégé	You have priority at junction ahead
Poids lourds	Heavy lorries
Priorité à droite	Traffic coming from right has priority
Prudence!	Drive with care
Ralentir, ralentissez!	Reduce speed now
Rappel	Reminder (that a previous traffic sign is still in force)
Route barrée	Road closed
Route en réparation	Road works
Sens interdit	No entry, no thoroughfare
Sens unique	One-way street
Serrez à droite	Keep in to the right
Sortie de camions	Lorries crossing
Tenez vos distances!	Keep your distance
Tourner interdit	No U-turns
Toutes directions	All directions
Travaux	Road works
Verglas	Black ice
Virage (dangereux)	(Dangerous) bend
Voie unique	Single-lane traffic
Zone blue	Parking only with parking disc
Zone rouge	"Red zone": parking prohibited
Mise en fourrière immédiate	Parked cars may be towed away

Speed limits

In built-up areas 50km ph (31 mph); outside built-up areas 100km ph (62 mph).
Motorists exceeding the speed limit can expect at least a fine.

Fuel

Standard-grade petrol (92 octane), premium grade (95 octane) and diesel fuel are readily available. Prices are rather lower than in Europe.
Lead-free petrol is difficult to obtain in Tunisia.

Petrol stations

Tunisian towns, large and small, are well supplied with petrol stations. There are few petrol stations in the steppe country, and in the desert motorists must carry their own supplies.
The opening hours of petrol stations vary from town to town and from season to season, but in general they are open from 7 or 7.30 in the morning to 10 o'clock at night. On Sundays opening hours are restricted. In large towns some petrol stations offer a 24-hour service.

Spare parts

In addition to a first aid kit, tools and a spare wheel motorists should have with them the most essential spare parts. It is also advisable to carry a solid board or something similar as a base for the jack.

Driving in the South

Clothing

Light clothing (preferably white cotton) should be worn during the day, with something warmer for the evening. Stout boots or shoes will give protection against snake-bites. Protection from the sun (cap or hat, sunglasses with green lenses, sun creams) is essential.

The car

Drivers should check that their car is in perfect working order before setting out on a journey.

Equipment

The fine sand of the desert can penetrate the smallest cracks and is unpleasant in itself and a danger to precision apparatus such as cameras. Suitable precautions should be taken.

Tent

It is also advisable to carry a tent. Care should be taken to shake it out before use in case it harbours scorpions or other creatures which become active at night. The same precaution should be taken with clothes, sleeping bags, etc.

Regulations on Travel in the Desert

Motorists intending to drive into the Sahara are required, for their own safety, to inform the police (Garde Nationale) of their proposed starting-point, route and destination and must obtain written permission for their trip.
The Tunisian Automobile Club (see above) can give advice and information about driving in the Sahara, and in particular the addresses of the police stations from which the necessary authority for the trip can be obtained.

Warning

Driving in the Sahara is dangerous and can cost lives. It is essential to take an experienced local guide.

Weather

In order to avoid unpleasant surprises it is advisable to check on the weather prospects before setting out.

Travel in convoy

Trips into the Sahara should always be made in convoy, never alone.

Vehicle; supplies

The best type of transport for the Sahara is a Landrover-type all-terrain vehicle with four-wheel drive. Adequate supplies of drinking water, petrol and oil, together with spare parts for the vehicle, *must* be carried.

Breakdown

In the event of a breakdown, stay with the vehicle: do not walk about in the desert. It is easier for a search party to locate a car than a number of separate individuals.
If the car sinks into the sand raise it with the jack, making sure that there is something solid and flat as a base for the jack (see above, Spare parts); then fill in the holes made by the car's wheels. If there is no firm base for the jack it may be possible to get the car away by laying branches under the wheels, starting the engine and engaging an intermediate gear. Often, however, a car stuck in the sand can be released only by being winched out by another vehicle.

Other precautions

Never drive off the marked track. On a corrugated track either drive very slowly (at less than 30km/20 miles an hour) or so fast that the car does not go down into the furrows between the ridges. This is a very testing process for the car, which may loosen screws or even cause welded joints to fail. Moreover the lack of grip of the tyres and the constant use of low gears considerably increase petrol consumption, making it all the more essential to carry sufficient reserves.

Reporting to military posts

It is important to report to any military post you encounter, so that the authorities can log the vehicle's movements.

Crossing the Chott el Djerid

Warning

Since the construction of the causeway over the Chott el Djerid (see entry) the crossing of this great salt lake is no longer the hazardous enterprise it once was, and there are now refreshment and souvenir stalls at intervals along the road. It is important, however, not to stray off the asphalted road: the verges of the road may look solid, but they might well give way under the weight of a vehicle, and then even a four-wheel drive vehicle might not be of any help.

Further information

See Breakdown Assistance, Emergencies, Excursions, Health, Medical Aid, Sahara Tourism

---

Museums

Opening times

Museums are usually closed on Mondays and on official public holidays; on other days they are open from 9am to noon and from 2 or 3 to 5.30pm.

The Bardo Museum in Tunis is open daily, except Fridays and public holidays, from 9.30am to 4.30pm. Other departures from the general rule are noted in the descriptive section of this guide.

Admission charge; photography

In addition to the charge for admission an extra ticket must be bought to take photographs. The use of flash and of a tripod is prohibited.

Guided visits

In most of the large museums there are guided visits in French and English.

National Parks

Since becoming independent Tunisia has made great efforts to protect its natural flora and fauna, and numerous National Parks, nature reserves and landscape reserves have been established. These are usually well away from the tourist centres and offer the interested and patient nature-lover fascinating insights into the natural beauties of Tunisia and the variety of its plant and animal life.

Information

Further information can be obtained from branches of the Tunisian National Tourist Office or from the Direction des Forêts (Forestry Commission) in Tunis, the authority responsible for the protection of nature in Tunisia.

National Parks
Bou Hedma

Situation: on the northern edge of the Sahel, 85km/53 miles south-west of Sfax and 85km/53 miles south-east of Gafsa. Area: 350sq.km/135sq.miles of upland country between Djebel Bou Hedma (790m/2592ft) in the north and Djebel Orbata (1164m/3819ft) in the south.
Features: over 139 species of plants, umbrella thorns and numerous desert animals (gazelles, golden eagles, scimitar-horned oryxes, chameleons, tortoises, etc.). Trips through the National Park in all-terrain vehicles (bookable through the larger travel agencies). Informative displays and publications.

Djebel Chambi

Situation: 15km/9 miles north-west of Kasserine in west central Tunisia. Area: 600sq.km/230sq.miles of forest in the Tunisian Atlas, with the country's highest peak, Djebel Chambi (1544m/5066ft).
Features: Aleppo pines, more than 100 species of plants, mountain gazelles, wild goats, wild pigs, moufflons, etc. Nature Museum. See Tunisia from A to Z, Kasserine, Surroundings.

Ichkeul

Situation: 75km/47 miles north-west of Tunis on the south side of Lake Ichkeul, near Bizerte. Area: 100sq.km/40sq.miles of lake, marsh and wetlands. The lake is only 1–3m/3–10ft deep and is well stocked with fish. Djebel Ichkeul (508m/1667ft) rises out of the centre of the lake.
Features: many migrant birds (duck, greylag geese, herons, storks, etc.); Tunisian water buffaloes, etc., etc. Museum of Ecology. See Tunisia from A to Z, Bizerte.

Zembra, Zembretta

Situation: two small islands 60km/40 miles north-east of Tunis off the Cap Bon peninsula. Area: 5.5sq.km/2sq.miles.
Features: interesting flora and fauna, with many migrant birds on their way to and from Europe, wild rabbits, goats, genets, tortoises and monk seals (a protected species). See Tunisia from A to Z, Cap Bon.

La Galite Is.

The La Galite island group, 85km/53 miles north-east of Bizerte, consists of six islands, only one of which has a small population who live by growing vines and catching crayfish. The little island of Le Galiton is a strictly protected reserve for the very rare monk seal.

Nature reserves

In addition to the National Parks there are a series of nature reserves and protected areas. One such reserve is El Feidja, near Ghardimaou, in the north-western corner of Tunisia, an upland region (area 350sq.km/135sq.miles), covered with great expanses of holm-oaks and cork-oaks, which is the home of Atlas deer, wild pigs and porcupines. The Kechem el Kelb nature reserve in west central Tunisia, near the Djebel Chambi National Park, is a well wooded area (Aleppo pines), the habitat of mountain gazelles.

In order to protect the flora and fauna of these nature reserves visitors are admitted only with special permission from the forestry authorities. Information can be obtained from local tourist offices and the Forestry Commission in Tunis (see above, Information).

Naturism

Naturism (nude bathing) is prohibited in Tunisia, and topless bathing on public beaches is frowned on. Out of consideration for the feelings of local people – and to avoid possible unpleasantness – visitors, and particularly women, should avoid provocative dress (or undress).

Further information

See Dress, Manners and Customs

Newspapers and Periodicals

Newspapers

Tunisia has a number of newspapers, in both Arabic and French, which circulate throughout the country. The two Arabic newspapers are "Al Amal" and "As Sabah"; the three French-language papers are "L'Action", "La Presse de Tunisie" and "Le Temps".

Periodicals

There are also a number of periodicals. "IBLA", founded in 1937 as the journal of the Institut des Belles Lettres Arabes, has the declared object of promoting knowledge of Tunisia and of Arab culture. Address: 12 rue Jamaa el Haoua, 1008 Tunis.

Tunisian Press Agency (RAP)

Tunis Afrique Presse (TAP)
25 Avenue Habib Bourguiba
1001 Tunis
Telex 13 400 (TAP)

English papers

The main British dailies and the "Herald Tribune" can be bought in the larger towns and tourist areas a day after publication.

Opening Times

See Business Hours

Photography

Insurance

Visitors who are taking valuable photographic equipment should make sure that it is covered by a travel insurance policy.

Video camera

Video cameras (camcorders) must be entered in the visitor's passport on entry into Tunisia.

Films

Films of the principal international brands are on sale in the large towns and tourist centres, but prices are higher than at home. It is advisable, therefore, to take in an adequate supply of films. The customs allowances

are generous (see Customs Regulations), and in practice there is not usually any check on the number of films brought in.
The strong sunlight and ultraviolet radiation on the coast make the use of an appropriate filter advisable. A powerful flash may also be found useful.

Photographing people

As in many Islamic countries, taking photographs of people in Tunisia may give rise to difficulty. Islamic religion bans the representation of the human figure, and Muslim believers regard having their photograph taken as degrading. In recent years, particularly as a result of the development of tourism, there has been some relaxation of attitudes; but photographers should still show the greatest tact in their choice of subjects.
In the large towns and tourist centres and at other places with tourist attractions many of the local people have come to terms with being photographed: they will put up with it if the photographer is not too intrusive and has asked for their agreement by a suitable gesture. Not infrequently, however, the photograph will be followed by a demand for payment.
There is usually no difficulty about photographing children, though in the large tourist centres they too may ask for money.
In the country areas, however, it is still difficult to take photographs of people. Most people will refuse to be photographed; and women in particular – who make especially tempting subjects for photographers with their picturesque costumes and jewellery – should be photographed, if at all, only with their express permission.
The photographing of Muslims engaged in the practices of their religion (prayer, ablutions, burials, pilgrims) is particularly undesirable. Since non-Muslims are banned from entering the prayer hall of a mosque, no question of photographing the interior arises.

Military zones

The photographing of military installations of any kind is strictly prohibited.

Post

Postal Services

Post offices

There are post offices (*bureaux de poste*) in all Tunisian towns of any size.

Post Office Headquarters:
Ministère des Communications
Direction Générale des Postes
1030 Tunis

Head post office in Tunis:
Rue Charles de Gaulle
Tel. (01) 24 60 09

Poste restante mail addressed to Tunis goes to the head post office.

Parcels in Tunis

Bureau de Poste Tunis-République
Avenue de la République
Tel. (01) 24 59 00
(Parcel = paquet; small packet = petit paquet; weight = poids)

Tunisian post-box

Other post offices

On the town plans in the main section of this guide post offices are indicated by the posthorn symbol.

Opening times

Beginning of July to mid September: Monday to Thursday 7.30am–12.30 (and emergency service from 5–7pm), Friday and Saturday

7.30am–1.30pm; mid September to end of June: Monday to Thursday 8am–noon and 2–5pm, Friday and Saturday 8am–12.30pm; during Ramadan: Monday to Saturday 8am–3pm.

Since there may be variations in opening times in some places it is advisable to post mail so far as possible in the morning.

Stamps

Tunisian stamps (*timbres*) are frequently designed by native artists and are much sought after. They can be bought in tobacconists', some kiosks and the larger hotels as well as in post offices.

Letters to Britain (sent by air mail at an extra charge) take about a week to arrive, letters to North America about two weeks.

Public Holidays

Weekly holiday

The religious holiday is Friday (Djemaa), but the official holiday, as in the West, is Sunday. On Fridays life continues normally, though there may be different opening times for offices and banks, since male Muslims go to the mosque for the communal Friday prayer in the early afternoon.

Official public holidays

New Year's Day (Jour de l'An): January 1st
Independence Day (Fête de l'Indépendance): March 20th
Youth Day (Jour de la Jeunesse): March 21st
Martyrs' Day (Jour des Martyrs): April 9th
Labour Day (Fête du Travail): May 1st
Republic Day (Fête de la Proclamation de la République): July 25th
Women's Day (Journée de la Femme): August 13th
New Era Day: November 7th

Religious holidays

Muslim religious festivals are determined by the Islamic calendar (see Calendars). The Islamic year is divided into twelve months, which – in contrast to the Gregorian calendar, which is based on the course of the sun – are related to the phases of the moon and are thus only 29 days long. As a result the Islamic year is 10–12 days shorter than the Gregorian year, so that Muslim religious festivals move 10–12 days back each year in the Gregorian calendar.

Aid es Seghir (end of Ramadan): April 4th–5th 1992
Aid el Kebir (pilgrimage to Mecca): June 11th–12th 1992
Ras el Am Hajri (Islamic New Year): July 2nd 1992
Mouled (birthday of the Prophet Mohammed): September 9th 1992

Ramadan

March 5th–4th April 1992
February 23rd–March 25th 1993
Ramadan, the month of fasting, is the ninth month in the Islamic year. "Fasting" implies leading an ascetic life, giving up all worldly pleasures – eating, drinking, smoking, taking *kif* (cannabis), sexual intercourse – and intensifying the religious observances of the five daily prayers and additional visits to the mosque.
Only children under 12, the aged, the sick, pregnant women and travellers are exempted from the duty of fasting.
The obligation to fast applies only during the day, from sunrise to sunset. As soon as the evening call to prayer at sunset is heard it is permissible to eat. Usually three meals are taken during the night, the last of them just before sunrise. Frequently these nocturnal meals are particularly lavish, taking on the form of a festival, with singing and dancing, which makes up for the privations of the day.
During Ramadan business life is much quieter than in the rest of the year, and public offices, shops and banks are open only in the mornings.

Jewish festivals

The island of Djerba still has the largest Jewish community in Africa, diminished though it may be by recent emigration to Israel. The Jews of

Djerba observe the Jewish festivals, in particular Yom Kippur, the Day of Atonement (September/October), which commemorates the wanderings of the Israelites in the desert.

Further information

See Business Hours, Calendars, Events, Manners and Customs, Night Life

Radio and Television

Information

Direction de la Télévision Tunisienne (TDT)
4 rue de Kenya
1002 Tunis
Tel. (01) 28 31 77

Radiodiffusion Télévision Tunisienne
71 Avenue de la Liberté
1002 Tunis
Tel. (01) 28 73 99

Radio

Tunis Radio transmits programmes in Arabic, French and sometimes Italian.
The BBC's World Service can be heard on short wave.

Weather reports for shipping

Weather reports are broadcast twice daily by radio stations at the ports of Bizerte, La Goulette, Mahdia and Sfax. These stations also transmit gale warnings, daily coastal weather forecasts and special warnings.

Television

Tunisian Television transmits programmes in Arabic and, mainly in the north of the country, French and Italian. Many of the larger hotels also receive American and German programmes by satellite.

Railways

Tunisia has a total railway network of some 2000km/1250 miles. Part of this is narrow-gauge, but it is planned to convert the whole system to standard gauge.

SNCFT

The railway system is run by the Société Nationale des Chemins de Fer Tunisiens (SNCFT), 67 Avenue Farhat Hached, Tunis.

Classes

There are three classes of carriage: luxury (L), 1st and 2nd. Some trains have restaurant cars, and on long journeys there are sleeping cars.

The network

See map on page 364. All the larger towns on the coast can be reached by rail; in the interior the coverage is less complete, and it may be necessary to continue a journey by bus (see Bus Services) or by communal taxi (see Taxis).

TM 1 and 2

The Trans-Maghreb Express (TM 1 and 2) provides fast connections with Algeria and Morocco.

Fares

Rail fares are low. There are reduced rates for return fares.
Children under four travel free; between four and ten they pay a quarter of the full fare; and over the age of ten they pay the full fare.

"Lézard Rouge"

See Tunisia from A to Z, Metlaoui

Air and Rail Services in Tunisia

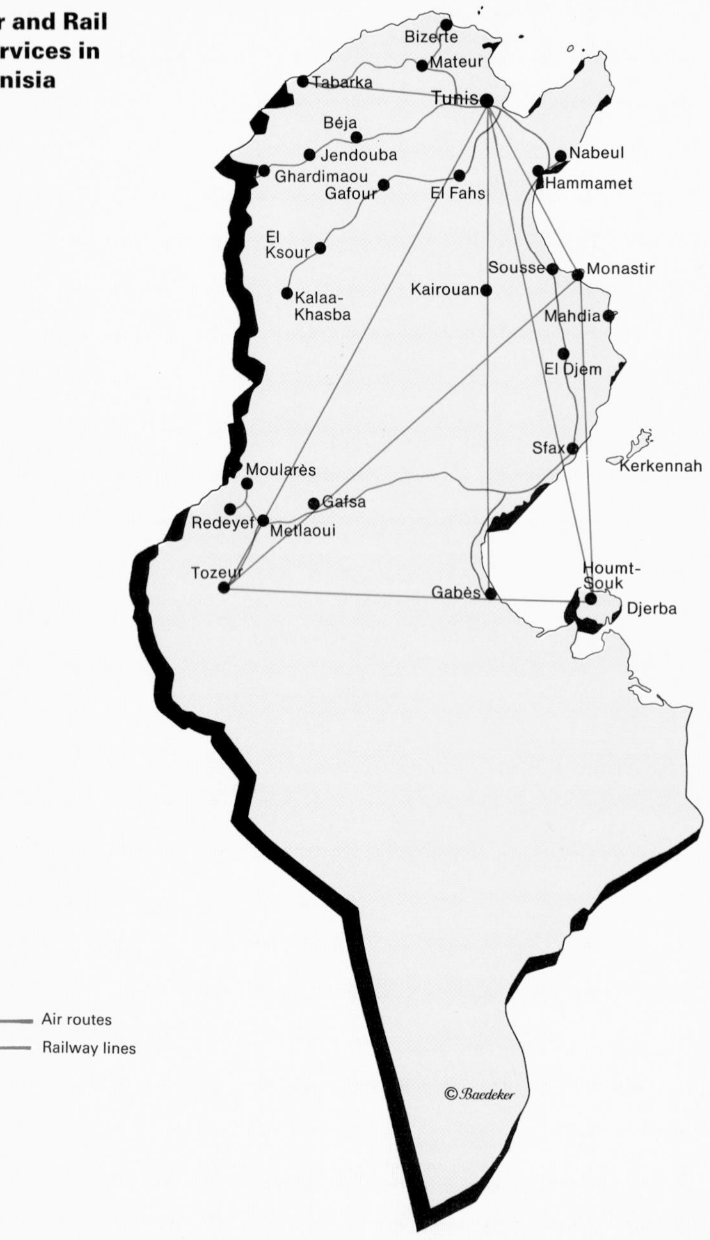

Ramadan

See Facts and Figures, Religion; Calendars; Manners and Customs

Restaurants

Once the body has adjusted to the climate it is well worth having a change from the international cuisine offered in hotels and restaurants in the tourist centres and trying some of the characteristic local dishes offered in speciality restaurants (see Food and Drink).

In addition to the restaurants in the tourist hotels there are a variety of high-quality restaurants, usually in the town centre or European quarter, as well pavement cafés and snack bars in the souks.

Bread is usually included in the price of a meal; it may be accompanied by olives, highly spiced sauces, etc.

Meal-times

Breakfast (petit déjeuner), is a frugal meal, usually taken fairly late. Lunch is served between 12.30 and 2 or 2.30, the evening meal (díner, souper) seldom before 8pm.

Tipping

It is usual in a restaurant other than a hotel restaurant to give a tip of 10–15%, which may – depending on the customer's degree of satisfaction – be rounded up.

Restaurants in Tunisia

The following is merely a brief selection. Most hotels also have restaurants.

Bizerte

Chez Antoinette, 6 rue de Bone, tel. 3 13 57; Le Petit Mousse, Corniche, tel. 3 21 85; Restaurant de la Plage, Corniche, tel. 3 18 17.

Djerba

Chez Baccar, Place Hedi Chaker, tel. 5 07 08; Blue Moon, Rue Med. Ferjani, tel. 5 05 59; Centre d'Animation, Hotel Al Jazira, tel. 5 01 42; Restaurant de l'Air, Aéroport International de Djerba-Zarzis, tel. 5 02 33; Restaurant de l'Ile, Rue Moncef Bey, tel. 5 05 68; Restaurant du Sud, Place Sidi Brahim, tel. 5 04 79; El Hana, Place Med. Ali, tel. 5 05 68; Méditerranéen, Place Moncef Bey, tel. 5 07 02; Neptune, Place Sidi Brahim, tel. 5 02 26; Haroun, Port de Houmt-Souk, tel. 5 03 92; Ecole Hotelière de Jerba, tel. 5 04 56; Tebsi, Avenue Abdelhamid el Cadhi, tel. 5 06 11.

Djorf

Jorf, tel. 5 50 55.

Gabès

L'Oasis, 34 Avenue Farhat Hached; El Mazar, 39 Avenue Farhat Hached, tel. 7 20 65; El Khalij, 114 Avenue Farhat Hached.

Gafsa

Gafsa, Rue Ahmed Snoussi, tel. 2 24 68 and 2 26 76; Samiramis, Rue Ahmed Snoussi.

Gammarth

Les Dunes, tel. 27 00 96.

Hammamet

Trois Moutons (grillroom), Avenue Habib Bourguiba, tel. 8 09 81; Pomodoro, 6 Avenue Habib Bourguiba, tel. 8 12 54.

Kairouan

Bir Barouta, Medina; Karawan, Rue Soukeine Bent el Houssein; Abbassia, Avenue Farhat Hached; Neptune, in Shopping Centre; Roi du Couscous, Medina; Splendid, Avenue du 9 Avril 1939.

Monastir

Bel Air, Aéroport International de Monastir-Skanès, tel. 6 13 14; Le Central, Port de Plaisance, Marina Cap Monastir, tel. 6 09 23; El Ferik, Route de la

Corniche, tel. 6 05 17; Le Flamand Rose, Dkhila-Monastir, tel. 3 18 53; Le Grill, Port de Plaisance, Marina Cap Monastir, tel. 6 09 23; Hannibal, Quartier Chraga, tel. 6 10 97; La Marina, Port de Plaisance, Marina Cap Monastir, tel. 6 09 23; La Plage, Place du 3 Août; La Pizzeria, Port de Plaisance, Marina Cap Monastir, tel. 6 09 23; Le Rempart, Avenue Habib Bourguiba, tel. 6 17 52; Le Sindbad, Port de Plaisance, Marina Cap Monastir, tel. 6 09 23; Snack Abou Nawas, Aéroport International de Monastir-Skanès, tel. 6 13 14.

Nabeul

L'Olivier, Rue Hedi Chaker, tel. 8 66 13; Bonheur, Avenue Habib Bourguiba, tel. 6 12 54.

Nefta

Chez Farid; Des Sources, tel. 5 70 51; Le Paradis, tel. 5 70 87; Les Amis (all in Souk de Nefta).

Port El Kantaoui

Ezzarda (Traiteur), tel. 4 17 99; Beach Club (summer only), tel. 4 17 99; Club House, at golf-course, tel. 4 17 56; L'Escale, tel. 4 17 91; Les Emirs, tel. 4 17 99; Yacht Club, tel. 4 17 99; Zitouna (Ezzarda), tel. 4 17 99.

Sfax

Bagdad, 63 rue Farhat Hached; tel. 2 38 56; Le Corail, 39 rue Habib Maazoun, tel. 3 73 01.

Sousse

Bonaparte, Avenue Taieb M'hiri, tel. 2 32 62; Café de Tunis, Avenue Habib Bourguiba, tel. 2 46 42; Capri, Rue Mongi Slim, tel. 2 82 71; Petit Marin, Avenue Habib Bourguiba, tel. 2 83 99; Flouka, Rue du 2 Mars 1934, tel. 2 89 10; Forum Grill, Avenue Habib Bourguiba, 2 83 99; Hong-Kong, Boulevard de Rabat, tel. 2 13 66; La Baraka, Rue Mongi Slim, tel. 2 76 81; La Calèche, Rue Remada, tel. 2 64 89; La Cave, Rue Mongi Slim, tel. 2 69 39; L'Albatros, Route de la Corniche, tel. 2 43 58; La Marmite, Rue Remada, tel. 2 67 28; L'Ambassadeur, Route de la Corniche, tel. 2 12 50; Le Bonheur, Place Farhat Hached, tel. 2 57 42; Le Gourmet, Rue Amilcar, tel. 2 47 51; Le Kandyl, Route de la Corniche, tel. 2 64 55; Le Lido, Avenue Mohamed V, tel. 2 53 29; Le Marrakech, Route de la Corniche, tel. 2 68 11; Le Pacha, Route de la Corniche, tel. 2 45 25; Le Phénicien, Boulevard de Rabat, tel. 2 30 12; L'Escargot, Route de la Corniche, tel. 2 47 79; Les Remparts, Rue de l'Eglise, Medina, tel. 2 63 26; Les Sportifs, Avenue Habib Bourguiba, tel. 2 51 18; Le Tunisien, Rue Ali Belhaouane, tel. 2 59 48; L'Olivier, Rue Mongi Slim, tel. 2 41 50; Malouf, Place Farhat Hached, tel. 2 65 08; Raphia, Avenue Habib Bourguiba, tel. 2 14 68; Régal, Boulevard Abdelhamid el Kadhi, tel. 2 63 66; Sélect Mokis, Rue Victor Hugo, tel. 2 80 11.
In Hammam-Sousse: El Mendia, tel. 42 77 77.

Tabarka

Barberousse; Le Pescadou; Le Pirate.

Tozeur

Chiraz, La République, Le Paradis, Le Petit Prince, Les Sportifs, all in Avenue Habib Bourguiba; Relais, in El Hamma (9km/6miles from Tozeur).

Tunis

Dar el Jeld, 5 rue El Jeld, La Kasbah, tel. 26 09 16; Brasserie Schilling, 93 Avenue Mohamed V; Brasserie Suisse, 43 Avenue Habib Bourguiba; Chez Nous, 5 rue de Marseille, tel. 24 30 43; Poisson d'Or, 5 rue Ibn Khaldoun; El Andalous, 13 rue de Marseille, tel. 24 17 50; Gaston's, 73 rue de Yougoslavie, tel. 34 04 17; La Baraka Saad, La Marsa, tel. 27 03 20; La Hungaria, 11 rue Ali Bach Hamba, tel. 24 54 69; La Maison Dorée, 6 bis rue de Hollande, tel. 24 06 31; La Mama, 11 bis rue de Marseille, tel. 24 12 56; Le M'rabet, Souk Ettrouk; L'Astragal, Cité Jardin, 6 rue Ryadh el Kadhi, tel. 89 04 55; Le Bagdad, 31 Avenue Habib Bourguiba; Le Cosmos, 7 rue Ibn Khaldoun, tel. 24 16 10; Le Golfe, Place Sidi Abdelaziz, La Marsa, tel. 27 02 19; Le Malouf, 108 rue de Yougoslavie, tel. 24 31 80; Le Milanais, 20 rue de l'Inde, tel. 28 80 64; Le Palais, 8 Avenue de Carthage, tel. 25 63 26; Le Strasbourg, 100 rue de Yougoslavie, tel. 24 11 39; L'Orient, 7 rue Ali Bach Hamba, tel. 24 20 58; Tchevap, 52 Avenue Habib Bourguiba, tel. 27 81 10.

Zarzis

Abou Nawas, in town centre, tel. 8 05 83; Les Palmiers, in town centre, tel. 8 01 14; L'Olivier, Route des Hotels, tel. 8 07 21; Souihel, Route des Hotels, tel. 8 03 45.

Riding

See Sports

Sahara Tourism

In recent years there has been a steady development of tourism in the Sahara: new airports have been established in southern Tunisia, hotel accommodation has been increased and new tracks have been laid in the desert.
Sahara tourism offers an alternative or a supplement to the standard seaside holiday, with trips into the interior of southern Tunisia in four-wheel-drive vehicles, visits to the palm-groves of the Djerid oases or the dune-like Nefzaoua oases, the ksars and the ghorfas, camel rides in the desert, the colourful festivals of Douz and Tozeur and much else besides.
Trips into the Sahara should be undertaken only under arrangements made by a local tour operator or through a travel agent before leaving home. Trying to do it alone could be, quite literally, fatal.

Further information

See Excursions, Motoring in Tunisia

Sailing

See Water Sports

Shooting

See Sports

Shopping · Souvenirs

Bargaining

All over Tunisia visitors will be tempted by a wide range of attractive souvenirs in the form of local artistic and craft products, and it is well worth taking time off in the souks to see what is available. Part of the process of buying anything in the souks is the haggling over the price: a contest of skills between the seller and the buyer. As a broad general rule the price first asked for by the seller should be countered by an offer of about half as much, and the price finally agreed on may be expected to lie between two-thirds and three-quarters of the original asking price. Although the process of bargaining can be regarded as a kind of game, it should be borne in mind that at the end of the day both parties must be satisfied with the transaction; and since, given the low wage levels in Tunisia, most things are relatively cheap visitors may not be inclined to press too hard for the lowest possible price.
To get some idea of price levels it is worth looking into the local ONAT shop (see below) before bargaining in the souks.

The following is only a brief selection from the wide range of possibilities: leather goods of all kinds (wallets, albums, book-covers, belts, cushions, etc.), ceramics (decorative plates, vases, flower-pots, etc.), brassware (mortars, etc.), copperware (coffee-pots and tea-pots, flower tubs), basket-work (bags, table runners, small chairs, etc.), embroidered fabrics (blouses, blankets, underwear).
In the towns there are perfumes made from jasmine oil and attar of roses.

As inexpensive souvenirs of the Sahara there are the "sand roses" or "desert roses" (crystals of gypsum in the form of flowers), found in a wide range of sizes. Other local products are drums and objects carved from olive-wood, palm-wood (Tozeur, Nefta) or oleander branches (Tabarka).

ONAT

The Tunisian National Handicrafts Organisation, ONAT (Organisation Nationale de l'Artisanat Tunisien), has showrooms in many towns and tourist centres throughout the country in which visitors can see a wide range of Tunisian artistic and craft products, including carpets. The articles on display are for sale, but even if nothing is bought a visit to an ONAT shop will give the visitor an excellent idea of what is available and of price levels before you venturing into the souks.

Tunis

Organisation Nationale de l'Artisanat Tunisien (ONAT)
Rue des Teinturiers
Tunis
Tel. (01) 22 04 22

Buying a Carpet

One of the finest and most valuable souvenirs of a visit to Tunisia is a carpet. On types of carpet, methods of manufacture, etc., see Carpets.

Guarantee of genuineness

The best guarantee of the genuineness of a carpet is the ONAT stamp on the underside, accompanied by a description of its quality.

Characteristics

When a carpet is bought all its characteristics (serial number, measurements, number of knots per square metre, weight, design, colour) should be specified in the bill. These particulars should be checked against the label on the underside of the carpet.

Price

The price of the carpet in Tunisian currency should be shown on the bill. ONAT shops allow a reduction in the price when payment is made in hard currency.
As a rule delivery will be free only to the nearest port, airport or post office.

Duty

Duty and VAT will be payable on the full value of the carpet. The receipt for the purchase must therefore be preserved for production to the customs authorities.

Local Specialities

Beni Khiar

In Beni Khiar, 5km/3 miles north-east of Nabeul, visitors can watch the local people spinning wool, weaving woollen carpets, blankets and garments, and working intricately patterned embroidery.

Dar Chaabane

In Dar Chaabane, a few kilometres north of Nabeul, the local stone-carvers create real works of art (wall decoration, etc.) in Moorish/Arab style.

Djara

The special products of Djara, north-west of Gabès, are articles woven from palm leaves and wrought-iron work.

Djerba

Djerba is, after Nabeul, the main Tunisian pottery centre. The widest range of choice is offered by Houmt-Souk and Guellala.
Er Riadh (formerly Hara Seghira) is noted for its beautiful filigree goldsmith's work.

Douz

In addition to the attractions of its Thursday market (see Markets, Souks) Daouz offers attractive camel-hair bags and felt shoes made from wool and lambs' fleeces.

Gafsa is famed for its vividly coloured woollen carpets in both geometric and representational designs. Gafsa

The Centre Commercial (Shopping Centre) in Hammamet offers an extensive range of attractive craft products in its numerous shops and galleries. Hammamet

Kairouan is world-famed as Tunisia's carpet-making town (see Carpets). Kairouan

Ksar Hellal, 10km/6 miles south-east of Monastir, has long been famed for the quality of its woven fabrics, and it now also has an efficient modern textile industry. Ksar Hellal

Ksibet el Médiouni, south-east of Monastir, has a famous carpet market. Ksibet el Médiouni

Mahdia is noted for its fine woollen fabrics, its embroidery and the making of traditional costumes. Mahdia

This little town 12km/7½ miles south-east of Monastir is famed for the manufacture of Berber clothing and jewellery. There are also a number of potters' workshops. Moknine

The pottery-making tradition of Nabeul goes back to Roman times, and its numerous potters produce a wide range of both glazed and unglazed ware – both ordinary pottery for everyday use and finely decorated tiles, jugs and vases, some of them based on antique models and decorated in the original colours (white, blue, green and yellow). Visitors can watch the potters at work. Nabeul

Nabeul also produces fine embroidery and lace (e.g., for brides' dresses) and perfumes made according to traditional recipes from orange, geranium and jasmine blossom.

Nabeul has a very picturesque Friday market, which in addition to everyday requirements, carpets and souvenirs sells a wide range of spices. A walk through the narrow streets and souks of the old town, with the workshops of all the various craftsmen (smiths, cobblers, carpenters, etc.), is a fascinating experience.

Oudref, 15km/9 miles north-west of Gabès, has a model weaving-shop which produces hambels (long strips of tent-cloth, gaily striped), mergoums (smooth-faced carpets in geometric designs), attractive saddle-cloths (bochts) and ladies' scarves (bakhnougs). Oudref

In Tozeur visitors can buy articles made from palm fibres (bags, wall hangings), woollen blankets, burnouses and "sand roses" (see above). Tozeur

Further information: See Carpets, Currency, Customs Regulations, Markets

Souks

See Markets, Souks

Spas

The hot springs in northern Tunisia have been used for medicinal purposes since Roman times, and the spas which have grown up around them, equipped with modern treatment facilities, attract many people, both from Tunisia and abroad, to "take the cure".

Information

Office du Thermalisme
11 Impasse de l'Aurore

The spa of Korbous

1002 Tunis-Mutuelleville
Tel. (01) 23 07 27, 28 81 50 and 28 74 57

Korbous
(Cap Bon)

Situation: 50km/31 miles east of Tunis. Altitude: 419m/1375ft.
Korbous (the Roman Aquae Calidae Carpitanae) has seven springs (50–60°C/120–140°F; containing chlorine, sodium and sulphur), including Ain Echiffa ("Spring of Healing"; for disorders of the metabolism), Ain Thalassira (chalybeate; skin conditions), Ain Atrous ("Goat Spring"), Ain el Kebira (the "Great Spring"; in a former summer residence of the Beys) and the underground steam baths of El Arraka ("Sweat-Maker"), Ain Sbia (the "Maiden's Spring") and Ain Fakroun ("Tortoise Spring").
Recommended for chronic inflammatory rheumatism, arthritis, inflammatory disorders of the nervous system, cellulitis, high blood pressure, obesity, periodontosis, children's diseases, gynaecological conditions.
Facilities: thermal baths, individual baths, underwater massage, foot baths and hand baths; healthy climate; international cuisine and diets; walking. It is planned to develop the infrastructure, lay out a golf-course, construct a marina and establish a centre of thalassotherapy.
Accommodation: see Hotels.

Ain Oktor
(Cap Bon)

Situation: a few kilometres south of Korbous. A cold mineral spring with low chlorine and sodium content.
Recommended for stones in the kidneys and inflammations of the urinary tract.
Facilities: drinking cures.
Accommodation: see Hotels, Korbous.

Djebel Oust

Situation: 30km/19 miles south-east of Tunis. Altitude: 130m/427ft.
Water containing sodium chloride and sulphate. There are remains of Roman baths with marble floors.
Recommended for chronic rheumatic inflammations, arthritis, disorders of the locomotor system, gout, cellulitis, obesity, periodontosis.

Facilities: therapeutic exercise in thermal water, massage, electrotherapy, physiotherapy.
Accommodation: see Hotels, Zaghouan.

Hammam Bourguiba

Situation: north-west of Tunis, 32km/20 miles from Tabarka. Altitude: 150m/490ft. The resort lies on the shores of the lake, surrounded by hills. Recommended for chronic inflammations of the respiratory passages, allergic inflammations, pneumonia.
Facilities: inhalations, baths, douches, massage; international cuisine.
Accommodation: Hotel ***Hammam Bourguiba, tel. (08) 4 71 06/227/300, 80 beds and 24 chalets.

Sport

In addition to the numerous activities laid on in the holiday villages of the Club Méditerranée, the Robinson Clubs and various hotels – ranging from early morning gymnastics, aerobics, archery, judo, volleyball and trampolining to late-night break dancing – Tunisia offers facilities for every kind of sport except winter sports. Visitors who are so inclined should therefore take their sports kit with them.

Ballooning

A number of resorts have facilities for hot-air ballooning. Information from hotel reception desks, travel agencies and local tourist offices.

Cycling

Cycles can be rented in many resorts for trips into the surrounding area. Information from hotel reception desks or the management of holiday villages.

Diving

See Water Sports

Fishing

The waters off Tunisia, with its Mediterranean coastline of over 1200km/750 miles, are well stocked with fish.

Tunisian anglers practise three methods of fishing – with rod and hook, with an invisible net and with vertical tackle. The SHTT diving school in Monastir, tel. (03) 6 01 56/633, offers trips on its boat "El Kahlia" (equipped with rods and net) on Fridays. Elsewhere visitors may be able to arrange to accompany a local fisherman in his boat.

Underwater hunting/fishing is subject to regulations issued annually by the Ministry of Agriculture. Before setting out, therefore, you should seek information about the current regulations from the Tunisian National Tourist Office (see Information) or from:

Centre Nautique International de Tunisie
22 rue de Médine
1001 Tunis
Tel. (01) 28 22 09 and 28 13 74

Gliding

There is a gliding area on Djebel Ressas, 25km/15 miles south-east of Tunis, tel. (01) 90 67 12.

Information from:

Centre Fédéral de Vol à Voile
17 Avenue Habib Bourguiba
1001 Tunis
Tel. (01) 25 57 61.

Golf

Foreign golfers are welcome in Tunisian golf clubs on presentation of the membership card of their own club. Some clubs also offer facilities for

Fishermen . . .

. . . at work

golfers who do not belong to a club. Information from the clubs listed below.

Country Golf Club (18 holes)
Tunis-Carthage
Tel. (01) 90 33 81

Tunis-La Soukra (18 holes)
Route de la Soukra
Tel. (01) 76 59 18

El Kantaoui Golf Course (27 holes)
Port El Kantaoui, Hammam Sousse (Sousse-Nord)
Tel. (03) 3 17 55

Monastir Golf Course (18 holes; 3-hole short course)
Route de Ouardanine (5 minutes from airport)
Tel. (03) 6 11 20

Hammamet (18 holes and 9 schooling holes)
Bir Bou Rekba
Tel. (02) 8 27 22

Tabarka Golf Course (18 holes)
Montazah Tabarka
Tel. (08) 4 43 21

Land-yachting

Land-yachting can be practised on the great expanses of the Chott el Djerid, the Great Salt Lake of central Tunisia. The land yacht is a three-wheeled board with a sail, a rudder and a seat for the yachtsman. Its speed is controlled by pedals, the brake and the position of the sail.

Information from Hotel El Jerid, Tozeur, tel. (06) 5 05 54.

Riding

There are two riding clubs in the Tunis area which offer introductory courses for beginners and rides in the country led by experienced instructors.
Information from:

Club Hippique
Kassar Said
(10km/6 miles from Tunis)
Tel. (01) 22 32 52 (daily, except Mondays, 8–11am and 2–5.30pm)

Club Hippique
La Soukra
(15km/9 miles north of Tunis)

The Baraket stud farm at Ghardimaou (9km/6 miles from the Algerian frontier), which breeds thoroughbred Arab horses, runs 14-day treks for small groups of riders. Information from Coopérative Baraket, Ghardimaou.

Rides on camels and Arab horses: see Excursions.

Sailing

See Water Sports

Shooting

At Ain Draham, Tabarka, El Haouaria, Zaghouan and Sbeitla there are facilities for shooting trips after wild boar, jackals and other game. Regulations for the shooting season (usually between December and February) are laid down annually by the Ministry of Agriculture; information about the current regulations can be obtained from tourist offices (see Information) or local shooting clubs.
There is a clay pigeon shooting club at Radès, south-east of Tunis. Information: tel. (01) 29 51 28.

Swimming

See Water Sports

Tennis

Visitors staying in the Tunis area can play tennis in the Belvédère Club, the Parc des Sports club (Avenue Mohamed V) or in Carthage.
Most hotels in the main tourist centres have their own tennis courts. The Tunisian government will in future require all new hotels to have their own tennis courts and swimming pool.

Water Sports

See entry

Taxis

There are three types of taxi in Tunisia: *taxis bébés, grands taxis* and *louages*.

Taxis bébés

These are small vehicles equipped with taximeters (make sure that the meter is switched on!), identified by numbers on the roof. They operate only within towns and can take a maximum of three passengers, with only light luggage.
Fares are very reasonable. There is an extra charge for night journeys, and in Tunis there is also a supplementary charge for journeys between the city and Tunis-Carthage airport or the port of La Goulette.

Grands taxis

These have a large "Taxi" sign on the roof. They can be picked up at taxi ranks in the town centre or hailed in the street. They operate both in towns and outside and can take up to four passengers, with luggage.

There is an extra charge for luggage and a 50% increase in the fare after 9pm. There is also a supplement if the taxi has to return empty from an outward journey.
These taxis can be hired by the day for sightseeing trips.
If the taxi has no meter the fare should be agreed before setting out.

Louages

These are communal taxis which run on fixed routes between towns and villages all over the country. They start from particular points in towns according to their destination (which is shown on the windscreen). As a rule they leave only when all five seats are occupied; if you cannot wait until then you must pay for the empty places. They do not usually pick up passengers en route.
Louages are popular with the Tunisian population, since they are only slightly dearer than the country buses, whose timetables cannot always be relied upon.

Telephone

International telephone calls can be made from all post offices. There are direct dialling facilities to Europe, North America and other countries from the larger Tunisian towns. Where direct dialling is not available, dial 17 for the operator for international calls, 15 for calls within Tunisia.

Payphones

There are payphones in all post offices in Tunis and its suburbs, in Avenue Habib Bourguiba in Tunis, at Tunis-Carthage Airport and in some hotels and cafés.

24-hour service

Centre d'Exploitation des Télécommunications
29 rue Gamel Abdel Nasser, Tunis

International dialling codes

To Tunisia from the United Kingdom: 010 216
To Tunisia from the United States or Canada: 011 216

From Tunisia to the United Kingdom: 00 44
From Tunisia to the United States or Canada: 00 1
From Tunisia to Australia 00 61; to New Zealand 00 64

After the international dialling code the zero of the local dialling code is omitted.

Some Local Dialling Codes and Post Codes

Bizerte	(02) 7000
Carthage	(01) 2016
Djerba	(05) 4180
Douz	(05) 4260
Gabès	(05) 6000 (town); 6071 (port)
Gafsa	(06) 2100 (town); 2111 (station)
Grombalia	(02) 8030
Hammamet	(02) 8050
Hammam-Lif	(01) 2050
Kairouan	(07) 3100

(07) 1200	Kasserine
(05) 4200	Kebili
(02) 8090	Kelibia
(08) 7100	Le Kef
(03) 5100	Mahdia
(05) 4100	Médenine
(03) 5000	Monastir
(02) 8000	Nabeul
(06) 2240	Nefta
(04) 3000	Sfax
(01) 2026	Sidi Bou Said
(03) 4000	Sousse
(06) 2200	Tozeur
(01) 1000	Tunis

(The various districts and suburbs of the city have different codes.)

Telegrams and Telex

Telegrams can be sent through the Telecommunications Centre in Tunis (15 rue Gamel Abdel Nasser): dial 14 for telegrams to foreign destinations, 15 for telegrams within Tunisia.
Telex messages can be sent from the same office.

Television

See Radio and Television

Tennis

See Sports

Time

Tunisia observes Central European Time, one hour ahead of Greenwich Mean Time.

Summer Time

Summer Time in Tunisia begins later than in most European countries. It lasts from the beginning of June to the end of September, so that during the early weeks of British Summer Time there is no difference between Tunisian and British time.

Tipping

Given the low wage levels and high unemployment in Tunisia, tipping (baksheesh, French pourboire) is a matter of some economic consequence, and many families depend on the additional income to be gained from performing various small services, selling souvenirs, etc. Muslims are also obliged by their religion to help the needy, and Tunisians as well as visitors are expected to give a suitable tip for any services rendered.

The general principle is that baksheesh is justified only in return for some help or service, but that when there has been such help or service it should always be given. Beggars should be turned away with the phrase "Allah yatik" ("May God give to you"), importunate adolescents with "Mafish baksheesh" ("Nothing doing!").

In view of the widespread expectation of baksheesh it is advisable to carry plenty of small change.

In hotels and restaurants it is usual to give 10–15% of the bill in tips.

Travel Documents

Personal papers

British, Canadian and United States nationals require only a valid passport (or British Visitor's Passport), without a visa, for a stay of up to three months (four months for US visitors).

Injections

There are no obligatory injections for British or North American visitors. A certificate of yellow fever injection is required only for visitors coming from an infected area.

Car papers

National driving licences and car registration documents (the *carte grise*) are accepted.
Third party insurance is obligatory, and an international insurance certificate ("green card") valid for Tunisia must be carried. It is advisable also to have comprehensive insurance cover.

Owners of trailer caravans should have an inventory of their contents.

Boat papers

Owners (or charterers) of sailing boats must have a sailing certificate and proof of membership of a recognised sailing club.

Turkish Baths

See Hammams

Water Sports

Diving

Centre International de Plongée (open throughout the year)
Port de Plaisance El Kantaoui
4000 Hammam-Sousse
Tel. (03) 4 17 99

Yachting Club de Tabarka
(open throughout the year; best time April 1st–October 31st)
Port de Pêche
8110 Tabarka
Tel. (08) 4 44 78

Those who pass the final examination at these diving schools are given a certificate which is recognised by the World Confederation of Underwater Activities (Confédération Mondiale des Activités Subaquatiques).

SHTT Diving School Monastir
Tel. (03) 36 01 56/633

Further information on diving in Tunisian waters can be obtained from the Tunisian National Tourist Office or from:

Centre Nautique International de Tunisie
22 rue de Médine
1001 Tunis
Tel. (01) 28 22 09 and 28 13 74

Parasailing

Parasailing over the sea has become increasingly popular in recent years. The parasailer, wearing a parachute, is towed out to sea by a motorboat, rises into the air as the speed increases and descends again as it falls. A trip lasts between 10 and 15 minutes. Protection from the sun is essential.

Sailing

The Tunisian coast, only between 100 and 400 sea miles from the principal European ports in the Mediterranean, offers attractive sailing conditions, with its beautiful coastal scenery, its excellent mooring facilities in the yachting harbours and marinas and the simplified process of customs clearance.
There are good, well equipped harbours at Tabarka, Bizerte, Ghar el Melh, Sidi Bou Said, La Goulette, Sidi Daoud, Kelibia, Beni Khiar, Hergla, El Kantaoui, Sousse, Monastir, Teboulba, Bekalta, Mahdia, Salakta, La Chebba, Sfax, Sidi Youssef, El Attaia and Sidi Fredj (Kerkennah Islands), Ennajet, La Louata, Mahrès, La Skhira, Gabès, Zarat, Adjim and Houmt-Souk (Djerba), Bou Grara and Zarzis.
There are special yachting harbours at Port El Kantaoui (300 moorings), Monastir (400 moorings), Sidi Bou Said (380 moorings) and Tabarka (at present 60 moorings; in course of development).

A helpful brochure, "Yachting in Tunisia", giving details of the facilities available at Tunisian yachting harbours, can be obtained from the Tunisian National Tourist Office.

Swimming

There are three municipal swimming pools in Tunis:

Piscine El Gorjani
Boulevard du 9 Avril

Piscine Municipale Belvédère
(heated in winter)
Place Pasteur

Piscine El Menzah
(heated in winter)
Cité Olympique

Many hotels in the tourist centres have their own swimming pools.

Water-skiing

There are facilities for water-skiing at many Tunisian coastal resorts.

Wind-surfing

At many resorts there are wind-surfing schools where surfboards can be rented.

Weather

See Facts and Figures, Climate; When to Go

Weights and Measures

The metric system is used in Tunisia.

When to Go

The best time for a visit to northern Tunisia is from April (the beginning of the bathing season) to the end of October; for central and southern Tunisia October to April.

Further information

See Facts and Figures, Climate; Dress; Health; Manners and Customs; Photography

Youth Hostels

Youth hostels in Tunisia (known variously as auberges de jeunesse, maisons des jeunes, centres de jeunesse, centres d'hébergement, centres de stages et de vacances) are open to all holders of an international youth hostel card, though preference is given to young people (minimum age 17).

Camping in tents at youth hostels is not permitted except in Nabeul.

Flowering meadows south-west of Tunis in May

Advance booking is advisable during the main holiday season and is obligatory for groups.

Youth hostels are open from 7am to 11pm.

Information

Association Tunisienne des Auberges de Jeunesse
10 rue Ali Bach Hamba
B.P. 320
1015 Tunis
Tel. (01) 24 60 00
Open Mon.–Sat. 8.30am–noon and 3–6pm

Addresses of youth hostels

Ain Draham
Tel. (08) 4 70 87
150 beds

Béja
Maison des Jeunes
Tel. (08) 5 06 21
80 beds

Bizerte
Auberge de Jeunesse, Route de la Corniche
Tel. (02) 3 16 08
100 beds

Djerba
Maison des Jeunes, Avenue Bourguiba, Houmt-Souk
Tel. (05) 5 06 19
60 beds;
11 rue Moncef Bey, Houmt-Souk
Tel. (05) 5 06 19
120 beds

Gabès
Centre de Stages et de Vacances, Rue de l'Oasis
Tel. (05) 2 02 71
80 beds

Gafsa
Tel. (06) 2 02 68
56 beds

Kairouan
Auberge de Jeunesse, Rue de Fès
Tel. (07) 2 03 09
70 beds

Kasserine
Maison des Jeunes, Cité Ouvrière (3km/2miles from Kasserine)
Tel. (07) 7 00 53
70 beds

Kelibia
Maison des Jeunes
Tel. (02) 9 61 05
80 beds

La Chebba
Centre de Jeunesse
Tel. (03) 8 38 15
60 beds

Le Kef
Maison des Jeunes
Tel. (08) 2 16 79
60 beds

Matmata Ancienne
Centre de Séjour et de Stages (in troglodyte dwellings)
6070 Matmata Ancienne
50 beds

Médenine
Maison des Jeunes
Tel. (05) 4 03 38
28 beds

Menzel Temime
Maison des Jeunes
Tel. (02) 9 81 16
80 beds

Monastir
Maison des Jeunes, Centre ville
Tel. (03) 6 12 16
60 beds

Nabeul
Auberge de Jeunesse, Centre ville
Tel. (02) 8 55 47;
Centre de Séjour et de Vacances "La Gazelle", Dar Chaabane el Fehri
Tel. (02) 2 13 66
70 beds

Nasrallah
Maison des Jeunes
Tel. (05) 2 02 71
80 beds

Remel (3km/2miles from Bizerte)
Tel. (02) 3 38 04
40 beds

Sfax (1km/¾mile out of town on road to airport)
Maison des Jeunes
Tel. (04) 4 32 07
70 beds

Sidi Bou Zid
Maison des Jeunes
Tel. (06) 3 00 88
27 beds

Siliana
Maison des Jeunes
Tel. (08) 7 08 71
45 beds

Sousse
Auberge de Jeunesse, Plage Boujaafar
Tel. (03) 2 12 69
56 beds

Téboursouk
Maison des Jeunes
Tel. (08) 6 50 95
40 beds

Tozeur
Maison des Jeunes
Tel. (06) 5 02 35
38 beds

Tunis
Centre d'Hébergement, Jelili ez Zahra, Oued Meliane Ezzahara, B.P. 1140
Tel. (01) 48 15 47
72 beds

Tunis-Medina (500m/550yds from Place de la Kasbah)
Maison des Jeunes, 23 rue Saida Ajoula

Tunis-Radès (10km/6miles south of Tunis)
Maison des Jeunes
Tel. (01) 48 36 31
56 beds

Zaghouan
Maison des Jeunes
Tel. (02) 7 52 65
85 beds

Zarzis
Maison des Jeunes
Tel. (05) 8 01 37
25 beds

Accommodation for students

During the summer students can obtain cheap accommodation in the University of Tunis on presentation of their student identity card.

Index